LANGUAGE AND POVERTY

Language and Poverty

Perspectives on a Theme

70681

Edited by

Frederick Williams

University of Texas at Austin

Institute for Research on Poverty Monograph Series

MARKHAM PUBLISHING COMPANY
Chicago

This book is one of a Series sponsored by the Institute for
Research on Poverty of the University of Wisconsin pursuant
to the provisions of the Economic Opportunity Act of 1964.

Preface

A basic aim of the Institute for Research on Poverty is the translation of knowledge gained through research into bases for policy making in attacking the problems of poverty in the United States. As a member of the Institute while preparing this volume, I felt the frustration of sensing the gap between what exists of research and theory in language behavior and the pressing practical questions about language raised by many of the persons working in antipoverty programs, particularly in those programs involving children. What appears in this volume is an attempt to transit some of this gap.

As the book goes to press, I consider that the practical goal of bringing together under one cover a range of perspectives pertinent to language and poverty has been achieved. But as readers of the papers will see, this collection heightens, rather than lessens, the sense of the gap which separates research from practice. Too often we have been the victim of the easy answer—e.g., that the poverty child's language is simply underdeveloped. Too often the research underlying such answers has taken little advantage of what the scientists of language—the linguist, psycholinguist, sociolinguist—have had to offer. Too often we have seen that research in language and poverty is fractionated in a way that sets an example akin to backyard iron making. Too often all of these shortcomings have culminated in efforts that have made the disadvantaged child even more disadvantaged.

Despite this frustration, I feel that a distinguishing mark of this collection of papers is, indeed, that different perspectives have been juxtaposed. That we see linguists, psychologists, sociologists, educators, and others exercising varying definitions of language and language behavior, is important to know. And that we understand the contrasts and similarities among these definitions is even more crucial to us.

One benefit of an eclectic collection is that when ideas are culled from multiple perspectives, they seem all the more worthy of our special consideration in policy making. Such ideas do transcend the papers of this volume. In capsule form, some of these include:

1. *We must avoid confusing language differences with deficiencies.* Careless interpretation of standardized tests has caused some of the problem on this point; bias on the part of researchers and their techniques may account for much of the rest. Children with true deficiencies of language require quite

different programs from those whose language mainly differs from that of the mainstream society. Moreover, children with language differences fall into a number of categories (bilingualism, dialect differences, radically different uses of language), each requiring different types of educational programs.

2. *It is a reasonable and desirable goal that all children in the United States be able to function linguistically in standard English in addition to whatever language or dialect they have learned in the home.* The reasons for this point are simple and practical—the language of our educational institutions (including its literature), and the language required for most better-paying occupations in this country, is standard English. But it is important that standard English be developed parallel, or built upon, the home language, rather than at the expense of it. It is important to realize also that "to function linguistically in standard English" means simply to be able to understand and to be intelligible to other speakers of this form of English. It does not mean sounding "right" or "white."

3. *We must develop new strategies for language instruction, as our existing ones are largely inadequate for use with children coming from varying language backgrounds.* Promising strategies include such characteristics as: (a) focusing upon the preschool child, even prior to Head Start age; (b) using instructional materials of an active and practical nature for the child, stressing communication development (i.e., how language is used to accomplish things); (c) using materials which build upon, show contrasts, or both, with what the child has already learned. The overall attempt is to incorporate the social context of language acquisition into the instructional context. Such programs would be different for different groups of children, and this imposes special demands upon teachers who should probably be as knowledgeable of the child's vernacular (or that of his environment) as they are of standard English. (This point has obvious implications for recruiting more minority group members into the teaching profession, and for the increased use of lay assistants.)

4. *We must increase our research efforts in the study of language differences in the United States, and the interrelation of these with different social and family structures.* Currently, we lack the necessary knowledge of the varieties of nonstandard English encountered in the kinds of needed program strategies described above. This knowledge can be gained by increasing our commitment to sociolinguistic field studies and to studies of the role of language in child socialization. Such research should not overlook the language habits and attitudes of the majority populations, particularly in how these attitudes are manifested in our institutions (by teachers, for example) and in how they affect the life and opportunities of the minority populations. We cannot expect the members of a single discipline to carry out such research; it requires large scale, centrally coordinated projects involving (even at their sometimes-mutual distrust) linguists, sociologists, psychologists, specialists in speech, and educators, to name a few.

5. *Language programs for the poor should incorporate research and evaluation components.* What we have seemed to lack the most in projects already undertaken on large scale bases are the objective indices and criteria for evaluating their effects. Our recent large-scale evaluations have mainly involved use of teacher-questionnaire and picture-vocabulary indices, which have left us with little more than nothing regarding the effects of educational intervention programs upon language. Programs proposed to have some effect upon the language development of children should devote as much emphasis to methods for research and evaluation as they typically do to the promises of effects. We need to concentrate upon the research and development of instructional strategies for different types of children, and upon the use of unified and objective criteria for evaluation of their effects. Only when given the benefits of such research should we dare to undertake new large-scale efforts, or at least to expect positive results from them.

I clearly recognize that these ideas move quite directly to the call for research. But rather than simply a call for more research, they call for better research and for more coordination of efforts. In a larger respect, they ask of our efforts in *social* technology the standards and coordination demanded of our research in the other sciences. As a technological society, we have paid the price of crowded cities, of depressed rural areas, and of the inverse correlation between economic opportunity and minority group membership. We should bring this same technology to bear upon a debt to the human element in our society.

ACKNOWLEDGEMENTS

The preparation of this book was supported by funds granted to the Institute for Research on Poverty by the Office of Economic Opportunity pursuant to the provisions of the Economic Opportunity Act of 1964. The conclusions are the sole responsibility of the authors.

As the editor, I am indebted to many people for their assistance on this volume. Professor Harold Watts and my colleagues in the Institute and in the Office of Economic Opportunity provided the encouragement and conditions for undertaking the project. Manuscript preparation, final editing, and publication would never have progressed on schedule without the assistance of the Institute editor, Jeanne DeRose; my research associate, Dr. Rita C. Naremore; the final draft typist, Lorraine Laufenberg (College Printing and Typing Co.); and, of course, the special help of my wife, Joan Williams. I must also thank the three evaluators of the final manuscript—Mrs. Franc Balzer of the Department of Health, Education, and Welfare; Dr. Susan Ervin-Tripp of the University of Calfornia–Berkeley, and Dr. Roger Shuy of the Center for Applied Linguistics.

Above all, the greatest credit must be given to the authors who contributed papers for the volume. Deadlines were set and met, and this, coupled with the quality of the papers, is testimony to the caliber of the people whose ideas appear on the pages that follow.

FREDERICK WILLIAMS

CONTENTS

Chapter 1

SOME PRELIMINARIES AND PROSPECTS

Frederick Williams*

Although *language and poverty* may seem a small fragment of a much broader problem, it is a theme that offers a wide range of perspectives associated with certain assumptions about poverty and its remediation in the United States. As the papers for this volume were gathered and their perspectives compared and contrasted, a most basic issue was revealed. Defined abstractly, this issue asks: In dealing with the language of the poverty child, are we essentially dealing with language which is deficient, or with language which is different? Obviously, such a question elicits contrasting perspectives on the definition of terms, on the interpretation of data, and even on the philosophic attitudes one has toward the proper workings of a society. Different perspectives on this issue constitute the papers of this volume.

In this introductory paper a sketch is first presented of the larger framework within which the deficit-difference issue can be seen relative to considerations of the causes of, and cures for, poverty. Next, some of the relations among the perspectives on the basic issue are outlined. Finally, it is proposed that the deficit-difference issue is one of the most fundamental questions challenging our society.

THE POVERTY CYCLE

As the War on Poverty has continued in the United States, it has become increasingly evident that the boundaries of poverty are often subcultural ones.

---

*Center for Communication Research, University of Texas

Individuals in a poverty group can be defined by their common socioeconomic problems, and these, in turn, are typically associated with an equally common range of sociocultural features—ways of life, education, attitudes, desires, and above all, language and the ways of using it. Much of the attention given to the sociocultural aspects of poverty can be seen in the kinds of causes and cures for poverty which are often linked as parts of an overall *poverty cycle* (Figure 1). In this cycle, the old and familiar, and less euphemistic, label of being *poor* is at the point which we now usually call being *economically disadvantaged*. This simple picture is broadened slightly, and a first part of the cycle recognized, when the causes of economic disadvantage are sought in some type of employment disadvantage. Backtracking from this point in the cycle was one of the key marks of the War on Poverty. Just as employment disadvantages underlay economic disadvantages, it was reasoned that educational disadvantages underlay those of employment. And when causes for educational disadvantage were explored, speculation led to a kind of developmental disadvantage associated with being reared in a home suffering from economic

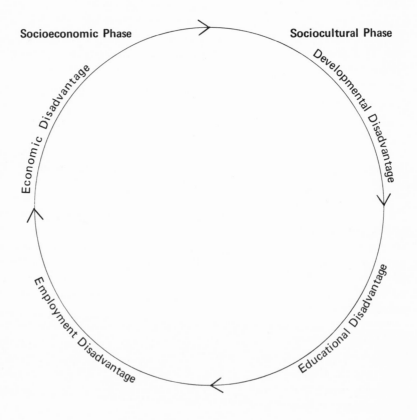

Figure 1. Poverty Cycle

disadvantage. Thus a cycle was fully defined—one which seemed logical and replete with interventional implications.

But this cycle also represents one account of the origin of the deficit-difference controversy—that is, where the concept of economic disadvantage was extended, by analogy, to create a concept of cultural disadvantage. Implicit in the concept of economic disadvantage are the ideas of "lack of necessary resources," "deficient," "underdeveloped," and the like. It is the extension of such ideas to include the concept of culture or subculture, or more properly to the people within it, that has given so much cause for concern. The contrast is captured in the following question: Are we talking about groups of individuals whose backgrounds, attitudes, and general capabilities have failed to equip them adequately for a life of opportunities or are we talking about minority cultures of a country where the attitudes of the majority have inhibited the participation of the minorities in these opportunities? The first version yields the definition of a *disadvantaged culture,* and the second, of a *culture at a disadvantage.* As we interpret evidence for purposes of assessing these alternatives, and as we may find ourselves faced with an interpretative blend of their extremes, we must cope theoretically and practically with what they imply about the nature of poverty in the United States. Moreover, we must consider what they imply about the ways in which we have chosen to fight poverty. Nowhere is this challenge more evident than in the contrasts between the deficit and the difference positions taken on the language of the poverty child.

PERSPECTIVES ON THE LANGUAGE OF THE POOR

The Deficit Argument

When reviewing the research on the sociocultural aspects of poverty published in the mid-1960s (Plumer, Chapter 14), one is immediately struck with the apparent coalescence of interpretations about the language of the poverty child. There are numerous individual reports, ranging from impressionistic descriptions to the use of standardized tests (Severson and Guest, Chapter 15), which point to shortcomings in the language capabilities of poverty children. Such evidence is usually gained by contrasting poverty children with their middle-class counterparts, and interpretations move from such contrasts to generalizations about the appearance of "developmental lags" in the language of the poverty child. All this fits quite well into the position that a poor home is an environment which retards a child's overall development, leading to his disadvantage in school. Failure in school leads in turn to lack of employment opportunities, and this sets the stage for economic disadvantage to perpetuate the cycle.

This is the type of picture which emerged, for example, from the work of Deutsch and his associates (1967), or from Hess and Shipman (1965; see Olim, Chapter 11), to name a few. Throughout such literature reference is made to restrictions and shortcomings of language development. Often such references are given a theoretical boost by citing the sociolinguistic speculations of Bernstein. Earlier, Bernstein (see esp., 1961) posed a theory of "restricted" and "elaborated" language codes, where such codes reflected the ranges of linguistic alternatives available respectively to members of the working and middle classes in Great Britain. His interpreters in the United States took the verbal performances of poverty children as symptomatic of the socalled restricted code, and identified it as a kind of underdeveloped, deficit style of speech, a view to which Bernstein (Chapter 3) currently objects.

This deprivation, or deficit, diagnosis of the poor suggests a kind of "cultural injection" as an antidote for poverty, and that the earlier it is given to the child, the better the results. Some have argued that the language portion of the cultural antidote for poverty is by far the most critical. The ideas of Bereiter and Engelmann (1966) are the best known on this point, and can be summarized as follows: Assuming that the poverty child lags behind his middle-class counterpart in preparation for school, then a preschool compensatory program will have to have this child learning at an even greater rate because his problem is essentially one of "catching up." Accordingly, a preschool program should concentrate directly upon the most critical of skills needed for school, and this is language. Rather than assume that language skills will be gained indirectly through a middle-class type nursery-school experience (as in Head Start), such skills should be taught by direct instruction. Unlike many contributors of the mid-1960s, Bereiter and Engelmann went on to present a concrete instructional program for disadvantaged children. Engelmann, in Chapter 6, describes the requirements for a concentrated program of language instruction. A program having similar ends, but different means, is described by Blank in Chapter 4.

A discussion of the deficit position would not be complete without mention of the argument that there may be a genetic variable rather than, or in addition to, environmental variables perpetuating a poverty class. Recently Jensen (1969) has argued the existence of a genetically based constraint on types of learning in individuals. Oppositions to his views are included in the Spring 1969 issue of the *Harvard Educational Review,* and in Labov's chapter (9) in this volume.

The Difference Position

Beginning also in the mid-1960s, but of interest to fewer researchers and with less immediate attention, were the roots of the now-current counterargument to the deficit position on language. Although recognition of a possible confusion of differences and deficits in the environmentalist literature was presented during this period in a paper by Cazden (1966), most of what we call the *difference position* has emanated from the writings of Stewart (Chapter 17), Labov (Chapter 9), Shuy (Chapter 16), and Baratz (Chapter 2).

Stewart has consistently argued that American Negro dialect should be studied as a linguistic system in itself rather than in terms of deviations from standard English. With others, such as Labov, he called for elimination of the bias inherent in the label *substandard English*—preferring instead the label *nonstandard,* and the idea that English, as most languages, has a variety of dialects, none of which should be viewed as any better than the other. Most of Stewart's research has centered upon historical and sociolinguistic aspects of American Negro dialect.

More strictly sociolinguistic in orientation is the research of Labov and Shuy, both of whom have pointed out the integrity of linguistic variations according to social stratification, ethnicity, and differences in speech situations. The admonition here is that speech variations among groups of people should not be assumed to be variations in degrees of linguistic complexity, sophistication, or development, nor capricious errors. Rather, such variations may reflect distinctions among quite normal and well-developed, but different, linguistic or dialect systems. This reasoning reflects the theoretical view of most linguists that no natural language or dialect can really be considered more primitive, rudimentary, or underdeveloped than another. In brief, as applied to the deficit position on the language of the poor, this group of linguists is arguing that what we are observing are often language differences, and if there is a discrepancy between the demands of the school, for example, and the performance of the child, we are seeing the consequences of forcing a child to perform in a linguistic system other than his primary one.

Like the proponents of the deficit position, the difference theorists agree that the poverty child is failing in our schools and that something has to be done. But where the former would focus much of the remediation upon the child's apparent unreadiness for school, the difference theorists tend to accuse the school of unreadiness. Thus, for example, Baratz argues that the urban black child's reading program should begin with primers in his vernacular, and then systematically work toward teaching the child the pragmatic and expressive contrasts between the two dialects. On a superficial level, some are quick to identify this position with the well-known "teaching-English-as-a-second-language." But the arguments of the difference theorists require far more than a teaching technique. They are arguing that the United States is a polycultural society with monocultural schools, and this is the first and perhaps most damaging inequity foisted upon the poverty child.

POTENTIAL BASES FOR RESOLUTION

Psycholinguistic Theory

Close to, if not at the nub of the evidence treated in the deficit-difference controversy are considerations of language development in children, particularly the issue of developmental lags. What theoretical grounds are there for deciding whether a child's progress in language acquisition is deficit or different? One basis can be developed from what is currently called *developmental psycholinguistics*. Although Osser (Chapter 13) and Menyuk (Chapter 10) describe this area in detail, a few main points will be sketched here.

Current thinking on developmental psycholinguistics centers mostly upon a nativist view of language acquisition which stresses that children are biologically predisposed to develop language and that the environment triggers rather than serves up the stages of development. This, of course, is contrary to the more traditional learning-theory-based, environmentalist views that a child's genetic asset in language acquisition is his superior learning capability, and that his linguistic knowledge and skills are solely the product of his experiences. The nativist position carries with it the concept of a distinction between a child's linguistic knowledge and all of the varied facets and factors of his actual speaking and listening behaviors, one factor of which is the aforementioned knowledge. Language acquisition is seen as the process by which this linguistic knowledge develops in the child. It is argued that this development can be described by discovering the types of linguistic rules operating in the child's repertoire and by correlations between the stages of such rule development and maturational factors (including brain development) of the organism. Should these maturational factors appear abnormal, and expectations in rule development not prevail, then there are grounds for expecting deficiency. This position, though theoretical and still being modified, does point the way toward a relatively rigorous developmental definition of linguistic deficiency, and one which can surmount dialect or outright language differences. Such classification of deficiency, moreover, should also have a direct and practical manifestation—if deficient, the child would not be functioning within the norm of *any* speech community. A final note is that if we take heed of the speech clinician's definition of *speech and hearing disorder* (Yoder, Chapter 19), then we should avoid some of the confusion wrought when it is suggested that the poverty child needs some type of speech therapy.

Sociolinguistic Theory

Given a relatively rigorous definition of linguistic deficiency, there is still the problem of describing linguistic differences. Here, contemporary research in sociolinguistics, particularly in urban language studies (Shuy, Chapter 16), seems to hold promise for dealing with the problem.

As already mentioned, an important generalization is that many of the variations in dialect can be reliably correlated with social stratification, ethnicity, and even the circumstances of speech situations. This generalization points to the position that many of what are referred to as deviations or errors or substandard features of language are in reality marks of consistent, well-ordered, grammatical systems exercised within the norms of some particular subgroup of speakers. As I have discussed in more detail (Chapter 18), the negative attitudes held by many toward such features is evidence of the strong prescriptionist tendencies for standard English perpetuated by our schools.

An emerging generalization in sociolinguistic theory is that the normal development of a child's language must be viewed relative to the demands of his primary speech community. Thus, one may see the linguistic problems of the Indian (Osborn, Chapter 12), Spanish-speaking American (John and Horner, Chapter 8), or Negro (Chapters 2, 9, 17) in a very different light when it is revealed that these are problems found, not within his speech community, but when he must meet the challenges of another community—typically, speakers of standard English. Additionally, Labov argues that many of the dialect differences that identify speakers of nonstandard English are trivial relative to meaning—that is, they are simply superficial alternatives for expressing the same things as could be said in standard English. However, even if a contrast in nonstandard-standard English does not differ in meaning, there is still the question of its social significance. As I have speculated in Chapter 18, these presumably superficial points of dialect contrast may serve an indexing and identifying role, marking the deeper boundaries which divide social structures within the larger community.

Added to the sociolinguistic perspective is the theorizing of Bernstein (Chapter 3) who has attempted to correlate different family organization types with styles of speech. That is, as a child is reared within a particular family structure, he internalizes some of its organizational and communication characteristics in the styles of speech he acquires. These styles in turn serve to perpetuate those kinds of organizational characteristics in families and, to some extent, also in the larger society of which the family is a part. One can reason from this type of picture to the concern for variables of the speech situation, a topic treated by Cazden in Chapter 5. It is within the range of such situations that the communicative demands of a given subculture are met by the performance capabilities of its members. Finally, and from a somewhat unique approach, there is the sociolinguistic research described by Entwisle in Chapter 7. In her studies of the correlations between the socioeconomic characteristics of parents and the kinds of word associations made by their children, the results surprisingly show a kind of linguistic-semantic advantage held by the poverty child over the middle-class child. Unfortunately, this advantage vanishes by third grade.

BREAKING THE POVERTY CYCLE

Even when returning to the larger issue of the sociocultural aspects of poverty, it is difficult to leave the deficit-difference controversy behind. Extension of its contrasts apply in any consideration of antipoverty strategies.

The deficit position puts the onus of the poverty problem on the poor— i.e., as one poverty population breeds another. The difference position puts the onus on all of society—as one segment has shut out another. Abstractly, both positions can be extended and interpreted within the poverty cycle. From the deficit point of view, populations stay in the cycle because of lack of capability to escape, whereas from the difference point of view, populations stay in the cycle because the majority society keeps them there. Strategies for breaking the cycle carry further salient contrasts. The deficit position would have the equalization of economic opportunity gained by intervening in the sociocultural development and education of the poverty child so as to make him a candidate for the majority society. Thus it is not unusual that at a vitriolic extreme, opponents of this position have used the term *racism*. The difference proponents would change society more than the individual in poverty, the goal being to equalize economic opportunity but at the same time respecting (and maintaining the opportunity for) sociocultural differences. Here the opponents' counter-invective has been the *noble savage* argument.

To pursue more practical contrasts in the two positions we can again consider the poverty cycle, but this time in terms of points for intervention. Where the two positions show most contrast in interventional strategies is in the sociocultural half of the cycle. Here the deficit position has led to a strong emphasis upon intervention into the preschool development of the poverty child so as to lessen the gap between his capabilities at school age and the requirements of the educational system. Such intervention is best known in the form of the preschool program Head Start. But additional programs have also been directed at the child-rearing practices of the family (Parent and Child Centers), a kind of head–Head-Start, and in supplementing school programs so as not to lose the "benefits" of Head Start (Program Follow Through). In brief the strategy is to prepare the child for candidacy into the economic mainstream, but the candidacy may be a sociocultural one, too.

The difference theorists would turn more to the schools than to the child. Here the argument is that schools should be designed to accept a polycultural input and to prepare these children for, hopefully, a full participation in a polycultural society. Some of the key assumptions and extensions of this position can be summarized as follows. The culturally different child has typically progressed normally, hence schools should be able to build upon what he does know, rather than starting from scratch. Building upon what he does know will avoid the cultural depreciation and eventual self-depreciation (or total alienation) now promoted by the schools. Making schools polyculturally oriented will be the first step in the reformation of a now-polycultural society with monocultural opportunity.

The two positions show contrast, too, when one considers the socioeconomic half of the cycle, particularly in view of current proposals for some type of direct economic equalization such as found in plans for a negative income tax or types of income guarantees. Such intervention is not welfare in the sense of temporarily aiding families in financial distress; it is instead a long range plan for control over economic equilibrium. Under the assumptions of the deficit position, such plans would also require continued intervention into the sociocultural phase of the poverty cycle, presumably because persons in poverty could not grasp opportunity even if it were given. By contrast, if the difference theorists are correct, families should be able to take advantage of economic righting without an additional major range of programs to compensate for sociocultural deficits.

The larger point to be made here is that even in the most recent theorizing about poverty and its alleviation we are again faced with the deficit-difference controversy. Thus while the topic of language and poverty may seem at first to be a very narrow view of a very major problem, it ultimately leads us to perhaps the most crucial question of all: *Whether the goal of economic opportunity for all carries with it the price of a monocultural society.*

REFERENCES

Bereiter, C., and Engelmann, S. *Teaching Disadvantaged Children in the Preschool*. Englewood Cliffs, N. J.: Prentice-Hall, 1966.

Bernstein, B. Social class and linguistic development: a theory of social learning. In A. H. Halsey, J. Floud, and A. Anderson, eds., *Education, Economy and Society*. New York: Free Press, 1961.

Cazden, Courtney B. Subcultural differences in child language: an inter-disciplinary review. *Merrill-Palmer Quarterly* 1966, 12: 185–219.

Deutsch, M., and associates. *The Disadvantaged Child*. New York: Basic Books, 1967.

Hess, R. D., and Shipman, Virginia. Early experience and the socialization of cognitive modes in children. *Child Development* 1965, 36: 869–86.

Jensen, A. R. How much can we boost IQ and scholastic achievement? *Harvard Educational Review* 1969, 39: 1–123.

Chapter 2

TEACHING READING IN AN URBAN NEGRO SCHOOL SYSTEM

Joan C. Baratz*

The inner-city Negro child is failing in our schools. His inability to read is a major challenge to contemporary educators because of its relationship to the child's self-esteem and his ultimate social effectiveness.

Failure to acquire functionally adequate reading skills not only contributes to alienation from the school as a social institution (and therefore encourages dropping out), but it goes on to insure failure in mainstream job success. There is certainly a relationship between reading success or failure on the one hand, and receptivity to or alienation from the society in which those reading skills are highly valued (Labov and Robins 1967; see Labov 1967, and Chap. 9 in this volume). It is almost impossible to underestimate the chain of reactions which can be touched off by the early and continued educational failure which so many disadvantaged Negro children experience in even the most well-intentioned schools. Because the educational system has been ineffective in coping with teaching inner-city children to read, it treats reading failure (in terms of grading, ranking, etc.) as if this failure were due to intellectual deficits of the child rather than to methodological inadequacies in teaching procedures. Thus the system is unable to teach the child to read, but very quickly teaches him to regard himself as intellectually inadequate, and therefore, of low self-worth and low social value.

---

*Education Study Center, Washington, D. C.
A slightly more technical version of this paper appeared under the same title in Joan C. Baratz and Roger W. Shuy, eds., *Teaching Black Children to Read* (Washington, D. C.: Center for Applied Linguistics, 1969). We are indebted to the Center for Applied Linguistics for permission to include this version in the present volume.

Despite the enormous expenditure of energy in remedial reading programs, children in the ghetto are still not learning to read. Although the difficulties of teaching reading to a portion of the population is a unique problem for the United States, the problem itself is not unique. The parallels are quite clear between the difficulty we are experiencing in teaching reading to the disadvantaged Negro child with those of emergent countries which are attempting to make a multicultured population literate in a single national tongue.

THE DEFICIT FALLACY

In his recent report on the Washington, D.C., school system, Passow (1967, p.4) indicated that the central question that must be answered is: "What are the educationally relevant differences which the District's pupils bring into the classroom and what kinds of varied educational experiences must be provided by the schools to accommodate these differences?" One major, educationally relevant difference for Washington, D.C., as for ghettos across the nation, is that of language. The Negro ghetto child is speaking a significantly different language from that of his middle-class teachers. Most of his middle-class teachers have wrongly viewed his language as pathological, disordered, "lazy speech." This failure to recognize the interference from the child's different linguistic system, and consequent negative teacher attitudes toward the child and his language, lead directly to reading difficulties and subsequent school failure. Understanding that the inner-city child speaks a language that is well ordered but different in many respects from standard English, is crucial to understanding how to educate him. Unfortunately, there is a tendency for the educator to think of the black child with his nonstandard speech as a "verbal cripple" whose restricted language leads to, or is caused by, cognitive deficits.

If we look briefly at the research and research assumptions concerning the language of Negro children, we can see how this erroneous notion of verbal inadequacy evolved.

When reviewing the literature, one finds three major professions concerned with describing the language and cognitive abilities of black children: educators, psychologists (mainly child development specialists), and linguists. Educators were the first to contribute a statement about the language difficulties of these children—a statement that amounted to the assertion that these children were, virtually, verbally destitute, i.e., they couldn't talk, and if they did, it was deviant speech, filled with errors. The next group to get into the fray, the psychologists, reconfirmed initially that the children did not talk, and then added the sophisticated wrinkle that if they did talk, their speech was such that it was a deterrent to cognitive growth. The last group to come into the

picture were the linguists who, though thoroughly impressed with the sophisticated research of the psychologist, were astonished at the naivete of his
pronouncements concerning language. The linguist began to examine the language of black children and brought us to our current conceptions of the
language abilities of these children, namely, that they speak a well-ordered,
highly structured, highly developed language system which in many aspects
is different from standard English.

We have a fascinating situation here where three professions are assessing
the same behavior—the child's oral language production and comprehension
—but with varying assumptions, so that they see different things. However, it
is not merely another example of the parable of the six blind men describing
the elephant and asserting than an elephant equaled that portion of the elephant that the blind man happened to be touching—for in the parable all men
were partially correct, and an elephant could be adequately described in the
sum total of their "observations." But when we look at the assumptions of the
educator, the psychologist, and the linguist, we find that there are actually
some premises held by one profession (for example, the psychologists' view
that a language system could be underdeveloped) that another profession sees
as completely untenable (for example, linguists, who consider such a view of
language so absurd as to make them feel that nobody could possibly believe
it and therefore to refute it would be a great waste of time). The educator
worked under the assumption that there is a single way of speaking and that
everyone who does not speak in this "grammar-book" fashion is in error.
(Indeed, although the psychologist may not recognize it, he tacitly adheres to
this principle when he defines language development in terms of "correct"
standard English usage.) This assumption also is untenable to the linguist, who
is interested in the structure and function of an utterance. To him the discussion of a hierarchial system that says that a double negative (e.g., *they don' have
none*) is inferior to a single negative (e.g., *they haven't any*) is meaningless. The
linguist simply wishes to describe the rules of the system that allow a speaker
of that system to generate a negative utterance—or any other complex structure—that is considered grammatical and understood as intended by the
speakers of the system.

THE LINGUISTIC VIEW

The linguist takes it as basic that all humans develop language. After all, there
is no reason to assume that black African bush children develop a language
and black inner-city Harlem children do not! Subsumed under this is that the
language is a well-ordered system with a predictable sound pattern, grammatical structure, and vocabulary (in this sense, there are no "primitive" lan-

guages). The linguist assumes that any verbal system used by a community that
fulfills the above requirements is a language and that no language is structurally better than any other language; that is, French is not better than German,
Yiddish is not better than Gaelic, Oxford English is not better than standard
English, and so on. The second assumption of the linguist is that children learn
language in the context of their environment. That is to say, a French child
learns French not because his father is in the home or his mother reads him
books, but because it is the language that he hears continually from whatever
source, and it is the language that individuals in his environment respond to.
The third assumption the linguist works with is that by the time a child is five
he has developed language; he has learned the rules of his linguistic environment.

What are those rules and how have they been determined? By using ghetto
informants, linguists such as Stewart (1964, 1965; see Chap. 17 in this volume,
or 1967, 1968), Dillard (1966, 1967), Bailey (1965, 1968), Labov (1967; see
Chap. 9 in this volume), Loman (1967) and Wolfram (1969) have described
some of the linguistic parameters of Negro nonstandard English. Differences
between standard English and Negro nonstandard occur to varying degrees in
regard to the sound system, grammar, and vocabulary.

Although Negro nonstandard has many phonemes similar to those of
standard English, the distribution of these phonemes varies from standard
English. For example, $/i/$ and $/e/$ may not be distinguished before nasals, so
that a " pin" in Negro nonstandard may be either an instrument for writing
a letter or something one uses to fasten a baby's diaper. Sounds such as $/r/$
and $/l/$ are distributed so that "cat" may mean that orange vegetable that one
puts in salads (standard English *carrot*) as well as the four-legged fuzzy animal,
or a "big black dude." The reduction of $/l/$ and $/r/$ in many positions may
create such homonyms as "toe" meaning a digit on the foot, or the church-bell
sound (standard English *toll*). Final clusters are reduced in Negro nonstandard so that "bowl" is used to describe either a vessel for cereal or a very brave
soldier (standard English *bold*).

These are but a few of the many instances where Negro nonstandard
sound usage differs from standard English. It is no wonder then, that Cynthia
Deutsch (1964) should find in her assessment of auditory discrimination that
disadvantaged black children did not "discriminate" as well as white children
from middle-class linguistic environments. She administered a discrimination
task that equated "correct responses" with judgments of equivalences and
differences in standard-English sound usage. Many of her stimuli, though
different for the standard English speaker (e.g., *pin-pen*) are similar for the
Negro nonstandard speaker. She attributed the difference in performance of
disadvantaged children to such things as the constant blare of the television
in their homes, and there being so much "noise" in their environment that the

children tended to "tune out." However, black children make responses based on the kind of language they consider appropriate. In the same way that *cot* (for sleeping), *caught* (for ensnared); or *marry* (to wed), *Mary* (the girl), and *merry* (to be happy) are not distinguished in the speech of many white people (so that they would say on an auditory discrimination test that *cot* and *caught* were the same), *pin* and *pen* are the same in the language of ghetto blacks. The responses that the black child makes are on the basis of the sound usage that he has learned in his social and geographical milieu, and do not reflect some difficulty in discriminating.

The syntax of low-income Negro children also differs from standard English in many ways (unfortunately the psychologist, not knowing the rules of Negro nonstandard has interpreted these differences not as the result of well-learned rules, but as evidence of "linguistic underdevelopment"). Some examples of the differences are provided below.

1. When you have a numerical quantifier such as 2, 7, 50, etc., you do not have to add the obligatory morphemes for the plural, e.g., *50 cent, 2 foot.*
2. The use of the possessive marker is different. For example, the standard English speaker says "John's cousin"; the nonstandard Negro speaker says *John cousin.* The possessive is marked here by the contiguous relationship of John and cousin.
3. The third-person singular has no obligatory morphological ending in non-standard, so that "she works here" is expressed as *she work here* in Negro nonstandard.
4. Verb agreement differs, so that one says *she have a bike, they was going.*
5. The use of the copula is not obligatory, e.g., *I going, he a bad boy.*
6. The rules for negation are different. The double negative is used: standard English "I don't have any" becomes *I don' got none* in Negro nonstandard.
7. The use of "ain't" in expression of the past; Negro nonstandard present tense is *he don't go,* past tense is *he ain't go.*
8. The use of "be" to express habitual action: *he working right now* as contrasted with *he be working every day.*

These are just a few of the rules that the nonstandard speaker employs to produce utterances that are grammatical for other speakers in his environment.

STUDIES OF DIFFERENCES

Baratz and Povich (1967) assessed the language development of a group of five-year-old black Head Start children. They analyzed speech responses to photographs and to Children's Apperception Test cards, using Lee's (1966) developmental-sentence-types model. A comparison of their data and Menyuk's (1964) on restricted and transformational types of white middle-class children was performed. Results indicated that the Negro Head Start child is not delayed in language acquisition. The majority of his utterances are on the kernel and transformational levels of Lee's developmental model. His transformational utterances are similar to those appearing above; he has learned the many complicated structures of Negro nonstandard English.

But how did the psychologist manage to come to the erroneous conclusion that the black child has an insufficient or underdeveloped linguistic system? The psychologist's basic problem was that his measures of "language development" were measures based on standard English (Bereiter 1965; Thomas 1962; Deutsch 1964; Klaus and Gray 1968). From these he concluded that since black children do not speak standard English, they must be deficient in language development.

Despite the misconceptions of the educator and psychologist concerning language and linguistic competence, the linguists for their part have described the differences between Negro nonstandard and standard English in some detail. The following is a list of some of the syntactic differences between the two systems.

VARIABLE	STANDARD ENGLISH	NEGRO NONSTANDARD
Linking verb	He *is* going	He . . . goin'
Possessive marker	Joh*n's* cousin	Joh*n* . . . cousin
Plural marker	I have five cent*s*	I got five cent . . .
Subject expression	John . . . lives in New York	John *he* live in New York
Verb form	I *drank* the milk	I *drunk* the milk
Past marker	Yesterday he walk*ed* home	Yesterday he walk . . . home
Verb agreement	He run*s* home	He run . . . home
	She *has* a bicycle	She *have* a bicycle
Future form	I *will* go home.	I*'ma* go home
"If" construction	I asked *if he did it*	I ask *did he do it*
Negation	I *don't* have *any*	I *don't* got *none*
	He *didn't* go	He *ain't* go
Indefinite article	I want *an* apple	I want *a* apple
Pronoun form	*We* have to do it	*Us* got to do it
	His book	*He* book
Preposition	He is over *at* his friend's house	He over *to* his friend house
	He teaches *at* Francis Pool	He teach . . . Francis Pool.

Be	Statement: He *is*	Statement: *He be*
	here all the time	here
Do	Contradiction: No,	Contradiction: No,
	he isn'.	he *don't*

But what of these differences? All the linguists studying Negro nonstandard English agree that these differences are systematized, structured rules within the vernacular. They agree that these differences can interfere with the learning of standard English, but they do not always agree as to the precise nature of these different rules. This leads to varied disagreements as to why a particular feature exists (e.g., phoneme deletion as against creolization), but it does not dispute the fact that the linguistic feature is present. No one would fail to agree that standard English has a grammatical structure and uniqueness, and many descriptions of that structure have been written. Yet it is probably true that no two linguists would agree in all details on how to write the grammar. This equally explains the current controversy among linguists as to how one writes the grammar of Negro nonstandard English.

This language difference, not deficiency, must be considered in the educational process of the black ghetto child. In 1953, the UNESCO report regarding the role of language in education stated that:

> It is axiomatic that the best medium for teaching a child is his mother tongue. Psychologically, it is the system of meaningful signs that in his mind works automatically for expression and understanding. Sociologically, it is a means of identification among the members of the community to which he belongs. Educationally he learns more quickly through it than through an unfamiliar medium. (UNESCO 1953, p. 17)

Since 1953, studies implementing the recommendations of the UNESCO report have clearly illustrated the importance of considering the vernacular in teaching reading in the national language (Modiano, 1968). It seems clear that a structural knowledge of nonstandard vernacular and the ways it can interfere with learning to speak and read standard English are indispensable to teaching ghetto Negro children. Goodman (1965) and Bailey (1965), along with Stewart (esp. 1969), have all discussed the possibility of interference from the dialect on acquiring the ability to read. Labov (1967) has also stressed that the ignorance of standard English rules on the part of the speakers of standard English and the ignorance of nonstandard English rules on the part of teachers and text writers may well be the cause for the reading failures that occur in the schools. In addition, Wiener and Cromer (1967) in their article on reading and reading difficulty discussed the need to determine the relationship between language differences and reading problems, because a failure to be explicit about the the relationship between reading and previously acquired auditory language often leads to ambiguities as to whether a particular difficulty is a reading problem, language problem, or both.

But does the black nonstandard speaker have to contend with interference from his own dialect on his performance in standard English? The following experiment clearly suggests that he does.

The subjects in this experiment were third- and fifth-graders from two schools in the Washington, D.C. area. One was an inner-city, impact-aid school; all the children in this school were Negroes. The other was a school in Maryland, located in an integrated low-middle-income community; all the children from that school were white. There were thirty-nine third graders (24 Negroes, 15 whites) and thirty-eight fifth graders (23 Negroes and 15 whites).

A sentence repetition test was constructed that contained thirty sentences, fifteen in standard English and fifteen in Negro nonstandard. The sentences were presented on tape to each child, who was asked to repeat the sentence after hearing it once. Examples of some of the sentences presented are:

STANDARD ENGLISH: Does Deborah like to play with the girl that sits next to her in school?

NONSTANDARD ENGLISH: Do Deborah like to play wid da girl that sit nex' ta her at school?

STANDARD ENGLISH: I asked Tom if he wanted to go to the picture that was playing at the Howard.

NONSTANDARD ENGLISH: I aks Tom do he wanna go to the picture that be playin' at the Howard.

STANDARD ENGLISH: She was the girl who didn't go to school because she had no clothes to wear.

NONSTANDARD ENGLISH: Dat girl, she ain' go ta school 'cause she ain' got no clothes to wear.

Each child was asked to repeat exactly what he heard as best he could. After the subject had responded to all the stimuli on the tape, he was asked to listen to two stimuli, one in standard English and the other in nonstandard English. After each of these stimuli, the subject was asked to identify who was speaking from among a group of pictures of Negro and white men, women, and children.

The data were analyzed to ascertain what had happened to the following constructions:

STANDARD CONSTRUCTION	NONSTANDARD CONSTRUCTIONS
Third person singular	Non-addition of third person -s
Presence of copula	Zero copula
Negation	Double negation; and *ain't*
If + subject + verb	Zero "If" + verb + subject
Past markers	Zero past morpheme

Possessive marker   Zero possessive morpheme
Plural   Use of *be*

Age did not appear to play an important role in identification of the speaker. Although the speaker of both the standard and the Negro nonstandard sentences was white, third-graders identified the standard sentence 73.3 percent of the time as being spoken by a white man, and the nonstandard sentence 73.3 percent of the time as being spoken by a Negro. Of the fifth-graders, 83.3 percent judged the standard sentence as being spoken by a white man, while 93.3 percent judged the nonstandard sentence as being spoken by a Negro. Eighty percent of the white children and 76.6 percent of the Negro children identified standard sentences as being spoken by a white man. Nonstandard sentences were judged to be spoken by a Negro 83.3 percent of the time by both Negro and white children.

As expected, the results of this sentence-repetition experiment indicated that whites were superior to Negroes in repeating standard English sentences, but on the other hand, Negroes were far superior to whites in repeating Negro nonstandard English sentences. Performance on the various sentences was influenced more by the race of the child than by his age.

Although white speakers did significantly better than black speakers in responding to standard English sentences, it is clear that the black child's responses to standard English were consistent. An examination of the black child's errors revealed that he did not fail utterly to complete the sentence; he did not jumble his response; nor did he use a "word salad." His error responses were consistent. For example, in response to the stimulus: "I asked Tom *if he wanted to* go to the picture that was playing at the Howard," 97 percent of the children responded with: "I aks Tom *did he wanna* go to the picture at the Howard." In response to: "*Does* Deborah like to play with the girl *that sits* next to her in school," 60 percent of the Negro children responded: "*Do* Deborah like to play wif the girl *what sit* next to her in school."

This same behavior was evident in the white children when asked to repeat Negro nonstandard sentences. Black children were superior to white children in repeating these stimuli. Here again the error responses followed a definite pattern. For example, in response to the stimulus: "I aks Tom do he wanna go to the picture that be playin' at the Howard," 98 percent of the white children said: "I asked Tom if he wanted to go to the picture that was playing at the Howard." Similar "translations" to standard English occurred on the other Negro nonstandard constructions.

The fact that the standard and nonstandard speakers exhibited similar translation behaviors when confronted with sentences that were outside of their primary code indicates quite clearly that the language deficiency that has so often been attributed to the low-income Negro child is not a language deficit so much as a difficulty in code switching when the second code (standard English) is not as well learned as the first (nonstandard English).

The kinds of errors the two groups made (e.g., white children adding the third person -s to nonstandard stimuli and Negroes deleting the third person -s on standard stimuli) represent an intrusion of one language code (the dominant system) upon the structure of the other code (the newly acquired system). If, indeed, nonstandard were not a structured system with well-ordered rules, one would not expect Negro children to be able to repeat the nonstandard structures any better than did the white children, nor would one expect nonstandard patterns to emerge systematically when lower-class Negroes responded to standard sentences. Neither of these expectations was upheld. The Negro children were in fact able to repeat nonstandard structures better than were the white children, and they did produce systematic nonstandard patterns when responding to standard sentences. The converse was true for the whites; they responded significantly better to standard structures and exhibited systematic standard patterns when responding to nonstandard stimuli.

The results of this research clearly indicate that (1) there are two dialects involved in the education complex of black children (especially in schools with a white middle-class curriculum orientation); (2) black children are generally not bidialectal; and (3) there is evidence of interference from their dialect when black children attempt to use standard English.

Since the disadvantaged Negro child, as this study suggests, like the Indian having to learn Spanish in Mexico or the African having to learn French in Guinea, has to contend with the interference from his vernacular in learning to read, how does his task of learning to read differ from that of the middle-class "mainstream American" child? When the middle-class child starts the process of learning to read, his problem is primarily one of decoding the graphic representation of a language which he already speaks. The disadvantaged black child must not only decode the written words, he must also "translate" them into his own language. This presents him with an almost insurmountable obstacle since the written words frequently do not go together in any pattern that is familiar or meaningful to him. He is baffled by this confrontation with (1) a new language with its new syntax; (2) a necessity to learn the meaning of graphic symbols, and (3) a vague, or not so vague (depending upon the cultural and linguistic sophistication of the teacher) sense that there is something terribly wrong with his language.

Although both the middle-class child and the disadvantaged Negro child are at the beginning faced with the task of relating their speech to a graphic representation that appears to be arbitrary and without a direct one-to-one correspondence to their speech (e.g., the silent *e* in *love*, the silent *k* in *knife*, the *k* as represented in *cut* and *kite*, and the *s* as represented in *Sue*, *cement*), the cards are stacked against the inner-city Negro child because his particular phoneme patterning is not considered in the curriculum at this early phase, so that when he reads "hep" for *help,* "men' " for *mend,* "boil" for *ball,* the teacher presumes that he cannot read the word. *Hep* and *help, men'* and *mend,* and *boil* and *ball* are homonyms in the inner-city child's vernacular.

IMPLICATIONS

Despite the obvious mismatching of the phoneme systems of the teachers and text writers and of the inner-city child, the difficulties of the disadvantaged Negro child cannot be simplified solely to the pronunciation and phoneme differences that exist in the two systems. There is an even more serious problem facing the inner-city child, namely, his unfamiliarity with the syntax of the classroom texts. Although the middle-income child also must read texts that are at times stilted in terms of his own usage, there is no question that the language of the texts is potentially comparable to his system. That is to say, although he does not speak in the style of his reading text, he has the rules within his grammar to account for the occurrence of the textbook sentences. However, the textbook style is more unfamiliar to the ghetto child than it is to his middle-class standard-speaking age-mate because much of the reading text is not a part of his potential syntactic system.

Because of the mismatch between the child's system and that of the standard English textbook, because of the psychological consequences of denying the existence and legitimacy of the child's linguistic system, and in the light of the success of vernacular teaching around the world, it appears imperative that we teach the inner-city Negro child to read using his own language as the basis for the initial readers. In other words, first teach the child to read in the vernacular, and then teach him to read in standard English. Such a reading program would not only require accurate vernacular texts for the dialect speaker, but also necessitate the creation of a series of "transition readers" that would move the child, once he had mastered reading in the vernacular, from vernacular texts to standard English texts. Of course, success of such a reading program would depend upon the child's ultimate ability to read standard English.

The advantages of such a program would be threefold; first, success in teaching the ghetto child to read; second, the powerful ego supports of giving credence to the child's language system and therefore to himself, and giving him the opportunity to experience success in school; and third, with the use of transitional readers the child would have the opportunity of being taught standard English (which cannot occur by linguistic swamping, since his schoolmates are all vernacular speakers) so that he could learn where his language system and that of standard English were similar and where they were different. Such an opportunity might well lead to generalized learning and the ability to use standard English more proficiently in other school work.

The continued failure of programs of reading for ghetto children that offer more of the same—more phonics, more word drills, and so on—have indicated the need of a new orientation toward teaching inner-city children to read. Any such program must take into account what is unique about the ghetto child that is impairing his ability to learn within the present system. This paper has suggested that one of the essential differences to be dealt with in teaching inner-city Negro children is that of language. The overwhelming evidence of the role that language interference can play in reading failure indicates that perhaps one of the most effective ways to deal with the literacy problems of Negro ghetto youth is to teach them using vernacular texts that systematically move from the syntactic structures of the ghetto community to those of the standard-English-speaking community.

REFERENCES

Bailey, B. Linguistics and nonstandard language patterns. Paper presented to the National Council of Teachers of English, 1965.

————. Some aspects of the impact of linguistics on language teaching in disadvantaged communities. *Elementary English* 1968, 45: 570–79.

Baratz, J., and Povich, E. Grammatical constructions in the language of the Negro preschool child. Paper presented at the national meeting of the American Speech and Hearing Association, 1967.

Bereiter, C. Academic instruction and preschool children. In R. Cobin and M. Crosby, eds., *Language Programs for the Disadvantaged*. Champaign, Ill.: National Council of Teachers of English, 1965.

Deutsch, C. Auditory discrimination and learning: social factors. *Merrill-Palmer Quarterly* 1964, 10: 277–96.

Dillard, J. The Urban Language Study of the Center for Applied Linguistics. *Linguistic Reporter* 1966, 8: 1–2.

————. Negro children's dialect in the inner city. *Florida Foreign Language Reporter*, 1967, Fall.

Goodman, K. Dialect barriers to reading comprehension. *Elementary English* 1965, 42: 853–60.

Klaus, R. and Gray, S. *The Early Training Project for Disadvantaged Children: A Report after Five Years*. Monograph of the Society for Research in Child Development, 1968, Vol. 33.

Labov, W. Some sources of reading problems for Negro speakers of nonstandard English. In A. Frazier, ed., *New Directions in Elementary English*, Champaign, Ill.: National Council of Teachers of English, 1967.

Labov, W., and Robins, C. A note on the relation of reading failure to peer-group status. Unpublished paper, 1967.

Lee, L. Developmental sentence types: A method for comparing normal and deviant syntactic development. *J. Speech and Hearing Disorders* 1966, 31: 311–30.

Loman, B. *Conversations in a Negro American Dialect*. Washington, D. C.: Center for Applied Linguistics, 1967.

Menyuk, P. Syntactic rules used by children from preschool through first grade. *Child Development* 1964, 35: 533–46.

Modiano, N. National or mother language in beginning reading: a comparative study. *Research in the Teaching of Reading* 1968, 1: 32–43.

Passow, A. *Toward Creating a Model Urban School System: A Study of the District of Columbia Public Schools*. New York: Teachers College, Columbia University, 1967.

Stewart, W. Foreign language teaching methods in quasi-foreign language situations. In W. Stewart, ed., *Non-standard Speech and the Teaching of English,* Washington, D. C.: Center for Applied Linguistics, 1964.

————. Urban Negro speech: sociolinguistic factors affecting English teaching. In R. Shuy, ed., *Social Dialects and Language Learning.* Champaign, Ill.: National Council of Teachers of English, 1965.

————. Sociolinguistic factors in the history of American Negro dialects. *Florida Foreign Language Reporter* 1967, Fall.

————. Continuity and change in American Negro dialects. *Florida Foreign Language Reporter* 1968, 6.

————. Negro dialect in the teaching of reading. In J. C. Baratz and R. W. Shuy, eds., *Teaching Black Children to Read.* Washington, D. C.: Center for Applied Linguistics, 1969.

Thomas, D. Oral language sentence structure and vocabulary of kindergarten children living in low socio-economic urban areas. *Dissertation Abstracts* XXIII (1962), 1014.

UNESCO. *The Use of Vernacular Languages in Education;* Monographs on Fundamental Education, VIII. Paris: UNESCO, 1953.

Wiener, M. and Cromer, W. Reading and reading difficulty: a conceptual analysis. *Harvard Educational Review* 1967, 37: 620–43.

Wolfram, W. A. *A Sociolinguistic Description of Detroit Negro Speech.* Washington, D. C.: Center for Applied Linguistics, 1969.

Chapter 3

A SOCIOLINGUISTIC APPROACH TO SOCIALIZATION: WITH SOME REFERENCE TO EDUCABILITY

Basil Bernstein*

Since the late 1950s in the United States there has been a steady outpouring of publications concerned with the education of children of low social class whose material circumstances are inadequate, or with the education of black children of low social class whose material circumstances are chronically inadequate. An enormous research and educational bureaucracy has developed in the United States, financed by funds obtained from federal, state, or private foundations. New educational categories have been developed—the *culturally deprived,* the *linguistically deprived,* the *socially disadvantaged,* and the notion of compensatory education was introduced as a means of changing the status of those children in the above categories. Ideas on compensatory education issued in the form of massive preschool programs (as in Head Start), large-scale research programs in the early 1960s (e. g., Deutsch and associates 1967), and a plethora of small-scale intervention or enrichment programs for preschool children (e. g., Bereiter and Engelmann 1966) or children in the first years of compulsory education (program Follow Through). Very few sociologists were involved in these studies. On the whole they were carried out by psychologists.

*Sociological Research Unit, University of London Institute of Education

The work reported in this paper was supported by grants from the Nuffield Foundation, Department of Education and Science, and from the Ford Foundation, to whom, gratefully, acknowledgement is made. A similar version of this paper is scheduled for publication under the same title in J. J. Gumperz and D. Hymes, *Directions in Sociolinguistics* (Holt, Rinehart & Winston).

The focus of these studies and programs was on the child in the poverty family and on the local classroom relationship between teacher and child. In the last few years one can detect a change in this focus. As a result of the movements toward integration and the opposed movement toward segregation (the latter a response to the wishes of the various Black Power groups), more studies in the United States have shifted the focus to problems of the schools. Rosenthal and Jacobson's classic study, *Pygmalion in the Classroom* (1968) drew attention to the critical importance of the teacher's expectations of the child.

Most studies or programs along the lines discussed above have dealt directly with the language of children, and among these a number have incorporated with varying degrees of accuracy some of the concepts of language and socialization which appeared in the author's early writings of the late 1950s and the early 1960s (e.g., Bernstein 1958, 1959, 1960a, b, 1961). Most notably, the reference has often been to the differentiation between *restricted* and *elaborated* language codes, and the consequences that these codes hold for the people who use them. The use (or abuse) of this distinction has sometimes led to the erroneous conception that a restricted code can be directly equated with linguistic deprivation, linguistic deficiency, or being nonverbal.

The error here seems largely due to the superficial focus upon the spoken details of the two codes rather than the broader conception of the codes as referring to the transmission of the basic or deep-meaning structures of a culture or subculture. This broader conception links code with communication context, and both with social structure. To emphasize this broader concept, consider the distinction between uses of language which can be called context-bound and uses of language which are less context-bound. This distinction can be seen in two stories constructed by Hawkins (1969), based upon his analyses of the speech of middle-class (story *A*) and working-class, (*B*), five-year-old children in London. The children were given a series of four pictures which portrayed the sequence of a story and they were invited to tell this story. The first picture shows some boys playing football near a house; the second shows the ball breaking a window; the third shows a man making a threatening gesture; in the fourth, the children are moving away, while watched by a woman peering out of the window.

> *(A)* Three boys are playing football and one boy kicks the ball —and it goes through the window—the ball breaks the window— and the boys are looking at it—and a man comes out and shouts at them—because they've broken the window—so they ran away—and then that lady looks out of her window—and she tells the boys off.
> *(B)* They're playing football—and he kicks it and it goes through there—it breaks the window and they're looking at it—and he comes out and shouts at them—because they've broken it—so they run away—and then she looks out and she tells them off.

With the first story the reader does not have to have the four pictures which were used as the basis for the story, whereas in the second story, the reader would require the initial pictures in order to make sense of the story. The first story is free of the context which generated it, whereas the second story is much more closely tied to its context. As a result the meanings of the second story are implicit, whereas the meanings of the first story are explicit. It is not that the working-class children do not have in their lexical repertoire the vocabulary used by the middle-class children. Nor is it the case that the children differ in their tacit understanding of the linguistic rule system. Rather what we have here are differences in the use of language arising out of a specific context. One child makes explicit the meanings which he is realizing through language for the person he is telling the story to, whereas the second child does not do this to the same extent. The first child takes very little for granted, whereas the second child takes a great deal for granted. Thus for the first child the task was seen as a context in which his meanings were required for explication, whereas the task for the second child was not seen as a task which required such explication of meaning. However, it would not be difficult to imagine a context where the first child would produce speech rather like that of the second.

What we are dealing with here are differences between children in the way they realize, in their language use, what is apparently the same context. We could say that the speech of the first child generated universalistic meanings in the sense that the meanings are freed from the context and so understandable by all. Whereas the speech of the second child generated particularistic meanings, in the sense that the meanings are closely tied to the context and would be only fully understood by others if they had access to the context which originally generated the speech. Thus universalistic meanings are less bound to a given context, whereas particularistic meanings are severely context-bound.

Let us take another example. One mother in controlling her child places a great emphasis upon language because she wishes to make explicit and to elaborate for the child certain rules and the reasons for the rules and their consequences. In this way the child has access through language to the relationships between his particular act which evoked the mother's control, and certain general principles, reasons, and consequences which serve to universalize the particular act. Another mother places less emphasis upon language in controlling her child; she deals with only the particular act and does not relate to general principles and their reasoned basis and consequences. Both children learn that there is something they are supposed (or not supposed) to do, but the first child has learned rather more than this. The grounds of the mother's acts have been made explicit and elaborated, whereas the grounds of the second mother's acts are implicit; they are unspoken. Our research shows just this: that the social classes differ in terms of the contexts which evoke certain linguistic realizations. Mothers in the middle class (but it is important to add, not all) relative to the working class (and again, it is important to add, not all), place greater emphasis upon the use of the language in socializing the child into the moral order, in disciplining the child, and in the communication and recognition of feeling. Here again we can say that the first child is oriented towards universalistic meanings which transcend a given context, whereas the second child is oriented towards particularistic meanings which are closely tied to a given context and so do not transcend it. This does not mean that working-class mothers are nonverbal, only that they differ from the middle-class mothers in the contexts which evoke universalistic meanings. They are not linguistically deprived, neither are their children.

We can generalize from these two examples and say that certain groups of children, through the forms of their socialization, are oriented towards receiving and offering universalistic meanings in certain contexts, whereas other groups of children are oriented towards particularistic meanings. The linguistic realization of universalistic orders of meanings (elaborated code) are very different from the linguistic realization of particularistic orders of meaning (restricted code), and so are the forms of the social relation (e.g., between mother and child) which generate these. We can say, then, that what is made available for learning, how it is made available, and the patterns of social relation are also very different.

If one is to apply these concepts in dealing with problems of social class, problems of education, and so on, it is necessary to avoid a superficial emphasis upon distinctions in speech, per se, and to broaden the focus to include the relations among the characteristics of social structures, their communication systems, and the linguistic demands of these systems. In the materials which follow I have attempted to examine these relations, beginning first with general relations which explain the social origins of linguistic codes, then turning to more specific relations between family-role systems and linguistic codes. Finally, I have included some of my current speculations on the consequences associated with attempts to change the linguistic codes of groups as well as my critical view of how the concept of compensatory education is misconceived as an agent for such change.

RELATIONS AMONG SOCIAL CLASSES, LINGUISTIC CODES, AND FAMILY ROLE SYSTEMS

If a social group, by virtue of its class relation—that is, as a result of its common occupational function and social status—has developed strong communal bonds; if the work relations of this group offer little variety, little exercise in decision making; if to be successful assertion must be a collective rather than an individual act; if the work task requires physical manipulation and control rather than symbolic organization and control; if the diminished authority of the man at work is transformed into an authority of power at home; if the home is overcrowded and limits the variety of situations it can offer; if the children socialize each other in an environment offering little intellectual stimuli—if all these attributes are found in one setting, then it is plausible to assume that such a social setting will generate a particular form of communication which will shape the intellectual, social, and affective orientation of the children.

If we look into the work relationships of this particular group, its community relationships, and its family-role systems, it is reasonable to argue that the genes of social class may well be carried less through a genetic code but far more through a communication code that a social class itself promotes. Such a communication code will emphasize verbally the communal rather than the individual, the concrete rather than the abstract, the substance rather than the elaboration of processes, the here-and-now rather than exploration of motives and intentions, and positional rather than personalized forms of social control. To say this about a communication system is not to disvalue it, for such a communication system has a vast potential, a considerable metaphoric range and a unique aesthetic capacity. A whole range of diverse meanings can be generated by such a system of communication. It so happens however, that this communication code directs the child to orders of learning and relevance that are not in harmony with those required by the school. Where the child is sensitive to the communication system of the school and thus to its orders of learning and relation, then the experience of school for this child is one of symbolic and social development. Where the child is not sensitive to the communication system at school, then this child's experience at school becomes one of symbolic and social change. In the first case we have an elaboration of social identity, and in the second case a change of social identity. Thus between the school and community of the working-class child there may exist a cultural discontinuity based upon two radically different systems of communication.

The Social Origins of Linguistic Codes

How do different forms of communication arise? The particular form of a social relation acts selectively upon what is said, when it is said, and how it is said; the form of the social relation regulates the options that speakers take up at both syntactic and lexical levels. For example, an adult talking to a child will use a form of speech in which both the syntax and vocabulary are relatively simple. The speech used by members of an army combat unit on maneuvers will clearly be different from the same members' speech with the unit's chaplain. To put it another way, the consequences of the form the social relation takes are transmitted in terms of certain syntactic and lexical selections (see, for example, Ervin-Tripp 1964, 1967; Hymes 1967; Blom and Gumperz in press). Thus different forms of social relation can generate very different speech systems or linguistic codes.

Different speech systems or codes create for their speakers different orders of relevance and relation. The experience of the speakers may then be transformed by what is made significant or relevant by different speech systems. As the child learns his speech—learns specific codes which regulate his verbal acts—he learns the requirements of his social structure. The experience of the child is transformed by the learning generated by his own apparently voluntary acts of speech. The social structure becomes, in this way, the substratum of the child's experience essentially through the manifold consequence of the linguistic process. From this point of view, every time the child speaks or listens, the social structure is reinforced in him and his social identity is shaped. The social structure becomes the child's psychological reality through the shaping of his acts of speech.

The same argument can be stated rather more formally. Individuals come to learn their social roles through the process of communication. A social role from this point of view is a constellation of shared, learned meanings through which individuals are able to enter stable, consistent, and publicly recognized forms of interaction with others. A social role can then be considered as a complex coding activity controlling both the creation and organization of specific meanings and the conditions for their transmission and reception. If the communication system which defines a given role is essentially that of speech, it should be possible to distinguish critical social roles in terms of the speech forms they regulate. By critical social roles is meant those through which the culture is transmitted. These roles are learned in the family, in the age or peer group, in the school, and at work. These are the four major sets of roles learned in the process of socialization. As a person learns to subordinate his behavior to the linguistic code through which the role is realized, then orders of meaning, of relation, and of relevance are made available to him. The complex of meanings, for example, generated within the role system of a family, reverberates developmentally in the child to shape his general conduct. Children who have access to different speech systems or codes—that is, children who learn different roles by virtue of their families' class positions in a society—may adopt quite different social and intellectual orientations and procedures despite a common developmental potential.

The concept of linguistic code, as used here, refers to the principle which regulates the selection and organization of speech events. Two fundamental types of linguistic codes may be defined in terms of the relative ease or difficulty of predicting the syntactic alternatives which speakers take up to organize meanings. If it is difficult to predict across a representative range the syntactic options or alternatives taken up in the organization of speech, this form of speech is called an elaborated code. In the case of an elaborated code, the speaker will select from a wide range of syntactic alternatives and these will be flexibly organized. By contrast, a restricted code is one where it is much less difficult to predict, across a representative range, the syntactic alternatives, as these will be drawn from a narrow range. Whereas there is flexibility in the use of alternatives in an elaborated code, in the case of a restricted code the syntactic organization is marked by rigidity. Notice that these codes are not defined in terms of vocabulary or lexical selection. Jargon does not constitute a restricted code. It is likely, however, that the lexical differentiation of certain semantic fields will be greater in the case of an elaborated code.

It is clear that context is a major control upon syntactic and lexical selections, consequently it is not easy to give general linguistic criteria for the isolation of the two codes. Derivations from the theory would be required in order to describe syntactic and lexical usage by any one speaker in a specific content.[1] The definitions given in the text would have increasing relevance to the extent that speakers could freely determine for themselves the nature of the constraints upon their syntactic and lexical selections. In other words, the less rigid the external constraints upon the speech the more appropriate the general definitions. The more rigid the external constraints then the more specific the criteria required. It is also important to point out that the codes refer to cultural, not genetic, controls upon the options speakers take up. The codes refer to performance, not to competence, in the Chomsky (1965, esp. pp. 3-15) sense of these terms. There may be different performances within every degree of competence. On the other hand, it is certainly the case that these codes can be seen as different kinds of communicative competence as this concept is expounded by Dell Hymes (in press).

If a speaker is oriented toward an elaborated code, then the code will facilitate the speaker in his attempts to make explicit (verbally) his intentions. If a speaker is oriented toward a restricted code, then this code will not facilitate the verbal expansion of the speaker's intent. In the case of an elaborated code the speech system requires more complex planning than in the case of a restricted code. For example, in the case of an elaborated code the time dimension of the verbal planning of the speech is likely to be longer (provided that the speaker in not quoting from himself) than in the case of a restricted code (Bernstein, 1962). It will be argued that the events in the environment,

---

[1]Research carried out by the Sociological Research Unit shows that there are considerable differences between middle-class and working-class children five years and seven years of age in their ability to switch grammar and vocabulary in accordance with the nature of the speech context (see Hawkins 1969; Henderson, in press; and Hakulinen, Lewis, and Taylor, in prep.).

which take on significance when these codes are used, are different whether the events be social, intellectual, or affective. These two codes, elaborated and restricted, are generated by a particular form of social relation. Indeed they are likely to be a realization of different social structures. They do not necessarily develop solely because of a speaker's innate ability.

We can now ask what is responsible for the simplification and rigidity of the syntax of a restricted code. Why should the language across certain semantic fields be drawn from a narrow range? Why are the speaker's intentions relatively unelaborated verbally? Why should the speech controlled by a restricted code tend to be fast, fluent, with reduced articulatory clues, the meanings often discontinuous, condensed, and local, involving a low level of syntactic and vocabulary selection where the "how" rather than the "what" of the communication is important? Above all, why should the unique meaning of the person be implicit rather than verbally explicit? Why should the code orient its speakers to a low level of causality?

A restricted code will arise where the form of the social relation is based upon closely shared identifications, upon an extensive range of shared expectations, upon a range of common assumptions. Thus a restricted code emerges where the culture or subculture raises the "we" above "I."[2] Such codes will emerge as both controls and transmitters of the culture in such diverse groups as inmates of prisons, the age group of adolescents, army personnel, friends of long standing, or between husband and wife. The use of a restricted code creates social solidarity at the cost of the verbal elaboration of individual experience. The type of social solidarity realized through a restricted code points toward mechanical solidarity, whereas the type of solidarity realized through elaborated codes points toward organic solidarity (Durkheim, 1933). The form of communication reinforces the form of the social relation rather than generating a need to create speech which uniquely fits the intentions of the speakers. Restricted codes do not give rise to the verbally differentiated first person, *I*, in communication. If we think of the communication pattern between married couples of long standing, then we see that meaning does not have to be fully explicit; a slight shift of pitch or stress, a small gesture, can carry a complex meaning. Communication goes forward against a backcloth of closely shared identifications and affective empathy which removes the need to elaborate verbal meaning and logical continuity in the organization of the speech. Indeed, orientation in these relationships is less towards the verbal but more towards the extraverbal channel; for the extraverbal channel is likely to be used to transmit intentions, purposes, and qualifications. It follows from this

---

[2]In different ways Vygotsky (trans. 1962), Sapir (1921), and Malinowski (1935) have drawn attention to the simplification of grammar and the lack of specificity in vocabulary where social relationships are based upon closely shared assumptions and identifications.

that speakers limited to a restricted code may well have difficulty in switching from this form of communication to other forms of communication which presuppose different role relations and so different social orientations. Thus a restricted code may limit certain kinds of role switching. However, it must be pointed out that a restricted code may be entirely appropriate for certain contexts.

An elaborated code will arise wherever the culture or subculture emphasizes the "I" over the "we." It will arise wherever the intent of the other person cannot be taken for granted. Insofar as the intent of the other person cannot be taken for granted, then speakers are forced to elaborate their meanings and make them both explicit and specific. Meanings which are discreet and local to the speaker must be cut so that they are intelligible to the listener. And this pressure forces the speaker to select among syntactic alternatives and encourages differentiation of vocabulary. In terms of what is transmitted verbally, an elaborated code encourages the speaker to focus upon the experience of others, as different from his own. In the case of a restricted code, what is transmitted verbally usually refers to the other person in terms of a common group or status membership. What is said here epitomizes the social structure and its basis of shared assumptions. Thus restricted codes could be considered status or positional codes whereas elaborated codes are person-oriented. An elaborated code, in principle, presupposes a sharp boundary or gap between self and others which is crossed through the creation of speech which specifically fits a differentiated "other." In this sense, an elaborated code is oriented towards a person rather than a social category or status. In the case of a restricted code, the boundary or gap is between sharers and nonsharers of the code. In this sense a restricted code is positional, or status-oriented, not person-oriented. It presupposes a generalized rather than a differentiated other.

In the case of an elaborated code, the orientation is toward the verbal channel, for this channel will carry the elaboration of the speaker's intentions. In the case of restricted codes, to varying degrees it is the extraverbal channels which become objects of special perceptual activity. It is important to point out that restricted code users are not nonverbal, only that the speech is of a different order from that controlled by an elaborated code. If an elaborated code creates the possibility for the transmission of individual symbols, then a restricted code creates the possibility for the transmission of communalized symbols.

Open and Closed Role Systems

What are the differences in the types of social roles realized through these two codes? Let us first consider the range of alternatives that a role system (say that of the family) makes available to individuals for the verbal realization of different meanings. Here we need to distinguish between two basic orders of meaning, one which refers to interpersonal and intrapersonal relationships (person meanings) and one which refers to relationships between objects (object meanings). We could call a role system which reduced the range of alternatives for the realization of verbal meaning a *closed type*. It would follow that the greater the reduction in the range of alternatives, the more communal or collective the verbal meanings and the lower the order of complexity and more rigid the syntactic and vocabulary selections—thus the more restricted the code. On the other hand, we could call a role system which permitted a range of alternatives for the realization of verbal meanings an *open type*. It would follow that the greater the range of alternatives permitted by the role system, the more individualized the verbal meanings, the higher the order, and the more flexible the syntactic and vocabulary selection and so the more elaborated the code.[3]

Note in Figure 1 that we can now take this simple dichotomy a little further by picking up the distinction between object and person orders of meaning. A role system may be open or closed with respect to the alternatives it permits for the verbal realization of object or person meanings.

In the area where the role system is open, novel meanings are likely to be encouraged and a complex conceptual order explored. In the area where the role system is closed, novel meanings are likely to be discouraged and the conceptual order limited. Where the role system is of the closed type, verbal meanings are likely to be assigned; the individual (or child) steps into the meaning system and leaves it relatively undisturbed. Where the role system is of the open type, the individual is more likely to achieve meaning on his own terms, and here there is the potential of disturbing or changing the pattern of received meanings. We can begin to see that in the area where the role system is open, there is an induced motivation to explore, to actively seek out, and to extend meanings. By contrast, where the role is closed there is little induced motivation to explore and create novel meanings.

Let us take this a little further. Where the role system is open, the individual or child learns to cope with ambiguity and isolation in the creation

---

[3]Our research shows that the speech of middle-class children, compared to working-class children, at five years of age is more likely to show greater differentiation in the open-set lexical choices within the nominal group, and that these children are more flexible in their use of the grammatical options they take up within the nominal group. The working-class children are more likely to select pronouns as heads (especially third person pronouns). Where pronouns are used as heads, the possibility of both modification and qualification is considerably reduced. Further, our research shows (as did Loban's 1966) that middle-class children are more likely, in certain contexts, to use more frequently than working-class children modal verbs of uncertainty or possibility. A detailed discussion of the above will be found in Hawkins's forthcoming monograph (in prep.).

Figure 1

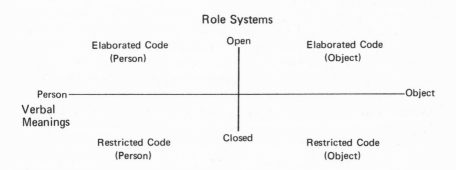

Role Systems

of verbal meanings; where the role system is closed, the individual or child foregoes such learning. On the contrary, he learns to create verbal meaning in social contexts which are unambiguous and communalized. Such an individual or child may experience considerable tension and role conflict if he persistently attempts to individualize the basis of his syntactic and vocabulary selections. In so doing, this member of a closed role system would be attempting to create or point toward an open role system. Notice that the source of strain here is precisely that which an individual or child learns to do if he is socialized into an open role system. Thus a source of role strain in restricted codes is precisely the role relationship appropriate to an elaborated code.

We have now outlined a framework which shows a causal connection between role systems, linguistic codes, and the realization of different orders of meaning and relevance. Emphasis has been laid upon the relationship between roles and codes. It is possible for a person to be able to write in an elaborated code but not to be able to speak it, for he may not be able to manage the face-to-face requirements of the role (over and above the matter of dialect). This may apply, for example, to a bright working-class boy whose early socialization has offered little training in the social role. In the same way, object and person forms of an elaborated code not only create different orders of meaning, they are realized through different role relations. It may well be that the cultural tension between the sciences—especially the applied sciences —and the arts reflects the different role relations which control object and person forms of the elaborated code.

The organization of education often produces cleavage and insulation between subject and levels, and this serves to reduce role and code switching between person and object modes of the elaborated code and from restricted to elaborated codes.

If we ask, what are the general social forces which influence the development of elaborated and restricted codes and their person and object modes, the answer is likely to be found in two sources. These shape the culture and role systems of the four major socializing agencies: the family, the age group (or peer group), the school, and work. One major source of the movement from restricted to elaborated codes lies in increases in the complexity of the division of labor. This changes both the nature of the occupational roles and their linguistic bases. The two modes of the elaborated code may well be affected by the movement of economies from goods to service types. The shift from a goods to a service economy may well promote the development of the person mode of an elaborated code. The second major source of code orientation is likely to be the character of the central value system. Pluralistic societies are likely to produce strong orientations toward the person mode of an elaborated code, whereas monolithic societies are likely to strengthen the orientation toward the object mode. (It should be remembered that persons can be treated as objects.)

Linguistic Codes and Educability

The nature of the division of labor and the character of the central value system affect linguistic codes through the way they affect the culture and role systems of the major socializing agencies, especially the family and school. Social-class position regulates the occupational function, the intrafamilial and interfamilial relationships, and responsiveness to the school. Thus we can expect, broadly speaking, to find both person and object modes of an elaborated code within the middle class, together with restricted codes. In the lower working class we could expect to find a high proportion of families limited to a restricted code. We might further expect that upwardly mobile working-class children would move toward the object rather than the person mode of the elaborated code.

Where children are limited to a restricted code, primarily because of the subculture and role systems of the family, community, and work, we can expect a major problem of educability whose source lies not so much in the genetic code but in the culturally determined communication code.

Children limited to a restricted code learn a code where the extraverbal (voice, gesture, facial expression, etc.) tends to become a major channel for the qualification and elaboration of individual experience. This does not mean that such children's speech output is relatively reduced. The verbal planning of the speech, relative to an elaborated code, involves a relatively low order and a rigidity of syntactic organization. The interpersonal and intrapersonal, although clearly perceived and felt, are less verbally differentiated. The concept of self which is developed through a restricted code does not itself become an area of inquiry as in the case of an elaborated code, particularly one where the orientation is toward persons. In the case of an elaborated code, such a code points to the possibilities which inhere in a complex conceptual hierarchy for the organization and expression of inner experience. This is much less the case where experience is regulated by a restricted code, for this code orients its speakers to a less complex conceptual hierarchy and so to a low order of causality. What is made available for learning through elaborated and restricted codes is radically different. Social and intellectual orientations, motivational imperative and forms of social control, rebellion, and innovation are different. Thus the relative backwardness of many working-class children who live in areas of high population density or in rural areas, may well be a culturally induced backwardness transmitted by the linguistic process. Such children's low performance on verbal IQ tests, their difficulty with abstract concepts, their failures within the language area, their general inability to profit from the school, all may result from the limitations of a restricted code. For these children the school induces a change of code and with this a change in the way the children relate to their kin and community. At the same time we often offer these children grossly inadequate schools with less than able teachers. No wonder they often fail—for those who have "more," tend to receive more and become more, while those who have "less," receive less and become less.

Lest the restricted code be misinterpreted as simply poor language, we must be aware that it contains a vast potential of meanings. It is a form of speech which symbolizes a communally based culture. It carries its own aesthetic. It should not be disvalued. We must ensure that the material conditions of the schools we offer, their values, social organization, forms of control and pedagogy, the skills and sensitivities of the teachers, are refracted through an understanding of the culture these children bring to the school. After all, we do no less for the middle-class child. The problem does not stop there. Housing conditions must be improved, social services extended, and preschool education developed.

We cannot say what a child is capable of, as we do not have a theory of what an optimum learning environment looks like. But even if such a theory existed, we (the British) seem unwilling to redirect national expenditure toward physically creating it for children on the scale required.

ON THE CAUSAL RELATION BETWEEN ROLE SYSTEMS AND LINGUISTIC CODES

Let us now look more closely at the relationships between role systems and linguistic codes, as the connection between social class and linguistic codes is too imprecise. Such a relationship omits the dynamics of the causal relationship. In order to examine these dynamics it is necessary to look at the nature of the role system of a family and its procedures of social control. The basic requirement of such an analysis is that it be predictive and so give rise to measurable criteria for evaluating the interrelationships among role systems, forms of social control, and linguistic orientations.

It is possible to evaluate family-role systems by reference to the principles which for any one family controls the allocation of decision making. Thus we could consider the effect of the allocation of decision making on the extent and kind of interactions among members of the family. Let us postulate two types of families—positional and person-oriented families.[4]

Positional Families

If the area of decision making is invested in the member's formal status (father, mother, grandfather, grandmother, age of child, or sex of child), this type of family will be called positional. (It is not necessarily authoritarian, or "cold" rather than "warm.") In such a family there would be a clear separation of roles. There would be formally defined areas of decision making and judgments accorded to members of the family in terms of their formal status. In such a family type we could expect close relationships and interactions between the parents and grandparents. Futher, we could expect that the parents would closely regulate the child's relationships with his age peers (if middle class) or that the child's relationship with his peers would be relatively independent of the parents' regulation (if working class). Thus, in certain positional families the socialization of the child might well be through his own age-mates. Positional families, it is suggested, would give rise to a weak or closed communication system.

Person–Oriented Families

By contrast we could consider a family type where the range of decisions, modifications, and judgments were a function of the psychological qualities of the person rather than a function of formal status. In such families there is clearly a limit to the interactions set by age development and status ascription. Status ascription would be reduced (age, sex, age relations) compared to positional families. Unlike certain positional families, the socialization of the children would never be left to the child's age group. The behavior of the child

---

[4]This distinction between positional and personal forms of control was set out by the author in a paper (Family Role Systems, Socialization and Communication) given to the Conference on Cross-Cultural Research into Childhood and Adolescence, University of Chicago, 1963. At that time the term *status* was used instead of *positional*. The terms *positional* and *personal* have also been used by Hanson (1965), although his discussion is somewhat differently focused, for he sees positional relationships as contractual and personal relationships as noncontractual.

in his peer group would be subject to discussion with parents rather than to their legislation. Person-oriented families would give rise to a strong or open communication system.

Positional–Personal Family Types and Open and Closed Communication Systems

Person-oriented Families—Open Communication System.   In person-oriented families the limits on the extent to which decisions may be open to discussion would be set by the psychological characteristics of the person rather than by his formal status. Simply, the ascribed status of the member, for many activities, would be weakened by his achieved status. Children, for example, would achieve a role within the communication system in terms of their unique social, affective, and cognitive characteristics. Clearly, if there is reduced segregation of role and less formal definition, then the parents and the children operate with a greater range of alternatives, that is, with greater role discretion. Inasmuch as the role discretion is wide (the range of alternatives of the role in different social situations), then individual choices can be made and offered. Verbal communication of a particular kind is generated. It is not just a question of more talk but talk of a particular kind. Judgments, their bases and consequences, would form a marked content of the communications. The role system would be continuously eliciting and reinforcing verbal signaling, making explicit individual intentions, qualifications, and judgments. The role system would be continuously accommodating and assimilating the different intents of its members. Looked at from another point of view, children would be socializing parents as much as parents would be socializing the children, for the parents would be very sensitive toward the unique characteristics of the children. These characteristics would be verbally realized and so enter into the communication system. Thus there would develop an open communication system which would foster and provide linguistic means and role learning for the verbal signaling and making explicit of individual differences, together with the explication of judgments, their bases and consequences. Of fundamental importance, the role system would promote communication and orientation toward the motives and dispositions of others.[5] Note also that in such a family the child learns to make his role rather than this being formally assigned to him. Children socialized within such a role and communication system learn to cope with ambiguity and ambivalence, although clearly there may well be pathological consequences if a sufficient sense of boundary is not provided.

Positional Families—Closed Communication Systems.   In this type of

---

[5]For more on this point, see Bernstein and Henderson (1969), Bernstein and Brandis (in press), and Kohn (1959a,b).

family judgments and the decision-making process would be a function of the status of the member rather than a quality of the person. There would be segregation of roles and a formal division of areas of responsibility according to age, sex, and age-relation status. Boundary areas, instead of generating discussion and accommodation, might well become border disputes settled by the relative power inhering in the respective statuses. The children's communication system might well be open only in relation to their age-mates, who would then become a major source of learning and relevance. If socialization is reciprocal in person-oriented families, it tends to be unilateral in positional families. The role system here is less likely to facilitate the verbal elaboration of individual differences and is less likely to lead to the verbal elaboration of judgments, their basis and consequences; it does not encourage the verbal exploration of individual intentions and motives. In a person-oriented family the child's developing self is differentiated by continuous adjustment to the verbally realized and elaborated intentions, qualifications, and motives of others. In positional families the child takes over and responds to status requirements. Here he learns what can be called a communalized role as distinct from the individualized role of person-oriented families. In positional families, the range of alternatives which inhere in the roles (role discretion) is relatively limited, consequently the communication system reduces the degree of individual selection from alternatives. Of course, within positional families there is sensitivity toward persons, but the point is that these sensitivities are less likely to be raised to a level of verbal elaboration so as to become objects of special perceptual activity and control. In positional families the child develops either within the unambiguous roles of his family, or within the clearly structured roles of his age-mate society, or both. Thus these children are less likely to learn to cope with problems of role ambiguity and ambivalence. They are more likely to avoid or foreclose upon activities or problems which carry this potential.

Social Control and Family Types. It is clear that the two family types generate radically different communication systems, which we have characterized as open and closed. It has been suggested that these systems have important socializing and linguistic consequences. Let us now examine differences in forms of social control with, again, special reference to uses of spoken language.

We have said that insofar as a role system is personal rather than positional in orientation, then it is a relatively more unstable system. It is continuously in the process of assimilating and accommodating the verbally realized but different intentions, qualifications, and motives of its members. Tensions arise which are a function of the characteristics of the role system. Special forms of arbitration, reconciliation, and explanation develop. These tensions only in the last resource are managed in terms of relative power which inheres in the respective statuses. Social control is based upon linguistically elaborated meanings rather than upon power. However, it is clearly the case that power is still the ultimate basis of authority.

In positional families where the status arrangements reduce the instability which inheres in person-oriented families, social control is affected either through power or through referring behavior to universal or particular norms which regulate status. In person-oriented families social control is likely to be realized through verbally elaborated means oriented to the person, while in positional families social control is likely to be realized through less elaborated verbal means, less oriented to the person but more oriented toward the formal status of the regulated (i.e., the child).

It is of crucial importance to analyze the procedures of social control so as to show, among other things, that person-oriented families very early in the child's life sensitize him and actively promote his language development in order that favored modes of control can be applied. In positional families the modes of social control depend less upon individually created and elaborated verbal meanings, and within these families there is less need to sensitize the child toward and promote the early development of verbally elaborated forms of speech.

Modes of Social Control[6]

We must now distinguish between imperative modes of social control and social control based upon appeals. Two forms of appeal will be further distinguished. Underlying these distinctions in modes of control is the role discretion (the range of alternatives) accorded.

Imperative Modes. The imperative mode of control reduces the role discretion accorded to the regulated (the child). It allows the child only the external possibilities of rebellion, withdrawal, or acceptance. The imperative mode is realized through a restricted code; for example, "Shut up," "Leave it alone," "Get out" (or extraverbally through physical coercion).

Appeals. Appeals are modes of control where the regulated is accorded varying degrees of discretion in the sense that a range of alternatives, essentially linguistic, are available to him. Thus social control which rests upon appeals does permit, to different degrees, reciprocity in communication and thus linguistically regulated learning. These appeals may be broadly grouped into two types, and each type further classified into subtypes. The two broad types are positional and personal appeals.

Positional appeals do not work through the verbal realization of the

---

[6]A coding manual for social control has been developed and applied to the speech of mothers and their children. It is available from the Sociological Research Unit, University of London Institute of Education.

personal attributes of the controllers (parents) or regulated (children). They do refer the behavior of the regulated (child) to the norms which inhere in a particular or universal status.

"You should be able to do that by now" (age-status rule).
"Little boys don't cry" (sex-status rule).
"People like us don't behave like that" (subcultural rule).
"Daddy doesn't expect to be spoken to like that" (age-relation rule).

Positional appeals are not necessarily disguised forms of the imperative mode. Consider the following situation where a child is learning his sex role. A little boy is playing with a doll.

MOTHER: "Little boys don't play with dolls."
CHILD: "I want the dolly."
MOTHER: "Dolls are for your sister."
CHILD: "I want the doll" (or he still persists with the doll).
MOTHER: "Here, take the drum instead."
As compared with a situation where the mother says:
"Why do you want to play with the doll—they are so boring—why not play with the drum?"

The essence of positional appeals is that, in the process of learning the rule, the child is explicitly linked to others who hold a similar universal or particular status. The rule is transmitted in such a way that the child is reminded of what he shares in common with others. Where control is positional the rule is communalized. Where control is positional the "I" is subordinate to the "we." Positional control is realized through a specific linguistic variant. As will be shown later, positional appeals can be given in restricted or elaborated codes. They can be complex linguistically and conceptually, as in the case of a West Point or public school boy who is reminded of his obligations and their origins. Where control is positional the child (the regulated) learns the norms in a social context where the relative statuses are clear-cut and unambiguous. Positional appeals may lead to the formation of shame rather than guilt. In the case of positional appeals, however, certain areas of experience are less verbally differentiated than in the case of personal appeals. Positional appeals transmit the culture or subculture in such a way as to increase the similarity of the regulated with others of his social group. They create boundaries. If the child rebels, he very soon challenges the bases of the culture and its social organization and this may force the controller (parent or teacher) into the imperative mode.

In personal appeals the focus is upon the child as an individual rather than upon his formal status. Personal appeals take into account interpersonal or intrapersonal components of the social relationship. They work very much at the level of individual intention, motive, and disposition and consequently are realized through a distinctive linguistic variant. This again can be within restricted or elaborated codes. Areas of experience verbally differentiated through personal appeals are very different from the experiences controlled by positional appeals. The following example might help to bring out the distinctions.

Imagine a situation where a child has to visit his grandfather who is unwell and the child does not like to kiss him because the grandfather has not shaved for some time. One mother says to the child before they go:

MOTHER: Children kiss their Grandpa (positional).
CHILD: I don't want to—why must I kiss him always?
MOTHER: He's not well (positional)—I don't want none of your nonsense (imperative).
Another mother says in the same context:
MOTHER: I know you don't like kissing Grandpa, but he is unwell and he is very fond of you, and it makes him very happy.

The second example is perhaps blackmail, but note that the child's intent is recognized explicitly by the mother and linked to the wishes of another. Causal relations at the interpersonal level are made. Futher, in the second example, there is the appearance of the child having a choice (discretion). If the child raises a question, more explanation is given. Thus the mother lays out the situation for the child, and rule is learned in an individualized interpersonal context. In this way the rule is achieved by the child. The child, given the situation and the explanation, opts for the rule. In the first example, the rule is simply assigned in a social relationship which relies upon latent power for its effectiveness. Here we see another difference between positional and personal appeals, in that rules are assigned in positional control but achieved in personal control.

Where control is personal, whole orders of learning are made available to the child which are not there if control is positional. Where control is personal, each child learns the rule in a context which, so to speak, uniquely fits him; moreover, he learns the language through which this is realized. Where control is positional, learning about objects, events, and persons is reduced, and the child comes to learn that the power which inheres in authority may soon be revealed. Where control is personal, as distinct from positional, status differences are less clear-cut and ambiguities and ambivalences are verbally realized. Finally positional appeals may lead to the development of shame, but personal appeals may lead to the formation of guilt.

In the case of person-oriented appeals, the rights of the controller or parent which inhere in his formal status are less likely to come under attack than in the case of positional appeals. For in the case of personal appeals, what may be challenged are the reasons the controller gives or even a specific condition of the controller or parent (e.g., the child asks: "Do you always have a headache when I want to play?"). Thus personal appeals may act to protect the normative order from which the controller derives his rights; for here there is an attenuation of the relationship between power and the role system. In the case of positional appeals which shift rapidly to the imperative mode of control, the formal rights of the controller or parent may well be challenged, and with this the whole normative order from which the controller derives his rights can come under attack. Imperative or positional forms of control under certain conditions may lead the socialized to turn to alternative value systems. Further, where control is personal the basis of control lies in linguistically elaborated, individualized meanings. This may lead to a situation where the child attains autonomy, although his sense of social identity may be weakened. Such ambiguity in the sense of social identity, the lack of boundary, may move a child toward a radically closed value system and its attendant social structure. On the other hand, where control is positional, and, even more, where it is imperative, the child has a strong sense of social identity but the rules which he learns will be tied to specific contexts and his sense of autonomy may well be reduced. Finally, a child socialized by controllers who favor positional or imperative procedures becomes highly sensitive to specific role relations in the context of control. Such a child may be bewildered, initially, when placed in a context of control where personal procedures are used, since he may lack the orientation and the facility to take up the different options or alternatives which this form of control makes available. Person-oriented forms of control may induce role strain where the child has been socialized through imperative or positional forms of control.

It is very clear that in any one family, or even in any one context of control, all three (imperative, positional, and personal) modes may be used. It is also likely that within a given family, parents may share control modes or each may use a different mode. We can, however, distinguish between families, or at a greater level of delicacy, between parents, in terms of their preferred modes of control. It follows that we could also distinguish the modes of control which are used in any one context. We can summarize the consequences for learning which inhere in the three modes as follows:

MODE	LEARNING	LEVEL OF LEARNING
Imperative	Hierarchy	Restricted Code
Positional	Role Obligation and differentiation	{ (Restricted Code { (Elaborated Code
Personal	Interpersonal Intrapersonal	{ (Restricted Code { (Elaborated Code

Family Types—Open/Closed Communication Systems— Modes of Control

We can now link positional families with closed systems of communication and with positional, imperative modes of control. We can, in principle, distinguish between positional families whose preferred mode of control is imperative (the lower working class?) from positional families where the preferred mode is positional with relatively little use of physical coercion. We can distinguish between positional families according to whether the dominant code is elaborated or restricted. In the same way we can link person-oriented families with open communication systems operating with personal appeals. We can again distinguish between such families in terms of the dominant general code, elaborated or restricted. The latter tells us about the degree of openness of the communication system and its conceptual orientation. Thus the roles which children learn in those various families, their conceptual orientations, their perception and use of language, will all differ.[7]

It may be that we can now speculate about the dynamics of the object and the person modes of the two general codes as these have been discussed here. We suggested that a communication system can be open or closed with reference to relationships between objects or relationships within or between persons. We should bear in mind that persons, if they are treated in their status capacity, may be likened to objects.

We can in principle distinguish between two variants of person- and object-oriented elaborated or restricted codes. Figure 2 will aid us in this task.

1. Object- or person-oriented codes can lead to the exploration of means or ends. Thus we might consider that an object code (means) is likely to be used by members of the applied sciences where individuals tend to work within established principles and derive from them specific applications. In the case of an object code (ends) the individual is less concerned with the specific application of established principles than with their explorations. Here we might expect the orientation to be toward objects at the level of ends.

2. If the form of control is personal and the code restricted, we might expect that the children would move initially toward a person-oriented restricted code of either the means or ends type. The predominant characteristic of the individuals in the quadrant would be their potentiality for change.

3. Families which use predominantly positional forms of control and elaborated codes are likely to socialize their children into an elaborated code object (means) where the code referents may be either relationships between

---

[7]It should be clear that in this discussion I have drawn upon a range of work in the literature of sociology and social psychology; in particular, Bott (1957), Foote (1961), Nye and Berardo (1966), and Bronfennbrenner (1958).

Figure 2

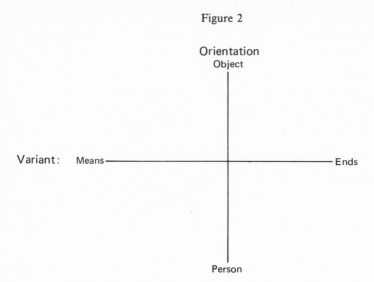

objects (future applied scientists?), or where the code referents are the status characteristics of persons (military, bureaucratic occupational positions).

4. Families which use predominantly personal forms of control are likely to develop an elaborated code person (means) where the referents emphasized are likely to be inner states and processes of the person. We might expect that such sociolinguistic socialization is likely to orient the children initially toward social positions which involve control relationships over persons.

5. It is difficult to speculate about the social origins of elaborated codes (ends), for the social psychology of creativity is still in its infancy. We might say that such socialization would induce: *(a)* marked egocentricity, *(b)* risk-taking, and *(c)* flexibility of boundary. In terms of the model used, we might then expect that where positional and personal forms of control are very much parent-specific, the child might be faced with a basic tension between inner and outer which he resolves by creative restructuring.

It is clearly the case that occupational functions are not simply given by primary socialization but are dominated by the nature of the educational and occupational systems. The point here is to emphasize the need for research to examine the linguistic consequences of role and control systems within families.

Social Class, Positional and Personal Families, and Social Change

In this analysis of class, family, and social change we might find positional families who are deeply imbedded in their community, operating essentially with imperative modes of control, where the children are socialized through

through unsupervised peers or age-mates. Here we could expect the development of restricted codes (object), and the hard core of the language and educability problem. It should also be possible to locate, within the working class, families who are moving toward personal forms of control within the general rubric of a restricted code. These families, we would expect, would be less tightly embedded within their local community, perhaps because of re-housing, or because the parents are actively confronting the complex relationships between their local subculture and the cultures of the wider society. Here we might find an orientation toward a restricted code (person) or a movement toward an elaborated code (person).

A further point is worth making. Within working-class positional (large) families, we should expect a marked difference between boys and girls in their use of language. Girls, especially older girls in such families, tend to take on mothering roles. Of equal relevance is the fact that they also mediate between parents and sibs. Their role, then, is more complex, as it combines a normal sib role with that of mediator and with that of controller. Further, girls are less tied to the activity-oriented, group-dominated, peer group social structure such as that of boys. Thus girls, especially older girls in such families, are likely to be person-oriented and to have to rely more upon forms of control based upon linguistically elaborated meanings than upon physical coercion. Finally, they are placed in situations involving a variety of role and code switching, e.g. girl-girl, girl-boy, girl controlling girls, girl controlling boys, girl mediating between parents and sibs. These factors are likely to develop a girl's orientation toward a more differentiated, more individualized use of language.[8]

Within the middle class we should be able to isolate positional and person-oriented families, who, according to this argument, should orientate their children initially (formal education could change this) to the two modes of object and person of an elaborated code. In the earlier section of this paper suggestions were made about the social origins of elaborated and restricted codes in terms of the increases in the complexity of the division of labor and

---

[8]Henderson's (in press) findings, as other research, indicate a marked superiority in the form-class usage of working-class girls compared to working-class boys. It is possible, however, that our eliciting techniques may well create contexts for girls in which they can demonstrate a socially promoted superiority. We have reason to believe that such superiority in girls is not wholly the result of earlier biological development. The girls (five years of age) of middle-class mothers who score low on an index of reported communication, offer speech where the vocabulary is less differentiated than the vocabulary of middle-class girls whose mothers score high on an index of reported communication. The findings of Bernstein and Brandis (in press) indicate that there is a subgroup of middle-class mothers (positional) who explain less and who are more coercive in the socializing of the girl than in the socializing of the boy. Thus, different uses of language by boys and girls may partly derive from family and age-group role learning. They may also be a function of the eliciting contexts constructed to obtain speech.

the character of the central value system. We shall now turn our attention to the social conditions which may produce positional and person-oriented families within the middle class and the working class.[9]

The literature strongly suggests that the traditional working-class family is of the positional type. For here, sustaining the transmission of the particular subculture, we find insulation between working-class and middle-class subcultures and social relationships (a product of the class system); high population density within limited territories; low rate of social mobility (through educational failure) producing intragroup marriage; social solidarity arising out of similarity of economic function and interests; unemployment; reciprocity of services and mutual help between families arising partly out of low income (and in the United States, a common ethnic origin and subculture). The weakening of the positional family type, with its closed system of communication limited to a restricted code, would result from the play of forces which would differentiate the family from its community and so weaken the transmission of collective beliefs and values, and the subsequent detailed regulation of behavior.

In England since the war, such weakening has begun as a result of: (1) greater affluence, greater geographical mobility, and therefore greater responsiveness to a wide range of influences which has been partly assisted by mass media; (2) rehousing into areas of relatively low population density; (3) a change in the power position of the wife through her independent earning capacity; (4) a change in attitude, towards both education and child development on the part of working-class groups, and therefore greater responsiveness to education and subsequent social mobility; (5) a change in the degree of solidarity among workers, arising, until recently, out of full employment and higher earnings; (6) a shift in the division of labor away from a goods, to that of a services, economy, part of a long term trend toward an economy which is now more person- than object-oriented. These different forces are beginning to weaken the transmission of the communally based, socially insulated, working-class subculture and have created the conditions for more individualized family systems.[10]

This is not to say that the working-class subculture has been eroded and replaced by middle-class beliefs, values, and norms; only that there now exist the conditions for more individualized and less communalized relationships.

In the United States (and we really are not entitled to discuss this fully

[9]A very interesting attempt to distinguish between entrepreneurial and bureaucratic families can be found in Miller and Swanson (1958).

[10]A good account of this movement is given by Goldthorpe and Lockwood (1963). For a general analysis of the effects of the interrelationships between the division of labor and the central value system upon the structure of socializing agencies, see Parsons (1964).

here) the situation is much more complex. Apart from attempts of the schools (which so far have not been outstandingly successful) the most important influence upon change of linguistic code is probably the Civil Rights movement. This movement and its various organizations are bringing about a change in the Negro's view of his own subculture, his relation to the white culture, and his attitude toward education. This movement has produced powerful charismatic leaders at both national and local levels, who are forcing Negroes to reassess and to reexamine their structural relationship to the society. This confrontation is likely to make new demands upon linguistic resources and to challenge the passivity of the old subculture and its system of social relationships. The language of social protest, with its challenging of assumptions, its grasping towards new cultural forms, may play an important role in breaking down the limitations of subculturally bound restricted codes.

On the other hand, middle-class changes in the orientations of family types might well reflect changes in the character of middle-class occupations —in particular, the movement from entrepreneurial to managerial, professional, and service-type occupations. At the same time, the indeterminancy of the value system has individualized choice and changed the basis of authority relationships within the family. The "science" of child development and its popularization through books, papers, and journals has also had an important influence, given the above conditions, in shaping role relationships and communication within middle-class families. It is likely that the personalizing of socialization agencies has gone further in the United States than in the United Kingdom. It is important to point out that family types may also be very much influenced by the nature of religious and political beliefs. On the whole, pluralistic societies like the United States and United Kingdom are likely to produce strong tendencies towards personalized socialization agencies, whereas societies with monolithic, centrally planned and disseminated value systems are likely to develop highly positional socializing agencies, generating object-oriented linguistic codes.

Summary

Let us now retrace the argument. We started with the view that the social organization and subculture of the lower working class would be likely to generate a distinctive form of communication through which the genes of social class would be transmitted. Second, two general types of linguistic codes (restricted and elaborated) were postulated and their social origins and regulative consequences analyzed. Third, it was suggested that the subculture of the lower working class would be transmitted through a restricted code while that of the middle class would realize both elaborated and restricted codes. This causal link was considered to be very imprecise and our discussion omitted the dynamics of the process. The fourth step entailed the construction of two types of family role systems, positional and personal, their causally related open and closed communication systems, and their procedures of social control. The fifth step established the causal link between restricted and elaborated codes and their two modes within positional and person-oriented family role systems. Finally, factors affecting the development and change of family types were discussed.

In the final sections of this paper we shall consider some possible consequences of linguistic code switching—that is, what is brought about when a segment of a society is undergoing change or is being changed—and summarize some views on the prospects of using compensatory education to facilitate such change.

SOME CONSEQUENCES OF CHANGE OF HABITUAL LINGUISTIC CODES

In contemporary societies, both in the West and in the newly developing societies, educational institutions are faced with the problems of encouraging children to change and to extend the way they normally use language. In the terms of this paper, this becomes a switch from restricted to elaborated codes. A change in linguistic code implies more than a change in syntactic and lexical selection. The view taken here and in other papers is that linguistic codes are basic controls on the transmission of a culture or subculture and are the creators of social identity. Changes in such codes involve changes in the means whereby order and relevance are generated, changes in role relationships, and in procedures of social control.

In another paper (Bernstein 1965) the author has distinguished his position from that of Whorf (see Carroll 1956), but believes that there are distillations or precipitations from the general system of meanings which inhere in linguistic codes and which exert a diffuse and generalized effect upon the behavior of speakers. Embedded in a culture or subculture may be a basic organizing concept, concepts, or themes, whose ramifications may be diffused throughout the culture or subculture. The speech forms through which the culture or subculture is realized transmit this organizing concept or concepts within their gestalt rather than through any one set of meanings. Figure 3 sets out the application of this essentially Whorfian thought to the linguistic codes and their social controls discussed in this paper. In this view an educationally induced change of code from a restricted code (object) to an elaborated code (person) involves a shift in organizing concepts from authority and piety toward one of identity—from an organizing concept which makes irrelevant

Figure 3

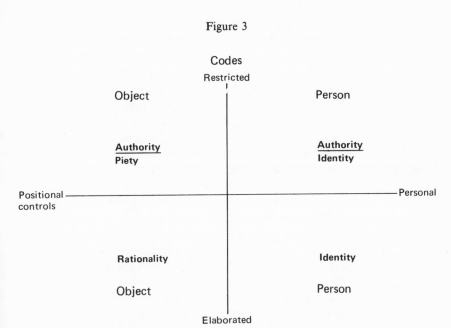

the question of personal identity to an organizing concept which places the notion of identity in the forefront of the personality. Individuals who are in the process of making such a switch of codes are involved in a basic cultural change at the level of meanings and at the sociological level of role. We need to know much more about the social and psychological consequences of radical shifts in linguistic codes.

It may be that the switch from a restricted code (object) is more likely to be toward an elaborated code (object) than toward the person mode of an elaborated code. In concrete terms, we might expect working-class children to move toward the applied sciences rather than toward the verbal arts. This shift from authority to rationality for working-class children may involve a less traumatic change in their role relations and systems of meanings and control than a shift from authority to identity. Authority and rationality are both positional in the sense that the individual works within a framework, within a system or structure, without a critical problem of ambiguity of ends. Where the organizing concept transmitted by the code is that of identity, the individual is faced with ambiguity at the level of ends, and often at the level of means. This speculation on no account should be taken to mean that it is more appropriate for individuals limited to a restricted code (object) to be guided toward the applied sciences or routine low-level supervisory functions, where persons are treated as objects. It means only that it may be expected that they may well make these choices rather than choose the verbal arts. They are more likely to be concerned with object processes than interpersonal and intrapersonal processes.

One might further expect the individuals starting from restricted codes (person) will move toward elaborated codes (person) rather than toward elaborated codes (objects). If they were to move toward the latter mode, it would be perhaps one where persons are treated as objects. Individuals in this quadrant, if they switch to elaborated codes, are likely to be restless in their search for belonging; or they might accept some belief system which creates it for them. Many may become teachers, writers, community protest leaders, or perhaps become involved in dropout movements or deviant groups. This code switch involves major problems of cultural conflict.

There are relatively few individuals who are capable of managing equally both modes of an elaborated code, although the social sciences perhaps may contain a number of these. The meanings, roles, and controls entailed in these two modes are somewhat antithetical. At the basis of the meanings of an elaborated code (object), is the notion of one integrated system which can generate order. In an odd way it is "objective-idealist" in character. At the basis of the meanings of an elaborated code (person) is a pluralism, a range of possibilities. It is "subjective-idealist" or romantic in character. Another way to see this might be to suggest that the major latent function of an elaborated code (object) is to remove ambiguity, while the major latent function of an elaborated code (person) is to create it.[11]

Obviously there is more to be thought about the matter of code switching; the ideas presented thus far are needed for such general discussion of how the sociolinguistic aspects of socialization apply in the consideration of the dynamics of social change.[12]

SOME COMMENTS ON COMPENSATORY EDUCATION

We have noted that both studies and programs focusing upon social change seem to mark an increasing concentration upon the school. Evidence of this in the United States can be seen in the writings of others (Passow 1963; Deutsch and associates 1967; Rosenthal and Jacobson 1968). In Great Britain we have been aware of the educational problem since the writings of Sir Cyril

---

[11]In this brief discussion I have not referred to the means/ends variants of object- and person-oriented linguistic codes. They should be borne in mind.

[12]The ideas presented in this section have been developed by M. Douglas, reader in social anthropology, University College, London, in her paper, "The Contempt of Ritual," given as the Acquinas Lecture, Black Friars, Oxford, March 1967.

Burt (1937) before the war. His book, *The Backward Child*, is probably still the best study we have. After the war a series of sociological surveys and public inquiries into education brought this educational problem into the arena of national debate, and so of social policy. In Wales there has been a large research unit financed by the Schools Council, concerned with compensatory education. Important research is taking place in the University of Birmingham into the problems of the education of Commonwealth children. The Social Science Research Council has given £175,000 for the development of special preschool programs concerned with introducing children to compensatory education.

It might be worth a few lines to consider the assumptions underlying this work and the concepts which describe it, particularly as the author's writings have sometimes been used (or, again, abused) to highlight aspects of the general problems and dilemmas.

To begin, the term compensatory education seems a curious one for a number of reasons. I do not understand how we can talk about offering compensatory education to children who in the first place have as yet not been offered an adequate educational environment. In Britain, the Newsom Report (*Half Our Future*, 1963) showed that 79 percent of all secondary modern schools in slum and problem areas were grossly inadequate, and that the holding power of these schools over the teachers was horrifyingly low. The same report also showed very clearly the depressed reading scores of these children compared with the reading scores of children who were at school in areas which were neither problem nor slum. This does not conflict with the findings that, on average for Britain as a whole, there has been an improvement in children's reading ability. The Plowden Report (*Children and Their Primary Schools*, 1966) was rather more coy about all the above points, but we have little reason to believe that the situation is very much better for primary schools in similar areas. Thus we offer a large number of children, both at the primary and secondary levels, materially inadequate schools and unstable teaching staff, and we further expect a small group of dedicated teachers to cope. The strain on these teachers inevitably produces fatigue and illness, and it is not uncommon to find, in any week, teachers having to deal with doubled-up classes of eighty children. And we wonder why the children display very early in their educational life a range of learning difficulties. At the same time, the organization of schools creates delicate overt and covert streaming arrangements which neatly lower the expectations and motivations of both the teachers and the taught. A vicious spiral is set up with an all-too-determinate outcome. It would seem then that we have as yet failed to provide on the scale required an initial satisfactory educational environment.

The compensatory education concept serves to direct attention away from the internal organization and the educational context of the school, and focus our attention upon the families and children. Compensatory education implies that something is lacking in the family, and so in the child, and that as a result the children are unable to benefit from schools. It follows, then, that the school has to compensate for the something which is missing in the family, and the children become little deficit systems. If only the parents were interested in the goodies we offer; if only they were like middle-class parents, then we could do our job. Once the problem is seen even implicitly in this way, it becomes appropriate to coin such terms as *cultural deprivation* and *linguistic deprivation*. Then these labels do their own sad work.

If the children are labeled *culturally deprived,* then it follows that the parents are inadequate, the spontaneous realizations of their culture, its images, and its symbolic representations are of reduced value and significance. Teachers will have lower expectations of the child, which the child undoubtedly will fulfill. All that informs the child, that gives meaning and purpose to him outside of the school, ceases to be valid or to be accorded significance and opportunity for enhancement within the school. He has to orient toward a different structure of meaning, whether it is in the form of reading books, in the form of language use and dialect, or in the patterns of social relationships. Alternatively, the meaning structure of the school is explained to the parents and imposed upon, rather than integrated within, the form and content of their world. A wedge is progressively driven between the child as a member of a family and community, and the child as a member of a school. Either way, the child (and his parents as well) is expected to drop his social identity, his way of life, and its symbolic representations at the school gate. For by definition his culture is deprived, the parents inadequate in both the moral and skill orders they transmit. By this we do not mean that no satisfactory home-school relations can take place or do not take place, but rather that the parents must be brought within the educational experience of the school child by doing what they can do, and particularly what they can do with confidence. There are many ways in which parents can help the child in his learning which are within the parents' spheres of competence. If this happens, then the parents can feel adequate and confident in relation to both the child and the school. This may mean that the content of the learning in school should be drawn much more from the child's experience in his family and community.

The compensatory education concept, then, distracts attention from the deficiencies in the school itself, and it focuses upon deficiencies within the community, family, and child. We can add to these criticisms a third. The concept of compensatory education points to the overwhelming significance of the early years of the child's life in the shaping of his later development. Clearly there is much evidence to support this view and thus its implication that we should create an extensive nursery-school system. However, it would be foolhardy indeed to write off the post-seven-years-of-age educational experience as having little influence. Minimally, what is required initially is to consider the whole age period up to the conclusion of the primary stages as a unity. This would require considering our approach at any one age in the context of the whole of the primary stage. This implies a systematic rather than a piecemeal approach—taking as the unit not a particular period in the life of the child, for example, from three to five years, or from five to seven years, but taking as the unit a stage of education, the primary stage. We should see all we do in terms of the sequencing of learning, the development of sensitivities within the context of the primary stage. In order to accomplish this, the present social and educational division between infant and junior stages must be weakened, otherwise gains at any one age in the child may well be vitiated by losses at a later age.

We should stop thinking in terms of compensatory education but consider instead most seriously and systematically the conditions and contexts of the educational environment.

The author's work may have inadvertently contributed to the formulation of the new educational concepts and categories; focusing upon the subculture and forms of familial socialization may also have diverted attention from the conditions and contexts of learning in school. The focus upon usage of language may have led some to divorce the use of language from the substratum of cultural meanings which are initially responsible for the language use, to equate the concept of restricted code with linguistic deprivation, or even with the nonverbal child.

If we return to the earlier discussed distinctions between restricted and elaborated codes and the corollary distinctions between particularistic and universalistic meanings, we can reason why the working-class child is likely to have difficulty in school. The school is necessarily concerned with the transmission and development of universalistic orders of meaning. It is concerned with making explicit and elaborating, through language, principles and operations as these apply to objects (the science subjects) and to persons (the arts subjects). One child through his socialization is already sensitive to the symbolic orders of the school, whereas another child is much less sensitive to the universalistic orders of the school. The second child is oriented toward particularistic orders of meaning which are context-bound, in which principles and operations are implicit, and toward a form of language use through which such meanings are realized. The school is necessarily trying to develop in this child, orders of relevance and relation as these apply to persons and objects which are not initially the ones he spontaneously moves toward. The problem of educability at one level, whether it is in Europe, the United States, or newly developing societies, can be understood in terms of a confrontation between the universalistic orders of meaning and the social relationships which generate them, of the school, and the particularistic orders of meanings and the social relationships which generate them which the child brings with him to the school. Orientations toward metalanguages of control and innovation are not made available to these children as part of their initial socialization.

We have suggested that the forms of an elaborated code give access to universalistic orders of meaning in the sense that the principles and operations controlling object and person relationships are made explicit through the use of language, whereas restricted codes give access to particularistic orders of meaning in which the principles and operations controlling object and person relationships are rendered implicit through the use of language. We have tried to explain the cultural origins of these codes and their change. If we now go back to our earlier formulation, we can say that elaborated codes give access to universalistic orders of meaning, which are less context-bound, whereas restricted codes give access to particularistic orders of meaning which are far more context-bound, that is, tied to a particular context.

Because his code is restricted does not mean that a child is nonverbal, nor is he in the technical sense linguistically deprived, for he possesses the same tacit understanding of the linguistic rule system as any child. It simply means that there is a restriction on the contexts and on the conditions which will orient the child to universalistic orders of meaning and to making those linguistic choices through which such meanings are realized and so made public. It does not mean that the child cannot produce at any time elaborated speech in particular contexts. Furthermore, it is critically important to distinguish between speech variants and a restricted code. A speech variant is a pattern of linguistic choices which is specific to a particular context: for example, talking to children, a policeman giving evidence in a court, talking to friends whom one knows well, and the rituals of cocktail parties or of train encounters. Because a code is restricted does not mean that a speaker will not, in some contexts and under specific conditions, use a range of modifiers or subordinations etc.; but it does mean that where such choices are made they will be highly context-specific. Because a code is elaborated does not mean that, in some contexts under specific conditions, a speaker will not use a limited range of modifiers, subordinations, etc.; but it does mean that such choices will be highly context-specific. For example, if an individual has to produce a summary (consider a precis), then it is likely that his linguistic choices will be affected.

Again, the concept code refers to the transmission of the deep meaning structure of a culture or subculture—the core meaning structure. It makes a distinction similar to the distinction which linguists make between surface and deep structure of the grammar. Thus sentences which look superficially different can be shown to be generated from the same rules. In the same way, although linguistic choices involved in a summary will be markedly different from the linguistic choices involved in a self-conscious poem, which in turn will be markedly different from linguistic choices involved in an analysis of physical or moral principles, or different again from the linguistic realization of forms of control, they may all, under certain conditions, point to the underlying regulation of restricted or elaborated codes.

This view is implicit in several papers (e.g., Bernstein 1965), but it has never been stated so explicitly in writing as here; the author must bear some of the responsibility for misinterpretations to which the series of papers has often given rise. It is also the case, however, that in 1959 the following was written:

> It is necessary to state at this point that the type of *public* language (*restricted* code) described and analysed here will rarely be found in the pure state. Even if such an "ideal" language use were to be spoken it would not be used in all situations within the local group (Bernstein 1959, p. 319).

Now, that the subculture or culture through its forms of social integration generates a restricted code, does not mean that the resultant speech and meaning system is linguistically or culturally deprived, that its children have nothing to offer the school, that their imaginings are not significant. It does not mean that we have to teach these children formal grammar, nor does it mean that we have to interfere with their dialect. There is nothing, but nothing, in dialect as such, which prevents a child from internalizing and learning to use universalistic meanings. But if the contexts of learning, the samples, the reading books, are not contexts which are triggers for the child's imaginings —are not triggers on his curiosity and explorations in his family and community, then the child is not at home in the educational world. If the teacher says continuously, "Say it again darling, I didn't understand you," then in the end the child may say nothing. If the culture of the teacher is to become part of the consciousness of the child, then the culture of the child must first be in the consciousness of the teacher. This may mean that the teacher must be able to understand the child's dialect, rather than deliberately attempt to change it. Much of the context of our schools is, unwittingly, drawn from aspects of the symbolic world of the middle class; when such a child steps into school he is stepping into a symbolic system which does not provide for him a linkage with his life outside.

It is an accepted educational principle that we should work with what the child can offer. Why don't we practice it? The introduction of the child to the universalistic meanings of public forms of thought is not compensatory education; it is education! In itself, this introduction does not make the child middle-class; how this introduction is effected, though the implicit values underlying the form and context of the educational environment, might do so. We need to distinguish between principles and operations; it is our task as teachers to transmit these implicit values and to develop them in the children, and in the contexts we create in order to do so. There is no one-to-one relationship between any given metalanguage and the content and the exemplars through which children gain an understanding of a given metalanguage. We should start to realize that the social experience the child already possesses is valid and significant, and that this social experience should be reflected back to him as being valid and significant. It can only be reflected back to him if it is part of the texture of the learning experience we create. If we spend as much time thinking through the implications of this as we do thinking about the implications of the Piaget developmental sequences, then possibly schools may become exciting and challenging environments for parents, children, and teachers.

Finally, the issues raised by the education of this disadvantaged group of the population demand a critical evaluation of the system, of the organization and knowledge properties of the institution of education, and of its relationships to the division of labor and the value orientations of society.

REFERENCES

Bereiter, C., and Engelmann, S. *Teaching Disadvantaged Children in the Pre-school.* Englewood Cliffs, N. J.: Prentice-Hall, 1966.

Bernstein, B. Some sociological determinants of perception. *British J. Sociology* 1958, 9: 159–74.

———. A public language: some sociological implications of a linguistic form. *British J. Sociology* 1959, 10: 311–26.

———. Socio-kulturelle Determinanten des Lernens. *Kölner Keitschrift Soziologie und Sozial-Psychologie* 1960, 4: 52–79.(a)

———. Language and social class. *British J. Sociology* 1960, 11: 271–76.(b)

———. Social class and linguistic development: a theory of social learning. In A. H. Halsey, J. Floud, and A. Anderson, eds., *Education, Economy, and Society.* New York: Free Press, 1961.

———. Linguistic codes, hesitation phenomena, and intelligence. *Language and Speech* 1962, 5: 31–46.

———. A sociolinguistic approach to social learning. In J. Gould, ed., *Penguin Survey of the Social Sciences.* Baltimore: Penguin, 1965.

Bernstein, B., and Brandis, W. Social class, communication and control. In W. Brandis and Dorothy Henderson, eds., *Social Class, Language and Communication.* Language, Primary Socialization and Education. Sociological Research Unit Mongraph Series, Vol. 1. London: Routledge & Kegan Paul, in press.

Bernstein, B., and Henderson, Dorothy. Social class differences in the relevance of language to socialization. *Sociology* 1969, 3: 1–20.

Blom, J., and Gumperz, J. J. Some social determinents of verbal behavior. In J. J. Gumperz and D. Hymes, eds., *Directions in Sociolinguistics.* New York: Holt, Rinehart & Winston, in press.

Bott, E. *Family and Social Network.* London: Tavistock Press, 1957.

Bronfennbrenner, U. Socialization and social class in time and space. In E. Maccoby, et al. eds., *Readings in Social Psychology.* New York: Holt, Rinehart & Winston, 1958.

Burt, C. *The Backward Child.* London: University of London Press, 1937.

Carroll, J. B., ed. *Language, Thought, and Reality: Selected Writings of Benjamin Lee Whorf.* Cambridge, Mass.: M. I. T. Press, 1956.

Children and their Primary Schools. (The Plowden Report). Vol. I., II. London: H.M.S.O., 1966.

Chomsky, N. *Aspects of the Theory of Syntax.* Cambridge, Mass.: M.I.T. Press, 1965.

Deutsch, M., and associates. *The Disadvantaged Child.* New York: Basic Books, 1967.

Durkheim, E. *On the Division of Labour in Society.* London: Macmillan & Co., 1933.

Ervin-Tripp, Susan. An analysis of the interaction of language, topic and listener. In J. J. Gumperz and D. Hymes, eds., *The Ethnography of Communication, American Anthropologist* 1964, 66: No. 6, Part 2, 86–102.

———. Sociolinguistics; Unpublished working paper, No. 3, University of California, Berkeley, 1967.

Foote, N. N., ed. *Household Decison-Making: Consumer Behavior.* New York: New York University Press, 1961.

Goldthorpe, J. H. and Lockwood, David. Affluence and the British class structure. *Sociological Review* 1963, 11: 133–63.

Hakulinen, A., Lewis, B., and Taylor, S. Seven year old children and the contextual use of language. Language, Primary Socialization and Education. Sociological Research Unit Monograph Series. London: Routledge and Kegan Paul (in prep.).

Half Our Future (The Newson Report). London: H.M.S.O., 1963.

Hanson, D. Personal and positional influences in informal groups. *Social Forces* 1965, 44: 202–10.

Hawkins, P. R. Social class, the nominal group and reference. *Language and Speech* 1969, 12: 125–35.

———. Social class, the nominal group and references. Language, Primary Socialization and Education. Sociological Research Unit Monograph Series. London: Routledge & Kegan Paul (in prep.).

Henderson, Dorothy. Social class differences in form-class usage. In W. Brandis and Dorothy Henderson, eds., *Social Class, Language and Communication.* Language, Primary Socialization and Education. Sociological Research Unit Monograph Series. Vol. 1. London: Routledge & Kegan Paul, in press.

Hymes, D. Models of the interaction of languages and social setting. *J. Social Issues* 1967, 23:8–28.

———. On communicative competence. In R. Huxley and E. Ingram eds., *The Mechanisms of Language Development.* London: C.I.B.A. foundation, in press.

Kohn, M. L. Social class and the exercise of parental authority. *American Sociological Review* 1959, 24: 352–66.(a)

———. Social class and parental values. *American J. Sociology* 1959, 64: 337–51.(b)

Loban, W. *Language Ability, Grades Seven, Eight and Nine.* Washington, D.C.: U.S. Government Printing Office, 1966.

Malinowski, B. *Coral Gardens and Their Magic,* Vol. 2. New York: American Press, 1935.

Miller, D., and Swanson, G.E. *The Changing American Parent.* New York: Wiley, 1958.

Nye, F.I., and Berardo, F.M. *Emerging Conceptual Frameworks in Family Analysis.* New York: Macmillan, 1966.

Parsons, T. *Personality and Social Structure.* New York: Free Press, 1964.

Passow, A.H., ed., *Education in Depressed Areas.* New York: Teachers College Bureau of Publications, 1963.

Rosenthal, R., and Jacobson, Lenore. *Pygmalion in the Classroom.* New York: Holt, Rinehart & Winston, 1968.

Sapir, E. *Language.* New York: Harcourt, Brace, 1921

Vygotsky, L.S. *Thought and Language.* Eugenia Hanfmann and Gertrude Vakar, eds. and trans. Cambridge, Mass.: M.I.T. Press, 1962.

Chapter 4

SOME PHILOSOPHICAL INFLUENCES UNDERLYING PRESCHOOL INTERVENTION FOR DISADVANTAGED CHILDREN

Marion Blank*

The question of preschool intervention, like all problems of applied research, places unusual demands on the basic sciences from which it must draw. Requisite to well-designed intervention programs is knowledge in some of the most central issues in psychology, including the answers to such questions as: How does learning occur? What is the role of language thinking? What is the effect of early environment on later development? Are there critical periods in human learning? Yet it is just because these issues are so basic and complex that we have no well defined answers to any of them. Nevertheless, because of the atmosphere of urgency and the attendant publicity with which the issue of intervention arose, psychology and education had to use the limited information they possessed to establish some guidelines for action.

This has meant that influences from such diverse frameworks as behaviorism, Freudian psychoanalysis, Piagetian epistemological psychology, and Chomsky's transformational grammar have formed an eclectic, or perhaps more correctly, a mosaic backdrop for deciding how to proceed in this area. In many cases, these theories are of questionable validity and relevance with

*Department of Psychiatry, Albert Einstein College of Medicine

A preliminary version of this paper was initially presented at the American Psychological Association meeting in Washington, D.C., in September 1967. The writing of this revised and expanded version was supported by USPHS grant #MH10,749.

reference to the functioning of the disadvantaged child. Nonetheless, they have played a major role in the establishment of intervention programs.

RATIONALE FOR PRESCHOOL INTERVENTION

The fact that preschool programs were established at all reflects the influence of several basic assumptions in our thinking. First, it mirrors our optimism about the almost endless modifiability and flexibility of human behavior (Hunt 1964; Feuerstein 1968). This view has been reinforced by the strong behaviorist influence in America where it is held that all aspects of learning and performance can be changed to a desired end through the proper manipulation of environmental events (Skinner 1953). Our faith in the importance of environmental factors seems well justified by a substantial body of literature concerning both animals and humans Ulrich, Stachnik, and Mabry 1966). There are, however, in almost all theories limitations to the degree of modifiability that can take place. In general, the major correlate for this limitation is age; that is, the older the organism, the less the change. The interpretations of this may vary. Thus, in a behaviorist model, slower learning in the adult may be seen as reflecting the need to unlearn previously established responses before new responses may be learned. In an ecological orientation, the change may be limited by what has been termed critical periods (Lorenz 1937). In this view, stages exist, particularly in early development, which allow rapid learning of certain skills. These skills may be learned at other ages, but only with much greater time and effort.

Thus, the hope for any modifiability rests strongly on the idea of early intervention. The problem remains as to what behavior is to be modified; this, in turn, rests on what is deemed to be the deficit in functioning. Our views here have been strongly affected by the developmental approach to behavior. Any developmental view has built-in expectations of increasing achievement with chronological growth. These expectations are clearly reflected in the institutions with which the child has contact. Thus, in the school situation we expect the average six- or seven-year-old to be able to read, write, and perform other symbolic operations. In this situation, disadvantaged children show poor progress (see Wilkerson 1967). Many other deficits may well exist—e.g., personality disorders, nutritional inadequacies, poor health. But the school situation, with its emphasis on scholastic achievement, has inevitably meant that learning disorders would appear most prominent.

Arguments, of course, can be and have been raised against this view. Learning in the school situation refers mainly to skills of literacy and it does not necessarily include all higher learning. Thus, it is suggested that perhaps the disadvantaged child may not be deficient in other cognitive skills. Evidence suggests, however, that the deficits may not be restricted to academic work but rather "characterize an entire approach and attitude towards life" involving such features as "inefficient problem solving, a chaotic outlook about world events marked by a lack of need for logical evidence, an episodic grasp of reality," and the like (Feuerstein 1968, p. 16).

There is perhaps another reason for the stress on learning. Man sees himself, in comparison with all other animals, as unique in his mental development, and, in particular, in his capacity for achieving high levels of symbolic activity. Thus the learning disorders of disadvantaged children are seen as representing a weakness in man's greatest strength.

Once one accepts the validity of a learning deficit, it inevitably follows that close attention be paid to all aspects of education. However, the influence of developmental theories as far apart as Piaget and Freud have meant that preschool intervention would perhaps receive the greatest attention. Despite their differing orientations, both these philosophies see early behaviors as laying the foundation for all subsequent growth. As a result, weaknesses in this initial structure leave the child not simply with a lag in development, but with an increasing disadvantage relative to his chronological age. This reasoning receives support in the finding of a cumulative deficit in which the discrepancy in IQ and achievement between middle-class and lower-class children increases with age (Deutsch and Brown, 1964).

FACTORS UNDERLYING THE LEARNING DEFICIT

Even with agreement as to the nature of the deficit, the problem remains of defining the course of remediation. Learning, even when limited to the academic situation, covers such a host of skills that it is essential to establish priorities of importance. In an effort to obtain a first approximation of some of the critical factors, comparisons have been made of the environments of children who did well in school and those who did not. Frequently, this meant comparing the home variables of lower-class and middle-class families since so much early learning occurs in the home (see Freeburg and Payne, 1967). Because of the myriad factors involved, attention was narrowed to those factors which "armchair analysis" indicated were logically related to poor school functioning. This method has been used at all levels of sophistication, from simple correlations (e.g., few books in the home associated with poor reading achievement) to much more involved analyses. For example, there have now been some studies documenting in specifics the kind of verbal interchange that occurs between mothers and children from different socioeconomic groups (Hess and Shipman 1965; Bernstein and Henderson 1969). For the most part, this selection of factors has been on a correlational basis, and therefore no cause and effect could be demonstrated.

PROGRAMS OF OVERALL ENRICHMENT

The pressure for immediate action, however, meant that correlation would have to serve the role that should have been filled by causal relation. Thus the correlational approach formed the basis for what is probably the most common type of intervention program—namely, that of overall enrichment. The general philosophy of such programs has been to select those environmental features which seem most central for cognition and to offer these, in varying doses, to the disadvantaged child. The premise of these programs is that one enriches or supplements the child's background by offering trips, equipment, stories, conversation, audio tapes, and any other presumably beneficial experience.

The value of this approach is questionable on many grounds. First, it involves major intervention in many aspects of the child's life and thus requires costly and extensive educational facilities. Second, even if gains in performance are obtained, it is not possible to determine which aspects of the program are responsible since so many areas of the child's life are affected. Third, perhaps the most serious concern is that even with this massive intervention, the cognitive gains are equivocal (Weikart 1967; Karnes 1968). This conclusion is, if anything, understated, because negative results are rarely reported. This does not mean, however, that we were overly optimistic in our goals, since some programs have achieved gains in learning rates and skills (Bereiter and Engelmann 1966a, b; Blank and Solomon 1968, Weikart and Wiegerink 1968). Rather, the limited success of overall enrichment may well rest in the inappropriateness of its philosophy which, like the materials offered, represents a melange of viewpoints. One is the developmental orientation, mentioned earlier, which stresses the continual emergence of new skills. A corollary to this approach, not previously noted, is that these skills will emerge in a uniform sequence in all children as they mature. The emphasis placed upon this uniformity has meant that the environment must be viewed as a force that can only affect the rate, but in no way alter the sequence. Thus the same techniques and materials can be offered to all children in the belief that they will foster the developmental sequence. As a result, aside from considering differences in the level of development reached, other individual differences are largely ignored. The basic idea seems to be that the presentation of enriched stimulation appropriate to a given level is bound to affect behavior and learning.

This reasoning is reinforced by the successful experimental work of the behaviorists in manipulating learning independent of any individual differences. The zeitgeist of this approach is so pervasive in our thinking that we are often unaware of its influence, and we may even label it by some other term. Thus, a nursery-school teacher may not recognize that she is not simply offering warmth and love but is also exerting control over her pupils with such verbal reinforcements as "that's a good job," "you're a big boy," "come on, try again." However, unlike the teacher, the laboratory experimenter has much greater control over his subject in terms of time, stimuli, rewards, sequencing, and the like. He can even control such highly motivating physiological states as hunger and thirst. Thus, the laboratory experimenter does not simply present appropriate stimuli; he has immense power to control the organism's response to the stimuli with the result that his procedures can guarantee a high degree of success. It goes without saying that teachers of children do not have such power and would hesitate to use it if they could. As a result, well-designed and potentially useful learning material may be presented by the teacher but be ignored by the child, with the result that it fails to serve as an effective stimulus.

In addition, the control that is available to the teacher is further limited by the permissive, activity-oriented nursery-school tradition focused on self-expression, social behavior, and emotional adjustment. Many of these aims represent the attempt to bring psychoanalytic principles to early childhood training. These programs may be successful with the well-functioning middle-class child who has already developed strong internal controls in the cognitive sphere. However, the literature on the disadvantaged is replete with descriptions of their failure to have developed such internal skills (Mattick 1965; Spaulding 1966), with the result that they frequently withdraw from cognitive demands. In such a situation, the tendency of most permissive orientations would be to leave the material and wait until the child is "ready" to deal with it. As a result, the organization of traditional nursery schools may not be appropriate for the disadvantaged child since it does not afford the control necessary for shaping the child's learning.

THE VIEWPOINT OF PERCEPTUAL DYSFUNCTIONING

Some investigators have taken a different approach from that of overall enrichment in that they have attempted to delineate specific factors that may be responsible for the learning disorder. One of the most important viewpoints relies heavily on the genetic approach of Piaget (1952) in which it is hypothesized that sensorimotor schema must be fully developed before higher-level concepts can be achieved. In this view, the IQ and achievement deficits at school age are seen as the result of earlier and perhaps even undiagnosed sensorimotor difficulties in early childhood (Hunt 1964; Kohlberg 1968). Surprisingly, although this view of hierarchical deficiencies is directed towards understanding weaknesses in man's unique language and cognitive abilities, support for this view has come mainly from research on animals. This research has shown that severe perceptual and sensorimotor deprivation in very young animals results in later distorted development. Thus, the lamb who is raised without its mother will turn out to be an isolate from other sheep, will prove to be an inadequate mother to her own young, and so on. Studies on human institutionalized infants strongly reinforce this view on the damaging effects of a restricted early environment (Spitz 1945; Goldfarb 1945; Dennis 1960).

Although this concept may be valid for particular groups of infants, the question nevertheless arises as to its usefulness in understanding the disadvantaged. This view is relevant to the disadvantaged child only if it can be demonstrated that he, in fact, is deprived of early basic opportunities for sensorimotor experience. Speculations have been raised as to whether different levels of stimulation exist in lower- and middle-class homes. The key question, however, concerns the significance of any such differences in the development of sensorimotor skills. Unfortunately there are almost no systematic data on this issue. Additionally, in contrast to the studies on institutionalized children, the data that are available suggest that disadvantaged children do not achieve lower developmental scores than middle-class children under two years of age (Dreger and Miller 1968; Bayley 1965). In many ways it is premature to raise this issue since, for the most part, we have not defined what are the essential stimuli for normal development in the human. As a result, except for extreme cases like severe isolation, we cannot even say with any certainty that a child has experienced perceptual restrictions.

In spite of the lack of evidence in support of a perceptual deficit, this approach has aroused a great interest and a variety of studies have been conducted to demonstrate perceptual dysfunctioning in older disadvantaged children. Research in our unit, however, has indicated the need for much more careful controls before one can state either that perceptual deficiencies do indeed exist in disadvantaged children, and if they do, what role, if any, they play in later school failure. For example, research on children with learning disorders had indicated difficulties in auditory perception (Olsen 1966; Deutsch 1964; Katz and Deutsch 1967). A test widely used in this research consists of pairs of highly similar words (e.g., *cat-cap*) which the subject is asked to judge as same or different (Wepman 1960). The finding that retarded readers did poorly on this task was of obvious interest since audition is the modality by which spoken language is learned. These results are intriguing since they raise the possibility that failure to learn written language (i.e., reading) is associated with some kind of failure in discriminating spoken language. In a study replicating and extending this work (Blank 1968), the correlation between an auditory discrimination task and reading performance did not appear to reflect auditory deficiencies per se. Rather, it reflected the deficiencies retarded readers experience in the seemingly simple cognitive demands imposed by this task (i.e., the ability to listen to a sequence, retain the sequence so as to judge one stimulus against the other, and then make a judgment as to their similarity or difference).

Another area of perceptual functioning which has aroused considerable interest is that of cross-modal integration (Birch and Belmont 1964; Beery 1967; Sterritt and Rudnick 1966). One of the tasks in this area requires the child to select a visual spatial dot pattern (e.g., ...) as representing a sequence of auditory signals (e.g., tap, tap, tap—long pause—tap, tap). The uniformly poor performance of retarded readers on this task has naturally attracted interest since the need to make equivalences between auditory (e.g., spoken words) and visual stimuli (e.g., written words) is vital to the reading process. Research done on cross-modal transfer (Blank and Bridger 1964, 1966), however, indicated that this task which is seemingly of a perceptual nature, actually requires a high level of abstract (verbal) conceptualization. The auditory stimuli used in all this research were, of necessity, temporally presented. We found that temporal stimuli, whether visual or auditory, could not be utilized unless coded in a number system. Since the retarded readers had significantly more difficulty in achieving this coding, they were unable to select the dot patterns representing these sequences. What appeared to be a cross-modal deficiency was in fact a failure to code accurately the temporally presented components of the task. These conclusions were reinforced by our findings (Blank and Bridger 1967; Blank, Weider, and Bridger 1968) that no differences existed between retarded and normal readers when the tasks were confined to nonabstract perceptual components (e.g., repeating temporal rhythms without having to convert them for use in another modality).

These results also indicated the need to differentiate among levels of verbal skills. For example the retarded readers were not deficient in applying verbal labels in certain situations, such as labeling spatially presented visual patterns. The difficulty they experienced was in using words to represent abstract concepts, such as temporal duration. These results suggested that a key deficiency in children with learning disorders was not simply a failure in language per se but rather in more abstract symbolic mediation. For brevity's sake, the deficiency might be called a limitation in the abstract attitude. As indicated in the work of theorists in this area (Goldstein 1959; Vygotsky 1962) language is intimately linked with higher-level abstract thinking, but language by itself is not to be equated with such thinking.

Even though the evidence for perceptual dysfunctioning is ambiguous, many programs, particularly those that are Montessori-based, have been established to compensate for this hypothesized deficit. As discussed by Hunt

(1964), this type of program has several potential advantages. The materials are well-designed and lend themselves to meeting individual differences (i.e., the children can work on their own, at their own rate, and with the material they select). The basic assumption of the program, however, remains open to question—namely, do the materials actually lead the child to develop the concepts for which they were designed? Although the research on this issue is meager, evidence suggests that disadvantaged children do not necessarily assimilate the information provided by self-didactic material (Gotkin et al. 1968). This concern receives support from the fact that contrary to the original philosophy, many Montessori programs have been altered to include more language training (Kohlberg 1968). As a result, these programs may differ little from those of overall enrichment.

THE CENTRAL ROLE OF LANGUAGE
IN LEARNING DEFICIENCIES

It should be noted that in all enrichment programs, regardless of orientation, language has emerged as a common denominator of the learning deficit. This has led many investigators to the belief that while other handicaps may exist, language is at the core of the difficulty for the disadvantaged child. The work of Bernstein (1959, 1960, 1961) on restricted and elaborated codes has been a major impetus to this approach. "In his definition, restricted codes are stereotyped, limited, and condensed, lacking in specificity and the exactness needed for precise conceptualization and differentiation. Sentences are short, simple, often unfinished; there is little use of subordinate clauses for elaborating the content of the sentence; it is a language of implicit meaning, easily understood and commonly shared. The basic quality of this mode is to limit the range and detail of concept and information involved" (Hess and Shipman 1968, p. 94).

Even if these conclusions are valid, the problem remains of determining which of the extremely broad range of language skills needs most to be fostered. Unfortunately here again we lack the necessary empirical foundation on which to build our teaching. The most logical source for such information would seem to be the psychological laboratory. However, much of the experimental research in psychology conducted in the United States has been influenced by the behaviorist tradition in which one deals only with external behaviors; internal mental processes are seen as either unkown or unknowable (Skinner 1953). This has meant that research on language has inevitably focused on those aspects of verbalization that can readily be observed and measured in the laboratory setting. As a result, emphasis has been placed on simple verbal labels as in discrimination learning (e.g., *red, large, man, chair,* etc.) and in paired-associate learning (e.g., *man-coat, window-bread, picture-happy*) (Kendler, Kendler, and Wells 1960; Spiker and Norcross 1962).

Research (John 1963; Blank and Bridger 1966, 1967), however, has suggested that disadvantaged children, while often lacking certain labels, are nevertheless not seriously deficient in this aspect of verbalization. Their difficulty seems to be in the use of more complex verbal structures (as in causal thinking, conditional statements, achieving deductions, retrieving past events, etc.). The aforementioned abilities involve internal mental processes and therefore they have received scant attention from the behavioral psychologists.

The limited view of language espoused by the behaviorists has been strongly criticized by linguists who use the transformational grammar model (Chomsky 1957, 1959). This view emphasizes the fact that meaningful language involves not simply the learning of discrete words, but rather the rules by which these words are organized. Thus, the words *boy, girl, ran, small, the, to, a,* tell us relatively little. These same words when organized into the form "A small boy ran to the girl" tell us a definite message. In recent years, work by psycholinguists using the transformational grammar model has led to considerable advances in our knowledge of the syntax (structure) of language and the way syntactic structures are mastered by the young child (Brown and Bellugi 1964; Ervin and Miller 1963).

This work has been largely responsible for one of the currently popular views about the language of the disadvantaged; namely, their language may not be the same as standard (middle-class) dialect, but that does not mean that it is a poorer language (Baratz 1968; Labov, Cohen, and Robins 1965). This view is extremely relevant to the many attempts in public education directed at altering any dialects simply because they differ from standard-middle-class. It should be noted, however, that much of the educational concern is not focused on dialect but on "the use of language for learning and communicating ideas" (Cazden 1968, p. 138). This distinction was well-illustrated in a study which found that lower-class Negro children utilized the verbal descriptions of middle-class white children more effectively than they utilized the verbal descriptions of their peers (Heider, Cazden, and Brown 1968). Thus, familiarity of dialect need not insure adequate use of language.

These results also suggest that the organizational principles governing the structure of a language may be quite distinct from the function that the language serves in thinking and problem solving. Thus, the question is not simply one of determining the similarities and differences in the structural components of various dialect systems but rather how effectively the child is using the language he already possesses. The work of Richelle and Feuerstein (1957) seems particularly relevant here since it was initially motivated by a desire to determine the differences in thinking among lower-class Israeli children from different cultural backgrounds. Contrary to expectations, they found few differences among children from various lower-class communities since they tended to have simple, undifferentiated concepts in which language was used in a primitive way. On the basis of these results it appeared that differences in thinking existed only when people possessed complex, well-developed mental skills. In the case of lower-class children, the necessary skills have not developed, resulting in a relative paucity of such differentiation. Thus, while attempts to preserve the language structures of the disadvantaged may well be valid, concentration on this aspect may cause us to overlook functional components of language. As a result, attention may unfortunately be drawn away from efforts to correct possible functional limitations.

INTERVENTION PROGRAMS FOCUSED ON LANGUAGE

The critical distinction between the form and function of language has been pointed out by many noted theorists including Piaget (1952), Sapir (1921), and Vygotsky (1962). Nevertheless, the work of the psycholinguists has concentrated almost solely on the structural and phonological rules of language (e.g., Does the child have the negative form? Does he have a means for indicating plurals? Does he use compound sentences? etc.). Almost no headway has been made towards defining the functions that language may serve (for poetry, for description, for propagandizing, for problem solving, for psychodynamic defenses, etc.). Thus, psycholinguists, like behaviorists, provide an extremely limited empirical basis from which to derive guidelines for teaching language skills to children, whether disadvantaged or otherwise. The result has been that in the teaching of verbal abilities there has been an orientation similar to that in overall enrichment; namely, try to offer every possible language skill that may be important. This ranges across such things as verbal labels, verbal descriptions of objects, rote repetition of sentences, listening to stories, facilitating dialogue, etc. Weikert and Wiegerink's (1968) description of *verbal bombardment* seems the most apt term for this approach. Although questions might be raised about the expense and redundancy of such a wide range of stimulation, the most serious questions concern the child's incorporation of the material. There is rarely adequate assurance that the child will partake of the verbalization or make it a meaningful part of his experience. At most, the child might be asked to respond to a specific item such as "Say what I say. . . . ," "What do you see in the picture?" and so on. Most teaching, however, is done in a group situation with the result that any overt response that is required is asked of only one child. It is assumed that in any dialogue that occurs, the other children will attend and comprehend even though they are not required to answer overtly. If the attention and comprehension are lacking, however, the children cannot follow the dialogue and the teaching, no matter how well organized, is lost.

The recognition of these difficulties has led to programs geared to require more active participation by the children. One of the first attempts to offer a program of more focused and directed language skills was that of Bereiter and Engelmann (1966a, b). Not only did they limit the type of verbalization to which the children were exposed, but they radically changed the behavior required of the child. For example, verbal responses were demanded of the children regardless of their interest in the material. In so doing, this program discarded the permissive orientation characteristic of nursery schools and adopted a more fully consistent behaviorist position.

Consistency does not necessarily yield success. However, in the case of the Bereiter-Engelmann program, the consistent behaviorist approach was ideally suited to the deficiencies of the disadvantaged child. Unlike so many other attempts at enrichment, the program demanded some level of response from the children. The material and teachers could not be ignored and thus the program refused to allow the children their well-documented mechanism of avoidance (Deutsch 1966; Mattick 1965).

Questions, nevertheless, remain as to the effectiveness of the material that the child is given to ingest, particularly since Bereiter and Engelmann have given scant attention to several key areas. First, their approach analyzes only the material to be taught; it ignores the cognitive processes in the child that may influence the way the material is incorporated. The hope is that with sufficient exposure to the minute components of any process, the child eventually is bound to learn. This philosophy is largely responsible for their almost total reliance on rote drill. Second, although they are interested in developing higher-level thinking, they feel that the most fruitful path is the development of language structures (e.g., prepositions, adverbs, full sentences, etc.). Research is needed to determine whether the rote repetition of language will lead to developing, eventually, the underlying cognitive structures that Bereiter and Engelmann wish to foster. Third, this program, like many others, ignores individual differences in functioning. By this, I do not mean simply rate of learning, but such factors as style of learning, personality factors, motivation, etc. (Kagan, Moss, and Sigel 1963; Witkin, et al. 1962).

It should be noted that almost no program in the sphere of public education grapples effectively with these issues. For example, we give lip service to the phrase *individual differences,* but almost sole reliance is placed on group teaching—at most, individual teaching means smaller groups or some degree of personalized attention in the group setting. This approach is then rationalized as representing egalitarian ideals since it is based on the assumption that all normal children are capable of achieving the same learning through the same techniques. As a result, one-to-one teaching becomes tinged with either antidemocratic overtones, or worse still, the connotation of illness (e.g., psychotherapy) since it must be used only for children who do not fit the norm. These assumptions may be applicable to older children who already have a large body of consensually validated information, language, and attitudes. However, even here, the large number of learning disorders makes group teaching a questionable method for many children. How much more questionable this method must be for introducing the precursors of abstract thinking to the young child who is distractible, egocentric, and limited in verbal skill. Another of the biases against individual teaching rests on the implicit assumption that individual teaching would or should occupy most of the teaching day. Little consideration has been given to the possible effectiveness of short periods of daily individual instruction, even though such instruction is widely and effectively used in the initial teaching of cognition to other language-deficient groups, for example, with deaf children (Blank 1965). In addition, the limited attention-spans of young children suggest that relatively brief sessions involving frequent reinforcement of new (cognitive) skills theoretically would be the most effective means of teaching.

Difficulties in teaching higher-level cognition in the group setting may not matter to the middle-class child who has numerous opportunities at home for a rich one-to-one verbal interchange. The latter may even allow the child to partake more fully of the group learning situation since he is developing the necessary fund of skills for this activity. This often is not the case with the disadvantaged child who has limited access to such individual attention. He can only rely on the group setting where the adult attention is diluted and sporadic. As a result, serious questions exist as to whether the group setting can provide the necessary opportunities for higher-level learning.

A LANGUAGE–BASED TUTORIAL PROGRAM

With these considerations in mind, the author developed a program of individual teaching designed to foster the precursors of abstract thinking that were needed by the preschool-age disadvantaged child (Blank and Solomon 1968, 1969; Blank 1968). The teaching was done daily, but occupied only a small part of the school day (i.e., about fifteen to twenty minutes per session). As in all intervention programs the teaching reflected underlying assumptions about the nature of learning. First, it contrasted with programs that view the learning deficit as resulting from the child's not having experienced sufficiently varied and extensive stimulation. Rather, the learning difficulties were seen as reflecting the children's failure to develop a symbolic system which would permit them to see the plentiful stimulation already available to them, as existing in a coherent, logical, and predictable framework. Second, it contrasted with programs which view learning as the acquisition of increasing numbers of facts and skills. Such information is obviously necessary if the child is to be familiar with the basic terms of the society (e.g., vocabulary). However, this view, which rests heavily on the concept of the mind as a *tabula rasa*, fails to recognize the active role played by the mind in organizing the input it receives. Recognition of the different levels of cognitive processing by the child stems in large measure from the work of Piaget wherein he documented the numerous errors made by children in seemingly obvious situations. These errors are comprehensible only if one recognizes that data are not simply imprinted as-is but are reorganized to make them congruent with already established mental structures. Gradually through the interplay of maturation and environment these limitations are overcome, and the child gains a more subtle and deeper understanding of reality.

Unfortunately, however, Piaget makes almost no effort to document the specific environmental opportunities that influence development. As a result, aside from trying to teach directly the particular concepts emphasized by Piaget (e.g., conservation of size, number, etc.) his theory does not delineate which factors will serve to facilitate the developmental sequence. A beginning may be made on this problem if one considers not the specific concepts in which the child makes errors, but the factors in his thinking that may have led to the error. Thus, in the classic experiment (Piaget 1968) on number conservation (e.g., a child says that six objects spread apart are "more" than six identical objects spaced close together) the error is caused in part by the child's being bound by the perceptual cues before him with the result that he fails to self-impose delay or to draw upon relevant skills which he may already have (e.g., counting).

One may attempt to overcome the difficulty by repeatedly exposing the child to this situation and explaining what he should do, requiring him to do it, or both (Lenrow 1968). Such training, however, may be self-defeating since it places the child in a situation in which his verbal and perceptual world are in conflict. He can learn to mouth the verbalization, but it does not represent his reality, with the possible result that illogical thinking is reinforced. An alternative course would be to train the child to use the cognitive and language skills in situations where no conflict exists. In such a case, the language may not necessarily be essential for solution, but it will be congruent with reality and may even aid problem solving (e.g., as in improved Porteus maze performance with self-directed verbal commands; see Palkes, Stewart, and Kahana 1968). In essence, this approach attempts to develop the set in the child of using higher-level cognitive skills even in situations where they may be redundant so that he may then be able to draw on these skills when they are essential for solution. Thus, the author's program was focused on developing a repertoire of cognitive skills which would help the child acquire strategies of thinking and information processing (e.g., selective attention, inner verbalization, ability to delay, imagery of future events, etc.) that would transfer to later, more complex learning situations.

To achieve these goals a common core of the program was the representation of reality through language. This meant using the words already in the child's repertoire so as to allow him both to see their relevance to particular situations and to extend their meaning to a wider framework. It also meant having the child test out the relevance of his verbalizations by giving him the opportunity to demonstrate whether his language reflected or differed from reality (e.g., if he said a piece of metal would break when it fell, he was asked to let the object fall and see if, in fact, it broke). As indicated by this example, these goals placed little emphasis on the acquisition of information independent of the context in which it might be relevant. Thus, it was felt that if sensory dimensions such as form, texture, and color were taught as independent facts, the children could learn to recognize and label them through building up a fund of associational learning. Such information, however, may contribute relatively little to helping the child organize his world on a more systematic basis. For example, one might teach the recognition of a large number of tactual sensations (e.g., rough, sticky, wet, sandy, smooth, heavy, etc.) and feel that grouping of "things that can be felt" unified these disparate bits of information. Such an abstract grouping exists largely in the mind of the adult, however, and may well be lost on the child. Much greater meaning can be gained if the child is asked not simply to recognize a particular stimulus, but rather is presented with a problem in which the tactual cues are necessary for solution (e.g., Which one of these could we use if we wanted to stick something on the wall: the rough sandpaper or the sticky tape? Which one of these will leave your hands wet: the milk or the flour?). Thus, the aim of the teaching was to offer common material and then pose many related questions about it which would require the child to reflect, seek information, maintain concentration, examine alternatives, and so on.

The unique opportunity afforded by the one-to-one teaching situation both helped the child to develop sustained sequential thinking and allowed the teacher to continuously diagnose difficulties and readjust the lesson to make it appropriate to the child's level. This is in marked contrast to the group setting where a child's errors (either wrong answers or failure to answer) are almost inevitably followed by didactic teaching or by turning to another child until the correct answer is supplied. In either case, the child who did not know the correct answer may often be left in ignorance since he must take the information on faith. There is little opportunity in the group setting for the teacher to pursue the reason for his failure and then to offer him the necessary experiences to help him understand the rationale for the correct answer.

The program of individual teaching was applied in a pilot program involving a group of 12 three- to four-year-old children (Blank and Solomon 1968, 1969). Thus far, promising results have been obtained and the progress has been dramatic and rapid. After three months, the mean IQ increases in groups tutored five and three times per week were 14.5 and 7.0 points respectively. In a group of three children given individual but not cognitively oriented sessions, gains in performance and IQ were not found. Comparable results were obtained in a replication of this study involving kindergarten-age children who had no previous preschool experience. Clinically, however, the changes in performance were more difficult to achieve at the five- to six-year range, reinforcing the belief in the greater efficacy of earlier intervention.

The program is in its initial stage of development and a great many problems must be explored. For example, a high degree of diagnostic skill coupled with ease in communicating with young children is demanded of the teacher. This makes the training of teachers quite exacting since they must develop insight rather than rely on methods such as programmed instruction. In addition, basic issues must be resolved concerning the length of time such a program must be kept up for the gains to be maintained, the relative effectiveness of different teaching techniques, the training of teachers and the like.

This program and others outlined above should be seen as preliminary attempts to establish focused programs of intervention. Even when their success is limited, such programs have the advantage of being based upon delineated, testable hypotheses which are necessary to help us go beyond the original approach of overall enrichment. In this way, the nursery school can assume the vital function of serving as the natural laboratory for studying the processes of thinking in early development. Thus, properly designed intervention programs may perform the dual function of advancing basic knowledge in human behavior as well as positively affecting the children under their aegis.

REFERENCES

Baratz, J. The assessment of language and cognitive abilities of the Negro. Paper presented at American Psychological Association, September 1968.

Bayley, N. Comparison of mental and motor test scores for ages one-fifteen months by sex, birth order, race, geographical location and education of parents. *Child Development* 1965, 36: 379–411.

Beery, J. Matching of auditory and visual stimuli by average and retarded readers. *Child Development* 1967, 38: 828–33.

Bereiter, C., and Engelmann, S. *Teaching Disadvantaged Children in the Preschool.* Englewood Cliffs, N.J.: Prentice Hall, 1966.(a)

———. An academically oriented preschool for disadvantaged children: results from the initial experimental group. Paper presented at Ontario Institute Studies in Education Conference on Preschool Education, 1966.(b)

Bernstein, B. A public language: some sociological implications of a linguistic form. *British J. Sociology* 1959, 10: 311–26.

———. Language and social class. *British J. Sociology* 1960, 11: 271–76.

———. Social class and linguistic development: a theory of social learning. In A.H. Halsey, J. Floud, and C.A. Anderson, eds.,*Education, Economy and Society.* New York: Free Press, 1961.

Bernstein, B., and Henderson, D. Social class differences in the relevance of language to socialization. *Sociology* 1969, 3: 1–20.

Birch, H., and Belmont, L. Auditory-visual integration in normal and retarded readers. *American J. Orthopsychiatry* 1964,34:852–61.

Blank, M. Use of the deaf in language studies: a reply to Furth. *Psychological Bulletin* 1965, 63: 442–44.

———. A methodology for fostering abstract thinking in deprived children. Paper presented at Ontario Institute Studies in Education Conference, March 1968.

———. Cognitive processes in auditory discrimination in normal and retarded readers. *Child Development* 1968, 39:1091–1101.

Blank, M., and Bridger, W. H. Cross-modal transfer in nursery school children. *J. Comparative and Physiological Psychology* 1964, 58: 277–82.

———. Deficiencies in verbal labeling in retarded readers. *American J. Orthopsychiatry* 1966, 36:840–47.

———. Perceptual abilities and conceptual deficiencies in retarded readers. In J. Zubin, ed., *Psychopathology of Intelligence.* New York: Grune & Stratton, 1967.

Blank, M., and Solomon, F. A tutorial language program to develop abstract thinking in socially disadvantaged preschool children. *Child Development* 1968, 39: 379–89.

————. How shall the disadvantaged child be taught? *Child Development* 1969, 40: 47–61.

Blank, M., Weider, S., and Bridger, W. H. Verbal deficiencies in abstract thinking in early reading retardation. *American J. Orthopsychiatry* 1968, 38: 823–34.

Brown, R., and Bellugi, U. Three processes in the child's acquisition of syntax. *Harvard Educational Review* 1964, 34: 133–51.

Cazden, C. B. Some implications of research on language development for preschool education. In R. D. Hess and R. M. Bear, eds., *Early Education.* Chicago: Aldine, 1968.

Chomsky, N. *Syntactic Structures.* The Hague: Mouton, 1957.

————. A review of B. F. Skinner's *Verbal Behavior. Language* 1959, 35:- 26–58.

Dennis, W. Causes of retardation among institutional children: Iran. *J. Genetic Psychology* 1960, 96: 47–60.

Deutsch, C. P. Auditory discrimination and learning: social factors. *Merrill-Palmer Quarterly* 1964, 10: 277–96.

————. Learning in the disadvantaged. In W. Harris, ed., *Analyses of Concept Learning.* New York: Academic Press, 1966.

Deutsch, M. Facilitating development in the preschool child: social and psychological perspectives. *Merrill-Palmer Quarterly* 1964, 10: 249–63.

Deutsch, M., and Brown, B. Social influences in Negro-white intelligence differences. *J. Social Issues* 1964, 20: 24–35.

Dreger, R. M., and Miller, K. S. Comparative psychological studies of Negroes and whites in the United States 1959-1965. *Psychological Bulletin* 1968, 70: monograph supplement No. 3, Part 2.

Ervin, S. M., and Miller, W. R. Language development. In H. W. Stevenson, ed., *Child Psychology.* Chicago : National Society For the Study of Education, 1963.

Feuerstein, R. The learning potential assessment device: a new method for assessing modifiability of the cognitive functioning of socio-culturally disadvantaged adolescents. Paper presented to the Israel Foundations Trustees, January 1968, Jerusalem.

Freeburg, N. E., and Payne, D. T. Parental influence on cognitive development in early childhood: a review. *Child Development* 1967, 38: 65–87.

Goldfarb, W. Effects of psychological deprivation in infancy and subsequent stimulation. *American J. Psychiatry* 1945, 102: 18–33.

Goldstein, K. Functional disturbances in brain damage. In S. Arieti, ed., *American Handbook of Psychiatry.* Vol. 1 New York: Basic Books, 1959.

Gotkin, L.S.; Caudle, F.; Gans, H.; Saggesse, V.; and Schoenfeld, L. Effects of two types of feedback on training and posttest performance in a visual discrimination task. Unpublished manuscript. Institute for Developmental Studies, New York, 1968.

Heider, E. R.; Cazden, C. B.; and Brown, R. Social class differences in the effectiveness and style of children's coding ability. Project Literacy Reports, No. 9, pp. 1–10. Ithaca, N.Y.: Cornell University, 1968.

Hess, R. D., and Shipman, V. C. Early experience and the socialization of cognitive modes in children. *Child Development* 1965, 36: 869–86.

———. Maternal influences upon early learning: the cognitive environments of urban preschool children. In R.D. Hess and R. M. Bear, eds., *Early Education.* Chicago: Aldine, 1968.

Hunt, J. McV. The psychological basis for using preschool enrichment as an antidote for cultural deprivation. *Merrill-Palmer Quarterly* 1964, 10: 209–48.

John, V. P. The intellectual development of slum children: some preliminary findings. *American J. Orthopsychiatry* 1963, 33: 813–22.

Kagan, J.; Moss, H.A.; and Sigel, I.E. Psychological significance of styles of conceptualization. In J. C. Wright and J. Kagan, eds., *Basic Cognitive Processes in Children.* Monograph of the Society for Research on Child Development, 1963, Vol. 28.

Karnes, M. B. The research program for the preschool disadvantaged at the University of Illinois. Paper presented at the American Educational Research Association, February 1968.

Katz, P. A., and Deutsch, M. The relationship of auditory and visual functioning to reading achievement in disadvantaged children. Paper presented at a meeting of the Society for Research for Child Development, March 1967, New York.

Kendler, T. S.; Kendler, H.H.; and Wells, D. Reversal and nonreversal shifts in nursery school children. *J. Comparative and Physiological Psychology* 1960, 53: 83–87.

Kimble, G.A., ed. E.R. Hilgard and D.G. Marquis' *Conditioning and Learning.* 2d ed. New York: Appleton-Century-Crofts, 1961,

Kohlberg, L. Montessori with the culturally disadvantaged: a cognitive-developmental interpretation and some research findings. In R. D. Hess and R. M. Bear, eds., *Early Education.* Chicago: Aldine, 1968.

Labov, W.; Cohen, P.; and Robins, C. A preliminary study of the structure of English used by Negro and Puerto Rican speakers in New York City. Final Report, U. S. Office of Education Cooperative Research Project No. 3091, 1965.

Lenrow, P. B. Preschool socialization and the development of competence. Project Evaluation Report, Institute of Human Development, University of California, Berkeley, March 1968.

Lorenz, K. Z. Imprinting. *The Auk* 1937, 54: 245–73.

Mattick, I. Adaptation of nursery school techniques to deprived children: some notes on the experiences of teaching children of multi-problem families in a therapeutically oriented nursery school. *J. American Academy Child Psychiatry* 1965, 4: 670–700.

Olsen, A. V. Relation of achievement test scores and specific reading abilities to the Frostig Developmental Test of visual perception. *Perceptual and Motor Skills* 1966, 22: 179–84.

Palkes, H.; Stewart, M.; and Kahana, B. Porteus maze performance of hyperactive boys after training in self directed verbal commands. *Child Development* 1968, 39: 817–26.

Piaget, J. *The Origins of Intelligence in Children.* New York: International Universities Press, 1952.

————. Quantification, conservation and nativism. *Science* 1968, 162: 976–79.

Richelle, M., and Feuerstein, R. Enfants Juifs Nord Africains Essai Psycho-Pedagogique a l'Intention des Educateurs. Mimeographed. Aliyah des Jeunes de l'Agence Juive Tel Aviv, 1957.

Sapir, E. *Language.* New York: Harcourt Brace, 1921.

Skinner, B. F. *Science and Human Behavior.* New York: Free Press, 1953.

Spaulding, R. L. The Durham Education Improvement program. Paper presented at Ontario Institute Studies in Education Conference on Preschool Education, 1966.

Spiker, C., and Norcross, K. Effects of previously acquired stimulus names on discrimination performance. *Child Development* 1962, 33: 859–64.

Spitz, R. A. Hospitalism: an inquiry into the genesis of psychiatric conditions in early childhood. *Psychoanal. Study of the Child* 1945, 1: 53–74.

Sterritt, G., and Rudnick, M. Auditory and visual perception in relation to reading ability in fourth grade boys. *Perceptual and Motor Skills* 1966, 22: 859–64.

Ulrich, R.; Stachnik, T.; and Mabry, J. *Control of Human Behavior.* Glenview, Ill.: Scott Foresman, 1966.

Vygotsky, L. S. *Thought and Language.* Eugenia Hanfmann and Gertrude Vakar, ed. and trans. Cambridge, Mass: M.I.T. Press, 1962.

Weikart, D. P. Preschool programs: preliminary findings. *J. Special Education* 1967, 1: 163–81.

Weikart, D. P., and Wiegerink, R. Initial results of a comparative preschool curriculum project. Paper presented at American Psychological Association, September 1968.

Wepman, J. M. Auditory discrimination, speech, and reading. *Elementary School J.* 1960, 60: 325–33.

Wilkerson, D. A. Selected readings on the disadvantaged. In J. Hellmuth, ed., *Disadvantaged Child.* Vol. I. Seattle: Special Child Publications, 1967.

Witkin, H. A.; Dyk, R. B.; Faterson, H. F.; Goodenough, D. R.; and Karp, S. A. *Psychological Differentiation.* New York: Wiley, 1962.

Chapter 5

THE NEGLECTED SITUATION IN CHILD LANGUAGE RESEARCH AND EDUCATION[1]

Courtney B. Cazden*

SOME CURRENT INADEQUACIES

Study of the acquisition of language has been based on the assumption that what had to be described and explained was the acquisition of a repertoire of responses (in the terminology of behaviorism) or the acquisition of a finite set of rules for constructing utterances (in the terminology of developmental psycholinguistics). On this assumption, the school language problems of lower-class children can have two explanations: either they have acquired less language than middle-class children, or they have acquired a different language. The less-language explanation has been given various names—*cultural deprivation, deficit hypothesis, vacuum ideology*—all with the same connotation of a nonverbal child somehow emptier of language than his more-socially-fortunate age-mates. The different-language explanation is forcefully argued by William Stewart and Joan Baratz.[2] It states that all children acquire language but that many children—especially lower-class black children—acquire a dialect of English so different in structural (grammatical) features that communication in school, both oral and written, is seriously impaired by that fact alone.

For different reasons neither of these explanations is adequate. Consider

*Graduate School of Education, Harvard University
[1]With thanks to Goffman (1964) for both title and ideas.
[2]Their positions can be seen in Chapters 17 and 2 in this volume. See also Stewart and Wilson (1969).

first the less-language explanation. There is growing evidence that if we are referring to what is called grammatical competence (the child's implicit knowledge of language structure), social-class differences are simply not great enough to explain the language problems which teachers report from the classroom. Four pieces of evidence can be offered.

First, LaCivita, Kean, and Yamamoto (1966) report a study in which lower-middle- and upper-class elementary-school children from three schools in Youngstown, Ohio, were asked to give the meaning of nonsense words in sentences such as the following:

"Ungubily the mittler *gimmled*." (grammatical signal *-ed* only cue)
"A twener *baikels* meedily." (grammatical signal plus position cue)

They hypothesized that lower-class children would have less understanding of grammatical structure and thus be less able to give a word that was the same part of speech as the underlined nonsense word (in the above instances, a verb). This hypothesis was not confirmed. Older children were better than younger children, and position cues aided comprehension, but the lower-class children were at no disadvantage.

Second, Shriner and Miner (1968) tested the ability of middle-class and lower-class white four-year-old children to generalize noun and verb endings (plural, possessive, and tense) to nonsense syllables, and found no difference between the two groups.

Third, Slobin (1968, p. 13) reports beginning returns from a cross-cultural study of the acquisition of language in Mexico, India, Samoa, Kenya, and the Negro ghetto in Oakland, California:

> Though we have not yet analyzed the language development of the children studied in these diverse groups, it is the impression of the field workers that they all appear to acquire language at a normal rate and are clearly not "linguistically deprived." This is certainly true of the Oakland children whom we have begun to study in some detail.

Finally, when measures of mean length of utterance (in morphemes, see Slobin 1967) as found in a study (Cazden 1965) of Negro children in a Boston day-care center are compared with the same measure as reported in studies of generally middle-class white children (Brown, Cazden, and Bellugi 1969; Bloom in press), the results indicate that the lower-class Negro children seem to be undergoing grammatical development at a similar rate. Although this comparison certainly may not apply to all lower-class children, it does raise questions about prior comparisons where such children were thought to have less language due to depressed test scores, but where their capabilities in spontaneous speech went unexamined. The speech of Gerald, one of the Negro children, is particularly interesting. At thirty three months, his average length of utterance is longer than that of any of the other Negro or white children. Following are the nine longest in his first two hundred utterances (unpublished speech samples from Cazden 1965):

"I'm looking for a cup."
"I waiting for a other cup."
"You put it up on there like dis."
"Look at what I made with this one."
"Den gon' put dis one back in here cause it fell out."
"I'm gonna knock dese things in."
"Soon I get finish I gon' do dat way."
"Can I take it off and put it on?"

Whatever Gerald's communication problems in any particular situation—and I will suggest later that a problem could arise—they are not caused by deficiencies in his grammatical competence.

Turn now to the different-language explanation. It is clearly true, but still inadequate. Dialects do differ in structural features, and these must be taken into account in planning curriculum materials and instructional techniques. Due largely to the work of Labov, et al. (1968, vol. 1; see also his Chapter 9 in this volume), we are now getting the kind of analyses of at least one dialect, which he calls nonstandard Negro English, that will make such planning possible.

Both the less-language and different-language views of child language are inadequate on two counts. First, they speak only of patterns of structural forms and ignore patterns of use in actual speech events. Second, they speak as if the child learns only one way to speak, which is reflected in the same fashion and to the same extent at all times. On both theoretical and practical grounds, we can no longer accept such limitations.

THE IMPORTANCE OF THE SOCIAL
CONTEXT OF SPEECH

When Kagan (1967) issued a call for "relativism" in psychology, Psathas (1968, p. 136) answered:

> When Kagan uses the term "relativistic," he says that it "refers to a definition in which context and state of the individual are part of the defining statement." The "neglected situation" as Goffman (1964) has called it and the state of the individual, particularly his internal symbol manipulating state, need to be considered. They

would involve Kagan in sociology and anthropology much more than he recognizes. The "context" that he refers to is one that has *socially* defined stimulus value. The social definitions for a situation are pregiven, i.e., exist before the psychologist or experimenter enters on the scene. He must, therefore, understand what these are and how they are perceived by the subject before he can claim to understand why the subject behaves the way he does. The "state of the individual" includes not only his biological and physiological state but his interpretive structuring of the world as he experiences it, based on his previous socialization experiences as a member of the culture.

Applied to language this means that we have to describe more than the child's grammatical competence; we have to describe what Hymes (in press) calls communicative competence—how the child perceives and categorizes the social situations of his world and differentiates his ways of speaking accordingly.

The important point here is not a contrast between competence or knowledge on the one hand, and performance or behavior on the other hand, though many people including the author (Cazden 1967) have formulated the question in this way. A child's manifest verbal behavior, or performance, has both grammatical and pragmatic aspects; such behavior is a reflection of implicit knowledge (or competence) both of a grammar and of its use.

The acquisition of competency for use, indeed, can be stated in the same terms as acquisition of competence for grammar. Within the developmental matrix in which knowledge of the sentences of a language is acquired, children also acquire knowledge of a set of ways in which sentences are used. From a finite experience of speech acts and their interdependence with socio-cultural features they develop a general theory of the speaking appropriate in their community, which they employ, like other forms of tacit cultural knowledge (competence) in conducting and interpreting social life. (Hymes in press)

We are a long way from understanding the range of communicative competences that different children have or how they develop. In fact, research on this enlarged question about the child's acquisition of language has only begun, as in the cross-cultural study mentioned earlier (Slobin 1967). Eventually, through such research, we will achieve a valid picture of social-class and ethnic differences in child language.

Practically, perhaps the best focus for attention is with the effect of the speech situation, since that is what we as educators, or social planners in some other sense, can change. At any one moment, a child decides to speak or be silent, to adopt communicative intent *A* or communicative intent *B*, to express idea *x* or idea *Y*, in form *1* or form *2*. The options the child selects will be a function of characteristics of the speech situation as he perceives it on the basis

TABLE 1 Studies of the Effects of Situation on Child Language

CHARACTERISTICS OF THE SITUATION

CHARACTERISTIC OF LANGUAGE	Topic	Task	Listener(s)	Interaction	Mixed
Fluency/ Spontaneity	Strandberg (1969) Strandberg and Griffith (1968) Williams and Naremore (1969a) Berlyne and Frommer (1966)	Heider, Cazden, and Brown (1968) Brent and Katz (1967)	Labov, et al.,(1968, vol. 2)		Cowe (1967) Cazden (1965) Kagan (1969) Jensen (1969) Labov, et al. (1968 vol. 2) Pasamanick and Knobloch (1955) Resnick, Weld, and Lally (1969)
Length/ Complexity	Strandberg and Griffith (1968) Cowan et al., (1967) Moffett (1968) Williams and Naremore (1969a,b) Labov, et al. (1968, vol 2)	Brent and Katz (1967) Cazden (1967) Lawton (1968) Robinson (1965) Williams and Naremore (1969a, b)	Cazden (1967) Smith (1935)	Plumer (1969)	Cowe (1967)
Content or Style		Labov, et al. (1968, vol. 2) Lawton (1968)			
Approximation to Standard English		Labov, et al. (1968, vol. 1)			

of his past experience.[3] We observe that a particular child in a particular situation either makes or fails to make a particular utterance. Traditionally, we have related that utterance only to some characteristics of the child, such as his social-class background, while ignoring characteristics of the situation which are at least equally influential. At a time when much attention is focused on how different children—for example, from middle- or lower-class groups —respond to a single situation—in an experiment or in school—it should be useful to focus attention on how the same children respond differentially in different speech situations. As Robinson (1968) points out, the tendency in child-language research has been to ignore situational (contextual) variables or to combine speech data from several contexts. Instead, he (p. 6), suggests "it may be wiser methodologically to accumulate the [social-class] differences within contexts and to see what higher-order generalizations can be made about them."

Although the research which we will report is all about monolingual children, the notions of a diversified speech repertoire and situational relativity apply even more obviously to bilinguals.[4]

SITUATION VARIABLES

The research literature on child language includes some descriptions of how language usage varies with characteristics of speech situation. Although not all of these studies deal with lower-class children, all do provide evidence of the situational relativity of children's speech, and each gives some idea of the variables which must be considered. These variables and the published studies in which they are reported are summarized in Table 1. The columns in the table represent a very gross categorization of situational differences (or the independent variables in the research): topic, task, listener(s), interaction, and situations with mixed characteristics. Rows represent more easily definable characteristics of language (the dependent variables): fluency and/or spontaneity; length and/or complexity; characteristics of speech content such as abstractness; and degree of approximation to standard English. Unless otherwise specified, all differences reported are differences in the way the same child or group of children speak in different situations; occasionally, differences between similar groups of children are reported. All but three (Moffet 1968; Robinson 1965, and my unpublished observations) deal with oral language.

---

[3]See Herman (1961) for an analysis of the three-fold influences on language choice of bilingual speakers: personal needs, the immediate situation, and the background situation.

[4]See Macnamara (1967) for papers on bilingualism, including one by Hymes on "Models of the Interaction of Language and Social Setting."

Topic

Four studies used different kinds of pictures. Strandberg (1969) found that four- and five-year-old children, above average in intelligence (with different children in each stimulus group), talked more about either a toy or a twenty-second silent film of that toy than they did about a still-color photograph of it. There was no difference, however, in either average length or complexity of the responses. Strandberg and Griffith (1968) gave four- and five-year-old children in a university laboratory school cameras loaded with color film. Later, they elicited conversations about the (remarkably successful) pictures the children took. The children talked more spontaneously (i.e., required fewer adult probes) and talked in longer and more complex utterances about the pictures they took at home of personally significant objects (e.g., a favorite climbing tree or a closeup of Mother's mouth) than they did about pictures taken under adult direction during the period of orientation to the camera. Since the pictures taken at home were also frequently of only one object, the authors conclude that the difference lies in the degree of personal involvement. Although topic is confounded with order in this study (since all the children told stories about the preselected objects first), it seems unlikely that this accounts for all the difference. Following are examples of one five-year-old's stories, first about an assigned picture and then about one of his choice:

> That's a horse. You can ride it. I don't know any more about it. It's brown, black and red. I don't know my story about the horse.

> There's a picture of my tree that I climb in. There's—there's where it grows at and there's where I climb up—and sit up there—down there and that's where I look out at. First I get on this one and then I get on that other one. And then I put my foot under that big branch that are strong. And then I pull my face up and then I get ahold of a branch up at that place—and then I look around. (Strandberg and Griffith, personal communication 1969)

Cowan, et al. (1967) presented elementary school children of mixed socioeconomic status with ten colored pictures from magazine covers. The effect of the particular picture on the mean length of response was strong across all age, sex, socioeconomic class, and experimenter conditions. One picture of a group standing around a new car elicited significantly shorter responses; one picture of a birthday party elicited significantly longer responses, while the other eight pictures were undifferentiated between the two extremes. Although the researchers cannot specify the source of the stimulus effect, they conclude that "the implicit assumption that magnitude of mean length of response is a property of the subject independent of his setting should be permanently discarded" (Cowan, et al. 1967, p. 202).

Finally, Berlyne and Frommer (1966) studied the properties of different pictures and stories in eliciting one particular form of speech: questions. They presented children from kindergarten and grades three, five, and six at a university laboratory school with stories, pictures, and stories accompanied by pictures, and then invited the children to ask questions about them. Novel, surprising, and incongruous items elicited more questions, and the provision of answers (an interaction characteristic) had little effect.

Two studies compare narratives about television programs with other topics. Williams and Naremore (1969a, b; see also, Williams in press) analyzed forty interviews with Negro and white fifth- and sixth-graders selected from the extremes of the socioeconomic distribution of children in the Detroit Dialect Study (Shuy, et al. 1967). All informants had responded to three topics: games ("What kinds of games do you play around here?"); TV ("What are your favorite TV programs?"); and aspirations ("What do you want to be when you finish school?"). Social-class differences were found in the proportion of utterances which went beyond a simple yes-no answer or naming, on a ranking of the degree of connectedness of the utterances in a response, and on verbal indices of specific grammatical features. For the most part, however, the social-class differences were found when children were talking on the television topic.

> Although it is at best a subjective interpretation, the concentration of status differences in three of the clause indices on the TV topic seem to be a reflection of the tendency of the H.S. [high-status] children to engage in story telling or narrative while the L.S. [low-status] children tended to itemize instances of what they had seen or preferred. . . . The language used by the child in an interview is as much a reflection of his engagement within the constraints of a communication situation as it is a reflection of his linguistic capabilities. (Williams and Naremore 1969b, p.791.)

Labov has collected narratives of television programs and personal experience from preadolescent boys attending vacation day camps in Central Harlem. Following are two such narratives, by two different eleven-year-old boys, the first about "The Man From Uncle" and the second about a personal fight (Labov, et al. 1968, vol. 2, pp. 298-99).

(First Boy)
a. This kid—Napoleon got shot
b. and he had to go on a mission.
c. And so this kid, he went with Solo.
d. So they went
e. And this guy—they went through this window.
f. and they caught him.

g. And then he beat up them other people.
h. And they went
i. and then he said that this old lady was his mother
j. and then he—and at the end he say that he was the guy's friend.

(Second Boy)
a. When I was in fourth grade—no it was in third grade—
b. This boy he stole my glove.
c. He took my glove
d. and said that his father found it downtown on the ground.
   (And you fight him?)
e. I told him that it was impossible for him to find downtown 'cause
   all those people were walking by and just his father was the only
   one that found it?
f. So he got all (mad).
g. So then I fought him.
h. I knocked him all out in the street.
i. So he say he give.
j. and I kept on hitting him.
k. Then he started crying
l. and ran home to his father
m. And the father told him
o. that he didn't find no glove.

Labov, et al. (1968, vol. 2, p. 297) summarize that the main difference
between the two sets of narratives is the absence of evaluation in the TV
narratives: ". . . the means used by the narrator to indicate the point of the
narrative, its *raison d'etre*, why it was told, and what the narrator is getting
at." Absence of evaluation in accounts of vicarious experience reduces structural complexity. Although the construction of the narrative clause in English
is a relatively simple construction, explanations (one of the devices for evaluation) may be exceedingly complex. Note, as an example, utterance *e* in the
second boy's narrative. It does not seem farfetched to suggest a common
element in the findings of Strandberg and Griffith (1968), and Labov, et al.
(1968): the greater the degree of affect or personal involvement in the topic of
conversation, the greater the likelihood of structural complexity.

Two final examples of the effect of topic on linguistic structure deal with
written language. First, Moffet's observations on a science lesson (1968, p.
180):

> While watching some third-graders write down their observa-
> tions of candle flames—deliberately this time, not merely in note
> form—I noticed that sentences beginning with if- and when-clauses
> were appearing frequently on their papers. Since such a construction
> is not common in third-grade writing, I became curious and then
> realized that these introductory subordinate clauses resulted directly
> from the children's *manipulation of what they were observing*. Thus:
> "If I place a glass over the candle, the flame goes out." And: "When
> you throw alum on the candle, the flame turns blue." Here we have

a fine example of a physical operation being reflected in a cognitive operation and hence in a linguistic structure. . . . The cognitive task entailed in the candle tests created a need for subordinate clauses, because the pupils were not asked merely to describe a static object but to describe changes in the object brought about by changing conditions (*if* and *when*).

Second are the author's observations of the written compositions by five-year-old children in two English Infant Schools in neighborhoods similarly mixed in socioeconomic status. In the first school, all the children were given their first writing books (blank, unlined pages for pictures and related stories), asked to draw a picture and then dictate a story for the teacher to write. All the resulting stories were simple sentences, and all but one was of the form "This is a＿＿＿＿" The exception was the sentence "This boy is dead." In the second school, children were using experimental beginning-reading materials developed by Mackay and Thompson (1968). Each child had a word folder with a preselected store of basic words plus some blanks for his personal collection. He also had a stand on which words from the folder could be set up as a text. These children composed sentences very different from those in the first school and (more importantly) very different from each other, for example, the following:

"My Mum takes me to school."
"Is my sister at school and is my baby at home?"
"My cousin is skinny."
"I like Sian she gave me one of David's doggies."
"On Tuesday the movie camera man is coming."
"I ask Helen to come to my birthday."

Whereas the presence of the pictures somehow constrained the first group of children to the simplest and most routine labels, absence of a picture seemed to free the second group of children to work with far more of their linguistic knowledge.

Task

In some studies, differences are found which seem to relate more to what the child is asked to do with the topic than to the topic itself. For instance, Brent and Katz (1967) asked white Head Start children to tell stories about pictures from the WISC (Wechsler Intelligence Scale for Children) picture-arrangement task, then removed the pictures and asked the children to tell the stories again. They found that the stories told without the pictures were superior. The children produced longer stories without prompting, and ideas were related more logically and explicitly. Brent and Katz (1967, pp. 4-5) suggest that:

. . . the actual presence of the pictures, which constitute a *spatially distributed* series of *perceptually discrete* events, may in fact, interfere with our younger subjects' ability to form a *temporally distributed* and *logically continuous* story—a task which required a conceptual and linguistic "bridging-the-gap" between discrete frames.

Since the order of story telling is confounded with the picture presence/absence, we cannot tell whether telling the story first with a picture present contributes to the more successful (and second) attempt when the picture is removed.

Lawton (1968), in a study of British boys aged twelve to fifteen years, tried to elicit both descriptive and more abstract speech by the instructions: "Describe your school and then answer: What do you think is the real purpose of education?" All the boys used more subordinate clauses and complex constructions on the abstraction task than on the description task.

Four studies report differences which result from different degrees of structure or constraint in the directions. With the same boys, Lawton (1968) also conducted a discussion of capital punishment, replicating an earlier study of Bernstein (1962). He also gave them assignments to write on four topics such as "My life in ten years time." In the more open, unstructured discussions, middle-class boys used more abstract arguments and hypothetical examples, while the working-class boys used more concrete examples and cliches or anecdotes. But in the abstract sections of the interviews, social-class differences were much smaller.

> The inference I would draw is that in an "open" situation the working-class boys tend to move towards concrete, narrative/descriptive language, but in a "structured" situation where they have little or no choice about making an abstract response, they will respond to the demand made upon them. They may have found the task extremely difficult, but it was not impossible for them. (Lawton, 1968, p. 138)

Comparable results were obtained by Williams and Naremore (1969a) and Heider, et al. (1968). One way in which Williams and Naremore (see the earlier description of the study) scored interviews on games, aspirations, and TV was by type of questions asked by the interviewer and the corresponding type of child response.

PROBE CONSTRAINTS:
simple: Do you play baseball?
naming: What television programs do you watch?
elaboration: How do you play kick-the-can?

RESPONSE STYLE:
simple: Yeah.
naming: Baseball
qualified naming: I usually watch the Avengers and lots of cartoons.
elaboration: Last night the Penguin had Batman trapped on top of this tower. . . .

Results show that following the first two probes, "the lower-status children had more of a tendency to supply the minimally acceptable response, whereas their higher-status counterparts had a greater tendency to elaborate their remarks" (Williams and Naremore 1969a, p. 86). The researchers' general interpretation held that:

> The mark of a lower status child was that he had some tendency to provide the type of response which would minimally fulfill the field worker's probe, [but] not go on to assume a more active role in the speech situation, including elaboration of more of his own experience. (Williams and Naremore 1969a, pp. 87-88)

The above differences, however, were not as evident when the field workers imposed a definite constraint for elaboration in their probes.

Heider, et al. (1968) report an experiment in which lower- and middle-class white ten-year-old boys were asked to describe a picture of one animal out of a large array. Criterial or essential attributes were the name of the animal, its number of spots, whether it was standing or lying down, and the position of its head. The frequencies of criterial attributes named by the children were almost identical for the two groups. However, there was a significant social-class difference in the number of requests the listener had to make for more information before the picture was adequately specified— nearly twice as many requests to the lower-class children as to the middle-class children. The lower-class children's performance was far superior to what it would have been if the amount of probing or feedback had been standardized for the two groups as it often is both in experiments and in classrooms.

Robinson (1965), another British researcher, gave two letter-writing assignments to middle-class and working-class twelve- and thirteen-year-old boys and girls in a comprehensive school. One assignment, to tell a good friend news of the past fortnight, presumably elicited informal language (or restricted code) from all subjects. The other assignment, advising a Governor of the school how some money he had donated might be spent, presumably elicited formal language (or elaborated code) from anyone who could use it. Contrary to expectations, there were no significant differences between the middle-class and working-class formal letters, and differences only in lexical diversity (number of different nouns, adjectives, and so on) between the informal letters where the topic was less constrained.

While the results of Lawton (1968), Williams and Naremore (1969a), Heider, et al. (1968), and Robinson (1965) suggest that working-class children display greater abstraction, elaboration, or informational analysis when it is demanded in a situation highly structured by an adult interviewer, one can find exceptions to the possible generalization suggested here. For example, in an earlier report (Cazden 1967), a lower-class Negro child of first-grade age provided the longest utterances (in morpheme count) in informal speech tasks, as against a middle-class white child who gave longest responses on highly structured tasks. Although this earlier study was only a pilot venture, it did reveal the strong potential interaction between children's backgrounds and the characteristics of speech situations. Presumably, there are more such interactions to be discovered if we knew where and how to look for them.

We can also differentiate speech situations on an informal-formal continuum from the least self-conscious and most excited speech in peer-group situations, to accounts of fights provided in interviews, to more usual interview materials, to reading sentences aloud, to reading lists of unconnected words (Labov, et al. 1968, vol. 1). As a speaker moves with increasing formality from the least self-conscious, excited speech to pronunciations of individual words, he tends to become more standard in his English usage.

Listener(s)

One important characteristic of the listener is age in relation to the speaker. In an early study, Smith (1935) found that children eighteen to seventy months old spoke longer sentences at home with adults than at play with other children. Presumably, this was because at home the children gave fewer answers to questions and fewer imperatives, and had greater opportunity for more connected discourse with less active play and less frequent interruptions. In the study cited above (Cazden 1967), it was found that both children spoke their shortest sentences, on the average, in two experimental situations with their peers—playing an arithmetic game, and in a telephone conversation.

In some recent unpublished research, two students at Harvard[5] found that children themselves modify their speech as they talk to different persons. One three-year-old spoke her longest utterances to her mother, her shortest utterances to her eighteen-month-old sister, while her speech to herself was between these in length. Three girls of nine, eleven, and thirteen years' modified the complexity of their speech to younger boys (roughly eighteen and thirty months) more according to their perception of the child's language ability than strictly according to his age. But younger listeners are not the only ones to inhibit speech complexity in a child. Labov, et al. (1968 vol. 2, p. 117) reports the following utterance from a boy who is typically very fast and fluent in

---

[5]M. J. Yurchak and E. Bernat.

speech, but in the presence of older (sixteen-year-old) gang members, appears at a loss for words: "He gon' getchyou with 'is li's . . . he got li-' he got leg like di- like . . . ."

Interaction

Here we have only one report from a pilot study and one hypothesis now being tested. Oliver Cooperman, a Harvard medical student working at the University of London on the effects of various conditions of residential care on preschool-age children, conducted a pilot study of various aspects of children's conversations. He found conversation more likely to occur and to include a greater number of exchanges with an adult when it was initiated by the child rather than by the adult, and adult commands to initiate action (to "do X") more frequently provoked verbal reply than commands to desist (to "stop doing X").

Plumer (1969) is currently conducting research on dialogue strategies within twelve families with children seven or eight years old—six with sons with high verbal ability (as measured on standardized tests) and six with sons with average verbal ability. Recording equipment is given to each family, and dialogue is recorded from a wireless microphone worn by the child under study. Each family records a total of seven hours during one week, including twenty-minute sessions at breakfast, supper, and bedtime. One measure used will be the length of a dialogue (the number of verbal exchanges between the initiation and termination of a topic) and one analysis will be the relation of length of dialogue to complexity of the child's utterances.

A major assumption underlying this study is that the longer the dialogue the more likely the child is to hear and use a wide range of the resources and strategies of his language. The ability to elaborate and qualify—or to follow elaboration and qualification—is most likely to be learned in an extended dialogue after an initial exchange has set up the need for clarification and elaboration. (Plumer 1969, pp. 7-8)

If either Cooperman's or Plumer's observation and expectations are borne out in further research, they would have important implications for planning classrooms for maximally productive conversation. For instance, initiation of conversation probably takes place more often in a classroom where children carry major responsibility for planning their activities. But this may only be productive for language usage if personal involvement, and thereby conversation on a topic, is sustained over some period of time.

Mixed Aspects of Situations

Two kinds of situations seem to contain a mixture of relevant aspects: various activities in any classroom and in testing situations themselves. Cowe (1967) has recorded the conversations of kindergarten children in nine activities. In both amount and maturity of speech, housekeeping play and group discussion held the greatest potential for language usage, while play with blocks, dance, and woodworking held least. She suggests that factors influencing speech are adult participation, something concrete to talk about, physical arrangements, and noise. I have made similar observations when selecting play materials for a tutorial language program (Cazden 1965).

Testing situations contain the effects of interpersonal formality and power relationship mixed with the cognitive demands of particular tasks. Pasamanick and Knobloch (1955) and Resnick, Weld, and Lally (1969) report evidence that the verbal expressiveness of working-class Negro two-year-olds is artificially depressed in testing situations. Even Jensen (1969 p. 100), arguing that social-class differences in intelligence are largely inherited, reports from his own clinical experience that he regularly raised IQ scores on the Stanford-Binet (largely a test of verbal performance) eight to ten points by having children from an impoverished background come in for two, three, or four play sessions in his office so that the child could get acquainted and feel more at ease. And Kagan (1969, p. 276), in answer to Jensen, reports the experience of Francis Palmer in New York City:

> Dr. Palmer administered mental tests to middle and lower class black children from Harlem. However, each examiner was instructed not to begin any testing with any child until she felt that the child was completely relaxed, and understood what was required of him. Many children had five, six, and even seven hours of rapport sessions with the examiner before any questions were administered. Few psychological studies have ever devoted this much care to establishing rapport with the child. Dr. Palmer found few significant differences in mental ability between the lower and middle class populations. This is one of the first times such a finding has been reported and it seems due, in part, to the great care taken to insure that the child comprehended the nature of the test questions and felt at ease with the examiner.[6]

Labov, and his colleagues (et al. 1968, vol 2, pp. 340-41) provide a dramatic example. Attacking the conditions under which much of the data on verbal deprivation is collected, he quotes an entire interview with a preadolescent boy in a New York City school, and contrasts it with his own methods and findings.

The child is alone in a school room with the investigator, a young, friendly white man, who is instructed to place a toy on the table and say "Tell me everything you can about this." The interviewer's remarks are in parentheses.

(Tell me everything you can about *this*) (*Plunk*).
[12 seconds of silence]

---

[6]See also Severson and Guest's Chapter 15 in this volume.

(What would you say it looks like?)
    [8 seconds of silence]
A space ship.
(Hmmmm)
    [13 seconds of silence]
Like a je-et.
    [12 seconds of silence]
Like a plane.
    [20 seconds of silence]
(What color is it?)
Orange (2 seconds) An' whi-ite. (2 seconds). An' green.
    [6 seconds of silence]
An' what could you use it for?
    [8 seconds of silence]
A je-et.
    [6 seconds of silence]
(If you had two of them, what would you do with them?)
    [6 seconds of silence]
Give one to some-body.
(Hmmm. Who do you think would like to have it?)
    [10 seconds of silence]
Cla-rence.
(Mm. Where do you think we could get another one of these?)
At the store.
(Oh ka-ay!)

The social situation which produces such defensive behavior is that of an adult asking a lone child questions to which he obviously knows the answers, where anything the child says may well be held against him. It is, in fact, a paradigm of the school situation which prevails as reading is being taught (but not learned).

We can obtain such results in our own research, and have done so in our work with younger brothers of the Thunderbirds in 1390 Fifth Avenue. But when we change the social situation by altering the height and power relations, introducing a close friend of the subject, and talking about things we know he is interested in, we obtain a level of excited and rapid speech.

NEW GOALS IN ORAL
LANGUAGE EDUCATION

Even if we had the kind of understanding of communicative competence among diverse groups of children which Hymes (in press) calls for, we would still be far from a theory of oral language education. That theory requires, in addition, decisions about which goals are important, what communicative competence we seek. Sociolinguistic interference from contrasting communicative demands both in and outside school is almost certainly more important than grammatical interference (Hymes in press; Labov, et al. 1968, vol 2). To reduce this interference, we have to know what communicative capabilities the child brings and what we want him to be able to do.

Discussions of the goals of education, like analyses of child language, too often focus on language form when they should be concerned with language use. In arguing against oral language programs for teaching standard English to speakers of a nonstandard dialect, Kochman (1969, p. 2) says:

> My first quarrel with such a program is that it does not develop the ability of a person to use language, which I would further define as performance capability in a variety of social contexts on a variety of subject matter. . . . Underlying this approach seems to be a misapplication of Basil Bernstein's terms which falsely equate *restrictive code* and *elaborated code* with, respectively, nonstandard dialect and standard dialect. It ought to be noted, as Bernstein uses the term, code is not to be equated with *langue*, but *parole*, not with *competence* but *performance*. What is restrictive or elaborated is not in fact the code as sociolinguists use the term, but the message.[7]

To reject attempts to teach a single, socially prestigious language form is not to reject all attempts at change. Cultural differences in language use can be interpreted as deficiencies when children confront the demands of particular communicative situations.

> Cultural relativism, inferred from an enormous variety of existing cultures, remains a prerequisite of objective analysis. . . . But the moral corollary of cultural relativism—moral relativism—has been quietly discarded, except as a form of intellectual indulgence among those who claim the privilege of non-involvement. (Wolf 1964, pp. 21-22)

Educators certainly cannot claim any privilege of noninvolvement, and they must decide what goals they seek. Taking as his goal the education of a person who knows enough not to remain a victim, Olson (1967, p. 13) says,

> A teacher must possess extraordinary knowledge and humanity if he is to distinguish what the school demands of children simply to symbolize its capacity for authority over them, from what it legitimately "demands" or "woos out of them" to equip them for a niche in a technological society.

Pieces of an answer can be suggested. On the basis of his experience as a teacher in a village school for Kwakiutl Indian children on Vancouver Island, Wolcott (1969) suggests teaching specific skills rather than trying to

---

[7](ED. NOTE) The distinction between *langue* and *parole* is meant to contrast between our description of the system of a language and the performance of that language in actual speech.

make over the child into one's own image. In Chapter 4 in this volume, Marion Blank argues for education in the use of language for abstract thinking. Kochman (personal communication 1969) recommends opportunity for the use of language in "low-context" situations where speaker and listener do not share a common referent and where a greater burden of communication falls on words alone, a skill that thirty-three-month-old Gerald needs help in acquiring.[8] Cazden and John (1969) argue for coordinate education for cultural pluralism, in which patterns of language form and use (and beliefs and values as well) in the child's home community are maintained and valued alongside the introduction of forms of behavior required in a technological society.

In the end, the goals of education are in large part matters of value, and decisions about them must be shared by educators and spokesmen for the child and his community. Such decisions, combined with knowledge of communicative competence and how it develops, will enable us to design more productive situations for oral language education in school.

---

[8]See also Erickson (1969).

REFERENCES

Berlyne, D.E., and Frommer, F.D. Some determinants of the incidence and content of children's questions. *Child Development* 1966, 37: 177-89.

Bernstein, B. Social class, linguistic codes and grammatical elements. *Language and Speech* 1962, 5: 221–40.

Bloom, L.M. *Language Development: Form and Function in Emerging Grammars.* Cambridge, Mass.: M.I.T. Press, in press.

Brent, S.B.; and Katz, E.W. A study of language deviations and cognitive processes. Progress Report No. 3, Office of Economic Opportunity Job Corps contract 1209, Wayne State University, 1967.

Brown, R.; Cazden, C.B.; and Bellugi, U. The child's grammar from I to III. In J.P. Hill, ed., *1967 Minnesota Symposium on Child Psychology.* Minneapolis: University of Minnesota Press, 1969.

Cazden, C. B. Environmental assistance to the child's acquisition of grammar. Doctoral dissertation, Harvard University, 1965.

———. On individual differences in language competence and performance. *J. Special Education* 1967, 1: 135–50.

Cazden, C.B., and John, V.P. Learning in American Indian children. In S. Ohannessian, ed., *Styles of Learning Among American Indians: An Outline for Research.* Washington, D.C.: Center for Applied Linguistics, 1969.

Cowan, P.A.; Weber, J.; Hoddinott, B.A.; and Klein, J. Mean length of spoken response as a function of stimulus, experimenter, and subject. *Child Development.* 1967, 38: 191-203.

Cowe, E.G. A study of kindergarten activities for language development. Doctoral dissertation, Columbia University, 1967.

Erickson, F.D. "F'get you Honky": A new look at Black dialect and the schools. *Elementary English* 1969, 46: 495-99.

Goffman, E. The neglected situation. In J.J. Gumperz and D. Hymes, eds., *The Ethnography of Communication, American Anthropologist* 1964, 66: No. 6, Part 2, 133–36.

Heider, E.R.; Cazden, C.B.; and Brown, R. Social class differences in the effectiveness and style of children's coding ability. Project Literacy Reports, No. 9, pp. 1–10. Ithaca, N.Y.: Cornell University, 1968.

Herman, S.R. Explorations in the social psychology of language choice. *Human Relations* 1961, 14: 149–64.

Hymes, D. On communicative competence. In R. Huxley and E. Ingram, eds., *The Mechanisms of Language Development.* London: CIBA Foundation, in press.

Jensen, A.R. How much can we boost IQ and scholastic achievement? *Harvard Educational Review* 1969, 39: 1–123.

Kagan, J. On the need for relativism. *American Psychologist* 1967, 22: 131–42.
————. Inadequate evidence and illogical conclusions. *Harvard Educational Review* 1969, 39: 274–77.
Kochman, T. Social factors in the consideration of teaching standard English. Paper read at convention of Teachers of English to Speakers of Other Languages (TESOL). March 1969, Chicago.
Labov, W.; Cohen, P.; Robins, C.; and Lewis, J. A study of non-standard English of Negro and Puerto Rican speakers in New York City. Final report, U.S. Office of Education Cooperative Research Project No. 3288, Vols. 1, 2. Mimeographed. Columbia University 1968.
LaCivita, A.F.; Kean, J.M.; and Yamamoto, K. Socioeconomic status of children and acquisition of grammar. *J. Educational Research* 1966, 60: 71–74.
Lawton, D. *Social Class, Language and Education.* New York: Schocken, 1968.
Macnamara, J., ed. Problems of bilingualism. *J. Social Issues* 1967, 23: No. 2.
Mackay, D., and Thompson, B. The initial teaching of reading and writing: some notes toward a theory of literacy. Programme in Linguistics and English Teaching, Paper No. 3. London: University College and Longmans Green, 1968.
Moffett, J. *Teaching the Universe of Discourse.* Boston: Houghton Mifflin, 1968.
Olson, P.A. Introduction. The craft of teaching and the school of teachers. Report of the first national conference, U.S. Office of Education Tri-University Project in Elementary Education, September 1967, Denver.
Pasamanick, B. and Knobloch, H. Early language behavior in Negro children and the testing of intelligence. *J. Abnormal and Social Psychology* 1955, 50: 401–2.
Plumer, D. Parent-child verbal interaction: a naturalistic study of dialogue strategies. Interim report, Harvard Graduate School of Education, 1969.
Psathas, G. Comment, *American Psychologist* 1968, 23: 135–37.
Resnick, M.B.; Weld, G.L.; and Lally, J.R. Verbalizations of environmentally deprived two-year olds as a function of the presence of a tester in a standardized test situation. Paper presented at the meeting of the American Educational Research Association, February 1969, Los Angeles.
Robinson, W.P. The elaborated code in working-class language. *Language and Speech* 1965, 8: 243–52.
————. Restricted codes in sociolinguistics and the sociology of education. Paper presented at Ninth International Seminar, University College, December 1968, Dar es Salaam, Tanzania.
Shriner, T.H., and Miner, L. Morphological structures in the language of disadvantaged and advantaged children. *J. Speech and Hearing Research*

1968, 11: 605–10.

Shuy, R.W.; Wolfram, W.A.; and Riley, W.K. Linguistic correlates of social stratification in Detroit speech. U.S. Office of Education Cooperative Research Project No. 6-1347, 1967.

Slobin, D.I., ed. A field manual for cross-cultural study of the acquisition of communicative competence (second draft). Berkeley, California: University of California, 1967.

Slobin, D.I. Questions of language development in cross-cultural perspective. Paper prepared for symposium on Language Learning in Cross-Cultural Perspective at Michigan State University, September 1968.

Smith, M.E. A study of some factors influencing the development of the sentence in preschool children. *J. Genetic Psychology* 1935, 46: 182–212.

Stewart, W.A., and Wilson, J.M.P. Anthology on educational problems of the disadvantaged. *Florida Foreign Language Reporter* 1969, 7: No. 1.

Strandberg, T. E. An evaluation of three stimulus media for evoking verbalizations from preschool children. Master's thesis, Eastern Illinois University, 1969.

Strandberg, T. E., and Griffith, J. A study of the effects of training in visual literacy on verbal language behavior. Unpublished paper. Eastern Illinois University, 1968.

Williams, F. Social class differences in how children talk about television: some observations and speculations. *J. Broadcasting,* in press.

Williams, F., and Naremore, R.C. On the functional analysis of social class differences in modes of speech. *Speech Monographs* 1969, 36: 77–102.(a)

———. Social class differences in children's syntactic performance: a quantitative analysis of field study data. *J. Speech and Hearing Research* 1969, 12: 777–93.(b)

Wolcott, H.F. The teacher as an enemy. Unpublished paper. University of Oregon, 1969.

Wolf, E.R. *Anthropology.* Englewood Cliffs, N.J.: Prentice-Hall, 1964.

Chapter 6

HOW TO CONSTRUCT EFFECTIVE LANGUAGE PROGRAMS FOR THE POVERTY CHILD

Siegfried Engelmann*

The child of poverty has language problems. These are problems far more crippling than mere dialect problems. Too frequently, a four-year-old child of poverty does not understand the meaning of such words as *long, full, animal, red, under, first, before, or, if, all,* and *not.* Too frequently, he cannot repeat a simple statement, such as, "The bread is under the oven," even after he has been given four trials (Engelmann, 1967a). Too frequently, he cannot succeed on a task in which he is presented with a picture of two boys and two girls and is asked to "Find the right ones: He is big . . . . She is not standing on the floor . . . . She is next to a chair" and so on (Engelmann 1967a). In brief, the child of poverty has not been taught as much about the meaning of language as a middle-class child of the same age.

A goal of the Bereiter-Engelmann project at the University of Illinois has been to teach young disadvantaged children the meaning of basic language. The focus of instruction has been not on teaching a broad spectrum of language skills but on teaching the language of instruction. What this means, briefly, is that throughout the elementary grades, teachers will try to teach concepts. Teachers will present objects, such as long, flat pieces of wood, and they will

*Bureau of Educational Research, University of Illinois

An earlier version of this paper was included in the proceedings of the National Conference on Educational Objectives for the Culturally Disadvantaged, held on September 7-8, 1967, in Hot Springs, Arkansas.

indicate what these objects are (e.g., "This is a yardstick"). They will then point out specific relationships ("See? The yardstick is three feet long . . . "). The teachers will classify the object presented ("A yardstick is a measuring instrument"). They will indicate how it differs from other measuring instruments ("It's used to measure length in inches, or feet, or in a yard"). Most of the teaching presentations the child will encounter in the elementary grades take a form similar to the yardstick demonstration. The teacher presents an instance of a concept and then uses language to describe that instance. She may use the same object as instances of different concepts. For example, she may use a toy truck as an instance of *truck, vehicle, red, on the table,* and so on.

For her instruction to succeed in teaching and not in merely confusing the child, a minimum understanding of language is implied. This minimum understanding is the focus of the Bereiter-Engelmann language program. The program is outlined in some detail in the book, *Teaching Disadvantaged Children in the Preschool* (Bereiter and Engelmann 1966).

Although the program has been demonstrated to be effective in compensating for the language deficits of poverty children (Bereiter and Engelmann 1968), it is considered a controversial program. Most of the controversy seems to be based on some confusion about what the role of a compensatory program is and how one is systematically developed. What follows is a sketch of the rationale underlying the ground rules used in the Bereiter-Engelmann program for systematically developing programs such as the language program.

CONSTRUCTING A PROGRAM

There is a system that more or less assures sound programs, but this system is used too infrequently by curriculum designers and educators. Most programs for the disadvantaged are based on fuzzy statements about the objectives of instruction and on a kind of magical notion about what teaching is and how teaching is related to the development of the child.

The basic rule for solving educational problems is that every phase of the teaching procedure from the establishment of objectives to the teacher's presentation—must be described in terms of specific concepts. Any departure from this rule results in varying degrees of chaos. The objectives must be set up in terms of the specific concepts the child is expected to master; the analysis of the tasks must be expressed in terms of specific concepts; the primary evaluation of the program must be expressed in terms of specific concepts; the performance of the children must be expressed in terms of mastery of specific concepts; and the teacher's presentation must be expressed in terms of specific concepts. The entire process, in other words, must be expressed in terms of what the children are expected to know, and what they do know as inferred from their behavior. The reason that the entire process must be expressed in these terms is quite basic: the educator, the curriculum designer, and the teacher deal only in concepts. They are expected to evaluate the child's behavior in terms of the concepts he has or has not been taught. We will outline program construction in terms of five basic steps.

Step 1: Objectives

The first step in constructing a program is to specify the objectives. The objectives represent an absolute criterion of performance that is to be achieved by the children through training. In other words, after training they are supposed to be able to do things they could not do before—not just anything, but very specific things. If the objective is to teach certain language skills, the children must be taught these skills. The children have no choice in the matter and the program is a failure if these skills are not taught. If a program to teach certain communication skills fails to teach these skills but succeeds in teaching the children how to do freehand sketches, the program failed to do what it set out to do and must be considered a failure, even though the children learned something. This point can be seen by considering a more obvious example. Suppose that every child in the class learned something, but no two children learned the same thing and none of the children could demonstrate at the end of the program that he had learned the skills he was supposed to have been taught. The program is a failure because if the objectives of the program are legitimate, the children will be expected to use what they were supposed to have been taught in working out future problems. If they have not been taught these skills, they will not be able to use them, which means that they will not be able to meet the next set of educational objectives. The program, therefore, was a failure.

Since objectives must be absolute, they cannot possibly be derived from a study of the child. They are imposed as statements of what we want all children to learn. The word *all* must be emphasized. We cannot have one objective for some children and another objective for others. It is possible that some children will not achieve all of the educational objectives that are established, and since children differ in their repertoire of skills, it is axiomatic that a greater amount of teaching will be required to bring some children to the desired criterion of performance. But the objectives hold for all children. Through education, we would like to be able to teach disadvantaged Negro children the same set of skills we require for middle-class white children.

For objectives to be acceptable in the educational setting, they must be stated in terms of specific tasks the children should be able to handle after training. This stipulation is introduced to avoid confusion. Let us say that the objective is presented as a general statement rather than a series of specific tasks—"The objective of this program is to teach children language skills."

The person who is charged with developing a program to meet this objective might interpret the objective in terms of language as used in social interaction or in terms of language skills used in the beginning instructional setting. He might even consider language broadly, interpreting it to mean any behavior in interpersonal situations. He might then provide instruction in general interpersonal behavior—verbal and nonverbal. These are a few of the options that are open to him. The fact that he has options means that he has a "floating standard" by which he can evaluate any program. He is not compelled to look at a program and note whether it actually succeeded in teaching the skills it set out to teach. He could always ask about a given program, "Does that program actually teach language?" a question which means, "I'm using a floating standard; I'm using language to mean something other than what you had intended it to mean when you constructed your program." It is always possible to criticize a program on what it did not teach the children. But the major question is: Did it teach what it set out to teach? Unless we know precisely what the children in a particular program are supposed to be able to do after instruction, we do not know whether a program is a success or not. In other words, the objectives of a program cannot be expressed simply in terms of teaching the children language. The objectives must be expressed far more concretely. For example, the child should be able to answer questions of the form "Is this a ———?" when presented with objects found around the home or neighborhood. If we were provided with a few hundred other statements about what the children should be able to do after instruction, we would have a relatively clear idea of what the investigator means when he states that he is teaching language.

By detailing the objectives in this manner, the educator makes it possible for the program to be rigorous. By examining the objectives, one knows what the child must learn. The objectives serve as the basis for testing children to see whether the instruction has succeeded. One can no longer legitimately introduce extraneous tests of language mastery. The definition of objectives serves as a basis for directing the activity of the teacher. She knows what the end product for her teaching is supposed to be.

Objectives that cannot be translated into specific tasks cannot be allowed in program construction. The objective of teaching the whole child, stimulating self-realization, and providing readiness can be accepted as objectives only if they can be translated into specific tasks. The argument, sometimes presented by educators, that not everything can be measured and that it does violence to such concepts as the "whole child" to try to gauge teaching by a series of specific tests is not convincing. Without such tests, the program advocate is never quite sure whether his program is actually the one that achieves the desired learning. It is quite possible, in the absence of specific measures, that the program he most strongly opposes is actually the most effective in teaching the whole child. In fact, unless specific measures are provided, every program can claim that it teaches the whole child. Similarly, the objective of providing "meaningful experiences" can be claimed by any program unless this objective is translated into a series of specific tasks.

There is another important point about objectives, which is that the objectives of a training program must be demonstrably consistent with the assumed priorities of skills valued in our society. Educators must recognize that they are not policy makers. They cannot make up objectives that are inconsistent with society's general commitment to make children competent in the academic arena. This stipulation, again, is introduced because of the confusion that can result if it were not introduced. If educators and teachers are allowed to make up policy, it is possible that they will introduce objectives that are not consistent with the general set of educational values espoused by society, or they may introduce objectives that cannot be realized through education. The objective of teaching the child to cope with his home environment probably cannot be achieved through classroom education, simply because the teacher has control in the classroom, but not in the home environment. Therefore, many of the problems encountered in the home environment cannot be demonstrated, and the rules of behavior necessary to handle certain situations cannot be reinforced. It would be possible to teach the child facts about how to cope with his home environment, but not the behaviors that constitute effective coping. The objective of focusing education on dance and basket-weaving is not consistent with society's general commitment to competence. The skills learned in dance and basket-weaving are not used in higher-order tasks, such as writing expositions on the college level, solving quadratic equations, or doing assignments in history. These objectives are therefore allowable only if adequate provisions for reaching the primary objectives have been included in the objectives.

Two questions must be answered affirmatively about the objectives of an educational program:

A. Does it provide a precise standard for evaluating the performance of the children?

B. Does it teach skills that will be used in future educational tasks?

Our commitment to competence dictates that all children should be taught a set of skills that is sufficient to allow them admittance to college. If they do not go to college it should not be because they have failed to learn the appropriate skills.

Step 2: Analysis

If the objectives are stated as legitimate tasks, the next step follows naturally; it is the step of breaking the objectives into the constituent concepts (the concepts that are used in a particular task). When the objective is stated as tasks, the concepts involved in these tasks can be rigorously analyzed. For example, the following may be one of several hundred criterion tasks for a unit in following instructions: "Draw a straight horizontal line on your paper."

To determine conceptual components of this criterion task, one simply specifies the concepts that are necessarily used in accomplishing it. If a verbal concept is used, it must be taught before it is introduced in the task. It therefore must be prerequisite to the task. This is not a mere empirical fact; it is a logical necessity.

The major concepts or operations involved in the task above are these:

The child must understand the word *draw;* he must know the kind of behavior that is demanded by the signal "Draw ———" and be able to demonstrate his understanding by following such instructions as "Draw a circle," "Draw a boy," "Draw a line."

The child must understand the word *line;* he must be able to identify things that are lines and distinguish between lines and things that are not lines (such as ropes, sidewalks, and other objects that may look like lines when they are represented in a drawing).

The child must be able to demonstrate that he understands what the words *a line* mean. He must demonstrate that he can discriminate between the singular *a line* and the plural *lines, three lines, some lines,* and so on.

The child must understand what *straight* means. He must be able to discriminate between things that are straight and things that are not-straight.

The child must understand that *straight, horizontal line* calls for a line that is both straight and horizontal. He must be able to demonstrate that he can discriminate between straight, horizontal lines, not-straight horizontal lines, and not-straight not-horizontal lines.

The child must understand the concept *on.* He must be able to demonstrate that he can point to things that are on something and things that are not on something. He must be able to tell what object the things are on. ("The coat is on [the floor, the table, John, etc.]").

The child must demonstrate that he understands the instructions, "Draw on ———." He must demonstrate that he can distinguish between "Draw on ———" and "Sit on ———" "Put your hand on ———" and "Push on ———" and the like. He must also demonstrate that he can handle the instructional form "Draw———on———" in which different object words are introduced in the blanks.

The child must understand the meaning of the word *paper.*

The child must demonstrate that he understands the word *your.* He must be able to discriminate between instructions containing *your, my, his, the, a, all, some, any,* and so on.

Although the procedure of analyzing the criterion task (objective) in terms of its constituent operations may seem laborious, it is necessary if the program is to be solid. Instruction is based on analysis. Unless the analysis accounts for the teaching of every skill required to handle the criterion task, the analysis will not imply adequate instruction. Stated differently, a child may fail the criterion task for many different reasons. He may not understand the word *straight*, for example. He may not understand what the teacher means by *Draw a line.* He may not know what *your paper* refers to. The training which the child receives must systematically eliminate each of the possible causes of failure. The training will be able to do this consistently only if all possible causes of failure are identified. They will be identified if the criterion task is carefully analyzed in terms of the concepts that are involved in it.

The analysis is only partially completed with the identification of the concepts that are used in the criterion task. To teach each of these constituent concepts, the teacher must use concrete demonstrations. That is, she must present specific objects and specific statements in connection with them. However, specific tasks are not implied by the analysis, which means, for example, that it is possible for one to make up more than one presentation for teaching the meaning of *straight, horizontal,* or other concepts. Futhermore, each of these presentations may contain words and operations that are not included in the criterion task. For example, in teaching the meaning of *straight*, the teacher may present the statement, "Show me the lines that are not straight." Thus new concepts such as, "Show me———" "lines," "that," and "not straight," are introduced in the task. Provisions must be made for the teaching of each of these concepts.

Since the teacher must demonstrate each of the constituent concepts, the curriculum designer must present every constituent concept as a task—a demonstration complete with statements and objects that are to be presented. In this way he will be able to see whether concepts that do not appear in the criterion problem must be taught, and he will be able to provide for the teaching of these new concepts. He will be able to analyze the constituent tasks in the same way he analyzed the criterion tasks. The ordering of the tasks comes about naturally from the type of concept analysis that is conducted. If a concept (operation, skill) is called for in a complex task, that concept preceded the complex task in the instructional sequence.

To assure that each constituent concept will be taught, each presentation specified in the analysis must be designed so that it is consistent with one and only one interpretation. If the presentation could possibly admit to more than one interpretation, it will probably fail to teach all children the desired skills. If the presentation calls for one object to teach the concept *red*, a child could legitimately conclude that *red* is another name for that particular object, that *red* has something to do with the shape or texture of the object, or that *red* refers to the color of the object. Unless the presentation rules out all possible incorrect interpretations by demonstrating, with a variety of objects, that the invariant referred to as "red" is the color and only the color, the presentation is not acceptable. Some incorrect interpretations may be ruled out with precise statements. However, physical demonstrations are usually necessary, especially when the curriculum designer is dealing with basic sensory concepts.

The specification of tasks that are to be presented to the children is governed by the principle of presentational economy. According to this principle, there are operations that are essential to the understanding of concepts and there are features that are not essential. For example, the ability to use syntactical forms is essential to successful performance on communication tasks; however, the ability to explain the usage in terms of syntax or grammar is not. The former ability would have to be incorporated in a program designed to teach communication skills; the latter would not because it is possible to teach all relevant skills involved in the criterion without referring to grammar or syntax.

Also, the principle of presentational economy would dictate that any procedure that can increase the potential rate of future teaching is preferable to techniques that are potentially slower. The potential rate of the presentation is determined by the amount of new teaching required for a set of tasks. Presentational economy is achieved by treating aspects of tasks that are the same in the same way. Since they are treated in the same way, less new learning is implied because elements are repeated from presentation to presentation. Stated differently, when one classifies tasks according to how they are the same, he is able to construct a basic set of procedures that apply to all instances included in the category. When one does not proceed in this manner, however, he must start from scratch on each problem and provide for a great deal more teaching. All opposites are the same in terms of the type of reasoning that is involved. If one is told that something is not wet, he knows that it is dry. He can draw this conclusion from the *not* statement. Since all opposites share this characteristic, they can be presented using variations of the same statement forms and variations of the same basic demonstrational procedures. A more detailed description of the procedures of concept analysis and task construction is contained in the author's paper, "Concepts and Problem Solving" (Engelmann 1969).

Using the procedure of analysis outlined above, one can work from any complex task down to its most minimal constituents. Futhermore, it is possible to determine precisely how close any individual is to criterion performance and to specify precisely what he must be taught if he is to handle the criterion task (or set of tasks). In other words, precise testing and teaching are implied by this method of analysis, and only by this method of analysis. The confusion of language and reading is a good example of what happens if the procedure is violated. There are a number of programs for the disadvantaged which are premised on the idea that the child will be taught how to read if he is taught a variety of language and perceptual skills. There is some relationship between language skills and reading skills, but a very specific and narrow one. As a generalization, reading will not be taught through language instruction (Engelmann 1967b).

Step 3: Tryout

The analysis of the objective or criterion task provides one with a list of prerequisite skills and the specification of tasks designed to teach each skill. However, the analysis does not tell anything about the relative "psychological difficulty" of each task. It does not tell him which tasks will be relatively easy for the children and which will be relatively difficult. The degree of difficulty for the tasks is discovered by presenting the tasks to children. What often happens is that the children will go through an entire sequence of tasks in a few minutes only to bog down on a further task for a few days, or even weeks. When such rough spots are encountered, the curriculum designer should first assume that his analysis is inadequate. He should blame himself, and assume that the children are having difficulties because he is asking them to learn more than one new concept at a time or that he is asking them to take more than one small step at a time.

Here is an example of the type of problem that may be encountered. The program calls for the teacher to teach number identification using the statement form, "This number is————." However, young disadvantaged children may fail to learn numbers partly because the task is requiring them to learn the names of the new objects. As a result, the children may not realize that the task calls for the same identification process they use in other situations. They may conclude that the statement is somehow a part of the identification procedure and that the exercise is a word game, not an identification task. This error can be corrected by changing the identification procedure so that it is more similar to the procedure the children are used to using—by requiring a single-word response: "What is this? . . . Three." Now the children can concentrate on the identification of the object, not on the compound task of concentrating on the identification and the production of an unfamiliar statement.

Through tryout the curriculum designer is able to give his program the refinements that do not come from the analysis of constituent concepts. If the children find the task he presents dull, he must do something to liven it up, perhaps changing the pace of tasks in the program so that children are not operating on the same level of intensity at all times. If the children are not serious about what is being taught, he must devise exercises in which there is a strong payoff for using the skills that are taught and no payoff for failing to use them properly. It may be that the curriculum designer fails to figure out how to lead children to certain constituent concepts without difficulties or extensive drill. This does not mean that the book is closed or that another curriculum designer will be unable to devise a series of tasks that works. It merely means that for the present, the educator must work with the program as it is, recognizing its specific shortcomings.

Step 4: Programming

The next step in the development of a program is to assure that the teacher can present concepts effectively and diagnose the children's responses in terms of precisely what they have been taught and what they have not been taught. The teacher must be thoroughly familiar with the steps a child must take to reach the criterion of performance set for a given task. Without detailed understanding, she may waste time and present tasks that are cumbersome. She may present questions that can be failed for a number of reasons, questions that contain words and concepts which have not been programmed.

If the program is adequate, the teacher should be able to test a child's mastery of a given concept by presenting a question or a direction to do something that can be failed for only one reason. If it can be failed for more than one reason, the teacher does not know precisely what to teach the child. She has options, and she may choose the appropriate option, or she may think that she knows why the child failed the task, but be quite wrong. She may have designed the question to get at the child's understanding of a particular concept, but unless the child understands everything in the question except that concept, he may fail for unsuspected reasons. For example, if the teacher asks the child, "Are there more red beads or are there more beads made of wood?" she may think that she is testing the child's understanding of class inclusion. But unless she knows that the child understands every constituent concept in the question—the concepts *more, beads,* or, *made of wood,* and so on—the child may fail the item for other reasons than the intended one. If she proceeds on the assumption that the child failed the item because he does not understand the concept of class inclusion, she is therefore operating from a position of ignorance.

The program that is adequate buttresses against such errors by programming the concepts one at a time, so that the teacher knows that the children understand all of the concepts in her statements except one—the one she is currently teaching. However, the program is never perfect, and the teacher must be able to diagnose the performance of the children in terms of what they do not know. She needs more than quantitative data. She must be able to infer from a child's responses to a series of questions what he thinks the concept is (or which concept is consistent with his behavior). She must then be able to provide a series of demonstrations that contradict his interpretation and point out to him the acceptable interpretation. For example, if his behavior is consistent with the interpretation that *red* is another word for *ball*, she must quickly demonstrate that things that cannot be called *ball* can be called *red* and that not all balls are called *red*. Inferring concepts from children's performance is not easy; it requires a great deal of practice in formulating tentative interpretations, providing appropriate questions to test these hypotheses, and then providing the demonstration that corrects the misinterpretation.

To teach properly, the teacher must hold her intuition in check. She must satisfy the requirements of the program in a way that comes naturally to her, but she must stifle the impulse to refer to operations and to use words that have not been programmed. She must learn to work fast, so that the children can receive as much practice as she can cram into a session, and so that the point is obvious when she is treating things in an analogous way. If the instances of an analogy are spaced several minutes apart, it may be some time before the child is able to get the point. If the instances follow each other at an interval of only a few seconds, however, the point is more obvious. There is less intervening noise for the child to deal with. Most important, the teacher must realize that the children she is working with—those complex beings—must be reduced to precise statements of what they know. Such statements are necessary if she is to bring every child to the desired level of performance in the least amount of time. In summary, the teacher must be a highly trained technician, not a combination of educational philosopher and social worker. She must recognize that she is responsible for a unique contribution to the child's welfare, that of teaching him essential concepts and skills. If she fails to satisfy this need, she will have failed, regardless of how well-meaning she is or how many visits to the home she makes. If she does not teach relevant skills, nobody will.

Step 5: Evaluation

The final step in constructing a program is to evaluate the results of the program. The most significant measure from an educational standpoint is the measure of whether the children achieved the desired criteria of performance. Such a detailed achievement evaluation is of primary importance because it comments on what the children know, which means that it provides a clear basis for formulating the next set of educational objectives. If children have mastered basic algebra by the end of the second grade, objectives in which basic algebra concepts are used can be established. The tasks in a program are presented because they teach concepts that are to be used in future tasks. The evaluation, therefore, must provide detailed information about whether the children met the criteria of performance. If the children have, then they are ready to move on to tasks in which they will use what they have learned. If they have not met the criteria of performance, they must work on these before proceeding.

The evaluation of the program in terms of IQ gain or some amorphous index of achievement is interesting to some but not particularly pertinent to the problem of teaching children, because these measures provide a gross indication of what happened during the training. But they are not useful in the present type of program since they do not relate the performance of each child to the specific criteria of instruction that had been established. The criterion-referenced measure evaluates the instruction in terms of the criteria of performance that grew out of the objectives.

ABUSES IN PROGRAM CONSTRUCTION

The educator who recognizes the necessity of the steps outlined above is able to operate from a position of strength. He knows where his ball park is and what it looks like. Consequently, he knows whether a given approach belongs in his ball park or belongs somewhere else. He rejects theoretical approaches unless they conform to the ground rules that obtain in his ball park. This is perhaps the most difficult point for some educators to understand. Merely because a theory or (in most cases) a series of organized observations seem plausible is no reason for accepting them. For them to be acceptable they must imply specific variables that can be manipulated. They must specify, not the whole child in a learning situation, but what must be done to change that child in a particular way. We will briefly examine some of the problems growing out of other approaches.

Developmental Approaches

The most common mistake that educators make is to work from theoretical explanations that are either irrelevant to or incompatible with the nature of the teaching situation. For example, educators often turn to theoretical explanations of how children develop. While it is possible for the educator to use developmental norms to arrive at some conclusion about what a particular child knows, developmental explanations are totally irrelevant to the act of teaching children. The tests of a child's cognitive development are merely samples of what he has learned. Like any other sample, they are subject to probability phenomena. If a child scores poorly on a series of "cognitive" tests, the chances are that he will score poorly on concepts that have not been tested. The environment that has not taught skills A through M to the child probably has not taught him skill N. Any broad sample of knowledge will therefore have a certain amount of predictive validity.

Although the information provided by developmental measures may be of some use in placing a child (especially a child who scores at the extremes of the range), the information cannot be used in the teaching or program development situations (except to indicate specific items that the child has failed). Teaching is based on the assumption that through the appropriate manipulation of environmental variables, the desired concepts can be taught and desired behavior can be induced. In order to know what kind of environmental manipulation is necessary, the educator must know precisely what the child knows in relation to specific criteria of performance. Regardless of what other information the educator has, he must have this information. Developmental tests usually do not provide such information, which in this respect makes them irrelevant to our needs.

This point is illustrated by the following example. Suppose that 90 percent of the children who passed a given developmental test knew the concepts *before* and *after* as they are used to describe events that are sequenced. The teacher who is given information on how her children performed on the developmental test would still have to test the children in the class on their knowledge of *before* and *after*. Possibly the test did not predict accurately with any of her children. The developmental test has no function in the teaching situation, because with it or without it, the teacher must test the concept understanding of every child in the class. The developmental test has neither provided a unique contribution nor has it served to eliminate a single step that the teacher would have to take if she did not have the test.

The weakness of the developmental approach can be stated in a different way. The analysis of criterion tasks reveals a minimum set of concepts the child must learn (and some additional concepts). It reveals the steps a child must take to reach the desired criterion of performance. Unless performance on a particular constituent task is revealed in the analysis to be essential to mastery of the criterion problem, it is irrelevant to us at this point. Therefore, unless a particular developmental task is revealed in the analysis, it is not one of the essential steps that a child must take to reach the desired criterion of performance. In the analysis of the instructions, "Draw a straight, horizontal line on your paper," one does not encounter such concepts as those involved in making judgments about the amounts of liquid in containers of different diameters. Therefore, the water-level task, although it may be of some normative significance, is not essential to the criterion of performance on the horizontal-line task and therefore tells us nothing about how ready the child is to be taught. His readiness is expressed only in terms of his performance on skills that are disclosed by an analysis of the task.

The major difficulty with developmental explanations is that they are based on the assumption that children learn. The teaching assumption is that children are taught. A child does not reach such specific criteria of performance as making correct judgments about liquid amounts unless he is taught.

He must be taught the various words in the instructions; he must be taught, through one type of demonstration or another, that liquids are composed of "fixed units." He must be taught that the changes in the height of the column of liquid are compensated for by changes in the width. The developmental explanation supposes that these concepts are learned. If they are learned, there is nothing we can do about the acquisition of "conservation" responses. If they are taught, however, we can treat the conservation responses like any other objective of training. That is, state the objective as a series of tasks, analyze these tasks into constituent concepts, and provide instruction that will teach these in a manner far less haphazard than the usual teaching procedure. It is an empirical fact that such teaching will succeed (Brison and Sullivan 1967).

Developmental norms imply that there is a fixed order of development. From a teaching-oriented standpoint, they imply that there is a fixed order of development under specific teaching conditions. A child's performance reflects nothing more than the relative effectiveness of the teaching that he has received. The culturally disadvantaged child is, according to developmental explanations, developmentally impaired. He scores poorly on developmental measures. Does this mean that we should give up on him or wait for him to mature? Not if we believe in the process of teaching. We must simply identify the relevant criteria of performance on which he is weak and provide the kind of careful instruction that will allow us to teach rapidly. If we teach rapidly enough, he will catch up.

The notion of readiness is based on the developmental assumption that something magical happens to a child with age. From the teaching-oriented view, nothing magical can happen. The child is simply taught concepts. The longer the period of time, the more concepts he is taught. Unless the child's performance is expressed in these terms, there is no remedy for the child who is not ready except to let time exert its magical influence on his development.

There is a test to determine whether developmental approaches are relevant to problems of teaching. That is to ask, "Does the approach tell what the child must learn to meet a specific criterion of performance?" As a rule, the answer will be "No." As a rule, therefore, developmental explanations do not imply the kind of remedy that can be provided through instruction.

The development approach is premised on the idea that objectives of education can be devised from a study of the child. Objectives, however, are basically "ought" statements —"The child ought to learn X." Statements about children's performance, are "is" statements—statements of fact—"The child is able to do X." It is impossible to derive "ought" statements from "is" statements, a fact that has been recognized for some time in philosophy, but which apparently has not been assimilated by the educator. To try to derive what children should learn from what they normally learn is to attempt the impossible and to commit gross reasoning errors in the process. The criteria of performance that are established as objectives of education are value judgments. They cannot be derived from a study of the child or from the "logic of the child." The "logic" is either acceptable or unacceptable in terms of specific criteria. If it is unacceptable, it must be changed through instruction.

The Linguistic and Psycholinguistic Approaches

One of the most unfortunate tendencies of some educators who deal with children's communication problems is to refer to explanations used in linguistics and psycholinguistics. The argument is that there is something to be learned from these approaches, since they present a somewhat rigorous analysis of speech sounds and written symbols. This argument, although popular, is not sound. A given criterion of performance may involve the use of language. For example, the investigator presents common objects such as balls, tables, and so on, and the child indicates what these objects are by using statements. Language is involved, but with definite restrictions. The language the child uses must be correct, that is, it must describe the object that is being presented. The child cannot pass the criterion test merely by using statements per se, such as, "This is a ball." He must use this statement only when the investigator presents a ball. If the child responds to a table by saying, "This is a ball," his production may be acceptable from a linguistic standpoint, but from an educational standpoint it is unacceptable.

Since the performance criterion for the task stipulates that the child must be able to use the statements appropriately, the kind of instruction that is implied is not merely one of learning sounds. It is one of learning the relationship between signals and observable aspects of reality. The child must understand what a ball is. He must be able to point to things that are balls and things that are not balls. In addition, he must be able to produce the statement that appropriately describes what he observes. The criterion militates against the possibility that the child receives instruction in sound production only. Yet, at best, sound production is all that linguistic theory can comment on, and even in this area, the comments would be extremely weak. This point is very obvious if one refers to any specific criterion of performance that is legitimately included in an educational program. The criterion usually considers language as a part of the child's successful performance, rarely as the entire criterion. From analysis of the criterion we can see what the child must learn and how a teacher would go about correcting specific mistakes. Linguistic analysis implies neither of these procedures.

That the linguistic approach is basically irrelevant to education is nicely illustrated by the linguist's description of the child's use of the open-and-pivot class constructions. It is interesting to note that children learn syntactical patterns, but it is not particularly astonishing, nor does it imply any educational remedy for children who do not use language appropriately. An adequate explanation of why children use open-pivot class constructions would have to include reference to the concepts the children are dealing with. On the linguistic level we cannot explain why children learn to use open-pivot class constructions. When one refers to concepts, however, it becomes evident that a given physical event represents the intersect of many concepts, and that each of these concepts can be found in other physical events. Given this fact, and the fact that a child learns to express these concepts, it follows that he has to deal in open-pivot class constructions of one sort or another. The combinations that are possible in reality are possible in the child's speech—"Green chair, green table, green grass"; "Truck bye-bye, Mommy bye-bye, Tommy byebye." To teach *green*, one must present various instances of green. These are open-pivot constructions. "This chair is green, this table is green, the grass is green." When a child uses open-pivot class constructions, therefore, it means merely that he has been taught some of the basic facts about the world of concepts. It does not mean that he has been taught in the most economical or efficient way.

The psycholinguist sometimes tries to bridge the gap between what he can legitimately conclude and what he would like to be able to say about teaching by introducing the notion of meaning. For the psycholinguist meaning is something that is personal—"You have your meaning and I have mine." By introducing this notion, the psycholinguist seems to believe that he is now able to comment on educational problems. But he cannot, for the simple reason that his notion of meaning has no educational application. All teaching deals with public meaning, the meaning that everybody agrees upon. The concept *red* is not merely something that one believes. It refers to something that can be found in the world, that can be observed by various people. If the educator did not operate from this basic notion of meaning, he could not sanction any type of education. The teacher may believe that an object is blue, but if she accepts the personal definition of *meaning*, she would have to recognize that this is her interpretation. Then a child who calls the same object *red* has his "meaning," and the teacher would have absolutely no basis for telling the child that he is wrong, so long as meaning is defined in terms of one's personal responses to stimuli.

There is a good test to demonstrate the irrelevant nature of linguistic and psycholinguistic attempts to set up educational programs. That is, one asks himself if it is possible, using the same statements that the program uses—the same theoretical premises—to develop a program that is different or even diametrically opposed to the proposed program. For example, if the linguist advocates the use of natural social situations to teach communication skills, see if it is possible to take his premises and derive a program based on precise programming of word sounds. In every case, opposite conclusions are possible, because it is not possible to imply statements about teaching from the premises upon which the linguist and the psycholinguist operate. Attempts to use linguistic analysis as the basis for teaching reading have produced the full range of programs, from paragraph reading to single-sound variations. The linguist's entire theoretical preamble, in other words, is nothing more than an appeal used to sanction an approach that derives from personal preferences, not from linguistic principles.

The Verbal/Nonverbal Dichotomy

Educators who turn to models of how children learn often draw spurious distinctions between verbal and nonverbal skills. The distinction arises because those who set up the tasks in a program do not follow the procedure of specifying the type of test which will be taken as an indication that the child has learned the skill being taught. These educators do not state that the objective is to have children learn such skills as sorting objects according to various criteria, and then specify precisely the type of test that will be given the child. Instead, they take a short circuit. They specify that the objective is to have the children demonstrate such skills as being able to sort objects, and then they classify the activity of object-sorting in some rationally derived category. They may conclude that block-sorting is an activity that involves visual-motor associations. Thus, since object-sorting is a nonverbal activity, they proceed to treat the task as a nonverbal task. They conclude that the task is nonverbal simply because it contains nonverbal components. If they had been more precise in the way they set up the objectives, however, they would have seen that this task cannot be legitimately called a nonverbal one because the test to be administered contains verbal (or receptive language) components. The child is given directions—"Put the blocks that are blue over here ———, Put the blocks that are big over here———," and so forth. If the program is to teach the child what he must know in order to handle the criterion task, the program must provide for teaching the behavior demanded by the language in these instructions. When the criterion task is used as the basis for analyzing constituent tasks, it becomes apparent that the child must have both the nonverbal awareness of the rules or operations in the problem and the understanding of how these relate to specific language signals.

If a task is treated as nonverbal, the verbal components may not be taught. The teacher may use language in an incidental manner and never test the child to see whether he understands the language she uses. She may hastily conclude that the child's inability to handle the task indicates that he needs new practice in object-sorting.

Another offspring of the verbal/nonverbal distinction is the teaching presentation that is merely consistent with a particular concept. Simply because a presentation is consistent with a particular concept does not mean that it is capable of teaching the concept. The teacher may present a ball and say, "This is red." Although her statement is true and is consistent with the concept she is trying to teach, it is also consistent with the interpretation that *red* is another name for the object she is presenting. Instead of calling it *ball*, we'll now call it *red*. Unless the teacher takes further steps to demonstrate clearly what *red* means (and not by having the child sniff an apple or mix red Kool-Aid) her presentation is incapable of consistently teaching the concept.

The Case–History Approach

Although case-history information may be useful to the school adminis-trator and may be of interest to the educator in his role as an informed citizen, this information is irrelevant to him in his role as a teacher or curriculum developer. Case-history data simply do not translate into what the child has learned. The fact that a child plays on a dirty floor tells the teacher nothing about how the child will perform on a specific criterion task. The test of case-history information is simply this: would the information lead the teacher to change one single element in the way she would appraise the child's reper-toire of relevant skills or teach new concepts? Most often it would not.

The case-history approach provides the educator with an inexhaustible number of options. It is possible to find causes for failure in the case histories of every child alive. By the time a child has reached the age of four, he has been traumatized and frustrated. He may have had illnesses, toilet-training traumas, perhaps even a difficult birth. It is therefore always possible, after the fact, to explain why a child failed. But the type of "why" used in case-history analyses does not translate into statements about what the child has been taught. There is nothing unique about a child who fails in school except that he has not been taught skills that are used in the instructional setting. Further-more, all of the information in the world about the child's history, his personal needs, and his problems does not imply educational remedy. For there to be educational remedies, the child's difficulties must be expressed in terms of what the child does not know, and his lack of knowledge must be evident in the classroom.

Educators rely heavily on case-history data because the case-history ap-proach is consistent with the notion that children differ and that education must meet each child's individual needs. Exactly what does this mean? The teaching process has as its goal absolute standards of performance. The child who indicates that seven times one equals one is not performing according to the standard. His responses, his individual difference in this area, cannot be accepted. So it is with behavior problems. If a child's classroom behavior is unacceptable and interferes with his learning and the learning of the others in the class, his individual needs cannot be accepted. His behavior must be changed. In short, education is not designed to satisfy the individual needs of the child if by needs we mean a child's desire to express himself in his own way or behave in his own way. The entire process is geared to make him behave in a conventionally acceptable way, both in handling concepts and in conducting himself in the classroom. The aim of the educational process is conformity (even when the criterion is expressed as divergent tasks, that is, tasks for which there is more than one correct answer). There is no way to have education without having conformity. Granted there are extreme differences in the type of rules to which conformity is demanded, but the process is generally one of modifying behavior to meet specified standards, and not necessarily standards that the child selects.

The individual differences that the teacher should concentrate on are differences in what children have been taught. When the teacher is provided with information about what the children have been taught, she can individualize instruction and begin teaching each child what he must learn, starting on his level and working up. Unless individual differences are limited to differences in what children have been taught, however, the teacher may use platitudes about satisfying the particular needs of the disadvantaged as she provides a combination of poor therapy and poor teaching.

IN SUM

The failure of education to teach language skills effectively to disadvantaged children and to provide them (and their teachers) with a quality education, stems from an almost appalling failure to recognize what education is and what it is designed to do, and from the theoretical limitations that are imposed by the nature of the teaching process. Too many educators are debating about the "aims of education" and borrowing theories from symbolic logic and psychology. They are searching for some kind of magic that will motivate the children or somehow stimulate children's cognitive processes. Too many educators have never seriously considered what teaching is all about. For them, it is a mysterious process in which the teacher somehow stimulates learning.

There are a great many evils in the poverty community. Some of these evils lead to despair, failure, poor health, and a defensive outlook. Many cannot be corrected through better school programs, but some can. School programs can recognize that their goal is to teach these children, to bring them to an acceptable standard of performance on academic skills. For the schools to succeed, they must abandon some of their cherished approaches and begin examining the problems with a realistic eye. Disadvantaged children can be taught, but the approaches that are used in many school programs will not work because they are not designed to work. They do not acknowledge that the disadvantaged child is different in terms of his motivation to work. To treat this child as one would treat a middle-class child is to deny that he is different. To put this child through programs designed for middle-class children is to commit oneself to lock-step teaching. It is in effect, to say, "These children will go through the same motions as the middle-class child goes through, regardless of how different these children may be." Disadvantaged children can be taught language and reasoning skills. But the process must begin with a sound evaluation of specifically what we want these children to be taught and an analysis of the steps that they must take. The instruction that follows from this procedure will be instruction, and not a mere sham that may have some appeal to our finer instincts.

REFERENCES

Bereiter, C. and Engelmann, S. *Teaching Disadvantaged Children in the Preschool.* Englewood Cliffs, N.J.: Prentice-Hall, 1966.

———. An academically oriented preschool for disadvantaged children: results from the initial experimental group. In D. Brison and Jane Hill, eds., *Psychology and Early Childhood.* Toronto: Ontario Institute for Studies in Education, 1968.

Brison, D. W., and Sullivan, E. V., eds. *Recent Research on the Acquisition of Conservation of Substance.* Toronto: Ontario Institute for Studies in Education, 1967.

Engelmann, S. *The Basic Concept Inventory.* Chicago: Follett Publishing Co., 1967.(a)

———. Teaching reading to children with low mental ages. *Education and Training of Mentally Retarded* 1967, 2: 190–92.(b)

———. Conceptual learning. In K. E. Beery and B. D. Bateman, eds., *Dimensions in Early Learning Series.* San Rafael, Calif.: Dimensions Publishing Co., 1969.

Chapter 7

SEMANTIC SYSTEMS OF CHILDREN: SOME ASSESSMENTS OF SOCIAL CLASS AND ETHNIC DIFFERENCES

Doris R. Entwisle*

LANGUAGE AND LIFE CHANCES

Topics which are of equal interest in the study of persons and in the study of societies are rare. Language, however, is a functional requisite both of selfhood and of social systems, and the study of language cannot therefore avoid an interdisciplinary emphasis. The process of language acquisition is certainly not yet well understood. Nevertheless the new generation acquires its native tongue, whatever it may be, and socialization in terms of language is the central pivot for all other socialization. Such socialization relates directly to social stratification and to social mobility.

Differential mobility can be conceived as a function of the relative opportunities (life chances) available to individuals who occupy various niches in the social structure. Money, specialized training, and prestigious contacts, are all relatively inaccessible to individuals in the lower social strata. When lower-class persons interact with persons from higher social strata under impersonal and public conditions, members of the lower class are identified primarily by dress and speech. Dress is fast fading as a source of social-class cues; the disparity between the type and quality of clothing worn by members of various

*Department of Social Relations, The Johns Hopkins University
Preparation of this paper was aided by support from the Center for the Study of the Social Organization of Schools, The Johns Hopkins University.

123

social classes lessens each year. Speech, however, continues to furnish reliable cues, for persons retain, to a surprising degree, linguistic habits and inflections learned in childhood. Ten to fifteen seconds of speech are sufficient to make reliable judgments of social status (Harms 1961). Pronunciation of a single word by an invisible speaker ("arrow" at the other end of a telephone line) is sufficient to establish the identity of the speaker as a Negro. Such an identification may have many consequences. If the caller is seeking a taxi, he might expect a longer wait than a Caucasian customer. If the caller seeks information from a branch of the city or state government he might find himself shunted from one extension to another or simply cut off.

Life chances may thus be directly shaped by linguistic habits that influence interpersonal relations, partly because speech instantaneously identifies members of a particular social group. Even more drastically, if cognition and language are as closely related as now supposed, life chances may be shaped more subtly by inadequate cognitive habits and skills. A lower-class person may fail to achieve upward mobility partly for motivational reasons—he is not socialized to strive for status or other goals the middle class prizes. But this may be also partly for cognitive reasons—he fails to perceive his environment in terms sufficiently differentiated so that he can recognize opportunities, or size up situations quickly and accurately, or even be aware in some cases that more than one alternative for action exists. In addition, if his speech identifies him as a member of an outgroup, when tagged as a member of that group he may be endowed with all the other modal attributes of that group—relatively low economic status, low educational status, values that emphasize immediate rather than delayed gratifications, relatively low power in the social hierarchy, or even having certain political leanings.

The main avenue for upward mobility of Americans, at least in folklore, has been the free public educational system. An overly simplistic view of this movement neglects, for one thing, the highly selective character of intercontinental migration. Only those especially strong in all ways would start for America in the first place or persevere once arrived, and the conclusion that education has proved so efficacious a socializing agent for immigrants from Europe over the past century may contain more fantasy than truth. Aside from motivational differences between European immigrants of a century ago and the present residents of the urban ghettos—and such differences may be of overriding importance—educational opportunities are perhaps more a consequence than a cause of upward mobility. Even for Jewish families, educational attainment typically occurs in subsequent generations, after financial and residential security has occurred. Be that as it may, evidence mounts that the educational system at present is not really meshing with the ghetto child.

Those who hope for the school to play a large role in overcoming the culture of poverty have cause for concern. Most strikingly, the ghetto child does not become functionally literate at an early age, and the deficit in literacy seems to increase as he progresses through school. Relative illiteracy is an obstacle to life chances that gets greater both within the life of the individual and within the cycle of society. If an individual fails to become sufficiently literate, all other parts of the educational process break down. The child who cannot read well acquires a scanty store of information; his ineptness in reading directions causes him to show up poorly on standardized tests, and then he is put into "slow" or "basic" sections in school; he is handicapped in assimilating and interpreting all the events in the world around him by his clumsiness in reading. In effect it is as though he reaps compound interest on his initial deficit; his skills of perceiving, of learning, and of attention are stunted because less and less success is experienced. Less and less success leads to less and less expectation of success by him and by his teachers, and the whole deficit snowballs. Thus within his own life cycle, illiteracy is an impediment that gets worse with time. Within the cycle of society as a whole, illiteracy is also an increasing barrier since the population is increasingly more urban and dependent upon a complex technology. Fewer jobs demand muscle power alone. Even the man who opens his own small business—the favorite strategy of the European immigrant in years gone by—needs to be literate to survive. He must report taxes on complicated forms, or deal with other business firms' invoices, bills of lading, and vouchers, or even estimate what kinds of liabilities he may fall heir to. It is not a question of "schoolroom" as opposed to "practical" knowledge. In today's society the worth of human muscle power is diminishing.

The central importance of language is acknowledged in the massive efforts now aimed at early education of the culturally deprived. Subcultural differences in language (and cognitive) development are assumed to be important, but documentation of this assumption is surprisingly sparse. It is astonishing —even somewhat frightening—how somewhat little solid information is available to guide these action programs. Much of what has already been said about educational deficits and about the role of language in life chances is based more on intuition than on hard data. What is called for is detailed mapping of both the dialects and the semantic structures of the culturally impoverished.

Workers in applied linguistics have addressed themselves to the dialect(s) of lower-class children, especially blacks, with a view toward teaching standard English as a second language. Inflections differ, or receive differential usage, among urban whites and blacks, and communication completely breaks down in some instances because of this. Clearly also, by pointing up the specific features of the dialect and by emphasizing that speech of inner-city blacks has an internal consistency and order of its own—it is not just wrong or ungrammatical—blacks can be taught another dialect more efficiently and at the same time their natural speech is not ignored or devalued. The black child internalizes a different linguistic code as a consequence of the cultural forces impinging on him. At the same time, because his subculture is an enclave within the larger white society, he is forced to internalize a second code, standard English. Baratz (in press; see Chapter 2) recently emphasized that if linguistic development is judged by proficiency in both codes, the black child is, if anything, linguistically advanced as compared to the white middle-class child. This is far different from concluding that a black child is linguistically deficient or incompetent. At times psychologists have seen "cognitive deficits" when in fact dialect differences ignored by, or unknown to, the investigator produce differences in behavior that get labeled as cognitive deficits.

THE CONCEPT OF SEMANTIC STRUCTURES

This paper reports a different kind of research on language. Its concern is not the formal structure of the code in terms of syntax or phonology, but in the semantic structures characteristic of black and white speakers, or of middle-class and lower-class speakers. Elements (simple words, for example) of a linguistic code that appear to be the same (neglecting some phonological differences) for two different cultural groups need not have identical semantic implications for speakers from these groups. Group differences in such semantic implications have received almost no attention, because the topic is an unwieldy one, both in terms of its theoretical underpinnings and in terms of its methodology. Nevertheless, the same life conditions that foster dialect differences would be presumed to lead to semantic differences. At simple levels of discourse, difficulties in communication may be minimal, but semantic differences, added to the phonological and dialect differences already mentioned, may have very serious consequences for the reading instruction of young children. In other words, differences on the semantic level could pose a further burden to the disadvantaged child, and yet so far little notice has been taken of these structures. As McNeill (1965) points out, the semantic component of children's grammar has repercussions for wide areas of cognition beyond language itself.

What kinds of problems do semantic differences produce? To take a well-worn example, the semantic associates (or semantic structure) of *apple* for a father might include shiny, red, sweet, nutritious, and so forth, and for his son (who had recently been made ill by eating green apples) might include nauseating, green, tough, and so on. The different semantic systems will not impede direct communication at the moment, for there need be no confusion on their parts about what is being discussed, and an apple may actually be present nearby. But if one assumed the son's associations to apple did not change he might eventually classify this word with *dogberries, elderberries,* and other inedible or unpleasant objects, rather than with *oranges* and *bananas*. If he were very young and just learning to read, he might guess from a picture in a reading primer that a boy was presenting his teacher with a red ball, or a tomato, rather than an apple. The point is that a different semantic structure does not necessarily impede communication at a simple level, but it seems very likely to me that it could greatly impede learning to read or other more complex forms of linguistic behavior. If semantic structures within subgroups of the population differ, then the semantic cues that are presumed to exist, and hopefully aid the teaching of reading and other language skills, may be much more visible to some children than to others.

Word Associations as a Strategy for Studying Semantic Structures

For some time, and for many reasons besides clarifying the interrelationships between language and poverty, the author has been studying the language of children from age four on (Entwisle, Forsyth, and Muuss 1964; Entwisle 1966a, b, c, 1968a, b). A very important concern in this work has been to contrast children from different subcultures and social classes where characteristics such as intelligence level, age, and sex are controlled. Most of the data have been obtained by asking children to give "the first word you think of" in response to a standard set of stimulus words (free associations).[1] The stimulus words represent different grammatical form classes (nouns, verbs, etc.) and different degrees of rarity (*table* as compared to *cocoon*, for instance). This very, very simple procedure, coupled with computer analysis of results, has produced a number of significant findings to be reviewed briefly here, because they aid in understanding results related to the main focus of this paper: how semantic systems vary by socioeconomic status.

First word associations by adults show a strong tendency to be of the same form class as the stimulus. An adult, asked to give a free association to *begin*, will say "start," "end," "stop," and the like. Children as young as four (the earliest age for which this kind of language sampling is practical) already show evidence of this kind of form-class matching, and a small percentage will give responses identical with high frequency adult responses. Thus, for example, some four-year-olds will say "chair" in response to *table*. The tendency to give matching responses gradually increases over the grade-school years. However, at the kindergarten level many more responses are determined by syntactic

---

[1]Before children can read, there is confusion about what a word is. Obviously, the spaces which separate words on the printed page are not available as the usual basis for definition. Certain words that occur together often are taken to be a single word —e.g., *once-upon-a-time*. To the word *belong*, young children will respond "be short," "be tall." This is important to bear in mind when interpreting responses.

patterning than by simple form-class matching tendencies. Kindergartners respond to *begin* with "building a house," "I just begin by puzzle," "to behave," "to cry," "to eat," "with," and the like. All of these responses reveal knowledge of how the word *begin* is used with other words. Most of the responses are words that follow *begin* in sentences. At ages four and five some responses are nonsense words—"selong" to *belong*, (*klang*, or rhyming responses)—where meaning is ignored (*begin* yields "lyn" or "chin"). But in spite of the occurrence of some nonsense responses, it is remarkable how well developed the semantic systems are for simple words, especially in the obvious awareness of how words are used in sequences.

Research of others testifies that grammatical development is already well along by age four, and grammatical cues are used efficiently in repetition or memory tasks by children at age five. Grammatical development is revealed by knowledge of pluralization, verb inflections, and so forth. The preponderance of syntagmatic responses in word-association data is another kind of evidence for this early grammatical maturity. McNeill (1965) cleverly demonstrates, however, that semantics—the structuring and elaboration of meanings—is acquired later. By asking children to repeat sentences immediately after hearing them, and by varying the semantic and syntactic consistency in the sentences, he shows that five-year-old children are not able to profit from the semantic consistency whereas eight-year-olds can. The five-year-old child is using syntactic cues just as well as the eight-year-old in his memory task.

This same trend in semantic development over ages five to ten is evidenced in word-association data by the gradual increase in the number of responses that match the form class of the stimulus word and in the convergence toward a few high frequency responses. Instead of giving as responses words that follow the stimulus word in a sentence (*begin*—"to cry"), as children advance in age they give as responses more words that could replace the stimulus word in a sentence (*begin*—"start") (Entwisle, et al. 1964). These are called *paradigmatic responses*. It is particularly noteworthy that these replacement words are not limited to synonyms; *begin* has "end" and "stop" as high-frequency adult responses, and most common adjectives have antonyms (*black*—"white," *tall*—"short") as high-frequency responses. Paradigmatic responses contain much evidence of semantic structures.

Some people would define *meaning* as the distribution of associative responses given to a word. Although the definition of meaning is no simple problem and we cannot thoroughly treat it here, the response-distribution is a useful operational definition for some purposes. Such a distribution seems especially apropos in research with young children, when it can be employed to yield comparative developmental data. The free-association responses of children show high overlap with responses obtained when the child is asked to give antonyms, synonyms, and so on. Recently, Rotberg (1968) has used responses to one set of words as stimuli to elicit further responses, and followed this process repeatedly. This has been shown to be a most effective method for studying meaning, and a particularly sensitive method for pointing up differences in semantic structures between adults and children.

To complete this description of how word associations provide useful data in the study of language development, a few comments should be made about how associative structures develop for rare—as compared with common—words and for words of one form class as compared to another (adjectives as against verbs, for instance). As stated earlier, high-frequency words such as *table* or *he* have associates for young children that strongly resemble adult associates; the main differences in associative patterns over age occur in the convergence toward a single high-frequency response. For adults, *table* produces "chair" in 65 percent of adult respondents, compared to about 30 percent at kindergarten and first grade, or 50 percent in the later years of elementary school (Entwisle 1966a). The word *cocoon*, however, yields "butterfly" in 30 percent of adults, in 15 percent of fifth-graders or third-graders, but is seldom given by first-graders. A low-frequency word, then, is distinguished developmentally by being later to develop strong associates and by approaching a lower asymptote of response commonality. (The pattern of associations, even for adults, is more varied.)

Words of various form classes have different rates of development. Verbs and adverbs develop later than pronouns and adjectives. Of course, different form classes occur with different frequencies and this alone would be expected to produce some differences in associative structuring. Pronouns, for example, occur more frequently than any other form class, particularly in informal discourse (see French, Carter, and Koenig 1930). Some verbs do occur frequently, verbs like *give, run,* and *sell.* It is noteworthy, however, that these most common verbs tend to be irregular verbs, so although they may occur often from the point of view of the grammarian, the occurrences in different formats may at first be interpreted by the child to be occurrences of different words. (Over the elementary-school years, past tenses of irregular verbs—e.g., "sold" in response to *sell*—are first given as associates and then eventually drop out. Past tenses of regular verbs—"add"-"added"—are never given as associates. This strongly suggests that past tenses of irregular verbs are being learned as separate words.) Also verbs are complicated because of auxiliaries. In brief, then, verbs may not have high frequency occurrence in the same sense as the other form classes.

Another factor that distinguishes verbs from nouns, adjectives, or pronouns, is in their being less often directly specifiable. That is, every noun on the list of stimulus words which I use can be defined ostensively (e.g., *bird, fruit, insect*). For nouns on this list, at least, there is no correlation between this property and the rarity of the word. *Cocoon* is just as well-defined ostensively as *table*, although it may take longer to find a cocoon than a table in one's immediate environment. For verbs the same cannot be said. Although *run* or *sit*, two very common verbs, can be defined ostensively, *maintain* or *restore* cannot (even though according to the Thorndike-Lorge 1944, word count both of these verbs occur much more often than *cocoon*). Apparently, ease of definition is correlated with frequency for verbs. It is not surprising, then, that verbs (and adverbs) appear to develop more slowly than adjectives or pronouns on the basis of conceptual complexity, frequency, or both. Our data suggest that adjectives and pronouns are well developed by third grade but that some verbs and adverbs are still in the process of development at fifth grade.

Much the same point is made by Roger Brown (1958), based on a different kind of data. He compared nouns and verbs of high frequency for adults (among the first thousand for each form class respectively) and not of high frequency for children, and also the converse (nouns and verbs of high frequency for children and not of high frequency for adults.) He concluded that nouns and verbs used by children have more consistent semantic implications than those used by adults. In fact, semantic elaboration may be a lifelong process and even common words may have their meanings altered or extended in adulthood (*soft sell*, for example).

It may be particularly difficult for the child in an impoverished environment to expand his semantic system. Word-association and other data reinforce this conclusion. Perhaps larger differences in semantic systems prevail between the adult slum dweller and the adult suburbanite than between children of the slum and suburbia. Concrete evidence in this area is badly needed. Some data on word associates of southern Negro college students (Belcher and Campbell 1968) suggest much lower commonalities for common words and show wide divergence from data for other college students.

SOME RESEARCH RESULTS

Word associations of black and of white elementary-school children reveal, contrary to expectation, that slum children are apparently more advanced linguistically than suburban children at first grade in terms of paradigmatic responses (Entwisle 1966a, b, c, 1968a, b). As mentioned earlier, paradigmatic responses are those of a form class matching that of the stimulus word and reflect very clearly a semantic structure for a word. White first-grade slum children of average IQ give paradigmatic responses to about the same extent as gifted (IQ 130) suburban children, and although inner-city black first-graders of average IQ lag behind inner-city white first-graders they give more paradigmatic responses than white suburban first-graders of average IQ. Thus, at first grade the white child is slightly ahead of the black child when both are reared in the inner city, but the black slum child exceeds the white suburban child. The superiority is short-lived, however, for by third grade, suburban children—whether blue-collar or upper-middle-class—have surpassed the inner-city children, whether black or white. According to 1960 census data the median income of the slum dwellers was around $3,000. In some schools where children were interviewed, principals estimated that as many as 75 percent of the families were on welfare. By contrast the suburban children came from homes with income more than double this, even for blue-collar families. Thus the temporary advance in linguistic development, and the subsequent decline, appears to be typical of the child in a poverty environment.

What features of this environment are most inimical to language development? Although there is no precise answer to this question, the early accelerated development and the later falling behind of inner-city children gives some clues. Television sets are almost universally present in even the poorest homes; whereas the middle-class parent may restrict his child's viewing in terms of time and in terms of content, the slum child has almost unlimited access to the TV set. This massive exposure to spoken discourse may account for the advanced status of the slum child at the time of school entrance.

To be more precise about the comparison across social-status groups, the low-IQ black child, the one who is most heavily represented in the urban beginning-school population, exceeds the medium-IQ white suburban child (whether middle-class or blue-collar) in paradigmatic rates for pronouns, and exceeds low-IQ blue-collar children in paradigmatic rates for adjectives (24.3 percent as against 21.7 percent). The medium-IQ inner-city black first-grader is far ahead of the medium-IQ suburban child for adjectives (40 percent as against about 30 percent for both middle-class and blue-collar). Pronouns and adjectives are the two classes showing the largest changes around this age. The black slum child also compares favorably on verbs (22.3 percent as against 19.2 percent for low-IQ, and 20.2 percent as against 19.9 percent for medium-IQ). Verbs would be expected to show small differences because paradigmatic rates for verbs are still low for all groups; they show changes later in the age scale. By third grade, however, the favorable position of the slum child has altered and suburban children lead in all paradigmatic measures. (But one must bear in mind that the average IQ of the suburban children is at least ten points higher.)

Even though paradigmatic rates are comparable for the blacks and whites, there is the very significant distinction that blacks give more different responses than whites to the same stimulus. The increased variability of response is most apparent at first grade. Furthermore, it is for words of highest frequency that the difference is most noticeable. For example, to the stimulus word *table*, fifty-four white first-graders and fifty-two Negro first-graders responded with a noun, but ten more different nouns were given by Negro children (with eighty children in each group). This finding emerged over words of all form classes. Low level of commonality (low total percentage of responses accounted for by primary, secondary, and tertiary associates) in other groups has been taken as an indicator of less mature individuals, or less educated individuals (Rosenzweig, 1964). In the present research with children, it seems best interpreted as evidence of a differently structured semantic system. It is very interesting, although problematic in interpretation, that white children of fifty years ago displayed much lower levels of commonality than modern (white) children. One cannot help speculating that recency of urban residency may be the factor in common between white children of former years and black children of today.

The most interesting differences between white and black, and between middle-class and poor children are those between semantic systems. If a stimulus word elicits an entirely different set of associations in one group from those it elicits in another group, the stimulus word can be considered to mean two different things. Using only the three most common responses for each stimulus word, one sees wide differences in response, especially at first grade, in the black and the white inner-city children (Entwisle and Greenberger 1968). Racial differences are greatest for the youngest children. The word *color*, for instance, yields "blue," "book," and "yellow" for white kindergarten children as the three most frequent responses. None of these is present for black kindergarteners; their three high-frequency responses are "crayon," "coloring books," and "tolor." Similarly, although the black and the white first-graders' responses look more alike than kindergartners', there are still rather remarkable differences between them. Comparison in terms of specific responses are difficult to make because the data are so voluminous. Two results, however, stand out:

1. The number of nonsense or klang responses is far greater in the black first-graders. Using only the three most frequent responses to the twenty-four adjectives, and recalling that adjectives are rather well developed by first grade, we note among black first-graders "mack," "bark," "mard," "nigh," "bond," "bean," "teasant," "mo," "mour," "birsty," plus some other words that are difficult to classify unambiguously but which are probably also nonsense or klang (like "hour" as a response to "sour"). Comparable responses made by white first-graders include only "hong." In other words, the twenty-four adjectives are, with one or two exceptions, already well on the way to being incorporated into the semantic systems of white children, but black youngsters are giving as high-frequency responses a minimum of eleven nonsense responses to these twenty-four adjectives at first grade. The reader will see the same patterns if he examines high-frequency responses to nouns (*sheep* yields "heap"), to adverbs ("mently" and "bently" are given to *gently*), and to verbs

("bad," "fad," and "mad" are given to *add*). Even for pronouns, where responses of both racial groups consist almost exclusively of other pronouns, Negro children give "mit," "hen," "bus" and "must," while all responses of white children seem to reflect expectations based upon English.

2. Even when primary responses are identical, as for instance, "hot" in response to *cold*, the frequency for black children is markedly lower (34 percent as against 13 percent). This comparison is more readily made among third-graders' responses, because by then, convergence toward a single high-frequency response has proceeded rather far. For eight high-frequency adjectives the strength of the primary response in white children ranges from 46 percent to 71 percent, whereas for black children corresponding figures are 34 percent to 58 percent.

All differences noted to this point have pertained to white or black children in the inner city. The next question is: Do slum groups differ in semantic systems from suburban children? Again, comparisons in terms of specific responses are awkward, but the overall impression is that white slum children possess semantic systems that overlap considerably systems of white suburban children at first grade. (We have no data for middle-class black children.) The differences already noted between disadvantaged white and black first-graders, then, also separate the black slum child from the suburban child.

At third grade there are more synonyms given by suburban children, which is consistent, of course, with their greater production of paradigmatic responses, and reflects a much more mature kind of semantic structure. For example, to the high-frequency verb *tell* suburban children respond "ask" 11 percent, and "talk" 8 percent. White slum children respond "me" 12 percent and "told" 9 percent; and Negro slum children give "well" 9 percent and "talk" 8 percent.

Differences between black and white respondents to the word *black* are particularly interesting. No responses that pertain to human beings are given by white children, whereas black children respond "child," "girls," "hand," "man," and even "yes" to the stimulus word *black*. Along the same lines the most frequent response among Negro third-graders to *sour* is "still good" (25 percent), and this response never occurs for white suburban children.

All responses given ten or more times by any race-grade group were compared across groups, but did not add much information to that already given.

Data for first-graders, then, show black children to be not far behind some white children and ahead of other white children, in general rate of development (Entwisle 1968a). At the same time the rate of development, primarily based on paradigmatic response, ignores differences in meaning itself between groups. For simple words—e.g., *table, run, black,*—where meanings are uncomplicated, there are minimal differences between groups. These are mainly the words for which any semantic structure that exists at all has been built up by first grade.

The relative developmental position of blacks and whites does shift with advancing age, however, and both inner-city blacks and whites show a slowed pace of development compared to suburban children by third grade. Again, however, the rate alone tells only a small part of the story, for while the semantic systems of white inner-city children overlap considerably the semantic systems of white suburban children, semantic systems of black children depart significantly from both white groups, especially for more complex words. Some examples will clarify this point. A common word like *add* suggests "subtract" or "arithmetic" to almost all children, suburban or city, white or black. A much less common word *examine* suggests "test" and "check," both verb synonyms, to suburban fifth-graders. It suggests "test," "x-ray," and "doctor" more frequently (in that order) than other words to white inner-city fifth-graders. To black inner-city fifth-graders it suggests "x-ray," "operate," and "doctor," not general words like "test" or "check" that will broaden its meaning beyond the medical examination situation, but words restricted to a very specific context. *Examine* therefore can be viewed as having a very constricted semantic structure for blacks.

In still another important respect inner-city children differ from suburban children. By fifth grade the paradigmatic response rate has leveled off for all groups so far studied, because most changes on this measure occur over the early elementary years. The variability of response at fifth grade, however, given the similar paradigmatic rates, is greater for suburban children than inner-city children for all the words that are well consolidated by this time (nouns, adjectives, more common verbs). One way to think of this is as greater stereotypy of response for the inner-city groups, which could be taken as evidence signifying a restricted code, the semantic structure of common words being less elaborate for slum children than suburban children. This kind of restriction may further hinder reading at later ages.

A clue as to the difficulties in semantics created by phonological differences, something we have no systematic evidence on, may be gleaned from third-grade black responses to *since*—e.g., "money," "dumb," "five." Obviously *since* is being heard as "cents" or "sense." By fifth grade "money" is still the most popular response for blacks, but "when" and "yesterday" are also frequent. Some of the phonological confusion has dissipated. At third grade suburban white children are responding "money" 1 percent of the time and white inner-city children are responding "money" 4 percent of the time. The Negro third-grade responses ("money," "dumb," "five") listed above cover 16 percent of responses, and the remainder of the responses seem mostly anomalous.

Since is a word that signifies logical relations between parts of a sentence.

Its misinterpretation would hinder unraveling the logic in sentences for a beginning reader. Other examples of semantic differences triggered by phonological problems can be given. *Allow* at kindergarten yields almost all unique responses with "to" and "people" as the most frequent responses, each accounting for only 2 percent of responses. At first grade there is real confusion about *allow*, for the responses "loud" and "quiet" appear often, and it is obvious that these are triggered by confusing *aloud* with *allow*. This confusion is most noticeable in black children who respond "soft" twice as often as white children. By third grade "let" is the most frequent response of white suburban children to *allow*, whereas inner-city black children are still giving "soft," "quiet," and "low" as the three most frequent responses. The kinds of confusions that are displayed in association data give some clue as to why semantic elaboration may be difficult for the urban child.

THE SEARCH FOR AREAS OF EXCELLENCE

Earlier in this chapter, the author cited Baratz' (in press) work demonstrating that black children have altogether become more proficient (considering linguistic status with respect to two codes) than white children by age five or six. Given that linguistic competence is defined in a reasonable way, black children are not behind white children. No one, Baratz points out, would define the linguistic competence of French children in terms of a code (English) to which they are not exposed, and by analogy it seems unreasonable to define the linguistic competence of black children solely in terms of standard English, which they may rarely hear. It seems extremeiy important, strategically speaking, to identify areas of excellence or areas of relative advancement (as, for example, their proficiency in different codes) in poor children of whatever color, for it seems obvious that for a child to engage himself with the educational system requires that he have genuine success experiences in the first two or three years of school. A poor child or a black child may find it virtually impossible to get any positive reinforcements for learning efforts, whether from himself or from his teachers, as matters now stand. A system that grinds out mostly failure experiences means at best a poorly educated child, and at worst a hostile child, alienated from society's institutions for communicating language and other cognitive skills. From this standpoint, a finding such as Baratz' has enormous importance, for it suggests ways to build success experiences into the system, even indirectly by improving teachers' opinions of their students.

In the same spirit, one can seize upon the finding from word-association research that first grade inner-city children are more advanced in some areas of linguistic competence than suburban children. An obvious first suggestion is that primers and basal readers should exploit these linguistic strengths with which the slum child enters school. Now, under the present system, apparently these strengths wither. Second, one would suggest revisions in the curriculum to devote more training to areas of specific weakness (verbs and adverbs) and to semantic enrichment over the early school years.

As a matter of fact, areas of excellence may already exist in the repertoires of poor children to a degree hitherto ignored. Weener (1967) notes, for instance, that black lower-class first-graders who lived in Detroit but who were born in the South did better on an immediate memory task with highly structured material than did white middle-class Detroit children born in the North. The superiority in black children declined as the structure of the materials declined. To display more awareness of structure, a child may be more advanced in terms of verbal associates (consistent with the word association data) and awareness of two codes would also probably help (consistent with Baratz' work). In working with white preschoolers from "very low income families" and from private nursery schools, Shriner (1968) also concludes that very poor children are not behind in language development. He tested their knowledge of morphological rules and found no difference between groups when mental age was controlled. Similarly, grammatical competence of older children—grades two, four, and six—is reported as unrelated to socioeconomic status (LaCivita, Kean, and Yamamoto 1966). There are several studies, then, suggesting that linguistic competence up to age five or six, and maybe thereafter, is not greatly different in lower-class (slum) and middle-class children. Osler (1967) has recently come to much the same conclusion regarding effects of social class on concept attainment and cites a number of other studies consistent with her own data.

Much evidence of another kind, however, including word-association data, suggests that from first grade on there are widening gaps between the language of children from poverty environments and those from middle-class groups. Word-association research suggests specific kinds of deficits, particularly in consolidation of verbs and adverbs. The word-association technique, used as a method for probing semantic systems, yields preliminary results suggesting very wide differences in semantic structure. Semantic systems appear to be elaborated mainly over the grade-school age range, and so may represent a particularly fruitful area for study in terms of action programs.

In kindergarten and first grade, word meanings, and therefore the cognitive role of words, overlap little for the black and the white child. Also, whereas suburban children seem to be making orderly progress in expanding their semantic systems to imbed less frequent words over the elementary-school years, slum children are making very limited progress toward use of language that is conceptually more elaborate than what they started school with (*maintain* produces "can," "retain" and "begin" for suburban third-graders but no response is the most frequent outcome for both white and black slum children; *seldom* yields "often" and "always" as the most frequent responses in suburban third-graders, but "sell" and no response as the two most frequent outcomes in both white and black slum children). Even more crucial, the high frequency responses of first-grade children, especially blacks, in the inner city, will occur less often even when responses are the same. The response strength is less even when the identical response occurs. In a practical situation, such as reading instruction where children are led to use contextual and grammatical cues to supply words whose configurations are unfamiliar, the inner-city child will less often come up with a correct response because of these weaker response strengths. This suggests very explicitly a reason for difficulties experienced in learning to read by inner-city youngsters. Their backgrounds (most notably television) have provided them with a knowledge of syntax and morphology, and perhaps even with a relatively high degree of linguistic competence in terms of several codes, when they reach school. Once in school where reading and cognitive enrichment are supposedly being fostered, there seems to be a deceleration in development. There may be a lack of environmental forces to encourage semantic development.

No single remedy is likely to be sufficient. Suggestions mentioned earlier for giving training in areas of particular weaknesses are worth trying but demand more knowledge than is available at the moment. Reading primers which emphasize word contingencies appropriate for the slum child should be considered. A very appealing idea is to invent games to be played in school that provide drill on particular skills, like building semantic structures, without eroding motivation. We have begun some work along these lines. Since television is so universal and so appealing to children, programs with specific content to aid in language development would require a relatively small investment but could yield enormous dividends.

Another remedy, probably the most fundamental, is obvious: more mixing of students in the school and in the community. Different semantic systems are no doubt a direct consequence of residential and educational segregation. With more mixing of students the semantic systems of all groups would tend to converge. This convergence would occur as a result of changes in all groups, not just the minority groups, and would thereby pose less of a burden for the underprivileged child. At present many differences between youngsters along social class lines are taken as deficits for lower-class youngsters, and lower-class youngsters are expected to modify their behavior to overlap the behavior of the more privileged. In some areas, particularly language, there seems to be small reason to force all the change in one direction. The benefits from having all groups change slightly rather than having one group change greatly, seem not to be overrated.

REFERENCES

Baratz, J. C. A bi-dialectal test for determining language proficiency. *Child Development* (in press).

Belcher, L. H., and Campbell, J. J. An exploratory study of word associations of Negro college students. *Psychological Reports* 1968, 23: 119–34.

Brown, R. *Words and Things.* New York: Free Press, 1958.

Entwisle, D. R.; Forsyth, D. F.; and Muuss, R. The syntactic-paradigmatic shift in children's word associations, *J. Verbal Learning and Verbal Behavior* 1964, 3: 19–29.

Entwisle, D. R. *Word Associations of Young Children.* Baltimore: Johns Hopkins Press, 1966.(a)

———. Form class and children's word associations. *J. Verbal Learning and Verbal Behavior* 1966, 5: 558–65.(b)

———. Developmental sociolinguistics: a comparative study in four subcultural settings. *Sociometry* 1966, 29: 67–84.(c)

———. Developmental sociolinguistics: inner city children. *American J. Sociology* 1968, 74: 37–49.(a)

———. Subcultural differences in children's language development. *International J. Psychology* 1968, 3: 13–22.(b)

Entwisle, D. R., and Greenberger, E. Report #19: Differences in the language of Negro and white grade-school children. Baltimore: Johns Hopkins University, Center for the Study of the Social Organization of Schools, 1968.

French, N. R.; Carter, C. W.; and Koenig, W. The words and sounds of telephone conversations. *Bell System Technical J.* 1930, 9: 290–324.

Harms, L. S. Listener judgments of status cues in speech. *Quarterly J. Speech* 1961, 47: 164–68.

La Civita, A.; Kean, J. M.; and Yamamoto, K. Socioeconomic status of children and acquisition of grammar. *The J. Educational Research* 1966, 60: 71–74.

McNeill, D. Is child language semantically consistent? Mimeographed. Harvard Center for Cognitive Studies, 1965.

Osler, S. F. Social class effects on concept attainment. Paper delivered at the American Psychological Association Symposium on Cognitive Development in Special Populations, September 1, 1967.

Rosenzweig, M. R. Word associations of French workmen: comparisons with associations of French students and American workmen and students. *J. Verbal Learning and Verbal Behavior* 1964, 3: 57–69.

Rotberg, I. C. A method for developing comprehensive categories of meaning. *J. Verbal Learning and Verbal Behavior* 1968, 7: 589–92.

Shriner, T. H. Social dialect and language. Paper presented at Eastern Illinois Conference on Dialectology, March 27, 1968.

Thorndike, E. L., and Lorge, I. *The Teacher's Word Book of 30,000 Words.* New York: Teachers College, Columbia University, 1944.

Weener, P. D. The effects of dialect differences on the immediate recall of verbal messages. Doctoral dissertation, University of Michigan, 1967.

Chapter 8

BILINGUALISM AND THE SPANISH-SPEAKING CHILD

Vera P. John and Vivian M. Horner*

The United States is akin to many nations in its multiethnic and multilingual character. The impact of ethnic and linguistic diversity upon national life is being studied increasingly, and such studies often emphasize the role of the national language in the unification of nation-states. Despite government policy and public belief to the contrary, ethnic minorities and their languages continue to survive in many nations. Indeed, the continuous existence of distinctive cultures and languages presents a challenge to the political hegemony of several nations in the world today.

BACKGROUND

In this country the widespread belief in the "melting pot" has obscured the complex history of our minorities, and still clouds understanding of their contemporary status. English may be the national language of the United States, but we must remember that it is not a native or indigenous language. It is one of the languages which, as was the case with French, German, Spanish, was exported in the process of colonization. With the notable exception of the brutality with which the language of African slaves was suppressed (see Frazier 1957), the pressure in this country against the use of languages other than English was limited, until the period after the First World War. At

*Ferkauf Graduate School of Humanities and Social Sciences, Yeshiva University
A note of thanks to Mr. Luis Fuentes for his help in delineating the critical issues of bilingual education as viewed by the Puerto Rican community of New York.

one time, for example, Spanish was one of the official languages of the state of New Mexico. Bilingual schools were not uncommon in nineteenth-century America. But the existence of many cultures and languages, both immigrant and native, was viewed as a threat in this country following the period of heightened nationalism born of World War I. The struggle to maintain "immigrant" languages in the face of restrictive legislation and pressure is well documented, in detail, by Fishman in his book, *Language Loyalty in the United States* (1966).

In spite of the commitment of some groups to their mother tongue, many immigrants have learned to conform to the political, educational, and language policies of their adopted nation as the price of citizenship. Indigenous Americans—e.g., Indians and Mexican-Americans (who are part Indian themselves) —of non-English background resist these pressures, although the history of their stance for cultural maintenance is poorly known. In part, this lack of information is due to an emphasis on documenting the relationship of minorities to the white majority, work which has been carried out mainly by scholars of Anglo-Saxon and immigrant backgrounds. Reflecting the conceptual framework born of their experience, researchers and writers have stressed the relationship of immigrant groups to the mainstream existing structure and government, and this has even been imposed upon the people whose language, whose knowledge of the land, and whose culture predates the formation of the American state. Indeed, a study of language loyalty among Indians, Mexican-Americans, and Puerto Ricans remains fragmentary without the recognition that many members of such groups consider themselves as conquered peoples whose attachment to their language is a bond to their past independence, and a continuous hope for a future of greater self-determination.

Until recently, acculturation and assimilation were the conceptual foci of literature on minorities. But with the decrease of immigration since World War II, and the dramatic increase of political activity among nonwhite and non-English-speaking minority groups, new models are explored. For example, Love (1969) discusses the recent agitation in New Mexico, by comparing it to a "primitive revolt . . . a kind almost always associated with developing nations."

The notion of cultural pluralism was not, according to Fishman (1966), part of the American dream. Thus a struggle toward a genuinely pluralistic society was not conceived of by members of European immigrant groups. The notion of an egalitarian and pluralistic society, in which ethnic minorities maintain and develop their cultural heritage, is now projected by many spokesmen of Negro, Indian, Mexican-American, and Puerto Rican groups as a hopeful alternative to the forced melting pot of yesteryear. This has had an effect which includes calling for self-determination in their rural and urban communities. It is in this context that current developments among non-

English-speaking groups in the United States are of particular interest for the student of language. A persistent demand for bilingual instruction in these communities is quite recent. Some are projecting for the rebuilding of a once-powerful educational system, such as the nineteenth-century academies developed by Cherokee Indians, who had a press and newspaper in their language. For other groups, the articulation of plans for bilingual education in the mother tongue as well as in the national language is a new concern.

Paradoxically, the pressures of migration of non-English-speaking ethnic groups to urban centers from rural areas, as brought about by the mechanization of America's farms, has increased their preoccupation with cultural and linguistic survival. The fear of being members of uprooted, alienated, and underemployed masses in the urban slums is a dread which is expressed by the young spokesmen of new movements. The returning Mexican-American veterans of World War II and subsequent wars were instrumental in forming political organizations in the *barrios* of Denver, Los Angeles, Albuquerque, San Antonio, and other cities (Galarza, Gallegos, and Samora 1966). Through the activities of such organizations,[1] a new pride in Spanish is being developed. Some of the political meetings are conducted in Spanish, and bilingual newspapers are being published in great numbers. Similarly, Indian war veterans, many of whom have attended college after demobilization, have formed pan-Indian organizations, and have joined the tribal governments of their people. In each of these settings they are projecting a new interest in their Indian heritage, and express revived interest in their tribal languages (Steiner 1968). The introduction of Navajo in a Gallup high school for Anglo as well as Navajo students is but one of the most recent expressions of programs in which an American Indian language is used in an instructional setting (see *New Mexico Foreign Language News Bulletin,* 1969). In New York City members of the Puerto Rican community are assuming an increasingly important role in the city's political life. Many mainland Puerto Ricans express the hope that New York City will become a genuinely bilingual area, in which Spanish and English are spoken by the majority of residents.

CAMPAIGNS FOR BILINGUAL EDUCATION

In a period of increasing political activity, the pressures for massive bilingual education have been mounting. The chairman of the Mexican-American Political Association, Bert Corona, expressed community sentiments to us in a recent personal interview:

---

[1]Among such organizations are: Crusade for Justice, Mexican-American Political Association (MAPA), Aspira, and the Puerto Rican Forum.

Now we are getting into a position where we are ready to mount a campaign in regard to the education, the *correct education,* of our children. We have many more educators. We have many people who can reach the mass media and make a valid argument for *bilingual* and *bicultural* education. We have good advocates now of pluralism in language and culture in America. And we have been able to define this, for ourselves, and to act upon this more effectively.

From non-English-speaking communities there is a wealth of testimony, some of it given in congressional hearings on bilingual educational legislation, in regard to the need for bilingual and bicultural education. Abelardo Delgado, Neighborhood Coordinator, El Paso Juvenile Project, expresses the needs of Mexican-Americans for a different approach to education in the following way:

> I have two daughters who talk of nothing else than finishing high school so that they can get a job as sewing machine operators in the local garment factories. Ladies and gentlemen, is that the true challenge for them? Does the State satisfy itself with turning out hundreds of sewing machine operators and bus boys, not that I have anything against either, but is the challenge enough? Unfortunately, whether it is enough or not, it is true and they know that the kind of discrimination that they are facing is hidden in a college entrance exam which they know for sure they will not pass. (Estes and Darling 1967, p. 137)

In his statement to the Texas Conference for Mexican-Americans, Delgado offered the following set of resolutions (Estes and Darling 1967, p. 138):

1. Let the poor speak out; provide conferences for them, too.
2. Let our cultures be dual if that is what we need to be effective citizens.
3. Educate us for college, and do not let the fact that none of us has any money to go influence the preparation.
4. Pay us well so that we can consider education in its perspective instead of worrying about the rent and the grocery bill.
5. Do not make school a marking-time institution for us by having us take shop or by throwing us into special education because we do not answer the IQ tests correctly when they are not for us.
6. Let those laws that so quietly discriminate against us, *such as the crime of speaking only English at school* [author's emphasis], be erased from the books.
7. Do not isolate education as a problem, but bring in the other factors involved, such as health, housing, employment.
8. Do not sit on funds, State or Federal, which would really help us to better ourselves, and release those that let the establishment maintain control.
9. Open up the good jobs for the few of us that manage to prepare ourselves for them.

10. Integrate our schools. I don't mean student-wise but teacher-wise. Why must all the Mexican schools have all the bad teachers and bad programs? Why don't we have those who understand our customs and what goes on?

Delgado emphasizes the economic and psychological plight of Mexican-Americans who need better education. He also expresses the feelings of parents, in the barrios, colonias, reservations, and ghettos, who view the schools as alien institutions. It is here that their children are attracted to a different way of life, while at the same time they experience a profound rejection by that way. In a moving article, Antonio Gomez (1968, pp. 8–9) wrote in a small Chicano (Mexican-American) magazine:

School is where it starts, and school can be a frightful experience for most Chicano children. It was for me. The subtle prejudice and the not so subtle arrogance of anglos came at me at a very early age, although it took many years to realize and comprehend what took place. The SPEAK ENGLISH signs in every hall and doorway, and the unmitigated efforts of the anglo teachers to eradicate the Spanish language, coupled with their demands for behavioral changes, clearly pointed out to me that I was not acceptable . . . . The association between being different and being inferior was quite difficult to resist, and it tortured me for many years.

The nearly universal rule against the use of the Spanish language, a rule which was enforced until very recently by many forms of punishment, is viewed by pupils and parents as but one example of Anglo hostility against that which they hold dear. The feelings of many Spanish-Americans are expressed in the statement that "language is people, they are one and the same, to know one is to know the other, to lose one is to lose the other, to destroy one is to destroy the other."[2] Knowlton (1966) has argued the need for better means of educating Spanish-speaking children. But he points out that the instructional use of the Spanish language, in the classrooms of New York and Los Angeles and the many smaller cities and towns in which Spanish-surnamed children study, is not sufficient to bring this about. Knowlton (1966, p. 4) emphasizes the cultural as well as the language aspects of what he conceives of as a needed curriculum in Spanish-American schools:

Before there can be an economic renaissance among the Spanish-Americans there must be a cultural revival. The Spanish-American people must recover their own history. They need to know that they have a historical and cultural background of achievement that is worthy of respect and admiration.

<hr>

[2]This statement is attributed to Professor S. R. Ulibarri, Chairman of the Department of Romance Languages, University of New Mexico.

The Spanish-Americans have been cut off from their own history and culture by the public school systems . . . . Spanish-American students coming out of the public schools . . . are completely
ignorant of the cultural developments of Spain, Portugal, and Latin
America. As a result they are filled with feelings of inferiority and
suffer from self-hatred. They look down upon their own families and
their own people.

This quote grows out of an attitude toward education which has been prevalent
since the introduction of compulsory public education in America, where the
schools are expected to serve as the crucial institution for socialization. This
society still functions under the assumption that socialization achieved before
entrance to school has to be undone and redone by the schools (save for the
"best families"), so that youngsters will turn out to be the kind of Americans
they should be.

The emphasis on character and citizenship training is of importance when
viewed in its historical context. At the turn of the century, when there was
available to immigrants and native born a great number of manual jobs, the
schools could afford to make but modest gains toward literacy. They were
hard-pressed to be successful in developing shared beliefs in children reared
in widely different homes. Psychological theory and educational practice during the period up to and inclusive of World War II stressed adjustment, the
team spirit, and good citizenship as the crucial outcomes of the teaching-
learning process.

Since World War II, however, the schools have been increasingly called
upon to prepare children for an altered job market in which literacy is crucial.
A shift in theoretical emphasis has occurred in psychology, where theories of
development with a heavy emphasis upon social and affective development
have been replaced by those stressing the cognitive (intellectual) development
of the child. At the same time, the values of a school system which considers
itself an arbiter of social and political beliefs for members of ethnic groups is
being challenged on all levels. The emerging emphasis, then, is upon an education which will prepare children of minority groups to compete equally for job
opportunities, a goal which requires a serious reexamination of the educational
experience of the nonwhite and non-English-speaking child currently in
school.

Figures compiled by Barrett (Brussell 1968, p. 22) in the Southwest are
illustrative in this regard. "The median for school years completed by Spanish-
surnamed individuals of both sexes fourteen years of age and over in 1960 was
9.0 years in California, 8.6 years in Colorado, 8.4 in New Mexico, 7.9 in
Arizona, and 6.1 years in Texas." It is interesting that the income of Spanish-
Americans, though universally low, shows a similar pattern of being relatively
higher in California than in Texas (Brussell 1968). The educational statistics

relevant to Indian children have also raised concern. Statistics of only twenty years ago indicate that fewer than half of all school-age Navajo children were in school (Holm 1969). As Holm (1969) has said:

> The need for more and better education is seen by many as of utmost importance, the real demand for better health and educational facilities comes now not so much from without as from within the tribe . . . . An education that will enable young Navajos, while continuing to perceive themselves as Navajo, to "cope" with, if not "compete" in, twentieth-century, urbanized, technological America.

Holm echoes for the Navajos a demand articulated for the education of Spanish-surnamed children, namely, that of bilingual education. He defines bilingual education as "the use of two languages as languages of instruction."

Support for bilingual education is not limited to spokesmen of non-English-speaking groups. The National Education Association-Tucson survey group, comprising educators drawn from majority and minority groups, in 1966 advanced a strong recommendation in favor of bilingual education. A handful of programs in the United States had been initiated in the fifties (e.g., the El Paso program, started in 1951). But a widespread and consistent campaign for bilingual education was not successful until the sixties. By the summer of 1967, hearings were being held by Senator Yarborough in the Southwest, and Senator Robert Kennedy in the East to gather testimony on the subject of bilingual education. "Representatives of all organized Mexican-American groups were at the Los Angeles hearing and were unanimous in support of federal subsidy for bilingual education" (*New Republic,* 1967, p. 9). In 1963, of nearly twenty-one thousand academic diplomas granted in New York City, only 331 went to Puerto Ricans (Hearings on Bilingual Education, 90th Congress, First Session, 1967). It was generally agreed that Spanish-speaking children in the East and in the West needed a more adequate education, and that bilingual instruction was a significant step toward this goal.

PSYCHOLOGICAL AND EDUCATIONAL REASONS FOR BILINGUAL EDUCATION

Much of the attention currently directed toward bilingual education has been sparked by the vocal demands of minority groups. Their political impact is increasingly heeded in the national scene, as they continue to struggle for the maintenance of their linguistic and cultural identities. While the motivation for these demands reflects social and political aspirations on the part of Spanish-speaking and Indian groups, the arguments put forth for bilingual education reflect educational concerns as well. The damage, both emotional and intellectual, inflicted upon the child who is forced to cope with an alien cultural and linguistic milieu for which he is unprepared is a first point in a rationale for bilingual teaching. Such teaching is often proposed as a more humane and enriched school experience for the non-English-speaking child, a means toward the development of a harmonious and positive self-image. Another argument stresses the pedagogical soundness, at least in the early years of the school experience, of teaching children basic subjects in their own tongue. Those who hold this view maintain that bilingual education is the most parsimonious means to better school achievement.

Common sense and the testimony of persons who have experienced the effects of having to relinquish their mother tongue to become educated in an English-speaking system support many of the social arguments put forth for bilingual education. Unfortunately, objective research on this issue is scant and is likely to remain so for some time. Given the present limitations in the social sciences, a research validation of the complex interaction of language with the individual in his many roles presents a task of formidable difficulty. Thus the claims for the social merits of bilingual education remain, for the moment, unproven from the strictly scientific point of view.

On the other hand, the claims for the pedagogical soundness of a bilingual approach in educating the child who is not a speaker of the national language are based on constantly accruing research evidence. A number of educational institutions, drawing upon the experience of other polylingual nations, are for the first time taking a serious look at the potential of bilingual education. In addition, some limited experimentation has begun in the United States as well.

One carefully evaluated demonstration project illustrating the value of a bilingual approach is the Iloilo experiment, begun in 1948 in the Philippines (Orata 1953). School children, native speakers of Hiligaynon, were introduced to their studies in the vernacular. During first and second grades, instruction proceeded in Hiligaynon while the children were learning English. In the third grade they were switched to instruction in English, and within six weeks their performance in all tested subjects, including oral English, surpassed that of a control group who had received all instruction in English, beginning in the first grade.

An experimental program in the teaching of reading, carried out with speakers of Pitean in Sweden, produced similarly effective results (Macnamara 1966). Children who received an initial ten weeks of reading instruction in Pitean before being switched into literary Swedish learned to read more rapidly than a control group of Pitean speakers taught from the outset in literary Swedish. By the end of the first year, the experimental group had surpassed the control group on a variety of language skills in literary Swedish.

In Chiapas, Mexico, an experimental literacy program introduced children to reading in their native Indian languages (Modiano 1968). When the children had mastered their vernacular primers, they were permitted to enter the first grade, where all subsequent instruction was carried out in Spanish. Subsequent test data on reading skills in Spanish revealed that those Indian children who had first been taught to read in their native tongues read Spanish better and with greater comprehension than their peers who had been instructed solely in Spanish.

Closer to home is a noteworthy bilingual program being carried out in Miami, Florida (Richardson 1968). This program includes both Spanish-speaking and English-speaking children, and has as its teaching goal the total mastery of both languages for all children. The evaluation data now available, which cover a three-year period, indicate that although children are not yet as fluent in their second language as their first, they learn equally well in either. In addition, the bilingual curriculum has been demonstrated to be as effective as the standard curriculum in all academic subjects.

In San Antonio, Texas, where there are large numbers of citizens who do not speak English, a somewhat newer bilingual program is achieving similar results (Pryor 1968). Children instructed in both Spanish and English during their first year in school were able at the end of first grade to read, speak, and write in both languages and scored better on measures of cognitive growth, communication skills, and social and emotional adjustment than did their control peers who began their school experience solely in English. Tests administered at the end of the second year of bilingual instruction indicate similar results.

These findings are of particular interest at a time when psychologists are probing the role of language in the intellectual development of children. We are witnessing a shift away from a preoccupation with the accumulation of information as the focus of learning to an emphasis upon basic processes. Cognitive theorists, such as Piaget (1967) and Bruner (1966), have been particularly influential in this trend. Instruction in the native language assumes a particularly important role in the context of this newly formulated stress upon learning to learn as the major task of education for young children. For so long, educators have believed that the earlier a child is exposed to a body of material to be learned (for example, the English language) the more likely he is to achieve lasting mastery. In this view, learning is additive, and the sooner the process of accretion is initiated, the better.

According to a cognitive view of early development, much early learning consists of the reduction of ambiguity, the ordering of the "buzzing of confusion" that surrounds the child. The child imitates and discovers ordering devices; he groups events and people into classes; he learns to recognize regularities in time, sequence, and routines. Language plays a critical role in this process of creating subjective order in the life of the young child, though language is not the only process available to him. Children as young as six months of age can engage in primitive abstraction without language, by systematically choosing similar shapes (Ling 1941). During the preschool years, children develop a variety of ways to conceptualize the world around them. Bruner (1966) speaks of enactive, iconic, and symbolic representations. But between the ages of five and seven, children's use of language accelerates; words become a medium of learning and problem solving (see White 1965). It is at this very age that the non-English-speaking child is ordinarily confronted with the demand to learn in English, and indirectly, to think in English. Macnamara's (1966) findings that such children who were instructed in a second language showed deterioration in arithmetic, particularly in the area of problem solving, are noteworthy in this regard.

It thus appears to us that one of the great benefits of bilingual instruction of young children may be in helping them to develop the use of language for problem solving in their native language. Once they have learned the value of words for memory and thought, they can apply this functional knowledge of language to the acquisition of a second language. The second language may then serve to extend the child's intellectual skills.

Some groups of bilingual children have been found to achieve better than their monolingual peers, in spite of long-held beliefs to the contrary. In a study of ten-year-old French-Canadian children in Montreal (Peal and Lambert 1962), bilingual children scored significantly higher on intelligence tests than monolingual children. According to the authors, the balanced bilingual (i.e. with mastery of both languages) children had a language asset, a greater ability in concept formation, and a greater cognitive flexibility, than their monolingual peers. The investigators (Peal and Lambert 1962, p. 14) conclude that "the bilinguals appear to have a more diversified set of mental abilities than the monolinguals."

Additionally, in light of an important finding of the Coleman (et al. 1966) report—that children's sense of control over their environment and self-image correlate highly with school achievement—it seems reasonable to expect that an educational experience based upon the language and culture of the child will contribute to strengthening his feelings of personal worth. Bilingual education may well be the means of eliminating or at least minimizing the confusion and shame created in the non-English-speaking child by the common educational practices of the day.

CONCLUSION

Present educational practice does not meet the needs of poor children generally; but it is especially inadequate for the non-English-speaking child. The individual with foreign-language skills at school entry, suggesting a richer potential than many children bring, all too often leaves as an individual with poorer prospects than most, his native language destroyed or carefully closeted, and his second language not well-enough developed to offer him even the narrow range of options open to the poorly educated monolingual.

In this paper we have attemped to place in a historical context some of the social and political issues involved in the current push for bilingual education. We have presented some arguments from the perspective of concerned participants, and we have explored some of the findings from research which suggest alternative educational objectives and the soundness of adopting such a bilingual and bicultural approach.

In its most highly developed form, this approach offers to the Spanish-speaking child the possibility to recognize and act upon the widest possible range of choices. The highly mobile Puerto Rican child can effectively function in either mainland or island schools. The child of the Southwest has the opportunity to participate in the broad cultural traditions of the Spanish-speaking world as a literate member, without paying the undue price of isolation from and unemployment in mainstream society.

This model also implies that children from English-speaking homes will increasingly be exposed to instruction in other languages, such as Spanish. Thus for society as a whole the bilingual and bicultural educative process can facilitate the move toward an open and pluralistic society which characterizes a mature democracy. Such an educational process can only be realized by the full and equal participation of all groups. Although some conceive of bilingual education as an efficient approach to the acquisition of the national language and culture on the part of minority children, others hold that bilingualism can only be successful as a mutually developed and mutually experienced process of learning and teaching, involving both majority and minority communities. We subscribe to this latter view.

REFERENCES

Bruner, J. S. *Studies in Cognitive Growth.* New York: Wiley, 1966.

Brussell, C. B. *Disadvantaged Mexican-American Children and Early Educational Experience.* Austin, Texas: Southwest Educational Development Corporation, 1968.

Coleman, J. S., et al. *Equality of Educational Opportunity.* Washington, D. C.: U. S. Government Printing Office, 1966.

Estes, D. M., and Darling, D. W., eds., *Improving Educational Opportunities of the Mexican-American; Proceedings of the First Texas Conference for the Mexican-American.* San Antonio, Texas: Southwest Educational Development Corporation, 1967.

Fishman, J. A. *Language Loyalty in the United States.* The Hague: Mouton, 1966.

Frazier, E. F. *Black Bourgeoisie.* Glencoe, Ill.: Free Press, 1957.

Galarza, E.; Gallegos, H.; and Samora, J. Mexican-Americans in the Southwest: a report to the Ford Foundation. Unpublished report. 1966.

Gomez, A. What am I about? *Con Safos* 1968, 1: 8–9.

Holm, W. The possibilities of bilingual education for Navajos. 1969. Mimeographed.

Knowlton, C. S. Spanish-American schools in the 1960s. Paper prepared for the 1966 Teacher Orientation Conference, East Las Vegas, New Mexico. Mimeographed.

Ling, B. Form discrimination as a learning cue in infants. *Comparative Psychology Monographs* 1941, 17: No. 2 (whole No. 86).

Love, J. L. La Raza, Mexican-Americans in rebellion. *Trans-Action* February 1969, 35–42.

Macnamara, J. *Bilingualism and Primary Education: A Study of Irish Experience.* Edinburgh: Edinburgh University Press, 1966.

Modiano, N. National or mother language in beginning reading: a comparative study. *Research in the Teaching of Reading* 1968, 1: 32–43.

New Republic. Bilingual education. October 21, 1967, 9–10.

Orata, P. T. The Iloilo experiment in education through the vernacular. In *The Use of Vernacular Languages in Education.* Monographs on Fundamental Education, VIII. Paris: UNESCO, 1953.

Peal, E., and Lambert, W. E. The relation of bilingualism to intelligence. *Psychological Monographs,* 1962, 76: No. 546.

Piaget, J. *Six Psychological Studies.* New York: Random House, 1967.

Pryor, G. C. Evaluation of the bilingual project of Harlandale Independent School District, San Antonio, Texas, in the first and second grades of four elementary schools during 1967-1968 school year. Mimeographed. San Antonio, Tex.: Our Lady of the Lake College, 1968.

Richardson, M. W. An evaluation of certain aspects of the academic achievement of elementary school pupils in a bilingual program. Mimeographed. Coral Gables, Fla.: University of Miami, 1968.

Steiner, S. *The New Indians.* New York: Harper & Row, 1968.

White, S. H. Evidence for a hierarchical arrangement of learning processes. In L. P. Lipsitt and C. C. Spiker, eds., *Advances in Child Development and Behavior,* Vol. 2. New York: Academic Press, 1965.

Chapter 9

THE LOGIC OF NONSTANDARD
ENGLISH

William Labov*

In the past decade, a great deal of federally sponsored research has been devoted to the educational problems of children in ghetto schools. In order to account for the poor performance of children in these schools, educational psychologists have attempted to discover what kind of disadvantage or defect they are suffering from. The viewpoint that has been widely accepted and used as the basis for large scale intervention programs is that the children show a cultural deficit as a result of an impoverished environment in their early years. Considerable attention has been given to language. In this area the deficit theory appears as the concept of verbal deprivation. Negro children from the ghetto area are said to receive little verbal stimulation, to hear very little well-formed language, and as a result are impoverished in their means of verbal expression. They cannot speak complete sentences, do not know the names of common objects, cannot form concepts or convey logical thoughts.

Unfortunately, these notions are based upon the work of educational psychologists who know very little about language and even less about Negro children. The concept of verbal deprivation has no basis in social reality. In fact, Negro children in the urban ghettos receive a great deal of verbal stimula-

_____

*Department of Linguistics, Columbia University

This paper was originally presented at the Twentieth Annual Georgetown Round Table meeting on Linguistics and Language Studies, Washington, D.C., March 14, 1969, where the theme was "Linguistics and the Teaching of Standard English to Speakers of Other Languages or Dialects." We are indebted to Prof. James Alatis, editor of the Round Table proceedings (Alatis, 1970) for permission to use this paper.

tion, hear more well-formed sentences than middle-class children, and participate fully in a highly verbal culture. They have the same basic vocabulary, possess the same capacity for conceptual learning, and use the same logic as anyone else who learns to speak and understand English.

The notion of verbal deprivation is a part of the modern mythology of educational psychology, typical of the unfounded notions which tend to expand rapidly in our educational system. In past decades linguists have been as guilty as others in promoting such intellectual fashions at the expense of both teachers and children. But the myth of verbal deprivation is particularly dangerous, because it diverts attention from real defects of our educational system to imaginary defects of the child. As we shall see, it leads its sponsors inevitably to the hypothesis of the genetic inferiority of Negro children that it was originally designed to avoid.

The most useful service which linguists can perform today is to clear away the illusion of verbal deprivation and to provide a more adequate notion of the relations between standard and nonstandard dialects. In the writings of many prominent educational psychologists, we find very poor understanding of the nature of language. Children are treated as if they have no language of their own in the preschool programs put forward by Bereiter and Engelmann (1966). The linguistic behavior of ghetto children in test situations is the principal evidence of genetic inferiority in the view of Jensen (1969). In this paper, we will examine critically both of these approaches to the language and intelligence of the populations labeled "verbally deprived" and "culturally deprived,"[1] and attempt to explain how the myth of verbal deprivation has arisen, bringing to bear the methodological findings of sociolinguistic work and some substantive facts about language which are known to all linguists. Of particular concern is the relation between concept formation on the one hand, and dialect differences on the other, since it is in this area that the most dangerous misunderstandings are to be found.

VERBALITY

The general setting in which the deficit theory arises consists of a number of facts which are known to all of us. One is that Negro children in the central urban ghettos do badly in all school subjects, including arithmetic and reading. In reading, they average more than two years behind the national norm (see

---

[1] I am indebted to Rosalind Weiner of the Early Childhood Education group of Operation Head Start in New York City, and to Joan Baratz of the Education Study Center, Washington, D.C., for pointing out to me the scope and seriousness of the educational issues involved here, and the ways in which the cultural deprivation theory has affected federal intervention programs in recent years.

New York Times, December 3, 1968). Furthermore, this lag is cumulative, so that they do worse comparatively in the fifth grade than in the first grade. Reports in the literature show that this poor performance is correlated most closely with socioeconomic status. Segregated ethnic groups seem to do worse than others—in particular, Indian, Mexican-American, and Negro children. Our own work in New York City confirms that most Negro children read very poorly; however, studies in the speech community show that the situation is even worse than has been reported. If one separates the isolated and peripheral individuals from members of central peer groups, the peer-group members show even worse reading records, and to all intents and purposes are not learning to read at all during the time they spend in school (see Labov et al. 1968).

In speaking of children in the urban ghetto areas, the term *lower class* frequently is used, as opposed to *middle class.* In the several sociolinguistic studies we have carried out, and in many parallel studies, it has been useful to distinguish a lower-class group from a working-class one. Lower-class families are typically female-based, or matrifocal, with no father present to provide steady economic support, whereas for the working-class there is typically an intact nuclear family with the father holding a semiskilled or skilled job. The educational problems of ghetto areas run across this important class distinction. There is no evidence, for example, that the father's presence or absence is closely correlated with educational achievement (e.g., Langer and Michaels 1963; Coleman, et al. 1966). The peer groups we have studied in south-central Harlem, representing the basic vernacular culture, include members from both family types. The attack against cultural deprivation in the ghetto is overtly directed at family structures typical of lower-class families, but the educational failure we have been discussing is characteristic of both working-class and lower-class children.

This paper, therefore, will refer to children from urban ghetto areas rather than lower-class children. The population we are concerned with comprises those who participate fully in the vernacular culture of the street and who have been alienated from the school system.[2] We are obviously dealing with the effects of the caste system of American society—essentially a color-marking system. Everyone recognizes this. The question is: By what mechanism does the color bar prevent children from learning to read? One answer is the notion of cultural deprivation put forward by Martin Deutsch and others (Deutsch and associates 1967; Deutsch, Katz, and Jensen 1968). Negro children are said to lack the favorable factors in their home environment which enable middle-

---

[2]The concept of nonstandard Negro English (NNE) and the vernacular culture in which it is embedded is presented in detail in Labov, et al. (1968, sections 1.2.3 and 4.1). See volume 2, section 4.3 for the linguistic traits which distinguish speakers who participate fully in the NNE culture from marginal and isolated individuals.

class children to do well in school. These factors involve the development of various cognitive skills through verbal interaction with adults, including the ability to reason abstractly, speak fluently, and focus upon long-range goals. In their publications, these psychologists also recognize broader social factors.[3] However, the deficit theory does not focus upon the interaction of the Negro child with white society so much as on his failure to interact with his mother at home. In the literature we find very little direct observation of verbal interaction in the Negro home. Most typically, the investigators ask the child if he has dinner with his parents, if he engages in dinner-table conversation with them, if his family takes him on trips to museums and other cultural activities, and so on. This slender thread of evidence is used to explain and interpret the large body of tests carried out in the laboratory and in the school.

The most extreme view which proceeds from this orientation—and one that is now being widely accepted—is that lower-class Negro children have no language at all. The notion is first drawn from Basil Bernstein's writings that "much of lower-class language consists of a kind of incidental 'emotional' accompaniment to action here and now" (Jensen 1968, p. 118). Bernstein's views are filtered through a strong bias against all forms of working-class behavior, so that middle-class language is seen as superior in every respect— as "more abstract, and necessarily somewhat more flexible, detailed and subtle" (p. 119). One can proceed through a range of such views until he comes to the preschool programs of Bereiter and Engelmann (1966; Bereiter, et al. 1966). Bereiter's program for an academically oriented preschool is based upon the premise that Negro children must have a language with which they can learn and the empirical finding that these children come to school without such a language. In his work with four-year-old Negro children from Urbana, Bereiter (et al. 1966, pp. 113 ff.) reports that their communication was by gestures, single words, and "a series of badly connected words or phrases," such as *They mine* and *Me got juice.* He reports that Negro children could not ask questions, that "without exaggerating . . . these four-year-olds could make no statements of any kind." Futhermore, when these children were asked "Where is the book?" they did not know enough to look at the table where the book was lying in order to answer. Thus Bereiter concludes that these children's speech forms are nothing more than a series of emotional cries, and he decides to treat them "as if the children had no language at all." He identifies their speech with his interpretation of Bernstein's restricted code: "the language of culturally deprived children . . . is not merely an under-developed version of standard English, but is a basically non-logical mode of

---

[3]For example, in Deutsch, Katz, and Jensen (1968) there is a section on Social and Psychological Perspectives which includes a chapter by Proshansky and Newton on "The Nature and Meaning of Negro Self-Identity," and one by Rosenthal and Jacobson on "Self-Fufilling Prophecies in the Classroom."

expressive behavior" (Bereiter, et al. 1966, pp. 112–13). The basic program of his preschool is to teach them a new language devised by Engelmann, which consists of a limited series of questions and answers such as "Where is the squirrel?" "The squirrel is in the tree." The children will not be punished if they use their vernacular speech on the playground, but they will not be allowed to use it in the schoolroom. If they should answer the question, "Where is the squirrel?" with the illogical vernacular form "In the tree" they will be reprehended by various means and made to say, "The squirrel is in the tree."

Linguists and psycholinguists who have worked with Negro children are apt to dismiss this view of their language as utter nonsense. Yet there is no reason to reject Bereiter's observations as spurious. They were certainly not made up. On the contrary, they give us a very clear view of the behavior of student and teacher which can be duplicated in any classroom. In our own work outside of adult-dominated environments of school and home, we have not observed Negro children behaving like this.[4] However, on many occasions we have been asked to help analyze the results of research into verbal deprivation conducted in such test situations.

Here, for example, is a complete interview with a Negro boy, one of hundreds carried out in a New York City school. The boy enters a room where there is a large, friendly, white interviewer, who puts on the table in front of him a toy and says: "Tell me everything you can about this." (The interviewer's further remarks are in parentheses.)

[12 seconds of silence]
(What would you say it looks like?)
[8 seconds of silence]
A space ship.
(Hmmmm.)
[13 seconds of silence]
Like a je-et.
[12 seconds of silence]
Like a plane.
[20 seconds of silence]
(What color is it?)
Orange. (2 seconds) An' whi-ite. (2 seconds) An' green.
[6 seconds of silence]
(An' what could you use if for?)
[8 seconds of silence]

A je-et.
[6 seconds of silence]
(If you had two of them, what would you do with them?)
[6 seconds of silence]
Give one to some-body.
(Hmmm. Who do you think would like to have it?)
[10 seconds of silence]
Cla-rence.
(Mm. Where do you think we could get another one of these?)
At the store.
(Oh ka-ay!)

We have here the same kind of defensive, monosyllabic behavior which is reported in Bereiter's work. What is the situation that produces it? The child is in an asymmetrical situation where anything he says can literally be held against him. He has learned a number of devices to avoid saying anything in this situation, and he works very hard to achieve this end. One may observe the intonation patterns of

$$^2 a ^{3} {}'o' {}^2 \text{ know}$$

and

$$a ^2 \text{ space } ^2 sh^{3} \text{ ip}$$

which Negro children often use when they are asked a question to which the answer is obvious. The answer may be read as: "Will this satisfy you?"

If one takes this interview as a measure of the verbal capacity of the child, it must be as his capacity to defend himself in a hostile and threatening situation. But unfortunately, thousands of such interviews are used as evidence of the child's total verbal capacity, or more simply his verbality. It is argued that this lack of verbality explains his poor performance in school. Operation Head Start and other intervention programs have largely been based upon the deficit theory—the notions that such interviews give us a measure of the child's verbal capacity and that the verbal stimulation which he has been missing can be supplied in a preschool environment.

The verbal behavior which is shown by the child in the situation quoted above is not the result of the ineptness of the interviewer. It is rather the result of regular sociolinguistic factors operating upon adult and child in this asymmetrical situation. In our work in urban ghetto areas, we have often encountered such behavior. Ordinarily we worked with boys ten to seventeen years old, and whenever we extended our approach downward to eight- or nine-year-olds, we began to see the need for different techniques to explore the verbal capacity of the child. At one point we began a series of interviews with younger brothers of the Thunderbirds in 1390 Fifth Avenue (Ed. Note: a preadolescent group studied in this research). Clarence Robins (CR) returned after an inter-

view with eight-year-old Leon L., who showed the following minimal response
to topics which arouse intense interest in other interviews with older boys.

> CR: What if you saw somebody kickin' somebody else on the
> ground, or was using a stick, what would you do if you saw that?
> LEON: Mmmm.
> CR: If it was supposed to be a fair fight—
> LEON: I don' know.
> CR: You don' know? Would you do anything? . . . huh? I can't
> hear you.
> LEON: No.
> CR: Did you ever see somebody got beat up real bad?
> LEON: . . . Nope . . .
> CR: Well—uh—did you ever get into a fight with a guy?
> LEON: Nope.
> CR: That was bigger than you?
> LEON: Nope . . .
> CR: You never been in a fight?
> LEON: Nope.
> CR: Nobody ever pick on you?
> LEON: Nope.
> CR: Nobody ever hit you?
> LEON: Nope.
> CR: How come?
> LEON: Ah 'on' know.
> CR: Didn't you ever hit somebody?
> LEON: Nope.
> CR: (incredulously) You never hit nobody?
> LEON Mhm.
> CR: Aww, ba-a-a-be, you ain't gonna tell me that!

It may be that Leon is here defending himself against accusations of
wrongdoing, since Clarence knows that Leon has been in fights, that he has
been taking pencils away from little boys, and so on. But if we turn to a more
neutral subject, we find the same pattern:

> CR: You watch—you like to watch television? . . . Hey, Leon
> . . . you like to watch television? (Leon nods) What's your favorite
> program?
> LEON: Uhhmmmm . . . I look at cartoons.
> CR: Well, what's your favorite one? What's your favorite pro-
> gram?
> LEON: Superman . . .
> CR: Yeah? Did you see Superman—ah—yesterday, or day
> before yesterday? When's the last time you saw Superman?
> LEON: Sa-aturday . . .
> CR: You rem—you saw it Saturday? What was the story all
> about? You remember the story?
> LEON: M-m.

CR: You don't remember the story of what—that you saw of
Superman?
Leon: Nope.
CR: You don't remember what happened, huh?
Leon: Hm-m.
CR: I see—ah—what other stories do you like to watch on TV?
Leon: Mmmm ? . . . umm . . . (glottalization)
CR: Hmm? (four seconds)
Leon: Hh?
CR: What's th' other stories that you like to watch?
Leon: Mi-ighty Mouse . . .
CR: And what else?
Leon: Ummmm . . . ahm . . .

This nonverbal behavior occurs in a relatively favorable context for adult-
child interaction. The adult is a Negro man raised in Harlem, who knows this
particular neighborhood and these boys very well. He is a skilled interviewer
who has obtained a very high level of verbal response with techniques developed for a different age level, and he has an extraordinary advantage over most
teachers or experimenters in these respects. But even his skills and personality
are ineffective in breaking down the social constraints that prevail here.

When we reviewed the record of this interview with Leon, we decided to
use it as a test of our own knowledge of the sociolinguistic factors which
control speech. In the next interview with Leon we made the following changes
in the social situation:

1. Clarence brought along a supply of potato chips, changing the interview into something more in the nature of a party.

2. He brought along Leon's best friend, eight-year-old Gregory.

3. We reduced the height in balance by having Clarence get down on the
floor of Leon's room; he dropped from six feet, two inches to three feet, six
inches.

4. Clarence introduced taboo words and taboo topics, and proved, to
Leon's surprise, that one can say anything into our microphone without any
fear of retaliation. The result of these changes is a striking difference in the
volume and style of speech. (The tape is punctuated throughout by the sound
of potato chips.)

CR: Is there anybody who says *your momma drink pee?*
{(Leon: (rapidly and breathlessly) Yee-ah!
{(Greg: Yup!
Leon: And *your father eat doo-doo for breakfas'!*
CR: Ohhh! ! (laughs)
Leon: And they say your father—*your father eat doo-doo for
dinner!*

GREG: When they sound on me, I say *C.B.S.*
C.B.M.
CR: What that mean?
{ (LEON: Congo booger-snatch! (laughs)
{ (GREG: Congo booger-snatcher! (laughs)
GREG: And sometimes I'll curse with *B.B.*
CR: What that?
GREG: Black boy! (Leon crunching on potato chips) Oh that's
a *M.B.B.*
CR: *M.B.B.* What's that?
GREG: 'Merican Black Boy.
CR: Ohh . . .
GREG: Anyway, 'Mericans is same like white people, right?
LEON: And they talk about Allah.
CR: Oh yeah?
GREG: Yeah.
CR: What they say about Allah?
{ (LEON: Allah—Allah is God.
{ (GREG: Allah—
CR: And what else?
LEON: I don' know the res'.
GREG: Allah i—Allah is God, Allah is the only God,
Allah . . .
LEON: Allah is the *son* of God.
GREG: But can he make magic?
LEON: Nope.
GREG: I know who can make magic.
CR: Who can?
LEON: The God, the *real* one.
CR: Who can make magic?
GREG: The son of po'— (CR: Hm?) I'm sayin' the po'k chop
God![5] He only a po'k chop God! (Leon chuckles).

(The "nonverbal" Leon is now competing actively for the floor; Gregory and Leon talk to each other as much as they do to the interviewer.)

We can make a more direct comparison of the two interviews by examining the section on fighting. Leon persists in denying that he fights, but he can no longer use monosyllabic answers, and Gregory cuts through his facade in a way that Clarence Robins alone was unable to do.

---

[5]The reference to the *pork chop God* condenses several concepts of black nationalism current in the Harlem community. A *pork chop* is a Negro who has not lost the traditional subservient ideology of the South, who has no knowledge of himself in Muslim terms, and the *pork chop God* would be the traditional God of Southern Baptists. He and His followers may be pork chops, but He still holds the power in Leon and Gregory's world.

CR: Now, you said you had this fight now; but I wanted you to tell me about the fight that you had.
LEON: I ain't had no fight.
⎰(GREG: Yes you did! He said Barry . . .
⎱(CR: You said you had one! you had a fight with Butchie,
⎰(GREG: An he say Garland! . . . an' Michael!
⎱(CR: an' Barry . . .
⎰(LEON: I di'n'; you said that, Gregory!
⎱(GREG: You did!
⎰(LEON: You know you said that!
⎱(GREG: You said Garland, remember that?
⎰(GREG: You said Garland! Yes you did!
⎱(CR: You said Garland, that's right.
⎧ GREG: He said Mich—an' I say Michael.
⎰(CR: Did you have a fight with Garland?
⎱(LEON: Uh-Uh.
CR: You had one, and he beat you up, too!
GREG: Yes he did!
LEON: No, I di—I never had a fight with Butch! . . .

The same pattern can be seen on other local topics, where the interviewer brings neighborhood gossip to bear on Leon, and Gregory acts as a witness.

CR: . . . Hey Gregory! I heard that around here . . . and I'm 'on' tell you who said it, too . . .
LEON: Who?
CR: about you . . .
⎰(LEON: Who?
⎱(GREG: I'd say it!
CR: They said that—they say that the only person you play with is David Gilbert.
⎰(LEON: Yee-ah! yee-ah! yee-ah! . . .
⎱(GREG: That's who you play with!
⎰(LEON: I 'on' play with him no more!
⎱(GREG: Yes you do!
LEON: I 'on' play with him no more!
GREG: But remember, about me and Robbie?
LEON: So that's not—
GREG: and you went to Petey and Gilbert's house, 'member?
Ah haaah!!
LEON: So that's—so—but I would—I had came back out, an' I ain't go to his house no more . . . .

The observer must now draw a very different conclusion about the verbal capacity of Leon. The monosyllabic speaker who had nothing to say about anything and cannot remember what he did yesterday has disappeared. Instead, we have two boys who have so much to say they keep interrupting each other, and who seem to have no difficulty in using the English langauge to express themselves. In turn we obtain the volume of speech and the rich array of grammatical devices which we need for analyzing the structure of nonstandard Negro English; for example: negative concord ("I 'on' play with him no more"), the pluperfect ("had came back out"), negative perfect ("I ain't had"), the negative preterite ("I ain't go"), and so on.

We can now transfer this demonstration of the sociolinguistic control of speech to other test situations, including IQ and reading tests in school. It should be immediately apparent that none of the standard tests will come anywhere near measuring Leon's verbal capacity. On these tests he will show up as very much the monosyllabic, inept, ignorant, bumbling child of our first interview. The teacher has far less ability than Clarence Robins to elicit speech from this child. Clarence knows the community, the things that Leon has been doing, and the things that Leon would like to talk about. But the power relationships in a one-to-one confrontation between adult and child are too asymmetrical. This does not mean that some Negro children will not talk a great deal when alone with an adult, or that an adult cannot get close to any child. It means that the social situation is the most powerful determinant of verbal behavior and that an adult must enter into the right social relation with a child if he wants to find out what a child can do. This is just what many teachers cannot do.

The view of the Negro speech community which we obtain from our work in the ghetto areas is precisely the opposite from that reported by Deutsch or by Bereiter and Engelmann. We see a child bathed in verbal stimulation from morning to night. We see many speech events which depend upon the competitive exhibition of verbal skills—sounding, singing, toasts, rifting, louding—a whole range of activities in which the individual gains status through his use of language (see Labov, et al. 1968, section 4.2). We see the younger child trying to acquire these skills from older children, hanging around on the outskirts of older peer groups, and imitating this behavior to the best of his ability. We see no connection between verbal skill in the speech events characteristic of the street culture and success in the schoolroom.

VERBOSITY

There are undoubtedly many verbal skills which children from ghetto areas must learn in order to do well in the school situation, and some of these are indeed characteristic of middle-class verbal behavior. Precision in spelling, practice in handling abstract symbols, the ability to state explicitly the meaning of words, and a richer knowledge of the Latinate vocabulary, may all be useful acquisitions. But is it true that all of the middle-class verbal habits are functional and desirable in the school situation? Before we impose middle-class verbal style upon children from other cultural groups, we should find out how much of this is useful for the main work of analyzing and generalizing, and how much is merely stylistic—or even dysfunctional. In high school and college, middle-class children spontaneously complicate their syntax to the point that instructors despair of getting them to make their language simpler and clearer. In every learned journal one can find examples of jargon and empty elaboration, as well as complaints about it. Is the elaborated code of Bernstein really so "flexible, detailed and subtle" as some psychologists (e.g., Jensen 1969 p. 119) believe? Isn't it also turgid, redundant, bombastic, and empty? Is it not simply an elaborated style, rather than a superior code or system?[6]

Our work in the speech community makes it painfully obvious that in many ways working-class speakers are more effective narrators, reasoners, and debaters than many middle-class speakers who temporize, qualify, and lose their argument in a mass of irrelevant detail. Many academic writers try to rid themselves of that part of middle-class style that is empty pretension, and keep that part that is needed for precision. But the average middle-class speaker that we encounter makes no such effort; he is enmeshed in verbiage, the victim of sociolinguistic factors beyond his control.

I will not attempt to support this argument here with systematic quantitative evidence, although it is possible to develop measures which show how far middle-class speakers can wander from the point. I would like to contrast two speakers dealing with roughly the same topic—matters of belief. The first is Larry H., a fifteen-year-old core member of the Jets, being interviewed by John Lewis. Larry is one of the loudest and roughest members of the Jets, one who gives the least recognition to the conventional rules of politeness.[7] For most readers of this paper, first contact with Larry would produce some fairly negative reactions on both sides. It is probable that you would not like him any more than his teachers do. Larry causes trouble in and out of school. He was put back from the eleventh grade to the ninth, and has been threatened with further action by the school authorities.

> JL: What happens to you after you die? Do you know?
> LARRY: Yeah, I know. (What?) After they put you in the ground, your body turns into—ah—bones, an' shit.
> JL: What happens to your spirit?
> LARRY: Your spirit—soon as you die, your spirit leaves you.

---

[6]The term *code* is central in Bernstein's (1966) description of the differences between working-class and middle-class styles of speech. The restrictions and elaborations of speech observed are labeled as codes to indicate the principles governing selection from the range of possible English sentences. No rules or detailed description of the operation of such codes are provided as yet, so that this central concept remains to be specified.

[7]A direct view of Larry's verbal style in a hostile encounter is given in Labov, et al. (1968, volume 2, pp. 39–43). Gray's Oral Reading Test was being given to a group of Jets on the steps of a brownstone house in Harlem, and the landlord tried unsuccessfully to make the Jets move. Larry's verbal style in this encounter matches the reports he gives of himself in a number of narratives cited in section 4.8 of the foregoing report.

(And where does the spirit go?) Well, it all depends . . . (On what?) You know, like some people say if you're good an' shit, your spirit goin' t'heaven . . . 'n' if you bad, your spirit goin' to hell. Well, bullshit! Your spirit goin' to hell anyway, good or bad.
    JL: Why?
    LARRY: Why? I'll tell you why. 'Cause, you see, doesn' nobody really know that it's a God, y'know, 'cause I mean I have seen black gods, pink gods, white gods, all color gods, and don't nobody know it's really a God. An' when they be sayin' if you good, you goin' t'heaven, tha's bullshit, 'cause you ain't goin' to no heaven, 'cause it ain't no heaven for you to go to.

Larry is a paradigmatic speaker of nonstandard Negro English (NNE) as opposed to standard English. His grammar shows a high concentration of such characteristic NNE forms as negative inversion ("don't nobody know . . ."), negative concord ("you ain't goin' to no heaven . . ."), invariant *be* ("when they be sayin' . . ."), dummy *it* for standard *there* ("it ain't no heaven . . ."), optional copula deletion ("if you're good . . . if you bad . . .") and full forms of auxiliaries ("I have seen . . . "). The only standard English influence in this passage is the one case of "doesn't" instead of the invariant "don't" of NNE. Larry also provides a paradigmatic example of the rhetorical style of NNE: he can sum up a complex argument in a few words, and the full force of his opinions come through without qualification or reservation. He is eminently quotable, and his interviews give us many concise statements of the NNE point of view. One can almost say that Larry speaks the NNE culture (see Labov, et al. 1968, vol. 2, pp. 38, 71–73, 291–92).

It is the logical form of this passage which is of particular interest here. Larry presents a complex set of interdependent propositions which can be explicated by setting out the standard English equivalents in linear order. The basic argument is to deny the twin propositions:
    (A) If you are good, *(B)* then your spirit will go to heaven.
    (~A) If you are bad, *(C)* then your spirit will go to hell.
Larry denies *(B)* and asserts that if *(A)* or *(~A)*, then *(C)*. His argument may be outlined as follows:
1. Everyone has a different idea of what God is like.
2. Therefore nobody really knows that God exists.
3. If there is a heaven, it was made by God.
4. If God doesn't exist, he couldn't have made heaven.
5. Therefore heaven does not exist.
6. You can't go somewhere that doesn't exist.
(~B) Therefore you can't go to heaven.
(C) Therefore you are going to hell.
The argument is presented in the order: *(C)*, because (2) because (1), therefore (2), therefore *(~B)* because (5) and (6). Part of the argument is implicit: the connection (2) therefore *(~B)* leaves unstated the connecting links (3) and (4),

and in this interval Larry strengthens the propositions from the form (2) "Nobody knows if there is . . . " to (5) "There is no . . . ." Otherwise, the case is presented explicitly as well as economically. The complex argument is summed up in Larry's last sentence, which shows formally the dependence of *(~B)* on (5) and (6):

An' when they be sayin' if you good, you goin' t'heaven, (The propostion, if *A*, then *B*)

Tha's bullshit, (is absurd)

'cause you ain't goin' to no heaven (because *B*)

'cause it ain't no heaven for you to go to (because (5) and (6)).

This hypothetical argument is not carried on at a high level of seriousness. It is a game played with ideas as counters, in which opponents use a wide variety of verbal devices to win. There is no personal commitment to any of these propositions, and no reluctance to strengthen one's argument by bending the rules of logic as in the (2)-(5) sequence. But if the opponent invokes the rules of logic, they hold. In John Lewis's interviews, he often makes this move, and the force of his argument is always acknowledged and countered within the rules of logic. In this case, he pointed out the fallacy that the argument (2)-(3)-(4)-(5)-(6) leads to *(~C)* as well as *(~B)*, so it cannot be used to support Larry's assertion *(C):*

JL: Well, if there's no heaven, how could there be a hell?

LARRY: I mean—ye-eah. Well, let me tell you, it ain't no hell, 'cause this is hell right here, y'know! (This is hell?) Yeah, this is hell right here!

Larry's answer is quick, ingenious, and decisive. The application of the (3)-(4)-(5) argument to hell is denied, since hell is here, and therefore conclusion *(C)* stands. These are not ready-made or preconceived opinions, but new propositions devised to win the logical argument in the game being played. The reader will note the speed and precision of Larry's mental operations. He does not wander, or insert meaningless verbiage. The only repetition is (2), placed before and after (1) in his original statement. It is often said that the nonstandard vernacular is not suited for dealing with abstract or hypothetical questions, but in fact speakers from the NNE community take great delight in exercising their wit and logic on the most improbable and problematical matters. Despite the fact that Larry H. does not believe in God, and has just denied all knowledge of him, John Lewis advances the following hypothetical question:

JL: . . . but, just say that there is a God, what color is he? White or black?

LARRY: Well, if it is a God . . . I wouldn' know what color, I couldn' say,—couldn' nobody say what color he is or really *would* be.

JL: But now, jus' suppose there was a God—
LARRY: Unless'n they say . . .
JL: No, I was jus' sayin' jus' suppose there is a God, would he
be white or black?
LARRY: . . . He'd be white, man.
JL: Why?
LARRY: Why? I'll tell you why. 'Cause the average whitey out
here got everything, you dig? And the nigger ain't got shit, y'know?
Y'unnerstan'? So—um—for—in order for *that* to happen, you know
it ain't no black God that's doin' that bullshit.

No one can hear Larry's answer to this question without being convinced that
they are in the presence of a skilled speaker with great "verbal presence of
mind," who can use the English language expertly for many purposes. Larry's
answer to John Lewis is again a complex argument. The formulation is not
standard English, but it is clear and effective even for those not familiar with
the vernacular. The nearest standard English equivalent might be: "So you
know that God isn't black, because if he was, he wouldn't have arranged things
like that."

The reader will have noted that this analysis is being carried out in
standard English, and the inevitable challenge is: why not write in NNE, then,
or in your own nonstandard dialect? The fundamental reason is, of course, one
of firmly fixed social conventions. All communities agree that standard English
is the proper medium for formal writing and public communication. Furthermore, it seems likely that standard English has an advantage over NNE in
explicit analysis of surface forms, which is what we are doing here. We will
return to this opposition between explicitness and logical statement in subsequent sections on grammaticality and logic. First, however, it will be helpful
to examine standard English in its primary natural setting, as the medium for
informal spoken communication of middle-class speakers.

Let us now turn to the second speaker, an upper-middle-class, college-
educated Negro man (Charles M.) being interviewed by Clarence Robins in
our survey of adults in Central Harlem.

CR: Do you know of anything that someone can do, to have
someone who has passed on visit him in a dream?
CHARLES: Well, I even heard my parents say that there is such
a thing as something in dreams some things like that, and sometimes
dreams do come true. I have personally never had a dream come
true. I've never dreamt that somebody was dying and they actually
died, (Mhm) or that I was going to have ten dollars the next day and
somehow I got ten dollars in my pocket. (Mhm). I don't particularly
believe in that, I don't think it's true. I do feel, though, that there
is such a thing as—ah—witchcraft. I do feel that in certain cultures
there is such a thing as witchcraft, or some sort of *science* of witchcraft; I don't think that it's just a matter of believing hard enough

that there is such a thing as witchcraft. I do believe that there is such a thing that a person can put himself in a state of *mind* (Mhm), or that—er—something could be given them to intoxicate them in a certain—to a certain frame of mind—that—that could actually be considered witchcraft.

Charles M. is obviously a good speaker who strikes the listener as well-educated, intelligent, and sincere. He is a likeable and attractive person, the kind of person that middle-class listeners rate very high on a scale of job suitability and equally high as a potential friend.[8] His language is more moderate and tempered than Larry's; he makes every effort to qualify his opinions, and seems anxious to avoid any misstatements or overstatements. From these qualities emerge the primary characteristic of this passage—its verbosity. Words multiply, some modifying and qualifying, others repeating or padding the main argument. The first half of this extract is a response to the initial question on dreams, basically:

1. Some people say that dreams sometimes come true.
2. I have never had a dream come true.
3. Therefore I don't believe (1).

Some characteristic filler phrases appear here: *such a thing as, some things like that,* and *particularly.* Two examples of dreams given after (2) are afterthoughts that might have been given after (1). Proposition (3) is stated twice for no obvious reason. Nevertheless, this much of Charles M.'s response is well-directed to the point of the question. He then volunteers a statement of his beliefs about witchcraft which shows the difficulty of middle-class speakers who (a) want to express a belief in something but (b) want to show themselves as judicious, rational, and free from superstitions. The basic proposition can be stated simply in five words:

"But I believe in witchcraft."

However, the idea is enlarged to exactly 100 words, and it is difficult to see what else is being said. In the following quotations, padding which can be removed without change in meaning is shown in parentheses.

(1) "I (do) feel, though, that there is (such a thing as) witchcraft." *Feel* seems to be a euphemism for 'believe.'

(2) "(I do feel that) in certain cultures (there is such a thing as witchcraft)." This repetition seems designed only to introduce the word *culture,* which lets us know that the speaker knows about anthropology. Does *certain cultures* mean 'not in ours' or 'not in all'?

(3) "(or some sort of *science* of witchcraft.)" This addition seems to have no clear meaning at all. What is a "science" of witchcraft as opposed to just

---

[8]For a description of subjective reaction tests which utilize these evaluative dimensions see Labov, et al. (1968, section 4.6).

plain witchcraft?[9] The main function is to introduce the word *science*, though it seems to have no connection to what follows.

(4) "I don't think that it's just (a matter of) believing hard enough that (there is such a thing as) witchcraft." The speaker argues that witchcraft is not merely a belief; there is more to it.

(5) "I (do) believe that (there is such a thing that) a person can put himself in a state of mind . . . that (could actually be considered) witchcraft." Is witchcraft as a state of mind different from the state of belief, denied in (4)?

(6) "or that something could be given them to intoxicate them (to a certain frame of mind) . . . ." The third learned word, *intoxicate*, is introduced by this addition. The vacuity of this passage becomes more evident if we remove repetitions, fashionable words and stylistic decorations:

> But I believe in witchcraft.
> I don't think witchcraft is just a belief.

A person can put himself or be put in a state of mind that is witchcraft. Without the extra verbiage and the "OK" words like *science, culture,* and *intoxicate,* Charles M. appears as something less than a first-rate thinker. The initial impression of him as a good speaker is simply our long-conditioned reaction to middle-class verbosity. We know that people who use these stylistic devices are educated people, and we are inclined to credit them with saying something intelligent. Our reactions are accurate in one sense. Charles M. is more educated than Larry. But is he more rational, more logical, more intelligent? Is he any better at thinking out a problem to its solution? Does he deal more easily with abstractions? There is no reason to think so. Charles M. succeeds in letting us know that he is educated, but in the end we do not know what he is trying to say, and neither does he.

In the previous section I have attempted to explain the origin of the myth that lower-class Negro children are nonverbal. The examples just given may help to account for the corresponding myth that middle-class language is in itself better suited for dealing with abstract, logically complex, or hypothetical questions. These examples are intended to have a certain negative force. They are not controlled experiments. On the contrary, this and the preceding section are designed to convince the reader that the controlled experiments that have been offered in evidence are misleading. The only thing that is controlled is the superficial form of the stimulus. All children are asked "What do you think of capital punishment?" or "Tell me everything you can about this." But the

---

[9]Several middle-class readers of this passage have suggested that *science* here refers to some form of control as opposed to belief. The science of witchcraft would then be a kind of engineering of mental states. Other interpretations can of course be provided. The fact remains that no such difficulties of interpretation are needed to understand Larry's remarks.

speaker's interpretation of these requests, and the action he believes is appropriate in response is completely uncontrolled. One can view these test stimuli as requests for information, commands for action, threats of punishment, or meaningless sequences of words. They are probably intended as something altogether different—as requests for display,[10] but in any case the experimenter is normally unaware of the problem of interpretation. The methods of educational psychologists such as used by Deutsch, Jensen, and Bereiter follow the pattern designed for animal experiments where motivation is controlled by simple methods as withholding food until a certain weight reduction is reached. With human subjects, it is absurd to believe that identical stimuli are obtained by asking everyone the same question.

Since the crucial intervening variables of interpretation and motivation are uncontrolled, most of the literature on verbal deprivation tells us nothing about the capacities of children. They are only the trappings of science, approaches which substitute the formal procedures of the scientific method for the activity itself. With our present limited grasp of these problems, the best we can do to understand the verbal capacities of children is to study them within the cultural context in which they were developed.

It is not only the NNE vernacular which should be studied in this way, but also the language of middle-class children. The explicitness and precision which we hope to gain from copying middle-class forms are often the product of the test situation, and limited to it. For example, it was stated in the first part of this paper that working-class children hear more well-formed sentences than middle-class children. This statement may seem extraordinary in the light of the current belief of many linguists that most people do not speak in well-formed sentences, and that their actual speech production, or performance, is ungrammatical.[11] But those who have worked with any body of natural speech know that this is not the case. Our own studies (Labov 1966) of the grammaticality of everyday speech show that the great majority of utterances in all contexts are complete sentences, and most of the rest can be reduced to grammatical form by a small set of editing rules. The proportions of grammatical sentences vary with class backgrounds and styles. The highest percentage of well-formed sentences are found in casual speech, and working-class speak-

---

[10]The concept of a request for verbal display is here drawn from a treatment of the therapeutic interview given by Blum (in press).

[11]In several presentations, Chomsky has asserted that the great majority (95 percent) of the sentences which a child hears are ungrammatical. Chomsky (1965, p. 58) presents this notion as one of the arguments in his general statement of the nativist position: "A consideration of the character of the grammar that is acquired, *the degenerate quality and narrowly limited extent of the available data* [my emphasis], the striking uniformity of the resulting grammars, and their independence of intelligence, motivation, and emotional state, over wide ranges of variation, leave little hope that much of the structure of the language can be learned . . . ."

ers use more well-formed sentences than middle-class speakers. The widespread myth that most speech is ungrammatical is no doubt based upon tapes made at learned conferences, where we obtain the maximum number of irreducibly ungrammatical sequences.

It is true that technical and scientific books are written in a style which is markedly middle-class. But unfortunately, we often fail to achieve the explicitness and precision which we look for in such writing, and the speech of many middle-class people departs maximally from this target. All too often, standard English is represented by a style that is simultaneously overparticular and vague. The accumulating flow of words buries rather than strikes the target. It is this verbosity which is most easily taught and most easily learned, so that words take the place of thoughts, and nothing can be found behind them.

When Bernstein (e.g., 1966) describes his elaborated code in general terms, it emerges as a subtle and sophisticated mode of planning utterances, where the speaker is achieving structural variety, taking the other person's knowledge into account, and so on. But when it comes to describing the actual difference between middle-class and working-class speakers (Bernstein 1966), we are presented with a proliferation of "I think," of the passive, of modals and auxiliaries, of the first-person pronoun, of uncommon words, and so on. But these are the bench marks of hemming and hawing, backing and filling, that are used by Charles M., the devices which so often obscure whatever positive contribution education can make to our use of language. When we have discovered how much of middle-class style is a matter of fashion and how much actually helps us express ideas clearly, we will have done ourselves a great service. We will then be in a position to say what standard grammatical rules must be taught to nonstandard speakers in the early grades.

GRAMMATICALITY

Let us now examine Bereiter's own data on the verbal behavior of the children he dealt with. The expressions *They mine* and *Me got juice* are cited as examples of a language which lacks the means for expressing logical relations, in this case characterized as "a series of badly connected words" (Bereiter, et al. 1966, p. 113). In the case of *They mine*, it is apparent that Bereiter confuses the notions of logic and explicitness. We know that there are many languages of the world which do not have a present copula, and which conjoin subject and predicate complement without a verb. Russian, Hungarian, and Arabic may be foreign, but they are not by that same token illogical. In the case of NNE we are not dealing with even this superficial grammatical difference, but rather with a low-level rule which carries contraction one step farther to delete single consonants representing the verbs *is, have* or *will* (Labov 1969). We have yet to find any children who do not sometimes use the full forms of *is* and *will*, even though they may frequently delete them. Our recent studies with Negro children four to seven years old indicate that they use the full form of the copula more often than preadolescents ten- to twelve-years-old, or the adolescents fourteen- to seventeen-years-old.[12]

Furthermore, the delection of the *is* or *are* in NNE is not the result of erratic or illogical behavior; it follows the same regular rules as standard English contraction. Wherever standard English can contract, Negro children use either the contracted form or (more commonly) the deleted zero form. Thus *They mine* corresponds to standard *They're mine*, not to the full form *They are mine.* On the other hand, no such deletion is possible in positions where standard English cannot contract. Just as one cannot say, "*That's what they're" in standard English, "*That's what they" is impossible in the vernacular we are considering. [Ed. Note: The asterisk indicates forms not permitted in the dialect.] The internal constraints upon both of these rules show that we are dealing with a phonological process like contraction—one sensitive to such phonetic conditions as whether the next word begins with a vowel or a consonant. The appropriate use of the deletion rule, like the contraction rule, requires a deep and intimate knowledge of English grammar and phonology. Such knowledge is not available for conscious inspection by native speakers. The rules we have recently worked out for standard contraction (Labov 1969) have never appeared in any grammar, and are certainly not a part of the conscious knowledge of any standard English speakers. Nevertheless, the adult or child who uses these rules must have formed at some level of psychological organization, clear concepts of tense marker, verb phrase, rule ordering, sentence embedding, pronoun, and many other grammatical categories which are essential parts of any logical system.

Bereiter's reaction to the sentence *Me got juice* is even more puzzling. If Bereiter believes that "Me got juice" is not a logical expression, it can only be that he interprets the use of the objective pronoun *me* as representing a difference in logical relationship to the verb—that the child is in fact saying that "the juice got him" rather than "he got the juice"! If on the other hand, the child means "I got juice" then this sentence shows only that he has not learned the formal rules for the use of the subjective form *I* and oblique form *me.* We have in fact encountered many children who do not have these formal rules in order at the ages of four, five, six, or even eight. It is extremely difficult to construct a minimal pair to show that the difference between *he* and *him,* or *she* and *her* carries cognitive meaning. In almost every case, it is the context which tells us who is the agent and who is acted upon. We must then ask: What

---

[12]This is from work on the grammars and comprehension of Negro children, four to eight years old, being carried out by Prof. Jane Torrey of Connecticut College in extension of the research cited above in Labov, et al. (1968).

differences in cognitive, structural orientation are signaled by the child's not knowing this formal rule? In the tests carried out by Jane Torrey, it is evident that the children concerned do understand the difference in meaning between *she* and *her* when another person uses the forms. All that remains, then, is that the children themselves do not use the two forms. Our knowledge of the cognitive correlates of grammatical differences is certainly in its infancy, for this is one of very many questions which we simply cannot answer. At the moment we do not know how to construct any kind of experiment which would lead to an answer; we do not even know what type of cognitive correlate we would be looking for.

Bereiter shows even more profound ignorance of the rules of discourse and of syntax when he rejects "In the tree" as an illogical, or badly formed answer to "Where is the squirrel?" Such elliptical answers are, of course, used by everyone. They show the appropriate deletion of subject and main verb, leaving the locative which is questioned by *wh* + *there*. The reply "In the tree" demonstrates that the listener has been attentive to and apprehended the syntax of the speaker.[13] Whatever formal structure we wish to write for expressions such as *Yes* or *Home* or *In the tree*, it is obvious that they cannot be interpreted without knowing the structure of the question which preceded them, and that they presuppose an understanding of the syntax of the question. Thus if you ask me, "Where is the squirrel?" it is necessary for me to understand the processes of *wh*-attachment, *wh*-attraction to front of the sentence, and flip-flop of auxiliary and subject to produce this sentence from an underlying form which would otherwise have produced "The squirrel is there." If the child has answered "The tree," or "Squirrel the tree," or "The in tree," we would then assume that he did not understand the syntax of the full form, "The squirrel is in the tree." Given the data that Bereiter presents, we cannot conclude that the child has no grammar, but only that the investigator does not understand the rules of grammar. It does not necessarily do any harm to use the full form "The squirrel is in the tree," if one wants to make fully explicit the rules of grammar which the child has internalized. Much of logical analysis consists of making explicit just that kind of internalized rule. But it is hard to believe that any good can come from a program which begins with so many misconceptions about the input data. Bereiter and Engelmann believe that in teaching the child to say "The squirrel is in the tree" or "This is a box" and "This is not a box" they are teaching him an entirely new language, whereas in fact, they are only teaching him to produce slightly different forms of the language he already has.

---

[13]The attention to the speaker's syntax required of the listener is analyzed in detail in a series of unpublished lectures by Prof. Harvey Sacks, Department of Sociology, University of California–Irvine.

LOGIC

For many generations, American school teachers have devoted themselves to correcting a small number of nonstandard English rules to their standard equivalents, under the impression that they were teaching logic. This view has been reinforced and given theoretical justification by the claim that NNE lacks the means for the expression of logical thought.

Let us consider for a moment the possibility that Negro children do not operate with the same logic that middle-class adults display. This would inevitably mean that sentences of a certain grammatical form would have different truth values for the two types of speakers. One of the most obvious places to look for such a difference is in the handling of the negative, and here we encounter one of the nonstandard items which has been stigmatized as illogical by schoolteachers—the double negative, or as we term it, *negative concord.* A child who says "He don't know nothing" is often said to be making an illogical statement without knowing it. According to the teacher, the child wants to say "He knows nothing" but puts in an extra negative without realizing it, and so conveys the opposite meaning, "He does not know nothing," which reduces to "He knows something." I need not emphasize that this is an absurd interpretation. If a nonstandard speaker wishes to say that "He does not know *nothing,*" he does so by simply placing contrastive stress on both negatives as I have done here ("He *don't* know *nothing*") indicating that they are derived from two underlying negatives in the deep structure. But note that the middle-class speaker does exactly the same thing when he wants to signal the existence of two underlying negatives: "He *doesn't* know *nothing.*" In the standard form with one underlying negative ("He doesn't know anything"), the indefinite *anything* contains the same superficial reference to a preceding negative in the surface structure as the nonstandard *nothing* does. In the corresponding positive sentences, the indefinite *something* is used. The dialect difference, like most of the differences between the standard and nonstandard forms, is one of surface form, and has nothing to do with the underlying logic of the sentence.

We can summarize the ways in which the two dialects differ:

	STANDARD ENGLISH, SE	NONSTANDARD NEGRO ENGLISH, NNE
Positive:	He knows something.	He know something.
Negative:	He doesn't know anything.	He don't know nothing.
Double Negative:	He *doesn't* know *nothing.*	He *don't* know *nothing.*

This array makes it plain that the only difference between the two dialects is in superficial form. When a single negative is found in the deep structure, standard English converts *something* to the indefinite *anything*; NNE converts it to *nothing*. When speakers want to signal the presence of two negatives, they do it in the same way. No one would have any difficulty constructing the same table of truth values for both dialects. English is a rare language in its insistence that the negative particle be incorporated in the first indefinite only. The Anglo-Saxon authors of the Peterborough Chronicle were surely not illogical when they wrote *For ne waeren nan martyrs swa pined alse he waeron*, literally, "For never weren't no martyrs so tortured as these were." The "logical" forms of current standard English are simply the accepted conventions of our present-day formal style. Russian, Spanish, French, and Hungarian show the same negative concord as nonstandard English, and they are surely not illogical in this. What is termed "logical" in standard English is of course the conventions which are habitual. The distribution of negative concord in English dialects can be summarized in this way (Labov, et al. 1968, section 3.6; Labov 1968):

1. In all dialects of English, the negative is attracted to a lone indefinite before the verb: "Nobody knows anything," not "*Anybody doesn't know anything."

2. In some nonstandard white dialects, the negative also combines optionally with all other indefinites: "Nobody knows nothing," "He never took none of them."

3. In other white nonstandard dialects, the negative may also appear in preverbal position in the same clause: "Nobody doesn't know nothing."

4. In nonstandard Negro English, negative concord is obligatory to all indefinites within the clause, and it may even be added to preverbal position in following clauses: "Nobody didn't know he didn't" (meaning, "Nobody knew he did").

Thus all dialects of English share a categorical rule which attracts the negative to an indefinite subject, and they merely differ in the extent to which the negative particle is also distributed to other indefinites in preverbal position. It would have been impossible for us to arrive at this analysis if we did not know that Negro speakers are using the same underlying logic as everyone else.

Negative concord is more firmly established in nonstandard Negro English than in other nonstandard dialects. The white nonstandard speaker shows variation in this rule, saying one time, "Nobody ever goes there" and the next, "Nobody never goes there." Core speakers of the NNE vernacular consistently use the latter form. In repetition tests which we conducted with adolescent Negro boys (Labov, et al. 1968, section 3.9), standard forms were repeated with negative concord. Here, for example, are three trials by two thirteen-year-old members (Boot and David) of the Thunderbirds:

> MODEL BY INTERVIEWER: "Nobody ever sat at any of those desks, anyhow."
> BOOT:
>> (1) Nobody never sa—No [whitey] never sat at any o' tho' dess, anyhow.
>> (2) Nobody never sat any any o' tho' dess, anyhow.
>> (3) Nobody as ever sat at no desses, anyhow.
> DAVID:
>> (1) Nobody ever sat in-in-in-in- none o'—say it again?
>> (2) Nobody never sat in none o' tho' desses anyhow.
>> (3) Nobody—aww! Nobody never ex— Dawg!

It can certainly be said that Boot and David fail the test; they have not repeated the sentence correctly—that is, word for word. But have they failed because they could not grasp the meaning of the sentence? The situation is in fact just the opposite; they failed because they perceived only the meaning and not the superficial form. Boot and David are typical of many speakers who do not perceive the surface details of the utterance so much as the underlying semantic structure, which they unhesitatingly translate into the vernacular form. Thus they have an asymmetrical system:

PERCEPTION	Standard	Nonstandard
PRODUCTION	Nonstandard	

This tendency to process the semantic components directly can be seen even more dramatically in responses to sentences with embedded questions; for example:

> MODEL:
>> I asked Alvin if he knows how to play basketball.
> BOOT:
>> I ax Alvin do he know how to play basketball.
> MONEY:
>> I ax Alvin if—do he know how to play basketball.
> MODEL:
>> I asked Alvin whether he knows how to play basketball.
> LARRY F:
>> (1) I axt Alvin does he know how to play basketball.
>> (2) I axt Alvin does he know how to play basketball.

Here the difference between the words used in the model sentence and in the repetition is striking. Again, there is a failure to pass the test. But it is also true that these boys understand the standard sentence, and translate it with extraordinary speed into the NNE form, which is here the regular Southern colloquial form. This form retains the inverted order to signal the underlying meaning of the question, instead of the complementizer *if* or *whether* which standard English uses for this purpose. Thus Boot, Money, and Larry perceive the deep structure of the model sentence (Figure 1). The complementizers *if* or *whether* are not required to express this underlying meaning. They are merely two of the formal options which one dialect selects to signal the embedded question. The colloquial Southern form utilizes a different device—preserving the order of the direct question. To say that this dialect lacks the means for logical expression is to confuse logic with surface detail.

   To pass the repetition test, Boot and the others have to learn to listen to surface detail. They do not need a new logic; they need practice in paying attention to the explicit form of an utterance rather than its meaning. Careful attention to surface features is a temporary skill needed for language learning —and neglected thereafter by competent speakers. Nothing more than this is involved in the language training in the Bereiter and Engelmann program, or in most methods of teaching English. There is of course nothing wrong with learning to be explicit. As we have seen, that is one of the main advantages of standard English at its best; but it is important that we recognize what is actually taking place, and what teachers are in fact trying to do.

   I doubt if we can teach people to be logical, though we can teach them to recognize the logic that they use. Piaget has shown us that in middle-class children logic develops much more slowly than grammar, and that we cannot expect four-year-olds to have mastered the conservation of quantity, let alone

Figure 1

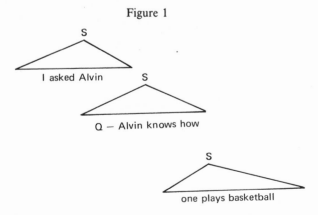

syllogistic reasoning. The problems working-class children may have in handling logical operations are not to be blamed on the structure of their language. There is nothing in the vernacular which will interfere with the development of logical thought, for the logic of standard English cannot be distinguished from the logic of any other dialect of English by any test that we can find.

WHAT'S WRONG WITH BEING WRONG?

If there is a failure of logic involved here, it is surely in the approach of the verbal deprivation theorists, rather than in the mental abilities of the children concerned. We can isolate six distinct steps in the reasoning which has led to positions such as those of Deutsch, or Bereiter and Engelmann:

1. The lower-class child's verbal response to a formal and threatening situation is used to demonstrate his lack of verbal capacity, or verbal deficit.

2. This verbal deficit is declared to be a major cause of the lower-class child's poor performance in school.

3. Since middle-class children do better in school, middle-class speech habits are seen to be necessary for learning.

4. Class and ethnic differences in grammatical form are equated with differences in the capacity for logical analysis.

5. Teaching the child to mimic certain formal speech patterns used by middle-class teachers is seen as teaching him to think logically.

6. Children who learn these formal speech patterns are then said to be thinking logically and it is predicted that they will do much better in reading and arithmetic in the years to follow.

In the preceding sections of this paper I have tried to show that the above propositions are wrong, concentrating on 1, 4, and 5. Proposition 3 is the primary logical fallacy which illicitly identifies a form of speech as the cause of middle-class achievement in school. Proposition 6 is the one which is most easily shown to be wrong in fact, as we will note below.

However, it is not too naive to ask: "What is wrong with being wrong? There is no competing educational theory which is being dismantled by this program, and there does not seem to be any great harm in having children repeat, "This is not a box" for twenty minutes a day. We have already conceded that NNE children need help in analyzing language into its surface components, and in being more explicit. But there are serious and damaging consequences of the verbal deprivation theory which may be considered under two headings: theoretical bias, and consequences of failure.

Theoretical Bias

It is widely recognized that the teacher's attitude toward the child is an important factor in his success or failure. The work of Rosenthal and Jacobson

(1968) on self-fulfilling prophecies shows that the progress of children in the early grades can be dramatically affected by a single random labeling of certain children as "intellectual bloomers." When the everyday language of Negro children is stigmatized as "not a language at all" and "not possessing the means for logical thought," the effect of such a labeling is repeated many times during each day of the school year. Every time that a child uses a form of NNE without the copula or with negative concord, he will be labeling himself for the teacher's benefit as "illogical," as a "nonconceptual thinker." Bereiter and Engelmann, Deutsch, and Jensen are giving teachers a ready-made, theoretical basis for the prejudice they already feel against the lower-class Negro child and his language (for example, see Williams, Chapter 18 in this volume). When teachers hear him say "I dont want none" or "They mine," they will be hearing through the bias provided by the verbal deprivation theory—not an English dialect different from theirs, but the "primitive mentality of the savage mind."

But what if the teacher succeeds in training the child to use the new language consistently? The verbal deprivation theory holds that this will lead to a whole chain of successes in school, and that the child will be drawn away from the vernacular culture into the middle-class world. Undoubtedly this will happen with a few isolated individuals, just as it happens for a few children in every school system today. But we are concerned not with the few but the many, and for the majority of Negro children the distance between them and the school is bound to widen under this approach.

Proponents of the deficit theory have a strange view of social organization outside of the classroom. They see the attraction of the peer group as a substitute for success and gratification normally provided by the school. For example, Whiteman and Deutsch (1968, pp. 86–87) introduce their account of the deprivation hypothesis with an eyewitness account of a child who accidentally dropped his school notebook into a puddle of water and walked away without picking it up: "A policeman who had been standing nearby walked over to the puddle and stared at the notebook with some degree of disbelief." The child's alienation from school is explained as the result of his coming to school without the "verbal, conceptual, attentional, and learning skills requisite to school success." The authors see the child as "suffering from feelings of inferiority because he is failing; he withdraws or becomes hostile, finding gratification elsewhere, such as in his peer group."

To view the peer group as a mere substitute for school shows an extraordinary lack of knowledge of adolescent culture. In our studies in south-central Harlem we have seen the reverse situation—the children who are rejected by the peer group are most likely to succeed in school. Although in middle-class suburban areas, many children do fail in school because of their personal deficiencies, in ghetto areas it is the healthy, vigorous, popular child with normal intelligence who cannot read and fails all along the line. It is not necessary to document here the influence of the peer group upon the behavior of youth in our society, but we may note that somewhere between the time that children first learn to talk and puberty, their language is restructured to fit the rules used by their peer group. From a linguistic viewpoint, the peer group is certainly a more powerful influence than the family (e.g., Gans 1962). Less directly, the pressures of peer-group activity are also felt within the school. Many children, particularly those who are not doing well in school, show a sudden sharp downward turn in the fourth and fifth grades, and children in the ghetto schools are no exception. It is at the same age, at nine or ten years old, that the influence of the vernacular peer group becomes predominant (see Wilmott 1966). Instead of dealing with isolated individuals, the school is then dealing with children who are integrated into groups of their own, with rewards and value systems which oppose those of the school. Those who know the sociolinguistic situation cannot doubt that reaction against the Bereiter-Engelmann approach in later years will be even more violent on the part of the students involved, and their rejection of the school system will be even more categorical.

The essential fallacy of the verbal deprivation theory lies in tracing the educational failure of the child to his personal deficiencies. At present, these deficiencies are said to be caused by his home environment. It is traditional to explain a child's failure in school by his inadequacy. But when failure reaches such massive proportions, it seems to us necessary to look at the social and cultural obstacles to learning, and the inability of the school to adjust to the social situation. Operation Head Start is designed to repair the child, rather than the school; to the extent that it is based upon this inverted logic, it is bound to fall.

Consequences of Failure

The second area in which the verbal deprivation theory is doing serious harm to our educational system is in the consequences of this failure, and the reaction to it. As failures are reported of Operation Head Start, the interpretations which we receive will be from the same educational psychologists who designed this program. The fault will be found not in the data, the theory, nor in the methods used, but rather in the children who have failed to respond to the opportunities offered to them. When Negro children fail to show the significant advance which the deprivation theory predicts, it will be taken as further proof of the profound gulf which separates their mental processes from those of "civilized," middle-class mankind.

A sense of the failure of Head Start is already in the air. Some prominent figures in the program are reacting to this situation by saying that intervention did not take place early enough. Caldwell (1967, p. 16) notes that:

. . . the research literature of the last decade dealing with social-class differences has made abundantly clear that all parents are not qualified to provide even the basic essentials of physical and psychological care to their children.

The deficit theory now begins to focus on the "long-standing patterns of parental deficit" which fill the literature. "There is, perhaps unfortunately," writes Caldwell (1967, p. 17), "no literacy test for motherhood." Failing such eugenic measures, she has proposed "educationally oriented day care for culturally deprived children between six months and three years of age." The children are returned home each evening to "maintain primary emotional relationships with their own families," but during the day they are removed to "hopefully prevent the deceleration in rate of development which seems to occur in many deprived children around the age of two to three years."

There are others who feel that even the best of the intervention programs, such as those of Bereiter and Engelmann, will not help the Negro child no matter when such programs are applied—that we are faced once again with the "inevitable hypothesis" of the genetic inferiority of the Negro people. Many readers of this paper are undoubtedly familiar with the paper of Arthur Jensen in the *Harvard Educational Review* (1969) which received immediate and widespread publicity. Jensen (p. 3) begins with the following quotation from the United States Commission on Civil Rights as evidence of the failure of compensatory education:

The fact remains, however, that none of the programs appear to have raised significantly the achievement of participating pupils, as a group, within the period evaluated by the Commission. (U.S. Commission on Civil Rights 1967, p. 138)

Jensen believes that the verbal-deprivation theorists with whom he had been associated—Deutsch, Whiteman, Katz, Bereiter—have been given every opportunity to prove their case, and have failed. This opinion is part of the argument which leads him to the overall conclusion (p. 82) that "the preponderance of the evidence is . . . less consistent with a strictly environmental hypothesis than with the genetic hypothesis." In other words, racism—the belief in the genetic inferiority of Negroes—is the most correct view in the light of the present evidence.

Jensen argues that the middle-class white population is differentiated from the working-class white and Negro population in the ability for "cognitive or conceptual learning," which Jensen calls Level II intelligence as against mere "associative learning" or Level I intelligence:

. . . certain neural structures must also be available for Level II abilities to develop, and these are conceived of as being different from the neural structures underlying Level I. The genetic factors involved in each of these types of ability are presumed to have become differentially distributed in the population as a function of social class, since Level II has been most important for scholastic performance under the traditional methods of instruction. (Jensen 1969, p. 114)

Jensen found, for example, that one group of middle-class children were helped by their concept-forming ability to recall twenty familiar objects that could be classified into four categories: animals, furniture, clothing, or foods. Lower-class Negro children did just as well as middle-class children with a miscellaneous set, but showed no improvement with objects that could be so categorized.

The research of the educational psychologists cited here is presented by them in formal and objective style, and is widely received as impartial scientific evidence. Jensen's paper has been reported by Joseph Alsop and William F. Buckley, Jr. (*New York Post*, March 20, 1969) as "massive, apparently authoritative . . . ." It is not my intention to examine these materials in detail, but it is important to realize that we are dealing with special pleading by those who have a strong personal commitment. Jensen is concerned with class differences in cognitive style and verbal learning. His earlier papers incorporated the cultural deprivation theory which he now rejects as a basic explanation.[14] Jensen (1968 p. 167) classified the Negro children who fail in school as "slow learners" and "mentally retarded" and urged that we find out how much their retardation is due to environmental factors and how much is due to "more basic biological factors." His conviction that the problem must be located in the child leads him to accept and reprint some truly extraordinary data. To support the genetic hypothesis Jensen (1969, p. 83) cites the following percentage estimates by Heber (1968) of the racial distribution of mental retardation (based upon IQs below 75) in the general population:[15]

---

[14]In Deutsch, et al. (1968), Jensen expounds the verbal deprivation theory in considerable detail, for example (p. 119): "During this 'labeling' period . . . some very important social-class differences may exert their effects on verbal learning. Lower-class parents engage in relatively little of this naming or 'labeling' play with their children . . . . That words are discrete labels for things seems to be better known by the middle-class child entering first grade than by the lower-class child. Much of this knowledge is gained in the parent-child interaction, as when the parent looks at a picture book with the child . . . ."

[15]Heber's (esp. 1968) studies of eighty-eight Negro mothers in Milwaukee are cited frequently throughout Jensen's paper. The estimates in this table are not given in relation to a particular Milwaukee sample, but for the general United States population. Heber's study was specifically designed to cover an area of Milwaukee which was known to contain a large concentration of retarded children, Negro and white, and he has stated that his findings were "grossly misinterpreted" by Jensen (*Milwaukee Sentinel*, June 11, 1969).

SOCIOECONOMIC STATUS	Percent of Whites	Percent of Negroes
1 (highest)	0.5	3.1
2	0.8	14.5
3	2.1	22.8
4	3.1	37.8
5 (lowest)	7.8	42.9

These estimates, that almost half of lower-class Negro children are mentally retarded, could be accepted only by someone who has no knowledge of the children or the community. If he had wished to, Jensen could easily have checked this against the records of any school in any urban ghetto area. Taking IQ tests at their face value, there is no correspondence between these figures and the communities we know. For example, among seventy-five boys we worked with in central Harlem who would fall into status categories 4 or 5 above, there were only three with IQs below 75. One spoke very little English; one could barely see; the third was emotionally disturbed. When the second was retested, he scored 91, and the third retested at 87.[16] There are of course hundreds of realistic reports available to Jensen. He simply selected one which would strengthen his case for the genetic inferiority of Negro children.

In so doing, Jensen was following a standing tradition among the psychologists who developed the deficit hypothesis. The core of Deutsch's environmental explanation of poor performance in school is the Deprivation Index, a numerical scale based on six dichotomized variables. One variable is "the educational aspirational level of the parent for the child." Most people would agree that a parent who did not care if a child finished high-school would be a disadvantageous factor in the child's educational career. In dichotomizing this variable Deutsch was faced with the fact that the educational aspiration of Negro parents is in fact very high, higher than for the white population, as he shows in other papers.[17] In order to make the Deprivation Index work, he therefore set the cutting point for the deprived group as "college or less." (see Whiteman and Deutsch 1968, p. 100). Thus if a Negro child's father says that he wants his son to go all the way through college, the child will fall into the "deprived" class on this variable. In order to receive the two points given to the "less deprived" on the index, it would be necessary for the child's parent

---

[16]The IQ scores given here are from group rather than individual tests and must therefore not be weighed heavily; the scores are from the Pintner-Cunningham test, usually given in the first grade in New York City schools in the 1950s.

[17]In Table 15-1 in Deutsch and associates (1967, p. 312), section C shows that some degree of college training was desired by 96, 97 and 100 percent of Negro parents in class levels I, II, and III, respectively. The corresponding figures for whites were 79, 95, and 97 percent.

to insist on graduate school or medical school! This decision is not discussed by the author; it simply stands as a *fait accompli* in the tables. This is the type of data manipulation carried on by those who are strongly committed to a particular hypothesis.

No one can doubt that the reported inadequacy of Operation Head Start and of the verbal deprivation hypothesis has now become a crucial issue in our society.[18] The controversy which has arisen over Jensen's article typically assumes that programs such as Bereiter and Engelmann's have tested and measured the verbal capacity of the ghetto child. The cultural sociolinguistic obstacles to this intervention program are not considered, and the argument proceeds upon the data provided by the large, friendly interviewers whom we have seen at work in the extracts given above.

THE LINGUISTIC VIEW

Linguists are in an excellent position to demonstrate the fallacies of the verbal deprivation theory. All linguists agree that nonstandard dialects are highly structured systems. They do not see these dialects as accumulations of errors caused by the failure of their speakers to master standard English. When linguists hear Negro children saying "He crazy" or "Her my friend," they do not hear a primitive language. Nor do they believe that the speech of working-class people is merely a form of emotional expression, incapable of expressing logical thought.

All linguists who work with NNE recognize that it is a separate system, closely related to standard English but set apart from the surrounding white dialects by a number of persistent and systematic differences. Differences in analysis by various linguists in recent years are the inevitable products of differing theoretical approaches and perspectives as we explore these dialect patterns by different routes—differences which are rapidly diminishing as we exchange our findings. For example, Stewart (see Chapter 17 in this volume) differs with me on how deeply the invariant *be* of "She be always messin' around" is integrated into the semantics of the copula system with *am, is, are,*

---

[18]The negative report of the Westinghouse Learning Corporation and Ohio University on Operation Head Start was published in the *New York Times* (April 13, 1969). The evidence of the failure of the program is accepted by many, and it seems likely that the report's discouraging conclusions will be used by conservative Congressmen as a weapon against any kind of expenditure for disadvantaged children, especially Negroes. The two hypotheses mentioned to account for this failure are that the impact of Head Start is lost through poor teaching later on, and more recently, that poor children have been so badly damaged in infancy by their lower-class environment that Head Start cannot make much difference. The third "inevitable" hypothesis of Jensen is not reported here.

and so on. The position and meaning of *have. . . ed* in NNE is very unclear, and there are a variety of positions on this point. But the grammatical features involved are not the fundamental predicators of the logical system. They are optional ways of contrasting, foregrounding, emphasizing, or deleting elements of the underlying sentence. There are a few semantic features of NNE grammar which may be unique to this system. But the semantic features we are talking about here are items such as "habitual," "general," "intensive." These linguistic markers are essentially *points of view*—different ways of looking at the same events, and they do not determine the truth values of propositions upon which all speakers of English agree.

The great majority of the differences between NNE and standard English do not even represent such subtle semantic features as those, but rather extensions and restrictions of certain formal rules, and different choices of redundant elements. For example, standard English uses two signals to express the progressive, *be* and *-ing*, while NNE often drops the former. Standard English signals the third person in the present by the subject noun phrase and by a third singular *-s;* NNE does not have this second redundant feature. On the other hand, NNE uses redundant negative elements in negative concord, in possessives like *mines*, uses *or either* where standard English uses a simple *or*, and so on.

When linguists say that NNE is a system, we mean that it differs from other dialects in regular and rule-governed ways, so that it has equivalent ways of expressing the same logical content. When we say that it is a separate subsystem, we mean that there are compensating sets of rules which combine in different ways to preserve the distinctions found in other dialects. Thus as noted above NNE does not use the *if* or *whether* complementizer in embedded questions, but the meaning is preserved by the formal device of reversing the order of subject and auxiliary.

Linguists therefore speak with a single voice in condemning Bereiter's view that the vernacular can be disregarded. I exchanged views on this matter with all of the participants in the Twentieth Annual Georgetown Round Table where this paper was first presented, and their responses were in complete agreement in rejecting the verbal deprivation theory and its misapprehension of the nature of language. The other papers in the report (Alatis 1970) of that conference testified to the strength of the linguistic view in this area. It was William Stewart who first pointed out that Negro English should be studied as a coherent system, and in this all of us follow his lead. Dialectologists like Raven McDavid, Albert Marckwardt, and Roger Shuy (see Chapter 16 in this volume) have been working for years against the notion that vernacular dialects are inferior and illogical means of communication. Linguists now agree that teachers must know as much as possible about Negro nonstandard English as a communicative system.

The exact nature and relative importance of the structural differences between NNE and standard English are not in question here. It is agreed that the teacher must approach the teaching of the standard through a knowledge of the child's own system. The methods used in teaching English as a foreign language are recommended, not to declare that NNE is a foreign language, but to underline the importance of studying the native dialect as a coherent system for communication. This is in fact the method that should be applied in any English class.

Linguists are also in an excellent position to assess Jensen's claim that the middle-class white population is superior to the working-class and Negro populations in the distribution of Level II, or conceptual, intelligence. The notion that large numbers of children have no capacity for conceptual thinking would inevitably mean that they speak a primitive language, for even the simplest linguistic rules we discussed above involve conceptual operations more complex than those used in the experiment Jensen cites. Let us consider what is involved in the use of the general English rule that incorporates the negative with the first indefinite. To learn and use this rule, one must first identify the class of indefinites involved—*any, one, ever,* which are formally quite diverse. How is this done? These indefinites share a number of common properties which can be expressed as the concepts "indefinite," "hypothetical," and "nonpartitive." One might argue that these indefinites are learned as a simple list, by association learning. But this is only one of the many syntactic rules involving indefinites—rules known to every speaker of English, which could not be learned except by an understanding of their common, abstract properties. For example, everyone knows, unconsciously, that *anyone* cannot be used with preterit verbs or progressives. One does not say, "*Anyone went to the party" or "*Anyone is going to the party." The rule which operates here is sensitive to the property [+ hypothetical] of the indefinites. Whenever the proposition is not inconsistent with this feature, *anyone* can be used. Everyone knows, therefore, that one can say "Anyone who was anyone went to the party" or "If anyone went to the party . . . " or "Before anyone went to the party . . . ." There is another property of *anyone* which is grasped unconsciously by all native speakers of English; it is [+distributive]. Thus if we need one more man for a game of bridge or basketball, and there is a crowd outside, we ask, "Do any of you want to play?" not "Do some of you want to play?" In both cases, we are considering a plurality, but with *any,* we consider them one at a time, or distributively.

What are we then to make of Jensen's contention that Level I thinkers cannot make use of the concept *animal* to group together a miscellaneous set of toy animals? It is one thing to say that someone is not in the habit of using a certain skill. But to say that his failure to use it is genetically determined implies dramatic consequences for other forms of behavior, which are not found in experience. The knowledge of what people must do in order to learn language makes Jensen's theories seem more and more distant from the realities of human behavior. Like Bereiter and Engelmann, Jensen is handicapped by his ignorance of the most basic facts about human language and the people who speak it.

There is no reason to believe that any nonstandard vernacular is in itself an obstacle to learning. The chief problem is ignorance of language on the part of all concerned. Our job as linguists is to remedy this ignorance; but Bereiter and Engelmann want to reinforce it and justify it. Teachers are now being told to ignore the language of Negro children as unworthy of attention and useless for learning. They are being taught to hear every natural utterance of the child as evidence of his mental inferiority. As linguists we are unanimous in condemning this view as bad observation, bad theory, and bad practice.

That educational psychology should be strongly influenced by a theory so false to the facts of language is unfortunate; but that children should be the victims of this ignorance is intolerable. It may seem that the fallacies of the verbal deprivation theory are so obvious that they are hardly worth exposing. I have tried to show that such exposure is an important job for us to undertake. If linguists can contribute some of their available knowledge and energy toward this end, we will have done a great deal to justify the support that society has given to basic research in our field.

REFERENCES

Alatis, J., ed. *Georgetown Monographs in Language and Linguistics, No. 22.* Washington, D.C.: Georgetown University Press, 1970.

Bereiter, C., and Engelmann, S. *Teaching Disadvantaged Children in the Preschool.* Englewood Cliffs, N.J.: Prentice-Hall, 1966.

Bereiter, C.; Engelmann, S.; Osborn, Jean; and Reidford, P.A. An academically oriented preschool for culturally deprived children. In F. Hechinger, ed., *Pre-school Education Today.* New York: Doubleday, 1966.

Bernstein, B. Elaborated and restricted codes: Their social origins and some consequences. In A.G. Smith, ed., *Communication and Culture.* New York: Holt, Rinehart & Winston, 1966.

Blum, A. The sociology of mental illness. In J. Douglas, ed., *Deviance and Respectability.* New York: Basic Books, (in press).

Caldwell, Bettye M. What is the optimal learning environment for the young child? *American J. Orthopsychiatry* 1967, 37: 8–21.

Chomsky, N. *Aspects of the Theory of Syntax.* Cambridge, Mass.: M.I.T. Press, 1965.

Coleman, J.S., et al. *Equality of Educational Opportunity.* Washington, D.C.: U.S. Office of Education, 1966.

Deutsch, M., and associates. *The Disadvantaged Child.* New York: Basic Books, 1967.

Deutsch, M.; Katz, I.; and Jensen, A.R., eds., *Social Class, Race, and Psychological Development.* New York: Holt, Rinehart & Winston, 1968.

Gans, H. *The Urban Villagers.* New York: Free Press, 1962.

Heber, R. Research on education and habilitation of the mentally retarded. Paper read at Conference on Sociocultural Aspects of Mental Retardation, June 1968, Peabody College, Nashville, Tenn.

Jensen, A.R. Social class and verbal learning. In M. Deutsch, et al., eds., *Social Class, Race, and Psychological Development.* New York: Holt, Rinehart & Winston, 1968.

———. How much can we boost IQ and scholastic achievement? *Harvard Educational Review* 1969, 39: 1–123.

Labov, W. On the grammaticality of everyday speech. Paper presented at the annual meeting of the Linguistic Society of America, December 1966, New York.

———. Some sources of reading problems for Negro speakers of nonstandard English. In A. Frazier, ed., *New Directions in Elementary English.* Champaign, Ill.: National Council of Teachers of English, 1967. Also reprinted in J.C. Baratz and R.W. Shuy, eds., *Teaching Black Children to Read.* Washington, D.C.: Center for Applied Linguistics, 1969.

————. Negative attraction and negative concord in four English dialects. Paper presented at the annual meeting of the Linguistic Society of America, December 1968, New York.

————. Contraction, deletion, and inherent variability of the English copula. *Language* 1969, 45: 715–62.

Labov, W.; Cohen, P.; Robins, C. A preliminary study of the structure of English used by Negro and Puerto Rican speakers in New York City. Final report, U.S. Office of Education Cooperative Research Project No. 3091, 1965.

Labov, W.; Cohen, P.; Robins, C.; and Lewis, J. A study of the nonstandard English of Negro and Puerto Rican speakers in New York City. Final report, U.S. Office of Education Cooperative Research Project No. 3288 Vols 1, 2. Mimeographed. Columbia University, 1968.

Labov, W., and Robins, C. A note on the relation of reading failure to peer-group status in urban ghettos. *The Teachers College Record* 1969, 70: 396–405.

Langer, T.S., and Michaels, S.T. *Life Stress and Mental Health.* New York: Free Press, 1963.

Rosenthal, R., and Jacobson, Lenore. Self-fulfilling prophecies in the class-room: teachers' expectations as unintended determinants of pupils' intellectual competence. In M. Deutsch, et al., eds., *Social Class, Race, and Pyschological Development.* New York: Holt, Rinehart & Winston, 1968.

United States Commission of Civil Rights. *Racial Isolation in the Public Schools,* Vol. 1. Washington, D.C.: U.S. Government Printing Office, 1967.

Whiteman, M., and Deutsch, M. Social disadvantage as related to intellective and language development. In M. Deutsch, et al., eds., *Social Class, Race, and Psychological Development.* New York: Holt, Rinehart & Winston, 1968.

Wilmott, P. *Adolescent Boys of East London.* London: Routledge & Kegan Paul, 1966.

Chapter 10

LANGUAGE THEORIES AND EDUCATIONAL PRACTICES

Paula Menyuk*

Linguistic and psycholinguistic descriptions of language and of language acquisition and development are largely theoretical descriptions or models derived from observational and experimental studies. Webster tells us that *theory* is "a doctrine or scheme of things which terminates in speculation without a view to practice." By definition, then, theory and practice are dissociated and it is the point of view of many educators and theorists that perhaps they should remain so. For some educators who are confronted with the task of "curing," "modifying," or "enriching" a child's linguistic performance, theory not only can be confusing, but also can interfere with getting on with the job by raising many unwanted questions. This is especially the case when theories (as they must) periodically change as new and different knowledge is acquired. In the area of language acquisition, as in all areas concerned with the structure and functioning of the human organism, our lack of knowledge leads us to comparatively more rapid change and perhaps greater speculation than is the case in other sciences. For some theorists who are concerned with devising simple and elegant models of the structure of language or the use of language, actual linguistic performance appears to be subject to too many random variables which becloud the underlying basis and structure of this performance.

*Research Laboratory of Electronics, Massachusetts Institute of Technology
This work was supported in part by the National Institutes of Health Grant No. 2R01 NB-04332-06 and by the U.S. Air Force Cambridge Research Laboratories, Office of Aerospace Research No. AF19(628)-5661. A part of this paper was presented at the American Association for Advancement of Science meeting, December 1967.

The situation could rest in this manner. Theorists and educators could continue in their independent pursuits without ever observing the necessity or even desire to have the two areas of experimental interest come in contact with each other. However, two factors have prevented some theorists and some educators from leading totally separate lives. The first is that the psycholinguistic scientist searches for models of language and language acquisition that describe and, perhaps, explain the ways in which language is perceived and produced. Therefore he must be concerned with human behavior and "clearly, the actual data of linguistic performance will provide much evidence for determining the correctness of hypotheses about underlying linguistic structure" (Chomsky 1965, p. 18). The second factor is that the educator (here, often the speech therapist) has been called upon to deal with a wide range of linguistic behaviors which have been labeled deficient or defective. Some of these behaviors appear to be primarily produced by physiological factors, others appear to be primarily produced by environmental factors, and still others by causative agents which are confounded or hidden. Despite the variety of linguistic behaviors, and although the etiology is often unclear, the child, nevertheless, performs in certain unsatisfactory ways, and the educator has been asked to modify this performance. To accomplish this task he must have a basic understanding of the ways in which a child's linguistic performance is unsatisfactory. That is, he must know the structure of this performance and how it deviates from the norm. A further goal of the educator would be an explanation for this deviant behavior. Linguistic descriptions of the grammar of the language and psycholinguistic descriptions of the developmental course of language acquisition may provide this basic understanding.

Because of these factors there have been expressions of mutual interest by language theorists and language educators in working together. Nevertheless, these are often merely tokens rather than acts, primarily because a credibility gap exists concerning the fruitfulness of mutual efforts. Before we can move from expressions of goodwill to mutual effort, it is necessary to explore those areas in which theory can and should affect educational practice and those areas in which theorist and educator should work together to achieve a better understanding of the human being's use of language.

A THEORY OF LANGUAGE AND LANGUAGE ACQUISITION

The language theorist wishes to provide a descriptive model which will account for all the significant linguistic generalizations that can be found in the language. The language acquisition theorist wishes to determine the mechanisms which the human organism uses to acquire a language and to engage in the communication process. A determination or understanding of this capacity could point the way to possible explanations for varying kinds of linguistic behavior. Thus, an area in which the theorist can contribute to the thinking, experimentation, and practices of the educator is by providing a model which fits the data (the language) and accounts for the facts of language development. Theories of language acquisition and development have been derived by both psychologists and linguists although the linguist may state that he is only interested in describing the data—that is, the language (Bloomfield, reprinted 1963). Nevertheless, claims about the human's linguistic capacity are implicit in the theory.

As was stated, the proposed goal of linguistic descriptions is to explicate as precisely as possible all the generalizations about his language that the native speaker has knowledge of, such as: (1) What is a sentence, and what are the functional relationships in sentences that the speaker is aware of ? (2) What is a word and how is it used in certain contexts? (3) What is a speech sound and how is it used in certain contexts? In sum, what is the speaker's knowledge of the rules in the grammar of his language?[1] This knowledge is what the native speaker uses to derive the meaning of an utterance and to express intended meaning. Linguists (Chomsky 1965) have termed this knowledge *competence* and they attempt to describe this competence by structural descriptions of the possible sentences of a language. These structural descriptions include syntactic information, semantic information, and phonological information.

Taking as an example the sentence, "Did the boy eat an apple?" the following are some limited examples of what the adult native speaker knows (or his linguistic competence) and what the child learns (because of his capacity to acquire his native language) about this sentence.
1. It is a sentence:
   The boy eats an apple = noun phrase + verb phrase
2. The functional realationships expressed in the sentence:
   The boy = subject, noun phrase of the sentence
   eat = main verb, verb of the verb phrase of the sentence
   an apple = object, noun phrase of the verb phrase of the sentence
3. Properties and features of morphemes in the sentence: syntactic, semantic and phonological:
   The = determiner, article, definite . . . consonant (having certain distinctive features)[2] + vowel (having certain distinctive features)
   boy = noun, animate, human, male, singular, young . . . consonant . . . + vowel . . .

---

[1]For descriptions of syntactic rules, see Chomsky (1965); for semantic rules, Katz and Postal (1964); and for phonological rules, Chomsky and Halle (1968).

[2]For a discussion of distinctive features, see Chomsky and Halle (1968).

Figure 1

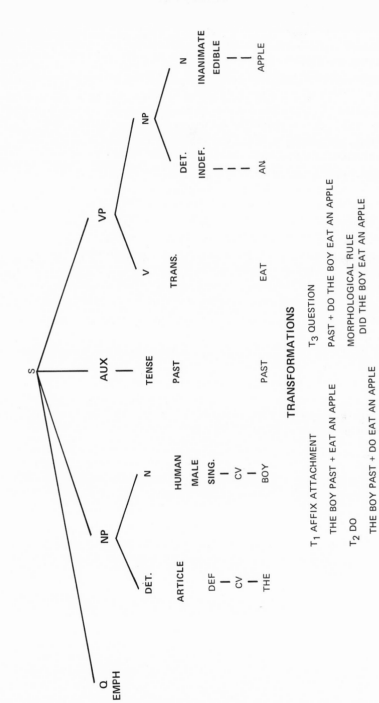

TRANSFORMATIONS

T₁ AFFIX ATTACHMENT
THE BOY PAST + EAT AN APPLE

T₂ DO
THE BOY PAST + DO EAT AN APPLE

T₃ QUESTION
PAST + DO THE BOY EAT AN APPLE

MORPHOLOGICAL RULE
DID THE BOY EAT AN APPLE

eat = verb, transitive, to partake of as food . . . consonant . . . + vowel
. . . + consonant.
4. Rules of cooccurrence:
   Subject of verb *eat* is + animate (i.e. "the apple eats the boy." is anomalous)
   Object of verb *eat* is + edible (i.e. "The boy eats a chair" is anomalous)
5. Morphological rules
   boy = 3rd person, singular
   did = *do* + past tense
6. Transformational rules
   The boy did eat an apple = *do* support transformation
   Did the boy eat an apple = Question transformation

A graphic representation of this information is presented in Figure 1.
These are just brief examples of what is known about the sentence—*Did the
boy eat an apple?*

In acquiring a language, then, a child must first comprehend the functional relationships of words in a sentence before he can establish the class
membership of these words. The category noun, for example, is established by
the nounlike role of words or phrases (subject or object in a sentence). The
child must learn the properties and distinctive features of words in sentences
and observe rules about their possible cooccurrences in sentences. He must
determine the rules in his language which are used to generate negations,
questions, imperatives, conjuctions, embeddings of sentences, and so on.

In proposing models to account for the acquisition and use of this information about language, some psychologists and linguists have been concerned
with observable behavior alone rather than attempting to describe the underlying structure or basis of this behavior.

> If the facts have been fully stated, it is perverse or childish to demand
> an explanation into the bargain. Explanation could serve only to
> facilitate filling out a fractional statement into a whole statement; or
> is explanation something magical? (Joos 1963, p. v.)

Psychologists have conceived of the language acquisition process as the
child's acquiring of larger and larger chunks of the stream of speech as he
matures. One observes that during the babbling stage the child produces
phonological sequences of consonants and vowels, then proceeds to combine
these sound segments into words, and, finally, combines these words into
sentences. These sentences grow longer as the child matures. Inappropriate
responses are eliminated, and words and sentences are classified by the conditioning effects of stimulus-response and reward (Salzinger 1967). Linguists
who stress this empirical approach have concerned themselves with the phonetic strings that speakers produce and the acoustic signals that listeners hear.
Their work consists primarily of attempts to segment and classify a stream of

speech into units that are uniquely identifiable, perhaps limited to a specific language or even dialect of a language in some instances. Syntax is, for the most part, ignored. Educators, in their turn, have spent a great deal of their time trying to establish correct response patterns by working on the correct production of phones (sounds) and then combination of these phones into words.

It is difficult for some psychologists to see, however, from this theoretical model how the classification process of words and sentences, deemed necessary for the acquisition of language, can take place simply from the stimulus-response-reward situation. One could perhaps learn from these situations the correct word response in the presence of appropriate stimuli, but language is not merely one-word responses. It has been felt that some higher level of organization is needed to account for the understanding and acquisition of classes of words and sentences. Linguists for centuries have been able to group together, under labeled headings, and in a very insightful manner, words and phrases that occur in a language. That is, the native speaker would agree that members of these classes should indeed go together on the basis of their functional role—nounlike, verblike, and so on (c.f. Jesperson 1938). Psychological theory has often proposed that words, phrases and sentences are classified by means of associations (c.f. Jenkins and Palermo 1964). For example, by observing the substitutions that occur in certain positions in sentences, a class is formed, and the membership of this class increases over time. Thus, by observing "boy likes," "boy eats," "boy jumps," "boy seems," etc., the membership of the class *verb* grows. Or by observing "boy seems," "girl seems," "table seems," etc., the membership of the class *noun* grows. Associations are formed between members of the classes so that possible sequences are determined. Some educators have found that they are often dealing with children who have, as it is termed, a language problem, rather than simply a speech-sound problem. For example, even if one could teach a child to articulate correctly a set of words, his language problem is far from resolved since he has still to learn how these words go together in sentences. Therefore, attempts have been made to teach language by giving the child exemplars of sentence frames. The slots or classes in the frame are established by substituting permissible words and the classes in the language are to be derived by this procedure. In essence, the stimulus-response-reward model is expanded now to include the acquisition of categories of sentences and words as well as the words themselves.

Some psychologists and linguists have found the above theoretical assumptions and descriptions inadequate in accounting for the facts of language and language use, and for what has been observed about language acquisition and development (c.f. Wales and Marshall 1966). Although it is correct to say that all languages have sentences—which are made up of phrases, which are made up of words, which are made up of sounds—it is incorrect to state that if we know a language, we know, or have stored in memory, a list of sentences which are made up of words which are made up of sounds, and so on. Given the fact that we are constantly creating unique sentences (that is, ones never exactly uttered before) and that the number of possible sentences in a language is infinite, it would be impossible to store such a list of utterances in our memory. Further, a great deal of what the native speaker knows about his language and what the child must learn does not physically appear in the stream of speech. For example, the listener understands and the child learns that the production of a word like "pit" by a child, by a female, or by a male represent the same word, although acoustically these productions may be very different. The listener understands and the child learns that an utterance such as "pick it up" should by segmented as (*pick*) (*it*) (*up*) and not (*pickit*) (*up*), although the acoustic signal may not segment the utterance in the former manner. The listener understands and the child learns that in the sentences (1) "The baby is crying" and (2) "The baby likes crying" the word *crying* is in two different grammatical classes despite the fact that it sounds alike (by some criteria) and appears in the same position in the sentence. (In the first instance the word is part of the verb and in the second instance it is a noun.) The listener understands and the child learns that in utterances which sound completely alike such as (1) "I am holding a pear" and (2) "I am holding a pair" the final words in these utterances have two different meanings. There are many in-stances in which word sequences, and sound sequences in words, which are heard as being completely identical and even appear in the same position in sentences, nevertheless play different roles in the sentence, have different meanings, or both.

Thus far, various theories of language acquisition have been briefly dis-cussed and their adequacy in accounting for the facts of language, language acquisition, and language use has been questioned. We will next discuss a theory of language acquisition which attemps to account for these facts, which is in the beginning stages of experimental use, and which seems to hold promise in terms of its adequacy for describing the structure of the changes that occur during language development. This theory makes a claim about the nature of the human organism, and this claim is very different from those made by some theorists. It is that the human organism does not simply have the capacity to learn and to generalize, but, rather, has the capacity to search for and store in memory abstract structural descriptions which fit his hypotheses about the language. What has been assumed by the linguist is that as the child acquires the grammar of his language, he detects and recognizes abstract features in the language (that he experiences) such as the functional relationships expressed in his language, the grammatical classes of the language, and the properties of members of a class. In some way he stores these abstract features as struc-

Figure 2

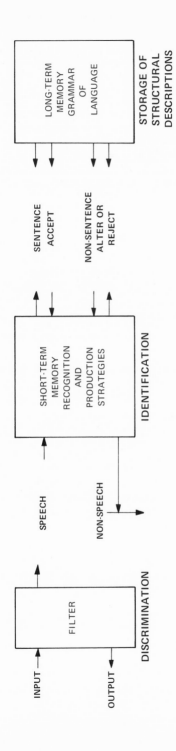

DISCRIMINATION

INPUT

FILTER

OUTPUT

SPEECH

NON-SPEECH

IDENTIFICATION

SHORT-TERM
MEMORY
RECOGNITION
AND
PRODUCTION
STRATEGIES

SENTENCE
ACCEPT

NON-SENTENCE
ALTER OR
REJECT

STORAGE OF
STRUCTURAL
DESCRIPTIONS

LONG-TERM
MEMORY
GRAMMAR
OF
LANGUAGE

tural descriptions for future reference. He rejects those descriptions which do not fit the linguistic data, and he increases the number of descriptions he has stored in memory as he matures. Not only does he add to the number of structural descriptions he has stored, but the types of descriptions which he adds change in nature as his analysis of the language deepens.

CAPACITY AND COMPETENCE

Psychologists are concerned with the ways in which the human organism uses his capacity to acquire a language, and his competence—or knowledge of the language—to understand and to produce utterances. Granted that the linguistic theory can adequately describe the facts of language acquisition and development, it is still the task of the psychologist to describe performance—that is, the use of this capacity and competence. This competence has been described by some psycholinguists as a process of reconstruction, or analysis-by-synthesis (Wales and Marshall 1966). That is, an utterance is heard, and by regenerating either partially or completely the phonological, syntactic, and semantic rules used to derive this utterance, the listener understands the utterance. Other theorists have suggested particular strategies rather than regeneration of an utterance to account for comprehension (Fodor and Garrett 1966). In either case it is held that the native speaker has available to him in storage the grammar of his language with all its possible descriptions. A possible model of the processing of an utterance is presented in Figure 2.

The child, in acquiring his language must, then, acquire these structural descriptions. The capacity to detect and recognize abstract features (structural descriptions), store them in some manner in memory, and to use them to understand and produce utterances is in itself dependent on the capacities of the peripheral mechanisms (both auditory and vocal) and central mechanisms of coding and storage. As was noted earlier, it has been hypothesized that the structural descriptions in a child's grammar change both in number and nature as he matures. This may then be due to increased storage capacity and reorganization of coding procedures.

Whether or not an utterance is perceived and understood, then, is presumably dependent on the structure of that utterance, and on both the capacity and competence of the speaker-listener. If the utterance of the speaker is grammatical and the listener is fully competent in his native language, the utterance will be understood. If the speaker or the listener is not fully competent in the grammar of the language the utterance will be produced or understood in a restricted or different manner. If the capacities, either peripheral or central, of the speaker or listener are limited, then either seriously deviant utterances will be produced or the utterance will be understood in a seriously deviant manner. Thus, the grammatical sentence "What I want, is your book" would be understood by the competent listener, and the nongrammatical sentences "What I wants is your book" and "Vat I vant is your book" would probably be understood by the competent listener, with some transformations performed to match structural descriptions. The following utterances would probably be either questioned or rejected because of the degree to which they deviate from the structural descriptions in the competent listener's grammar.

1. Who I want, is your book
2. Vat I dant, is your book
3. I want who, is you book
4. Bat I bant, i ya doot

Sentences (1) and (3) vary from our structural descriptions in terms of syntactic rules, and sentences (2) and (4) in terms of phonological rules. It is possible of course for utterances to vary in terms of both types of rules and also in terms of semantic rules, as in the sentence "Me no wide fee," which was taken from the language sample of a three-year-old child described as using infantile speech, and which was eventually interpreted as, "I ride without using my feet" (Menyuk 1964a). These latter types of utterances vary so widely from our internalized structural descriptions that we cannot apply our grammatical knowledge to interpret them.

Application to Studies of Normal and Deviant Language Development

We will next discuss the ways in which the above theoretical assumptions and methods of description have and can be experimentally used to describe language development, both normal and deviant, and to obtain possible explanations for the deviancy.

By examining the structures that the speaker-listener uses to produce utterances and the structures that he can understand, we can obtain some measure of his language competence. By examining these factors in a variety of experimental situations such as recall, following verbal instructions, solving problems based on understanding of utterances, etc., we can gain some insight into how a child might deviate in basic capacities.

It would follow from the linguistic model just described that there would be some operations on underlying sentences that the child would be able to perform before others in order to produce different types of sentences. He should be able to produce sentences which involve fewer operations on single underlying sentences before those which would involve more operations. An example of this is verb phrase expansion in which forms such as *be* + verb ("I *am* thinking about that") are expanded to *have* + *be* + verb ("I *have been* thinking about that"). In analyzing the sentences of preschool, kindergarten and first-grade children (Menyuk 1964b), one finds that although all the preschool children are using the *be* + verb form, only 14 percent of these children are using the expanded form, and the number increases at each grade level (19 percent in the kindergarten group and 41 percent in the first-grade group). The child should also be able to produce sentences which involve operations on single underlying sentences before he produces sentences which involve operations on more than one underlying sentence. In analyzing the sentences produced by children from three to seven years old (Menyuk 1969, Chap. 3), one finds that although the percentage of children at the beginning of the age range, using simple transformations (operations on one sentence), is very high (81 percent) and does not change very much over this age range (85 percent at the end), the percentage of children using structures involving operations on more than one underlying string does change dramatically as an increasingly older group is observed (from 47 percent at the beginning to 77 percent at the end of the age range). These are some examples of how linguistic structural descriptions of the language can be used to describe the structure of the child's production of sentences at various stages of development, and thus can lead to an understanding of the kinds of linguistic operations that the child can perform at various stages of development. These descriptions can also be used to predict developmental trends in terms of the structures that are produced earlier or later in the developmental course. These developments are not simply indications that the child can produce longer utterances as he grows older. For example, the child is producing utterances such as "I am playing a game with Jimmie" before he produces "I have been playing." Or he produces utterances such as "The boy is playing in the yard" before he produces "I see a boy who's playing." In fact, some structures that are acquired after others introduce economies in the length of utterances. Conjunction operations, as in "I ate some steak last night and I liked it," are used before relative clause operations, as in "I ate some steak last night that I liked," or "I liked some steak I ate last night."

In analyzing the structures produced by children who are developing language normally, one finds that most of the deviations from our internalized model that are produced by these children occur in alternation with completely grammatical structures and do not create any problems in communication with other members of the child's linguistic community, once a certain level of competence is reached. The following are examples of (1) declarative, (2) negative and (3) question sentences used by some children aged two years, ten months (Menyuk 1969, Chap. 3):

1. "He making me wet"
2. "I not a bad boy"
3. "How you fix that?"

Most of the usual phonological deviations produced by children (for example, "I wan dat pwitty dwess" and "I wide in a tar") also do not create problems in communication and can usually be decoded and transformed by the listener to match his own descriptions. This process of transforming deviant utterances, of course, depends on the listener's willingness to participate in the game. If these same deviations were produced by a ten-year-old, other barriers besides linguistic ones might prevent communication.

If the speaker-listener is not fully competent in the grammar of his language, which is the case of the child who is in the process of acquiring the language, it would follow from the theoretical model that at the beginning stages of the acquisition of a syntactic structure (or of the properties of a lexical item or of a phonological rule), approximations to the structure, based on previously acquired rules, may be produced. A very familiar example of this is the child's acquisition of the past form of strong verbs. He proceeds from such forms as *goed* (past derived from present form + past tense as in "played") to *goeded* (previous past form + past) or *wented* (strong verb past form + past tense marker) to *went*.

It would also follow that the child, in the process of acquiring the language, understands utterances in terms of his level of competence. That is, he understands them in terms of the structural descriptions in the grammar that he has acquired. When a group of normal-speaking children are asked to repeat grammatical sentences, their success in repetition is very much dependent on the structures in their grammar. Most of their incomplete repetitions are, in fact, modifications of the structure in terms of the descriptions in their grammar, as, for example, converting the verb form in the sentence "I've been here for a long time" to "I was here for a long time." That the modifications which occur change at various age levels ("I been," "I was," "I have been," etc.) also reflect changes which are occurring in the spontaneous everyday speech of these children, further indicates that an utterance is understood in terms of the child's own grammar. Another indication is that nongrammatical utterances presented for repetition are frequently corrected and that the structures of these corrections change at various grade levels as well (Menyuk 1969, Chapter 4). For example, "He wash his dirty face" is first corrected as "He washes . . . " and then as "He washed . . . ."

If the child deviates in some marked manner in the basic capacities which underlie the acquisition of language, the structural descriptions he acquires may differ so radically from those of his linguistic community that communication becomes difficult and in some instances impossible. His descriptions may differ on the phonological level, or syntactic level or semantic level of the grammar or any combination of these. By examining the structures that the child produces and understands, we can obtain some measure of his language competence. A careful analysis of the structures he can produce and understand will describe his linguistic behavior or language disorder and provide some measure of the degree of deviancy of the language he uses, in precise rather than intuitive (moderate, mild, severe, etc.) terms. By examining the structures the child uses in a variety of experimental situations some insight may be gained into how he might deviate in basic capacities from the child acquiring language normally.

The foregoing descriptive model was used to analyze the spontaneous utterances of a group of children who used language in a sufficiently deviant manner so as to interfere with communication between themselves and other members of their linguistic community but who also showed no hard evidence of physiological damage (Menyuk 1967). It was found that the number of structural descriptions in these children's grammar was significantly smaller than those of the normal-speaking children of the same ages, that a number of the structural descriptions were different from those of normal-speaking children, and that the children did not exhibit any significant changes in the acquisition of new structures over an age range of three years. In sum, we can describe in detail a language disorder by describing which structural descriptions are missing from a child's grammar, which structural descriptions are different, and how they are different as compared to the grammars of normal-speaking children.

When the foregoing children were given the task of repeating sentences of differing structures, both grammatical and nongrammatical, it was found that their performance in this task not only differed markedly from normal-speaking children, but also differed markedly from their own spontaneous generation. The normal-speaking children in some instances reproduced sentences which contained structures they did not use in their spontaneous utterances. They were structures that these children were probably on the brink of using since they were being used by children who were just slightly older. Although the structure of the utterance did affect the response of the children in the deviant speaking group, in many instances they could not reproduce structures which they used in their spontaneous speech, and unlike normal-speaking children their performance in the repetition task was significantly correlated with the length of the utterance.

A possible conclusion to be drawn from these findings is that short-term memory storage capacity for these children is much narrower than for normal-speaking children. It is necessary for the child to be able to scan the utterance to determine its structural description. He can then form hypotheses about its structure, match them against those stored in long-term memory or add them to those already stored, for future reference. If the child has a narrow short-term memory capacity, he is unable to analyze an utterance in depth, or is unable to add to the number and nature of the structural descriptions he has in his grammar by extensions of previous hypotheses, until he has had many, many more samplings of the language than is required by the child with normal capacity. His hypotheses about structural descriptions would be different, since his samplings of the language are different or distorted. His repetition capacity would be restricted both by the length of the utterance and the complexity of the utterance he is asked to repeat. In fact his repetition capacity would be worse than his spontaneous generation capacity. All these behaviors were observed with this group of children.

These types of explanations about linguistic behavior are obviously highly tentative. Nevertheless, the descriptive model provided a tool for the analysis of linguistic performance and the question can be further explored by examining in detail the performance of these children in various linguistic tasks.

Previously, it was noted that the age of a child is a factor in determining whether or not a child's linguistic competence deviates markedly from the norm. Certain deviations produced by a three-year-old, which create no interference in the communication process, may do so if they are produced by a child who is ten. Other factors may also cause interference in the communication process. A child may produce utterances that the educator may intuitively label as deviant because they depart, in terms of underlying structure, from the structural descriptions in his grammar. However, they may be perfectly consistent with the rules of grammar in the child's own linguistic community. The following are some examples taken from Stewart (see Chapter 17 in this volume) of verb forms in a Negro dialect.

1. "He busy" (He is busy—for the moment)
2. "He workin" (He is working—right now)
3. "He be busy" (He is habitually busy)
4. "He be workin" (He is working steadily)

One might, on listening to a child produce these utterances, leap to the conclusion that there are deficiencies in basic language capacity, and this would obviously be an incorrect conclusion. If one analyzes the structure of utterances being used (as Stewart does), one finds that a quite-complex verb-tense system is being used, although tense is not marked in the manner to which we, as users of standard English, are accustomed. Further, if one asks children around age eight who are using this dialect, which is the most acceptable, the next acceptable and the nonacceptable verb form, they rank order as most acceptable the standard English form, as next acceptable, the verb form from their own dialect, and as nonacceptable, a form that is nongrammatical in both dialects.[3] This is, of course, true of children who have been exposed to another linguistic environment, that of standard English. Younger children, not having been exposed to this other environment, or having been exposed for only a short period of time, might have only two categories: grammatical and nongrammatical.

[3]Personal communication with W. A. Stewart, Center for Applied Linguistics.

Few studies have been undertaken to examine the linguistic performance of children in ghetto environments, and fewer still to describe the language development of these children over some maturational period, or to describe the grammar of their linguistic community. However, even a cursory glance at some data that have been collected indicates that, indeed, the ghetto child goes about the business of acquiring the grammar of his language in exactly the same manner as do children in middle-income communities.

TABLE 1. MODEL SENTENCES CHARACTERISTIC OF CHILD AND ADULT SPEECH FROM DIFFERENT SOCIAL STRATA

Grammatical Feature	Low Income Strata	Middle Income Strata
Auxiliary Verb	They playin a game	They are playing a game
	He be playin	
	They were playin a game	They were playing a game
	He was playin	He was playing
	*He was hit him	*The boy running away
Copula	She a girl	She's a girl
	Jane be pretty	
Person-Tense	My sista wash duh dishes	My sister washes the dishes
Markers	He have a book	He has a book
	They went away	They went away
	She didn take that	She didn't take that
	*Mary play with me last night	*Mary play with me last night
	*The boy runned away	*The boy runned away
Question	That a new dress?	Is that a new dress?
	What you gon do?	What are you going to do?
	Where you goin?	Where are you going?
	Why you have that?	Why do you have that?
Negation	He don' have no book	He doesn't have any book
	Don' let him do nuthin	Don't let him do anything
	He ain good	He isn't good
	*You not makin nuthin	*You're not making nothing

*Sentences marked with an asterisk appear to be limited to the children's grammar at a commensurate age, and represent a stage in the development of their grammar.

If we examine the syntactic structures which appear to most markedly differentiate the dialects of children from two differing communities, black low-income and white middle-income, we find that these are structures which are also part of the fully developed grammar of the community and can be found in the sentences produced by adults in the community. Some of the syntactic differences that have been observed are the use of auxiliary and modal verbs, tense markers and copulas. These differences, in turn, lead to differences in question formation and negation. The other outstanding differentiating structure is the double negative. Table 1 presents some model sentences based on the structures produced by a preschool child (age forty-three to forty-four months) and an adult from the inner city,[4] and some model sentences based on the structures produced by children and adults in a middle-income community. These are only some examples of the differences in syntactic rules used by children and adults in two linguistic communities which generate differences in the utterances produced. It should be noted that in addition to syntactic differences, there are differences in phonological rules (for example, no final stop consonant in don', won', etc.) and probably some differences in lexical items and the properties of lexical items as well. More importantly, it should also be noted that although rules may differ, tense, person, negation, and question are marked in both dialects. Person and tense markers, and question and copula structures are marked nonredundantly in the low-income dialect but they are, nevertheless, marked. Further, one finds in the sentences produced by the children in the inner city both conjunction and syntactic embedding although, again, there are instances of rule difference. It may be true, as has been stated, that there is proportionately less elaboration in the everyday language of the ghetto environment (c.f. Baratz in press), but one must be careful to observe rule differences in an estimation of this factor. The following are some model sentences (1-3) of these constructions in the grammar of the inner-city child described above and some sentences (4-6) of inner-city children in another community (Baratz and Povich 1968).

1. "A baby was playin in the house and somebody feed her."
2. "If you don' listen I'm o hit you."
3. "I know he don' hurt us cause we good friends to him."
4. "Dey gon fall down hurt dereself."
5. "Dey go way up dere dey go fall."
6. "Muvver was beat him for he didn' go outside."

Presumably in this latter community, clauses which define subjects are not marked by the relative *wh* but by a prosodic feature (pause) and pronoun (Baratz in press). The following are some of the examples given.

"That girl, she" *v.* "The girl, who"
"My aunt, she" *v.* "My aunt, who"

---

[4] The actual sentences on which these models are based were collected by Claudia Mitchell (Kernan) during the progress of her dissertation research.

It is also clear from a brief examination of the data obtained in the two different inner-city communities that, just as so-called standard English may vary in some ways from community to community, so does the grammar of low-income communities. The results obtained in a study (Shriner and Miner 1968) of the morphological structures understood and used by children from low-income and middle-income families also raises this question. In this study no significant differences were found in the competence of both groups of children to apply morphological rules (including third-person-singular and present participle forms) to nonsense stems, and the use of these rules developed for both groups in the expected direction over the age range sampled. Although the grammar of the adults in the low-income community was not examined it may be that the use of morphological structures was not very different from the morphological structures used by adults in the middle-income community. Or it is possible that children whose performance grammars do not contain third-person-singular markers or auxiliary verbs in present participle forms still have the competence to observe these structures in the standard English they hear and to apply these rules in an experimental situation.

If school children (grades three and five) are asked to repeat utterances which contain structures from both grammars, the children from each linguistic community are significantly better able to reproduce sentences containing structures restricted to their own grammar (Chapter 2). It should be stressed that there is no similarity in the performance of ghetto children in the repetition task, and the performance of the children who were described previously as perhaps deviating in short-term memory capacity from children who develop language normally.

If preschool children (aged twenty-eight to thirty-seven months) from the ghetto environment are exposed to a standard English dialect for a short period of time, the structure of their spontaneous utterances and their repetition of certain structures changes (Cazden 1965). Some of the changes that occur in repetition are concerned with verb forms that appear to mark the ghetto dialect. After exposure, some of the children are adding in repetition the past-tense marker *(drop* goes to *dropped)*, the third-person-singular marker *(go* goes to *goes)* and the copula *(broken* goes to *are broken)*, Some of the children are also making changes in phonological rules *(won* goes to *won't)* but in many instances they are not. A particular case is that of the pronoun *they* and the determiners *the, this,* and *that.* The number of children using the voiced dental *(dey, duh, dis, dat)* increases.

All of the studies cited clearly show that inner-city children display an undisturbed linguistic capacity by being able to determine how abstract features (tense, for example) are marked in their language and by marking it correctly in terms of their own speech.

One must examine the structures children understand and produce in terms of the primary linguistic data which they hear, and observe how linguistic universals such as tense, number, negation, question, conjunction, embedding, etc., are marked in their grammar. In essence, if the educator wishes to modify linguistic behavior he must first have a basic understanding of the speaker-listener's linguistic capacity and competence. He must also have some knowledge of what occurs in the course of normal development.

IMPLICATIONS FOR EDUCATIONAL PRACTICES

Familiarity with both structural descriptions by linguists of the grammar of the language, and structural descriptions by psycholinguists of the developmental course in language acquisition can be extremely useful in planning curriculum. These descriptions can point the way to the range of what is simple and what is complex in the grammar, and to what structural descriptions are precursors to others both in the language and in the acquisition of language. They will also point the way to those aspects of the grammar that are basic and those that are just surface generalizations. Curriculum can then be planned which is logically consistent with the structure of language and its developmental course in children, as well as with the nature and degree of language deviancies which may be encountered. Answers to the questions— At what stage do we find him? and, Where should we take him next?—have to be obtained. To sum up, the theorist can provide descriptions of the structure of the language and the developmental sequence in the acquisition of language. The theorist and educator together, through experimentation, can observe how adequately these descriptions define and differentiate language deviancy and degrees of deviancy. The theorist and educator can, through experimentation possibly derive some explanations for the language behavior observed in any instance or group of instances of language deviancy. The educator can then plan a program which is based on the facts of language and language acquisition and a particular child's linguistic capacity and competence. The educator can evaluate the effectiveness of this program by measuring the changes in the degree of deviancy in terms of the structural descriptions at the phonological, morphological, and syntactic levels of the grammar that a child is using after a period of time. The theorist and educator together, through experimentation, may be able to devise particular measurement techniques based on linguistic descriptions of language competence which can be used to define language deviancy, to plan a curriculum, and to evaluate progress in an educational program.

What of methodology? As was observed previously, it has been hypothesized that in the normal acquisition of language, the child detects and recognizes abstract features in the language he hears. These features are the structural descriptions that make up his grammar at various stages of development. He does this without specific instructions to mark these features. Would it then be correct to state that a manipulation of the linguistic environment is sufficient to modify the behavior of the child whose linguistic performance is deviant? The answer to this question must, of course, be a multiple one. In the case of the child who has the capacity to acquire language normally (which he exhibits by acquiring the language of his environment), but who uses structural descriptions which are different from the "standard," and thus suffers in the many school tasks which require reading and understanding of the code, this approach would probably be correct. However, manipulation of the natural environment may mean that peers, siblings, parents and other adults in the child's environment, as much as is possible use the dialect which the teacher wishes him to acquire. Moreover the child must be exposed to this linguistic environment during the critical years of his development. This alternative obviously raises absurd and infeasible demands.

It is often suggested that the techniques of teaching a second language be used. Again, in that case, it is necessary to understand the rules of the child's grammar to determine which new rules he must acquire or which he must modify, which will cause conflict and difficulty, and which may be easily acquired. For this approach, the current reasoning about capacity and competence would certainly apply.

In the case of the child who does not have the capacity to acquire language normally, a manipulation of the natural linguistic environment is obviously not the answer, since if it were acquisition would already have occurred. Again, one must think in terms of the linguistic competence and capacity of the child. Since these children will differ in competence and capacity, there is no one method of presentation, or a learning model which will meet every child's needs. Therefore, not only is it necessary to evaluate a child's linguistic competence and capacity to determine the content of a program of intervention, but also to determine methodology (concerning method hypotheses, see Grimes and Allinsmith 1966). The area in which the educator can contribute most is in taking into consideration the various theoretical assumptions that have been made about the techniques for modifying behavior, and applying these in the classroom or clinic situation keeping in mind that what is taught and the order in which it is taught may be as critical as how it is taught. However, it is insufficient merely to apply. The attitude must be one of hypotheses testing. That is, an application will be tried, and how well it works in modifying—on a permanent basis—the linguistic behavior of the child will be systematically evaluated.

Before any of these tasks is undertaken a statement is required about the vital necessity of sharing an attitude. *Investigative* and *critical* are perhaps good adjectives for this attitude. Theory, the experimentation which may be motivated by theory, and the application of experimental results in further experimentation do not guarantee panaceas. An outstanding characteristic and the most fruitful aspect of experimentation is that it not only may resolve some questions, but may raise further questions. By a series of many, many experiments and hopefully a few sudden leaps of insight, experimentation may lead us closer to our goals of understanding the structure and basis of both normal and deviant language acquisition and development and of devising methods for successfully "curing," modifying, and enriching linguistic behavior. For those who wish immediate answers since the problem exists now, this is a frustrating procedure. However, unless there is some time set aside in some concerted effort to approach these problems with this attitude, the educator will perhaps sacrifice the possibility of obtaining better answers to his questions and the child's needs, in order merely to gain immediate answers.

REFERENCES

Baratz, Joan. A bi-dialectical test for determining language proficiency. *Child Development* (in press).

Baratz, Joan, and Povich, E. Grammatical constructions in the language of Negro preschool children. Unpublished manuscript. Center for Applied Linguistics, Washington, D.C., 1968.

Bloomfield, L. A set of postulates for the science of language. In M. Joos, ed., *Readings in Linguistics.* New York: American Council of Learned Societies, 1963.

Cazden, Courtney B. Environmental assistance to the child's acquisition of grammar. Doctoral dissertation, Harvard University, 1965.

Chomsky, N. *Aspects of the Theory of Syntax.* Cambridge, Mass.: M.I.T. Press, 1965.

Chomsky, N., and Halle, M. *The Sound Pattern of English.* New York: Harper & Row, 1968.

Fodor, J., and Garrett, M. Some reflections on competence and performance. In J. Lyons and R. J. Wales, eds., *Psycholinguistic Papers.* Chicago: Aldine, 1966.

Grimes, J. W. and Allinsmith, W. Compulsivity, anxiety and school achievement. In J. Rosenblith and W. Allinsmith, eds., *The Causes of Behavior, II.* Boston: Allyn & Bacon, 1966.

Jenkins, J. J., and Palermo, D. S. Mediation processes and the acquisition of linguistic structures. In Ursula Bellugi and R. Brown, eds., *The Acquisition of Language,* Monograph of the Society for Research in Child Development, 1964, Vol. 29.

Jesperson, O. *Growth and Structure of the English Language* (9th ed.) New York: Doubleday, 1938

Joos, M., ed. Preface. *Readings in Linguistics.* New York: American Council of Learned Societies, 1963.

Katz, J. J., and Postal, P. M. *An Integrated Theory of Linguistic Descriptions.* Cambridge, Mass.: M.I.T. Press, 1964.

Menyuk, Paula. Comparisons of grammar of children with functionally deviant and normal speech. *J. Speech and Hearing Research* 1964, 7: 109–121.(a)

————. Syntactic rules used by children preschool through first grade. *J. Child Development* 1964, 35: 533–46.(b)

————. Linguistic descriptions and what they may tell us about the nature and role of memory in language acquisition. Paper presented at the national meeting of the American Speech and Hearing Association, 1967.

————. *Sentences Children Use.* Cambridge, Mass.: M.I.T. Press, 1969.

Salzinger, K. The problem of response class in verbal behavior. In K. Salzinger and S. Salzinger, eds., *Research in Verbal Behavior.* New York: Academic Press, 1967.

Shriner, T. H., and Miner, L. Morphological structures in the language of disadvantaged and advantaged children. *J. Speech and Hearing Research* 1968, 11: 605–10.

Wales, R. J., and Marshall, J. J. The organization of linguistic performance. In J. Lyons and R. J. Wales, eds., *Psycholinguistic Papers.* Chicago: Aldine, 1966.

Chapter 11

MATERNAL LANGUAGE STYLES AND COGNITIVE DEVELOPMENT OF CHILDREN

Ellis G. Olim*

Among the many variables that contribute to the creation and maintenance of poverty is maternal language style.[1] In brief, the argument is this: The behavior which leads to social, educational, and economic poverty is learned; it is socialized in early childhood. This socialization takes place in large measure by way of language. Since the mother is the primary socializing agent in most instances, the learning takes place in the context of the mother-child communication system. The deprivation that leads to poverty is a lack of cognitive meaning and cognitive and linguistic elaboration in this communication system. The family control system of the socially deprived is one in which appeals to status and role predominate and this type of system, by offering the child predetermined solutions and a narrow range of alternatives of action and thought, limits the child's cognitive development.

The converse of the foregoing situation suggests one way of ameliorating some of the problems of poverty. In culturally advantaged families, the family control system more often includes an orientation towards persons rather than to status, and/or an orientation towards consequences, viewing behavior as antecedent to more or less predictable outcomes. In person- and consequence-oriented families, the dominant language code is more particular, more differ-

*Department of Human Development, University of Massachusetts
[1] I believe the concept of maternal language style was originated by Professor Robert D. Hess.

entiated, and more precise. It permits and encourages in the child a wider range of alternatives of action and thought, leading toward greater elaboration, discrimination, and differentiation of cognitive and affective content.

However, cognitive development alone is not enough to guarantee the elimination of social inequity. In both types of family control systems there exist language codes in which meanings are transmitted primarily through extraverbal and nonverbal channels. These codes emphasize the communal rather than the individual, the concrete rather than the abstract, the present rather than the future. Such codes have the potential of enhancing the aesthetic, of encouraging the development of interpersonal sensitivity.[2] In the present condition of our schools, this type of code is largely dysfunctional.

Before we develop the general argument presented above, however, let us delineate some of the dimensions of the problem and underscore the urgency of its solution.

DIMENSIONS OF THE PROBLEM

For the foreseeable future, it seems clear that society, culture, and human behavior will continue to move toward ever greater elaboration, complexity, and subtlety. The dreams of even the most utopian among us can no longer contemplate seriously a return to pristine simplicity. If we do have a vision of finding the good life and of solving the problems created by the incredible growth of our cities, the seething new nationalism over half the earth's surface, and the destructive potentialites of our technology, such a vision is likely to embrace the conviction that man cannot retreat but must press ever harder toward the goal of expanding his potential as a human being and of maximizing the opportunities of all for optimal growth and development.

We have little reason to suppose that the accumulation and dissemination of knowledge and information will abate.[3] The economy is expanding most rapidly in those service industries that demand high educational attainment and highly developed skill in the use of symbol systems. At the same time, as a result of increased productivity, there has been only moderate expansion in manufacturing employment in the United States in the past twenty years. Unskilled jobs are rapidly disappearing as more and more physical work is assigned to machines. The economy is being converted from one in which

---

[2] I am not sure that Professor Bernstein (see essay in this volume) would accept my description of certain aspects of what he has called a restricted code. However, my partial description is intended to include at least some of the features of this code.

[3] This is not to overlook the serious assimilation gap between knowledge and our use of it. There seems to be an overproduction of trivial knowledge and an underconsumption of important knowledge.

workers produce physical products to one in which they produce services. Many of the new services deal with the management of information. Society, therefore, is accelerating its need and demand for persons who have developed highly skilled and elaborate methods of processing information and who are able to manipulate the environment, not directly as in factory work, but representationally, by symbolic means—the means essential for coping with the conditions of an advanced technological civilization.

Even if we assume that technological advances will decrease the manpower needs of the information industries or if we assume that, for whatever the reason, society learns to become a learning society, in which people will spend most of their time in the cultivation of leisure (in the Greek sense of that concept), the need for high levels of symbol-processing skills will continue to increase.

It is disturbing that while the movement toward information gathering and processing is proceeding at an exponential rate, a large segment of the population is being left further and further behind. These are the poverty people, the socially disadvantaged, the people who have been migrating from rural areas to swell the densely crowded metropolises. Most of these reside in the ghettos, where they are not being acculturated to urbanism. These new migrants must bridge a far wider cultural gap than their predecessors—European immigrants who had to be assimilated by the manufacturing industries in which the demand was for physical labor at standardized tasks. Some of these earlier migrants responded to the need for the establishment of small businesses. Often in a rapidly expanding economy, such enterprises became large. Because readily accessible avenues of economic mobility were available to many second- and third-generation Americans, they were able to acquire the social and cognitive skills that a less-sophisticated urbanism then demanded, thereby rising to political, governmental, managerial, and professional occupations.

The task facing the new migrants is far more difficult, the cultural gap far greater, because life and society have become far more complex than for the earlier immigrants. This enormous expansion and elaboration of the physical and social worlds must be accompanied by a correlative expansion of the cognitive world of the new migrants, if they are to adapt successfully to the conditions of modern life.

In the search for the elimination of poverty and disadvantage in general many solutions are being offered: educational, economic, social and psychological.

Since the schools traditionally have been the major means for socializing children to the mores of our society, it is understandable that early attention would be directed to the schools, their possibilities for improvement, and their failures. The schools have indeed lagged behind in adapting to the changing needs of a changing society. One indispensable condition of educability today is the achievement of abstract, conceptual intelligence and a stance that encourages an ever-expanding level of intellectual competence. For those interested in improved education for the socially and culturally disadvantaged child, the challenge to the educational system takes on particular poignancy because this kind of competence has never been achieved by a majority of our children, let alone the underprivileged. Even after we prevented the majority of children from becoming early dropouts by extending the number of years of mandatory school attendance, most of them remained intellectual dropouts —they have not been educated by any reasonable definition of that term. Hence, the current concern with improving opportunities for the underprivileged has laid bare a problem that has been for a long time latent. We are now observing that in the great urban centers a large proportion of the children in the early grades are not being adequately educated even by traditional standards and are being grossly undereducated in relation to the demands which society will place upon them when they reach late adolescence and enter the labor market.

However, it would be an oversimplification to place primarily on the schools blame for the failure of the socially disadvantaged to achieve adequate levels of intellectual competence. Even after all the inadequacies of the American school system are acknowledged, there still remains the stubborn fact that in economically depressed areas of the large metropolitan cities a sizeable proportion (sometimes estimated to be as high as two-thirds) of the children arrive at the first grade without the basic cognitive, motivational, and social skills necessary to undertake the tasks ordinarily presented in a first-grade curriculum. It is too early to evaluate correctly the effects of intervention and remediation programs (such as Head Start and Follow Through)—particularly the long term effects—but to date there is not sufficient evidence for self-congratulation on the success of such programs.

Some feel that the solution to poverty is essentially economic—that rising employment in the context of an ever-expanding economy is the answer. Economists of this persuasion hold that there must be a continuous increment in the gross national product in order to create employment opportunities and purchasing power for the expanding population and the presently unemployed.

But not all agree that continuous increments in the gross national products or in the provision of services are unmixed blessings. Some would wish to slow down or call a halt to the continuous production of commodities and the emphasis on sustained technological innovation. Some would prefer to devote a major share of the nation's energy to eliminating air and water pollution, conserving natural beauty, beautifing the environment in which we live, advancing medical knowledge, expanding the role of education, eliminating poverty, attaining world peace, and cultivating leisure. And it may be argued that the knowledge explosion is not an explosion of wisdom so much as it is an explosion of information gathering and processing to achieve more and more effects without too much attention to the value for humanity of such effects. The predominant view in the Ninteenth century was that scientific research, by unlocking the secrets of nature, would usher in the abundant life for all and provide the opportunity for the cultivation of leisure. Contrary to this expectation, the explosion of scientific knowledge has created an ironical situation in which much of technology is engaged in trying to find solutions to problems brought about by the continued application of science to society.

An even more serious consequence of the unbridled technological application of science to the expansion of the economy has been the resulting alienation of man both from himself and from others. It is more than a metaphor to say that man is becoming more and more like the computers he has invented. It is a truism that our culture has tended for a long time to promote conformity, triviality, and dehumanization. In an affluent society, things have become the measure of man. Why are so many persons, brought up with elaborated and complex language and cognitive structures, turning to extraverbal and nonverbal channels of communication, both intrapersonally and interpersonally?

This is not to suggest that linguistic impoverishment and mindlessness are the antidote to dehumanization and alienation. On the contrary, I would contend that maximization of one's human potential, by which I include intrapersonal and interpersonal sensitivity and nonverbal and extraverbal communication, is contingent upon the development of an elaborated language code. The dehumanization and alienation of today's society argue, additionally, for the encouragement of greater sensitivity of human beings in extraverbal and nonverbal channels of communication.

In turning to the problems of the socially and culturally disadvantaged, we see, then, that there are two problems, not one. The first is that social and cultural disadvantage are correlated with retardation and restriction in intellectual growth. The second is that the disadvantaged suffer also from the evils of dehumanization and alienation that characterize society as a whole. Important as it is to alleviate and eliminate cognitive underdevelopment, it is important also to find ways of increasing intrapersonal and interpersonal sensitivity, affective development, motivation, and an awareness of what it means to be human in a community of human beings—not only for the disadvantaged but also for the socially and economically advantaged.

LANGUAGE AND COGNITIVE DEVELOPMENT

Let us return, now, to the development of the argument set forth at the outset. It is not sufficient to say that social and cultural disadvantage (with its attendant psychological constriction) depresses the underprivileged child's academic potential. This is true enough. But the more basic problem is to understand how cultural experience is translated into cognitive behavior and educability. We need to know how cultural disadvantage acts to shape and depress the potential of the human mind and when cultural disadvantage exercises its most critical influence (Hess and Shipman, 1965).

One of the views implicit in the summary argument I presented at the outset is that language, in some way, has a determining influence on cognitive development. This view has been advanced by a number of theorists. Vygotsky (1962, p. 51) states:

> Thought development is determined by language, i.e., by the linguistic tools of thought and by the sociocultural experience of the child . . . . The development of logic in the child, as Piaget's studies have shown, is a direct function of his socialized speech. The child's intellectual growth is contingent on his mastering the social means of thought, that is, language.

According to Vygotsky, the process of intellectual development starts with a dialogue of speech and gesture between child and parent. One of the most important roles adults play in promoting the child's cognitive development is to demarcate the relevant and important dimensions of experience (Luria and Yodovich, 1959; Vygotsky, 1962). From significant adults in his environment, the child learns what is important for him to attend to; how to give order, structure, and meaning to the relevant environmental stimuli; and how to process, both directly and representationally (symbolically), the information he attends to. The mother's first words, when she shows her child objects and names them, have a decisive influence on the formation of the child's mental processes. The word isolates the essential features of an object or event and inhibits the less essential properties (Luria and Yodovich 1959). Berlyne (1963) has summarized the Soviet position on the nature of the child's intellectual development. As children acquire language, they test their tentative notions about the meanings of words chiefly through verbal interaction with more-verbally-mature speakers (John and Goldstein, 1964). Excellent discussions on the mediating role of language have been presented by Brown (1958; 1965). Bloom, Davis, and Hess (1965, p. 13) describe the usefulness of affixing labels to objects as follows:

> As the child comes to perceive the world about him, he is able to "fix" or hold particular objects and events in his mind as he is given words or other symbols to "attach" to them. "Mama" and "Dadee" become representations of the important adults in his life. "Bottle," "cup," "dog" become symbols for appropriate objects in the environment.

This view of the language-thought relationship draws upon the work of those anthropologists who have affirmed a determinative relationship between language and cognitive development, notably, Sapir (1929) and Worf (1956), and upon the work of Bernstein (1965), who has advanced a sociolinguistic approach to social learning. Thus Sapir (1959, pp. 209–10) has stated:

> Language is a guide to "social reality" . . . . It is quite an illusion to imagine that one adjusts to reality essentially without the use of language and that language is merely an incidental means of solving specific problems of communication or reflection. The fact of the matter is that the real world is to a large extent unconsciously built up on the language habits of the group . . . . We see and hear and otherwise experience very largely as we do because the language habits of our community predispose certain choices of interpretation.

This is a reversal of the older, traditional view that all languages deal with the same "reality" and that thought is independent of, and prior to, language. Worf (1956, pp. 212–213), a student of Sapir, explicates the Sapir-Whorf hypotheses as follows:

> . . . the background linguistic system (in other words, the grammar) of each language is not merely a reproducing instrument for voicing ideas but rather is itself the shaper of ideas, the program and guide for the individual's mental activity . . . . Formulation of ideas is not an independent process, strictly rational in the old sense, but is part of a particular grammar . . . . We dissect nature along lines laid down by our native languages. The categories and types that we isolate from the world of phenomena we do not find there because they stare every observer in the face; on the contrary, the world is presented in a kaleidoscopic flux of impressions which has to be organized by our minds—and this means largely by the linguistic systems in our minds. We cut nature up, organize it into concepts, and ascribe significances as we do, largely because we are parties to an agreement that holds throughout our speech community and is codified in the patterns of our language . . . .

Brown and Lenneberg (1954, p. 454) have stated the Sapir-Whorf hypothesis succinctly:

> The world can be structured in many ways, and the language we learn as children directs the formation of our particular structure. Language is not a cloak following the contours of thought. Languages are molds into which infant minds are poured.

A caveat is in order. Brown (1965, p. 315) points out that for concepts that are universal, "social mediation is not likely to be important," that is, they are learned from direct commerce with the physical world. Nevertheless, he agrees that the most important form of concept learning is probably socially and linguistically mediated.

Let us summarize the argument to this point. Much of reality is not what is "out there," independent of conceptualization of reality, but consists of what is verbally schematized. Central, therefore, to the individual's grasp of reality is the use of language. Without it, complex information could not be processed since such processing requires (1) abstraction, from the infinite welter of events in the world, of catergories of events sharing common defining attributes, (2) a code to enable recovery (recollection) of concepts pertinent to the processing of information, and (3) a constant reshuffling of events into different categories with different focal-defining attributes. The necessity for this constant development of new categorizations of experience apparently is embedded in the fact that some of reality is capable of being restructured (conceptualized) in an infinite number of ways. Without categorization the ongoing stream of events would have to be ignored or, if perceived, handled individually (as infrahuman animals must). By means of a limited number of words standing for concepts and by means of the combinatorial possibilities of words, it is possible for man to assimilate experience in manageable ways that are far beyond the reach of animals.

SOCIAL STRUCTURE AND LANGUAGE

In Whorf's view, the language habits (integrated fashions of speaking) of a community are seen as acting directly upon the individuals, rather than being mediated through the social structure. "On the contrary, they are seen as determiners of social relations through their role in shaping the culture" (Bernstein 1965). Bernstein (1965, p. 149) offers a sociological modification of the Whorfian view:

. . . a number of fashions of speaking . . . are possible in any given language and . . . these fashions of speaking, linguistic forms, or codes, are themselves a function of the form social relations take. According to this view, the form of the social relation or—more generally—the social structure, generates distinct linguistic forms or codes and *these codes essentially transmit the culture and so constrain behavior.*

Bernstein's view is that in the context of a common language there will arise distinct linguistic forms—fashions of speaking—which induce in the speakers different ways of relating to objects and persons. Language "is a set of rules to which all speech codes must comply, but which speech codes are generated is a function of the system of social relations" (Bernstein 1965, p. 151).

Bernstein (1959, 1960, 1961a, 1961b, 1964, 1965) has expounded the view that the language code of a specific social structure conditions what the child learns and how he learns, and sets limits within which future learning may take place.

Different social structures will emphasize or stress different aspects of language potential, and this in turn will create for the individual particular dimensions of relevance. As the child learns his speech, so he will learn his social structure, and the latter will become the sub-stream of his innermost experience through the effects of linguistic processing. (Bernstein 1961a, pp. 322–23)

Many investigators have shown that the structure and level of the language which a child acquires are related to variables associated with social class (Anastasi 1958; Cazden 1966; Irwin 1948; John 1963; Lawton 1963; Milner 1951, Templin 1957). Jensen (1968), Gordon (1965), and Raph (1965) have summarized much of the work in this area.

Bernstein has discussed these "different aspects of language potential" in terms of differential codes. He has identified two kinds of communication codes, or styles of language, which have a direct bearing on how language helps shape thought: restricted and elaborated codes. Restricted codes are stereotyped, limited, and condensed, lacking in specificity and the exactness for precise conceptualization, differentiation, and discrimination. The individual limited to a restricted code is sharply constricted in range and detail of concepts and information processing. A major purpose of restricted codes is to promote solidarity and to ease tensions within a group—not to promote cognitive elaboration. Restricted codes arise where the form of the social relation is based upon closely shared identifications and common assumptions. Restricted codes reinforce the form of the social relation rather than explicit meanings and intentions of the speakers. Orientation is less toward the verbal and more toward the extraverbal channel of speech. Restricted codes are status-oriented. But, as Bernstein (see chapter 3 in this volume) has indicated, they should not be disvalued. A restricted code contains a vast potential of meanings, particularly metaphorical. It is a form of speech which symbolizes a communally based culture.

In elaborated codes, communication is individualized and the message is specific to a particular situation, topic, or person. It is more differentiated, more precise, permitting expression of a wider and more complex range of thought. Meanings are elaborated and more explicit and specific. Intelligibility of the message is important. An elaborated code is person- or object-oriented rather than status-oriented. Verbal planning requires a high level of syntactic organization and lexical selection since the conveyance of relatively explicit meaning is the major function of an elaborated code (Bernstein 1965). Though meanings are not necessarily abstract, abstraction is facilitated. Also, the code facilitates the verbal transmission and elaboration of the individual's unique experience.

Now, the significance of these two forms of code in terms of socioeconomic status level is this: Restricted codes are available to both upper and lower socioeconomic groups. But lower socioeconomic groups tend to be limited in their language styles mainly to restricted codes. As previously mentioned, the mechanism by which the child is socialized to his language code or codes is in the communicative interaction between mother and child. It follows therefore, that the mother's language style has decisive consequences for the language development of the child.

FAMILY CONTROL SYSTEMS AND LANGUAGE STYLES[4]

How does the mother's language style—that is, whether her mode of communication to the child is based primarily on an elaborated or a restricted code —manifest itself in different family control systems and how are these systems related to socioeconomic status? Following Bernstein (1964), Hess and Shipman (1965) hold that the kind of family control and regulation used determines the type of code used. Three types of family control have been distinguished by Hess (Hess et al. 1968). One type is oriented toward control by status or position appeal or by appeal to ascribed role norms. A second type is oriented toward the subjective states of individual persons. A third is oriented toward consequences, toward rational considerations involving antecedent conditions and consequent effects. Families differ in the extent to which they use each of these types of regulatory appeal. We might say that the relative proportion of each of the three types of orientation used defines (in principle, at least) the style of the family.

In status-oriented families, behavior is generally regulated in terms of role expectations. The appeal to the child is based on tradition and authority (as publicly defined). This approach is essentially imperative and status-normative in character. ("You must do this because I say so," or "Girls don't act like that" [Bernstein 1964]. Mothers in status-oriented families tend to favor inhibitory and input-control techniques in the control of the child. Inhibitory techniques are intended to prevent a response from recurring or to prevent the child from considering or selecting certain types of alternatives for action and thought. Input-control techniques are used to restrict information and alternatives open to the child. Where intentional, its purpose is to prevent certain types of response from happening by preventing the initial stimulating circumstances from occurring. In the deprived family, this type of control is likely to be inadvertent, rather than intentional, stemming from the disadvantaged mother's inability to provide the symbols and patterns of thought and com-

---

[4]The material in this section draws heavily on the ideas of Professor Hess (et al, 1968). If there are deviations in any respect from his published views, those expressed are mine, not his.

munication necessary for developing the cognitive potential of the child. This is because she has a limited fund of ideas and information on which to draw in her attempts to cope with the environment. The result is the oft-noted paucity of linguistic and symbolic interaction in culturally deprived families.

The consequences for the child of the mother's use of inhibitory and input-control techniques are to promote the development of a nonrational, nonverbal stance toward the environment. By cutting off the opportunity of the child to engage in linguistic and symbolic interaction the results for the child are a limited repertoire of information and ideas, a low level of differentiation and complexity in his linguistic and cognitive structure, a failure to develop a sense of competence and pleasure in the use of his mind as a way of coping with the environment, and an inability to deal with situations and problems that call for the use of abstract concepts and complex problem-solving strategies (Olim, Hess, and Shipman, 1967).

A third type of technique, whose effect is to internalize cognitive control in the child, consists of the attempt to regulate the child's behavior through appeal to logical considerations and consequences ("If you run out into the street, you may get hurt"), and to subjective consequences and feeling states ("If you go to bed late, you will be tired and sleepy tomorrow"). This approach involves the presentation to the child of a wide range of logical alternatives to thought and action and, by pointing out the rationale of various courses, it encourages the child to choose correctly or wisely among the alternatives that are open to him.

Internalizing techniques are more likely to be associated with families who modify and moderate their appeals to status and role by the frequent use of techniques based upon personal-subjective or cognitive-rational orientations. In the personal-subjective orientation, the family is oriented more toward personal and individual considerations than toward group considerations. The individual characteristics of the child are taken into account. In situations of conflict, the feelings, preferences, reactions, and viewpoint of the child are given careful consideration. In the cognitive-rational orientation, justification of behavior is sought in the elements of the situation, emphasizing antecedent-consequent considerations. This orientation is not necessarily inconsistent with the personal-subjective approach, but need not include personal considerations in its appeal to logical considerations.

The consequences for the child of the use of personal-subjective and cognitive-rational approaches is to orient the child away from external standards as reference points and away from uncritical acceptance of authority and existing institutions. They orient the child, rather, towards an awareness of the existence of more options for thought and action, exploration of the environment in order to maximize comparisons among possibilities, and the development of elaborated and complex language and cognitive structures. Where the status-orientation approach is dominant, the child is led to attend to authority figures for direction, to develop a compliant, passive approach to learning (until he learns, as a result of failure and frustration in school, either to tune out the school or to adopt a defiant, rebellious attitude toward it), and to reach solutions to problems impulsively rather than reflectively. In personal-subjective-oriented systems, the child is directed toward expressive, subjective responses in others and in himself and toward greater responsivity to interpersonal aspects of behavior. The cognitive-rational approach tends to orient the child to logical principles as a guide to behavior. Both the personal-subjective and the cognitive-rational approaches encourage the child to develop a more active stance toward engagement with the environment and a more assertive approach to learning.

The various family control systems and strategies described above are related to maternal language styles and to socioeconomic status level. Mothers who are predominantly status-normative oriented are likely to come from the lower socioeconomic levels and to be limited to restricted codes. Status-oriented statements are often imperative in form, are arbitrary, and restrict the range of alternatives of thought and action. The mother-child communicative interaction system does not require an elaborated code since the systen is designed to promote role-conforming rigidity. It is a system that promotes group and status solidarity rather than individuation of personal development. Mothers who are predominantly oriented toward personal-subjective and cognitive-rational approaches are more likely to come from the higher socioeconomic status levels and will manifest elaborated language styles because these orientations not only permit but demand an elaborated code to deal with the wide range of alternatives of behavior and thought that are involved.

IMPLICATIONS FOR CHILDREN'S COGNITIVE DEVELOPMENT

If the arguments presented in this essay are sound, there are a number of practical implications and applications for those engaged in attempting to eliminate poverty and its attendant evils. First, on a psychological level, any program of remediation or change must start in the preschool years and be related to the mother-child communication interaction system. The child is exposed to a great deal of potential information in his environment. What he assimilates and accommodates to, how he interprets the stimuli to which he attends, and the responses he develops are learned in interaction with the environment, which in most instances is the maternal environment. Patterns of linguistic and cognitive activity are developed which become the basis upon which further cognitive development proceeds. The opportunity and encouragement to begin the process of developing an elaborated code are usually available to the higher-socioeconomic-status child but generally denied to the lower-socioeconomic-status child (i.e., the socially and culturally deprived). Bloom (1964) concludes that as much intellectual growth is achieved between birth and age four as is achieved between age four and age seventeen. Remediation, then, should begin in the home. Some efforts have been made along this line. However, there is considerable ground for pessimism that the problem can be handled on an individual basis (Bloom, Davis, and Hess 1965, p. 16) when "the total syndrome of poverty, broken homes, slum living, large families, and illiteracy all conspire against the intellectual development of the child." How can a mother, who is limited to a restricted code, be the means for making it possible for her child to develop an elaborated code? And if the social structure and the structure of the disadvantaged family shape and promote the development of restricted codes and if "language is used by participants of a social network to elaborate and express social and other interpersonal relations" (Hess and Shipman 1965, p. 871), how can the bind be broken? Two obvious solutions come to mind.

The first is to extend the school age downward to the early critical years of language and cognitive development. Preschool and early childhood programs, preservice and in-service teacher training for disadvantaged areas, and development of more effective instructional materials for use with the disadvantaged are all being tried. Whether such programs can rescue the disadvantaged child from the crushing effects of the total syndrome of poverty is a moot question.

The second solution would call for drastic social reform. Since the structure of the family and the attendant family control systems are embedded in the larger structure of society, it may be that nothing short of a major transformation in the economic and social world of the disadvantaged will suffice to bring about a major change in their cognitive world.

Of course, one need not back either of these alternatives to the exclusion of the other. Since behavior and social structure interact, those interested in the eradication of poverty may work at various levels simultaneously—educational, economic, social, and psychological.

Earlier in this paper, I indicated that the socially and culturally deprived suffer from a serious disadvantage cognitively but that they also suffer from what may be a far worse problem—one that is shared by the whole society—that is, the problem of dehumanization and alienation. Although elaborated codes maximize the range of alternatives of thought and action, and the possibility of this maximization should be open to all, the acquisition and use of an elaborated code does not require that the user have either an exquisite sense of his own identity and worth as a human being, or a highly developed sense of community. What else can we conclude from the litany of troubles besetting us today: an unpopular war, social unrest, the repolarization of racial attitudes, the disarray and underfinancing of our public school system and public health services, student revolts, dissent and civil disobedience, the pollution of our air and water supplies, experimentation with drugs, and experimentation with new forms of social structure? Surely, those responsible for these troubles are not those limited to a restricted code. On the contrary they are the responsibility of those who have developed an elaborated code and complex cognitive strategies. We should also ask ourselves how it has come about that the young who have mastered an elaborated language code and who have been reared in relatively open family systems—open both in the Bernstein sense (see essay in this volume) and in the Rogerian sense (Rogers 1961)—are sometimes just those who are most sensitive to their alienation from themselves and from other human beings.

The growth of Black Power and racial separatism in America is, I believe, symptomatic of the unwillingness of the disadvantaged black to give up his (admittedly tenuous) grip on what little identity and community he has in exchange for the alienated depersonalization of the white society. Bernstein (1961b, pp. 308–09) indicates that the solution for the person limited to a restricted code is not to eliminate it but to create for him the possibility of utilizing an elaborated code as well. For survival and success in an advanced society, this prescription seems unassailable. But Bernstein (1961b, p. 308) also points out that a restricted code:

. . . contains its own aesthetic—a simplicity and directness of expression, emotionally virile, pithy, and powerful, with a metaphoric range of considerable force and appropriateness. It is a language which symbolizes a tradition and a form of social relationship in which the individual is treated as an end, not as a means to a further end.

Is it not appropriate to conclude that it is just as important for the socially advantaged to develop to a high degree the use of restricted codes and concomitantly to develop a sense of community with their fellow human beings? Is it not just as important to construct social relations in which persons are not treated as objects and commodities, where competition and conquest are not the dominant values, and where affective intrapersonal and interpersonal development are as important as the development of proficiency in scientific-rational-symbolic thought? The current emphases on human development (as opposed to merely cognitive competence) reflect the tremendous dissatisfaction many feel with the underdevelopment of extraverbal and nonverbal channels of communication and modes of relationship (see, for example, *Psychology Today*, December 1967).

Insofar as we rely on our educational system to be the vehicle for overcoming some of the effects of poverty, we must face the fact that to provide remedial and compensatory education for the socially disadvantaged is not enough. From the standpoint of developing human potential, it is necessary to face up to the fact that we have failed in all our institutions (including the school) to see the urgency of fostering the humanness of citizens. Hutchins (1965) has posed the question as to whether we are not educating our children for the wrong future. With ever-increasing technological efficiency and productivity, are we not confronted with the terrifying prospect that, no matter how much we increase the complexity and level of our training, there may still be a declining number of job opportunities for which even complex skills will be needed? In a society which is evolving toward less work and more leisure, educating, not training, should be the proper goal of our schools. It is a truism that education requires attention to the total man—his aesthetic and moral aspects as well as his cognitive. To these ends, our schools should emphasize the development of human sensitivity as well as cognitive competence, though the latter should not be disvalued since the future society may be a learning society (Hutchins 1965). To the extent that the schools and, indeed, our society do not engage in such emphases, all our children may progressively become culturally disadvantaged.

REFERENCES

Anastasi, Anne. *Differential Psychology.* New York: Macmillan, 1958.

Berlyne, D. E. *Soviet Research on Intellectual Processes in Children.* Monograph of the Society for Research in Child Development 1963, Vol. 28.

Bernstein, B. A public language: some sociological implications of a linguistic form. *British J. Sociology* 1959, 10: 311–26.

———. Language and social class. *British J. Sociology* 1960, 11: 271–76.

———. Aspects of language and learning in the genesis of the social process. *J. Child Psychology and Psychiatry* 1961, 1: 313–24.(a)

———. Social class and linguistic development: a theory of social learning. In A. H. Halsey, J. Floud, and A. Anderson, eds., *Education, Economy, and Society.* New York: Free Press, 1961.(b)

———. Family role systems, communication. and socialization. Paper presented at Conference on Development of Cross-National Research on Education of Children and Adolescents, February, 1964. University of Chicago.

———. A socio-linguistic approach to social learning. In J. Gould, ed., *Penguin Survey of the Social Sciences.* Baltimore: Penguin Books, 1965.

Bloom, B. S. *Stability and Change in Human Characteristics.* New York: Wiley, 1964.

Bloom, B. S.; Davis, A.; and Hess, R. D. *Compensatory Education for Cultural Deprivation.* New York: Holt, Rinehart & Winston, 1965.

Brown, R. W. *Words and Things.* New York: Free Press, 1958.

———. *Social Psychology.* New York: Free Press 1965.

Brown, R. W., and Lenneberg, E. H. A study in language and cognition. *J. Abnormal and Social Psychology* 1954, 49: 454–62.

Cazden, Courtney B. Subcultural differences in child language: an interdisciplinary review. *Merrill-Palmer Quarterly* 1966, 12: 185–219.

Gordon, E. W. Characteristics of socially disadvantaged children. *Review of Educational Research* 1965, 35: 377–88.

Hess, R. D., and Shipman, Virginia. Early experience and the socialization of cognitive modes in children. *Child Development* 1965, 36: 869–86.

Hess, R. D.; Shipman, Virginia; Bear, Roberta M.; and Brophy, J. *The Cognitive Environments of Urban Preschool Children.* Chicago: University of Chicago Press, 1968.

Hutchins, R. M. Are we educating our children for the wrong future? *Saturday Review,* September 11, 1965, 66–67, 83.

Irwin, O. C. Infant speech: the effect of family occupational status and of age on use of sound types. *J. Speech and Hearing Disorders* 1948, 13: 224–26.

228 Maternal Language Styles

Jensen, A. R. Social class and verbal learning. In M. Deutsch, et al., *Social Class, Race, and Psychological Development.* New York: Holt, Rinehart, & Winston, 1968.

John, Vera. The intellectual development of slum children: some preliminary findings. *American J. Orthopsychiatry* 1963, 33: 813–22.

John, Vera, and Goldstein, L. S. The social context of language acquisition. *Merrill-Palmer Quarterly* 1964, 10: 265–75.

Lawton, D. Social class differences in language development: a study of some samples of written work. *Language and Speech* 1963, 6: 120–43.

Luria, A. R., and Yudovich, F. *Speech and the Development of Mental Processes in the Child.* London: Staples Press, 1959.

Milner, Esther. A study of the relationships between reading readiness in grade one school children and patterns of parent-child interaction. *Child Development* 1951, 22: 95–112.

Olim, E. G.; Hess, R. D.; and Shipman, Virginia. Role of mothers' language styles in mediating their preschool children's cognitive development. *The School Review* 1967, 75: 414–24.

Raph, Jane B. Language development in socially disadvantaged children. *Review of Educational Research* 1965, 35: 389–400.

Rogers, C. The implications of client-centered therapy for family life. In *On Becoming a Person.* Boston: Houghton Mifflin, 1961.

Sapir, E. The status of linguistics as a science. *Language* 1929, 5: 207–14.

Templin, Mildred C. *Certain language skills, in children, their development and interrelationships.* Institute for Child Welfare Monograph Series, No. 26. Minneapolis: University of Minnesota Press, 1957.

Vygotsky, L. S. *Thought and Language.* Eugenia Hanfmann and Gertrude Vakar, ed. and trans. Cambridge, Mass.: M.I.T. Press, 1962.

Whorf, B.L. Science and linguistics. In J.B. Carroll, ed., *Language, Thought, and Reality: Selected Writings of Benjamin Lee Whorf.* Cambridge, Mass.: M.I.T. Press, 1956.

Chapter 12

LANGUAGE, POVERTY, AND THE NORTH AMERICAN INDIAN

Lynn R. Osborn*

The conditions, symptoms, and results of poverty-level existence in the United States during the last several decades have hardly anywhere been more appalling than among the nation's first citizens, the North American Indians. Although both the present picture and the future outlook are brighter today, their poverty problems are still the most serious faced by any group in this country during the latter half of the twentieth century.

Contrary to the widely held myth of the "vanishing Americans," the Indian population of the United States actually is increasing at a markedly faster rate than the general population. The 1960 census reported well over a half-million Indian citizens. It is estimated that this figure currently has risen to approximately six hundred thousand with two-thirds of this population living on or near government reservations in twenty-five states. Should the present rate maintain during the decade of the '70's, the number will have risen to over eight hundred thousand by 1980. This projected growth would reflect a population expansion of well over 300 percent in less than a century from the reported low of two hundred forty thousand in the 1890's. Thus the future concern is not only one of degree, but of numbers as well.

The circumstances of contemporary Indian poverty on the reservations have been well-summarized by Nash (in a press release dated in 1964):

1. Unemployment on the reservations runs between 40 and 50%—seven or eight times the national average.

---

*The Communication Research Center, University of Kansas

2. Family income on the reservations averages between one-fourth and one-third the national average.
3. Nine out of ten Indian families live in housing that is far below minimum standards of comfort, safety, and decency.
4. Average schooling of young adults on the reservations is only eight years—two-thirds of the national average.
5. The average age at death on the reservation is 42 years, two-thirds the figure for the national population.

As the primary focus of this paper is upon the relationships existing between language and the state of poverty among Indians, we will not detail the literature concerning Indian poverty in general. One study, however, which is representative of the kinds of research undertaken in this regard is that reported by Roy (1962). The results of this investigation indicated that, with respect to the items that constitute a high level of living in white society, Indians have acquired these items only about half as often as whites. As a group they have acquired only about half the material goods that would give them an equal level of living in the adjacent white society.

Among recent volumes to which the reader may refer for both historical and contemporary orientations to Indian life today are those of Brophy and Aberle (1966), Farb (1968), Levine and Lurie (1968), Owen, Deetz, and Fisher (1967), and Spencer, Jennings, et al. (1965). Additional sources of information are included in the bibliography prepared by Gordon (1967). It should be noted, though, that as one examines the overall treatment of poverty in the United States, it is apparent that the plight of the North American Indian has not received its due share of scholarly attention. Gordon (1967, p. 1) perceptively reported:

> The development of an extensive literature on disadvantaged populations in the United States has been greatly influenced by historic and episodic concern with the civil rights of the Negro people —so much so that although the Negro people do not constitute the largest number of poor people in this country, the representation of this group in this literature suggests that they account for a larger proportion of the poor than is consistent with fact . . . . A review of this literature clearly indicates that poor whites, migrant workers, poor families of Spanish-speaking backgrounds, American Indians, etc., as special groups have received somewhat less attention than have Negroes . . . . The majority of investigators who have worked in this field have viewed disadvantaged populations as a great homogeneous mass. Insufficient attention has been given to the wide variety of persons, conditions, problems, and potential assets which are represented by these groups.

These observations nowhere are illustrated better than in that segment of the literature concerned with the ways in which language acquisition, mastery, and

usage relate to the incidence and intensity of poverty conditions. We will turn
now to a discussion of some of the most salient aspects of this perspective.

INDIAN LANGUAGES AND THEIR CULTURAL IMPLICATIONS

Despite the fact that many individuals often speak of *Indian* in the same
manner as they speak of *English, French,* or *German,* there is no single Indian
language as such. Nor did all of the original inhabitants of this continent speak
in mutually intelligible dialects of a single mother tongue. Voegelin (1941)
counted 149 native languages, exclusive of local and regional dialects, still
spoken by Indians north of Mexico. Although the passage of time has marked
the extinction of certain of these with the death of their last surviving speakers,
most still are living languages—some, such as Navajo, with several thousands
of speakers.

Precise statistics regarding the numbers of native users of the several
languages and dialects are not available. Ohannessian (1967, p. 10) and her
associates reported these findings:

> There are no accurate figures on the number of speakers of the
> various Indian languages, nor is there reliable information on the
> proportion of monolinguals in these languages, bilinguals (either in
> English or another European language, usually Spanish or French,
> or in other Indian languages), or non-speakers, that is, Indians who
> no longer speak their tribal language. A shift in language is appar-
> ently taking place in at least some Indian communities, but at present
> there are few accounts of the settings in which Indian languages are
> used and those in which English is used, whether Indian languages
> are becoming less frequently used, and whether there are genera-
> tional differences in language use and language fluency.

That such generational differences as alluded to above do in fact exist is in part
substantiated by the report of Fishman (1966) that approximately 55 percent
of the extant Indian languages and dialects are spoken only by the older
members of the communities.

The ties between Indian languages and cultures were examined early in
this century by Boas (1911). Sapir (1929, p. 209), for example, offered his views
concerning these ties in what is considered an initial statement of the Sapir-
Whorf hypothesis:[1]

---

[1]Other published materials on the language-culture relation and its study relative
to the North American Indian include Hoijer (1948, 1951, 1953, 1954, 1959); Whorf
(1941, 1950, 1952, 1956); Goddard (1930); Thompson (1963, 1965); and Hymes (1964),
which includes a useful bibliography.

Language is a guide to social reality. Though language is not ordinarily thought of as of essential interest to the students of social science, it powerfully conditions all our thinking about social problems and processes. Human beings do not live in the objective world alone, nor alone in the world of social activity as ordinarily understood, but are very much at the mercy of the particular language which has become the medium of expression for their society. It is quite an illusion to imagine that one adjusts to reality essentially without the use of language and that language is merely an incidental means of solving specific problems of communication or reflection. The fact of the matter is that the real world is to a large extent unconsciously built up on the language habits of the group. No two languages are ever sufficiently similar to be considered as representing the same social reality. The worlds in which different societies live are distinct worlds, not merely the same world with different labels attached.

ENGLISH AS A SECOND LANGUAGE

As one turns from the more general issue of the language-culture relation to the immediate language problems of the North American Indian, the focus usually becomes centered on the consideration of English as a so-called second language. Thompson (1965, p. 1), for example, has clearly stated a basic link between the Indian's mastery of the English language and his success in the dominant, mainstream society:

Certain aspects of life in traditional Indian groups, especially in the economic sector, no longer adequately serve Indian needs. Indians like the rest of us, but to a greater extent, are faced with making rapid adjustments. A good command of the English language today, more than ever before, is the master key to Indians' successful transition to 20th-century living.

In the case of the Indian citizen who lacks this master key, what might be termed a deficiency syndrome may be evidenced in the problems described by Hopkins (1966, pp. 2–3):

Essentially, he has difficulty meeting basic English language requirements in society. He has trouble talking with sales clerks. He has trouble discussing problems held in common with other Indian peoples and with the society as a whole. He may not read adequately and may find it difficult to understand and follow citizenship requirements associated with voting, registering an automobile, or making purchases on the installment plan . . . . He does not often understand the social role of language in an English-speaking society. He may know some English utterances but be uncertain as to where to apply them in a social setting. He may identify strongly with a preliterate language and society and therefore does not understand the importance of a literary heritage. He may attach a different set of values to language and perceive its function to be different from that of the English-speaking society.

We should, however, note that the other extreme does exist within the Indian population. Indeed, there exists an extremely broad spectrum of literacy in English among contemporary North American Indians. This varies from full-blooded Indian students who have no grasp of their tribal tongues and who speak English as well or better than their white peers, to tribes such as the isolated Miccosukee of the Florida Everglades who did not have a school in which English was taught until 1962. Some recent statistics on the problem have been reported by Coombs (1967, p. 2):

> . . . the greatest problem exists among several of the tribes of the Southwest, whereas most Oklahoma Indian children learn English as a first language . . . recent research findings . . . from both Bureau and public schools in five administrative areas of the Bureau, show from 55 to 77 percent of the pupils reporting that English is not the language ordinarily spoken in their homes.

Indian Education and English as a Second Language

The early days of English as a second language in schools for American Indian children, particularly during the latter years of the nineteenth century and the first quarter of the twentieth, were marked by a deliberate and concerted effort to obliterate completely any traces of the native tongue. It was this and similar practices, which Gaarder (1968, p. 12) labeled "attempted assimilation by alienation," that triggered much criticism of the conduct of Indian education in this period. The present writer has often listened to firsthand accounts by Indian men and women of punishment they received as young school children accidentally slipping back into the use of their native languages, including having their mouths scrubbed with laundry soap so strong it left blisters for many days thereafter.

The late 1920s and the 1930s marked a turning point in Indian education generally, and specifically in regard to English as a second language. The famed Meriam Report released in 1928 was quite critical of the boarding-school scheme and its attendant system of teaching English with attempted total removal of the child's original Indian language. The ensuing four decades have been marked by significant changes in philosophy, methodology, and motivational practices with regard to teaching English to Indian children. Commentary concerning this transitional period may be found in the writings of such authors as Havighurst (1957), Officer (1965), and Thompson (1964a, b; 1967).

The "Both-And" Approach

Recent years have brought great interest on the part of many Indian educators in what Roessel (1968) identified as the *both-and* concept of Indian education relative to the retention of native philosophies, mores, art forms, and languages. In a description of this innovative approach at the Rough Rock Demonstration School on the Navajo Reservation, Roessel (quoted by Conklin 1967, p. 4) cited these objectives:

> Indians have begun to question whether it is necessary for them to lose their heritage in order to become citizens of the United States, and so the 'Both-And'—both white and Indian—approach to Indian education was born . . . . Rough Rock is the first school to have the tools and resources to see whether this new approach can be effective. We want to instill in our youngsters a sense of pride in being Indian. We want to show them that they can be Indian and American at the same time, that they can take the best from each way of life and combine it into something viable.

Some of the program is described as follows (Conklin 1967, pp. 6–7):

> At one time in most Indian schools the children were punished if they spoke Navajo. At Rough Rock they are encouraged and even forced to use their own language. Navajo is taught in the fourth, fifth, and sixth grades for one hour three days a week. Also, for the first time on the reservation, portions of regular classes, such as arithmetic and social studies are held in Navajo. The purpose is to see whether students find it easier to retain subject matter when taught in their native language, as research has suggested may be the case . . . . English is taught formally twice a day, informally at all times. For example, as the children pass through the cafeteria line at noon they must ask for their food in English.

For additional information regarding English instruction at Rough Rock, see papers by Pfeiffer (1968), Roessel (1967), or Witherspoon (1968).

Scholastic Achievement and English Instruction

Thompson et al. (1964, p. 188), in describing the language problems of the more than forty-one thousand Indian children enrolled in Bureau of Indian Affairs schools during the 1960–61 school year, noted:

> All of these children were in Federal schools because of some particular needs that did not apply to other children. They lived in isolated communities or they did not speak English or they had no opportunities to go to school until they were nine, ten, or even sixteen to seventeen years of age . . . . Most of these Indian children spoke only their Indian tongue when they entered school.
> If Indian children enter at six, they are already six years behind in spoken English by comparison with children who enter school at six speaking English.

The language problem, however, has its greatest impact upon scholastic performance when the Indian child is in the upper elementary grades. Thompson (1966a, p. 2) has summarized this problem as follows:

> Indian children . . . achieve at levels comparable to the national norms until the English language becomes an essential tool for further learning, usually around grade four. At that point they begin to fall behind, and the gap grows wider as they advance upward through the grades.

This decline in achievement has been found to be accompanied by a corresponding decrease in both frequency and length of pupil responses in classroom discussions. A study by Orata (1953) at the Little Wound Day School on the Pine Ridge Indian Reservation in South Dakota revealed a drop from 62 to 46 percent in frequency of pupil participation in class discussion between the first grade and junior high school. Pupil usage of one- and two-word responses rose from 15 and 8 percent respectively to 50 and 12 percent. At the same time, usage of three-, four-, and over four-word responses fell from 10, 14, and 53 percent to 7, 4, and 27 percent. This reticence in speech behavior in the intermediate and upper grades often is referred to as the *silent sitter phenomenon* (see, for example, Beatty 1944, Ohannessian 1967, or Timmons 1965). The studies by Ohannessian and Timmons present data on the attitudes of Indian students toward the acquisition, mastery, and use of spoken English.

As are the problems involved in gauging the scholastic and linguistic performance of any group whose language and culture is different from the so-called norm, this phenomenon has been a recognized factor in dealing with the Indian. It can be seen in an early guide for teaching English as a second language (Reel 1904), as well in more recent observations (e.g., Hopkins 1967) that what Indians have been taught about English often has been tied to agricultural tasks rather than to the linguistic requirements of a technological society. For some of the problems involved in gauging the success of language instruction with Indian children, see Anderson, et al. (1953), Coombs, et al. (1958), Howe (1966), and Peterson (1948). Havighurst (1957) has summarized the arguments against there being hereditary deficiencies contributing to the scholastic problems of Indian children.

The Dropout Phenomenon

Another problem in Indian education which first begins to manifest itself in the upper elementary grades when the English language becomes a crucial educational factor is that of pupil dropout. Boyce (1964a, p. 79) has reported that:[2]

---

[2]Figures released after the preparation of this chapter indicate a dropout rate of slightly more than 42 percent for Indian youth as against 27 percent for all American pupils (*Indian Record*, July 1969, 3).

. . . dropouts among Indian youngsters begin to take on serious proportions as early as the fifth and sixth grades. In some regions relatively few Indian children even cross the bridge from elementary to secondary school. Of those who do make the grade, reports indicate that on a national basis fully 60 per cent of Indian high school youths drop by the way before graduation.

Perhaps the most outstanding study of the Indian dropout in recent years was that of Bryde (1966) which deals with Oglala Sioux children. Among other things, he reported a decline in scholastic achievement and an increase in dropout rates at that particular level in the upper elementary and intermediate grades when English became a critical variable affecting academic success. Although he observed that on achievement variables Indian students scored significantly higher than national test norms from the fourth through the sixth grade, at the eighth-grade level the Indian students were significantly below the national norms. (For another study dealing with the Oglala Sioux, see Wax and Wax 1968.) More information on the Indian dropout problem in the elementary and secondary grades can be found in sections of an extensive survey by Coleman et al. (1966), brief papers by Hand (1963), Maloy (1963), Miller (1965), Monacchio (1964), Muehe (1966), and Thompson 1964a, b), as well as the previously mentioned writings of Anderson et al. (1953), Coombs et al. (1958), and Havighurst (1957).

The dropout problem becomes even more pronounced for the Indian at the college level. After suffering the 60 percent attrition rate in the secondary school before graduation (Boyce 1964a), only slightly more than one-fourth of those who do graduate enroll in institutions of higher education. In a survey of twelfth-grade Indian pupils, Coleman et al. (1966, p. 284) reported only 27 percent definitely planning to enroll in college the following year. At a hearing held before the Special Subcommitte on Indian Education of the United States Senate, Montoya (1967, p. 107) reported that there were only six college seniors who, it was hoped, would graduate in 1968 from the entire nineteen tribes of the All-Indian Pueblo Council in New Mexico, which comprise a population well in excess of twenty-five thousand.

The relationships between proficiency in English and the Indian's success in college are treated by such writers as Salisbury (1965, 1967) and Thompson (1964a, b, 1966b). Salisbury (1967, pp. 8–9) discusses the communication difficulties experienced by Alaskan Indian and Eskimo freshman students at the University of Alaska:

. . . his imperfect use of English is due to the fact that, although he has received 12 years of formal western education, he has not lived within the western culture. His only contacts with Caucasians have been teachers, missionaries, and various public health and

social workers he may have had occasion to meet. He has no *concrete* idea of the culture which his new language expresses . . . .
Compounding the native's communication problem is the fact that he has come from a culture where he has been reinforced for reticence. Although he may have come from a high school where the students were encouraged to discuss and debate certain issues, if his classmates were all natives, it is unlikely that he has developed any real skill in expressing his ideas clearly and directly. He has never seen the lively exchange of opinions which (hopefully) characterizes the western college classroom.

In examining factors thought to be responsible for the extremely high dropout rate among Indian freshmen enrolled at Northern Arizona University, Thompson (1966b, p. 2) found lack of proficiency in the English language to rank at the top of the list:

English for these students had to be learned in the elementary and high-school grades as a second language, which means that these students have acquired their formal education in what to them is a foreign language. A few of them may have been fortunate enough to have had teachers well prepared in teaching English as a second language, but in all probability most did not . . . . Some Indian college students still find it difficult to think in English, and some are attempting to handle college subject matter with less than high-school reading tools. On the other hand, evidence points to the fact that most of these same college students if tested with instruments that eliminate English language factors score average or better with respect to potential ability. Nevertheless, struggling with the language problem has a damaging effect on their confidence in themselves. . . . the failing grade problem complicated by financial problems and sub-standard capability in the English language forms a web more frustrating than many students can take . . .for many of them, walking away is the only solution they know.

Jackson (1964, pp. 195–196) comments on the different reactions to problems in adjusting to the college environment on the part of Indian and non-Indian students and the relationship of English proficiency to these reactions:

Good communication skills are essential for all college students; however some Indian students are set apart from non-Indian students because of differences in cultural and environmental background . . . . Perhaps all college students experience that feeling of inadequacy and insecurity during the first few days of their freshman year. In many cases, the beginning non-Indian student overcomes his feeling of inadequacy by over-verbalizing and participating in attention-getting activities, while many Indian students simply withdraw from this unfamiliar and frustrating experience. The temptation to withdraw, unfortunately, is greater than the will to face what appears to be an insurmountable obstacle. In addition, in many cases, family censure for dropping out of school is negative. The student does not fear family or community rejection. Here again, cultural background proves to be a disadvantage . . . . Without a doubt, the most common criticism expressed by Indian students is that they were not taught enough English in high school.

Vocational Success and Urbanization

Another set of relationships between language and problems of the North American Indian which has received some attention in professional literature is that dealing with vocational success. Perhaps the most succinct and appropriate statement on English and vocational success is this one from Thompson (1962, p. 3):

> There was a time in the on-going program of Indian schooling that a simple skill and a meager command of English was sufficient to place Indians in a favorable position for employment. This is no longer true. Indians today must have a good command of English and further they must be highly skilled. In the words of the Commissioner of Indian Affairs, Philleo Nash, "English capability is the best vocational preparation we can give this generation . . . ."

A revealing study conducted by Baker (1959) dealt with problems faced on the job by young Indian men in their first year of employment after high-school graduation. Sixty Navajo graduates of the Intermountain School operated by the Bureau of Indian Affairs in Brigham City, Utah, who had found positions in Denver, Los Angeles, Salt Lake City, San Francisco, and other western locations, were queried concerning their assessments of job success and satisfaction. Baker found that the vocational inadequacies identified by members of the group were linked closely with lack of proficiency in English. His findings further indicated that the Indians themselves felt that they would have been in a much better situation for employment had they received more and better instruction in English usage while in school.

Closely allied with the language difficulties encountered by the Indian as he endeavors to attain vocational success are those related to his concurrent movement in increasing numbers away from the essentially rural and isolated setting of the reservation to the larger population centers of the United States. There are, for example, some forty-five thousand Indians in the Los Angeles area alone (Belindo 1967, p. 188). Similarly increasing concentrations of Indian populations may be noted not only in those metropolitan areas geographically close to the reservations, but in such distant cities as Chicago as well.

An excellent long-range examination of Indian urbanization was the five-year project conducted by Hurt (1966) in South Dakota. Included in his findings is a discussion of the relative usage of the native Dakota language and of English by groups of Indians exhibiting varying degrees of assimilation into the culture of an urban community. Related studies concerning urbanization among the Indians of South Dakota include those of Lovrich (1951) and White (1959). The work of Ritzenthaler and Sellers (1953) with Indians in the city of Milwaukee and that of Roy (1962) in the Spokane, Washington, area also falls in this category.

CONCLUSIONS AND IMPLICATIONS

This paper has first presented a broad overview of the literature which treats those relationships which have been identified between language and the state of Indian poverty in America. It seems obvious, even to the most casual critic, that there yet remains much research to be done before the gaps in this literature have been filled. Currently, the bulk of the writings which concern the language-poverty relationships among contemporary Indian cultures are limited to two primary areas: that of education and that of vocational preparation and success, coupled with its related phenomenon of urbanization. Scattered here and there, one occasionally finds studies in tangential areas. Unfortunately, however, these are the rare exceptions rather than the rule. One such exception is the recent report of Dizmang (1967) concerning the high incidence of suicide among the Cheyenne. A significant segment of his paper is centered upon the language and communication difficulties of these Indians.

Prevention and Remediation

Although it would require another paper, indeed most likely another volume, to summarize the large number and wide variety of programs being undertaken to help the Indian overcome his educational and vocational handicaps—including those of language—the following programs are noted here for purposes of illustration:
1. The innovative three-year College Orientation Program for Alaskan Natives (COPAN) recently concluded at the University of Alaska (Salisbury 1965, 1967).
2. The pioneering work of Roessel and his associates, first at the Rough Rock Demonstration School (Conklin 1967; Pfeiffer 1968; Roessel 1967, 1968, and Witherspoon 1968) and more recently at the new community college on the Navajo Reservation.
3. The landmark survey, *The Study of the Problems of Teaching English to American Indians*, by the Center for Applied Linguistics for the Bureau of Indian Affairs (Ohannessian, 1967).
4. The developmental conference, Speech Communication and the American Indian High School Student, cosponsored by the Communication Research

Center of the University of Kansas and the Institute of Indian Studies at
the University of South Dakota (Osborn, 1968).

5. The new "family residential training" programs at Madera, California,
Roswell, New Mexico, and Pearl River, Mississippi, initiated in 1967 by the
Bureau of Indian Affairs (Bennett, 1968).

Research Needs

In summary, there are a number of general inferences and a few conclusions which may be drawn from that body of literature which treats the
language-poverty relationships in contemporary North American Indian culture. First and foremost, there is a discouraging scarcity of well-designed,
well-controlled, well-administered, and well-interpreted research studies from
which meaningful predictions may be made concerning these relationships.
The following excerpts from the general observations of Boyce (1964b, pp.
82–84) with regard to Indian research are most fitting in this instance:

> There is a tremendous lack of working data about almost every
> Indian tribe today, and there is a tremendous need for research about
> Indians. . . . In view of the many years of dealing with the baffling
> problem of incorporating the Indian into our society, there should
> be available a large body of germane data on every Indian tribe.
> . . . It is next to impossible to run down reliable data about the
> nature of the Indian himself. This is a serious handicap . . . . In the
> case of Indian affairs, there have been plenty of investigations and
> surveys. A superabundance of them. Unfortunately, from the scien-
> tific point of view, these have largely been compilations of opinion
> —of various degrees of expertness . . . . Perhaps the greatest unmet
> need today in Indian affairs is sustained, scientific social research.

One of the most promising responses to this need is the National Study of
American Indian Education being conducted by Havighurst and his associates
under the auspices of the U. S. Office of Education (1968).

Summary and Overview

As one attempts to examine relationships between the language capabilities of the Indian and his state of poverty, this examination must take into
account an imposing array of disparate languages and dialects—some of which
are disappearing and, in contrast, others in which the number of potential
speakers is increasing. It also is apparent, to repeat the words of Thompson
(1965, p. 1), that "a good command of the English language today, more than
ever before, is the master key to Indians' successful transition to twentieth
century living." The degree of acquisition and usage of this "master key" varies
widely from those older Indians who speak little or no English at all to some
of the younger generation who learned English as their first language and are

totally unfamiliar with their native languages. The manner and form in which English as a second language has been taught have evolved from an earlier philosophy of total obliteration of the native language to the current belief of many that the Indian child should be educated for productive citizenship in both the Indian and non-Indian communities and, hence, must be literate in both languages.

Several of the better studies concerning Indian education have dealt with scholastic ability and acheivement. The results of these have indicated that the Indian child has no inherited educational disadvantage when compared with his non-Indian peers. When measures not dependent upon knowledge of the English language have been utilized, the Indian child has been found to perform within the national norms. In some instances, indeed, the Indian pupil has exhibited certain performances superior to those of the non-Indian (Havighurst 1966).

It has been shown that the Indian child seems to compensate for his language differences in the early elementary grades. However, from about the fourth grade, when English proficiency becomes a crucial factor in academic success, he frequently begins to fall behind his non-Indian classmates in scholastic performance.

Closely linked with this lag in academic achievement is a progressively higher incidence of dropouts among Indian school children. The rate steadily increases through the upper elementary, intermediate, and secondary grades until it ultimately is manifested in the extremely small number of Indian young people who graduate from college. Surveys of vocational success and satisfaction among employed Indians also have revealed close ties to employee proficiency in English. Similar links have been observed in the relatively few studies reported which deal with the urbanization of Indian populations.

At this point in time, perhaps the safest generalization which may be offered is that all signs point to very significant relationships among Indian poverty, the native American languages, and the degree to which English has become a workable social, economic, and educational tool of our first citizens. In far too few instances have these relationships been subjected to precise measurement and evaluation. When and where such research has been undertaken, it often has lent support to many of the subjective observations and hunches which have guided our thinking and action concerning the Indian over the years. Without question, there remains today a great body of pioneering work yet to be done. Conscience dictates and scholarly responsibility demands that far greater investments of time, effort, and money be devoted to the elimination of those barriers to full citizenship in space-age America which still plague the Indian and often relegate him to a second-class, primitive existence (see, for example, the remarks on this subject by former President Johnson 1968, p. 2).

As a closing thought, an observation from the pen of a young Navajo man who has traveled the long road from youthful sheepherder to college student seems most fitting. The writer is Emerson Blackhorse (Barney) Mitchell, and the words are drawn from the conclusion of his captivating autobiography, *Miracle Hill: The Story of a Navajo Boy* (Mitchell and Allen 1967, p. 222). As he thinks upon his recent graduation from the Institute of American Indian Arts in Santa Fe, New Mexico, and contemplates the significance of the English language which he has learned to use so eloquently—even though this usage is flavored strongly by his native tongue—Mitchell reflects:

> At last, I know a little, I have accomplished, and achieve the knowledge and wisdom of my distance (*sic*) friends. Ever I shall use their tongue to understand and to communicate, exchange gifts, for their tongue is the barrier of destruction to my people.

***

As this volume goes to press, the United States Senate Special Subcommittee on Indian Education has just released its final report, "Indian Education: A National Tragedy—A National Challenge." The document, Report No. 91–501 of the 91st Congress, contains certain data concerning the North American Indian more current than those available at the time this chapter was written.

REFERENCES

Anderson, K., et al. *The Educational Achievement of Indian Children.* Lawrence, Kan.: Haskell Press, 1953.

Baker, J. E. Problems of Navajo male graduates of Intermountain School during their first year of employment. Master's thesis, Utah State University, 1959.

Beatty, W. W. *Education for Action.* Chilocco, Okla.: Printing Department, Chilocco Agricultural School, 1944.

Belindo, J. Statement. *Report of Proceedings of Hearing Held before Special Subcommittee on Indian Education of the Committee on Labor and Public Welfare, United States Senate.* Washington, D.C.: Ward and Paul, Official Reporters, December 14, 1967, pp. 186–204.

Bennett, R. L. *Indian Affairs 1967.* Washington D.C.: U. S. Government Printing Office, 1968.

Boas, F. Introduction. *Handbook of American Indian Languages.* Part I. Washington, D.C.: Smithsonian Institution, 1911.

Boyce, G.A. Why do Indians quit school? In H. Thompson, ed., *Education for Cross-cultural Enrichment.* Lawrence, Kan.: Haskell Press, 1964. (a)
———. What we don't know about Indians. In H. Thompson, ed., *Education for Cross-cultural Enrichment.* Lawrence, Kan.: Haskell Press, 1964.(b)

Brophy, W. A., and Aberle, S. D. *The Indian: America's Unfinished Business*. Norman, Okla.: University of Oklahoma Press, 1966.

Bryde, J. F. *The Sioux Indian Student: A Study of Scholastic Failure and Personality Conflict*. Pine Ridge, S. D.: Holy Rosary Mission, 1966.

Coleman, J. S., et al. *Equality of Educational Opportunity.* Washington, D.C.: U. S. Government Printing Office, 1966.

Conklin, P. Good day at Rough Rock. *American Education* 1967, 3: 4–9.

Coombs, L.M. The educational needs of Indian students. Paper presented at the workshop for directors of NDEA institutes for educators of American Indian pupils, March 1967, Lawrence, Kansas.

Coombs, L. M., et al. *The Indian Child Goes to School: A Study of Interracial Differences.* Lawrence, Kan.: Haskell Press, 1958.

Dizmang, L. H. Suicide among the Cheyenne Indians. *Bulletin of Suicidology* July 1967, 8–11.

Farb, P. *Man's Rise to Civilization As Shown by the Indians of North America from Primeval Times to the Coming of the Industrial State.* New York: Dutton, 1968.

Fishman, J. A. *Language Loyalty in the United States.* The Hague: Mouton, 1966.

Gaarder, A. B. Education of American Indian children. Paper presented at the annual round table meeting on linguistics and language studies of the School of Languages and Linguistics, March 1968, Georgetown Univer-· sity, Washington.

Goddard, S. A. The Zuni language as a means of interpreting Pueblo Indian culture. Master's thesis, University of New Mexico, 1930.

Gordon, E. W. A bibliography on disadvantaged populations. *I. R. C. D. Bulletin: Publication of the ERIC Information Retrieval Center on the Disadvantaged* 1967, 3: No. 4, 2–6.

Hand, N. Improving school attendance. *Indian Education* 1963, No. 388, 7–8

Havighurst, R. J. Education among American Indians: individual and cultural aspects. *Annals of the American Academy of Political and Social Sciences* 1957, No. 311, 105–15.

———. Who are the disadvantaged? In S. W. Webster, ed., *Knowing the Disadvantaged.* San Francisco: Chandler, 1966.

Hoijer, H. Linguistic and cultural change. *Language* 1948, 24: 335–45.

———. Cultural implications of some Navajo linguistic categories. *Language* 1951, 27: 111–20.

———. The relation of language to culture. In A. L. Kroeber, et al., eds., *Anthropology Today.* Chicago: University of Chicago Press, 1953.

———. The Sapir-Whorf hypothesis. In *Language in Culture.* Chicago: University of Chicago Press, 1954.

———. Semantic patterns of the Navajo language. In Helmut Gipper, ed., *Sprache-Schlüssel zur Welt.* Düsseldorf: Pädagogischer Verlag Schwann, 1959.

Hopkins, T. R. Problems the Indian student faces today. Paper presented during the NDEA Institute for Advanced Study for Secondary Teachers of Speech to American Indian Pupils, June 1966, Lawrence, Kansas.

———. *Language Testing of North American Indians.* Washington, D.C.: Bureau of Indian Affairs, 1967.

Howe, H. Breaking the language barrier. In *A Chance for a Change.* Washington, D.C.: U. S. Government Printing Office, 1966.

Hurt, W. R., Jr. The urbanization of the Yankton Indians. In S. W. Webster, ed., *Knowing the Disadvantaged.* San Francisco: Chandler, 1966.

Hymes, D., ed. *Language in Culture and Society.* New York: Harper & Row, 1964.

Jackson, K. Communication skills needed by college-bound students. In H. Thompson, ed., *Education for Cross-cultural Enrichment.* Lawrence, Kan.: Haskell Press, 1964.

Johnson, L. B. The President's message to the Congress on goals and programs for the American Indian; March 6, 1968. *Indian Record* 1968, special issue, No. 2.

Levine, S., and Lurie, N. O., eds. *The American Indian Today.* Delano, Fla.: Everett & Edwards, 1968.

Lovrich, F. The assimilation of the Indian in Rapid City. Master's thesis, State University of South Dakota, 1951.

Maloy, T. C. The child who isn't there. *Indian Education* 1963, No. 388, 6–7.

Miller, R. E. One by one. *Indian Education* 1965, No. 419, 3–4.

Mitchell, E. B., and Allen, T. D. *Miracle Hill: The Story of a Navajo Boy.* Norman, Okla.: University of Oklahoma Press, 1967.

Monacchio, G. School record of isolates. *Indian Education* 1964, No. 405: 6–7.

Montoya, D. Statement. *Report of Proceedings of Hearing Held before Special Subcommittee on Indian Education of the Committee on Labor and Public Welfare, United States Senate.* Washington, D.C.: Ward and Paul, Official Reporters, December 14, 1967, pp. 102–18.

Muehe, R. P. Improving school attendance on the Yakima reservation. *Indian Education* 1966, No. 428, 7–8.

Officer, J. E. English in the education of Indian children. In V. F. Allen, ed., *On Teaching English to Speakers of Other Languages: Series I.* Champaign, Ill.: National Council of Teachers of English, 1965.

Ohannessian, S., ed. *The Study of the Problems of Teaching English to American Indians.* Washington, D.C.: Center for Applied Linguistics, 1967.

Orata, P. T. *Fundamental Education in an Amerindian Community.* Lawrence, Kan.: Haskell Press, 1953.

Osborn, L. R. Speech communication and the American Indian high school student. *The Speech Teacher* 1968. 17: 38–43.

Owen, R. C.; Deetz, J. J. F.; and Fisher, A. D., eds. *The North American Indians.* A Sourcebook . New York: Macmillan, 1967.

Peterson, S. *How Well are Indian Children Educated?* Lawrence, Kan.: Haskell Press, 1948.

Pfieffer, A. Educational innovation. *J. American Indian Education* 1968, 7: No. 3, 24–31.

Reel, E. *Teaching Indian Pupils to Speak English.* Washington, D.C.: U. S. Government Printing Office, 1904.

Ritzenthaler, R. R., and Sellers, M. Indians in urban situation, a preliminary report. Mimeographed. Milwaukee: 1953.

Roessel, R. A., Jr. A new dimension in the education of American Indian children: the Rough Rock story. Paper presented at the workshop for directors of NDEA institutes for educators of American Indian pupils, March 1967, Lawrence, Kansas.

———. An overview of the Rough Rock Demonstration School. *J. American Indian Education* 1968, 7: No. 3, 2–14.

Roy, P. The measurement of assimilation: the Spokane Indians. *American J. Sociology* 1962, 67: 541–51.

Salisbury, L. H. The speech education of the Alaskan Indian student as viewed by the speech educator. *J. American Indian Education* 1965, 4: No. 3, 1–7.
———. Teaching English to Alaska natives. *J. American Indian Education* 1967, 6: No. 2, 1–12.
Sapir, E. The status of linguistics as a science. *Language* 1929, 5: 207–14.
Spencer, R. F.; Jennings, J. D.; et al. *The Native Americans.* New York: Harper & Row, 1965.
Thompson, H. The language laboratory. *Indian Education* 1962, No. 378, 1–3.
———. Cultural empathy. *Indian Education* 1963, No. 387, 1–3.
———. Another look at dropouts. In *Education for Cross-cultural Enrichment* . Lawrence, Kan.: Haskell Press, 1964.(a)
———. Goals for the future. In *Education for Cross-cultural Enrichment.* Lawrence, Kan.: Haskell Press, 1964.(b)
———. Culture and language. *Indian Education* 1965, No. 418, 1–3.
———. Calling all education employees. *Indian Education* 1966, No. 429, 1–3.(a)
———. A survey of factors contributing to success or failure of Indian students at Northern Arizona University. *Indian Education* 1966, No. 439, 1–8.(b)
———. A review of present policies and practices in teaching oral English (speaking and listening) to Indian pupils in grades 7-14. Paper presented during the conference on speech communication and the American Indian high school student, May 1967, Vermillion, South Dakota.
Thompson, H., et al. Teaching English to Indian students. In *Education for Cross-cultural Enrichment.* Lawrence, Kan.: Haskell Press, 1964.
Timmons, B. J. Z. An exploratory investigation of attitudes toward certain speech communication variables found among male post-high school vocational students at Haskell Indian Institute, Lawrence, Kansas. Doctoral dissertation, University of Kansas, 1965.
U. S. Office of Education. USOE sponsors national study of Indian education. *Indian Education Newsletter* 1968, 1: No. 3, 1.
Voegelin, C. F. North American Indian languages still spoken and their genetic relationships. In L. Spier; A. J. Hallowell; and S. S. Newman, eds., *Language, Culture, and Personality.* Menasha, Wis.: Banta, 1941.
Wax, R., and Wax, M. Indian education for what? In S. Levine and N. O. Lurie, eds., *The American Indian Today.* Delano, Fla.: Everett & Edwards, 1968.
White, R. The urbanization of the Dakota Indians. Master's thesis, St. Louis University, 1959.
Whorf, B. L. The relation of habitual thought and behavior to language. In L. Spier; A. J. Hallowell; and S. S. Newman, eds., *Language, Culture, and Personality.* Menasha, Wis.: Banta, 1941.

————. An American Indian model of the universe. *International J. American Linguistics* 1950, 16: 67–72.

————. *Collected Papers on Metalinguistics.* Washington, D.C.: Department of State, Foreign Service Institute, 1952.

————. A linguistic consideration of thinking in primitive communities. In J. B. Carroll, ed., *Language, Thought and Reality. Selected Writings of Benjamin Lee Whorf.* Cambridge, Mass.: M.I.T. Press, 1956.

Witherspoon, G. Navajo curriculum center. *J. American Indian Education* 1968, 7: No. 3, 36–41.

Chapter 13

BIOLOGICAL AND SOCIAL FACTORS IN LANGUAGE DEVELOPMENT

Harry Osser*

Presumably, many of the language problems of the so-called disadvantaged child should be susceptible to interpretation relative to comtemporary research and theory in the area of language acquisition. On the contrary, however, what this appeal to research and theory reveals to us is that the contemporary picture is in a state of substantial flux. If we are to benefit at all from consulting this changing picture, it is important to have some knowledge of the various positions which it incorporates. In this paper, we will review some of these positions, and at the same time show how they lead to contrasting emphases and implications regarding the language of the disadvantaged child.

In contemporary psycholinguistics a predominant point of view is that the child is "prewired" for language behavior, so that his linguistic abilities depend largely on the unraveling of maturational processes. This clearly nativistic view is postulated by a number of linguists and psycholinguists, including, for example, Chomsky (1965), Lenneberg (1967), and McNeill (1966). The theoretical counterpart of their views appears in the work of Skinner (1957) and Mowrer (1960) who, in stressing the role of environmental, or social, factors, argue that the child acquires language by being reinforced for imitating the speech patterns of the people around him. A somewhat different environmentalist position, which is neutral with respect to the controversy between the nativists and empiricists over the origin of language behavior, is derived from the research and theorizing of the sociolinguists (Grimshaw, in press)

*Department of Psychology, San Francisco State College

who are primarily interested in the role of social structural factors, such as social-class membership, type of family structure, and role relations between speaker and listener, on the use of language in particular situations. We will next consider these positions in some detail.

THE NATIVIST POSITION

A Biolinguistic Viewpoint

One of the most detailed arguments in support of the nativist position is presented by Lenneberg (1967), who proposes that language development is a function of maturational factors, and that human language is a species-specific phenomenon. He argues that nonhumans can never be trained to use language in a human manner because underlying speech there are a number of anatomical and physiological features that do not exist in species below the level of man. These include differences in oropharyngeal morphology, cerebral dominance, specialization of cerebrocortical typography, special coordination centers for motor speech, specialized temporal pattern perception, special respiratory adjustment, and tolerance for prolonged speech activities. All of the special features together permit speech reception and the precise and very rapid movements of the articulators that are necessary for speech production.

In arguing that language development is a function of maturational factors, Lenneberg (1967, pp. 128-130) refers to the parallels between language and motor development in children from twelve weeks through four years. His interpretation of this information is that there is a synchrony between the attainment of each language milestone and the development of particular motor skills. Language cannot begin to develop until the child has attained a certain level of physical maturation and growth. This view is vulnerable, of course, to the discovery of a lack of synchrony between the two types of development in individual cases.

Language development is often divided into two major stages, prelinguistic and linguistic. During the prelinguistic stage, approximately from birth up to twelve months, the infant produces a number of different kinds of vocalizations, e.g., cooing, chuckling, and babbling. When the child enters the linguistic stage (at about 12 months), he begins to use individual words. Lenneberg, Rebelsky, and Nichols (1965) have studied the prelinguistic sound making of both deaf and hearing infants. The deaf infants not only went through the same sequence of vocalizations as the hearing infants, but they also produced as much noise. This suggests that the emergence of prelinguistic behavior does not depend upon social factors such as training or reward, but instead is a function of maturational factors.

Lenneberg also argues that the transition from prelinguistic to linguistic behaviors occurs as a function of maturational processes. He states that there is no evidence that the onset of speech in the child is correlated with the initiation of any special language training by the mother. In support of this claim, Lenneberg refers to the research results of Morley (1957), who carried out a large-scale longitudinal study of the language development of children whose backgrounds were heterogeneous. She found that notwithstanding considerable differences in social milieu, the onset of speech occurred at about the same time for the great majority of the children. Lenneberg may be correct in his statement that the onset of language is unrelated to training, but since our information on the verbal interactions between parents and children is very sparse, the opposite argument could, of course, be proposed. That is to say, there is no evidence to suggest that the onset of speech is independent of social factors, for as Morley observed, not all children begin to speak at the same time. Lenneberg's view would probably be that individual differences in time-of-speech onset are correlated with individual differences in rate of motor development; that is, he would explain such differences as biologically based.

Not only is the onset of speech a very regular event for most children, but according to Lenneberg's (1967, pp. 133-134) own research, children also attain other milestones of language development in a fixed sequence and at a relatively constant chronological age. He found that 450 out of 500 children were able, at thirty nine months, to name a large number of objects in their houses, to comprehend spoken instructions, and to prcduce structurally complex sentences spontaneously and fairly intelligibly.

Lenneberg derives additional evidence for the maturational viewpoint from studies of abnormal children. He found, for example, that in mongoloid children, as in normal children, there was the same synchrony between motor and language milestones of development. The difference between the two groups was that the developmental process was stretched out beyond the usual time limits for the mongoloid group. Lenneberg interprets such evidence as the strongest support for the argument that language development is regulated by maturational phenomena.

Lenneberg argues that speech acquisition is unlike the acquisition of many skills where large individual differences exist which depend upon genetic factors, yet considerable training is also necessary before the skill develops maturely. He claims that language as a skill is different from, say, piano playing, in that equal aptitude for it is exhibited in a much larger number of individuals than for the latter. In addition, the onset of language skill occurs very early, and appears not to need particular training.

There is a problem with Lenneberg's argument that language as a skill is unlike many other skills in that many more prople show equal aptitude in it; this is that the term *language skill* remains undefined. A similar problem exists in the psycholinguistic and linguistic literature where the statement is made that by three years (or in some instances by four, or five, or six years) the child has acquired the basic structures of his language; again a key term remains undefined. There are probably a large number of language skills, and the question is whether there are small or large differences in such skills.

Lenneberg's argument, in summary form, is that the child's capacity to learn language is a consequence of maturation. The evidence he provides is that the milestones of language development are normally interlocked with stages of motor development which are themselves distinctly related to physical maturation. Such synchrony is preserved even when the whole maturational schedule is slowed down, as in cases of pathology. There is no evidence that the onset of language is related to special training. The capacity for language acquisition is intimately related to the maturation of uniquely human anatomical and physiological characteristics. Language is a species-specific behavior.

Lenneberg acknowledges the existence of individual differences in language ability, and he suggests that they relate to complex interactions between biological and social factors. He offers two interpretations of the frequent experimental finding that disadvantaged (i.e., lower-class) children exhibit poorer language performances than middle-class children. Lenneberg (1967, p. 136) speculates that such observed differences may be a function of nutritional factors, or due to the experimenter's inadequate sampling techniques.

Lenneberg's interest in the commonalities of language performance, rather than individual and group differences, has not led him to examine closely the role of social factors in language development. The two major research suggestions relating to the language problems of the disadvantaged that derive from Lenneberg's biolinguistic viewpoint are: (1) to search for biological factors (e.g., early nutritional deficiencies) that may account for such problems, and (2) to obtain more adequate speech samples in contrastive studies of lower-class and middle-class children than has previously been the case. There are only limited suggestions in the biolinguistic viewpoint for the remedial treatment of the disadvantaged child.[1] Perhaps the main suggestion is to ensure adequate nutritional support for the child's physical development. The value of such a suggestion is severely curtailed by our ignorance of the role of nutritional factors in language development.

---

[1]We should acknowledge the feeling currently expressed by some that intersections between a biolinguistic perspective and Jensen's (1969) arguments about genetically-based restrictions upon intellectual development should be explored. As of this writing, however, most of the concern with this issue is focused upon Jensen's position itself, and until some of the questions on this are resolved it will probably not be profitable to explore the significance of his position relative to biolinguistic theory, let alone to combine the two when considering the disadvantaged child.

A Linguistic Viewpoint

The linguist Chomsky (1965) maintains that the child's ability to produce and understand novel sentences can only be understood by assuming that he has an innate language capacity. In particular, Chomsky posits the existence of a language acquisition device, which is, of course, an abstraction, so that he can account for the disparity between the linguistic input to the child, and his ouput. This device therefore refers to a hypothetical set of innate mechanisms that permit the child to analyze incoming linguistic data, and to produce messages. Chomsky asserts that linguistic principles are not learned at all, but are simply part of the innate conceptual capacities brought to the language-learning situation by the child.

Chomsky asserts that the child acquires language by discovering its underlying system of grammatical rules. The processes characterized by the language acquisition device incorporate a built-in set of specifications for correct grammars, plus a testing capability which permits the child to discover which particular grammar, from out of a small set of correct grammars, is appropriate for the language he is exposed to. The device receives a sample of the possible sentences in the language, and the child abstracts the regularities from them; or, in other words, he acquires the rules of the language. Once the child has done this, he can now go far beyond the particular sample of sentences he has heard, so that he can produce and understand novel sentences.

The role of experience in Chomsky's model of language acquisition is quite limited. The child uses language input solely to eliminate his false hypotheses about the rules of a language. This position is that all the child requires for developing language is exposure to a small amount of the language he is to learn. That which is defined as the language acquisition device provides him with a preknowledge of language universals, i.e., the rules and constituents which underlie all languages. The child's remaining task is to learn the unique rules of his own language. It is clear that Chomsky's model of language acquisition provides only a passive role for environmental, or social, factors, whereas the child is assigned a very active role in his own language development.

Chomsky (1965) asserts that the child inevitably acquires the language of his culture. Such learning relates to his intrinsic cognitive resources, and is only minimally dependent upon extrinsic supports. Chomsky emphasizes the basic human equality with regards to linguistic competence (i.e., knowledge of the language) by contrast to linguistic performance (i.e., actual behavior).[2] Chomsky's position contains virtually no suggestions for the remediation of

---

[2]This theoretical distinction of competence-performance is treated in more detail by Menyuk (Chapter 10) in this volume. Its application to subcultural differences in children's language was earlier posed by Cazden (1967), but as can be seen from her chapter (5) in the present volume, she has modified her ideas on this application.

the language problems of disadvantaged children. He does suggest one general direction which research on children's language should take, and this suggestion has implications for studies of both advantaged and disadvantaged children. Chomsky (1964) argues that valid assessments of language development require the use of many different kinds of measurements. One example of recent research on disadvantaged children which attempts to meet requirement is that of Osser, Wang, and Zaid (1969), who compared the linguistic performances of a group of lower-class Negro preschoolers with those of a group of middle-class white children. Two tasks were employed, including one of speech imitation and one of speech comprehension. These tasks were designed to evaluate the child's control over different syntactic structures of standard English. It was assumed that there were differences in the linguistic environments of the two groups, which would result in differences being observed in their performances on the experimental tasks. In general, the findings were consistent with this expectation. However, on one of a number of different indicators of performance—namely, 100 percent correct responses to a syntactic structure for either the imitation task or the comprehension task —the differences between the two groups, with regard to control over the test structures, were insignificant. Does this evidence allow the interpretation that both groups are equal in linguistic development, at least with respect to the test structures? The answer depends upon the definition of *linguistic control*. Some investigators may accept the single use of a grammatical structure as evidence of control, whereas others may demand more stringent conditions be met before the child is assumed to exhibit control over that structure. However this definitional dilemma is resolved, it seems clear that Chomsky's suggestion concerning multiple measurements of language performance is extremely valuable.

A Psycholinguistic Viewpoint

Chomsky's (1965) formulation of the major features of child language acquisition is accepted by McNeill (1966) who looks at the theoretical problems of language development from the different perspective of a psycholinguist. He is concerned, for example, with specifying the child's innate linguistic rules, and also with the description of the particular set of rules that the child uses at different stages of his development. McNeill, like other developmental psycholinguists, is interested in the convergence of the child's language system onto the adult model.

McNeill views the language acquisition device as necessarily highly structured, because the input to it is unstructured (e.g., incomplete sentences, typically disfluent speech), yet its output, which conforms to grammatical rules, is highly structured. He envisages the internal organization of the device as being made up of two components. One component consists of certain kinds of linguistic information in the category of language universals, and the other is a set of procedures that enable the child to analyze his linguistic input.

By this view the child knows the ways in which a language can be structured; that is, he has knowledge of language universals, which are the general forms of human language. Such general forms have presumably developed to match human capacities, and if this is in fact the case, then it is reasonable to expect that a description of language universals would illuminate the character of the acquisition device. Every language uses the same syntactic categories, arranged in the same way—the syntactic categories of sentences, noun phrases, and verb phrases. The same grammatical relations obtain among these categories as, for example, the subject and predicate of a sentence, verb and object of a verb phrase, and so on. These basic grammatical relations correspond to the traditional grammatical functions of subject, predicate, verb, object modifier, and head. If such relations are universal, what is the evidence that they are present in children's early speech?

If all children are endowed with language universals, then their early linguistic outputs should be very similar, and only later would they show divergence toward their particular grammars. The examination of cross-cultural data would therefore provide a direct test of McNeill's view that the child who begins to learn a language already knows the major syntactic categories, which appear universally in human languages. There is a small amount of supportive information for this position. It has been observed that children from several different language communities use two similarly functioning form classes when they begin to speak in two-word sentences, notwithstanding large differences in the respective adult languages. Slobin (1966) refers to a Russian child who had a pivot class (P) and an open class (O) that coincided with the same classes of words that were used by an English-speaking child investigated by Brown and Fraser (1964). Both children included in their P-class, demonstratives, personal pronouns, various adjectives, and several determiners. The P-class seems to subserve a modifier function, and there is no single class of modifiers in Russian or English which corresponds to the two children's P-class. McNeill suggests that children come equipped to notice a general function of modification when it occurs in the speech of adults, so that they learn to categorize words which serve this function.

McNeill (in press) later offered a more elaborate view of the development of the P- and O-classes. He thought originally that each represented a very generalized grammatical category, but he now views the construction of the two classes as evidence of the child's learning of syntactic features. This change in interpretation was necessary to take into account the occasional finding that adjectives, as well as members of other form classes, have been found in both P- and O-classes (the O-class consists usually of nouns only), and was also

attributable to changes in linguistic theory regarding the nature of word categorization. These views consist of a discussion of the syntactic features of
various categories and subcategories of words. For example, nouns can be
cross-classified in terms of many distinguishing features, such as common,
proper, inanimate, so that words in the same form class can have different
syntactic features.

McNeill's proposal is that the very young child responds perhaps to one
syntactic feature of a word, and places all words with this syntactic feature into
the same class. McNeill assumes that in very early speech, children have two
categories, one of which is a modifier category (the P-class) and the other is
a modified category (the O-class). If the child also responds to another feature
of the same word, he may then place it into more than one category. In order
to develop the modifier and modified categories, the child must, according to
McNeill, be able to understand the basic grammatical relations between them,
which then permits him to identify which of the two words has the modifier
function and which one has the modified function. Such knowledge, according
to McNeill's interpretation, depends upon the innate characteristics of the
language acquisition device.

McNeill's view of the process of language acquisition has led him, like
Lenneberg (1967), to focus upon the similarity in linguistic performance
among very young children, and, of course, the confirmation that similarities
do exist in the early syntax of Russian and American children has buttressed
his theoretical viewpoint. McNeill's stress on nativistic factors does not offer
any obvious suggestions either for research into the linguistic problems of the
disadvantaged, nor for programs of remediation.

Evaluation of the Nativist Position

It has not been customary in psychology to posit a great deal of internal
organization as the basis for behavior, although some innate mechanisms are
postulated by most theorists. The behaviorists, for example, have accepted the
capacities of association formation, and stimulus and response generalization
as native properties of the organism. The nativists go much beyond this description of innate capacities and claim many more endowments for the child.
Their view is that the child has available unlearned procedures for analyzing
speech input, and abilities for hypothesis testing, as well as an inborn preknowledge of the universal features of language structure. Without such capacities, the nativists assert, the child could not acquire a language. They argue
that without the postulation of such capacities there cannot be developed any
adequate explanation for what we observe as the child's productive use of
language.

The evidence for the nativist position is, with the exception of the information provided by cross-cultural comparisons of early speech, largely of an indirect nature. There is one kind of support in Lenneberg's arguments that language is a species-specific phenomenon and is genetically determined. Another type of supportive evidence derives from the study of language universals. The nativist view of language universals is that all human languages share these features because all humans share specific learning capacities.

None of the arguments put forward by the nativists proves their case for elaborate language-information-processing abilities. The nativists however, provide the basic question that any substantial theory of child language acquisition will have to answer: How does a child go beyond the examples of sentences he hears in the speech around him?

THE ENVIRONMENTALIST POSITION

Psychologists who work within the framework of behaviorism (e.g., Skinner 1957; Mowrer 1960) have taked about language development in terms of the traditional categories of explanation derived from learning theory—namely, reinforcement and generalization—rather than invoking the learning of rules and innate supportive mechanisms. The beginning of language behavior, as described by Mowrer (1960), can be summarized as follows: The infant begins to learn language by associating the sounds of the human voice, particularly his mother's, with need-satisfying circumstances (e.g., milk drinking). The result of this is that when he hears his own random babbling, he is more likely to repeat those sounds that are similar to the pleasurable sounds made by his mother. Thus the pleasure associated with the mother's voice now becomes transferred to the child's own vocalizations. Mowrer's argument may be extended as follows: As the mother tends to reward the infant's sounds, particularly if they approximate adult speech patterns, the child learns that his imitations are generally reinforced, and thus he is on his way to learning those speech patterns. This model of language acquisition may be designated the imitation-reinforcement model. So far the explanation is only applicable to the child's acquisition of sounds, words, and sentences that he has heard. Since a child produces for the most part novel sentences (ones that he has not heard or produced before), an additional explanation is necessary.

The problem of explaining novel behaviors has usually led behaviorists to suggest that the speaker is reinforced for certain behaviors, so that he generalizes his responses to new stimulus situations. There is a major problem in using the explanatory concept of generalization in the interpretation of novel linguistic behavior. In a typical generalization experiment, an organism is said to have shown generalization when after being trained to respond to one stimulus, it also responds to a second stimulus. Response transfer is usually explained by referring to the similarity between the two stimuli, where the similarity is specifiable along a physical dimension, such as intensity of sound, and so on. In trying to use the generalization argument to explain, say, the child's acquisition of the plural forms for English, it is not only extremely difficult to define the stimulus situations which result in such learning, but it is equally difficult to see how arguments that relate to responses based on physical similarities can be carried over to situations where physical similarity is not involved. The morphological signals for the noun plural in English are physically quite different, for example, glass*es*, boy*s*, doughnut*s*, and pant*s* (which has no singular form, so is considered to embody a "zero-morpheme").

Newer views of generalization have been propsed by Jenkins and Palermo (1964), and Braine (1963a, b). They explain novel linguistic behavior as a contextual generalization phenomenon, which means basically that a child learns to use a word in a particular position, and then generalizes the use of this word to similar sentence positions. This viewpoint has some very serious defects, as Bever, Fodor, and Weksel (1965) have pointed out. In essence, the contextual generalization hypothesis does not take into consideration that the same word can appear in a large number of different contexts, so that if the child had to acquire language by contextual generalization, he would probably need considerably longer than he seems to take in achieving mature usage.

What is the role of reinforcement in language acquisition? The Lenneberg, Rebelsky, and Nichols (1965) study of the prelinguistic vocalizations of deaf children strongly suggests that at least for the first few months of vocalization no social reinforcement is necessary. Can the same be said for the development of linguistic behavior? Brown, Cazden, and Bellugi (1969) have evidence that bears upon this question. They analyzed the conversations between mother and child to determine whether there is anything like grammatical training by the mother going on. In inspecting the grammatical correctness of the child's utterances which were followed by some expression of approval (positive social reinforcement), they found that grammatical contingencies did not govern the mother's approval or disapproval of the child's speech. Instead, the truth or falsity of the utterance defined such approval or disapproval. For example, when Eve said, "Mama isn't boy; he a girl," the mother answered, "That's right." Eve used the wrong pronoun, but her mother knew what she meant, and what she meant was in fact true. However, when Adam said in perfectly grammatical English, "Walt Disney comes on, on Tuesday," his mother said "That's not right," because the child was wrong about the day of the week. Brown, Cazden, and Bellugi note that the parents they studied typically rewarded true statements and punished false ones, which results paradoxically in speakers who are highly grammatical, but not notably truthful. Even if the child were reinforced for grammatical statements, and punished for nongrammatical statements, such parent behavior only provides the child with information on the acceptability of particular sentences. The fact that the child can generate novel sentences for which he has not been rewarded remains unexplained.

What is the role of imitation in language acquisition? There is evidence that imitation is not necessarily involved in speech comprehension. Lenneberg (1962) describes a child who could not talk because of a congenital disability that affected the development of motor speech skills. This child nevertheless could understand elaborate instructions, for example, "Take the block and put it on the bottle"; "Is it time to eat breakfast now?" and (after being told a story), "Was the black cat fed by the nice lady?" This child obviously could not imitate speech, nor could he have ever been reinforced for speech production.

Does imitation have any role in language development? In a general sense the answer has to be yes, for without being provided with samples of the language to be learned, and unless he operated on these samples in some way, the child could not learn his language. Slobin (1968) suggests a specific role for imitation in language development. He examined the child's imitations of the parent's expansions, where an expansion is the parent's imitation of what the child says, but with additional elements supplied. For example, the child says, "Papa name Papa," the mother expands this to "Papa's name is Papa, uhhum," and the child imitates the mother's utterance, and in doing so adds something not in his original sentence, for example, "Papa name *is* Papa." Slobin found that Adam and Eve (children studied by Brown and Fraser 1964) in imitating expansions added something to their original utterances 50 percent of the time. The new items added included articles, the copula, a pronoun, a preposition, an inflection—that is, the forms that were missing from their spontaneous speech. Slobin argues that such imitation very likely helps the child advance in his grammatical development, although Slobin acknowledges that there is no direct evidence that adult expansions of children's speech play an essential or even a facilitative role in normal grammatical development.

Other evidence suggests that the imitation-reinforcement position cannot provide an adequate interpretation of language development. Children's speech, particularly in the early stages of development, contains examples which deviate from the adult model of the language, for example, "The child*ren*s are here," and We went*ed*," as well as other combinations which never occur in adult speech, and which therefore could never have been heard and imitated, such as "All gone shoe" and "More car" (Braine 1963b). Such deviations from adult usage are more parsimoniously interpreted as instances of linguistic productivity which derive from the child's acquisition of a rule system, or in other words, they illustrate the child's implicit grammatical theory.

THE SOCIOLINGUISTIC POSITION

Psycholinguists have been preoccupied with studing the child's acquisition of grammatical structures—that is, the forms of language—and have neglected the set of equally important questions of how the child learns the social uses of language. The developing subdiscipline, sociolinguistics, does concern itself with such questions. One of the articles of faith to the sociolinguist is that a considerable diversity exists in the way in which language can be used to meet needs demanded by individual social structures (Grimshaw in press). Many of the central problems in developmental sociolinguistics have been summarized in the statement that in addition to the child's acquisition of the structural rules of his language, he also must learn another set of rules which refer to when he should speak, when he should remain silent, which linguistic code he should use, and to whom. (Hymes 1967)

The major theoretical work in developmental sociolinguistics has been carried out by Bernstein. (1964, see Chap. 3 in this volume) He assumes that linguistic output, or certain kinds of linguistic output, are not as highly valued in some subcultures and in some family structural types as in others. Bernstein describes two general kinds of linguistic codes, the restricted and the elaborated that are isomorphic to social subgroups. The habitual restricted-code user usually but not always comes from a lower social class than the elaborated-code user, and by contrast to the predominantly elaborated-code user, is quite limited in the range of his possible selections from the total population of lexical and structural options. Bernstein suspects that social groups differ significantly in the range of situations in which they use elaborated speech.

Hess and Shipman (1965) have reported an experiment that derives directly from and supports Bernstein's theorizing. They analyzed the content of mothers' communication to their children, where the mothers came from different social-class backgrounds. Findings indicated that whereas the middle-class mothers tended to give their children informationally adequate messages, with occasional supportive statements, the lower-class mothers, by contrast, tended not to be explicit, and conveyed very little information in their messages.

The main directions of research on the language of the disadvantaged child suggested by the various environmentalist positions can be summarized as follows. One direction is the necessary closer examination of the child's environment in order to locate possible sources of support for details of his language development. For example, in analyzing the verbal interchanges between a child and his parents, one needs a detailed specification of the kinds of linguistic information (both structural and functional) being provided for the child; then one also needs to specify the child's use (or lack of use) of such information. A second direction is the analysis of the correlations between communicative demands in certain situations and the language used to meet such demands. Williams and Naremore (1969) have carried out one of the first major studies on this problem. They investigated the way in which children brought language to bear upon specific situations to meet the different communicative demands imposed by a linguistic field worker. Language samples in this research had been obtained from the corpus of the Detroit Dialect Study (Shuy, et al. 1967) and included the responses to questions (e.g., "What games do you play around here?") given by fifth- and sixth-grade children of varying socioeconomic status and ethnicity. Social-class differences in the elaboration of responses were greatest when a field worker's question could be answered minimally but adequately by a simple yes or no (or "uh huh"); here the lower-status children tended to give such minimal (but communicatively acceptable) responses as against the middle-class children's going beyond this minimum. Status differences in the incidence of elaboration, however, all but vanished when the question required elaboration (e.g., "Tell me how you play baseball?"). Also as might be expected, but seldom studied, there were substantial within- and between-group variations according to the topics (games, television, aspirations) discussed. On a more general level, the lower-class child had a tendency to talk in the first person, communicating from his own perspective, thus using a self-focused mode of discourse. The middle-class child, by contrast, tended to employ a variety of perspectives in his remarks. He used the third person more frequently than the lower-class child, which increased his options in constructing subject-noun phrases, so that he could incorporate many communication perspectives in one message. Williams and Naremore found that maximal differences in modes of communication were obtained for the two social-class groups when they responded to the television topic (see also, Williams, 1969).

The environmentalist position is sharply differentiated from the nativist position with regard to remediation of the language problems of the disadvantaged. To begin with, the environmental position usually assumes that such problems actually exist, and that observed social-class differences are not totally explainable by referring to faulty sampling techniques, which is the suggestion offered by many nativists. The environmentalist position, in addition, implies that language behavior can be changed by developing appropriate training procedures. It is the case, however, that so far most research has been concerned with diagnosis of problems rather than with their remediation.

INTEGRATION OF NATIVIST AND ENVIRONMENTALIST POSITIONS

The nativist position, as exemplified in the work of Chomsky (1965), Lenneberg (1967), and McNeill (1966, in press), focuses our attention on what is assumed to be a set of indisputable facts, namely that prelinguistic behavior and early linguistic behavior unfold under the influence of maturational processes, and are relatively independent of experiential influences. The nativists propose that an adequate explanation of language development must be predicated upon a range of sophisticated innate structures. They claim that models of language acquisition which rest upon the explanatory concepts of imitation and reinforcement (e.g., that of Mowrer 1960), or word position learning (e.g., that of Braine 1963a) fail to account for the complexity of linguistic knowledge. The nativists argue that the child is not taught language but learns it rather effortlessly, largely because the general features of language structure reflect the general character of the human capacity to acquire knowledge.

The environmentalists, in sharp contrast to the nativists, assume environmental factors exert considerable influence on language development, so they suspect that careful analysis of these factors will reveal important information on the nature of the processes of language acquisition. Given that the environmentalist and the nativist positions seem to be radically different, the question is whether there is any common ground between them.

One point of convergence between the two positions is that both agree that language is acquired in a social context. A second point of agreement is on the existence of individual and group differences in linguistic performance. Among the nativists, Lenneberg (1967) makes the most explicit statements about such differences. He remarks that they occur at the time of speech onset, as well as at the time the various speech milestones are reached. His interpretation of these differences is that they result from complex interactions between social and biological factors in development. On the environmentalist side, there is much literature related to the role of environmental factors in determining individual and group differences (McCarthy 1954; Cazden 1966).

Yet another point of intersection between the two positions concerns the appropriate methods to study child language. Chomsky (1964) and the sociolinguists (e.g., Bernstein 1964; Hymes 1967) would all agree that a broad spectrum of tasks, situations, and linguistic analytic procedures are necessary to validly assess the child's language capabilities. Novel modes of assessment have recently been developed by Williams and Naremore (1969), and Osser, Wang and Zaid (1969), among many others.

In explaining language development the environmentalists stress the role of forces acting upon the child, i.e., external agents; whereas the nativists stress internal mechanisms of the speaker-listener himself. These two viewpoints are in conflict but are not necessarily irreconcilable. It is clearly possible to integrate these two models so that the coexistence of both social factors and biological factors in determining linguistic behavior would be admitted. It is possible, for example, to hold the view that all humans are by their nature equal with respect to language competence, and simultaneously to accept the existence of individual and group differences in language performance.

The information that has been collected thus far in studies of language development suggests that no single position, nativist or environmentalist, can explain all developmental language phenomena. There are four kinds of problems for which explanations have to be developed; we need to account for: (1) the development of prelinguistic vocalization; (2) the acquisition of basic language structures; (3) the acquisition of elaborated language sequences; (4) the acquisition of different modes of communication (the ability to use different styles of speech, such as a narrative, or an explanatory style, when it is appropriate in a particular social situation).

It is quite possible that social factors play a lesser role in the development of the skills represented in (1) and (2), but a greater role in those skills defined by (3) and (4). There is, at present, very little evidence on the precise role of either social or biological factors in the acquisition of linguistic structures and their use. The promise shown by such research as that of Bernstein (1964) and Hess and Shipman (1965) suggests that our knowledge of the role of social factors in language development will be vastly improved as more fine-grained analyses are carried out on child-adult verbal interactions. It is assumed by those who propose a nativist view on language development that the child need only be provided with a small sample of sentences and he will "invent" the remainder of the language. It is therefore very likely that the study of child-adult verbal interactions will permit the definition of the characteristics of the linguistic input to the child, which together with studies of the child's output will provide insights into the role of biological and social factors and their interactions in language development.

REFERENCES

Bernstein, B. Elaborated and restricted codes: their social origins and some consequences. In J. J. Gumperz and D. Hymes, eds., *The Ethnography of Communication, American Anthropologist* 1964, 66: No. 6 Part 2, 55–69.

Bever, T. G.; Fodor, J. A.; and Weksel, W. On the acquisition of syntax: a critique of "contextual generalization." *Psychological Review* 1965, 72:467–82.

Braine, M. D. S. On learning the grammatical order of words. *Psychological Review* 1963, 70:323–48. (a)

———. The ontogeny of English phrase structure: the first phase. *Language* 1963, 39:1–13.(b)

Brown, R. and Fraser, C. The acquisition of syntax. In Ursula Bellugi and R. Brown, eds., *The Acquisition of Language.* Monograph of the Society for Research in Child Development, 1964, Vol. 29.

Brown, R.; Cazden, Courtney; and Bellugi, Ursula. The child's grammar from I to III. In J. P. Hill, ed., *The 1967 Minnesota Symposium on Child Psychology.* Minneapolis: University of Minnesota Press, 1969.

Cazden, Courtney B. Subcultural differences in child language: an interdisciplinary review. *Merrill-Palmer Quarterly* 1966, 12:185–219.

———. On individual differences in language competence and performance. *J. Special Education* 1967, 1: 135–150.

Chomsky, N. Formal discussion. In Ursula Bellugi and R. Brown, eds., *The Acquisition of Language.* Monograph of the Society for Research in Child Development, 1964, Vol. 29.

———. *Aspects of the Theory of Syntax.* Cambridge, Mass.: M.I.T. Press, 1965.

Grimshaw, A. D. Sociolinguistics. In W. Schramm, I. Pool, N. Maccoby, E. Parker, F. Frey, and L. Fein, eds., *Handbook of Communication.* Chicago: Rand McNally, in press.

Hess, R. D., and Shipman, Virginia C. Early experience and the socialization of cognitive modes in children. *Child Development* 1965, 36:869–86.

Hymes, D. Models of the interaction of languages and social setting. *J. Social Issues* 1967, 23:8–28.

Jenkins, J. J., and Palermo, D. S. Mediation processes and the acquisition of linguistic structures. In Ursula Bellugi and R. Brown, eds., *The Acquisition of Language.* Monograph of the Society for Research in Child Development 1964, Vol. 29.

Jensen, A. R. How much can we boost IQ and scholastic achievement? *Harvard Educational Review* 1969, 39: 1–123.

Lenneberg, E. H. Understanding language without ability to speak: a case report. *J. Abnormal and Social Psychology* 1962, 65: 419–25.

———. *Biological Foundations of Language.* New York: Wiley, 1967.

Lenneberg, E. H.; Rebelsky, F. G.; and Nichols, I. A. The vocalization of infants born to deaf and hearing parents. *Vita Humana* 1965, 8:23–37.

McCarthy, Dorothea, Language development in children. In L. Carmichael, ed., *Manual of Child Psychology.* New York: Wiley, 1954.

McNeill, D. Developmental psycholinguistics. In F. Smith and G. A. Miller, eds., *The Genesis of Language: A Psycholinguistic Approach.* Cambridge, Mass.: M.I.T. Press, 1966.

———. The development of language. In P. A. Mussen, ed., *Carmichael's Manual of Child Psychology.* New York: Wiley, in press.

Morley, Muriel, E. *The Development and Disorders of Speech in Childhood.* London: Livingstone, 1957.

Mowrer, O. H., *Learning Theory and the Symbolic Processes.* New York: Wiley, 1960.

Osser, H.; Wang, Marilyn D.; and Zaid, Farida. The young child's ability to imitate and comprehend speech: a comparison of two sub-cultural groups. *Child Development* 1969, 40:1063–75.

Shuy, R. W.; Wolfram, W. A.; and Riley, W. K. Linguistic correlates of social stratification in Detroit speech. U. S. Office of Education Cooperative Research Project No. 6-1347, 1967.

Skinner, B. F. *Verbal Behavior.* New York: Appleton-Century-Crofts, 1957.

Slobin, D. I. The acquisition of Russian as a native language. In F. Smith and G. A. Miller, eds., *The Genesis of Language: A Psycholinguistic Approach.* Cambridge, Mass.: M.I.T. Press, 1966.

———. Imitation and grammatical development in children, in N. S. Endler, L. R. Boulter, and H. Osser, eds., *Contemporary Issues in Developmental Psychology.* New York: Holt, Rinehart & Winston, 1968.

Williams, F. Social class differences in how children talk about television: some observations and speculations. *J. Broadcasting* 1969, 13:345–57.

Williams, F., and Naremore, Rita C. On the functional analysis of social class differences in modes of speech. *Speech Monographs* 1969, 36:77–102.

Chapter 14

A SUMMARY OF ENVIRONMENTALIST VIEWS AND SOME EDUCATIONAL IMPLICATIONS

Davenport Plumer*

Researchers have long been aware that differences in language are consistently associated with groups and individuals who are economically disadvantaged or otherwise out of the mainstream of American life. However, the nature of the association and the possibility of remediation have until recently been unclear. A great deal remains to be done, but there is a growing body of literature dealing with the language problems of disadvantaged children and a strong commitment to remediation on the part of the federal government and university researchers.

Tracing the very real and important political antecedents of this change would have to consider the impact of the civil rights movement, of books such as Conant's *Slums and Suburbs* (1961) and Harrington's *The Other America* (1962), and the vast federal support of education and educational research in the Kennedy and Johnson administrations. These trends and forces, however, explain only part of the increased research interest in disadvantaged children generally and in their language problems in particular. If these problems can be attributed to racial or other hereditary factors, the best that research can

*Graduate School of Education, Harvard University

The research reported herein was performed pursuant to a contract OE 5-10-239 with the U. S. Department of Health, Education and Welfare, Office of Education, under the provisions of the Cooperative Research Program, as a project of the Havard Center for Research and Development on Educational Differences.

expect is to catalogue them and describe their relationships. If, on the other hand, these problems can be shown to have their roots in the early experiences and environments of disadvantaged children, then research becomes an enquiry into causes and, at least theoretically, a basis for remediation. It is, of course, impossible to specify the extent of a given researcher's commitment to an environmentalist position or to claim that this commitment influenced him to undertake a certain piece of research. Nevertheless it is useful to note some of the characteristics and implications of a point of view that implicitly or explicitly informs the bulk of the recent work on language problems of disadvantaged children.

A variety of reasons can be offered for the scope of the present paper. Perhaps weakest but most practical among them is that much of the environmentalist literature on the topic of language and poverty is found in scattered sources, in little known research journals, and in research reports of limited circulation. In short, one goal of this paper is to bring together some of this literature in a single presentation. A stronger yet still practical reason is that hopefully from the collation of this literature will come some bases for decision making, both in terms of needed future research and in the formulation of policy for dealing with the problems of poverty.

For the most part, the individual papers subsumed in this review have dealt with some aspect of language, and it has seemed most efficient to organize this report in terms of those aspects. Though artificial when considered in terms of linguistic theory, these categories do provide some bases for structuring what has been reported. They include: dialect, vocabulary and syntax, reading, and language codes and styles.

DIALECT

Dialect and Social Mobility

There seems to be the presumption, both now and in the past, that every American ought to be able to speak standard English, and the schools have long taken the responsibility for teaching it. Some thirty years ago, Fries (1940, p. 14) characterized the problems associated with this position:

> The schools . . . have assumed the responsibility of training every boy and girl, no matter what his original social background and native speech, to use this "standard" English, this particular social or class dialect . . . . Many believe that the schools have thus assumed an impossible task. Certainly the widespread and almost unanimous condemnation of the results of their efforts convinces us that either the schools have not conceived their task adequately or they have chosen the wrong materials and methods to accomplish it.

Fries goes on to claim that the crux of the problem is that the form of standard English toward which the schools hope to move their students is a "make-believe" standard, much more formal and artificial than the actual language used to conduct the affairs of the country. This fault has been more or less overshadowed by another important problem stressed by Fries (1940, p. 15):[1]

> The first step in fulfilling that obligation is the making of an accurate and realistic survey and description of the actual language practices in the various social or class dialects. Only after we have such information in hand can we know what social connotations are likely to attach to particular usages.

Conflicting Views on the Teaching of Standard Dialect

Fries's remarks give us a good approximation of the current state of standard dialect teaching. Despite some politically motivated reluctance to acknowledge the existence of a Negro dialect (see Labov, 1967, p. 143), there is a general agreement that culturally disadvantaged children do use consistent forms of nonstandard English and there is an increasing commitment to the ideal of bidialectilism for these children. That is, they should be able to use standard English on appropriate occasions yet be able to retain their original dialect unstigmatized by the school (McDavid 1965, pp. 257–258).

Although a considerable body of opinion seems to favor teaching standard English to nonstandard speakers, we should also look at the opposition to this view. James Sledd (1965) offers the purist's vision when he comments that English teachers should be spending their time teaching individual responsibility and dignity, not facilitating the student's entrance into a middle class whose values are at best uncertain. Others, such as Riessman (1962) and Brewer (1966), do not directly oppose standard-dialect teaching but stress the power and vitality of disadvantaged children's home and street language.

More substantial and direct opposition comes from those who assert that it is naive to consider teaching the standard dialect on a large scale to students for whom social mobility may be a matter of chance or currying favor, and for whom there are few convincing role models (see Rosenthal, 1966, p. 22). The skeptics base their arguments primarily on the assumption that "Change of speech will accompany or follow, not precede, his (the disadvantaged child's) decision to make his way out of the world into which he was born" (Lloyd 1964, p. 113; c.f. Labov 1965, p. 85).

Lloyd (1964, p. 113; c.f. Green 1965) gives another objection to teaching standard dialect, at least to young children:

---

[1]See McDavid (1965) for a comparable statement.

. . . Each person must *at all times* read his own speech off the page of standard English print, and put his own speech on the page when he writes. To change his speech in the process of leading him to literacy is to multiply the problems of literacy beyond his ability to cope with them.

From a somewhat more sophisticated viewpoint, Loban (1963, pp. 225–26) argues the same way, also with respect to elementary school children. In the same vein Labov (1967) cautions against jumping to conclusions about the relationship between a child's failure to pronounce an inflection like the past tense, *-ed*, when it appears in his reading, and the need for someone to try to change his dialect. Labov (1967, pp. 163–64) explains:

We have two distinct cases to consider. In one case, the deviation in reading may be only a difference in pronunciation on the part of a child who has a different set of homonyms from the teacher. Here, correction might be quite unnecessary. In the second case, we may be dealing with a boy who has no concept of *-ed* as a past tense marker, who considers the *-ed* a meaningless set of silent letters. Obviously the correct teaching strategy would involve distinguishing these two cases, and treating them quite differently.

In other words, Labov wants to be certain that teachers can distinguish between mistakes in reading and mistakes in pronunciation. If the problem is genuinely associated with reading, remediation may involve spending time teaching an inflection like *ed* with the same systematic concentration that is generally reserved for silent letters like *b* in "lam*b*." Labov (1967, pp. 163–65) concludes:

On the face of it there is no reason why a person cannot learn to read standard English texts quite well in a nonstandard pronunciation. Eventually the school may wish to teach the child an alternate system of pronunciation. But the key to the situation in the early grades is for the teacher to know the system of homonyms of nonstandard English, and to know the grammatical differences that separate her own speech from that of the child . . . . Thus the task of teaching the child to read 'ed' is clearly that of getting him to recognize the graphic symbols as a marker of the past tense, quite distinct from the task of getting him to say /paest/ for "passed."

These cautions or demurs say essentially, "do not jump to conclusions about the effectiveness or value of standard dialect teaching, and be particularly chary about introducing it in the early grades." There is another more direct argument that opposes any and all attempts to change a person's dialect by school instruction. Though this case has not been made in print, it is raised often enough informally to warrant making it explicit here. The argument is primarily a moral one and says that teaching the standard dialect to nonstandard speakers is fundamentally wrong because of what it says and does to those who are obliged to be taught. Despite protestations about bidialectalism and the fact that teachers are not to denigrate the student's home dialect, the argument runs, the fact is that the student will unavoidably come to disparage his home dialect and those who use it. The opponents of standard-dialect teaching would grant that this is not an inevitable consequence for all children, but believe that it is too great a risk for the children so affected. Assuming that a child does learn the standard dialect, those who oppose it on moral grounds claim that this has a damaging effect on the child's relationship to his family, that this damage was in fact done to large numbers of European immigrants whose acquisition of English made them in effect strangers to their own culture and families before they could be sustained and guided by the traditions and associations of American culture. Despite its gaps this argument has adamant, articulate adherents. It is important to recognize, however, that this argument assumes that the standard dialect can be taught. We shall see that this assumption is open to question.

The majority of the proponents of teaching standard dialect emphasize its relationship to socioeconomic mobility (Golden 1960; Temple 1967; Pederson 1965; Center for Applied Linguistics 1966). But other arguments have been offered. In opposition to, and with less persuasiveness than Labov, Loban, or Lloyd, some teachers will argue that speech therapy or some other systematic treatment of the student's dialect should accompany early training in reading for speakers of nonstandard dialects. These assertions generally rest upon intuition, common sense, or personal bias and should be treated with some skepticism (see Yoder, Chap. 19).

Standard Dialect and Teacher-Pupil Communication

The idea that the teacher's rejection of the student's nonstandard dialect cuts him off from oral communication in the school must be taken very seriously. It implies that there may be a serious communication breakdown between the lower class student and middle-class teacher, mainly on the level of encoding-decoding, rather than on the level of emotional support, though that too is an obvious problem. The research relating to this question is limited and conflicting. Cloward (1966), in his report of tutoring done under the auspices of the Neighborhood Youth Corps in New York, points out that when tutor and pupil exceed a certain optimum degree of age or class difference from each other, the effectiveness of the tutoring diminishes, but he does not specify these differences in terms of dialect.

Peisach (1965) has studied this question directly, but even her work does not much clarify the effect of a child's dialect on his communication in school. Using the cloze technique[2] she investigated the child's comprehension of teacher and peer speech across age, sex, and race lines. Peisach's findings, though somewhat clouded by shortcomings in her definition of comprehension, indicated that: (1) Negro and white children of the same social class and matched by IQ did not differ in their comprehension of teacher speech. (2) Lower-class children did as well as middle-class children in comprehending lower-class and Negro children's speech passages, but did worse than middle-class children on white, middle-class children's passages. (3) Fifth-grade Negro students showed differentially poorer comprehension than Negro middle-class first-graders, which Peisach (1965, p. 479) interprets rather broadly:

> It may be that Negro SES III (middle-class) children can be considered to speak two dialects with subsequent diminished efficiency in each dialect. Diminished efficiency due to conflicting dialects might then explain both the relatively poorer IQ achievement and cloze performance of the Negro SES III children.

One of two implications for improved within-school communication for speakers of nonstandard English seems possible. They should learn to comprehend the teachers' standard dialect better, or teachers need to learn to speak the dialect of disadvantaged children. In short, what evidence exists suggests that disadvantaged students may have trouble understanding their teachers, and, by extension, teachers may have trouble understanding students. At present, however, this evidence provides only a weak basis for remedial efforts directed primarily at students' speech production.

Research on Nonstandard Dialect

The final chapter of Fries' *American English Grammar* (1940) points to a necessary prerequisite to teaching standard dialect: that is, finding (p. 287) "those language items in which standard English and vulgar English differ." Whereas Fries puts most of his emphasis on the need to describe accurately the features of informal standard English, dialectologists and linguists such as McDavid, Stewart, Pederson, or Labov stress the need for a contrastive analysis, which would provide detailed knowledge of the nonstandard dialect onto which the standard forms are to be grafted (see, for example, Labov 1965; Pederson 1965). They stress, in other words, the need for thorough description of whatever semantic, phonological, and syntactic features distinguish a particular nonstandard dialect from the standard.

Before looking at some of the problems of contrastive analysis and assess-

---

[2]In cloze technique, a person attempts to replace words deleted from a language sample. In this application, as a child correctly replaced words, his "comprehension" of the sample was assumed reflected.

ing its role in the process of dialect teaching, we must note that the analysis entailed by the description above is far more detailed and specific to a particular speech community than Fries anticipated. A study such as Loban's *Problems in Oral English* (1966a) which categorizes the departures from standard English in the speech of four representative groups of children (Caucasian-high language proficiency; Caucasian-low language proficiency; Negro-low language proficiency; and random) suggests some of the gross deviant features common to the many local versions of nonstandard English. Such a study cannot, however, provide the richness and specificity being reported in more recent and linguistically sophisticated studies of urban language (see Shuy Chapter 16 in this volume).

Labov's (1965, p. 101) comments indicate the kind of specificity and close analysis required for a workable contrastive description:

> In order to make intelligent decisions about which forms of language require correction or suppletion with alternate forms, we have to know which markers of linguistic behavior have serious effects upon the life chances of the individual. In different areas, we might find the same nonstandard forms, but with radically different social significance. For example, one can hear stops and affricates used for θ and $\eth$ in the Southwest, but there this feature does not seem to have the same strong social impact as in Chicago or New York.

Labov points out, moreover, that even within an otherwise seemingly homogeneous speech community there are at least semantic differences that set one group apart from another. Temple (1967), for instance, refers to the large "hip" or "cool" vocabulary of Negro adolescents in Washington, D.C., which often serves to exclude their elders as well as white outsiders. Brewer (1966) notes the same characteristic of the speech of younger children in New York. My own observations in Boston point to a noticeable phonological difference between the recent arrivals from the South and Negroes born in the area. All of these intragroup differences complicate both the completion of a contrastive analysis for a given group and the subsequent decisions about how and at what age to begin introducing the standard dialect.

Labov's work (1966; Chapter 9 in this volume) on nonstandard speech—white and Negro—in New York indicates the kinds of complexity involved in dialect acquisition and dialect change, and the research methods required to isolate the critical variables inhibiting natural or forced dialect change.

One of Labov's principal methods involves revealing a speaker's full range of speech behaviors, as opposed to only his formal or his informal speech. Another way of putting this is to say that Labov takes seriously the idea that speakers of all classes vary their speech in accordance with their perception of a particular social context—just as they vary their clothes (see Fries 1940, pp. 9–11 for an early but very full development of this metaphor). Thus Labov sets the language-gathering tasks so that his respondents will demonstrate their full range of styles: casual speech, careful speech, reading style, and a more formal style evoked by reading individual words. The finding that four classes of speakers lower class, working class, lower-middle class, and upper-middle class—differed most on casual speech but were the most similar when saying individual words is not unexpected (Labov 1965, pp. 80–83). But it does underline the importance of context and strongly suggests that at least part of the problem in changing dialects is getting people to do something that they presently do not do—rather than something that they presently cannot do.

In his work in Harlem, Labov (1966, 1967) presses this issue more closely, raising questions that resemble those associated with grammatical competence and performance. In order to determine whether speakers have the past inflection /-ed/ or whether they invariably delete final /r, l, s, z, t, d/, he uses an especially formal situation to elicit careful speech or uses the effect of grammatical conditioning to determine, for example, what happens when final /r/ in "car" appears before a vowel. In the case of final /r, l, s, z, t, d/ Labov finds that under the most formal conditions, a final consonant that was not apparent in informal speech is often "there" in some sense, and not entirely inaccessible to the speaker.

Another of Labov's (1965) contributions is to suggest a model of the stages in an individual's acquisition of standard English and to point to the nonlinguistic, noncognitive stimuli and constraints operating on the child's gradual approximation to this standard. The configurations of the trend toward the standard form are the same for children from all the social strata in Labov's study, but the lower-class families differed from those in the middle class in that they began and ended with less resemblance to the adult standard form. As a critical milestone in the process of change in the direction of standard English, Labov cites changes in perception—particularly during what he calls Stage 3, social perception, occurring in early adolescence when the speaker begins to hear other speech forms but is still limited to the style of his own vernacular. Also revealed by Labov's self-evaluation test is another perceptual feature which may, at least potentially, affect dialect change. That is the way a speaker "hears himself as speaking the norm that he considers correct" (Labov 1965, p. 85). Add to these variables the fact that a significant proportion of disadvantaged students may have auditory discrimination problems (C. Deutsch 1964) and these factors alone would go far toward explaining the problems encountered thus far with schemes for teaching bidialectilism.

The problems of describing a nonstandard dialect are, then, compounded when we look at the way actual speakers use this dialect in different contexts and at different ages. Moreover, the problem of dialect change itself is further compounded when we realize that natural changes in the direction of the standard form are more than likely tied to the speaker's awareness of the standard form as distinct from his own and to his perception or judgment of his own approximation to that form.

Labov (1965, p. 103) cites three additional nonlinguistic barriers to the acquisition of standard English.

1. *Opposing motivations.* Labov claims that, though most New Yorkers endorse the value of standard English, the prestige of Negro and southern dialect forms is rising and may militate against efforts to change these dialects. These observations are particularly important now that black people are getting much greater TV coverage, and the slogan "black is beautiful" is becoming the focus of many profound changes within black communities. This combination of factors means that the larger society is hearing the so-called Negro dialect more often, and it is spoken by men and women of considerable prestige and presence. One obvious result is the currency of such expressions as "baby," "man," and "tell it like it is." In short, there appears, on the one hand, a growing familiarity with and acceptance of Negro dialects among whites. On the other hand, among blacks there is a clearly growing pride and sense of self that will resist attempts to get black children to talk like "whitey."

2. *Resistance in the peer group.* It appears that adolescent and prea-dolescent peer pressure will either have to be overcome or mobilized if students are going to alter their dialect away from peer-group standards.

3. *Teacher-student interaction.* Labov speculates that the pattern of teacher-student interaction may have so biased nonstandard dialect speakers, especially boys, that they will resist any efforts at change—particularly under the auspices of the school—that would make their speech resemble that of their teachers.

The final word on this aspect of the dialect-teaching controversy should go to Labov (1965, p. 94), who says:

> One can hardly imagine a theory of mechanical constraints which could account for the dilemma proposed at the beginning of this paper: How is it that young people who are exposed to the standard English of their teachers for twelve years cannot reproduce this style for twelve minutes in a job interview . . . ? Those who feel that they can solve this problem by experimenting with the machinery of the learning process are measuring small causes against large effects. My own feeling is that the primary interference with the acquisition of standard English stems from a conflict of value systems.

Teaching Standard Dialect

Apparently undeterred by reservations about "experimenting with the machinery of learning process," teachers and researchers have devised programs for teaching the standard dialect, following by and large the principles of second-language learning formulated by Fries in *Cumulative Pattern Practices* (1954): (1) the primary importance of shaping speech behavior, (2) the use of an audiolingual approach, and (3) the use of structural substitution frames.

By adapting these principles, several experimenters have worked out programs for hearing and practicing the standard dialect. For example, Barrows (1956) has developed oral games for junior-high students requiring the repetition of standard English patterns; Golden (1964) has designed a series of fourteen instructional tapes for the tenth grade in Detroit's Central High School.

The most complete, long-term project was carried out at Claflin College in Orangeboro, South Carolina, by Lin (1965), whose work covered three academic years. She devised tapes, role-playing schemes, and a variety of supplementary materials to provide pattern practice to freshmen four days a week in the academic year. The students participating in the experiment were drawn on the basis of their "averageness" rather than upon their desire to learn standard dialect. The exercises were based upon a sample of the students' errors. Much of the material stressed problems of verb and noun inflection and agreement. Although the analyses were incomplete at the time of reporting on evaluation, Lin (1965) recognized that group results were inconclusive, and that even individual case histories showed mixed reactions and results. In particular, she noted that a nine-month period was insufficient to produce a single completely bidialectical student. Golden's (1963) somewhat less-detailed evaluation of her taped language lessons did favor an experimental group, and this included evaluation of extempore speech, a business interview, and two specific oral tests.

Having personally heard samples from pattern practice drills used by Lin and those used by Golden, I think that one can attest to their monotony and sympathize with black students who reject similar materials originally prepared to teach English to foreign students. However, some of these materials have been revised and are complete with jazz background and "cool talk" (Temple 1967, p. 11). Unfortunately, the effectiveness of this revised material has not yet been determined.

Some Current Questions

We are left, then, with some agreement that public schools have traditionally considered one of their roles to be teaching standard English and that poor children generally speak a nonstandard dialect which may restrict their socioeconomic mobility. At this point agreement stops and some major unresolved questions begin:

How can we best use the contrastive studies of structural interferences between dialects?

How important is the contrast in value systems cited by Labov?

What is the importance for dialect change of the ratio of nonstandard to standard speakers in, say, a newly integrated school?

What is the optimum age for children to begin learning standard dialect?

With foreign languages the answer to the last question may be, the sooner the better. However, if Labov's model of the stages in the natural acquistion of standard English is accurate, then waiting until adolescence may be better for dialect teaching. This may also be true because successful bidialectalism seems to depend upon knowing which setting or person requires which dialect, a social sophistication perhaps beyond the reach of an elementary school child who would be able to learn a foreign language quite successfully.

In a larger perspective, these questions simply beg the more important question of priorities—where should a school concentrate its greatest time and effort? Though such questions should, ideally, be answered in terms of the individual student, it seems generally indefensible, given the general lack of success in planned dialect change, to take time from a student's academic program to work on changing his dialect. If indeed the primary motive for teaching functional bidialectilism is social and economic mobility, it seems that this cause would be better served by improving the student's academic performance and providing him with improved guidance toward higher education or employment. (But we still might have the employer to worry about.)

Given the close association between dialect change and a speaker's perception of himself and his role in society, it is also clear that dialect change without an accompanying awareness of opportunities for social mobility is unrealistic and impractical. The same observation also applies to the groups for whom English is truly a second language—Indians, Mexican-Americans, Puerto Ricans, and French-Canadians. The relation between knowing English and the ability to perform in school is clearly much more vital and complex for these groups, but the general point is the same. If they see themselves locked out of the society anyway, then their motivation to learn English will be understandably low, especially if in doing so they risk cutting themselves off from associations they already have, namely their peers and families. It is possible, in other words, to apply what seems to be a theoretically and empirically sound method to the teaching of English to Mexican-Americans and still have it fail because they consider the whole idea of learning English irrelevant. This is much the same way that a ladder lying in the middle of a desert might be irrelevant. It is not inherently useful. It becomes so only in a particular context—when there is something desirable and attainable but just out of reach.

VOCABULARY AND SYNTAX

Although many of the language problems of the disadvantaged child can be subsumed under the general heading of dialect, some of the literature in this area refers specifically to problems of vocabulary or of syntax. Again, the division of materials into separate categories of vocabulary and syntax or even separating these from dialect may be artificial, but it facilitates their review.

Vocabulary

While few writers would confidently draw a clear line between learning or knowing a word[3] on the one hand and learning or knowing a concept on the other, there are even fewer who would claim that disadvantaged children are notably strong in either one. The evidence from large- and small-scale standardized testing is that poor children have generally limited vocabularies (Ausubel 1964; Figurel 1964; McCarthy 1954; Newton 1960); their labeling vocabularies seem limited to items found in homes and schools (John and Goldstein 1964); their categorizing behavior is reportedly immature with respect to adult or middle-class norms (Carson and Rabin 1960; John 1963; M. Deutsch 1964a); and their store of concepts (Ausubel 1964), as well as their ability to form or recognize new concepts are reported limited (M. Deutsch 1964a).

The majority of researchers reporting these deficits attribute them to some inadequacy in the children's homes, some lack of parental models, stimulation, or corrective feedback. However, there is presently no large or informative collection of direct evidence to support these attributions. A number of writers have called for direct studies of lower-class or disadvantaged home environments (e.g. Gordon 1965, Bernstein and Henderson 1969), and some researchers have taken steps in this direction (Dave 1963; Hess and Shipman 1965; Wolf 1963). However, being restricted to questionnaires, interviews, and laboratory tests these studies, though certainly valuable, have not been able to pinpoint reliably the set of variables which inhibit vocabulary development in disadvantaged homes.

Types of interpretations. Lacking precise environmental data but feeling some obligation to interpret their findings, some researchers have turned to a modified operant-conditioning model of vocabulary and concept learning. One particularly concise description of this model is what Brown (1958) calls the Original Word Game:

---

[3]See Lorge and Chall (1963) for a discussion of some problems associated with judging a child's vocabulary size or his knowledge of a given word. See also Carson and Rabin (1960) for one attempt to get beyond the information derived from tests of simple word recognition.

The Original Word Game has three component processes: the categorization of speech, the categorization of referents, and the speaking skill. Invariance in speech signals some invariance outside of speech, some referent invariance. Because speech has a systematic structure it is easier to learn to recognize it in other behavior. For the player of the Original Word Game (the child) a speech invariance is a signal to form some hypothesis about the corresponding invariance of referent. The speech form may guide him to a very probable hypothesis through phonetic symbolism, methaphor, or the part of speech to which the form belongs. The hypothesis can be made almost certainly correct by giving the superordinate of the new form or by naming the critical attributes of its referent category. Whether or not his hypothesis about the referent is correct the player speaks the name where his hypothesis indicates that it should be spoken. The tutor (teacher or parent) approves or corrects this performance according as it fits or does not fit the referent category. In learning referents and names the player of the Original Word Game prepares himself to receive the science, the rules of thumb, the total expectancies of his society. (Brown 1958, pp. 227–28)

This summary does not mention either the player's perceptions or the quality of the signal he receives from others in his home and school, though the model does predict that in a noisy environment or one with inarticulate speakers, the child will probably have difficulty establishing speech invariance. With the notable exceptions of investigations by John (1963) or by C. Deutsch (1964), studies of vocabulary problems in disadvantaged children bypass these perceptual origins and concentrate on the causal role of other features of the Word Game. Figurel (1964, p. 164), for example, stresses the small number and the limited variety of a deprived child's experiences: "the meagre experiential background children have had in developing an adequate vocabulary." Ausubel (1964), John (1963), and Deutsch (1965), on the other hand, look to a different feature of word and concept acquisition, and stress the poor quality of home language as the primary causal factor. In a later article, John and Goldstein (1964) shift the emphasis to adult, or tutor, feedback and reinforcement. Their analysis of errors on a Peabody Picture Vocabulary Test administered to four-year-old lower-class Negro children illustrates one way the Word Game model can be used to interpret a consistent pattern of vocabulary weakness. They found that the children failed on three categories of words: words associated with rural living, words whose referents may be rare in lower-class homes, and action words. Restricted experience would explain failure in the first two categories. Marked failure to identify action words, John and Goldstein (1964, p. 268) argue, results from the fact that, "Children from low-income homes have relatively little opportunity to engage in active dialogue when learning labels." John and Goldstein's emphasis on dialogue stems from their view that label-learning requires the interaction of two variables: word-referent relationship and corrective feedback.

John and Goldstein's (1964, p. 269) description of these two key variables clearly flows from a Word Game model:

> One, the stability of the word-referent relationship, refers to the specificity of the features of the referent and the degree of its invariance within the learning context in the natural environment. The second variable, derived from the frequency and type of verbal interaction during language acquisition, refers to the amount of corrective feedback the child receives while learning a new label, i.e., the consistency with which his speech is listened to, corrected, and modified.

Based on this formulation, John and Goldstein's full explanation for action-word problems runs as follows. Accepting the notion that there is quite likely a paucity of parent-child verbal interaction in a lower-class Negro home, they conclude that children in these homes must rely on the frequency of co-occurrence of label and referent and the invariance between them much more than do middle-class children. Frequency and invariance are allegedly both in short supply in most lower-class homes, but even if they could be counted on to facilitate the learning of simple labels, they are of considerably less value in learning action words whose referents are constantly shifting and appearing in different contexts. Hence the learning of action words requires increased amounts of corrective feedback from adults, a requirement which is allegedly seldom met in low-status homes.

John and Goldstein's comments on the role of adult reinforcement illustrate both the function and the insufficiency of the Word Game model. They specify that adult reinforcement is particularly important at the time when a child is shifting from a labeling to a categorizing use of words. Though their description of this shift may be somewhat overprogrammatic, it points up the importance of seeing word and concept learning as a changing, fluctuating process, one in which the relative importance of the components varies with, at least, the developmental stage of the learner and with the kind of learning. Their observation implies, in other words, that a component of the Game that is simply necessary at one stage can become sufficient at another. Or, as the researchers also suggest, when one component of the Game, frequency of word-referent cooccurrence, is lacking or in limited supply, another, invariance of word-referent relationship, must become more influential. Until this shifting relationship between the several components of the Game has been more accurately described—until the theoretical model has been supplanted by an accurate description—attempts to improve the way deprived children and their teachers, parents, or both play the Original Word Game can have only limited potential for success.

Implications. One means of improving language learning starts not from a detailed analysis of the process but from a consideration of the content. The list of labeling words that children can learn and that they may encounter in oral or written work in school is virtually limitless. Also, the reward for learning some specific set of these words is very small. Hence the question arises: Are there other kinds of words that are more powerful in terms of their frequency of occurrence and their function in a sentence? One answer to this question may be to experiment with teaching a limited set of so-called operational terms. For the most part, these are easily spelled and pronounced words that appear often and signal relationships that are crucial to following oral instructions or understanding a story. Such words include: *in, on, before, during, while, outer, higher, smaller, more, least,* and so on. This approach is similar in its assumptions to Bereiter's (1965, Bereiter and Engelmann 1966) preschool program. The idea cannot be considered to have had a fair or informative test in Bereiter's program, however, since his classes introduce experimentally uncontrolled and controversial teaching methods.

In sum, we have seen evidence of what might best be called vocabulary weakness in disadvantaged children. Here weakness refers to capability relative to the demands for school and eventually job success. Although it can be argued that the vocabularies of many of these children are adequate or even quite well adapted for everday needs in the home or peer environments, this does not solve the problem that these children have relative to the standards of our society. It should be noted, too, that much of what is written about the disadvantaged child's vocabulary problems can be viewed in conjunction with research in concept learning (e.g., Gordon 1965; Siller 1957; Ausubel 1964), a topic beyond the scope of the present review.

Syntax

Studies dating back to 1947 (see McCarthy 1954) show group differences between lower- and middle-class children on measures of oral and written sentence structure. In the years since 1947 these measures have included sentence length and complexity (Templin 1957, 1958), frequency of occurrence of certain structural types (Strickland 1962), counts of grammatical errors (Loban 1966b), and counts based on a modified transformational analysis of clause and subclause units (Mellon 1967). Such studies cover a wide age and geographical distribution, using a variety of definitions for social class. For the most part, the evidence provided by these studies has been interpreted to indicate more developed, elaborated, or complex syntactic usage among middle-class compared to lower-class children. In no case has the reverse been reported. Frazier's (et al., 1964 p. 70) generalization that some deprived children "truly have less language than other children" sums up the position that many have taken in regard to this area of research.

Evaluation of the "less-language" interpretations.   Assume for the moment the most extreme interpretation of Frazier's statement: Disadvantaged children's language performance leads to the conclusion that they simply cannot produce or understand certain types of English sentences (e.g., a passive sentence or sentence with an embedded relative clause). Some theoretical reservations about this view appear below. The empirical work is also subject to the following reservations. First is that a number of the often-cited studies of grammar either do not include children defined in this paper as "disadvantaged" (Fries 1940; Strickland 1962) or they attempt to get a socioeconomically representative sample but do not report any status correlations (Loban 1963, 1966b). Thus, the major studies of syntax pay so little attention to disadvantaged children that they do not provide grounds for evaluating Frazier's claim. Nor are they designed, for example, to support or deny the conflicting hypothesis that although disadvantaged children may produce a relatively smaller number of certain structures or transformations, their production includes sentences that indicate mastery of all the important rules of the grammar. Since disadvantaged children are not adequately defined in the above studies, there is little possibility of even considering Frazier's claim.

A second difficulty is the way the data are gathered. Even if, as Loban (1963, pp. 3, 26–27; 1966b, pp. 15–16) claims, his whole sample is slightly biased toward the low end of the status scale and "those ranked low in language proficiency are of predominantly low socioeconomic status . . ." (1966b, p. 61), this does not permit a careful generalization about the performance of low-status children relative to higher-status ones. Unfortunately, Loban's treatment of his data also loses all the low-status children who are not rated low in language proficiency. Additionally, the problem of grammatical data gathered from production alone would militate against applying the findings of Loban's study to Frazier's point about poor children having less language. In other words, it seems virtually impossible for a large correlational study of the kind cited above to speak to the question of what kinds of sentences a child can produce or understand. To get beyond the question of what he does produce, it is necessary to adapt the kinds of suggestions made by Chomsky (1964) and by Brown and Frazier (1964) in the monograph, *The Acquisition of Language*. Brown and Frazier observe that a child's correct sentences cannot be the basis for assuming mastery of a particular rule because there is no way of knowing that these are not simply imitations of adult models rather than "orginal" sentences generated by the child's system of rules. Following Chomsky's suggestion, Brown and Frazier (1964, p. 72) state:

> It seemed to us that systematic errors and manipulation of invented words were better evidence (for the child's command of particular rules), as a child is not likely to have had exact models for these.

This problem reduces to one that confronts all researchers—whether to use a test that reveals optimum or representative performance. A test of optimum performance is the only sound basis on which to conclude what a child can do, what abilities he has or does not have (see Severson and Guest, Chapter 15 in this volume).

Gauging optimum performance. Some research on disadvantaged children's syntax has involved the use of techniques that promise increased insight into what a child can do rather than stressing the opposite. Among these would be Osser's research (1966; Osser and McCaffrey 1965; Osser, Wang, and Zaid 1969) which is discussed elsewhere in this volume (Chapter 13) and the study reported by Baratz, also described in this volume (Chapter 2). In these studies much more attention has been devoted to specification of the particular structures under study as well as what is required of the child in using them (e.g., sentence creation, comprehension, imitation). Such attention has yielded dividends in approaching the problem of gauging syntactic performance. For example, in the research of Osser and his associates cited above, lower-status children appeared less able to process selected complex sentence structures (Osser 1966) as compared with evidence reported in studies of other children. However, these distinctions varied as a function of whether the child had to imitate or comprehend the sentences and whether certain dialect features were included in the scoring procedures (Osser, et al. 1969). Baratz's (Chapter 2) study draws attention to the point that children's performances in sentence reproduction are highly biased in favor of language materials in their own dialects. Thus, a white child will do as poorly (sometimes even more poorly) when reproducing Negro dialect as a Negro child will do in reproducing standard English.

Even with the availability of techniques like the ones discussed above, there are still major problems to be solved when trying to gauge optimum performance or even to use it as a basis for considering programs of intervention or remediation. One of these is the situational problem such as described by Labov (Chapter 9 in this volume) relative to conducting linguistic interviews, by Severson and Guest (Chapter 15) relative to the environment for standardized testing, or by Cazden (Chapter 5) and Hymes (in press) relative to the overall setting of a child's speech. In brief, even if the social class or ethnic difference between a field worker and a child is lessened, if the environment for a standardized test is made as nonthreatening as possible, or the language materials approximate his primary dialect, a child may still perform less than optimally because of gross situational factors. All existing data on social class differences in language are currently susceptible to criticism on this point.

A final point on the studies of optimum performance is that, like the more straightforward linguistic studies of lower-class children's speech (Labov,

Chapter 9; Shuy, Chapter 16), they reveal that deviations from standard English are not typically capricious or random, but are systematic and predictable. They usually indicate that the child is functioning in an organized, logical manner, but he is doing this relative to what he has learned of a language or dialect. Nevertheless, it still remains that the lower-class child's language is different from that of the school, and that something must be done to alleviate this discrepancy. Studies incorporating the idea of optimum performance may reveal to us where the discrepancies are the least, and thus provide a more systematic basis for dealing with those discrepancies which may affect most the child's academic performance. Some of the techniques described in the studies cited above should be of value in this approach, and so should such techniques as reported in studies by Berko (1958), Berko and Brown (1967), and Cazden (1968).

Similar to the presumed relation between vocabulary development and concept learning, there is an often-cited or assumed relation between syntactic mastery and intellectual development. Much of this refers to type and complexity of constructions, such as Piaget (trans., 1955) used in the twenties as a gauge of a child's cognitive development; or is currently interpreted in terms of what Bernstein purportedly means by restricted and elaborated codes (based esp. upon Bernstein 1961, 1962, but see Chapter 3 in this volume). Although space limits our delving into this relation as exercised in the study of disadvantaged children, it has been cited in the large-scale correlational studies such as those by Deutsch (1965) and Loban (1966b, p. 66) and has been a point discussed in educational intervention programs with preschoolers (e.g., Bereiter 1965; Bereiter and Engelmann 1966).

READING

Incidence of Reading Problems

We have already noted that a disadvantaged child may have a particularly difficult time learning to read if he speaks nonstandard dialect, either because he does not have certain sounds and relationships signaled by particular letters or because his teachers have failed to grasp his system of homonyms. However, neither the complex etiology nor the extent and significance of reading problems found among disadvantaged children and youth are suggested by a discussion of nonstandard dialect alone. Gordon and Wilkerson (1966, p. 76) give one indirect indication of the scope of disadvantaged children's reading disability:

> No area of the curriculum has received as much attention in compensatory programs as reading and language development. Indeed, the

attention given to all other subjects combined in compensatory programs does not equal the attention that is given to reading alone.
. . . Remedial reading ranks with guidance as the most widely used
single approach to compensatory education.

This kind of concentration of effort is a natural response to well-estab-
lished correlations between reading disability and social class on the one hand
(M. Deutsch 1964b; Sexton 1964) and delinquency or dropping out on the
other (e.g., Findley, 1964). These studies characteristically report reading
retardation in terms of national norms for standardized testing, using for
example, Science Research Associates Reading Test, Stanford Paragraph
Meaning, Iowa Silent Reading Test, and so on. Despite the limitations inherent
in this practice, it does provide a basis for some gross though revealing comparisons, such as that offered by Deutsch (1964a, p. 236): ". . . it is estimated
that up to 60 per cent of lower class children are retarded two years or more
in reading by the time they leave the elementary school." Standardized testing
in Boston (Menzies and Forman, undated) and Atlanta (Findley 1964) has
produced similar findings.

Analysis of the Problem

Consideration of the reading problems of disadvantaged children in these
global terms can, however, do little more than assert their existence. An
observation by Cohen (1964, p. 6) offers a way of looking more closely at the
problem:

Stated concisely, socially disadvantaged, retarded readers have two
basic problems: (A) They can't break the code. They have trouble
moving from the visual symbol (printed word) to the oral-aural
symbol (spoken or heard word) to the experience. (B) Even when
they break the code and move from the visual to the oral-aural, they
cannot reach final closure to the experience. The word is meaningless
because the original experience is lacking. The printed word "lawn"
may be eventually pronounced, but it will never be "read" unless
"lawn" symbolizes an experience for the reader.

The picture remains incomplete without a third feature—the extent to
which the content of the disadvantaged child's reader-texts or his own view
of himself as a reader affects his desire to learn to read. It is important, in other
words, to consider the possibility that what Labov calls a conflict of values may
prejudice the student against learning to read.

What factors of the disadvantaged child's background would help to
explain his trouble with breaking the code? There is some research, both in this

country and in England (e.g., Pringle 1965), that points to the quality of the child's early verbal interaction in his home as a source of reading difficulty. For example, Milner's (1951) small but often-quoted study reported a correlation between a student's performance on tests of reading and the amount and the affective quality of his parents' reading to him, as well as their conversation with him.

A somewhat related association between the quality of a child's speech and his reading ability also appears in Strickland's (1962) study of children's language and reading which showed that second-graders with high and low reading scores differed only in that children with above-average reading age tended to use longer phonological units. Sixth-graders, on the other hand, showed a different pattern of relationships: students with high silent reading comprehension used fewer short utterances, a higher average number of movables ("there" plus adverbial words, clauses and phrases) and elements of subordination.

Loban's (1963) longitudinal study of elementary-school children produced a similar finding which stressed the apparent long-term influence of early oral language stimulation; he reported (p. 57):

> . . . those who are proficient in oral language (the basis of group selection) are also those who are superior in reading achievement; in all qualities, the high subjects are above their chronological age in reading achievement. By grade six they are all above their age expectation . . . . Virtually all subjects in the low group are reading significantly below their chronological age in each of the years studied. The performance of the low group is almost identical in each successive year except that the median and upper quartile are shifting slightly to the left (lower). Considering the shift and the fact that the high group is shifting to the right (higher), the picture as a whole apparently is a widening reading gap from year to year between those rated high and those rated low in language ability.

Dave (1963), in his study of fifth-graders' home environment and school achievement, reported a related though not identical finding. This was a high correlation between reading achievement and six environmental process variables taken together. He noted that the second-highest correlation is between reading achievement and language models, i.e., (a) the quality of the parents' language usage (b) opportunities for enlargement and use of vocabulary and varied sentence patterns, as in talking to adults, watching television or seeing movies or plays, and (c) keenness of the parents for correct and effective language usage, as indicated by the frequency of parents reading to the child. It is important to note, however, that the most influential of the six environmental variables was achievement press, an index of the way a family pushes a child toward achievement.

With few exceptions (e.g., Whiteman, Brown, and Deutsch 1967), then, what might be called a verbal-fluency hypothesis has some support. That is, researchers and theorists tend to agree on the need for rich and varied language experience as an essential condition for successful reading. But the existence of this apparent link and the extensiveness of reading problems among poor children does not justify the general conclusion that poor children's reading deficiencies are caused by a language-poor home environment. This caution is particularly appropriate since the research cited above does not deal directly with disadvantaged children.

The evidence regarding perceptual origins of reading disability is on a somewhat firmer footing. In general terms there are three perceptual problems, any one of which might be sufficient to affect a child's learning to read. First, he may have some organic sensory disorder which prevents him from seeing or hearing letters or sounds adequately. Studies of Negro children by Pasamanick and Knobloch (1955, 1958), observations of low-status white children by Cohen (1964), and medical reports cited by Sexton (1964) all indicate that the percentage of perceptual disorders is greater among disadvantaged children. Hence it is possible to predict that without some remediation by the school, at least this percentage of children is destined for reading retardation even before they enter school.

The second potential problem concerns not an organic malfunction but a learned inability to make fine auditory discriminations which prevents the child from hearing, for example, the differences between the vowel sounds in *pit, pot, put, pet,* and *pat.* Though this problem is not peculiar to disadvantaged children, Cynthia Deutsch (1964) suggests that it may be more prevalent among this group and that this can be explained by the poor quality of the urban slum child's sensory environment. Her paper is built around two related hypotheses. The least interesting of these—because it has been generally accepted for some time before this research (DeBoer 1965; Durrell and Murphy 1953)—is that of the relation between poor reading and poor auditory discrimination. Deutsch examined this hypothesis by administering tests of verbal skills and of auditory discrimination to lower-class white and Negro children in the first and fifth grades. Roughly half of the children were retarded in reading, and these showed the expected low auditory discrimination scores. However, the analysis did indicate that this relationship diminished as one separately examined it from the first through the fifth grades, a finding that seems contrary to the cumulative-deficit hypothesis posed by Martin Deutsch (1965) and Klineberg (1963).

Though persuasively argued, Cynthia Deutsch's second hypothesis—i.e., a noisy urban slum contributes to the development of poor auditory discrimination—has not really been tested. The research part of her study (C. Deutsch 1964) was not intended to test this thesis, which rests, instead on citations of other sources. She refers to: (1) animal research on the reticular system which lies at the base of the brain and serves to maintain a kind of sensory homeostasis, based on optimum levels of sensory excitement established in infancy and early childhood; (2) the information-theory finding that "the signal-to-noise ratio is influential in the stimulus perceived and in the response evoked" (p. 279). The message or signal may, in other words, get lost in the welter of noise and the repeated struggle to attend to it may discourage careful listening. Finally, (3) there is Myklebust's observation that we are unable to avoid the impingement of sound, and thus, according to Deutsch, "auditory stimuli are particularly prone to a 'tuning-out' process, to a learned inattention" (p. 280).

Martin Deutsch's (1963) analysis of his Verbal Survey of first and fifth grade children in New York City also revealed a significant correlation between low auditory-discrimination scores and low social-class status for the first grade but not for the fifth; by then the low discrimination scores correlated with low reading scores. Though this difference or change seems plausible enough, it leaves tantalizingly open the question of how some of the low-status children improved enough (or how the middle-status children declined enough) to upset the correlation between first-graders' status and discrimination scores. Findings of this kind are a clear call for longitudinal studies designed to uncover the critical features of the schools and homes where change does seem to occur. With the information from his survey, Deutsch can go no further than he has, but two of Deutsch's students, Sher and Horner (1967), have developed wireless transmission and recording techniques that promise useful insights into the actual home and school environments that influence the development of, among other things, auditory discrimination. But until these techniques have been applied and perfected we are obliged to accept Cynthia Deutsch's (1964 p. 280) summary, the steps of whose logic may be questioned (see Bereiter 1965, pp. 26–28)) but whose conclusion is persuasive.

> Granting, for the moment, the accuracy of . . . [the research on reticular function, etc., above] one could expect that a child raised in a very noisy environment with little directed and sustained speech stimulation might well be deficient in his discrimination and recognition of speech sounds. He could also be expected to be relatively inattentive to auditory stimuli, and further, to have difficulty with any other skill which is primarily or importantly dependent on good auditory discrimination. The slum child does indeed live in a very noisy environment and he gets little connected and concentrated speech directed to him. If indeed he does show poor auditory discrimination, and if for the most part sensitivity of the end-organ ear is normal, then the hypothesized process by which poor discrimination is produced would point to methods of alleviation. . . . [Thus for slum-dwelling retarded readers] alleviation of difficulties in auditory discrimination would appear to be potentially highly important.

Cracking the code requires an additional step beyond making the initial auditory or visual discrimination. When the student is learning to read he must shift rapidly from one sensory modality to another, from the visual to the aural and vice versa. When the teacher points to a letter on the board or in a book and tells the student what the letter says, what sound it represents, he must shift quickly to make the necessary connection between sight and sound. Birch and Belmont (1964) reported a significant group difference between normal and retarded readers (nine- and ten-year-old boys in Aberdeen, Scotland) on a test of audiovisual integration. They found that audiovisual integration performance differentiates strong and weak readers within the normal and retarded groups. The experiment carefully controlled for the effects of IQ,- short-term auditory memory, age, sex, and defects in sight and hearing, but it neglected to mention social status. Thus while this study points to a relationship between poor audiovisual integration and poor reading, it offers no grounds for concluding that this set of conditions is any more or less severe among low-status students.

Katz and Deutsch (1967), working with a slightly smaller sample of first-, third-, and fifth-grade low-status Negro boys in Harlem, reported a positive relation between problems of attention, memory, and discrimination and reading difficulties. Their emphasis, however, was on the differential roles and patterning of these three processes, particularly with regard to the sensory mode involved. They considered, in other words, questions about which modality the students have the greatest trouble attending to, and whether memory or attention vary with the complexity of the task and with the modality involved.

On the basis of the research cited above we can posit that: (a) Urban slum children do live in an environment characterized by a high noise-to-signal ratio. (b) As a group these children do show marked problems of auditory and visual discrimination, of auditory and visual memory and of attention to auditory and visual stimuli. (c) These problems of perception, memory, and attention are associated with reading retardation, as is the problem of audiovisual integration.

One way of joining the separate links of this chain would be to teach visual or auditory discrimination and observe the effect on reading performance. The work or Bogar (1952) and Covington (1962) suggests the possibilities of such research with disadvantaged children. In both studies the hypothesis was tested that IQ and performance scores of low-status children would be improved by training in visual discrimination. Covington's (1962) work, based on only a two-week training period, revealed that after discrimination training, the low-status children made greater relative gains in performance than did the higher-status ones. Bogar (1952) took five months to train rural Negro and white children, and in the post-tests both groups showed gains in IQ measures. Although Brazziel and Terrell (1962) also claim to have raised the scores of a group of Negro children to national norms in a six-week training period, one cannot tell whether their discrimination training was necessary, sufficient, or even unrelated to these gains.

Like Deutsch's work, these three studies point to a perceptual skill that has a significant relationship to school performance. Clearly, though, the perceptual discriminations are sufficient rather than necessary causes of low reading performance; furthermore, the precise nature of the relationship between perception and reading remains obscure. We need to know more about the way the low-status child catches up in auditory discrimination relative to his middle-class age-mate. Does learning to read or simply being in school improve his auditory discrimination? We also need longitudinal studies of what happens to individual low-status students who show poor auditory discrimination when they begin to read. Does their reading improvement correlate with their (improved?) auditory discrimination, or can some students learn to read in spite of apparently inadequate auditory discrimination? Part of Cynthia Deutsch's testing indicates that retarded readers show an unexpectedly high auditory discrimination in a continuous performance test. This finding, which she explains away, relates interestingly to my own teaching experience where I have seen low-status students "turn off" the sounds of a noisy class and apparently attend quite carefully to their own reading or writing. Investigation is needed to discover whether a person reading in a noisy, or perhaps even a signal-filled environment, is not somehow better off if he has learned to tune out one sense modality.

Even if it were possible to remedy a disadvantaged child's perception problems, a child, according to Cohen's (1964) formulation (discussed earlier), would still be disabled by the presumed restrictions in his experiences. That is, he would be able to break the code to the extent that he would be able to pronounce or sound out most printed words, but his understanding of these words would be limited by his lack of direct experience with their referents. (This is of course questionable, since highly advantaged, sophisticated readers read with understanding, words whose referents are not part of their direct experience—for example, *colitus, liquid oxygen, nirvana*, and so on.)

Assuming, however, that a child's experience is important to his reading ability, the question arises: What kind of experience, and what is the process whereby the experience might influence the child's reading ability? Some clarification of these questions is afforded by two studies that indicated a correlation between a family's so-called cultural activities and the children's reading achievement—Dave (1963), and Whiteman, et al. (1967). Whiteman's conclusions are particularly interesting to us because he makes a point of distinguishing between simple family activities and those activities that he calls cultural. He finds that the former do not correlate significantly with reading achievement but that the latter do. One critical feature of Whiteman's cultural activities may be that they confront the child with new experiences which require some explanation, thus thrusting the parent quite naturally into the role of tutor in language learning. If this were so, an intact family might engage in many activities together but not thereby enhance the child's reading ability because the settings and activities were always familiar and required no prior or subsequent discussion or explanation. I am suggesting, in other words, that from the standpoint of verbal development togetherness is not the key feature of family activity; rather the kind and the length of dialogue that the activity promotes or requires are the critical variables.

The Schools and Reading Problems

If the above interpretation of the function and significance of cultural activities is correct, then it follows that a school cannot, without drastic restructuring, offer this kind of experience on a regular basis. School field trips, in other words, may have value for the student's self-concept and general familiarity with the world, but they should not be thought of as the equivalent of the same trip taken by a family. A good Head Start or Higher Horizons program might closely approximate the experience of a family trip, but most schools come nowhere near it.

In approaching the reading problems of disadvantaged students more directly, schools have taken two related approaches: they have attempted modifications of the process of reading instruction, and modifications of the contents of reading texts, or both. Chall (1967) reviews the bulk of the reports on using these approaches in her three-year study, *Learning to Read: the Great Debate.* She (p. 311) draws this conclusion with regard to methods of reading instruction and the contents of early readers:

> The producers of some beginning reading programs (especially the conventional basal-reading series) are in a dilemma about content above all for the first grade. These programs emphasize meaning and appreciation, while their rigid vocabulary control makes possible only content that contains little to be understood or appreciated. If meaning is pursued, then a meatier content is needed.
>
> What should this content be like? Should the emphasis be, as now, on familiar experiences? And should these familiar experiences be broadened to include all kinds of children—nonwhite as well as white, urban as well as suburban, poor as well as middle class?
>
> If the stories are to be built around familiar experiences, the only possible answer to the second question is "yes." Whether such broadening of content will help urban, poor children learn to read better,

however, I do not know. The children's attitudes may be improved. This is desirable. But a reading program that improves attitudes only and does not improve the teaching of reading is just not enough.

At the moment, many people are pinning their hopes for helping culturally disadvantaged children to read better on a change in content rather than in method. They are assuming that these children do poorly in reading because they lack the necessary concepts and cannot identify with the surburban, white, well-to-do children in their readers.

This assumption has gone untested. Raising the reading attainment of culturally disadvantaged children is too important a problem for us to concentrate all our efforts on one solution—namely, a change in content—whose effectiveness is as yet unsubstantiated. On the other hand, our inquiry indicates that the reading standards of culturally disadvantaged children can be improved by a change in method. The evidence points to a code-emphasis start for them. A change in method, I believe, should accompany any modifications in content for these children.

Chall's conclusions about method, which have not gone unchallenged (e.g., Serwer in press), are based on an extensive sifting of most of the available evidence. It is important to note, however, that most of the research that Chall has combed through has not dealt specifically with disadvantaged students. Hence it is imperative that her research suggestions be adapted to this population and carried out in order to produce conclusions more sharply focused on the disadvantaged child as a reader.

The question of content has raised a somewhat more public storm than that of method, but has not been subjected to notably careful research. The assumption that disadvantaged children's experience is limited (i.e., to their area of a ghetto or rural community, to people of their own minority group in combination with the assumption that these children prefer to read about events and people familiar to them have influenced reading texts for disadvantaged children. Style to some extent and content to a much greater extent have been changed to bring the stories closer to what publishers and their consultants believe to be the experience of disadvantaged children, closer to what they believe disadvantaged children want to read about (see Gordon and Wilkerson 1966, pp. 81–83). Though some persons have observed privately that these books are little more than *color-me-brown* versions of Dick and Jane, there are texts which do include urban settings, minority group characters, and conflicts presumably familiar to both disadvantaged and advantaged children.

Two studies dealing with the effects of the so-called multiethnic readers have given rather mixed support to these editorial efforts. Rowland and Hill (1965) investigated the preferences of Caucasian and Negro children for reading and creative-writing materials accompanied by either Negro or white illustrations. On only one measure, the proportion of Negro as against white children committed to combined reading and writing materials with Negro illustrations, did the black students prefer the Negro-illustrated material. Such a finding could be attributable to many causes, the presence of a white examiner, for example. Even without this explanation, the Roland and Hill study does not seem to go much beyond Clark's early investigation of Harlem children's low self-concept with respect to the roles they assign to black dolls (see Pettigrew 1964, pp. 6–8).

Using a relatively large sample of children and looking at the effect of multiracial preprimers on tests of vocabulary mastery as well as children's preference for the materials and individual characters, Whipple (1963, 1966) found that all classes preferred a City Series over a Standard Series. The students, regardless of race, gave highest preference to a black character as most desirable of all characters in the City Series as playmate and schoolmate. Whipple also found that students using City Series books achieved 68 percent complete mastery of their vocabulary as opposed to the controls who achieved 50 percent complete mastery of the Standard Series vocabulary. Anecdotal material also pointed to a high degree of student and faculty interest. Taken together, however, these two studies are ambiguous at best. They are at odds on students' preference for characters of their own or other races. One study was an in-house evaluation that neither controlled for differences in vocabulary content or presentation in the primers nor showed significant differences between overall mean scores. Moreover, neither study was able to isolate specific differences in content which would account for the reported differences in student performances. Until subsequent studies do this kind of difficult but vital analysis, we can only guess that some multiethnic readers are quite interesting to various students (other readers are not necessarily bad; they simply remain untested) and may for a variety of reasons actually improve these students' vocabulary test scores and their reading.

One other project deserves mention because of what it indicates about a phenomenon that recurs almost invariably in discussions of what some disadvantaged students can do as opposed to what they do. *Hooked on Books* (1966) by Fader and Shaevitz tells of a project at the Maxey Boys Training School, near Ann Arbor, Michigan. The heart of the report lies in the fact that delinquent boys (whose delinquency so often has been found to correlate with low-reading scores, e.g. Findley 1964, p. 46) became eager readers when they found paperback books and magazines on drugstore-type racks. They exhausted the supply of these paperbacks, which later had to be confiscated to insure redistribution. These and other instances of rapid improvement are admittedly exceptions, but are, nevertheless, common enough to warrant careful study of their causes (see Karnes et al 1966; Mackler et al 1965; and

McCabe 1964 for some preliminary findings regarding successful disadvantaged children).

LANGUAGE "CODES" AND "STYLES"

More sociolinguistic than psycholinguistic in approach is a body of research literature which refers not only to social-class distinctions in language but in its uses and manner of uses. This literature expands the view of language to its functioning in social systems, and such systems may range all the way from parent-child communication to the uses of language within a given subculture.

Bernstein's Restricted and Elaborated Codes

Bernstein, whose current views are presented in Chapter 3 of this volume, is most frequently linked with his contributions to the idea that different classes have their own language codes—i.e., the particular ranges of linguistic selection characteristic of communication within given social structures. Bernstein theorizes that members of the lower classes (or in Great Britain, the working classes) have access only to a style of language (restricted code) characteristic of their social structures but different from that of the middle class and the language used by the schools (elaborated code). Obviously, then, this distinction carries substantial implications concerning social mobility, educational intervention programs, and the like.

Much of the empirical research into this theory has been focused upon isolation and definition of the two codes. This work dates back to studies conducted on the language and IQ of teen-age boys from different social classes (see Bernstein 1961, 1962). Although this research has been carried further by Bernstein and his associates (see esp. Lawton 1968), three fundamental problems are yet to be resolved. The first refers to a suitably objective definition of the linguistic distinctions between restricted and elaborated codes (see Bernstein 1961, pp. 297–99; 1964; 1965; 1966; and 1967, pp. 94–95 for his attempts at this). The definitions of these distinctions have varied substantially according to researcher and project. The items listed by Lawton (1963, 1968) differ from Bernstein's lists, and all of these differ somewhat from distinctions described by Loban (1966b) and Robinson (1965). Thus when we speak of restricted and elaborated codes we are, in fact, referring to a varying configuration of characteristics rather than a consistent set. Part of this problem is that Bernstein's statement of the characteristics that constitute both codes is imprecise—for example one characteristic is "a discriminitive selection from a range of adjectives and adverbs" (Bernstein 1967, p. 95).

A second major problem—more important than inconsistency or imprecision but probably underlying both—is the lack of consistent theoretical grounding for the individual items or the full code. This problem is illustrated in Lawton's (1968) treatment of passive verbs. Bernstein found (1962) that his middle-class subjects used a higher proportion of passive verbs than did his working-class subjects. This finding was later supported for both writing and speech by Lawton (1963). This is an interesting finding only if it can be related to something else—a theoretical notion or some set of empirical data like reading performance, family size, disciplinary pattern, or a developmental scheme showing the use of passive verbs at certain ages. When Lawton (1968) attempts to give some theoretical account for this finding he refers to three grammarians with divergent points of view and concludes (p. 119): ". . . although it might be argued that in theory anything could be expressed in English without ever using the passive voice, in practice its absence or low frequency is probably symptomatic of a limited control over language use." This kind of support (and this is not atypical) is insufficient to establish the significance of the individual feature or its relation to the rest of the features of the code.

That there are class-related differences in speech and writing has been clear for some time. What is needed now is greater attention to what these differences mean. Does the difference in the proportion of passive verbs signify, for example, a developmental lag? Is it related to verbal or nonverbal IQ? How does it relate to the other revealed differences in language or language usage? In short, what do we know when we have found such a difference in the proportion of passive verbs used?

A third problem is the representative-optimum argument discussed earlier. Although Lawton (1963, 1964) reported class differences roughly similar to those earlier found by Bernstein—i.e., restricted code used by lower-class subjects, elaborated by higher—attempts to get at the heart of the social implications of this thesis have been inadequate. That is, the main problem is whether a lower-status person can use an elaborated code, or even whether he has one. As Robinson (1965) has argued, the earlier findings may show only a choice (representative) in codes typical of the lower-status speaker, rather than what he actually can do (optimum). Lawton (1968) has more recently concluded that when pushed, working-class boys will attempt a linguistic adjustment toward an elaborated code, but that (p. 140) "they lack practice and therefore facility." Data and interpretations reported by Williams and Naremore (1969) tend to support this position, although these researchers have yet another definition of the code differences.

Despite these problems, Bernstein's theories are richly suggestive, particularly in the way he explains the social and family-group patterns of organization and communication that give rise to the two codes. His chapter in this book outlines his theory around the following components:

Social Class	Family Role System	Family Communi- cation System	Language Code	Characteristic perception and reaction to tasks set by the school

Rather than go over material appearing in the present volume, I will mention briefly a recent study by Bernstein and Henderson (1969) which deals with the orientation toward use of language for various kinds of socialization. The subjects were working-class and middle-class mothers who were asked questions about the relative difficulty that a mother who could not talk would encounter in socializing her children in interpersonal relations and in certain rudimentary skills. The results showed both groups wanting to use language more for interpersonal socialization than for teaching children skills. The between-group differences, however, are marked. Bernstein and Henderson (1969, p. 21) conclude:

> The results show that the middle class, relative to the working class, place a greater emphasis upon the use of language in dealing with situations within the person area. The working class, relative to the middle class, place a greater emphasis on the use of language in the transmission of various skills.

These preferences are not due to a difference in the relevance of the skill area as opposed to the person area for the two groups, but rather to different implicit learning theories which in turn shape the language codes of the children of the two groups (Bernstein and Henderson 1969, p. 13):

> It would appear then that the difference in the response of middle class and working class mothers to the relevance of language in the acquisition of various skills is more likely to arise out of differences in the concept of learning than out of differences between social classes in terms of the value placed upon the learning of such skills. The socialization of the middle class child into the acquisition of skills is into both operations and principles which are learned in a social context which emphasizes *autonomy*. In the case of the working class child his socialization into skills emphasizes operations rather than principles learned in a social context where the child is accorded *reduced autonomy*.

Although it is clearly impossible to do more than suggest the richness of Bernstein's views on language and education, we can at least note the kinds of research needs that his work has generated. First, we need to consider the feasibility of teaching elaborated code: What is the optimum age for this teaching to begin; what aspects of the code should come first? Second, we need to study the families that may characteristically use the two codes. That is, we need to look naturalistically at families of different social classes and describe the social relations within them. Such a study would emphasize those topics that have appeared in Bernstein's and his colleague's theoretical work and interview research—mother's control behavior, socialization in the areas of skill training, and learning about interpersonal relations. This research would produce a much-needed picture of the specific conditions in the two types of homes which give rise to different codes and the educational assets and liabilities associated with them.

Family Language Styles

Bernstein has not been alone in studying language and communication within family structures. Some pertinent ideas have been reported in papers by Dave (1963), Strodtbeck (1965), and Gordon and Wilkerson 1966). However, the best known recent study which deals with social-class differences in family language styles was conducted by Hess and his colleagues in Chicago. Since the major ideas on maternal language styles are reported in Olim's chapter (11) in this volume, only a few features of the research will be discussed here.

As reported in various places (Hess and Shipman 1965; Hess, Shipman, Bear, and Brophy 1968; Olim, Hess and Shipman 1967), the project involved administering a variety of tests to Negro mothers selected from a range of social strata; among the data were interview and selected verbal-task materials. The researchers cite four major correlations that support Bernstein's notion of language as the mediating variable between a mother's social-class orientation and her child's perceptions and abilities. First is a significant relationship between a mother's control behavior and her language. If she uses status-normative controls—if she presents rules in an assigned manner where compliance is the only rule-following possibility—then she will also use imperatives frequently and she will use a restricted code in telling her child a story in an experimental situation. Second is the correlation between a mother's status-normative, imperative controls and her child's performance on the Binet, the Sigel Sorting Task, and a block-sorting task. The performance of the children with status-normative mothers was significantly lower on seven out of eight tasks than that of children whose mothers used so-called cognitive-rational controls. The third major correlation related mother's language styles to children's performance on the cognitive tasks above. Again the relationship is in the expected direction, the children of elaborated code mothers doing significantly better than children whose mothers used the restricted code. Finally, the researchers report that the mothers who use elaborated code, cognitive-rational controls, and who use instructions rather than imperatives are most likely to be members of the middle class, while the mothers who use less-option-opening language and controls are to be found in the lower two classes in this sample.

Although the language measures used in this study are not always clear and uncontroversial, the research as a whole suggests that Bernstein's point about the importance of a mother's control behavior and speech patterns certainly merits more intensive investigation. However, the emphasis on the options which the mother's control behavior opens for the child raises the additional question that will be harder to investigate but which is vital to any plans for systematic remediation. The question centers on the relation between the kinds of real options that exist in the life of the child, the way these options are reflected in the behavior of the family, the extent to which the child can select among options for his own behavior, and the language of the mother which sets up these options. Stated another way, this question concerns the relation between so-called fate-control, which seems to be positively correlated with academic success (Coleman, et al. 1966), and the speech codes characteristic of those families in which there exists this sense of fate control.

The rough scheme in Figure 1 suggest one way of visualizing this relationship, based on the way a family would perceive its ability to shape its own destiny and the way that perception might be related to its customary patterns of speech performance.

From the research discussed above, the apparent conclusion seems to be that quadrants *A2* and *B1* would represent social-status extremes and also

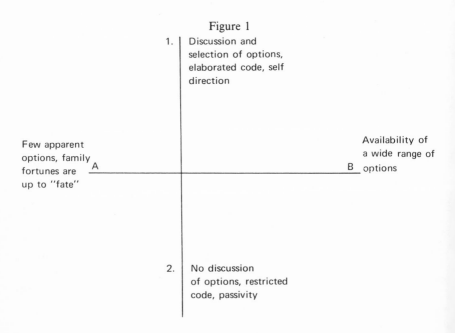

Figure 1

either end of the restricted-elaborated code spectrum. This is a conclusion we can infer from the work of Bernstein and Hess (see also Strodtbeck 1965). It is, of course, important to investigate in detail the possible exceptions represented by quadrants A1 and B2—the elaborated-code speakers with few viable options and the restricted-code speakers with many options. On a much broader scale, Stodolsky and Lesser (1967) have proposed that some of the alleged relationships between language, school success, and life style should be studied by means of a very direct, large scale experiment.

> Would poor people, given jobs and money (and the counselling necessary to see and act upon options) change in their behaviors relevant to the child's educability? Would parental behaviors such as cognitive level, teaching style, values and attitudes change with a change in economic conditions? (Stodolsky and Lesser 1967, p. 581)

Without these two kinds of studies a great deal of time and money may be spent ministering to a symptom—the child's inability to use the elaborated code—that may itself resist treatment and may, even if improved, not affect the underlying problem, that is, poor performance in school and the resulting inability to make a satisfying, dignified life for himself.

IMPLICATIONS

A book with the title *Language and Poverty* must consider the implications of research in quite broad terms. Let us begin with four conclusions that emerge with considerable force from this research.

1. The five preschool years are the most important in a child's language development.

2. Hence, poor children who spend these five years in homes which lack the conditions necessary for full language development enter schools poorly prepared for the challenges of the traditional school curriculum. There is, in short, a consistently high correlation between poverty (and often race) and poor language performance.

3. This correlation persists throughout a child's schooling. In other words, schools have, at best, a very modest impact in terms of their ability to educate poor children. That is, a poor child who begins school with submedian tests scores will, in all likelihood, end his school career even further below the median score for his age and grade. The Coleman report (1966) indicates that this is true for middle-class as well as lower-class children. Irrespective of the child's social status, schools do not account for much of the variance in achievement scores.

4. Finally, there are exceptions to the poverty cycle (and to the prosperity cycle). The poor children who "make it" may be genetically superior, or they

may have had an unusually supportive environment. Thus far, however, research has not been able to distinguish between these causes or to specify in detail the characteristics of a supportive environment.

These four points can be incorporated into a circular relation as shown in Figure 2—a version of the poverty cycle. This circular representation of the problem recommends itself because it invites multiple solutions, and because it represents the magnitude of the problem. Cohen (1968, p. 339), reviewing the Plowden Report on elementary education in Great Britain, comments forcefully on both of these points:

> Thus, if the Council (which sponsored the research) is to be faulted, perhaps it should not be for making such policy suggestions as it did, but rather for not more fully exploring the other lines of inquiry and policies which seem to be suggested in its data. Chief among these were the findings on school social class, and quasi-

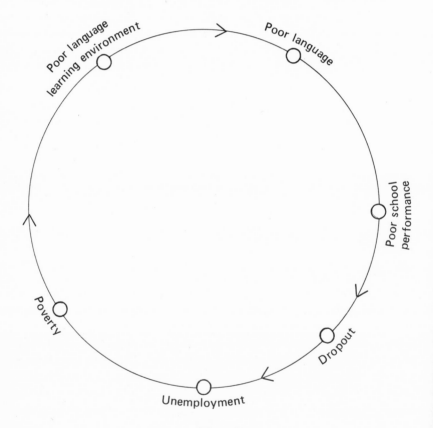

Figure 2

experimental research to more directly and competitively test various policy alternatives.

The Council's report invites one other reflection on the relation between research and policy in this area. It is that efforts to provide equality of educational opportunity will be enormously costly, in whatever terms we choose to compute cost. In the last analysis it is the low social and political priority assigned to equality of opportunity in both England and America—not the absence of adequate research—which is the chief obstacle to effective policy. The pity is not that the Plowden research was less than perfect, or less than conclusive, for given the constraints of time it is remarkably good and useful. The pity is that were the research much more perfect and conclusive we would be a little closer to schools that would remove, rather than reflect, the educational consequences of social and economic inequality.

Another way of putting Cohen's point is to emphasize that there is nothing in the logic of this review that compels us to cut into the cycle of language and poverty at the language segment rather than the poverty segment. In one sense we may be seen as taking a timid, conservative approach that may—even if carried to a successful conclusion—not result in breaking the poverty cycle. If our highest priority is to break this cycle, it would probably be more productive to devote all of the money and man-hours now devoted to language study to achieving full employment and an adequate income for all families. Thus it should be clear that the educational implications spelled out below are not meant to indicate that education is the way, or the only way, to break the poverty cycle. These implications are offered to an audience of professional researchers and educators whose commitment is to those aspects of a child's immediate home and school environment which can be changed so as to achieve the goal of fully realizing each child's intellectual potential. However, they are offered with the understanding that educational effort alone cannot achieve that goal.

Educational Implications: Negative

Consider first what we should not do. First, we should not spend further time and money on methods, texts, and so on for teaching grammar in schools as a means for language improvement. Braddock's (et al., 1963) review has shown unequivocally that teaching grammar does not improve students' writing. There is, then, no practical justification for teaching grammar. For students with high language ability, the study of grammar does little serious harm, except that it takes time from more valuable activities. My own observations suggest that children in inner-city schools suffer most from studying grammar simply because they study it more. In many such schools, sophomores, juniors, and seniors spend half to three-quarters of their language-arts time studying grammar—that is, between sixty and ninty hours a year that they could be using more profitably. Assuming these sixty and ninty hours were to be suddenly made available for some other purpose, how should they be used? What would an English teacher teach during that time?

One negative answer is clear; this time should not be spent on attempts to change disadvantaged students' dialect. Students do not drop out of school because of dialect problems unless, of course, they leave out of frustration with the school's efforts to change their dialect. However, they do leave because they can't read. Hence, one simple recommendation: drop grammar study and let students read, or teach them to read better, for sixty to ninty hours per year. This may be a difficult change to bring about, given the expectations of parents, students, and teachers with respect to grammar study. Until such a change has been accomplished, however, no school should, in good conscience, apply for Federal or other money for a compensatory language program.

A third, and perhaps obvious, change that should not be made is that suggested by Davis (1965): Make school less verbal, less language-oriented for the children who come to school with underdeveloped language skills. The implication of lowered teacher expectations makes this suggestion difficult to accept in light of recent research on expectations (Rosenthal and Jacobson 1968). It is difficult to imagine how the sixty to ninty hours we might allocate to a nonverbal program might be spent, but any alternatives that come to mind would do little to help the language-poor student.

Educational Implications: Positive

We have emphasized the need to focus on reading. The emphasis must be on basic reading skills, not a peripheral issue like developing taste. A student will not come to share a teacher's taste by being required to read a nineteenth-century novel. He may simply not read. Whether or not the student reads should be the final judgment. To this end, he might be encouraged to read Brown's *Manchild in the Promised Land* (1965), Miller's *The Cool World* (1964), or magazines on karate or automechanics. Children learn to read by reading; thus, the school must somehow provide them with books they can and will read. *Hooked on Books* (Fader and Shaevitz 1966) presents one way of getting around a small (under $10 in many school systems) per-pupil book budget. A school should exhaust these approaches before looking into a compensatory or remedial reading program.

What else does this review suggest about school practice? The most prominent theme running through all of the literature on language development is that children learn language through verbal interaction with more mature speakers. They learn language by using it. This does not mean simply listening to more mature speakers—otherwise poor children who have attended school regularly and listened to television more than middle-class children would be on a par with their middle-class counterparts.

To improve language performance by using language, a student has to talk, write, and read in school. The younger the child, the more he should be allowed and encouraged to talk to mature speakers. The interaction must be frequent, structured, and systematic, through not necessarily without humor or "soul," as the Bereiter (1965) dialogues often appear to be. This kind of interaction is hard to achieve. However, older students and nonprofessional adults can be trained to work with young students as tutor-conversationalists. Several programs based on Vygotsky's (trans. 1962) theories about dialogue being the germ of inner thought have been tried and these should provide a basis for programs adapted to the particular needs of a given school (see, for example, Blank and Solomon 1968, Chapter 4 in this volume; Bereiter 1965; Karnes 1966, 1969).

Schools, no matter who their clientele, are at a disadvantage when attempting to supplement or enrich a child's home experience. The child enters school as the period of fastest language development is ending. If a school is to offset any disadvantage in the child's home language environment, it must concentrate on providing for his language development not just in a single class but throughout the day. An excellent language-arts class can be wiped out by two periods of sitting and listening, even to a well-intentioned, competent teacher. Every class or activity must develop the child's language ability in some way. If it does not, the school cannot hope to overcome the effects of a language-poor environment.

The kinds of changes proposed may help to overcome some of the language disabilities stemming from a language-poor home environment. They will, however, be seen by the child and his parents as irrelevant if the child's schooling appears to lead nowhere except onto the front stoop and into the street. If the disadvantaged child and his parents do not see schooling as a means of achieving equal opportunity, if the society is not able to demonstrate the relevance of education, its relation to a man's life chances, then no educational changes are sufficient to alter the charge that education is irrelevant to the lives of disadvantaged children.

REFERENCES

Ausubel, D. P. How reversible are the cognitive and motivation effects of cultural deprivation? Implications for teaching the culturally deprived child. *Urban Education* 1964, 1: 16–38.

Barrows, Marjorie W. *Good English Through Practice.* New York: Henry Holt, 1956.

Bereiter, C. Academic instruction and preschool children. In *Language Programs for the Disadvantaged.* Champaign, Ill.: National Council of Teachers of English, 1965.

Bereiter, C., and Engelmann, S. *Teaching Disadvantaged Children in the Preschool.* Englewood Cliffs, N. J.: Prentice-Hall, 1966.

Berko, Jean. The child's learning of English morphology. *Word* 1958, 14: 150–77.

Berko, Jean, and Brown, R. Word acquisition and the acquisition of grammar. In J. P. DeCecco, ed., *The Psychology of Language, Thought, and Instruction.* New York: Holt, Rinehart & Winston, 1967.

Bernstein, B. Social class and linguistic development: a theory of social learning. In A. H. Halsey, J. Floud, and A. Anderson, eds., *Education, Economy, and Society.* New York: Free Press, 1961.

————. Social class, linguistic codes, and grammatical elements. *Language and Speech* 1962, 5: 221–40.

————. Aspects of language and learning in the genesis of the social process. In D. Hymes, ed., *Language in Culture and Society.* New York: Harper & Row, 1964.

————. A socio-linguistic approach to social learning. In J. Gould, ed., *Penguin Survey of the Social Sciences.* Baltimore: Penguin, 1965.

————. Elaborated and restricted codes: their social origins and some consequences. In A. Smith, ed., *Communication and Culture.* New York: Holt, Rinehart & Winston, 1966.

————. Social structure, language and learning. In J. P. DeCecco, ed., *The Psychology of Language, Thought, and Instruction.* New York: Holt, Rinehart & Winston, 1967.

Bernstein, B., and Henderson, Dorothy. Social class differences in the relevance of language to socialization. *Sociology* 1969, 3: 1–20.

Birch, H. G., and Belmont, L. Auditory visual integration in normal and retarded readers. *American J. Orthopsychiatry* 1964, 34: 852–61.

Blank, Marion, and Solomon, Frances. A tutorial language program to develop abstract thinking in socially disadvantaged preschool children. *Child Development* 1968, 39: 379–89.

Bogar, J. H. An experimental study of the effects of perceptual training on group IQ test scores of elementary pupils in rural ungraded schools. *J. Educational Research* 1952, 46: 43–52.

Braddock, R.; Lloyd-Jones, R.; and Schoer, L. *Research in Written Composition.* Champaign, Ill.: National Council of Teachers of English, 1963.

Brazziel, W. F., and Terrell, Mary. An experiment in the development of readiness in a culturally disadvantaged group of first grade children. *J. Negro Education* 1962, 31: 4–7.

Brewer, J. M. Ghetto children know what they're talking about. *New York Times Magzine,* December 28,1966.

Brown, C. *Manchild in the Promised Land.* New York: Macmillan, 1965.

Brown, R. *Words and Things.* New York: The Free Press, 1958.

Brown, R. and Fraser C. The acquisition of syntax. In Ursula Bellugi and R. Brown eds., *The Acquisition of Language.* Monograph of the Society for Research on Child Development, 1964, Vol. 29.

Carson, A. S., and Rabin, A. I. Verbal comprehension and communication in Negro and white children. *J. Educational Psychology* 1960, 51: 47–51.

Cazden, Courtney B. The acquisition of noun and verb inflections. *Child Development* 1968, 39: 433–48.

Center for Applied Linguistics. Description of the Urban Language Survey. Mimeographed. Washington, D. C.: Center for Applied Linguistics, 1966.

Chall, Jeanne S. *Learning to Read: The Great Debate.* New York: McGraw-Hill, 1967.

Chomsky, N. A review of B. F. Skinner's *Verbal Behavior.* In J. A. Fodor, and J. J. Katz, eds., *The Structure of Language.* Englewood Cliffs, N. J.: Prentice-Hall, 1964.

Cloward, R. D. Studies in tutoring. Mimeographed. New York: Columbia University School of Social Work, 1966.

Cohen, S. A. Diagnosis and treatment of reading difficulties in Puerto Rican and Negro communities. Paper delivered at Fairleigh Dickinson University Reading Conference, December 1964.

Cohen, D. Children and their primary schools. *Harvard Educational Review* 1968, 38: 329–40.

Coleman, J. S., et al. *Equality of Educational Opportunity.* Washington, D. C.: U. S. Government Printing Office, 1966.

Conat, J. B. *Slums and Suburbs.* New York: McGraw-Hill, 1961.

Covington, M. V. Some effects of stimulus familiarization on discrimination. Doctoral dissertation, University of California, Berkeley, 1962.

Dave, R. H. The identification and measurement of environmental process variables that are related to educational achievement. Doctoral dissertation, University of Chicago, 1963.

Davis, A. *Social Class Influence upon Learning.* Cambridge, Mass.: Harvard University Press, 1965.

DeBoer, J. J., and Dallmann, Martha. *The Teaching of Reading.* New York: Holt, Rinehart, & Winston, 1965.

Deutsch, Cynthia P. Auditory discrimination and learning: social factors. *Merrill-Palmer Quarterly* 1964, 10: 277–96.

Deutsch, M. The disadvantaged child and the learning process: some social, psychological, and developmental considerations, In A. H. Passow, ed., *Education in Depressed Areas.* New York: Teachers College Bureau of Publications, 1963.

———. Social and psychological perspectives on the development of the disadvantaged learner. *J. Negro Education* 1964, 33: 232–44. (a)

———. Early social environment: its influence on social adaptation. In D. Schreiber, ed., *The School Dropout.* Washington, D. C.: The National Education Association, 1964. (b)

———. The role of social class in language development and cognition. *American J. Orthopsychiatry,* 1965, 35: 77–88.

Durrell, D. C., and Murphy, Helen A. The auditory discrimination factor in reading readiness and reading disability. *Education* 1953, 73: 556–60.

Fader, D. N., and Shaevitz, M. H., *Hooked on Books.* New York: Berkeley Medallion Books, 1966.

Figurel, J. A. Limitations in the vocabulary of disadvantaged children: a cause of poor reading. In *Improvement of Reading Through Classroom Practice.* Newark, Del.: International Reading Association, 1964.

Findley, W. G. Language development and dropouts. In D. Schreiber, ed., *The School Dropout.* Washington, D. C.: National Education Association, 1964.

Frazier, A.; Jewett, A.; Mersaud, J.; and Gunderson, Doris B. A research proposal to develop the language skills of children with poor background. In *Improving English Skills of Culturally Different Youth.* Washington, D. C.: U. S. Office of Education, 1964.

Fries, C. C. *American English Grammar.* New York: Appleton-Century-Crofts, 1940.

———. *Cumulative Pattern Practices.* Ann Arbor, Mich.: University of Michigan, 1954.

Golden, Ruth I. *Improving Patterns of Language Usage.* Detroit: Wayne State University Press, 1960.

———. Effectiveness of instructional tapes for changing regional speech patterns. Doctoral dissertation, Wayne State University, 1963.

———. *Changes Dialects.* Instructional record for changing regional speech patterns. New York: Folkways Records, 1964.

Gordon, E. W. Characteristics of socially disadvantaged children. *Review of Educational Research* 1965, 35: 377–88.

Gordon, E. W., and Wilkerson, D. A. *Compensatory Education for the Disadvantaged.* New York: College Entrance Examination Board, 1966.

Green, W. D. Language and the culturally different. *English J.* 1965, 54: 724–33, 740.

Harrington, M. *The Other American—Poverty in the United States.* New York: Macmillan, 1962.

Hess, R. D., and Shipman, Virginia. Early experience and the socialization of cognitive modes in children. *Child Development* 1965, 36: 869–86.

Hess, R. D.; Shipman, Virginia; Bear, Roberta M.; and Brophy, J. *The Cognitive Environments of Urban Preschool Children.* Chicago: The University of Chicago Press, 1968.

Hymes, D. On communicative competence. In R. Huxley and E. Ingram, eds., *The Mechanisms of Language Development.* London: CIBA Foundation, in press.

John, Vera P. The intellectual development of slum children: some preliminary findings. *American J. Orthopsychiatry* 1963, 33: 813–22.

John, Vera P., and Goldstein, L. S. The social context of language acquisition. *Merrill-Palmer Quarterly* 1964, 10: 265–75.

Karnes, M. B.; Zehrback, R. R.; Studley, W. M.; and Wright, W. R. Culturally disadvantaged children of higher potential: intellectual functioning and educational implications. Mimeographed. Champaign, Ill. 1965.

Karnes, M. B., et al. Activities for developing psycholinguistic skill with preschool culturally deprived children. Mimeographed. Urbana, Ill. Institute for Research on Exceptional Children, 1966.

Karnes, M. B. A new role for teachers: involving the entire family in the education of preschool disadvantaged children. Mimeographed. Urbana, Ill. University of Illinois College of Education, 1969.

Katz, Phyllis A., and Deutsch, M. The relation of auditory and visual functioning to reading achievement in disadvantaged children. In M. Deutsch and associates, *The Disadvantaged Child.* New York: Basic Books, 1967.

Klineberg, O. Negro-white differences in intelligence test performances: a new look at an old problem. *American Psychologist* 1963, 18: 198–203.

Labov, W. Stages in the acquisition of standard English. In R. W. Shuy, ed., *Social Dialects and Language Learning.* Champaign, Ill. National Council of Teachers of English, 1965.

———. *The Social Stratification of English in New York City.* Washington, D. C.: Center for Applied Linguistics, 1966.

———. Some sources of reading problems for Negro speakers of nonstandard English. In A. Frazier, ed., *New Directions in Elementary English.* Champaign, Ill. National Council of Teachers of English, 1967.

Lawton, D. Social class differences in language development: a study of some samples of written work. *Language and Speech* 1963, 6: 120–43.

———. Some class language differences in group discussions. *Language and Speech* 1964, 7: 182–204.

———. Social Class, Language and Education. New York: Schocken, 1968.

Lin, S. C. *Pattern Practice in the Teaching of Standard English to Students with a Non-standard Dialect.* New York: Teachers College Bureau of Publications, Columbia University, 1965.

Lloyd, D. Subcultural patterns which affect reading development. In *Improving English Skills of Culturally Different Youth.* Washington, D. C.: U. S. Government Printing Office, 1964.

Loban, W. *The Language of Elementary School Children: Research Report No. 1.* Champaign, Ill.: National Council of Teachers of English, 1963.

———. *Problems in Oral English.* Champaign, Ill.: National Council of Teachers of English, 1966.(a)

———. *Language Ability, Grades Seven, Eight and Nine.* Washington, D. C.: U. S. Government Printing Office, 1966.(b)

Lorge, I., and Chall, Jeanne. Estimating the size of vocabularies of children and adults: an analysis of methodological issues. *J. Experimental Education* 1963, 32: 147–57.

Mackler, B.; Catalana, Thelma P.; and Holman, W. D. The successful urban slum child: a psychological study of personality and academic success in deprived children. Unpublished report. Columbia University, 1965.

McCabe, Alice R. The intellectually superior child in a deprived social area. Unpublished report. Harlem Demonstration Center, Community Service Society of New York, 1964.

McCarthy, Dorothea. Language development in children. In L. Carmichael, ed., *Manual of Child Psychology.* New York: Wiley, 1954.

McDavid, R. I. Jr. American social dialects. *College English* 1965, 26: 254–60.

Mellon J. C. Transformational sentence-combining: a method for enchancing the development of syntactic fluency in English composition. Doctoral dissertation, Harvard University, 1967.

Menzies, I., and Forman, I. *The Mess in Bay State Education.* Undated pamphlet.

Miller, W. *The Cool World.* New York: Fawcett, 1964.

Milner, Esther. A study of the relationship between reading readiness in grade one school children and patterns of parent-child interaction. *Child Development* 1951, 22: 95–112.

Newton, Eunice S. Verbal destitution: the pivotal barrier to learning. *J. Negro Education* 1960, 29: 497–99.

Olim, E. G.; Hess, R. D.; and Shipman, Virginia. Role of mother's language styles in mediating their preschool children's cognitive development. *The School Review* 1967, 75: 414–24.

Osser, H., and McCaffrey, A. Language control in a group of headstart children. Unpublished research report. 1965.

Osser, H. The syntactic structures of five-year-old culturally deprived children.

Paper read at the symposium on the concept of structure in language and thinking, Eastern Psychological Association, 1966, New York.

Osser, H.; Wang, Marilyn D.; and Zaid, Farida. The young child's ability to imitate and comprehend speech: a comparison of two sub-cultural groups. *Child Development* 1969, 40: 1063–75.

Pasamanick, B. and Knobloch, Hilda. Early language behavior in Negro children and the testing of intelligence. *J. Abnormal and Social Psychology* 1955, 50: 401–2.

Pasamanick, B. and Knobloch, Hilda. The contribution of some organic factors to school retardation in Negro children. *J. Negro Education* 1958, 27: 4–9.

Pederson, L. A. Some structural differences in the speech of Chicago Negroes. In R. W. Shuy, ed., *Social Dialects and Language Learning*. Champaign, Ill.: National Council of Teachers of English, 1965.

Peisach, Estelle C. Children's comprehension of teacher and peer speech. *Child Development* 1965, 30: 467–80.

Pettigrew, T. F. *A Profile of Negro America*. Princeton, N. J.: Van Nostrand, 1964.

Piaget, J. *The Language and Thought of the Child*. Marjorie Gabain, trans. Cleveland: Meridian, World Pub., 1955.

Pringle, M. L. K. *Deprivation and Education*. London: Longmans Green, 1965.

Riessman, F. *The Culturally Deprived Child*. New York: Harper & Row, 1962.

Robinson, W. P. The elaborated code in working class language. *Language and Speech* 1965, 8: 243–52.

Rosenthal, R. The world across the street. *Harvard Graduate School of Education Bulletin* 1966, 11: 4–24.

Rosenthal, R. and Jacobson, Lenore. *Pygmalion in the Classroom*. New York: Holt, Rinehart & Winston, 1968.

Rowland, M., and Hill, Patricia. Race, illustrations, and interest in materials for reading and creative writing. *J. Negro Education* 1965, 34: 84–87.

Serwer, Blanche. Linguistic support for a method of teaching reading to black children. *Reading Research Quarterly,* in press.

Sexton, Patricia C. *Education and Income*. New York: Compass Viking, 1964.

Sher, Abigail and Horner, Vivian. A technique for gathering children's language samples from naturalistic settings. Paper read at a meeting of the Society for Research in Child Development, March 1967, New York.

Siller, J. Socioeconomic status and conceptual thinking. *J. Abnormal and Social Psychology* 1957, 55: 365–71.

Sledd, J. On not teaching English usage. *English J.* 1965, 54: 698–703.

Stodolsky, Susan A., and Lesser, G. S. Learning patterns in the disadvantaged. *Harvard Educational Review* 1967, 37: 546–93.

Strickland, Ruth G. The language of elementary school children: its relationship to the language of reading textbooks and the quality of reading in selected children. *Bulletin of the School of Education, Indiana University* 1962, 38: 1–131.

Strodtbeck, F. L. The hidden curriculum in the middle-class home. In J. D. Krumboltz, ed., *Learning and the Educational Process.* Chicago: Rand McNally, 1965.

Temple, T. R. A program for overcoming the handicap of dialect. *The New Republic,* March 25, 1967.

Templin, Mildred C. *Certain Language Skills in Children, Their Development and Interrelationships.* Institute of Child Welfare Monograph Series, No. 26. Minneapolis: University of Minnesota Press, 1957.

Templin, Mildred C. Relations of speech and language development to intelligence and socio-economic status. *Volta Review* 1958, 60: 331–34.

Vygotsky, L. S. *Thought and Language.* Eugenia Hanfmann and Gertrude Vakar, ed. and trans. Cambridge, Mass.: M.I.T. Press, 1962.

Whipple, Gertrude. Appraisal of the City Schools Reading Program. Unpublished report. Detroit, 1963.

————. Multicultural primers of today's children. In J. Frost and G. Hawkes, eds., *The Disadvantaged Child.* Boston: Houghton Mifflin, 1966.

Whiteman, M.; Brown, B. R.; and Deutsch, M. Some effects of social class and race on children's language and intellectual abilities. In M. Deutsch and associates, *The Disadvantaged Child.* New York: Basic Books, 1967.

Williams F., and Naremore, Rita C. On the functional analysis of social class differences in modes of speech. *Speech Monographs* 1969, 36: 77–102.

Wolf, R. M. The identification and measurement of environmental process variables related to intelligence. Doctoral dissertation, University of Chicago, 1963.

Chapter 15

TOWARD THE STANDARDIZED ASSESSMENT OF THE LANGUAGE OF DISADVANTAGED CHILDREN

Roger A. Severson and Kristin E. Guest*

Any sensitive person who has worked with disadvantaged children—as teacher, as social worker, or even as a Head Start volunteer—can testify that differences in language separate these children from those whose families enjoy membership in the socioeconomic mainstream of American life. Despite the major attention given to this observation, however, there is continuing confusion regarding the accurate description of these differences. A considerable part of this confusion has been created in the effort to transform these impressionistic descriptions into more exact descriptions through the use of standardized tests. Such tests involve description in the form of measurement, where reliability and validity of measurement have been assessed, and where norms have been established as a basis for interpretation of the results. It is not easy to be sensitive to this confusion, let alone to find one's way out of it, without considering some of the basic assumptions involved in creating and using standardized tests, examining problems in the standardized assessment of certain populations, and finally, looking at innovative methods for measuring language. In this paper we have tried to outline some of the issues in this problem area, at least enough of an outline to provide some basis for answering the question: How should one approach standardized assessment of the language of disadvantaged children?

*Department of Educational Psychology, University of Wisconsin

CONCEPTUAL ISSUES AND TEST GOALS

Although standardized measurement with the use of individually administered tests has acquired a great deal of acceptance in the behavioral sciences, there are several problems which must be resolved, or at least clearly seen, before such instruments can be of true value in any new area. Consideration of these issues will alert persons to the limitations of some of the standardized or nonstandardized findings which researchers have reported about disadvantaged children.

One largely unresolved problem involves the differentiation of measures of language behaviors from measures of other behaviors. In this paper, we will use the general term *language* to refer to the extended network of behaviors which affect verbal communication, such as auditory discrimination, articulatory competencies, verbal fluency, receptive and expressive capacities, and the various abilities which we assume reflect one's knowledge of his language. Since tests requiring language responses provide the vehicle for measuring many other psychological behaviors, measurement devices of specific language behaviors must be carefully constructed to avoid duplication in test function.

With regard to the desirability of avoiding test overlap (or ambiguity), the contrast between measures of intelligence and measures of language will serve to illustrate the difficulties of definition and measurement. Intelligence is historically the most valuable construct in the history of measuring psychological behavior.[1] Since Binet's breakthrough in creating an effective IQ test in the first decade of this century, one trend has been away from the global measurement of IQ toward the measurement of more specific areas of ability. In part, this has involved differentiating the place of language in intellectual functioning, as in the distinction between verbal IQ and nonverbal IQ, where the latter measures require no oral language responses. Although this distinction reduces the confounding between language behaviors and intellectual behaviors, measures of verbal IQ still necessarily employ language responses to assess intellective abilities. For example, in one of the most popular individually administered IQ tests, the Wechsler Intelligence Scale for Children (or WISC), most of the verbal intelligence subtests require complex language skills, but correct responses do not take into consideration qualitative differences in several important facets of language (Wechsler 1949).

---

[1] A construct is a theoretical dimension created to explain behavior. It can only be related to actual behavior by means of predicted relationships which are subject to empirical assessment. A new construct acquires utility when visible behaviors seem better explained by using it in addition to, or instead of, existing explanations, and where measurements confirm these better predictions. Intellectual behaviors, as measured by numerous IQ tests, have generated very significant relationships with a wide variety of human behaviors, both theoretical and practical.

Although high correlations between global measures of IQ and language behaviors are found, some language tests (e.g., Crabtree 1958, 1963; Spradlin 1963) show a definite shift in organization away from verbal IQ tests. Thus, the Stanford-Binet may employ a single item to measure word production because this meets the general requirements of an IQ test, but a new language test might develop a whole subtest around the area of verbal fluency. Whether specific measures of language do in fact generate important new information regarding language (and, thus, better serve the needs of theorists, clinicians, and educators) can only be demonstrated by empirical information not now available.

A consideration of the development of standardized testing itself is required to see that even now the issues are far from settled in the standardized assessment of any area of behavior. Major confusion arises when test constructors and users are unclear over the purposes to which measurement instruments are put. Three essentially different purposes exist in the standardized assessment of human behaviors, and each purpose calls for a different kind of measurement instrument. These three objectives are understanding (theory building), prediction (classification), and control (change of behavior).

Measurement instruments based upon a single behavioral construct (e.g., tests designed to measure anxiety or need-achievement) should have certain qualities in order to be most useful for establishing the value of the construct. It should be clear why each test item is thought to be a measure of the construct and, as much as possible, the items should be measures of the same thing. The test should relate highly to established measures of the same construct (convergent validity) and be as unrelated as possible to established instruments where the broader theory predicts such independence (discriminant validity; Campbell and Fiske 1959). Finally, gathering empirical data on large numbers of homogeneous populations, both normal and deviant, together with measurements of groups receiving varying treatments, helps to fulfill the purpose of the test.

The second major purpose for measurement instruments is classification or behavioral prediction. For example, when persons are to be selected from a larger group for differential placement in subgroups, then instruments are sought which best define, according to some criterion, the selection of those persons for the various subgroups. Such instruments may be used for selecting vocational candidates (Anastasi 1968; Cronbach 1969) or for placing certain children in special classes for language remediation. A single classification decision is called for, and therefore the best test items for these instruments will correlate as highly as possible with the criterion (e.g., with ultimate vocational or classroom success). Greater efficiency is obtained if the test items have low intercorrelations, but the test items may not necessarily have interpretable connections with the content of the programs into which the people will go. In both classification and construct measurement, the search is for tests with high stability (test-retest reliability) which maximally differentiate people being tested (the tests should result in as large a spread of scores as possible).

The third major application of measurement instruments involves the detailing of remedial strategies. This involves providing information about the kinds of experiences and the learning environments which will be most profitable in changing the person from his present functioning to a desired criterion level of functioning. Such instruments should provide for the standardized observation of behavior under both natural and controlled environments, together with observation of behavior change when systematic modifications are made in the stimulus or reinforcement qualities of the environment. The qualities of tests which best serve this latter purpose largely remain in the process of development (Beery 1968; Engelmann 1967; Glaser 1963).

The careful distinctions among the purposes of test users and the types of tests which best serve these purposes are not sufficiently made in current practice. Many tests in the areas of intelligence and language assessment involve a compromise among these various purposes, both at the level of construction and the level of application. Test designers in most commercial areas try to serve all masters by offering subtest scores for diagnostic-remedial purposes, and a summed score deemed reputedly most useful for classification purposes. McNemar (1964) has presented a caustic attack against this confusion of claims by those who market tests. Until test designers can refine the measuring instruments, we are faced with using existing measures which are often less than adequate.

The adequacy of language measures obtained in highly structured testing situations has itself been increasingly questioned. One alternative involves gathering samples of language in relatively natural situations (free speech) with no effort to standardize the environmental conditions. Although relatively few studies are yet available, those reporting standardized scores on a sample of individuals where free speech samples are also obtained show very little correlation between test scores and free speech scores when both are supposed to reflect usage of a given type of language behavior (Dever 1968; Jones and Wepman 1965). Such comparisons, however, are plagued by the lack of comparable scoring standards and the lack of consistency in the methods for obtaining and describing samples of free speech.

Another problem with standardized tests of language is the assumption that only one version of language is correct—that is, a child's responses to a standardized instrument are scored relative to responses presumed to be the right ones. In defining what we mean by *right*, we are faced with a choice between normative language usage in the community of the tested individual and some set of standards judged as the desired language capabilities for the person. Even if we settle for an individual's community language standards, the sheer variation in the use of English in the United States confronts the test constructor with the formidable task of presenting regional norms, if his objective is to construct a test with national relevance. Increasingly, test constructors are placing the responsibility of gathering norms onto test users within the settings which employ the test, but this solution is feasible only if the specific items included have clear relevance for language behaviors in these settings.

In many current studies of subcultural dialects, what have previously been reported as linguistic deficiencies, based on the norms of standardized language measures, are now sometimes being defended as linguistic differences of a systematic nature (see Cazden 1966; Baratz, Chapter 2, and Stewart, Chapter 17, in this volume). Efforts to circumvent this problem in language testing have involved the use of two language versions of tests—one in the person's own dialect and one in whatever other dialect is being considered (e.g., standard English; see Baratz, Chapter 2 in this volume; McCaffrey 1969).

AN APPROACH TO STANDARDIZED MEASURES OF LANGUAGE BEHAVIOR: THE ILLINOIS TEST OF PSYCHOLINGUISTIC ABILITIES

Certainly there has been no shortage of attempts to measure language behavior, but among these only a few—and particularly one, The Illinois Test of Psycholinguistic Abilities (ITPA)—reflect the goals of a standardized test. We will use the ITPA as the basis for our discussion of an actual test and to show some of the results obtained when using it with disadvantaged populations.

Scope of the Test

The ITPA, now in a revised edition (Kirk, McCarthy, and Kirk 1968), has evolved through numerous editions in the past fifteen years, mainly under the leadership of Professor Sam Kirk of the University of Illinois. Although the theoretical bases of the ITPA have been extensively discussed elsewhere (Kirk 1968; Kirk and McCarthy 1961), its theoretical scope can be described here in terms of three dimensions of psycholinguistic abilities:

1. *Channels of Communication.* Conceivably, these channels would involve all possible combinations of sensory input and response output (auditory, visual, and tactile input; auditory and motor output), but the ITPA limits itself, for practical reasons, to measuring auditory-vocal and visual-motor channels.

2. *Psycholinguistic Processes.* The distinction is maintained between

receptive processes ("that ability necessary to recognize and/or understand what is seen or heard"), expressive processes ("those skills necessary to express ideas or to respond either vocally or by gesture or movement"), and organizing processes ("the internal manipulation of percepts, concepts, and linguistic symbols"; Kirk, McCarthy, and Kirk 1968, p. 7).

3. *Levels of Organization.* The complexity of response is seen to vary from an automatic level to a representational level. The former includes psycholinguistic behaviors which are highly organized and require relatively automatic responding, such as visual and auditory closure, perceptual speed, rote recall, and rote learning. The representational level involves the more abstract manipulation of the meaning presumably associated with the symbols.

The revised ITPA contains ten regular subtests and two alternate subtests. The following six subtests are found at the representational level (labels in parentheses identify the corresponding names on the earlier Experimental Edition):

1. *Auditory Reception (Auditory Decoding).* This is a measure of the child's ability to comprehend verbally presented material. A simple yes or no response is required, or even a nod or shake of the head in response to questions such as "Do dials yawn?"

2. *Visual Reception (Visual Decoding).* A picture of a single item, such as a doll, is presented first. Then a second picture, with four objects (such as a cat, pig, girl and doll), is presented and the child is asked to select the object closest to the first in structural qualities.

3. *Auditory-Vocal Association.* This is a verbal analogies test consisting of items such as "I cut with a saw; I pound with a———."

4. *Visual-Motor Association.* A picture of a single item, such as a bone, is shown, surrounded by a set of four other pictures (such as a pipe, a rattle, a pencil, and a dog). The child is asked which of the four is closest to the first in functional or conceptual qualities.

5. *Verbal Expression (Vocal Encoding).* This gauges the child's capacity to describe verbally several familiar objects. For example, he is given a ball and asked to, "Tell me all about this." His responses are scored for the number of concepts expressed, as represented by the spontaneous reporting of name, color, shape, usage, size, and other classifying qualities.

6. *Manual Expression (Motor Encoding).* This requires the child to make gestural representations of the correct way to manipulate pictorially presented objects such as a violin or telephone.

At the automatic level there are four regular tests, and two supplementary tests are included for use with children manifesting reading or spelling difficulties; these are:

1. *Grammatic Closure (Auditory-Vocal Automatic).* This requires the

child to present the correct grammatic completion of an incomplete phrase; for example, "Here is a dog; here are two————."

2. *Auditory Closure.* This is a supplementary test which assesses the child's capacity to fill in deleted parts of spoken words in order to produce a complete word; for example, "What am I talking about—bo———le?", "tele———one?"

3. *Sound Blending.* This is a supplementary test requiring the child to produce words whose parts are spoken to him consecutively at half-second intervals. For example, "Listen. D-OG. What word is that?"

4. *Visual Closure.* This measures the child's ability to locate figures (e.g., bottles) partly hidden behind various objects in a cartoon drawing.

5. *Auditory Sequential Memory (Auditory-Vocal Sequencing).* This assesses capacity to orally reproduce number series presented at the rate of two digits per second.

6. *Visual Sequential Memory (Visual-Motor Sequencing).* This measures the child's ability to reproduce sequences of nonmeaningful geometric figures after five seconds exposure to a model. The figures are on the face of plastic chips for the child to place in order.

The Revised Edition of the ITPA is similar to the Experimental Edition published in 1961 except for changes in subtest labels, considerable modification of items to make the test easier to administer, extension of the floor age from two years and six months down to two years and four months, extension of the ceiling age from nine years and three months up to ten years and three months, and the addition of three subtests. An excellently prepared test manual describes all of the requirements for proper test administration, including the extent of examiner training required. Kirk and his associates have also been conscientious about publishing information concerning standardization procedures (Paraskevopoulos and Kirk 1969; McCarthy and Kirk 1963), and providing information on validity (McCarthy and Olson 1966). Two reviews of studies on the Experimental Edition of the ITPA have been published by Bateman (1965, 1968). Due to the basic similarity of the Experimental Edition and the Revised Edition, we can assume that the research and clinical findings based on the two versions are likely to be very similar.

Recognizing the intricate relationship between intellectual and linguistic abilities, Kirk and his associates (et al. 1968) have described the test as a molar assessment of intelligence. They also refer to it as a measure of specific cognitive abilities. There are also claims that one of the major objectives of the test is to identify the existing pattern of abilities in a child with a learning disability. The subtests are claimed to have primary value in identifying the areas requiring specific remediation, but the primary purpose of the test is not claimed to be providing a basis for placing children into special classes.

Some Examples in the Use of the ITPA with the Disadvantaged

Perhaps the most extended information on ITPA performances of disadvantaged groups has come from the Early Training Project in Murfreesboro, Tennessee, where approximately eighty children were followed from ages three to seven (Klaus 1965; Klaus and Gray 1968). All of the children were defined as culturally disadvantaged Negroes, and half were involved in various treatment programs designed to modify several kinds of behaviors thought to be related to cultural disadvantage. Despite significant gains in mean subtest scores, the repeated testings and treatment programs did not lead to changes in the group subtest patterns obtained on the ITPA. The profile continued to show the highest relative scores on the Auditory-Vocal Sequential (an immediate memory for number series) and Visual-Motor Association (knowledge of functional relationship between objects) subtests. This contrasted with a consistently low score on Auditory-Vocal Automatic (capacity to complete words and phrases with standard grammatical form). Klaus and Gray (1968) and Bateman (1968) both underscore the fact that the assessment of grammatical correctness may be particularly influenced by differences in the cultural backgrounds of the Negro children, when compared to the predominantly white sample used for standardization of the test. Klaus and Gray also speculate on the general preference of these Negro culturally disadvantaged groups for visual as against auditory channels of communication.

One study, also from Tennessee but from a different group of experimenters (Ivey, Center, and Tanner 1968), involved four groups of ten children, selected to represent high- and low-social-class backgrounds for both Negroes and whites. These researchers also found low scores for Negroes of both social-class levels on the Auditory-Vocal Automatic subtest (word and phrase completion), suggesting this is a subcultural consistency in ITPA patterning. Only the high-social-class white sample showed no depression on this subtest. Once again, the Auditory-Vocal Sequencing (digit reproduction) was one of the highest scores in both Negro samples.

A few other studies have reported data which allow a separate inspection of the ITPA profiles of different races and social-class levels. Bateman (1968) reported profile information on kindergarten children, which once again reflected the selectively low score in the Auditory-Vocal Automatic and the selectively high score in the Auditory-Vocal Sequiential for the Negro children. The social-class differences were not analyzed statistically, and marked IQ and age differences render her interpretations of subtest differences somewhat questionable. With an even younger Head Start group, Leventhal and Stedman (1967) found significant differences on six of the nine subtests. Interestingly, two of the three subtests showing no significant differences required no language usage at all (Visual-Motor Sequential and Visual-Motor Automatic), and the third merely required repetition of spoken numbers. This latter Auditory-Vocal Sequential subtest score was again clearly superior to all other subtest scores for the Negroes, and the lowest subtest score was the Auditory-Vocal Automatic.

In contrast to these somewhat consistent findings of racial differences where social class is controlled, comparisons between different social-class levels have not yet revealed a definite pattern of subtest scores. In fact, in one study which considered the overall test differentiation, a general language factor was thought to best separate the social-class levels within an all-Negro sample (Ryckman 1967). Although the few studies which have reported profiles separately for different social-class levels do not show consistent subtest pattern differences (Bateman 1968; Ivey, Center, and Tanner 1968), a challenging question is raised since there is a consistent difference between total scores.

In studies where IQ scores are also reported, the discrepancy between different groups is quite similar on both the summed ITPA subtest scores and the IQ measure (Bateman 1968; Ivey, Center, and Tanner 1968). Unfortunately, in none of the previous studies have the authors reported correlational information between IQ and the individual ITPA subtests, nor made efforts to partial out the influence of IQ to see if residual and unique language differences remain. We have found only one study where efforts to control for the effect of IQ was made. Giebink and Marden (1968) examined differences between Head Start children and middle-class children on the Vocal Encoding and Auditory-Vocal Automatic subtest of the ITPA, as well as on Peabody Picture Vocabulary Test scores (PPVT). A significant difference favoring the middle-class children was found only for the Auditory-Vocal Automatic subtest; this difference remained when the influence of PPVT–IQ was held constant. Whether significant differences would remain if the full ITPA and a more adequate IQ test were used (such as the WISC or Stanford-Binet) can only be determined empirically. It is possible that when comparing groups differing only in social class (where race is controlled), the ITPA is primarily useful as a measure of global intelligence.

In the absence of more and better studies, it is difficult to put the various findings together meaningfully. With the exception of Klaus and Gray (1968), most researchers have made little effort to interpret profile differences with regard to implications for actual language functioning, both between and within the groups tested. Klaus and Gray's (1968) conclusion, that the Negro culturally deprived children were more disposed to visual than to auditory reception, was based on a sophisticated statistical analysis and seems to us to deserve much further study. This distinction, and the consistently low Auditory-Vocal Automatic scores, raise the question whether the language difference between examiners and children may have resulted in the auditory channel being avoided by the children. A recent study (McConnell, Horton, and Smith 1969), using a culturally deprived sample of preschool children heavily composed of Negro children, reported a selective lag in auditory development across several tests, including the ITPA, Stanford-Binet, and other extensive, individually administered tests. Unfortunately, no separate findings were reported by race or subtests, and it is not possible to know at this point whether the selective impairment is racially or experientially related.

High scores on the Auditory-Sequential Memory subtest by Negro children is an intriguing finding worthy of further study, particularly since it runs counter to the general pattern of depressed auditory performance. In a recent controversial article, Jensen (1969) has noted the superiority in lower-class Negroes of rote learning (such as immediate memory for digits) when compared to other more abstract kinds of learning tasks (such as concept learning). Jensen has interpreted this as a deficit pattern in the Negro because of the presumably greater importance of abstract learning skills. The ITPA pattern, where this same rote-learning skill is found to be superior at both lower-class and middle-class levels, casts the general question of the significance of the rote-learning skills into a new light. It is possible that in a general pattern of experiential deficit, rote learning in the Negro emerges as an intact facility. While it is not possible to determine at this point whether the ability is genetically or subculturally related, it does seem to suggest that the quality of rote learning is an unsuspected asset.

Evaluation of the ITPA

It is unfortunate that such a conscientious effort at designing a standardized language test should take place at a time when so much ferment is occurring, both in the area of psycholinguistic theory and in the field of behavioral assessment. However, it is a testimony to the extensive psychometric work which has been done on this test that it will probably survive despite earlier and anticipated future attacks upon its rationale and validity (e.g., Weener, Barritt, and Semmel 1967). If the major proponents of the test continue to revise it when demands of the field suggest a need for improvement, then the ITPA should indefinitely continue as the most important general language test with children.

The test constructors have placed considerable emphasis on the theory-based nature of the test. This position is ironic for several reasons. Psycholinguistic theory is evolving so rapidly that even the most recently developed theory is likely to find several critics (See Dixon and Horton 1968). Second, even the original theory (see Osgood 1957) did not cover all language behaviors considered important by Kirk and his associates, and it was deemed necessary to draw partly from another theoretical position (Wepman, Jones, Bock, and Pelt 1960) in order to achieve a satisfactory theoretic scope for the test. Our most serious criticism of this test, however, is the observation made earlier that differing purposes require different kinds of assessment instruments.

Even if one accepts the concept of a test-based diagnostic approach, certain questions can be raised with regard to criteria used in selecting a standardization group. The test authors decided to limit the selection of children to those with Stanford-Binet IQs within one standard deviation on each side of the established national average of 100. The samples were chosen from five average communities (representative of national social-class characteristics) in the Middle West, and excluded children manifesting various deviant behaviors, such as physical impairment, probable organic involvement, or emotional disturbance. One possible embarrassment in this standardization is that an average of 100–IQ may well be very close to a full standard deviation below the actual average of the communities used. An abundance of evidence is available to show that national IQs are rising, and even the description of the standardization process shows that a much larger proportion of children above the 116–IQ cut off on the ITPA sample were discarded than those below an 84–IQ (Paraskevopoulos and Kirk 1969). With regard to one community used, the senior author has considerable empirical support for the validity of this conclusion, largely through data obtained in several projects.

The philosophy involved in the ITPA norm-group choice has never been adequately presented or discussed in the research literature; thus it is difficult to criticize on a more detailed level. The general idea is that of selecting a homogeneous average group in terms of psycholinguistic functioning. If persons are functioning in any setting significantly below the standards set by this midline of functioning, it is presumed that the deficit revealed by the test is an adequate recommendation for focusing remediation on that general area. An individual's performance on a subtest is gauged relative to its deviation from the mean of his own performances on all of the subtests. Since the effect of omitting persons with relatively high or low IQs from the original standardization sample is to magnify (in a relative sense) the deviations among the persons left in the group, there is the question of whether this effect will bias interpretation of test results in general. Moreover, there is the question of whether the patterns of deviations based upon the original sample for standardization are appropriate for groups of people (particularly the disadvantaged) who are unlike the original sample.

With regard to the adequacy of the ITPA for representing the important areas of language competency, Spradlin (1967) has noted that all Experimental Edition subtests but one (and the same could be said of the Revised Edition) can be answered with one or two words; the remaining subtest (Verbal Expression) is not scored for linguistic features in a child's response. Thus, any psycholinguistic features which are solely related to extended oral language will not be assessed by the ITPA.[2]

Where do these limitations leave the ITPA? It is without a doubt the major standardized instrument in the area of language functioning. By trying to serve multiple purposes, however, it is seriously weakened. Despite its psychometric elegance, further development is essential if the test is to survive. If it is to focus on psycholinguistic parameters, then it needs to broaden its scope into either theoretical or practical areas. If it continues to try to do both, it may eventually be replaced by more useful instruments in both areas. With the addition of supplementary tests which relate more to practical areas of academic functioning, there is a suggestion that the test comstructors wish to remain practical in scope. If so, they will need at some point to create subtests reflecting some of the increasing attention given to aspects of grammar in free speech samples and in a person's capacity to reproduce grammatical passages. Secondly, they will need to build in more systematic assessment of the environmental influences affecting differential language performance.

If the instrument is meant to be primarily a measure of competence in the area of learning disabilities, and be truly useful for prescribing academic remedial information, then it must abandon the more focal psycholinguistic ties and give increased attention to criterion-oriented qualities of the academic process existing in the classroom (Glaser 1963; Englemann 1967). While recent philosophies are increasingly tending to break down the artificial distinction between reading, spelling, and other skills of the language arts, no single test can effectively assess the wide range of behavioral problems which impair academic functioning. The ITPA has certainly provided new information about learning disorders, and may eventually establish itself as a permanently useful test in this area, but it cannot continue for long to lay claim to serving well in so many roles.

SOME FURTHER KEY CONSIDERATIONS ABOUT TESTS AND TESTING

Until now we have concentrated on the qualities and aims of standardized tests and have considered the ITPA as an example of a standardized test of lan-

---

[2]Such a simple procedure as taping the child's responses to the Verbal Expression subtest of the ITPA (or the Vocabulary and Comprehension subtests of the WISC), and scoring it later for linguistic qualities, can add useful data for making a clinical judgment of the language qualities not systematically tested by the ITPA. Clinicians who wish to employ free-speech samples as a supplementary assessment of language behaviors could profit from reading about techniques already available for gathering and scoring free speech in natural settings or under standardized conditions (Brottman 1968; Spradlin 1963, 1967).

guage. Here we turn to several more general and practical, yet highly important, factors to be considered in test selection, administration, and interpretation. Although most test users are generally cognizant of these factors, the
debate over their influences in standardized tests of disadvantaged groups has
become so heated that in some cases traditional testing programs have been
abandoned because of them (e.g., some tests in New York City schools; see
Wasserman 1969).

One common criticism holds that tests are culturally unfair to disadvantaged populations. This criticism bears on the issue of validity, or the degree
to which the test measures what it claims to measure. Critics assert that to the
degree that test content reflects cultural influences (usually leading to lower
scores for disadvantaged children than for their middle-class counterparts), it
is an unfair test for disadvantaged persons. But this charge can be answered
by returning to the criterion question. All psychological tests measure behavior
samples, and if the test is to have predictive validity, it should differentiate
culturally to the same extent that criterion measures differentiate culturally.
In sum, if the behaviors one is attempting to predict are tied to cultural
differences, then the test should reflect these differences in order to be a good
predictor. Put another way, eliminating the cultural influences in tests may
also eliminate their criterion validity. A test becomes biased, however, and the
stated criticism justified, when the instrument differentiates between disadvantaged and advantaged groups more sharply than does the criterion (Anastasi
1968).

When individuals' test scores are used only to describe their relative
standing with respect to a specified norm group, disadvantaged status may be
accurately reflected by relatively low performance. But it is important to know
the defining characteristics of the population which was used for establishing
the norms. If disadvantaged individuals' scores are interpreted as pure measures indicating ability vis-a-vis those factors based upon norms obtained from
settings involving only middle-class native-born Americans, the interpretation
may be incorrect because of a number of test-extraneous influences (e.g. motivation) on test validity.

Some of these influences may attenuate a test's predictive validity because
they affect test scores, but do not necessarily affect the criterion. For example,
Fishman, Deutsch, Kogan, North, and Whiteman (1964, p. 160) point out that
a disadvantaged child's test performance may be affected by poor skills in
test-taking, a disruptive level of anxiety, lowered motivation to perform well
on tests, less concern with speed, poorer understanding of test instructions,
unfamiliarity with format, and poorer rapport with the examiner.

> . . . it may be hypothesized that in contrast to the middle-class child
> the lower-class child will tend to be less verbal, more fearful of
> strangers, less self-confident, less motivated toward scholastic and

academic achievement, less competitive in the intellectual realm, more "irritable," less conforming to middle-class norms of behavior and conduct, more apt to be bilingual, less exposed to intellectually stimulating materials in the home, less varied in recreational outlets, less knowledgeable about the world outside his immediate neighborhood, and more likely to attend inferior schools. (Fishman, et al. 1964, p. 158)

Dreger and Miller (1968), in particular, have discussed motivational factors in intelligence testing. They point out that a relatively small number of studies are available where specific motivational incentives have been employed, and among these the results are often conflicting. Several studies specifically concerned with motivation and intelligence (Burt 1961; Burt and Williams 1962; Zigler and Butterfield 1968) suggest that motivation does affect intelligence-test performance. For example, Zigler and Butterfield (1968) employed intelligence-testing procedures which attempted to separate motivational from cognitive-achievement determinents of IQ. Scores of a group of culturally deprived children who attended nursery school increased significantly more than those of a group of disadvantaged children who did not attend nursery school. More important for our purposes, however, the results indicated that the increase in IQ which resulted from the nursery school experience was due to a reduction in the effects of debilitating motivational factors rather than to changes in the rate of the children's intellectual development.

We must also recognize that motivational factors are tied to a wide range of personality variables. Some investigators report that culturally deprived children are more wary of adults than are middle-class children (McCoy and Zigler 1965; Schallenberger and Zigler 1961). Others suggest that disadvantaged children are less motivated to be correct for the sake of correctness alone (Terrell, Durkin, and Wiesley 1959), and are willing to settle for lower levels of achievement success than are middle-class children (Gruen and Zigler 1968). If, for instance, a child's experiences have led him to be frightened and wary, he may know the answer to a test item, but respond "I don't know" in order to end as soon as possible the trauma or unpleasantness of being examined by an unfamiliar and demanding adult.

A growing body of literature is reported where such factors as examiner differences (including race of examiner), and their effects on test or task performance are assessed (e.g., DiLorenzo and Nagler 1968; Forrester and Klaus 1964; Katz 1964; Katz and Benjamin 1960; Katz and Cohen 1962; Katz, Epps, and Axelson 1964; Katz and Greenbaum 1963; Smith and May 1967). Several investigators are also studying the effects of various types of reinforcement or feedback on performance (e.g., Allen 1966; Berlin and Dill 1967; Rosenhan 1966; Rucinski 1968). Conflicting evidence is presented on some of these points. For example, Tiber (1963) and Tiber and Kennedy (1964) report expected class and color differences on an IQ test but no differential performance on the basis of measures of incentive.

A few recent studies present evidence regarding the influence of dialectal and syntactical features on ability to process and remember spoken language. Weener (1967), for example, argues that a person's ability to process natural language is directly related to the degree to which the phonetic, syntactic, and semantic features of a message match these same features of his own dialect. Frequency characteristics of syntactic structure reportedly affect immediate memory for word sequences, and differences exist between lower-class Negroes and middle-class whites with respect to the absolute recall of verbal as against similar nonverbal sequences (Salzinger, Salzinger, and Hobson 1967). These studies suggest the operation of another test-related factor—understanding of test instructions, which may accrue to the detriment of persons whose language is characterized by different structural and dialectal features than that of the examiner.

Although it is difficult to make definitive or sweeping statements, the possibility that a number of test-related factors affect test performance of disadvantaged children looms large. Such factors may impair the predictive validity of tests, and the possibility of their influence should be recognized when interpreting test results. Fishman, et al. (1964) also point out that some test-related factors may even be prejudicial to middle-class groups rather than disadvantaged groups. For example, some middle-class groups may experience greater test-taking anxiety of a disruptive nature (Sarason, Davison, Lighthall, Waite, and Ruebush 1960) than lower-class groups. In general, however, biases resulting from test-related factors are more likely to have a depressing effect on the performance of disadvantaged groups.

The types and quality of intervening experiences and environmental factors constitute a second set of conditions which may differentially lower the predictive validity of tests for disadvantaged populations. The longer the time period elapsing between a test and the point of criterion assessment, the more important become the events occurring during the time interval. A multitude of experiential, motivational, and maturational changes may affect individuals in ways that decrease the validity of a test which predicts future behavior. Some research indicates a decline, for example, in academic, aptitude and achievement test scores of disadvantaged children over time (Masland, Sarason, and Gladwin 1958). If such a decline does occur, or if any marked changes in behaviors are observed consistently over a given time period, they must be taken into account in any attempt to predict future behavior from scores derived at an earlier point in time. For example, an intensive language-training program for disadvantaged children could have an impact which would render invalid any normative language-test data obtained prior to the training period.

That is, normative interpretations of test results cannot predict how much the language of disadvantaged individuals might change if their environmental opportunities, motivation, and the like, were to be changed significantly.

The concept of test reliability, or the consistency of scores obtained by the same individuals on the same or equivalent test on repeated occasions, also presents difficulties when standardized tests are used with disadvantaged populations. In general, the reliability estimate increases (i.e., test results are increasingly consistent) with a greater spread of scores. There is evidence that children from disadvantaged populations have a smaller spread of scores on many tests than do middle-class children, largely due to the clustering of scores in the lower range of the test, and this lowers the test reliability (Anastasi 1968; Fishman, et al. 1964; Tyler 1956).

Although test publishers generally describe the age, sex, race, grade-level composition, and so on, of the group used for determining the test's reliability, little attention has been given to possible dependence of test reliability on subcultural differences. There is a growing tendency to report subgroup reliabilities, but this is not always done, nor are separate reliability data provided for specific minority groups. Therefore, unless, separate reliability studies are conducted by groups or institutions which use standardized tests with specific minority groups, we have no way of assuming the adequacy of the tests' reliabilities when used with these groups.

SUGGESTED DEVELOPMENTS IN STANDARDIZED LANGUAGE ASSESSMENT

Those who wish to introduce an increasing degree of rigor into tests for language distinctions in disadvantaged groups find themselves in a special bind. As things currently stand, most of the claims of deficient language patterns come either from day-to-day impressions by observers, or from research instruments administered without known standards of psychometric precision or interpretation. Yet the rapid introduction of individually administered standardized tests is delayed by severe warnings of their considerable limitations as valid and reliable measures with disadvantaged populations. It seems particularly important to convince both clinical and theoretical workers in this area that nothing is to be gained by avoiding more exact measurement. Impressionistic data are inevitably laden with individual biases of selective perception and erroneous interpretation, although the insights of skilled observers are always valuable as initial leads. Before major strides can occur in the use of standardized measurement instruments with disadvantaged groups, progress will have to be made in solving several problems.

Criterion Problems

Those who build tests should continue to examine linguistic theories for facets of language which can be measured, but which currently are not. Of particular importance is the need to obtain more adequate, but measurable, criteria of language functioning in natural and realistic settings. Such criteria as communicative effectiveness and grammatical competence readily occur, although they must obviously be broken down into more specific and measurable dimensions before they will achieve genuine utility.

Not only must there be a better determination of areas where language functioning is important, but some further consideration should be given to the problem of what kinds of variations constitute what we can genuinely call deficiencies. As currently employed, language tests put forth a statistical criterion of deficiency by using a format which compares an individual's score with the spread of scores in the normative sample. Is, for example, the comparative judgment of two standard deviations below average an appropriate criterion for instituting remedial efforts? Perhaps it would be useful to examine such additional aspects of the criterion problem as the degree to which language variations approximate standards of minimum, average, and optimum functioning in a given setting. These levels could be determined by a nonstatistical criterion, such as the use of competent professional judgments. The selection of standards for determining the need for intervention might then depend upon whether one is dealing with a criterion where language is only minimally required for effective communication and functioning, as against being crucially required.

Measurement Problems

It is clear that the current approach to individual assessment of language competence introduces unnecessary penalties for those groups who have not been trained in taking such tests, or for whom the situation is frightening or unpleasant. One does not wish to remove assessment of behaviors which add to prediction in a nontest setting, but one of the major purposes of one-to-one assessment is to determine competency of functioning under presumably optimum conditions. The term *competence* is used here in a different way than the competence-performance distinction made by Chomsky (1965) and his interpreters (relative to our topic, see Cazden 1967). These theorists consider linguistic competence as referring (in a mentalistic sense) to the knowledge which enables an individual to comprehend and to produce the language of his community. By contrast, the strongly behavioristic position of those who employ psychological tests uses *competence* to refer (in a performance sense) to skills which an individual will display under nearly optimum environmental conditions. In determining remediation strategy, it is important to know if a person cannot perform a desired response under such conditions of measurement.

This conception of the purpose of standardized individual assessment obviously goes awry when optimum conditions do not, in fact, prevail. In the interest of retaining the value of individual assessment, one must determine what modifications in the measurement situation will actually allow us to measure more accurately the basic competence (in our sense) of a given person. In the case of standardized language assessment with disadvantaged children, current modifications under review include the use of examiners from the same subculture, the use of additional incentives to enhance performance, the use of adapted linguistic content in the presentation of items, and others. Such changes, however, may not come close to the kinds of ultimate modifications which will prove of greatest value.

One very strong challenge posed against assessment in contrived situations comes from the operant school (Honig 1966; Skinner 1938; Sloane and MacAulay 1968) which replaces this with assessment in the actual settings where change is desired. By examining the person's behavior as a function of both individual and environmental stimuli, they argue they have a more useful form of diagnosis than that which occurs in contrived settings. By adjusting environmental reaction in a systematic way, they try to arrive at the kinds of changes which will modify the behavior of the person in the direction desired (see Guess, Sailor, Rutherford, and Baer 1968; Reynolds and Risley 1968; Hart and Risley 1968).

One probable development lies in an examination of the relative effectiveness of systematically sampling different environmental conditions and their associated effects on the behavior of the person. Do disadvantaged children use language more effectively when the (communicating) examiner is an impersonal machine, rather than a person of any kind? One specific modification might involve the use of a standardized movie which samples across dialects and individuals. The task would require the person both to carry out directions and to attempt a meaningful conversation with each presented model, and the individual's responses could be video taped and evaluated.

A different approach would be to develop measures which have standardized qualities, but which assess behavior in the setting where change is desired. For example, a teacher could be trained on the administration of a test in the classroom where each child was systematically presented with standardized stimuli under normal-group, small-group, and individual conditions, and where presumed differences in the reinforcement of language behavior could also be manipulated. Such a test need not be given all at once, but could be gradually plotted in cumulative records. If the performance could not be changed in the classroom as a function of stimulus- or reinforcement-modifications, the next step might be to remove the child from the classroom into progressively less-demanding or more-reinforcing situations until it was determined that language behavior was sampled under as nearly optimum conditions as possible. Then remediation could proceed toward restoration of desired language competency in the classroom. Considerable imagination is needed if we are to salvage the value of standardized assessment in assisting children who are integrated into different social systems but who appear seriously challenged by the communication requirements of those systems.

Problems of Minimum Data

Currently so little objective information is available on standardized language behaviors of specific subcultural groups, both advantaged and disadvantaged, that pressures to make social decisions and support theoretical positions result in the acceptance of impressionistic findings or the uncritical acceptance of findings based on single studies and small samples. We need not only an increase of objective information, but also improved conditions of measurement and the reporting of findings. The reports of Bereiter and Engelmann (1966) provide one example of work which has had considerable impact but where the bases of the impact have lacked desired standards of scientific rigor (see Friedlander 1968).

Those who hope to extend our knowledge of language functioning would benefit the field considerably if all samples were more carefully described with respect to race, socioeconomic status, background experiences, family constitution, and extended data on the environmental circumstances surrounding the groups studied. In addition to obtaining this information, language behaviors should not be assessed in the absence of an IQ control, or the investigator may be rediscovering the fact that populations differing in social class or quality of background experience also differ in intelligence, as incidentally measured by a language test.

We also need extended statistical evaluation of the relationships between measures of language and measures of other behavior. In the current attention focused on learning within Head Start populations, it is not entirely clear whether the various deficits being studied and worked with are actually independent. Factor-analytic studies, which investigate the communalities among various behaviors, could at least help us to see if such currently assessed behaviors as visuomotor skills, perceptual skills, cognitive skills, and language skills are actually independent areas of functioning. There is good reason to believe we are dealing with heavily overlapping areas of ability in these populations and are too often considering them as independent abilities in the absence of necessary definitive measurements. Without trustworthy evidence of such independence, we are left with an unfortunate level of imprecision and a lack of coordination of effort among professionals in various specialties.

Perhaps most important is an expanded knowledge of the specific influence of various environmental factors upon language behavior, which will begin to emerge only when techniques are available and used for the conjoint evaluation of both environmental and individual factors as they influence the language process. At this point the longitudinal study of changes in language behaviors which occur with changes in environment would seem to have a high priority. A particularly useful longitudinal study might involve the examination of language changes as a child moves from home to school for the first time, and include a careful examination of environmental factors such as interpersonal reactions to the language of the child.

Finally, it would be extremely useful to introduce standardized assessment of process-learning variables into the language field. These variables involve determination of the amount a child learns when presented with a given number of experiences, or conversely, the amount of time it takes a child to reach an established criterion of mastery. Up to now the study of process learning has been largely confined to the human-learning laboratories, but persons are beginning to see that these procedures have a place in extending the clinical information that can be gained under standardized assessment conditions. In the area of articulation, for example, a start has been made in this direction by the use of the Carter-Buck Tests of Stimulability (Kisatsky 1967). In this study children who made articulation errors were given practice in correcting these errors. Those children who gained the most during testing also showed the most intervening improvement when tested six months later. This tentative approach might be extended, by examining the child's capacity to master various psycholinguistic abilities such as grammatical structure, to an initial criterion of learning. Further information might then be gained by inspecting retention over standardized intervals of time, spontaneous transfer to new communicative settings, and so on. These approaches, which are standard aspects of the laboratory-learning paradigm, are directed to the kinds of questions asked by persons charged with the systematic change of a child's behavior in a school setting.

It is an irony of our current clinical approach to inadequate behaviors in learning situations such as the schools that we lean most heavily on the IQ test, which is a blend of past learning and current learning abilities, but which allows no useful separation of the two. Jensen (1961, 1968) has underscored the importance of looking at these two areas separately, particularly for disadvantaged populations. For too long we have conceived of diagnosis and treatment as separated operations, and thereby neglected the potential value of standardized observations of behavior change for the definition of the most effective kinds of learning environments.

CONCLUSION

One must accept with considerable caution the current use of standardized language tests with disadvantaged children, as well as the value of published findings. Yet the ultimate promise of standardized measures should stimulate active seeking of imaginative and more useful techniques for language assessment, together with insistence upon certain elements of quality control in gathering data and drawing conclusions from them. The trend, however, seems to be in the direction of individual and fragmented research efforts among theoreticians, test constructors, and test users. This trend runs counter to what is needed if massive programs of social intervention are pursued with the disadvantaged. A crucial part of such programs should be the unification and coordination of efforts to develop measurement instruments in the areas where behavior is to be affected. Only the availability and use of better tests and standards of measurement can lead social interventionists and basic researchers out of the current state of generalized speculation regarding the significance of language deficiencies or differences in the lives of disadvantaged persons. More rapid advance may also come as the individual researchers and project leaders accept the model of a consortium of researchers, where data are gathered under identical conditions of measurement and analyzed at a central place. This approach might be particularly useful in the area of language, where regional variations in this country limit the value of findings obtained from small numbers of diverse communities.

To summarize the answers to our main question: How should one approach standardized assessment of the language of disadvantaged children?

1. We need increased sensitivity to the different goals and criteria pertinent to standardized testing, and their application to language behavior.

2. The ITPA, though an admirable effort at standardized assessment, is evidence that we have a long way to go in this area, particularly in assessment of disadvantaged populations.

3. Extratest factors, which affect test results and interpretations, loom as particularly influential in the case of disadvantaged populations.

4. A substantial and concerted effort is needed to develop standardized procedures for language assessment and to increase our knowledge of how language capabilities fit into the larger context of an individual's other abilities and his environment.

REFERENCES

Allen, S. A. Children's performance as a function of race of experimenter, race of subject and type of verbal reinforcement. *J. Experimental Child Psychology* 1966, 4: 248–56.

Anastasi, A. *Psychological Testing*, 3d ed. New York: Macmillan, 1968.

Bateman, B. D. *The Illinois Test of Psycholinguistic Abilities in Current Research: Summaries of Studies.* Urbana, Ill.: University of Illinois Press, 1965.

———. *Interpretation of the 1961 Illinois Test of Psycholinguistic Abilities.* Seattle: Special Child Publications, 1968.

Beery, K. E. Comprehensive research, evaluation, and assistance for exceptional children. *Exceptional Children* 1968, 35: 223–28.

Bereiter, C., and Engelmann, S. *Teaching Disadvantaged Children in the Preschool.* Englewood Cliffs, N. J.: Prentice-Hall, 1966.

Berlin, C., and Dill, A. C. The effects of feedback and positive reinforcement on the Wepman Auditory Discrimination Test scores of lower-class Negro and white children. *J. Speech and Hearing Research* 1967, 10: 384–89.

Brottman, M. A., ed. *Language Remediation for the Disadvantaged Preschool Child*, Monograph of the Society for Research in Child Development 1968, No. 33.

Burt, C. Intelligence and social mobility. *British J. Statistical Psychology* 1961, 14: 3–24.

Burt, C., and Williams, E. L. The influence of motivation on the results of intelligence tests. *British J. Statistical Psychology* 1962, 15: 129–316.

Campbell, D. T., and Fiske, D. W. Convergent and discriminant validation by the multitrait-multimethod matrix. *Psychological Bulletin* 1959, 56: 81–105.

Cazden, C. B. Subcultural differences in child language: an interdisciplinary review. *Merrill-Palmer Quarterly* 1966, 12: 185–200.

———. On individual differences in language competence and performance. *J. Special Education* 1967, 1: 135–50.

Chomsky, N. *Aspects of the Theory of Syntax.* Cambridge, Mass.: M.I.T. Press, 1965.

Crabtree, M. The Houston Test of Language Development, I. Houston, Tex. 1958.

———. The Houston Test for Language Development, II. Houston, Tex. 1963.

Cronbach, L. J. *Essentials of Psychological Testing*, 3d ed. New York: Harper & Row, 1969.

Dever, R. A comparison of the results of a modified version of Berko's test of morphology with the free speech of mentally retarded children. Doctoral dissertation, University of Wisconsin, 1968.

DiLorenzo, L. T., and Nagler, E. Examiner differences on the Stanford-Binet. *Psychological Reports* 1968, 22: 443–47.

Dixon, T.R., and Horton, D.L. *Verbal Behavior and General Behavior Theory,* Englewood Cliffs, N.J.: Prentice-Hall, 1968.

Dreger, R. M., and Miller, K. S. Comparative psychological studies of Negroes and whites in the United States: 1959-1965. *Psychological Bulletin* 1968, 70: monograph supplement No. 3, Part 2.

Engelmann, S. *The Basic Concept Inventory; Teacher's Manual.* Chicago: Follett Publishing Co., 1967,

Fishman, J. A.; Deutsch, M.; Kogan, L.; North, R.; and Whiteman, M. Guidelines for testing minority group children. *J. Social Issues* 1964, 20: 129–45.

Forrester, B. J., and Klaus, R. A. The effect of race of the examiner on intelligence test scores of Negro kindergarten children. *Peabody Papers in Human Development* 1964, 2: 1–7.

Friedlander, B. Z. The Bereiter-Engelmann approach. *The Educational Forum* 1968, 32: 359–62.

Giebink, J. W., and Marden, M. Verbal expression, verbal fluency, and grammar related to cultural experience. *Psychology in the Schools* 1968, 5: 365–68.

Glaser, R. Instructional technology and the measurement of learning outcomes: some questions. *American Psychologist* 1963, 18: 519–21.

Gruen, G., and Zigler, E. Expectancy of success and the probability learning of middle-class, lower-class, and retarded children. *J. Abnormal Psychology* 1968, 73: 343–52.

Guess, D.; Sailor, W.; Rutherford, G.; and Baer, D. M. An experimental analysis of linguistic development: the productive use of the plural morpheme. *J. Applied Behavior Analysis* 1968, 1: 297–306.

Hart, B. M., and Risley, T. R. Establishing use of descriptive adjectives in the spontaneous speech of disadvantaged preschool children. *J. Applied Behavior Analysis* 1968, 1: 109–20.

Honig, W. K. *Operant Behavior: Areas of Research and Application.* New York: Appleton-Century-Crofts, 1966.

Ivey, S. M.; Center, W. R.; and Tanner, N. Effect of cultural deprivation on language development. *Southern Speech J.* 1968, 34: 28–36.

Jensen, A. R. Learning abilities in Mexican-American and Anglo-American children. *California J. Educational Research* 1961, 12: 147–59.

————. Social class, race, and genetics: implications for education. *American Educational Research J.* 1968, 5: 1–42.

————. How much can we boost I.Q. and scholastic achievement? *Harvard Educational Review* 1969, 39: 1–123.

Jones, L. V., and Wepman, J. M. Language: a perspective from the study of aphasia. In S. Rosenberg, ed., *Directions in Psycholinguistics.* New York: Macmillan, 1965.

Katz, I. Review of evidence relating to effects of desegregation on the intellectual performance of Negroes. *American Psychologist* 1964, 19: 831–99.

Katz, I., and Benjamin, L. Effects of white authoritarianism in biracial work groups. *J. Abnormal and Social Psychology* 1960, 61: 448–56.

Katz, I., and Cohen, M. The effects of training Negroes upon cooperative problem solving in biracial teams. *J. Abnormal and Social Psychology* 1962, 64: 319–25.

Katz, I.; Epps, E. G.; and Axelson, L. J. Effect upon Negro digit-symbol performance of anticipated comparison with whites and with other Negroes. *J. Abnormal and Social Psychology* 1964, 69: 77–83.

Katz, I., and Greenbaum, C. Effects of anxiety, threat, and racial environment on task performance of Negro college students. *J. Abnormal and Social Psychology* 1963, 66: 562–67.

Kirk, S. A. The Illinois Test of Psycholinguistic Abilities: its origin and implications. In J. Hellmuth, ed., *Learning Disorders,* Vol. 3 Seattle: Special Child Publications, 1968.

Kirk, S. A., and McCarthy, J. J. The Illinois Test of Psycholinguistic Abilities: An approach to differential diagnosis. *American J. Mental Deficiencies* 1961, 66: 399–412.

Kirk, S. A.; McCarthy, J. J.; and Kirk, W. D. *Illinois Test of Psycholinguistic Abilities, Revised Edition, Examiner's Manual.* Urbana, Ill.: University of Illinois Press, 1968.

Kisatsky, T. J. The prognostic value of Carter-Buck tests in measuring articulation skills of selected kindergarten children. *Exceptional Children* 1967, 34: 81–85.

Klaus, R. A. The Murfreesboro Project: cognitive approaches to culturally disadvantaged children. *Selected Convention Papers, 43rd Annual Council for Exceptional Children Convention.* Washington, D. C.: Council for Exceptional Children, 1965, pp. 249–55.

Klaus, R. A., and Gray, S. W. *The Early Training Project for Disadvantaged Children: A Report after Five Years.* Monograph of the Society for Research in Child Development 1968, No. 33.

Leventhal, D. S., and Stedman, D. J. A factor analytic study of the performance of 340 disadvantaged children on the Illinois Test of Psycholinguistic Abilities. Unpublished manuscript, Department of Psychiatry, Duke University and The Education Improvement Program, Durham, North Carolina, 1967.

Masland, R.; Sarason, S.; and Gladwin, T. *Mental Subnormality.* New York: Basic Books, 1958.

McCaffrey, A. Convergent methodologies and the study of language usage by children from differing sub-cultural environments. Paper presented at a meeting of the Society for Research in Child Development, March 1969, Santa Monica, Calif.

McCarthy, J., and Kirk, S. A. *The Construction, Standardization and Statistical Characteristics of the Illinois Test of Psycholinguistic Abilities.* Urbana, Ill.: University of Illinois Press, 1963.

McCarthy, J. J., and Olson, J. L. *Validity Studies on the Illinois Test of Psycholinguistic Abilities.* Urbana, Ill.: University of Illinois Press, 1966.

McConnell, F.; Horton, K. B.; and Smith, B. R. Language development and cultural disadvantage. *Exceptional Children* 1969, 35: 597–606.

McCoy, N., and Zigler, E. Social reinforcer effectiveness as a function of the relationship between child and adult. *J. Personality and Social Psychology* 1965, 1: 604–12.

McNemar, Q. Lost: our intelligence? why? *American Psychologist* 1964, 19: 874–79.

Osgood, C. E. Motivational dynamics of language behavior. *Nebraska Symposium on Motivation.* Lincoln, Neb.: University of Nebraska Press, 1957.

Paraskevopoulos, J. N., and Kirk, S. A. *The Development and Psychometric Characteristics of the Revised Illinois Tests of Psycholinguistic Abilities.* Urbana, Ill.: University of Illinois Press, 1969.

Reynolds, N. J., and Risley, T. R. The role of social and material reinforcers in increasing talking of a disadvantaged preschool child. *J. Applied Behavior Analysis* 1968, 1: 253–62.

Rosenhan, D. L. Effects of social class and race on responsiveness to approval and disapproval. *J. Personality and Social Psychology* 1966, 4: 253–59.

Rucinski, P. R. The motivating effect of two reinforcers upon lower- and middle-class fifth-grade children. *J. Educational Research* 1968, 61: 369–71.

Ryckman, D. B. A comparison of information processing abilities of middle- and lower-class Negro kindergarten boys. *Exceptional Children* 1967, 33: 545–52.

Salzinger, S.; Salzinger, K.; and Hobson, S. The effect of syntactical structure on immediate memory for word sequences of middle- and lower-class children. *J. Psychology* 1967, 67: 147–59.

Sarason, S. B.; Davison, K. S.; Lighthall, F. F.; Waite, R. R.; and Ruebush, B. K. *Anxiety in Elementary School Children.* New York: Wiley, 1960.

Schallenberger, P., and Zigler, E. Rigidity, negative reaction tendencies, and feebleminded children. *J. Abnormal and Social Psychology* 1961, 63: 20–26.

Skinner, B. F. *The Behavior of Organisms.* New York: Appleton, 1938.

Sloane, H. N., Jr., and MacAulay, B. D., eds. *Operant Procedures in Remedial Speech and Language Training.* Boston: Houghton Mifflin, 1968.

Smith, H. W., and May, W. T. Influence of the examiner on the ITPA scores of Negro children. *Psychological Reports* 1967, 20: 499–502.

Spradlin, J. E. Language and communication of mental defectives. In N. Ellis, ed., *Handbook of Mental Deficiency.* New York: McGraw-Hill, 1963.

———. Procedures for evaluating processes associated with receptive and expressive language. In R. L. Schiefelbusch, R. H. Copeland, and J. O. Smith eds., *Language and Mental Retardation.* New York: Holt, Rinehart & Winston, 1967.

Terrell, G., Jr.; Durkin, K.; and Wiesley, M. Social class and the nature of the incentive in discrimination learning. *J. Abnormal and Social Psychology* 1959, 59: 270–72.

Tiber, N. The effects of incentives on intelligence test performance. Doctoral dissertation, Florida State University, 1963.

Tiber, N., and Kennedy, W. A. The effects of incentives on the intelligence test performance of different social groups. *J. Consulting Psychology* 1964, 28: 187.

Tyler, L *The Psychology of Human Differences*. New York: Appleton, 1956.

Wasserman, M. Planting pansies on the roof: a critique of how New York City tests reading. *Urban Review* 1969, 3: 30–35.

Wechsler, D. *Manual for the Wechsler Intelligence Scale for Children.* New York: Psychological Corporation, 1949.

Weener, P. D. The influence of dialect differences on the immediate recall of verbal messages. *Studies in Language and Language Behavior* 1967, 5: 364–65.

Weener, P.; Barritt, L. S.; and Semmel, M. I. A critical evaluation of the Illinois Test of Psycholinguistic Abilities. *Exceptional Children* 1967, 33: 373–80.

Wepman, J. M.; Jones, L. V; Bock, R. D.; and Pelt, D. V. Studies in aphasia: background and theoretical formulations. *J. Speech and Hearing Disorders* 1960, 25: 323–32.

Zigler, E., and Butterfield, E. Motivational aspects of changes in I.Q. test performance of culturally deprived nursery school children. *Child Development* 1968, 39: 1–14.

Chapter 16

THE SOCIOLINGUISTS AND URBAN LANGUAGE PROBLEMS

Roger W. Shuy*

It is often the case that new academic entities are created out of the increasing territorial overlaps of old ones. Thus biology and physics create biophysics, or a mixture of history with fiction yields the historical novel. That the creation of sociolinguistics is very recent is a tribute to neither of the parental disciplines involved. For years sociologists have avoided language as an aspect of their territory, possibly because they were ill-trained to handle it. Linguists, meanwhile, were relatively oblivious to the contributions which sociology could make to their own territory, all the while making naive statements about social class and engaging in less-than-adequate sampling procedures.

TOWARD A SOCIOLINGUISTIC PERSPECTIVE

Although for many years linguists have been interested in the larger phenomenon of language and culture (where whole systems of language and whole systems of culture are seen in relationship to each other) it has been only recently that anyone but dialectologists have systematically observed linguistic variation within the smaller social groups of a culture. Linguistic geographers, of course, have long been observing small-group language dynamics based on geography and history. In addition, Hans Kurath (1939) introduced the dimension of the social group to the Linguistic Atlas of the United States and Canada, even though his criteria for social marking are hardly acceptable by current standards.

*Center for Applied Linguistics, Washington, D. C.

From the sociologists there were a few articles in the forties by C. Wright Mills (1940) and in the fifties by Joyce Hertzler (1953), largely borderline reflections on language rather than linguistically acceptable analyses. Thus, both the linguists and sociologists who were committed to studying the language behavior of groups within a culture were relatively free from the kind of cross-fertilization necessary for a truly effective sociolinguistics.

Access to this field has been varied, even among linguists. We have already noted the entrance of dialectologists through Linguistic Atlas methodology, relying heavily on citation forms dealing with lexical and phonological features. Recently specialists in Caribbean languages (e.g., Stewart 1967, 1968; Chapter 17) have begun to see a relationship between creole speech and the dialects of certain Negroes in the United States, particularly in matters of grammar. A third entry has been from the field of linguistic theory, exemplified in the work of William Labov (1966, 1968, Chapter 9), who approaches the study of language in society in order to solve linguistic problems such as the description of continuous variations, overlapping phonemic systems, and the mechanism of linguistic change. Some of Labov's work moves toward sociological phenomena per se, as for example, the discreteness of socioeconomic stratification, the relation of normative values to social behavior, and the nature of social control.

In sum, among the topics of sociolinguistics are dialect geography, languages in contact (including bilingualism and problems of interference), social dialectology (including studies of social stratification and minority-group speech), language situations (language rivalries, standardization, language as a means of group identification and functional styles), and attitudes toward language. The field of sociolinguistics, then, is quite broad, involving a rather complicated intersection of the study of language in relationship to geography, social status, sex, age, race, style and situation, other languages, psychology, and pedagogy.

Sociolinguists are generally concerned with the social implications of the use of the language, and some are especially concerned with the varieties of English in urban areas. They carry out basic research on language variation and acquisition among social groups (e.g., Shuy, Wolfram, and Riley 1967), on standard language in relation to nonstandard varieties (Labov, et al 1968), and on attitudes toward the use of language by speakers of all social levels (Shuy, Baratz, and Wolfram 1969). Some (e.g., Feigenbaum 1970; Fasold 1970) are particularly interested in the nonstandard English of the urban Negro and are preparing teaching materials for elementary and secondary schools, as well as participating in teacher training to provide the necessary skills for dealing with nonstandard speech.

One important branch of sociolinguistic study in urban areas has been focused in particular upon the language problems of the poor. Some of the

Figure 1

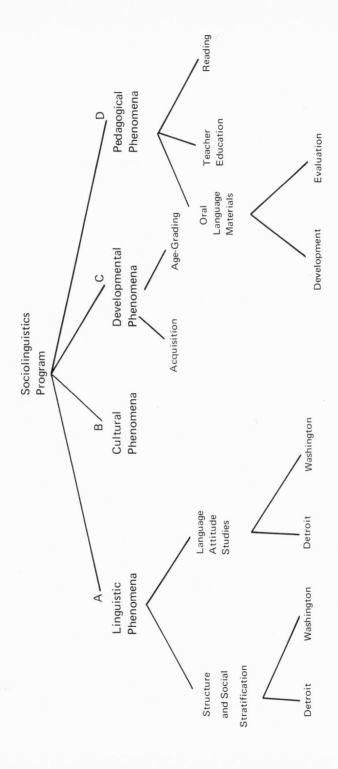

concern for this problem was formalized during the summer of 1964 at the Conference on Social Dialects and Language Learning, a report of which was subsequently published under the title of *Social Dialects and Language Learning* (Shuy 1965). Although several important articles along these lines had been written in the forties and fifties by Raven I. McDavid, Jr. and others (e.g., McDavid 1958; McDavid and McDavid 1951), it was not until the sixties that the language situations of urban populations were widely approached. Primary research in this area has been done by linguists such as William Labov (1966), Raven I. McDavid, Jr. (1966), William A. Stewart (1967, 1968; Chapter 17), Lee A. Pederson (1965) and myself, and by sociologists such as Lewis Levine and Harry J. Crockett (1966), and Basil Bernstein (1964). Current research projects are well under way or are largely completed in New York City (by Labov), in Detroit (by Shuy, Walter A. Wolfram and William K. Riley), in Washington, D.C. (by Ralph Fasold, William Stewart, Joan Baratz, and Shuy), in Chicago (by McDavid, Alva Davis and Lee Pederson) and in Los Angeles (by Stanley Legum and Clyde Williams).

These projects are furthering existing knowledge of the linguistic characteristics of nonstandard English and are shedding considerable light on the correlation of language and social behavior.

Although professional contact between the major linguists in the field of sociolinguistics has been relatively open, the research in urban sociolinguistics runs the risk of becoming too narrow and inbred unless care is taken to insure the exchange of information between linguists and researchers in related disciplines. It is for this reason that the study of urban language has taken the appearance of truly interdisciplinary research. The organizational structure of the Sociolinguistics Program at the Center For Applied Linguistics, for example, is as shown in Figure 1. It should be clear from this structure that the special expertise of the linguist *(A)*, the anthropologist and the sociologist *(B)*, the psychologist *(C)*, and the educator *(D)* are all required for an action program involving both basic and applied research. Nor are these people confined to their specialized areas. The linguist is involved in all areas, the psychologist in language attitudes as well as in the study of language development and pedagogical matters. The anthropologist provides important cultural interpretations from which the linguistic phenomena can be better understood. The sociologist's demographies and background profile studies provide useful settings in which the linguistic data can be appropriately viewed.

When discussing a broad topic such as social dialects, one chooses a level of abstraction rather arbitrarily and focusses his attention only on it. Linguists frequently focus on language as a whole just as anthropologists may focus on a culture as a whole, while temporarily overlooking the parts from which it is constituted. When we deal with contrasts between standard and nonstandard urban language, however, we can ignore neither the cultural wholes nor the interrelated parts. For our subject is both at the same time and neither alone.

SOME CONCEPTS IN SOCIOLINGUISTIC ANALYSIS

In order to analyze the data provided by urban language, the concepts of the linguistic continuum, the linguistic variable, and the linguistic situation must be recognized.

1. The Linguistic Continuum

The first concept reflects the observation that variations in the speech of any given person, or a society as a whole, can often be characterized in terms of a continuum of usage. Stewart's (1965) theoretical concepts of *acrolect* (a topmost dialect in a sociolinguistic hierarchy) as against *basilect* (the other extreme in the hierarchy) reflect this concept. Presumably, no person speaks a pure acrolect or basilect, but his speech may be seen to cover some portion of this continuum, and this portion may vary with such factors as race, age, sex, status, and speech style.

At this point, then, we may refer to speakers of English, standard or nonstandard, as though they were locatable between two points on a continuum which ranges from absolute basilect to absolute acrolect. The continua of most speakers of English overlap extensively. It is where they do not overlap that we can point to marked features of dialect. Where these nonoverlapping areas may be attributed to social phenomena (rather than to, say, geographical matters), the marked features may be called those of social dialect.

2. The Linguistic Variable

The basilect-acrolect continuum enables us to conceive of the individual or of groups of individuals with similar or identical coinciding areas of continua. It is William Labov's (1966, p. 15) formulation of the linguistic variable, however, which enables us to account for continuous ordered variation within linguistic features. In the past, linguists have made careful descriptions of the distributions of various allophones of phonemes, which worked most but not all of the time. The exceptions, the nonworking times, were said to be matters of free fluctuation or free variation. That is, they were said to be legitimately varying in a way which was not possible to describe by using only linguistic criteria. In formulating the concept of the linguistic variable, Labov sought to correlate matters hitherto dismissed as free fluctuation with such social characteristics as social status, race, age, sex, and style. This would provide a more complete explanation for linguistic behavior although it would not eradicate totally the notion of free variation, for certain irreducible fluctuations in language would continue to exist.

This concept, then, refers to the speaker's variation between variants of a linguistic variable. That is, suppose he produces both voiced and voiceless alveolar stops in word final position in words like *good* and *word.* One might say that for some speakers there is free variation of /d/ and /t/ in this position. Another approach would be to try to identify, as closely as possible, the situational contexts in which this variation takes place (close friends, classroom, cocktail party, etc.), or to identify the style of language in which the features appeared (narrative, reading, listing, etc.). Still another approach would be to compare the frequency distributions of speakers of one social group with those of another (on the bases of economic status, education, age, sex, race, etc.).

It may be appropraite to point out here that speakers of low-prestige dialects in America have very few linguistic features which are totally alien to prestige dialects. Our experience has shown that a person of school age who is said to have no -*s* in noun plurals can and will produce an -*s* on a noun plural somewhere, sometime in the course of his oral language experience. If the past findings of serious sociolinguistics research continue to be born out, then if we observe such a speaker long enough and under a sufficient variety of circumstances, we will hear the -*s* at some time—perhaps even frequently.

Since linguistic theory has not been greatly concerned with systematic variation, linguists interested in establishing norms of either standard or nonstandard dialects have not been concerned with establishing procedures for finding them. Instead they have assumed that any variation in a speech community is a mixture of standard and nonstandard and that the latter is that which is different from their own concept of the standard norm. This is as true of linguists as it is of laymen, for past research has shown that speakers hear themselves as using the norm which they have adopted rather than their unedited but realistic variations from that norm (Labov 1966, p. xii). Another rationalization used by linguists when confronted with the problem of dealing with speech variation is to consider such variation *ideolect* (the individual characteristics of a given person's speech at a given time) and let it go at that. This explanation limps badly and instead seems to say only that the answer is too hard to find. Nor can we pass it off as mere dialect borrowing, at least not without having first clearly described and separated the dialects which are being mixed (noting overlap as well).

If the concept of the linguistic variable is to be used in dealing with variation in language, linguists will have to broaden considerably the scope of their realm of professional abstraction. In the past they have avoided quantitative judgments, generally favoring the notion of the whole of the language, which was based on a discretely contrasting qualitative model. They were interested essentially in code rather than behavior. However adequate the qualitative model may be for the important task of analyzing the cognitive function of language, it is simply inadequate for describing its social functions.

3. The Linguistic Situation

Although a workable taxonomy for discussing a well-defined social situation has not yet been developed, linguists have done some preliminary study in this area. John Gumperz (1964), for example, utilized the concept of a communication network, particularly a friendship network, to investigate linguistic code-switching between a local dialect and a higher prestige dialect in India. He noted that the choice of dialect was based on a number of situational constraints such as whether the setting was transactional or personal, whether the network was open or closed, and whether the topic was local or nonlocal.

Labov (1966), noting that most field work in urban-language research itself paradoxically defines the speech context as *careful*, suggests that linguists seek out several contexts (speech with a third person, emotionally charged speech, and speech to outsiders before, during, or after the interview, for example) in order to get at *casual* speech. To isolate the phonological variables from situation to situation, he observed channel cues, modulations of the voice production which affect speech as a whole. These cues included a change in volume, a change in the rate of breathing, and the presence of laughter. The presence of any one of these cues (except laughter) marks the speech as casual rather than careful.

Taking a clue from Labov's field work design, the researchers on the Detroit Dialect Study (Shuy, Wolfram, and Riley, 1967) sought four loosely defined speech contexts within the interview situation: emotionally charged speech, narration and description, citation forms, and oral reading. Comparison of a given speaker's production of certain linguistic features in several of these styles showed an increase in normativeness from emotional speech to narration, from narration to citation, and from citation to oral reading.

But research in sociolinguistics can be narrowed even further. The field may also include studies of the components of face-to-face interaction as these relate to speech structure. Susan Ervin-Tripp (1967) observes that these components may include the personnel, the situation, the function of the interaction, the topic and message, and the channel, along with a series of sociolinguistic rules which account for alternations.

SOME RESEARCH STRATEGIES

At this point, the author has noted the historical setting in which urban sociolinguistics has been developing, has pointed out the interdisciplinary nature of the research, and has noted some of the important concepts upon which many current analyses are based. Now it will be useful to observe a small example of how an urban sociolinguist handles his research.

The major differences between standard and nonstandard urban English are, in number, relatively few (when seen in relationship to the many points of similarity) and the speakers of nonstandard who are of school age or older have the ability to produce standard forms in some style or in some degree of frequency. One may wonder, then, why all the fuss? Even though nonstandard urban English seems to be not greatly separated from standard, the fact remains that these apparently slight differences carry tremendous social weight.

The exact nature of this weight is the study of much current research in urban sociolinguistics. Linguists have been studying these matters from the viewpoints of the objective language phenomena, subjective reactions to language, what happens to the conflicting language systems in contact, and how a person switches from one to the other. Although research in the field is still very modest in quantity, the general character of difference between standard and nonstandard can be briefly described.

Correlation Studies

Although linguists have not been known, in recent years, to join linguistic forms with social context, there is a rather strong current movement to expand the focus on linguistic form in isolation (idealized language) to linguistic form in social context (realistic language). In an effort to set the linguistic data in appropriate sociological contexts, the staff of the Detroit Dialect Study calculated a social-status index for each informant in that study (Shuy, Wolfram, and Riley 1968). The distribution of assigned social-status indexes was then quartiled. Having established a tentative social population, the next task was to extract relevant linguistic data from the some seven hundred tape-recorded, hour-long interviews of randomly selected Detroit residents and to display these data with the social classes in which they occurred. Figures noting such displays are found in Shuy, Wolfram and Riley (1967) and in Wolfram (1969). Figure 2, modified from Shuy, Wolfram and Riley (1967) is illustrative of these displays. For each informant, all instances of negatives cooccurring with indefinites were tabulated (e.g., "He didn't hit nobody"). This procedure gave a total number of potential occurrences for multiple negation. From this total the number of actual occurrences of multiple negation was tabulated. The percentage of actual multiple negatives in relation to potential multiple negatives was then computed and displayed as in Figure 2.

Similarly, Wolfram (1969) has tabulated the relative absence of the final member of word-final monomorphemic consonant clusters (e.g., *test, mask,*

Figure 2. Multiple Negation: Social Stratification

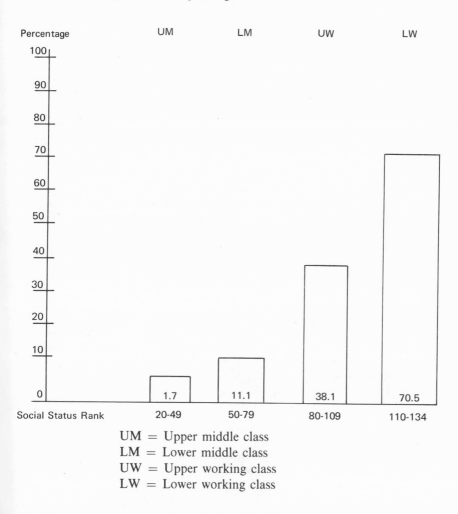

UM = Upper middle class
LM = Lower middle class
UW = Upper working class
LW = Lower working class

mind, cold, etc.) among Detroit Negroes by social class. His data revealed contrasts illustrated in Figure 3.

The examination of both Figures 2 and 3 should provide some idea of how we have worked quantitatively with a linguistic variable in terms of relative percentages, and how these percentages have been correlated with differences in social class (as defined by quartiles in the distribution of the index). In particular, the point should be stressed that unlike more traditional analyses, where a feature is assessed for its presence as against absence, here we have been concerned with frequency data. Thus we have felt that many of the major

Figure 3. Absence of Final Cluster Member in Monomorphemic Clusters, Negroes

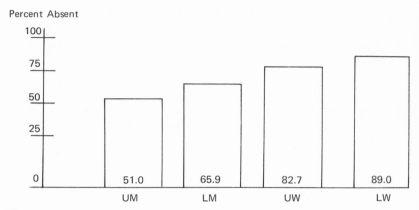

Key:
UM = Upper middle class
LM = Lower middle class
UW = Upper working class
LW = Lower working class

linguistic differences across social-class boundaries are more a case of relative frequency of usage than of some highly consistent presence or absence of a feature. Further research may reveal, however, some structural differences across dialects that would reflect such things as clear differences in rules and the like, rather than simply relative frequencies.

Attitude Studies

Although people make assumptions about other people on the basis of speech characteristics, there has been relatively little systematic research concerning the linguistic variables upon which the listener bases these assumptions. Language attitude studies have been done by Lambert, et al. (1960), Harms (1961), Labov (1966), Buck (1968), Williams (in press; Chapter 18) and Shuy, Baratz, and Wolfram (1969). The latter may serve as an example.

The Shuy, Baratz and Wolfram study was primarily concerned with the ability of Detroit residents to identify the race and socioeconomic status of adult males on the basis of a small sample of their speech. A part of the taped stimulus included twenty one passages of discourse of between 20 and 30 seconds in length from three adult white males from the upper-middle class, lower-middle class and upper working-class of Detroit. Also included were three adult males from the upper-middle class, lower-middle class, upper working-class and lower working-class of the Detroit Negro population. All passages were taken from the corpus of the Detroit Dialect Study. The respondents totaled 620 Detroit residents—286 were sixth-graders, 170 were eleventh-graders, and 164 were adults. Of these, 256 subjects were Negroes and 364 were whites, 305 were male, and 315 female. In terms of social class, 167 were upper-middle class, 173 lower-middle class, 140 upper working-class and 140 lower working-class.

There were several research questions asked in the study but, for our purposes here, let us note only one or two examples. In response to the question, "Can individuals correctly identify the social class of a person from a sample of his spoken language?" the following results were obtained. The social class of the taped stimulus was correctly identified by all respondents as follows: that of upper-middle class 29.6 percent, lower-middle class 31.8 percent, upper working-class 40.8 percent, and lower working-class 60.8 percent. Thus it appears that overall ability to identify socioeconomic status from these speech samples increased as socioeconomic status decreases.

Another research question asked in the preceding study was, "What is the effect of the socioeconomic status of the listener on identification of the socioeconomic status of the speaker?" Not surprisingly, lower-working-class speakers are most often correctly identified regardless of the socioeconomic status of the respondent, and upper-middle-class respondents appear to perform significantly better than lower-working-class respondents on all identifications.

Several other research questions were posed in this study, including the ability of individuals to identify ethnicity, the relationship of the sex of the respondent to his ability to make such identifications, the differences in the identification abilities of children and adults, the relative merits of the grammatical or phonological indices and the utility of semantic-differential testing in such studies.

Language Systems in Contact

Urban sociolinguistics is also involved in the dynamics of language change when two or more language systems come into contact, whether from inmigration, immigration, colonialization, desegregation, or any other stimulus. The linguistic problems which one frequently faces are matter of *language assimilation* ("studies of the nature and rate of changes made in the language system of the outsider as he develops mastery of the new system"), *swamping* ("changes worked on the extant systems by the newcomers"), and *creolization* ("a new language system restructured from a pidgin language"). The latter is especially relevant to the language situation of many American Negroes today and is treated elsewhere (Stewart, Chapter 17) in this volume.

Actually, there has been relatively little research done in the study of urban sociolinguistics in America with respect to any of the foregoing problems of studying language systems in contact. Linguists have observed that recent black in-migrants from the South are noticeably different in their speech behavior from long-time Negro residents in Northern cities, even though some may share a certain number of Southern-Negro speech features. Despite this observation, no study has been made of the nature and rate of linguistic assimilation processes for blacks or for in-migrant whites. Likewise, even though much of our current knowledge of Negro nonstandard English seems to indicate a historical relationship with Gullah and perhaps with Caribbean creole, we need to know more about the effects of creolization on learing standard English.

Language System Switching

One of the clear products of almost all research in American urban sociolinguistics is that the major task of the English teacher is not just to teach his pupils their own language. It is, rather, to help students understand that a language has a number of different social dialects, each of which as acceptability within the sphere of its influence. Second, speakers must be helped to use several different social dialects (or parts of these dialects) on different occasions, depending on such nonlinguistic phenomena as the speaker's emotional involvement, his real or conceptualized audience, his intention, his understanding of stylistic requirements and other factors.

If we are willing to accept the speaker's need to switch social dialects for different social involvements and stylistic requirements, then we must discover not just the items which characterize social differences but also the processes by which this switching takes place. One of the important research questions in American urban sociolinguistics, then, is: How is language switching accomplished?

Extensive observation of style-shifting and code-shifting should yield a description of the process in relation to the social situations in which such switching takes place. We now know, for example, that people engage in style shifts within or crossing social dialects. A sudden shift in subject matter, for example, may bring about emotional overtones causing phonological or grammatical shifts. The following example will illustrate this principle. The speaker is a twelve-year-old Detroit Negro boy whose father has overcome tremendous obstacles to become a successful police administrator. The family is upwardly mobile even though they live in a lower-middle-class community (a fact which is not surprising in terms of current residential segregation patterns in America). The boy's speech is neither noticeably lower class or Negro throughout most of the interview, suggesting that his home language and, perhaps, his friendship-group language are somewhat similar. When the field worker (FW) asked him (INF) a question which involved him emotionally with school, however, he shifted social dialects quite vividly as follows:

> INF: . . . but sometimes when I want to do some procrastinat-
> ing, I go out to the playground and swing around the swings or walk
> down to Hamilton and get an ice cream cone. Nothing much.
> FW: Did you ever have a teacher who hollered a lot?
> INF: Gosh, I have one that always hollers at me.
> FW: About what?
> INF: Sometimes we thinks she's absolutely crazy. She *come* in
> the classroom *she be* nice and happy, she never *have* a smile though
> cause *she be* nice and happy . . . the next minute *she be hollering* at
> us for no reason, she'd be giving us a lecture on something that
> happened twenty years ago. And we have another one that well,
> that's not like that, she at least wears a smile some of the times but
> she does holler."

At no other time during the ninety minutes our field worker spent with this boy did he use these grammatical forms again. Whether his use of *she come, she be nice, she never have a smile, she be nice,* and *she be hollering* are considered a lapse or a systematic shift, the fact remains that there is an associated social situation that apparently correlates with certain linguistic features which can be identified with a known social dialect.

A CLOSING NOTE

There are undoubtedly many avenues to the problems of language in the urban areas of our country. As I have indicated here, the approach of the sociolinguist is but one of many. Scholars from some other disciplines often begin with quite different assumptions (c.f. Baratz 1969) about language and the language user. Sociolinguists assume that language, or a variety of a language, used by a given speech community is adequate to meet the needs of its user relative to the demands of that community. They assume, furthermore, that children learn the language of their peer group, and that dialects, even nonstandard dialects, are systematic in nature. Their fundamental assumptions prevent sociolinguists from accepting some of the beginning points held by scholars in other disciplines, for example, that poor black children are somehow universally nonverbal or have some sort of consistent cognitive deficit. The linguists have learned, perhaps from their long tradition of data gathering, that unresponsiveness of the informant is as likely to be a consequence of the interview situation and the interviewer, as a reflection of the informant himself. Sociolinguists usually begin by describing the dialect in question with all of the scientific rigor available to them. They then compare this dialect with the description of any other dialect of interest, typically the one which is the target (and vehicle) for formal education. To scholars from other disciplines, this may seem like a long and a wasteful way to approach the problem. Perhaps they are right. But sociolinguists are more ecumenical than most people, partly because of the vastness of their job, the interdisciplinary character of their view of the problems, and the varied nature of their training.

Lest it be thought that sociolinguists are close to solving the major problems in the field of urban language, it should be stated emphatically that we have only begun to see the nature of our task. With good reason, there has been great emphasis on the language of the economically disadvantaged Negro, but this is not to say that Negroes are the only people in need of attention. We need answers to a number of large and pressing questions before extensive pedagogical assistance can be accomplished. We need to know considerably more about sex differences in language. We need to study linguistic change across age groups. We need to study the influence of peer groups, even friendship groups, on language acquisition. We know very little about style shifting, about language assimilation and swamping by large groups on in-migrants or immigrants. And these only begin to list the vast number of problems in need of contemporary sociolinguistic research.

REFERENCES

Baratz, J. C. Language and cognitive assessment of Negro children: assumptions and research needs. *ASHA* 1969 11: 87–91.

Bernstein, B. Elaborated and restricted codes: their social origins and some consequences. In J. J. Gumpenz and D. Hymes, eds., *The Ethnography of Communication, American Anthropologist* 1964, 66: No. 6, Part 2, 55–69.

Buck, J. F. The effects of Negro and white dialectal variations upon attitudes of college students. *Speech Monographs* 1968, 35: 181–86.

Ervin-Tripp, S. Sociolinguistics. Unpublished working paper, No. 3. Language Behavior Research Laboratory, University of California at Berkeley, 1967.

Fasold, R. W. Grammatical features of black English. In R. W. Fasold and R. W. Shuy, eds., *Teaching Standard English in the Inner City.* Washington, D. C.: Center for Applied Linguistics, 1970.

Feigenbaum, I. Using nonstandard to teach standard: contrast and comparison. In R. W. Fasold and R. W. Shuy, eds., *Teaching Standard English in the Inner City.* Washington, D. C. : Center for Applied Linguistics, 1970.

Gumperz, J. J. Linguistic and social interaction in two communities. In J. J. Gumperz and D. Hymes, eds., *The Ethnography of Communication, American Anthropologist* 1964, 66: No. 6, Part 2, 137–53.

Harms, L. S. Listener judgments of status cues in speech. *Quarterly Journal of Speech* 1961, 47: 164–68.

Hertzler, J. Toward a sociology of language. *Social Forces* 1953, 32: 109–19.

Kurath, H. *Handbook of the Linguistic Geography of New England.* Vol. 1, *Linguistic Atlas of New England.* Providence, R.I.: Brown University Press, 1939.

Labov, W. *The Social Stratification of English in New York City.* Washington, D.C.: Center for Applied Linguistics, 1966.

Labov, W.; Cohen, P.; Robbins, C.; and Lewis, J. A study of the non-standard English of Negro and Puerto Rican speakers in New York City. Final Report, U. S. Office of Education Cooperative Research Project No. 3288, Vols 1, 2. Mimeographed. Columbia University, 1968.

Lambert, W. E.; Hodgson, R. C.; Gardner, R. C.; and Fillenbaum, S. Evaluational reactions to spoken language. *J. Abnormal and Social Psychology* 1960, 60: 44–51.

Levine, L., and Crockett, H. J., Jr. Speech variation in a Piedmont community: postvocalic r. *Sociological Inquiry* 1966, 36: 204–26.

McDavid, R. I., Jr. American English dialects. In W. N. Francis, ed., *The Structure of American English*. New York: Ronald, 1958.

McDavid, R. I., Jr. and Austin, W. M. Communication barriers to the culturally disadvantaged. U. S. Office of Education Cooperative Research Project No. 2107, 1966.

McDavid, R. I., Jr., and McDavid, V. G. The relationship of the speech of American Negroes to the speech of whites. *American Speech* 1951, 26: 3–17.

Mills, C. W. Methodological consequences of the sociology of knowledge. *American J. Sociology* 1940, 46: 316–30.

Pederson, L. A. *The Pronunciation of English in Metropolitan Chicago*. Tuscaloosa, Ala.: University of Alabama Press, 1965, 44.

Shuy, R. W., ed. *Social Dialects and Language Learning*. Champaign, Ill.: National Council of Teachers of English, 1965.

Shuy, R. W.; Wolfram, W. A.; and Riley, W. K. Linguistic correlates of social stratification in Detroit speech. U. S. Office of Education Cooperative Research Project No. 6–1347, 1967.

————. *Field Techniques in an Urban Language Study*. Washington, D. C.: Center for Applied Linquistics, 1968.

Shuy, R. W.; Baratz, J. C.; and Wolfram, W. A. Sociolinguistic factors in speech identification. National Institutes of Mental Health Research Project No. MH–15048–01, 1969.

Stewart, W. A. Urban Negro speech: sociolinguistic factors affecting English teaching. In R. W. Shuy, ed., *Social Dialects and Language Learning*. Champaign, Ill.: National Council of Teachers of English, 1965.

————. Sociolinguistic factors in the history of American Negro dialects. *Florida Foreign Language Reporter* 1967, Spring. Also in this volume, Chap. 17.

————. Continuity and change in American Negro dialects. *Florida Foreign Language Reporter* 1968, Spring. Also in this volume, Chap. 17.

Williams, F. Psychological correlates of speech characteristics: on sounding "disadvantaged." *J. Speech and Hearing Research* (in press).

Wolfram, W. A. *Sociolinguistic Description of Detroit Negro Speech*. Washington, D. C.: Center for Applied Linguistics, 1969.

Chapter 17

TOWARD A HISTORY OF AMERICAN NEGRO DIALECT

William A. Stewart*

The two articles (Stewart 1967, 1968) on Negro dialect history which are reprinted here are in a sense belated products of the Conference on Social Dialects and Language Learning held at Bloomington, Indiana, in the summer of 1964. Although the topic does not appear in the published papers from that conference (Shuy 1965), there was considerable disagreement among participants as to the facts of Negro dialect history, as well as to the relevance to educators of whatever those facts might be. Beryl L. Bailey and the author took the position that American Negro dialects probably derived from a creolized form of English, once spoken on American plantations by Negro slaves and seemingly related to creolized forms of English which are still spoken by Negroes in Jamaica and other parts of the Caribbean. Bailey and the author held the opinion that, although most American Negro dialects have now merged enough with white speech to preclude their still being considered truly creole dialects, the apparent survival of some creole features in many of them was a likely explanation of their more unique (vis-a-vis white speech) structural characteristics. Without prior examination of historical evidence on early American Negro speech, we merely came to our conclusions (arrived at quite independently) from some striking similarities between American Negro speech and Caribbean Negro speech. In addition, it seemed likely that the greater structural deviation of Negro dialects from the standard English superposed on all Americans created a situation in which Negro speech communities might resemble more the "diglossic" creole-plus-standard speech

---

*Education Study Center, Washington, D. C.

communities of the Caribbean than they would white American speech communities. That, in fact, was the whole purpose of Bailey's paper on the Jamaican language situation; it was meant to serve as one possible pedagogical model for teaching English in American Negro speech communities.

In the course of the discussion following Bailey's paper, it became apparent that some of the participants had already come to a quite different set of conclusions concerning the history of American Negro speech. In their view, there never was any pidgin or creole stage through which the English spoken by early American Negro slaves might have passed. Instead, the acquisition of colonial English by Negro slaves on the early North American plantations was believed to have been both rapid and successful, so that within one or two generations American Negro speech evidenced the same inventory of structural features as white speech. Consequently, there could be no instances of creole features appearing as survivals in present-day American Negro speech —no matter how nonstandard this might be. (Gullah was admitted to constitute a notable exception, but its creolization was held to be a fairly recent and isolated phenomena.) Any apparent similarities between American Negro dialects and Caribbean creole English would therefore be fortuitous. Thus, the creole historical model and the Caribbean pedagogical model were irrelevant to American Negro speech and (it was implied rather directly) a slur on the "American-ness" of all American Negroes.

When it became clear that these two positions were at loggerheads, the historical issue was wisely shelved by the chairman, and the conference moved on to other (and only slightly less controversial) matters. Yet, long after the conference was over, the author continued to think about the problem of historical evidence (with which, incidentally, our opponents proved to be similarly unfamiliar). Was it really true, for example, that there were no written samples of early American Negro slave speech? Or did such samples exist, and did they all show the slaves speaking the same kind of English as local whites of a comparable social-class level? Having begun to look into the colonial and antebellum records, the author was amazed to find how much evidence there actually was in support of the creole hypothesis. The only question which remained was: Is an understanding of the creole origin of American Negro dialects of any use to today's educators, faced as they are with pressing classroom problems? But the classroom problems in part are there because nonstandard dialect-speaking Negro children have had difficulties with standard English which white children (even nonstandard-dialect-speaking ones) do not have to the same degree; the difference is due to the relatively greater nonstandard-ness of Negro speech, and this is to no small extent a result of its particular historical background. So it was that, in early 1967, the author contributed the first of these articles on Negro dialect history, as an aspect of nonstandard speech, to *The Florida Foreign Language Reporter.*

SOCIOLINGUISTIC FACTORS IN THE HISTORY OF AMERICAN NEGRO DIALECTS[1]

Within the last few years, the increased national commitment to bettering the lot of socially and economically underprivileged groups of Americans—the so-called disadvantaged—has caused educators to consider ways in which the schools may involve themselves in this task. Of the many possibilities, certainly one of the most obvious is to deal with the chronic language problems associated with many of the disadvantaged. Yet, although there is a general awareness that certain of the disadvantaged do have language problems, there is at the same time a lack of agreement as to what these problems entail, and therefore what to do about them. Some investigators (often educational psychologists) have maintained that the disadvantaged characteristically do not use verbal communication to the extent that members of the middle class do, and are thus impoverished in communicative skills. To alleviate this situation, they have recommended programs aimed at encouraging the use of verbal communication of a variety of kinds by disadvantaged pupils. A few investigators have theorized that members of disadvantaged groups may even engage less in abstract thinking than do middle-class persons. For this there have been suggested programs designed to teach more perception and conceptualization on the part of the disadvantaged pupils.

On the other hand, linguists have tended to emphasize one other type of language problem which some disadvantaged groups often have, and for which evidence is quite accessible—being encountered every day in the nation's classrooms. This is the purely structural conflict between on the one hand the patterns of a nonstandard dialect which an individual may have learned at home or in peer-group interaction, and on the other hand the equivalent patterns of standard English—the language of modern technology and of the middle class. This is one kind of problem which many of the nation's schools ought to be ready and willing to cope with. One indication of the readiness of the schools is the fact that traditional English teachers are rapidly abandoning the older "sloppy speech" and "lazy tongue" views of nonstandard speech in favor of a realization that it usually represents the speaker's use of some language system which, though it may differ from standard English in form

---

[1] *The Florida Foreign Language Reporter* (Spring 1967); reprinted by permission. Copies of this and the following paper in their original forms are available for purchase in quantity from *The Florida Foreign Language Reporter* (801 N.E. 177th St., North Miami Beach, Fla. 33162). For a fuller discussion of the creole hypothesis as it relates to the study of American Negro speech, see William A. Stewart, "Sociopolitical issues in the linguistic treatment of Negro dialect" and "Historical and structural bases for the recognition of Negro dialect"; both in James E. Alatis, ed., *Monograph Series on Languages and Linguistics, No. 22* (Georgetown University, 1969).

and sometimes even in function, is nevertheless logical, coherent, and (in its own way) grammatical. Another indication of the readiness of schools to cope with the problem of dialect differences is the growth of a cadre of specialists in the teaching of English to speakers of other languages. With them, there has come into being a set of new techniques for teaching English to persons coming from different language backgrounds.

Just as they are ready, America's schools certainly ought to be willing to deal with dialect-based problems, since there are a number of ways in which, by themselves, such problems can render a nonstandard speaker dysfunctional in exchanges with standard-English-speaking members of the middle class. One way is for minor pronunciation differences between a nonstandard dialect and standard English—each one perhaps trivial by itself—to pile up in an utterance to such an extent that the nonstandard version becomes unintelligible to a middle-class listener, even though in grammar and vocabulary it may be quite similar to its standard equivalent. Thus, a nonstandard version of "I don't know where they live" might, in one dialect, become cryptic to the standard-speaking listener, merely because of its being pronounced something like *Ah 'own know wey 'ey lib.* Or, a standard-English speaker may misunderstand a nonstandard utterance, even though he thinks he has deciphered it correctly, because it contains nonstandard grammatical constructions which are unknown to him. For example, a middle-class listener may take a nonstandard sentence *Dey ain't like dat* to mean "they aren't like that," when it really means "They didn't like that." The standard-English speaker is simply unaware that *ain't* is this particular dialect's way of negating verbs in the past tense, as he is unaware that the usual equivalent in the same dialect of "They aren't like that" would be either *Dey not like dat* or *Dey don't be like dat* (the two variants indicating a difference in meaning which is not easily expressed in standard English). Of course, similar breakdowns in intelligibility may also occur in the other direction, when the nonstandard speaker tries to understand standard English. Finally, even when he does succeed in making himself understood by his middle-class listeners, the nonstandard speaker may still fall victim to the difference in social prestige between his dialect and standard English. In other words, although middle-class persons may understand what he is saying, they may still consider him uncouth for saying it the way he does.

Professionally able though the schools now may be to embark on programs which would deal effectively with this kind of problem, the likelihood of their actually doing so in the near future certainly is not increased by the unwillingness of many educators and even some applied linguists to approach the problem in any but the most general terms. For, unfortunately, the technical know-how necessary to teach standard English to speakers of nonstandard dialects is not simply embodied in an awareness of the problem at the level of

"Some children should probably be taught standard English as a second dialect"—no matter how true such statements may be. The necessary know-how will begin to be adequate when and only when applied linguists can give, and educators will take seriously, details of the type "The verb system of such-and-such a nonstandard dialect operates in such-and-such a way, and the verb system of standard English operates in such-and-such a way, so that structural interference is most likely to occur at points a, b, and c. Therefore, the following lessons and drills in the standard English verb system is what children who speak this nonstandard dialect will need" (see Stewart 1964).

One reason why there is now being taught little remedial English based upon a systematic comparison of the differences between nonstandard dialects and standard English, is that information about one of the pedagogically most important features of nonstandard dialects—their grammatical systems—is still largely lacking. This lack is due in great part to the fact that American dialect studies have traditionally emphasized differences in pronunciation and vocabulary, at the expense of information on systematic grammatical differences.

Now that linguists have begun to fill this information gap, however, they are finding their observations on language variation among the disadvantaged received with uneasiness and even hostility by many teachers, administrators, and community leaders. The reason for this is undoubtedly that the accurate description of dialect variation in American communities—particularly in urban centers—is turning out to show a disturbing correlation between language behavior on the one hand and socioeconomic and ethnic stratification on the other.[2] The correlation is particularly controversial insofar as it involves the speech of large numbers of American Negroes, since at the present time Negro leadership (and this includes most Negro educators) is probably more achievement-oriented than any other. Because of this orientation, Negro elites tend not to welcome any evidence of uniform or stable behavioral differences between members of their own group (even lower-class ones) and those of the white-dominated middle class. Yet the fact is that Negroes account for most of the most pedagogically problematic nonstandard-dialect speakers in the larger cities, and also include within their group speakers of the most radically

[2]The American Dream notwithstanding, it is well known to social scientists that American society is stratified into a number of social classes and ethnic groups, and that each of these exhibits a characteristic configuration of customs, attitudes, roles, life-ways and, as it turns out, speech patterns. The literature on social and ethnic stratification is extensive, but good introductions are Egon Ernest Bergel, *Social Stratification* (1962), and Tamotsu Shibutani and Kian M. Kwan, *Ethnic Stratification* (1965). For an exhaustively documented study of the correlation between language variation and social class, ethnicity, and age in an American metropolis, see William Labov, *The Social Stratification of English in New York City* (1966).

nonstandard dialects of natively spoken English in the entire country.[3] Furthermore, de facto segregation in housing has caused nonstandard-dialect-speaking Negroes to predominate in many schools; these Negroes appear in many cases to have different kinds of problems with standard English than nonstandard-dialect-speaking whites have (even in the same area). Therefore the sweeping for political purposes of Negro dialect descriptions under the white-oriented geographic-dialect rug would probably be more detrimental to disadvantaged Negro children than it would be advantageous to Negro elites.[4]

On the other hand, linguists should realize that the fears and anxieties of Negro leaders about public discussion of ethnically correlated behavioral differences may have some foundation. It is possible, for example, that quite objective and innocently made statements about dialect differences between whites and Negroes might be interpreted by white racists as evidence of Negro cultural backwardness or mental inferiority, or even seized upon by black racists as evidence of some sort of mythical Negro "soul." Linguists should not censor their data, but they should make sure that their statements about Negro-white differences are not divorced from an awareness of the historical, social, and linguistic reasons why such differences may have come into existence and been maintained. Perhaps it would serve that end to point out here some of the sociolinguistic factors involved in the evolution of American Negro dialects, factors which explain why certain kinds of American Negro dialects are both different from the nonstandard dialects of American whites, and also more radically deviant from standard English.

Although the linguistic history of the Negro in the United States can be reconstructed from the numerous literary attestations of the English of New World Negroes over the last two-and-a-half centuries, and by comparing these with the English of Negroes in the United States, the Caribbean, and West Africa today, this has never been done for the English-teaching profession. In presenting a historical sketch of this type, the author realizes that both the facts presented and his interpretations of them may embarrass or even infuriate those who would like to whitewash American Negro dialects by claiming that they do not exist—that (in spite of all sorts of observable evidence to the contrary) they are nothing but southern white dialects derived from Great Britain.

---

[3]These two facts may not be entirely unrelated. For a graphic indication of the relatively-more-nonstandard grammatical norms of Negro children over white children in a single city, see Figure 18 in Walter Loban, *Problems in Oral English: Kindergarten Through Grade Nine* (1966).

[4]For a discussion of Negro dialect in one urban community, see Stewart (1965). The nonstandard dialect patterns cited earlier in the present article are also Negro dialect.

Of those Africans who fell victim to the Atlantic slave trade and were
brought to the New World, many found it necessary to learn some kind of
English. With very few exceptions the form of English which they acquired
was a pidginized one, and this kind of English became so well established as
the principal medium of communication between Negro slaves in the British
colonies that it was passed on as a creole language to succeeding generations
of the New World Negroes, for whom it was their native tongue.[5] Some idea
of what New World Negro English may have been like in its early stages can
be obtained from a well-known example of the speech of a fourteen-year-old
Negro lad given by Daniel DeFoe in the *The Family Instructor* (London,
1715). It is significant that the Negro, Toby, speaks a pidginized kind of
English to his boy-master, even though he states that he was born in the New
World. A sample of his speech is:[6]

> Toby. Me be born at Barbadoes.
> Boy. Who lives there, Toby?
> Toby. There lives white mans, white womans, negree mans,
> negree womans, just so as live here.

---

[5]In referring to types of languages, linguists use the terms *pidgin* and *creole* in a
technical sense which has none of the derogatory or racial connotations of popular uses
of these terms. When a linguist says that a variety of language is pidginized, he merely
means that it has a markedly simplified grammatical structure compared with the
normal (i.e., unpidginized) source language. This simplification may be one way in
which speakers of different languages can make a new language easier to learn and use
—particularly if they have neither the opportunity nor the motivation to learn to speak
it the way its primary users do. In addition, some of the unique characteristics of a
pidgin language may be due, not to simplification, but to influences on it from the native
languages of its users. What is important to realize, however, is that pidginized languages do have grammatical structure and regularity, even though their specific patterns may be different from those of the related, unpidginized source language of higher
prestige. Thus, the fact that the sentence *Dem no get-am* in present-day West African
pidgin English is obviously different from its standard-English equivalent "They don't
have it " does not necessarily indicate that the pidgin-English speaker "talks without
grammar". In producing such a sentence, he is unconsciously obeying the grammatical
rules of West African pidgin English, and these determine that *Dem no get-am* is the
right construction, as opposed to such ungrammatical or wrong combinations as *No
dem get-am, No get dem-am, Get-am dem no,* etc. If a pidgin finally becomes the native
language of a speech community (and thereby becomes by definition a creole language),
it may expand in grammatical complexity to the level of normal, or unpidginized,
languages. Of course, the resulting creole language may still exhibit structural differences from the original source language, because the creole has gone through a pidginized stage. For more details, see Robert A. Hall, Jr.,*Pidgin and Creole Languages*
(1966).

[6]The same citation is given in a fuller form, along with a number of other attestations of early New-World Negro speech, in George Philip Krapp,*The English Language in America* (1925). Other attestations are cited in Tremaine McDowell, "Notes
on Negro dialect in the American novel to 1821" (1930).

Boy. What and not know God?

Toby. Yes, the white mans say God prayers,—no much know God.

Boy. And what do the black mans do?

Toby. They much work, much work,—no say God prayers, not at all.

Boy. What work do they do, Toby?

Toby. Makee the sugar, makee the ginger,—much great work, weary work, all day, all night.

Even though the boy-master's English is slightly nonstandard (e.g. *black mans),* it is still quite different from the speech of the Negro.

An idea of how widespread a pidginized form of English had become among the Negro population of the New World by the end of the seventeenth century can be gathered from the fact that it had even become the language of the coastal plantations in the Dutch colony of Surinam (i.e., Dutch Guiana), in South America. In an early description of that colony, the chapter on the Negro ends with a sample conversation in the local Negro English dialect as *Me bella well* "I am very well," *You wantee siddown pinkininne?* "Do you want to sit down for a bit?", and *You wantee go walka longa me?* "Do you want to take a walk with me?"[7] In these sentences, the use of the enclitic vowel in *wantee* recalls the same in DeFoe's example *makee.* Also, the speaker, like Toby, uses *me* as a subject pronoun. In the first Surinam sentence, we see an early example of a construction without any equivalent of the standard English verb "to be." Toby also would probably have said *Me weary,* since the *be* in his first sentence was in all likelihood a past tense marker (as it is in present day West African pidgin English)—the sentence therefore meaning "I was born in Barbadoes." In the last Surinam sentence, a reflex of English *along* is used with the meaning of standard English "with." It may or may not be accidental that in the Gullah dialect, spoken by the Negroes along the South Carolina coastal plain, the same phenomenon occurs, e.g., *Enty you wantuh walk long me?* "Do you want to take a walk with me?" Some Gullah speakers even still use *me* as a subject pronoun, e.g., *Me kyaan bruk-um* "I can't break it", and enclitic final vowels seem to have survived in such Gullah forms as *yerry, yeddy* "to hear."

Early examples of Negro dialect as spoken in the American colonies show it to be strikingly similar to that given by DeFoe for the West Indies and by Herlein for Surinam. In John Leacock's play, *The Fall of British Tyranny*

---

[7] J. D. Herlein, *Beschryvinge van de volksplantinge Zuriname* (1718, pp. 121–23). Herlein gives the Negro-English dialogues in Dutch orthography. I have retranscribed these sentences in the kind of spelling which his English contemporaries would have used in order to show better the relationship between the Surinam dialect and the other examples. In the Dutch spelling, these sentences appear as *My belle wel, Jou wantje sie don pinkinine?,* and *Jo wantje gaeu wakke lange mie?*

(Philadelphia, 1776), part of the conversation between certain "Kidnapper" and Cudjo, one of a group of Virginia Negroes, goes as follows:[8]

> KIDNAPPER . . . what part did you come from?
> CUDJO. Disse brack man, disse one, disse one, disse one, come from Hamton, disse one, disse one, come from Nawfok, me come from Nawfok too.
> KIDNAPPER. Very well, what was your master's name?
> CUDJO. Me massa name Cunney Tomsee.
> KIDNAPPER. Colonel Thompson—eigh?
> CUDJO. Eas, massa, Cunney Tomsee.
> KIDNAPPER. Well then I'll make you a major—and what's your name?
> CUDJO. Me massa cawra me Cudjo.

Again, the enclitic vowels (e.g., *disse*) and the subject pronoun *me* are prominent features of the Negro dialect. In the sentence *Me Massa name Cunney Tomsee* "My master's name is Colonel Thompson," both the verb "to be" and the standard English possessive suffix -*s* are absent. Incidentally, Cudjo's construction is strikingly similar to sentences like *My sister name Mary* which are used by many American Negroes today.

One possible explanation of why this kind of pidginized English was so widespread in the New World, with widely separated varieties resembling each other in so many ways, is that it did not originate in the New World as isolated and accidentally similar instances of random pidginization, but rather originated as a *lingua franca* in the trade centers and slave factories on the West African coast (cf., e.g., Davidson 1961, particularly p. 218). It is likely that at least some Africans already knew this pidgin English when they came to the New World, and that the common colonial policy of mixing slaves of various tribal origins forced its rapid adoption as a plantation *lingua franca*.

In the course of the eighteenth century, some significant changes took place in the New World Negro population, and these had their effect on language behavior. For one thing, the number of Negroes born in the New World came to exceed the number of those brought over from Africa. In the process, pidgin English became the creole mother tongue of the new generations, and in some areas it has remained so to the present day.[9]

In the British colonies, the creole English of the uneducated Negroes and the English dialects of both the educated and uneducated whites were close enough to each other (at least in vocabulary) to allow the speakers of each to

---

[8] This citation also occurs in Krapp (1925) and with others in Richard Walser, "Negro dialect in eighteenth-century American drama" (1955).

[9] In the West Indies, creole English is usually called *patois*, while in Surinam it is called *Taki-Taki*. In the United States, the only fairly pure creole English left today is Gullah, spoken along the coast of South Carolina.

communicate, although they were still different enough so that the whites could consider creole English to be "broken" or "corrupt" English, and evidence, so many thought, of the mental limitations of the Negro. But in Surinam, where the European settlers spoke Dutch, creole English was regarded more objectively. In fact, no less than two language courses specifically designed to teach creole English to Dutch immigrants were published before the close of the eighteenth century.[10]

Another change which took place in the New World Negro population primarily during the course of the eighteenth century was the social cleavage of the New-World-born generations into underprivileged field hands (a continuation of the older, almost universal lot of the Negro slave) and privileged domestic servants. The difference in privilege usually meant, not freedom instead of bondage, but rather freedom from degrading kinds of labor, access to the "big house" with its comforts and civilization and proximity to the prestigious "quality" whites, with the opportunity to imitate their behavior (including their speech) and to wear their clothes. In some cases, privilege included the chance to get an education and, in a very few, access to wealth and freedom. In both the British colonies and the United States, Negroes belonging to the privileged group were soon able to acquire a more standard variety of English than the creole of the field hands, and those who managed to get a decent education became speakers of fully standard and often elegant English. This seems to have become the usual situation by the early 1800s, and remained so through the Civil War. In Caroline Gilman's *Recollections of a Southern Matron* (1838), the difference between field-hand creole (in this case, Gullah) and domestic-servant dialect is evident in a comparison of the gardener's "He tief one sheep—he run away las week, cause de overseer gwine for flog him" with Dina's "'Scuse me, missis, I is gitting hard o' hearing, and yes is more politer dan no" (page 254). A more striking contrast between the speech of educated and uneducated Negroes occurs in a novel written in the 1850s by an American Negro who had traveled extensively through the slave states. In Chapter 17, part of the exchange between Henry, an educated Negro traveler, and an old "aunty" goes as follows.[11]

> "Who was that old man who ran behind your master's horse?"
> "Dat Nathan, my husban'."

---

[10]These were Pieter van Dijk, *Nieuwe en nooit bevoorens geziende onderwijzinge in het Bastert Engels, of Neeger Engels* (undated, c1780), and G. C. Weygandt, *Gemeenzame leerwijze om het Basterd of Neger-Engelsch op een gemakkelijke wijze te leeren verstaan en spreeken* (1798).

[11]Martin R. Delany, Blake; or the Huts of America, published serially in *The Anglo-African Magazine* (1859). The quotation is from Vol. 1, No. 6, (June 1859), page 163.

"Do they treat him well, aunty?"
"No, chile, wus an' any dog, da beat 'im foh little an nothin'."
"Is uncle Nathan religious?"
"Yes, chile, ole man an' I's been sahvin' God dis many day, fo yeh baun! Wen any on 'em in de house git sick, den da sen foh 'uncle Nathan' com pray foh dem; 'uncle Nathan' mighty good den!"

After the Civil War, with the abolition of slavery, the breakdown of the plantation system, and the steady increase in education for poor as well as affluent Negroes, the older field-hand creole English began to lose many of its creole characteristics, and take on more and more of the features of the local white dialects and of the written language. Yet this process has been just one way, for as it is true that the speech of American Negroes has not been strongly influenced by the speech of whites with whom they came into contact, it is probably also true that the speech of many whites has been influenced in some ways by the speech of Negroes (see McDavid and McDavid 1951).

Over the last two centuries, the proportion of American Negroes who speak a perfectly standard variety of English has risen from a small group of privileged house slaves and free Negroes, to persons numbering in the hundreds of thousands, and perhaps even millions. Yet there is still a sizeable number of American Negroes—undoubtedly larger than the number of standard-speaking Negroes—whose speech may be radically nonstandard. The nonstandard features in the speech of such persons may be due in part to the influence of the nonstandard dialects of whites with whom they or their ancestors have come in contact, but they also may be due to the survival of creolisms from the older Negro field-hand speech of the plantations. To insure their social mobility in modern American society, these nonstandard speakers must undoubtedly be given a command of standard English; that point was made in the early part of this paper. In studying nonstandard Negro dialects and teaching standard English in terms of them, however, both the applied linguist and the language teacher must come to appreciate the fact that even if certain nonstandard Negro dialect patterns do not resemble the dialect usage of American whites or those of the speakers of remote British dialects, they may be, nevertheless, as old as African and European settlement in the New World and therefore quite widespread and well established. On various occasions, it has been pointed out that many speakers of nonstandard American Negro dialects make a grammatical and semantic distinction by means of *be,* illustrated by such constructions as *he busy* "He is busy (momentarily)" or *he workin'* "he is working (right now)" as opposed to *he be busy* "he is (habitually) busy" or *he be workin'* "he is working (steadily)," which the grammar of standard English is unable to make.[12] Even this distinction goes

---

[12]See, for example, *The Florida Foreign Language Reporter,* Vol. 4, No. 2, (Winter

back well over a century. One observer in the 1830s noted a request by a slave for a permanent supply of soap as "(If) Missis only give we, we be so clean forever," while *be* is absent in a subsequent report of someone's temporary illness with "She jist sick for a little while."[13]

Once educators who are concerned with the language problems of the disadvantaged come to realize that nonstandard Negro dialects represent a historical tradition of this type, it is to be hoped that they will be less embarrassed by evidence that these dialects are very much alike throughout the country, while different in many ways from the nonstandard dialects of whites; less frustrated by failure to turn nonstandard Negro dialect speakers into standard-English speakers overnight; less impatient with the stubborn survival of Negro dialect features in the speech of even educated persons; and less zealous in proclaiming what is right and what is wrong. If this happens, then applied linguists and educators will be able to communicate with each other, and both will be able to communicate with the nonstandard-speaking Negro child. The problem will then be well on its way toward a solution.

CONTINUITY AND CHANGE IN AMERICAN NEGRO DIALECTS[14]

In the foregoing paper, I cited examples of the kind of literary and comparative evidence which exists for determining earlier stages of these dialects, and which practically forces the conclusion that the linguistic assimilation of the Afro-American population to the speech patterns of English-speaking American whites was neither as rapid nor as complete as some scholars have supposed.[15] Of the Negro slaves who constituted the field labor force on American

---

1965-1966), p. 25.

[13]Frances Anne Kemble, *Journal of a Residence on a Georgian Plantation in 1838-1839*(1862). The first quotation is from page 52, and the second is from page 118.

[14]This paper originally appeared in *The Florida Foreign Language Reporter,* Spring 1968, reprinted by permission.

[15]For example, "The Negroes born in this country invariably used, according to these records, good English." Allen Walker Read, "The speech of negroes in colonial America" *The Journal of Negro History* (1939, p. 258). The records which Read refers to are for the most part runaway-slave advertisements published before the American Revolution. Of course, the evidence which they supply on slave speech is indirect (i.e., they give impressions of the particular slave's competence in English, but no examples of that English), since the information was merely intended to help identify the runaway. If these indirect records say what Read interprets them as saying, then they are certainly at variance with what direct evidence (quotations in slave dialect) is available from the same period. Furthermore, the far larger number of attestations of slave speech during the nineteenth century which show widespread use of nonstandard

plantations up to the mid-nineteenth century, even many who were born in the New World spoke a variety of English which was in fact a true creole language —differing markedly in grammatical structure from those English dialects which were brought directly from Great Britain, as well as from New World modifications of these in the mouths of descendants of the original white colonists.[16] And, although this creole English subsequently underwent modification in the direction of the more prestigious British-derived dialects, the merging process was neither instantaneous nor uniform. Indeed, the nonstandard speech of present-day American Negroes still seems to exhibit structural traces of a creole predecessor, and this is probably a reason why it is in some ways more deviant from standard English than is the nonstandard speech of even the most uneducated American whites.

For the teacher, this means that such Negro patterns as the zero copula,[17] the zero possessive,[18] or undifferentiated pronouns[19] should not be ascribed to greater carelessness, laziness, or stupidity on the part of Negroes, but rather should be treated as what they really are—language patterns which have been in existence for generations and which their present users have acquired, from parent and peer, through a perfectly normal kind of language-learning process.[20]

---

dialect, together with a similar situation observable today, would mean that American Negro speech generally became less standard after that first generation of American-born slaves. Needless to say, such a process would be very difficult to explain either structurally or historically. The trouble with Read's conclusion seems to be that, in interpreting such advertisements, he did not consider the possibility that in the parlance of slave owners a term like "good English" might have meant something very different when applied to Negroes than it would have if applied to whites. Indications that this was probably the case seem to exist in the advertisements quoted on pages 252-53.

[16]The Gullah (or Geechee) dialect, spoken by many Negroes along the South Atlantic coast, appears to be a fairly direct descendant of the older kind of plantation creole.

[17]The term *zero copula* refers to the absence of an explicit predicating verb in certain dialect constructions, where standard English has such a verb (usually in the present tense). Compare nonstandard Negro dialect *He old, Dey runnin'*, and *She a teacher* with standard English "He is old," "They are running" and "She is a teacher".

[18]The term *zero possessive* refers to the absence of an explicit suffix in noun-noun constructions, where standard English has such a suffix. Compare nonstandard Negro dialect *My fahver frien'* with standard English "My father's friend."

[19]The term *undifferentiated pronoun* refers to the use of the same pronoun form for both subject and object, and sometimes for possession as well. The pronominal form used may be derived from either the standard English object form, or the subject form. Compare such nonstandard forms as *Him know we, Him know us* (beside *He know us)* with the standard English "He knows us" to which they are equivalent. Or compare *He fahver* (beside *his fahver*) and *We house* (beside *Our house*) with standard English "His father" and "Our house."

[20]If the term *Negro dialect* is understood to refer to nonstandard varieties of

Since the main purpose of the earlier article was to document the use of creole English by native-born American Negroes during the colonial and ante bellum periods, almost nothing was said about the course of Negro dialects since Emancipation. But, as anyone can see who compares written samples of Negro dialect from around the time of the Civil War with Negro dialect today, there have been changes. And, equally interesting, one can also see that there are still many similarities between the two. An overview of the interacting processes of continuity and change in American Negro dialects as they relate to one important aspect of language variation—grammatical structure—will help educators to put the classroom language problems of today's disadvantaged Negro children into a clearer perspective.

One of the more important changes which has occurred in American Negro dialects during the past century has been the almost complete decreolization of both their functional and lexical vocabulary. Although this process actually began long before the Civil War (particularly in areas with a low proportion of Negroes to whites), the breakdown of the plantation system apparently accelerated it considerably, even in the coastal areas of South Carolina and Georgia. In the process, overt creolisms which were so common in early attestations of slave speech, such as *been* for marking past action (with no basic distinction between preterite and perfect), undifferentiated pronouns for subject and object (e.g., *me, him* and *dem* also as subject pronouns, *we* as an object pronoun), a single subject-pronoun form (usually *him* or *he*) for masculine, feminine, and neuter in the third person singular, *-um* (or *-am*) as a general third-person (all genders and numbers) object suffix, *no* as verbal negator, and *for* as an infinitive marker, became quite rare in even the non-standard speech of Negroes born after Emancipation.[21]

_____

American English whose more unique (i.e., nonwhite and non-British) structural features are simply due to the historical influence of an earlier plantation creole, then it should be clear that such a term does not imply any direct genetic determination of speech patterns, in spite of its ethnic reference. *Negro* in "Negro dialect" is merely a recognition of the fact that the creole predecessor for such structural features was itself the result of African migration to and acculturation in Anglo-Saxon America, and that those present-day dialects which show the greatest influence from such a creole are precisely those which are used by the descendants of the Negro field hands who originally spoke it. In addition, the speech of American Negroes is often characterized by special kinds of syllable and breath dynamics, as well as unique used of pitch, stress, and volume. But even these language habits are always socially-learned and transmitted ones, although it is difficult to tell whether they represent survivals of African speech habits or creole speech habits, or are more recent innovations. That they are not the product of any special Negro vocal physiology should be obvious from the fact that some whites can mimic such features quite well, and that there are some Negroes in whose speech the same features are not normally present.

[21]Judging from the literary treatment of Negro dialect, these features were charac-

However, the speed and thoroughness with which the plantation field-hand dialects were thus made more "proper" varied both according to the region and according to the social characteristics of the speakers themselves. Because people learn most of their language forms from others, the change took place more rapidly and completely in areas where speakers (white or Negro) of more-or-less standard varieties of English were present in numbers, than it did in areas with a high concentration of field laborers. On the other hand, because children generally are more affected by the language usage of other children than by that of grown-ups, and because lower-class child-peer groups tend to remain rather isolated from the stylistic innovations of adult discourse, the change took place more slowly and less thoroughly in the speech of young children than it did in that of adolescents and adults.

The result of this uneven correction of the older plantation dialects was that, while they seemed to have died out by the end of the nineteenth century (particularly outside the South Atlantic coastal area and the Mississippi basin), juvenile versions of them actually continued to survive in many Negro speech communities as baby-talk or small-boy talk.[22] That is, the older nonstandard

---

teristic of the nonstandard speech of even New England Negroes up to the close of the eighteenth century. Within the first decades of the nineteenth century, however, the northern limit of their common occurrence in adult speech appears to have receded to the Delaware region, and to somewhere in the Carolinas by the middle of the same century. Of course, most of these creolisms still occur in Gullah—at least sporadically. And it is likely that the *for to* infinitives of some Deep South Negro dialects are the result of incomplete decreolization (the adding of noncreole *to*, without giving up the creole *for*), rather than the borrowing of a white nonstandard dialect pattern, as some might suppose. In the first place, such white dialects (Appalachia, Georgia, etc.) usually have a contrast between *to* and *for to*, e.g. *I come to see it* (i.e., "It dawned on me") vs. *I come fer to see it* ("I came in order to see it"), while many Negro dialects in which *for to* occurs do not make such a distinction. In the second place, there is piecemeal evidence of the addition of *to* after *for* along the South Atlantic coast, where the change has been relatively recent. For example, in *Drums and Shadows: Survival Studies Among the Georgia Coastal Negroes* (1940, p. 144) a team of the Georgia Writers' Project interviewed an old lady (then approximately one-hundred years old) who, speaking of an African-born slave whom she knew in her youth, recalled "I membuh he say 'Lemme cook sumpm fuh nyam.' He mean sumpm fuh tuh eat." Notice also her decreolization of the Gullah and Caribbean creole English verb *nyam* "to eat." In some areas, the changeover was not so complete, c. f. a literary reflection of a Gullah Negro's alternation between the same two verbs, in Ambrose E. Gonzales, *The Captain: Stories of the Black Border* (1924, p. 149), "You hab mout' fuh nyam da' haa'd hoecake you juntlemun gi' you fuh eat."

[22] The impression that the rustic and creole features of the older plantation dialects died out entirely during this period is easy to get, considering that the speech of children hardly appears at all in the records of folklorists or dialectologists, or even in the fictional use of dialect, since the main concern of the social scientist and the novelist

(and sometimes even creole-like) dialect features remained in use principally by younger children in Negro speech-communities—being learned from other young children, to be given up later in life when small-boy talk was no longer appropriate to a more mature status.[23] And even though the adult dialects which these child dialects were ontogenetically given up for, were also structurally nonstandard and identifiably Negro in most cases, they were still more standard—enough, at least, so that conspicuous retentions of child-dialect forms in the speech of an adult could sometimes result in the accusation that he or she was "talking like a child" or simply "talking bad."[24]

Interestingly enough, the use of an older, more conservative form of Negro dialect as child-speech was not always limited to Negroes. In the Old South, many upper-class whites went through a similar linguistic metamor-

alike has been the adult. Evidence that the older dialects have in fact survived in the speech of children is only now coming to light through recent studies of present-day Negro speech communities. See Stewart (1965), particularly pages 16-18, and Dillard (1967). It would seem that the preservation of a more conservative dialect by young children in communities where the older language forms are being encroached upon by imported ones is not limited to Negro communities. During a recent sociolinguistic survey of the Appalachian region, I found full-fledged mountain dialect still being used by preschool-age white children in communities where it had been abandoned by all but the oldest adults.

[23]Like Dillard (1967), I feel that this constitutes the plausible explanation of the sporadic but not infrequent occurrence in the speech of lower-class Negro children of such "mistakes" as *been* as a general past-time marker (e.g., *He been hit me*), pronominal forms which are undifferentiated for case or gender (e.g., *Me gonna try* and *He out playin'*—the latter said in reference to a girl), etc., since these same features were quite normal in older forms of Negro dialect (and still are in Gullah) and since there is, after all, an uninterrupted chain of language transmission from those earlier speakers to Negro children of the present day. Because some of the features are similar (at least superficially) to ones which are characteristic of certain stages of language development in virtually all English-speaking children, most specialists have attributed the Negro-child patterns to developmental causes. However, since the Negro patterns are sometimes used by children who are well beyond the developmental stage (which normally ends at age 3.6 or or 4 years for whites), this would imply that Negroes develop linguistically more slowly than do whites. And, since there are even Negro octogenarians who use these forms, one would be forced to the absurd conclusion that some Negroes must not have completed the development process at all.

[24]In Washington, D.C., I know of an adolescent Negro who for some reason had retained many child-dialect features in his speech. His peers characterized his speech by saying that "He talk just like a small boy." And in her *Folk-Lore of the Sea Islands, South Carolina* (1923), Elsie Clews Parson gives a Negro folktale (No. 148, "The Girl Who Learned to Talk Proper") in which the speech of a young lady who was said to "talk very bad" is marked by the use of creole pronominal forms (e.g., "Me ain' col', suh!"). It is interesting that the conclusion of this tale also shows popular recognition of the effect of out-migration on speech habits, since the same girl did finally "learn to talk proper" when an outsider married her and "kyarried her to his country."

phosis from the nonstandard dialect of their Negro playmates to the relatively standard English of their adult station in life. As John Bennett (1908, p. 339; see also 1909) described the situation for the Charlestonian aristocracy of his day:

> It is true that, up to the age of four, approximately, the children of the best families, even in town, are apt to speak an almost unmodified *Gullah*, caught from brown playmates and country bred nurses; but at that age the refinement of cultivation begins, and "the flowers o' the forest are a' weed awa!"[25]

It was undoubtedly in this manner that such white southern writers as Joel C. Harris and Ambrose E. Gonzales first acquired their knowledge of the Negro dialects which they immortalized in print.[26]

Today, genteel southern whites no longer learn nonstandard Negro dialects as children, since the social conditions which once prompted them to do so have now become part of history. In their preschool childhood, however, many Negroes still learn and use such dialects, and although they may modify these in later life, few ever attain anything like the elegant standard English which was the familial and social heritage of the older white aristocrats. Yet, when they enter the standard-English milieu of the school, Negro children from this kind of language background are expected to compete linguistically with children (usually white) who have known and used standard English all

---

[25]This same process had evidently been going on for at least a century and a half before Bennett's time. It was noted during the first half of the eighteenth century by G. L. Campbell, a British traveler to the American colonies. "One Thing they are very faulty in, with regard to their Children," he wrote of the white planters in the July 1746 number of *The London Magazine*, "which is, that when young, they suffer them too much to prowl amongst the young Negroes, which insensibly causes them to imbibe their Manners and broken Speech" (quoted in Read 1933, p. 329). Since even the most aristocratic British children probably picked up nonstandard English or Scottish dialects from children of the servant class, it must have been the "broken" (*i.e.,* creolized) character of the colonial Negro speech which Campbell found so disagreeable in the North American situation.

[26]Elsewhere (Stewart 1965, p. 13, fn. 7), I have taken Ambrose E. Gonzales to task for his racistic explanation of some of the structural characteristics of the Gullah dialect. At the same time, one can see how he would come to such a point of view, since he was obviously unaware of pidginization as a linguistic phenomenon, and therefore unable to account scientifically for its operation in the speech of the Gullah Negroes. In addition, a genetic explanation of language differences fitted quite comfortably into the rhetoric of the caste-cloven society of which Gonzales was so much a product. This theoretical weakness notwithstanding, Gonzales' literary rendition of Gullah was superb. Considering the accuracy of his dialect phonology and syntax, and the ease with which he handled subtle dialect differences and even individual switching behavior, he can certainly qualify as America's greatest dialect writer. For a similar opinion of Gonzales, see Ann Sullivan Haskell (1964, pp. 238–41).

their lives. Of course, a few of these Negro children do succeed, not because of good teaching, but because of their own exceptional abilities. But a far greater proportion of these children—the average ones, as well as the few who are truly below average—fail conspicuously. And, because there is obviously some sort of ethnic correlation between pupil success and failure in newly integrated school situations, the embarrassed educational establishment and the frustrated public enter into a crisis relationship. Some whites charge (privately, at least) that the schools are being given the impossible task of teaching unteachable Negroes. And some Negroes charge (not so privately) that white educators are involved in a conspiracy to deliberately keep Negro children from learning. Parents protest blindly and school administrators run helter-skelter, holding councils of despair with colleagues who understand the problem no better.

A basic reason why so many Negro children fail in school is not that they are unteachable, but that they are not being taught efficiently or fairly. And this fact may have little or nothing to do with a white conspiracy against integrated schools. Rather, it may be the result of a far-less-deliberate yet equally devastating insensitiviiy of the educational process to the social and cultural characteristics of the school population. This is probably nowhere more striking than in the area of language since, as speakers largely of nonstandard dialects which are among the most deviant from standard English now being used in America, many Negro children are burdened at every turn with achievement barriers in the form of extra (and uncompensated for) language-learning requirements. For example, all children are expected to learn how to read in school. But for many Negro pupils the problem is made more difficult by the fact that they are unfamiliar not only with the sound-spelling-meaning correspondences of many of the words, but even with the grammatical patterns which these words make up in their reading lessons. Consequently, the reading achievement of these children becomes dependent upon their own success in deciphering standard-English sentence structure. And the same type of problem is reflected in other subject areas in the schools. The irony here is that the traditional educational system is itself creating much of the pedagogical disadvantagement of its linguistically different pupils by requiring them to accomplish, on their own, as much again as middle-class pupils from a standard English background are expected to accomplish with expert help.

In many ways, the plight of the Negro child who enters school speaking a nonstandard dialect is similar to that of a foreign-language-speaking child entering an American school. And, while it can be argued that no Negro dialect is as different from standard English as is, say, Spanish, this does not necessarily mean that the linguistically different Negro's task is that much easier. For, while the boundaries between a full fledged foreign language and English are usually clear-cut (the Spanish-speaking child, for example, will usually know at any given point whether Spanish or English is being used, and so will the teacher), the many similarities between any Negro dialect and standard English make it difficult to tell exactly where one leaves off and the other begins.[27] Thus, even the linguistic similarities between a nonstandard dialect and standard English can be pedagogically and psychologically disadvantageous, since they can camouflage functional differences between the two linguistic systems. Furthermore, while a wealth of linguistic knowledge and pedagogical know-how is currently brought to bear on the language problems of the child who speaks a foreign language such as Spanish, no similar competences have yet been developed to help the child who speaks a nonstandard dialect, although his needs are just as great—and his numbers greater. Considering his educational prospects as they stand at present, the linguistically different Negro child might well say "I look down de road an' de road so lonesome."

Although English teachers, speech therapists and other language-oriented educators are now dedicating themselves more than ever to the task of helping disadvantaged children—and especially disadvantaged Negro children—acquire proficiency in standard English, very few of these dedicated professionals have demonstrated any real understanding of the language characteristics of the communities from which these children come. For their part, teachers of English to Spanish-speaking Mexican, Puerto Rican or Cuban children know that an understanding of the structure of Spanish will give insights into the problems which such children have with English, and these teachers would be shocked by any suggestion that a comparative approach to the language of the school and the language of the child is unnecessary. In contrast, teachers of English to disadvantaged Negro children have generally remained aloof from the serious study of nonstandard Negro dialect.

This lack of interest on the part of many English teachers in the nonstandard language of Negro children is in large part the product of a normative view of language which has long been the mainstay of traditional teacher training. Either overtly or by implication, the teacher-to-be is taught that the kind of usage which is indicated in grammar books, dictionaries, and style manuals (and which is presumably followed by educated speakers and writers) represents a maximum of structural neatness, communicative efficiency, esthetic taste, and logical clarity. Once this normative view has been inculcated in the prospective teacher (and it must be admitted that popular beliefs about correct and incorrect language practically guarantee this), then the teacher will quite

---

[27]Because the structural relationships which hold between the two dialects in such a case are in part like those between completely foreign languages and in part like those between two style-levels of a single language, I have coined the term *quasi-foreign language situation* to describe it. See my "Foreign language teaching methods in quasi-foreign language situations" (Stewart 1964).

naturally regard departures from the norms of standard English as departures from structure, clarity, taste, and even logic itself.[28]

Of course, there have always been exceptional teachers who have seen that chronic deviations from standard-English usage on the part of their pupils may indicate simply their normal use of some other variety of English, with its own structure and logic. William Francis Allen was an early example of a teacher who who not only discovered this, but came to realize that even apparent ignorance in coping with logical or experiential problems could sometimes be traced to mere difficulty with the language in which the problems were posed. He recorded the following incident, which occurred while he was teaching Gullah Negro children on Port Royal Island, South Carolina, during the Civil War (Allen, Ware, and Garrison 1867, p. xxvii).

> I asked a group of boys one day the color of the sky. Nobody could tell me. Presently the father of one of them came by, and I told him their ignorance, repeating my question with the same result as before. He grinned: "Tom, how sky stan'?" "Blue," promptly shouted Tom.[29]

But in attempting to teach standard English to children who speak a nonstandard dialect, even those teachers who understand that there is a language conflict involved, and who would accordingly like to borrow techniques from foreign-language-teaching methodology, are likely to find their efforts hampered by too limited a knowledge of the structural characteristics of whatever nonstandard dialect the children speak. For, in all too many cases, the best pedagogical grasp of the structural features of a particular nonstandard dialect will consist of little more than a list of certain "folk" pronunciations and an awareness of the use of such grammatical shibboleths as *ain't* and the double negative. Unfortunately, this kind of superficial knowledge of the structural details of the speech of disadvantaged children will not only prevent the teacher or therapist from understanding the reasons for many of these children's mistakes in standard English, but it is also likely to lead to an inadvertent lumping together of children who speak different dialects (and therefore who have different kinds of problems with standard English) under a generalized remedial English approach which would not take these differences into account. In the likely event that both Negroes and whites make up the disad-

---

[28]Linguistic and cultural relativists will be pleased to learn that the dialect tables have been turned on the normativists at least once. In his essay, John Bennett (1908, p. 350) reports that Gullah-speaking Negroes passed judgment on visiting Yankees with "Dey use dem mout' so funny!"

[29]What the father of the boy knew was that, in Gullah, observable characteristics are usually indicated by means of the verb *stan'* (or *'tan'*) which can be translated roughly as "look," "seem" or "appear."

vantaged student population of a school system, this egalitarian approach to
their language problems may prove almost irresistible in the face of a particularly unsophisticated kind of social liberalism, currently in vogue among
educators, which regards it as a manifestation of racism to entertain even the
most well-qualified hypothesis that differences in ethnicity (such as being
"white" or "Negro" in America) might possibly correlate with differences in
behavior (in language usage, for example). In fact, so strong is the hold upon
today's educators of this sociologically simplistic philosophy, with its "all
children are the same" credo, that many educators and teachers even find
uncomfortable the anthropologist's contention that correlations between ethnicity and behavior are not only possible but probable when one considers that
ethnicity is more of a social phenomenon than a physiological one, and that
so much of human behavior is socially conditioned rather than genetically
determined. And instead of seeing the chronic failure of disadvantaged
Negroes in integrated school situations as a strong indication that this same-
ness-credo is inadequate and counterproductive in terms of the real goals of
education, many educators let such unpleasant realities force them into cling-
ing all the more blindly and tenaciously to their simplistic views of the matter.

But the failure to perceive structural differences between the nonstandard
dialects of American Negroes and those of American whites has not been
unique to English teachers and speech therapists. Some prominent dialectologists also have claimed that Negro dialects represent, at the most, a minor
statistical skewing of white dialect features.[30] And still others have passed over
the subject altogether.[31]

---

[30]As one dialect geographer expressed his view of the matter, "the range of
variants is the same in Negro and in white speech, though the statistical distribution
of variants has been skewed by the American caste system" (McDavid 1965, fn. 7). In
an even more recent article, McDavid (1967, p. 122) rejects the idea of a pidgin or creole
background for American Negro dialects, saying "To a native social scientist, what is
generally known about the operations of the domestic slave trade should be sufficient
to refute such an argument." In view of the numerous attestations of the actual use of
of pidgin and creole forms of English by American Negro slaves in the contemporary
literature (see the first section of this paper, "Sociolinguistic Factors . . . ," for a few
references), it is difficult to imagine any historical basis for McDavid's statements. Since
he must have seen at least the reprintings of some of these in scholarly books and
articles, it can only be that he has not considered the linguistic implications of their
rather non-European grammatical structure. Furthermore, if there is anything in what
is known about the slave trade, slave life, or plantation social stratification in America
which would call into question these early attestations of pidgin and creole English, it
is strange that it has never been articulated in such standard works on American Negro
slavery as Philip Alexander Bruce, *Economic History of Virginia in the Seventeenth
Century* (1895); Ulrich B. Phillips, *American Negro Slavery* (1918), and his *Life and
Labor in the Old South* (1929); Marcus William Jernegan, *Laboring and Dependent
Classes in Colonial America: 1607-1783* (1931); Frederick Bancroft, *Slave-Trading in
the Old South* (1931); Kenneth M. Stampp, *The Peculiar Institution: Slavery in the*

One further reason why both language teachers and dialectologists have failed to appreciate the extent to which nonstandard Negro dialects may differ from nonstandard white dialects (even in the Deep South) may simply be that such differences now remain mostly in syntax (i.e., grammatical patterns and categories) rather than in vocabulary or lexicophonology (i.e., word forms), and are thus not normally uncovered by the word-comparison techniques which dialectologists and nonlinguists rely on so heavily. Yet, a comparison of the grammatical details of white and Negro nonstandard dialects suggests a very different kind of historical relationship than is evident from a comparison of words alone. This can be illustrated by a comparison of a standard English (STE) conjunctive sentence like "We were eating—and drinking, too" together with its equivalents in representative varieties of southern-white nonstandard basilect (WNS), Negro nonstandard basilect (NNS), and Gullah basilect (GUL):[32]

STE: We were eating—and drinking, too.

WNS: We was eatin'—an' drinkin', too.

NNS: We was eatin'—an' we drinkin', too.

GUL: We bin duh nyam—en' we duh drink, too.

If one compares only the forms of the equivalent words in these sentences, NNS (Negro nonstandard) appears to be virtually identical to WNS (white nonstandard), with both of them about equally different from STE (standard English).[33] Judged by the same criteria, GUL (Gullah) appears to be radically different from all the others, including NNS.

Because of such word-form similarities and differences, many dialectologists have concluded that, while Gullah itself may be a creolized form of English (rather than a direct descendant of any British dialect or dialects),

---

Ante-Bellum South (1956); and Herbert S. Klein, *Slavery in the Americas: A Comparative Study of Virginia and Cuba* (1967).

[31]None of the four recent publications on American dialects which have been written for the use of English teachers contain any substantive reference to Negro dialect—not even a simple statement of the historical and definitional issues involved in the concept. This omission is probably due to the tacit acceptance on the part of the various authors of the theory that most Negro speech is identical to southern varieties of white speech, and therefore that the description of the latter in their manuals takes care of Negro speech as well. These four publications are: Jean Malmstrom and Annabel Ashley, *Dialects—USA* (1963); Jean Malmstrom, *Language in Society* (1965); Carroll E. Reed, *Dialects of American English* (1967); and Roger W. Shuy, *Discovering American Dialects* (1967).

[32]The term *basilect* refers to that variety of a particular dialect which is structurally the most deviant from standard English. See Stewart (1965, particularly pp. 15–17).

[33]The literary dialect spellings which I have used in these examples may well make the individual words in WNS and NNS seem more alike than they actually are when pronounced. But, for the sake of argument, I would just as soon allow for the possibility that some words might have identical phonological forms in the different dialects.

there is no evidence that other kinds of American Negro speech are related to it in any direct way.[34] For, according to the same kind of word-form comparisons, these represent little more than the use by Negroes of dialect patterns which are also used by (and presumably borrowed from) whites in the Deep South.

However, a comparison of the sentence structure of these dialects shows a somewhat different kind of relationship. In the foregoing equivalent sentences, this is evident in the treatment of the subject pronoun and the tense-marking auxiliary (or copula). For, although STE, WNS, NNS, and GUL can all repeat the subject pronoun and auxiliary in a conjunctive clause (e.g., STE "We were eating—and we were drinking, too"), this is not generally done in any of them. Instead, one or both will usually be omitted (provided, of course, that the subject and temporal referents remain the same). But in terms of what they omit, these dialects split along lines which are different from those indicated by word-form similarities and differences. Both STE and WNS normally omit both the subject pronoun and the auxiliary in a conjunctive clause, although the tense-marking auxiliary must be present if the subject is not omitted. But NNS, like GUL, often repeats the subject pronoun in a conjunctive clause while omitting the auxiliary—even when this indicates past tense.[35]

An example of the same phenomenon in American Negro speech at the beginning of the nineteenth century is to be found in A. B. Lindsley's play, *Love and Friendship* (New York, 1807). A Negro says: "I tink dey bin like sich a man de bess, for dey like for be tumel 'bout'." Side by side with *dey bin like* in the first clause is *dey like* in the second one, even though the context makes it reasonably clear that both mean "they liked" (quoted in Krapp 1925, pp. 258–59).

If, in such features as the omission of a redundant auxiliary (while retain-

---

[34]This concession as to the creole nature of Gullah was largely forced upon an intensely Anglo-centric American-dialect-studies tradition by Lorenzo Dow Turner's *Africanisms in the Gullah Dialect* (1949) which, though it concentrated more on African survivals than on creole influences and dealt more with naming practices than with linguistic structure, did at least make the point rather strongly that Gullah is a creolized form of English.

[35]Those who have had enough contact with Negro nonstandard dialects to know that constructions like *We tryin'* usually indicate the present tense (i.e., STE "We are trying") might assume that the superficially similar construction *we drinkin'* in the NNS sentence *We was eatin'—an' we drinkin', too* also indicates the present tense—the whole thereby meaning "We were eating—and we are drinking, too", with an erroneous lack of tense agreement between the two clauses. Although it is true that *we drinkin'* does mean "we are drinking" in most circumstances (c. f. NNS *We drinkin' right now*), in the sentence cited the phrase really represents *we was drinkin'* with the past tense marker *was* omitted. By the same token, GUL *we duh drink* can mean "we are drinking" as well, but represents *we bin duh drink*, with the past tense marker *bin* omitted, in the sentence cited.

ing the redundant subject pronoun), Gullah and other nonstandard Negro dialects part company with standard English and nonstandard white dialects (of both America and Great Britain), they do have counterparts in a number of pidgin and creole forms of English, all of which, though used far from the shores of the United States and in widely separated places, are the legacy of the African slave trade. To illustrate how much these forms of English resemble Gullah and other nonstandard Negro dialects with respect to auxiliary omission, the same equivalent sentences are given in Jamaican Creole (JMC), Sranan (SRA)—the creole English in Surinam in South America, and West African pidgin English (WAP):[36]

JMC: We ben a nyam—an' we a drink, too.
SRA: We ben de nyang—en' we de dringie, too.
WAP: We bin de eat—an we de dring, too.

In addition to the grammatical correspondences, the word-form similarities of these languages with Gullah will be apparent.[37]

These correspondences are much too neat to be dismissed as mere accident. Rather, they seem to indicate that at least some of the particular syntactic features of American Negro dialects are neither skewings nor extensions of white dialect patterns, but are in fact structural vestiges of an earlier plantation creole, and ultimately of the original slave-trade pidgin English which gave rise to it.

This kind of evidence—existing in abundance for those who will admit it—calls for a complete reassessment of the relationships between British dialects, white American dialects, Negro American dialects (including Gul-

---

[36]For comparative purposes, I have written these languages in a spelling which is as close to that of standard English as the literary dialect spellings used in the preceding set of equivalent sentences. Scientific (phonemic) orthographies have been devised for these languages, however, and in them the same sentences would appear as—JMC: *We ben a nyam—an we a dringk, tu;* SRA: *We ben de njan—en we de dringi, toe;* WAP: *Wi bin de it—an we de dring, tu.* See Frederic G. Cassidy, *Jamaica Talk* (1961), Beryl L. Bailey, *Jamaican Creole Syntax* (1966); A. Donicie, *De Creolentaal van Suriname* (1959); Gouvernement van Suriname, Bureau Volkslectuur, *Woordenlijst van het Sranan-Tongo* (1961); Gilbert D. Schneider, "West African pidgin English" (1966); David Dwyer, *An Introduction to West African Pidgin English* (1967).

[37]The past tense markers in this series are *ben* (JMC, SRA) and *bin* (WAP), the latter having a common variant—*be.* The preverbal *a* in JMC is a modern reduction of an older *da,* obviously related historically to GUL *duh,* as well as to SRA and WAP *de.* In fact, the preverbal *a-* in some southern Negro dialects (e.g., *he a–workin'*) may well derive from just such a source, rather than from the verbal prefix *a-* of many white dialects. This seems likely in view of the fact that, in those white dialects in which such a prefix is used functionally, there is usually a contrast between its presence and its absence (e.g., *he's workin'* "he is working within view" vs. *he's a–workin'* "he is off working somewhere"), while Negro dialects with preverbal *a-* use it as Gullah uses preverbal *duh*—for the simple durative. Finally, Gullah actually has *a* (or *uh*) as a variant of *duh,* especially after *bin.*

lah), and the pidgin and creole English of Africa and the Caribbean. In particular, a new and more careful look at the question of American Negro dialects needs to be taken by those working within orthodox American dialectology—most of all by those who have made an almost exclusive use of American dialect Atlas materials and techniques. High on the list of priorities for determining Negro and white dialect relationships should be: (1) the relationship between Gullah and other Negro dialects, and (2) the relationship between Negro dialects (other than Gullah) and white dialects. In such a reassessment, many new insights into the history of these relationships will be gained from studies of the syntax, not only of present-day dialects, but also of literary attestations of early Negro and white nonstandard dialect, and by comparative studies of European, pidgin, and creole dialects of English.

All-in-all, it looks very much like the word-form similarities between nonstandard Negro dialects and nonstandard white dialects are the result of a relatively superficial merging process, in which creole-speaking Negroes tried to make their broken (i.e., creole) English become more like that of the whites by means of minor pronunciation changes and vocabulary substitutions. But the creole grammatical patterns of these Negroes' speech, being less amenable to conscious manipulation, remained more resistant to this substitution process.[38] In an earlier article (Stewart 1965, p. 17) on urban Negro dialect in Washington, D.C., the author pointed out how Negro children who reach school age speaking a radically nonstandard dialect often modify it in the direction of standard English in a similarly superficial fashion as they grow older. It is interesting to consider that, in the language-socialization process of their individual lifetimes, many American Negroes may actually repeat something of the larger process of Negro dialect history.

Now, the pedagogical implications of a historical relationship of this kind between Negro and white nonstandard dialects and, more particularly, between nonstandard Negro dialects and standard English ought to be clear. For, if American Negro dialects have evolved in such a way that structural similarities with other dialects of American English (including standard English) are

---

[38]Even persons who are quite familiar with American Negro dialects may be led, by dissimilarities in word forms, to overestimate the difference between them. For example, as keen an observer of dialect as E.C.L. Adams stated in *Nigger to Nigger* (1928, p. viii), that the speech of the Congaree Negroes of inland South Carolina was "absolutely distinct" from the coastal Gullah. Actually, the many striking syntactic similarities between the two dialects would suggest that the former is only a slightly decreolized form of the latter. Observers of Gullah, from John Bennett (1908, 1909) on, have all remarked on how the older "pure" form of the language has been undergoing modification (i.e., decreolization), particularly in the cities and towns. Seeing this modified Gullah always as a new phenomenon, they never expressed any awareness of the possibility that they might have been watching a continuation of the same process which earlier gave rise to the contemporary forms of other American Negro dialects.

greatest at the superficial word-form level, then it is possible for these similarities to mask any number of grammatical differences between them. And the teacher, concentrating on the more obvious word-form differences, is quite likely to miss the grammatical differences in the process—thereby leaving them to persist as apparent malapropisms, awkward turns of phrase, and random mistakes in speech and composition through grade school, high school, and frequently even through higher education.

As the grammatical study of nonstandard Negro dialect progresses, it is quite probable that many more differences will be found between Negro and white speech patterns, and it may well turn out that at least some of these will also be traceable to a creole English, pidgin English, or even African language sources. Of course, such discoveries are bound to cause embarrassment to those superficially liberal whites who will accept the Negro for what he is only if his behavioral patterns prove to be as European as their own, and they will be disquieting to those racial-image-conscious Negroes who are so often preoccupied with the question "What will the white folks think?" But quite apart from whether he thinks they are a help or a hindrance in integration, good or bad for the Negro's racial image, the dedicated educator should welcome the discovery and formulation of such ethnically-correlated dialect differences as do exist. For, only when they are taken into account in the teaching process will the linguistic cards cease to be stacked against the disadvantaged Negro pupil in the nation's classrooms.

REFERENCES

Adams, E. C. L. *Nigger to Nigger.* New York: Scribner, 1928.

Allen, W. F.; Ware, C. P.; and Garrison, Lucy McKim. *Slave Songs of the United States.* New York: A. Simpson & Co., 1867.

Bailey, Beryl B. *Jamaican Creole Syntax.* London: Cambridge University Press, 1966.

Bancroft, F. *Slave-Trading in the Old South.* Baltimore: J. H. Furst Co., 1931.

Bennett, J. Gullah: A Negro patois. *The South Atlantic Quarterly* 1908, vol. 7, and 1909, vol. 8.

Bergel, E. E. *Social Stratification.* New York: McGraw-Hill, 1962.

Bruce, P. A. *Economic History of Virginia in the Seventeenth Century.* New York, 1895.

Cassidy, F. G. *Jamaica Talk.* London: Macmillan & Co., 1961.

Davidson, B. *Black Mother: The Years of the African Slave Trade.* Boston: Little Brown, 1961.

Dillard, J. L. Negro children's dialect in the inner city. *The Florida Foreign Language Reporter* 1967, Fall.

Donicie, A. *De Creolentaal van Suriname.* Paramaribo: N. V. Varekamp, 1959.

Drums and Shadows: Survival Studies among the Georgia Coastal Negroes. Georgia Writers' Project. Athens, Ga.: University of Georgia Press, 1940.

Dwyer, D. *An Introduction to West African Pidgin English.* East Lansing, Mich.: African Studies Center, Michigan State University, 1967.

Gilman, Caroline. *Recollections of a Southern Matron.* New York, 1838.

Gonzales, A. E. *The Captain: Stories of the Black Border.* Columbia, S. C.: The State Co., 1924.

Gouvernement van Suriname, Bureau Volkslectuur. *Woordenlijst van het Sranan-Tongo.* Paramaribo: N. V. Varekamp, 1961.

Hall, R. A., Jr. *Pidgin and Creole Languages.* Ithaca, N. Y.: Cornell University Press, 1966.

Haskell, Ann S. The representation of Gullah influenced dialect in twentieth century South Carolina prose: 1922–30. Doctoral dissertation, University of Pennsylvania, 1964.

Herlein, J. D. *Beschryvinge va de volksplantinge Zuriname.* Leeuwarden, 1718.

Jernegan, M. W. *Laboring and Dependent Classes in Colonial America: 1607–1783.* Chicago: University of Chicago Press, 1931.

Kemble, Frances A. *Journal of a Residence on a Georgian Plantation in 1838–1839.* New York, 1862.

Klein, H. S. *Slavery in the Americas: A Comparative Study of Virginia and Cuba.* Chicago: University of Chicago Press, 1967.

Krapp, G. P. *The English Language in America.* New York: Century Co., 1925.

Labov, W. *The Social Stratification of English in New York City.* Washington, D. C.: The Center for Applied Linguistics, 1966.

Loban, W. *Problems in Oral English: Kindergarten through Grade Nine.* Champaign, Ill.: National Council of Teachers of English, 1966.

Malmstrom, Jean, and Ashley, Annabel. *Dialects—USA.* Champaign, Ill.: National Council of Teachers of English, 1963.

Malmstrom, Jean. *Language in Society.* New York: Hayden Book Co., 1965.

McDavid, R. I., Jr., and McDavid, Virginia G. The relationship of the speech of American Negroes to the speech of whites. *American Speech* 1951, 26: 3–17.

McDavid, R. I., Jr. Needed research in southern dialects. In E. T. Thompson, ed., *Perspectives on the South: Agenda for Research.* Durham, N.C.: Duke University Press, 1967.

———. American social dialects. *College English* 1965, 26: 254–60.

McDowell, T. Notes on Negro dialect in the American novel to 1821. *American Speech* 1930, 5: 291–96.

Parson, Elsie C. *Folk-Lore of the Sea Island, South Carolina.* Cambridge, Mass.: American Folklore Society, 1923.

Phillips, U. B. *American Negro Slavery.* New York: D. Appleton and Co., 1918.

———. *Life and Labor in the Old South.* Boston: Little Brown, 1929.

Read, A. W. The speech of Negroes in colonial America. *J. Negro History* 1939, 24: 247–58.

———. British recognition of American speech in the eighteenth century. *Dialect Notes* 1933, no. 6.

Reed, C. E. *Dialects of American English.* Cleveland: World Pub., 1967.

Schneider, G. D. West African pidgin English. Doctoral dissertation, Hartford Seminary Foundation, 1966.

Shibutani, T. and Kwan, K. M. *Ethnic Stratification.* New York: Macmillan, 1965.

Shuy, R. W., ed. *Social Dialects and Language Learning.* Champaign, Ill.: National Council of Teachers of English, 1965.

———. *Discovering American Dialects.* Champaign, Ill.: National Council of Teachers of English, 1967.

Stampp, K. M. *The Peculiar Institution: Slavery in the Ante-Bellum South.* New York: Knopf, 1956.

Stewart, W. A. Foreign language teaching methods in quasi-foreign language situations. In *Non-Standard Speech and the Teaching of English.* Washington, D. C.: Center for Applied Linguistics, 1964.

———. Urban Negro speech: sociolinguistic factors affecting English teaching. In R. W. Shuy, ed., *Social Dialects and Language Learning.* Champaign, Ill.: The National Council of Teachers of English, 1965.

———. Sociolinguistic factors in the history of American Negro dialects. *Florida Foreign Language Reporter* 1967, Spring.

———. Continuity and change in American Negro dialects. *Florida Foreign Language Reporter* 1968, Spring.

Turner, L. D. *Africanisms in the Gullah Dialect.* Chicago: University of Chicago Press, 1949.

van Dijk, P. *Nieuwe en nooit bevoorens geziende onderwijzinge in het Bastert Engels of Neeger Engels.* Amsterdam, undated (*c* 1780).

Walser, R. Negro dialect in eighteenth century American drama. *American Speech* 1955, 30: 269–76.

Weygandt, G. C. *Gemeenzame leerwijze om het Basterd of Neger-Engelsch op een gemakkelijke wijze te leeren verstaan en spreeken.* Paramaribo, 1798.

Chapter 18

LANGUAGE, ATTITUDE, AND SOCIAL CHANGE

Frederick Williams*

THE FLOWER GIRL (with feeble defiance) I've a right to be here if I like, same as you.

THE NOTE TAKER. A woman who utters such depressing and disgusting sounds has no right to be anywhere—no right to live. Remember that you are a human being with a soul and the divine gift of articulate speech: that your native language is the language of Shakespeare and Milton and The Bible; and don't sit there crooning like a bilious pigeon.

THE FLOWER GIRL (quite overwhelmed, looking up at him in mingled wonder and depreciation without daring to raise her head) Ah–ah–ah—ow–ow–ow–oo!

Although this brief exchange illustrates much of what this paper is about, the issue to be explored runs more deeply than speech such as Eliza's or attitudes such as held by Professor Higgins. It centers upon how language and attitudes reflect the dynamics of a society, the point which made *Pygmalion* more than entertainment.

BASES FOR THEORIZING

Our everyday experiences, like the excerpt from Shaw, provide us with an abundance of anecdotal evidence about language and attitude. Recently, as will be discussed, we have had the benefits of some systematic research, which,

*Center for Communication Research, University of Texas

This chapter was prepared while the author was a member of the senior research staff of the Institute for Research on Poverty at the University of Wisconsin.

among other things, has indicated that listeners will provide a range of reliable cultural, social class, and personality associations upon hearing speech samples. On the one hand, this research has served to verify some fragments of what we have already assumed about language and attitudes. But in a more important way, it points to a thesis which links speech, attitudes, and social structure:

That our speech, by offering a rich variety of social and ethnic correlates, each of which has attitudinal correlates in our own and in our listeners' behaviors, is one means by which we remind ourselves and others of social and ethnic boundaries, and is thus a part of the process of social maintenance (or change).

The Stereotype Hypothesis

Stated briefly, there is an hypothesis which holds that one's evaluational reactions to speech are a stereotyped or generalized version of his attitudes toward the users of that speech (Lambert, Hodgson, Gardner, and Fillenbaum 1960). In simpler terms, this says that we associate types of speech with types of people. By types of speech, we could mean something as broad as a language itself (e.g., English as against French), we could mean dialect (variations of English by region, community, even social status), and, as we shall speculate, even the way the uses of speech may vary from situation to situation.

Considerable support for the stereotype hypothesis comes from the research of Wallace Lambert and his associates working at McGill University in Canada. Most of this has been based upon a technique whereby listeners are presented with stimulus tapes representing speakers of some dialect or language, then are requested to rate the speakers on a series of traits. Illustrative of this research is the Lambert, et al. (1960) study of attitudes in Canada toward speakers of French and English. Tapes of perfectly bilingual speakers, each once speaking English and once French, were presented for speaker evaluation by groups of French-speaking or English-speaking college students. Ratings on a scale ranging from "very little" (*fort peu*) to "very much" (*beaucoup*) were obtained for these fourteen traits: height, good looks, leadership, sense of humor, intelligence, religiousness, self-confidence, dependability, entertainingness, kindness, ambition, sociability, character, and likability. Interestingly, the results showed that both French and English students evaluated the English speakers more favorably on most traits—e.g., on good looks, intelligence, dependability and the like—even though the French and English speakers were the same (bilingual) persons. Similar studies have since been conducted on "flawless," as against Jewish-accented, English (Anisfeld, Bogo, and Lambert 1962), and on bilingual and monolingual children's evaluations of French as against English speech (Anisfeld and Lambert 1964; see Lambert 1967, for a review of these).

Consequences of Stereotyping

Assuming the tenability of the stereotype hypothesis, there are corollary hypotheses on how such stereotypes have an effect upon speaker and listener behavior toward one another—how they perceive one anothers' messages, how they hold expectations of one another, and so on. Perhaps first suggested would be the many studies[1] of how speaker- and listener-attitudes enter into message perception, behavioral changes, and the general process of persuasion. Although this is no doubt a rich area for extension of the stereotype thesis as it relates to speech attitudes, the more recently considered thesis of self-fulfilling prophecies will offer more for our speculations of how maintenance of social structure is incorporated into this picture. As stated by Rosenthal and Jacobson (1968, p. vii), the self-fulfilling prophecy is " . . . how one person's expectation for another person's behavior can quite unwittingly become a more accurate prediction simply for its having been made."

We have long had anecdotal evidence and more recently research evidence of the circumstances of self-fulfilling prophecies. In Rosenthal's (1966) earlier work, these circumstances were illustrated in how the outcomes of experiments are often unwittingly and inaccurately in the direction of the researcher's attitudes—not in how an experimenter might directly try to bias results but in how his attitudes would inadvertently bear themselves out by affecting the behavior of experimental subjects. Later (Rosenthal and Jacobson 1968), this line of reasoning was extended to an experimental situation where teachers were told that certain students were "spurters" or "bloomers," but where the selection of such students was actually upon random basis. In accord with the thesis, gains (IQ scores and other indexes) were shown to favor the students who had been designated as mentioned above, as compared with the remaining students. Among other things, one of the generalizations from this research was that part of the dynamics of a child's being disadvantaged was in the attitudes of those in life around him, and if this is extended to teachers, we are faced with the prospect of how the self-fulfilling prophecy works against the poverty child in our schools.[2]

As generalized to our thesis, linking speech, attitude, and social structure, self-fulfilling prophecy leads us to expect that the stereotypes associated with speech types in a situation would in turn become predictions of the types of behaviors and social attitudes exercised in that situation. In other words, in

---

[1]A good survey of literature on this topic may be found in Insko (1967).

[2]It must be borne in mind that the Rosenthal and Jacobson study involved manipulation of an attitude of advantage ("bloomer," etc.) rather than disadvantage. The opposite was not undertaken for ethical reasons. Their school population was one from an area of depressed socioeconomic status, thus giving some basis to talk about the consequences of such attitudes toward poverty children.

a situation, (1) speech types serve as social identifiers. (2) These elicit stereotypes held by ourselves and others (including ones of ourselves). (3) We tend to behave in accord with these stereotypes, and thus (4) translate our attitudes into a social reality. That is, we perpetuate, or again reaffirm, those distinctions of social structure stored in our stereotypes and manifested in our actions. Speech provides us with an index of such stereotypes, thus giving us a way to catalog what we have generalized about the status of others, and at the same time provide us with a basis for hypothesizing very quickly (along, say, with cues of dress, etc.) the status of a newly encountered individual. If such reasoning has a measure of validity, then we would expect to see not only that attitudes toward speech are highly tied to attitudes toward people, but that differences in these attitudes should vary with linguistic and dialect distinctions, perhaps even to the level of how people use speech in different situations. We can see evidence of this from research conducted in the United States.

SPEECH ATTITUDES IN THE UNITED STATES

White and Negro Speech

As might be expected when considering the attitudinal contrasts between English and French Canadians, there is the suggested analogy in the attitudinal contrasts separating the speech of whites and blacks in the United States. One study of this comes again from Lambert's group (Tucker and Lambert, unpublished). Among the findings were that although northern and southern white college students as well as southern Negro students rated a (standard English) broadcaster style of speech as most favorable relative to other samples of Negro and white speech, there were reversals in how whites and Negroes evaluated each other. All whites evaluated a Mississippi style of Negro speech least favorably. On the other hand, Negro students rated educated-white-southern speech least favorably, which was the reverse of what the southern-white raters assigned to themselves.

These findings coincide somewhat with results of a study by Hurst and Jones (1966), although in this study only a type of speaker was rated, not his actual speech. Hurst and Jones had identified groups of relatively high- and low-proficiency speakers from the freshman class (Negro) at Howard University. Proficiency was defined by a pooling of scores on a word intelligibility test and judges' ratings of the students' oral readings and impromptu speeches. Students in the two groups were found to agree substantially with the judges' distinctions, usually rating their own speech as excellent or very good (high-proficiency group) as against fair or poor (low group). Additionally, they extended these high or low ratings of speech to their family and to their friends.

A study by Buck (1969) involved the attitude responses of white college girls to samples of white and Negro New York speech of "standard" or "substandard" quality. Although the standard-quality tapes were judged more favorably by the students than the substandard ones, the Negro's tape (standard) was almost always identified as that of a white speaker. There was no such confusion in differentiating the "substandard" Negro and white speakers, although the listeners did rate the Negro more favorably than the white. Included with the attitude scales were ratings of competence and trustworthiness, thought to be two dimensions of a speaker's credibility. Competence ratings favored the standard speakers over the nonstandard ones and showed no race differences. Trustworthiness, however, showed a mixed-rating pattern. The Negro and white speakers using standard dialect were judged more trustworthy than the nonstandard white speaker, but not more so than the Negro nonstandard speaker. My own interpretation of this finding is that the white student raters had less tolerance for nonstandard speech from a person whom they knew as a white speaker, thus rating him less competent and less trustworthy. In short, in these girls' attitudes if a white speaks substandardly, he is probably viewed as "worse" than a black speaker of nonstandard English. We might speculate, too, that since the listeners, being from the urban area, were probably familiar with Negro nonstandard English, they may have considered it more as a legitimate dialect as judged against the nonstandard speech spoken by the white informant.

It is not difficult to argue that these studies show black-white attitude differences which exist along subcultural lines, at least at the time data were gathered. Here, somewhat parallel to the Canadian research, we see whites and Negroes agreeing upon the favorability of the white standard dialect (save perhaps for the southern-white dialect version) as compared with Negro dialect. An important reservation, however, is that these data may now be seriously dated in view of the attitudes illustrated in the black-is-beautiful campaign, coming first from the "black revolution" in America and subsequently having had its effect on segments of the white population as well. In brief, as this campaign has changed attitudes, both in the black toward himself and in the white's attitudes toward the black, we would expect to find changes in speech attitudes. We will have more to say on this at a later point.

Attitudes about Social Status

The assumption that a person's speech reveals his social status to listeners has been borne out in a number of studies, dating back mainly to the report by Putnam and O'Hern (1955) who gathered social-status ratings in response to brief recordings of Negro speakers (Washington, D. C.) telling the story of the "Lion and the Mouse." Added to this as evidence is Harms's (1963) study, where using Putnam and O'Hern's recordings he found that midwestern college students could make status differentiations very similar to the Washington, D. C. respondents. Harms (1961) also reported an earlier study where the tapes of white adult speakers (Ohio) were classified by college students into three status levels. Results indicated "correct" status differentiations and the generality of these across different levels of social status of the listeners themselves.

Although the above studies are typically cited as the basis for the generalization about speech and social-status attitudes, they by no means have closed the matter.[3] Obviously, the correlation between such ratings and the actual social status of speaker[4] is subject to the variability and distinctiveness among the speech samples, and in none of these studies were the speakers chosen in such a way as to give us some reflection of the distribution of such differences in the actual population. Although we can probably agree that these studies provide some evidence of the validity and reliability of social-status ratings relative to a contrived distribution of speech differences, the relatively high correlations, the generalizations on listener consistency, and the like, could be quite misleading in terms of the population distribution of speakers. Thus it becomes obvious that to gain some useful generalizations from such studies we have to specify what varies in the speech samples themselves, and to know its degree of variation. Some research in this direction has come from the work of Labov (1966, pp. 405 ff.).

Whereas in the studies just described, the differentiation of speech samples in the research design was based upon the speakers' statuses, Labov's strategy was to vary the individual speech features thought to serve as cues for status recognition. At the time, this strategy fitted well into the context of Labov's (1966) overall project of studying the social stratification of English in New York City. After he had found certain phonological features which varied in relative incidence across social strata, it was logical that such features might serve as cues for the listener in differentiating a speaker's social status. Para-

---

[3]We can add to these some unpublished studies described by Ellis (1967), which were conducted as follow-ups to the work of the persons just mentioned. Among his findings are the following points: (1) when college students tried to sound "upper class," they were not typically rated as such, although the correlation of status and ratings did diminish as compared with earlier studies; (2) even when speakers were only counting from one to twenty, their social status could be reliably guessed; and (3) this obtained even when the sample was for a twenty-second duration.

[4]One should bear in mind too, that the concept of actual social status is often misleading. Many researchers have defined status upon the bases of education, occupation, and residence factors (often after Hollingshead 1958), whereas in the eyes of the members of a community, status is a much more relative thing, particularly when we get away from middle-class white standards. This discrepancy points to the futility of trying to study too closely the correlation between social-status ratings and some presumably objective index of social status.

phrasing Labov (1966, pp. 50–55), these features included: (1) presence of final and preconsonantal /r/ in selected words; (2) height of vowel in words such as *bad, bag, ask, pass, cash, dance;* (3) the realization of the mid-back rounded vowel in *caught, talk, awed, dog, off, lost, all;* and (4, 5) realization of voiceless and voiced dental fricatives in words like *thing* and *then.*

Listeners heard the variants of these features so arranged in individual sentence contexts that a single sentence would include a variant and would be spoken by a particular speaker, another sentence would contain another variant and a different speaker, and so on. For each sentence presentation the listener was asked to rate the speaker on an occupational scale which was ordered from "television personality," "executive secretary," and so on to "factory worker," and "none of these." Although Labov's response data are presented mainly in graphic form as averages for listener groups and the stimulus variants, they do show patterns across the occupational scale that generally conform to the social stratification of the variant itself. In short, there was a substantial agreement between finding a phonological feature which correlated with social stratification in his linguistic survey, and finding the same correlation presumably present in the evaluative behavior of listeners in a rating situation.[5] Whereas Labov had pointed to the cues for speech evaluation and Lambert had pointed to the evaluative process itself, an obvious next step was to put these two ends together. The next section describes such an attempt undertaken in our own research program at the Institute for Research on Poverty.

Teachers' Attitudes toward Children's Speech

Among the reasons for conducting a study of teachers' speech attitudes was the prospect that a child's speech should offer a salient range of status cues to a teacher, thus eliciting attitudes and consequences as described in the self-fulfilling prophecy thesis of Rosenthal and Jacobson (1968). This study, the technical details of which are published elsewhere (Williams, in press), can be sketched as follows.

From a series of studies (Williams and Naremore 1969a,b;), we had available forty children's speech tapes, obtained from the corpus of the Detroit Dialect Study (Shuy, Wolfram, and Riley 1967), where twenty of the children were from families rated as from middle to high socioeconomic status, and

---

[5]Although the work described here shows an admirable combination of linguistic and quantitive techniques, the generality of his findings would have benefitted substantially if he had assessed the psychometric qualities of his occupational scale relative to his judge population, and if he had presented more of the distributional statistics of the response data, even perhaps testing the judged-status differences in a probability model.

twenty were from relatively low-status families. Within each subgroup of twenty children were ten black and ten white matched on the status index, and within these subgroups were equal numbers of boys and girls. The children were a mixture of fifth- and sixth-graders and their tapes were segments where the field worker had encouraged them to talk freely about games ("What games do you play around here?") and television ("What are your favorite television programs?"). Although our initial question was whether teachers, as listeners, could estimate the child's social status, we eventually tried to meet the challenge of incorporating some of Lambert's and Labov's strategies into the same research design.

One of the first steps was to develop a technique for eliciting and eventually recording teachers' attitudes toward the children. This was done by conducting a series of interviews with teachers—having them hear a sample tape, asking them to guess the child's social status, then to tell us the basis for the guess. From recordings of these interviews we obtained a list of items that the teachers typically mentioned and the evaluative adjectives used to describe them. Eventually these were cast into a series of twenty-two scales, each having a form similar to:

Sentences are: fragmentary__:__:__:__:__:__:__complete

Included among these were scales referring to a child as being "disadvantaged," sounding "white-like" or "Negro-like," sounding "confident," "eager," and a variety of scales referring to language characteristics (vocabulary, pronunciation, sentence construction, grammar).

Using these scales, we had a group of inner-city teachers from Chicago respond to the tapes.[6] By translating their responses into numerical form and by a series of statistical analyses, we were able to gain some views of the kinds of judgments the teachers as a group seemed to make. Main among these was that the teachers tended to evaluate the children in terms of two gross dimensions, which we later labeled as *confidence-eagerness* and *ethnicity-nonstandardness.* This interpretation was based upon how teachers had used certain scales in common, suggesting that rather than assessing, say, individual traits of confidence, fluency, or eagerness as separate dimensions, these ratings were reflections of a single, more basic, evaluative dimension, which we called

---

[6]As described elsewhere (Williams, in press), this involved a detailed testing design whereby each teacher heard sixteen of the tapes, these representing all combinations of the children's and speech-topic characteristics. A recognized problem was that the tapes were from Detroit and the teachers from Chicago. This problem, however, seemed alleviated when no teachers inquired about this, and a topic of conversation among them after testing was to try to guess the child's school in the Chicago area.

confidence-eagerness. The ethnicity-nonstandardness dimension told us that as a child's speech was rated as nonstandard, the children were rated as Negro-like, and other language features were rated less favorably. These dimensions were more gross than we had expected, thus suggesting to us that the teacher may have some type of overall reaction rather than one tied to individual and detailed speech characteristics.

Separate ratings of the children's statuses by the teachers were found to be related to the aforementioned judgmental dimensions, but, as might be expected, more to the dimension of ethnicity-nonstandardness than to confidence-eagerness. Thus a kind of stereotype was suggested to us—that the teachers' image of a low-status or disadvantaged child was one whose speech they would rate in the direction of being nonstandard and ethnic and whose general performance may seem somewhat unsure and reticent to them. To be sure, there were exceptions to this, for example, a speaker rated as nonstandard would sometimes be rated as confident and eager.

A number of further interpretations arose when we began to assess for differences due to race of teacher and child. After separating the teachers whom we had classified as Negro or white during the original testing sessions, we found that among the white teachers there was a markedly higher correlation between ratings of ethnicity-nonstandardness and status than was found among Negro teachers. This finding can lead to a number of interpretations, among which is the suggestion that white teachers have a less differentiated stereotype for Negro children than the stereotype held by Negro teachers. In brief, white teachers were less inclined to rate a child as nonstandard and also rate him as high status, whereas Negro teachers allowed for this to some extent in their evaluations.

This kind of interaction between teacher and child race also emerged when we found that the white teachers, when rating an actual Negro child as high-status, had more of a tendency to also rate him as white. Neither teacher group made any errors in guessing the race of white children. But, on the other hand, their differentiations of the white childrens' statuses were far less "accurate" than for the Negro children.

In a further portion of this same study we made an attempt to predict mathematically the teachers' ratings, based upon measures of the characteristics of each speech sample.[7] From earlier research, some eighty measures were available for each tape, including (1) production phenomena (e.g., rate, hesitations), (2) amount of speech (various word-counts), (3) syntactic elaboration (type and frequency of syntactic divisions in sentences; see Williams and Naremore 1969b), (4) functional characteristics (relations between the type

---

[7]The mathematical model was the (linear) regression of the attitude variable upon the array of stimulus measures.

and form of field workers' questions and the childrens' responses; Williams and Naremore 1969a), and (5) nonstandard characteristics (e.g., nonstandard realizations of certain phonemes, verb constructions; see Williams, in press).

Relative to predicting ratings on the two gross judgmental dimensions, the most salient correlate of confidence-eagerness ratings was the incidence of pausal behavior, the relation being that as a tape had fewer pauses the child had been rated as more confident and eager. For both Negro and white teachers nonstandard realizations of *s* and *th* sounds were salient correlates of ratings of ethnicity-nonstandardness. Status ratings were correlated with the above types of variables, but more so with those reflecting nonstandard realizations than pausal behavior. In brief, the above presented a quite interpretable picture for us, but being correlational and in this context, it could not be a basis for concluding cause-effect relations. Conservatively and objectively, the best we could say is that children with a relatively high incidence of pausal phenomena and nonstandard realizations were usually rated as relatively low in social status.

By seeing this study in context with previous ones, and at the hazard of some speculation, we can venture a tentative account of the teachers' behavior. The suggestion is that upon hearing a very brief portion of the child's speech a stereotype was elicited in the teacher and she used this, more than her detailed perception of the child's speech, as a basis for marking our scales. My speculation is that a teacher (or most any listener) will be highly alert for cues, but given a few (perhaps only one) the stereotype will be elicited and attendance to further details will diminish. In other words, the teachers' detailed responses to the scales are not isomorphic to the detailed characteristics of speech. Support for this speculation came from these data in three ways: (1) When scale responses were analyzed, there was evidence of a gross rather than detailed array of evaluations. (2) Inspection of the individual response data suggested that when marking a child as high- or low-class, a teacher sometimes had a rather consistent set of ratings (based on a gross stereotype) on other scales.[8] (3) In the prediction equation, one speech characteristic, alone, would be sufficient as a basis to predict status ratings beyond a chance level (although the addition of further predictor variables improved this). Support also comes from Labov's (1966) research where a variant in a single sentence prompted reliable estimates of occupational status; and from Harms (1963) who obtained reliable and accurate status judgments based upon as few as ten seconds of speech. My further speculation, but a point far beyond the data of this study, is that the teacher bases much of her instructional behavior toward a child upon this kind of a stereotype. All of this, it could be maintained, is a concrete proposition for how a child's speech characteristics and a teacher's stereotypes

---

[8]This is the topic of study by Naremore (1969).

could easily fit into the dynamics of self-fulfilling prophecies in the classroom, as described by Rosenthal and Jacobson (1968). Or in broader terms, it is an illustration of how attitudes toward speech, and hence, social stereotypes, are perpetuated by our institutional agents of socialization—the schools.

The General View

Given some thought, one can easily visualize the many types of studies that are needed in this area, particularly if we want to fill in the picture for the United States. We need to broaden this picture to incorporate other minority groups and social distinctions, some of the practical ramifications of such attitudes, and also to look for evidence of change. For present purposes, however, the point to be made is that ethnic and social-status differences in the United States have their correlates in speech attitudes, and presumably social stereotyping. The studies just described seem good evidence of this.[9]

FURTHER THEORETICAL CONSIDERATIONS

The Variable of Context

Thus far in our discussion we have focused upon a one-to-one relation between race and attitudes or social status and attitudes. If, however, speech serves as an indexer and identifier of social stereotypes, we must incorporate a concern for the kinds of contexts within which this takes place. Let us reconsider, for example, what was described about Negro dialect. Many Negroes, particularly in middle-class urban areas, are clearly bidialectical, and it seems unnecessary to emphasize how closely tied the choice of dialect is to the context of speech. Negro nonstandard English is expected of blacks by blacks in the inner city, whereas a Negro's use of standard English is expected, mainly by whites, for participation as a member of certain social or occupational structures (say, as a schoolteacher). For the speaker to violate such expectations elicits drastically revised stereotypes—the black male being considered a traitor (or sometimes a homosexual) when speaking standard English in the inner city, or being considered militant or "uppity" when using black speech in situations where standard English is expected. The point here seems obvious: We cannot talk about speech and stereotypes without including context as a variable.

This reasoning casts a shadow on the studies previously discussed. All, except for Labov (1966), who had his listeners play "personnel manager," were relatively ambiguous relative to speech context. Given the task of rating speech

---

[9]Other studies would include research recently conducted by the Center for Applied Linguistics (see Shuy Chapter 16) and a replication of the teacher project, but involving southern schools, by Wayne Shamo of Purdue University and myself.

in an isolated context—one perhaps most associated by persons with their school experiences (say, in English or speech classes)—may have resulted in respondents' giving a prescriptionist array of attitudes, and perhaps even ones that they thought the researcher (identified with the middle-class teacher) wanted from them.

The challenge in incorporating context as a variable in the stereotyping process is to gain a basis for developing generalizations about types of context, lest we be faced with unwieldy inventories of speech situations. In the examples just discussed, context became somewhat self-defining as a particular array of stereotypes, as, for example: when one expects speech in standard English; when Negro nonstandard is expected; or when we are ready to engage in cross-class communication, and so on. On the other hand, we can consider context in terms of another dimension—that is, the degree to which the actual context of speech is a part of the communication, thus making the stereotypes of speaker and listener less relevant, as against situations where context is less a part of the communication but makes speaker and listener stereotypes more relevant. This distinction can be illustrated in the difference between such utterances as "look out," "hand me that," or "this one costs more than that," as compared with "You should vote Democratic because this is the party of the common man." In the former example, stereotyping of and by speaker and listener are presumably far less relevant to interpretations and actions than in the latter. As speech becomes itself less context-bound, context becomes more abstract and such abstraction may be realized by us in the form of our stereotypes. A corollary is that the more we have experienced speech which transcends immediate context, the more we will have developed a repertoire of stereotypes, including potential variation in our own role. In an even more general sense, this is part of the knowledge that moves us from candidacy to membership in a given social structure.

Developmental Speculations

Much of what is currently written about language development in children stresses their psycholinguistic development (see Osser Chapter 13; Menyuk Chapter 10)—that is, how a child acquires his grammatical competence, the knowledge which allows him to create and understand the sentences used in his speech community. A basic point in the present line of discussion is that a child's developing knowledge of the uses of speech—his generalizations about how to use his grammatical competence, and his expectations of others—is a reflection of sociolinguistic development.[10] That a three-year-old child will readily and consistently vary his own styles of speech when addressing his

---

[10]My thinking on this has been most affected by Dell Hymes's (in press) concept of communicative competence and somewhat by the ideas of Lewis (1963) and Cazden (1967; Chapter 5).

mother, baby brother, dog, or teddy bear, is evidence of a developing sociolinguistic knowledge. Upon his entering school, we see marked differentiations among a child's ways of speech with parents, peers, and teachers. Later, as described by Labov (1965), we see the development of variations in uses of the vernacular such as are tied to values, social perceptions, and styles of speech. Eventually, we witness the complex interaction of the variables of topic, participants, setting, purposes, and so on, that mark the sociolinguistic variations of adult speech (c.f. Ervin-Tripp, 1964).

The point is that such variations in how we use our grammatical capabilities develop systematically in children; the proposition is that this systematicity evolves along the lines of the stereotype thesis where speech serves both indexing and identifying processes. Elsewhere (Williams and Naremore 1969a), the argument was advanced that a child's communication development could be seen in terms of his learning the forms of speech which increasingly enabled him to transcend immediate contexts of communication. As a child's speech developed from, say, impulsive cries, to minimal greetings, to rudimentary conversation, to description or direction-giving (or taking), and eventually to topic-centered discourse, one requirement for transcending context was a greater fund of grammatical knowledge. In the author's current thinking, the role of grammatical knowledge would be restricted to the word *requirement,* for it seems more likely that it is the child's sociolinguistic knowledge that is the main mediator in how he behaves as a speaker-listener in situations. That is to say, psycholinguistic ability endows the child with the capability to be a speaker-listener, whereas what he learns sociolinguistically mediates in how he exercises this capability.

Lest the description become too obtuse at this point, it can be paraphrased much more simply. As candidates for membership in a social structure, children learn the uses of speech characteristic of that structure. Their own personal linguistic reality is a pragmatic one—what speech will do for them or to them. A form of this reality is the range of stereotypes held by the child of himself and of others. Sociolinguistic development can be viewed in terms of a child's increasing differentiation of stereotypes, including those of himself. Although this summary puts the focus on the child, it is also a way of explaining how the developing child, as an agent of a parent social structure, internalizes it in his attitudes, manifests it in his behaviors, and thus contributes to its maintenance.

THE DISADVANTAGED CHILD

Much has been written (see Plumer Chapter 14) about the types of underdeveloped language so often reported in poverty children. As is argued in other chapters of this volume (Labov Chapter 9; Baratz Chapter 2), it is maintained that dialect differences in these children have been mistaken for linguistic deficiencies. My thesis is that much of the problem can be defined and evaluated in terms of the current theorizing about sociolinguistic development. Let us consider, for example, how the stereotypes held by researchers and poverty children have been so effectively self-fulfilled.

Although researchers have long been aware of the hazards of cross-class interviewing (see Strauss and Schatzman 1955), we perhaps have been victims of this in language interviews with children. The interviewer's expectation of the poverty child is one of nonstandardness, reticence, uncertainty (as with our teachers); the child's expectation of the interviewer is one of dominance, confidence, verbosity. It is not unusual that so often they have fulfilled their joint prophecies. Labov (Chapter 9) has provided some excellent examples of how the reticence of an inner-city Negro boy, even in the presence of a well-trained field worker, varied drastically with the factors of the speech setting—everybody on the floor instead of two sides of a desk, very casual dress, eating potato chips, opening the interview on a taboo topic. In terms of the present concern, what happened was that the field worker immediately transformed his role, and thus his stereotype to the child, into being one of the group and not an interviewer (save when the potato chips ran out).

One of our own studies (Williams and Naremore 1969a) offers evidence along a similar line. We found that the differences between middle- and lower-class children relative to elaboration in their responses to a field worker all but vanished when such comparisons were made in instances where the field worker had specifically requested elaboration ("Tell me how you play baseball") as against a request that could be fulfilled in a more minimal fashion ("Do you play baseball?"). The most salient social-class difference found in this study seemed to reflect not the lower-class child's incapability to meet the minimal communicative demands imposed by the field worker but the higher-status child's tendency to go beyond this minimal demand and to say more than he had to. As Labov (Chapter 9) suggests in the analysis of the language sample of an educated black adult from Harlem, perhaps this is one of the characteristics of the middle-class way of speech, and hence, a part of a stereotype—that is, verbal display, the adherence to a single set of prescriptive standards.

The point in these brief illustrations is that, when we engage a child in an interview, we are witnessing as much a sociolinguistic response as a psycholinguistic one. The child will have a repertoire of sociolinguistic knowledge, a basis for hypothesizing a stereotype of the interviewer and of himself in that situation. Presumably, this repertoire even offers the child some choice in the stereotypes or roles that he can assume in the interview; he will likely choose the one least threatening to him. One safe role is to stay close to context, to make a minimal commitment verbally in the situation, for the more that the child's speech transcends context the more he is committing himself to behavior based upon not only psycholinguistic but also sociolinguistic knowledge, and the greater is the potential for failure. A context-bound type of speech offers the guarantee of shared referents for speech, less reliance upon stereotypes, and the context even assumes part of the communicative load. This line of speculation is one way of unravelling the puzzle about an oft-cited observation of the speech of poverty children—that they employ a highly concrete style of speech. The usual extension of this observation is that due to this style of language they are incapable of properly connecting thoughts (due to fragmented language) or thinking in abstractions (due to having only concrete language).[11]

Consider the thesis that the more the two individuals do not share a knowledge of one another's social structure, especially in its abstractions (a knowledge of what and what not to do, ideals, threats, myths, and so on), the more likely they are to initiate and to focus speech upon what they do share, that is, experience of the speech context.[12] Speech under these circumstances is context-bound, that is, about the mutual experience of speaker-listener in that specific situation, or if one step removed, about the details of direct experiences. By its referents, context-bound speech is linked to that which is immediately sensed, and creates no pressure to transcend the details of the situation. In brief, such speech is naturally concrete. Additionally, context-bound speech allows us some linguistic efficiencies. Why create a complex subject-noun phrase in a situation where a pronoun will suffice? Why repeat the sentential kernel of a question ("Do you watch Gunsmoke?") when in the time span of the immediate context, a single word ("No") will suffice? In short, context itself often serves in our messages, and in context-bound speech, language need only add what the context cannot communicate. Fragmented speech under such circumstances is efficient, not incomplete. This reasoning prompted me to return to the corpus assessed in an earlier study (Williams and Naremore 1969b) where we had puzzled over the distinctively concrete speech of the lower-class children. My interpretation now is that these children, as compared with their higher-status counterparts, often chose the safe alternative of a context-bound style to insure their own favorability of performance in a cross-class situation. Although I have only observed this informally, it appeared, too, as if the field worker had some, perhaps inadvertent, inclination to help them take this alternative. The field worker would ask a question which

---

[11]See, for example, Schatzman and Strauss (1955), Hess and Shipman (1968), Williams and Naremore (1969a), Bereiter and Engelmann (1966).

[12]For an extreme example of contextual reliance, consider the dilemma of scientists who now have the capability to send signals far out into the universe, but who must figure out how to start the conversation.

required elaboration ("How do you play kickball?"), but then after a very brief silence would sometimes cancel this requirement by adding a yes-no option for answer ("You do play it, don't you?"). To sum up, the argument is that the concrete style of speech so often observed in the lower-status individual in cross-class interviews is a more sociolinguistic than psycholinguistic phenomenon.

The above still does not answer the question whether the lower-status individual has the psycholinguistic and sociolinguistic capabilities for the communication of relations and abstractions. Labov argues that he does, but that we must see through the barrier of dialect differences to find it (see his analysis in Chapter 9). Much of one's response to this depends, no doubt, upon what would qualify as an abstraction or a relation. If we are talking about that which is beyond one's store of actual experiences, if it includes hypothesizing about processes, relations, and so on, then a small ghetto boy's theories about how women have babies could no doubt qualify. The point to be made is that abstractions and relations are so typically tied to the milieu and requirements of social structures that one cannot fully sense them without being a linguistic member of that structure (or else an ethnographer) and certainly will be hard-pressed to comprehend or communicate them under conditions of cross-class speech. Thus although I think that I understand and can discuss the concepts of Zipf's law or linguistic relativity, I am no more inclined to make them a topic of conversation in inner-city Chicago than a member of the Black P. Stone Nation will be to engage me in conversation about the nature of his abstractions and relations conveyed in calling a girl, a *mink*; a homosexual, an *AC-DC*; his landlord, *teach;* police, *pigs;* or me, *Micky Mouse* (all of which, I'd make the mistake of saying, are marvelous examples, of linguistic relativity and Zipf's law). Lest the point not be clear, this example is given to argue the foolishness of expecting people from markedly different social structures to have common types of abstractions, let alone to share them easily in their speech with one another.

CIRCUMSTANCES FOR SOCIAL CHANGE

Let us first summarize from a sociolinguistic viewpoint, the special dilemma of the poverty child in America. He is reared in ways of speech which mark his social status and his ethnicity, or so often the combination of the two. In a centripetal sense, these ways of speech hold him to his group allegiance; they are manifested in his self-stereotype as an identification to his parent social structure. Yet these are the same ways of speech which, in a centrifugal sense, hold him outside of a majority culture in his country. They are manifested in the negative stereotype which the mainstream culture holds of him. It is no wonder, then, that the poverty child's language has been so much the center of attention for it marks the deeper social boundaries which divide the American population.

Much of the research into the language of the poverty child has revealed little of his ways of speech as they may be richly exercised to meet demands of the social structure within which he was reared and within which he must daily exist (school is a small segment of this). Instead this research has cast mainly a reflection of the attitudes of the researchers and the social structure of which they are a part. This is an attitude of ethnocentrism—of cultural superiority—which is manifested at its utmost when distinctions are made between standard and substandard English. It is in the strongly prescriptive attitudes found in the textbooks, the testing materials, and curricula of our schools. It is found in teachers' attitudes.

To build upon a generalization stated by Lambert (1967), the more children are reared in a rigidly defined, monocultural setting, the more they will come to differentiate social stereotypes only in an evaluative sense, and to do this relative to the prescriptive stereotypes of their monoculture. Under these circumstances, they will less and less be able to understand that cultural distinctions do legitimately exist among people and that to be different is not necessarily to be disfavored. Or relative to the dilemma of the poverty child —that to be different is not to be deficient. A consequence of this ethnocentric bias is an increase in the forces which impose the contrast of unfavorability upon the outsider and serve to keep him outside. In other words it may not be that the poverty child himself contributes totally to his difference from the mainstream society, but that the mainstream society itself magnifies this difference, and, eventually, serves to fulfill its own prophecy.

Contributing monumentally to the problem in the United States is the strong correlation between economic opportunity and being able to function in the mainstream society. Here, we can equate at least part of being-able-to-function with being able to exercise the language of the society. But this kind of linguistic candidacy brings with it a role candidacy. That is, as we ask a person to learn and use a way of speech, we are at the same time asking him to function (if sometimes only to a small degree) in that society. One of the problems associated with such candidacy is the strain put upon a person who, because he is trying to assume a role in a new social structure, feels regret at leaving behind his parent structure and also feels uncertainty about being accepted in the new structure. Lambert (1967) calls this feeling *anomie*. It is a challenge to the candidate's stereotypes of himself. Will he reject the old roles as the price of gaining new ones? Will he try to maintain both? Will he reject the proposed new role and return to the old? Closely tied with the answers to these questions is the candidate's motive for learning the language—whether instrumental (learning it for a specific task) or integrative (learning it mainly for candidacy into the society). Is the candidate's proposed self-stereotype one of only being a visitor in the social structure, that is, being able to exercise a required portion of the language but still mainly in the role of an outsider? Or is the proposed self-stereotype one of candidacy for full membership, not only of moving into the society, but once in, having mobility within it? These are the challenges put to the individual in the process of linguistic candidacy; they are the circumstances he faces in the process of social change. They are also the circumstances directly set by the mainstream society.

If the mainstream society is not hypocritical about increasing the spectrum of participatory opportunity, then there are actions it can take upon itself rather than focusing all actions so often upon the outsider. Main among these is a reduction of the circumstances which perpetuate and increase ethnocentrism—one of which is child-rearing in a rigid monocultural environment. This point is remindful of one of the lesser-heard arguments about school desegregation, namely, that the child of the mainstream society can thus learn to recognize and to respect cultural differences rather than perceive them on a single evaluative continuum. The evidence seems to be that the more a child has witnessed a spectrum of cultural differences, the less he will come to tolerate ethnocentrism in his own group and in others. Such a generalization has important consequences for the antipoverty preschool programs in America (e.g., Head Start). Perhaps these programs should incorporate the full range of children in American society, rather than segregating minority-group children and treating them in the customary stereotype of the disadvantaged child. The point here is that among all of the circumstances of social change, one of the most challenging to modify is the attitude of the majority class. Just as we started this paper with Professor Higgin's attitudes as an illustration of this problem, we can aptly close with Eliza's summary of the dilemma:

> . . . the difference between a lady and a flower girl is not how she behaves, but how she's treated. I shall always be a flower girl to Professor Higgins, because he always treats me as a flower girl, and always will; but I know I can be a lady to you, because you treat me as a lady, and always will.

REFERENCES

Anisfeld, M.; Bogo, N.; and Lambert, W. E. Evaluational reactions to accented English speech. *J. Abnormal and Social Psychology* 1962, 65: 223–31.

Anisfeld, E., and Lambert, W. E. Evaluational reactions of bilingual and monolingual children to spoken languages. *J. Abnormal and Social Psychology* 1964, 69: 89–97.

Bereiter, C., and Engelmann, S. *Teaching Disadvantaged Children in the Preschool.* Englewood Cliffs, N. J.: Prentice-Hall, 1966.

Buck, J. F. The effects of Negro and white dialectal variations upon attitudes of college students. *Speech Monographs* 1968, 35: 181–86.

Cazden, Courtney B. On individual differences in language competence and performance. *J. Special Education* 1967, 1: 135–50.

Ellis, D. S. Speech and social status in America. *Social Forces* 1967, 45: 431–37.

Ervin-Tripp, Susan. An analysis of the interaction of language, topic, and listener. In J. J. Gumperz and D. Hymes, eds., *The Ethnography of Communication, American Anthropologist* 1964, 66: No. 6. Part 2, 86–102.

Harms, L.S. Listener judgments of status cues in speech. *Quarterly J. Speech* 1961, 47: 164–68.

———. Status cues in speech: extra-race and extra-region identification. *Lingua* 1963, 12: 300–6.

Hess, R. D., and Shipman, Virginia C. Maternal influences upon early learning: the cognitive environments of urban preschool children. In R. D. Hess and Roberta M. Bear, eds., *Early Education.* Chicago: Aldine, 1968.

Hollingshead, A. B. *Two Factor Index of Status Position.* New Haven: Yale University Press, 1957.

Hurst, C. G., Jr., and Jones, W. L. Psychosocial concomitants of sub-standard speech. *J. Negro Education* 1966, 35: 409–21.

Hymes, D. On communicative competence. In Renira Huxley and Elisabeth Ingram, eds., *Mechanisms in Language Development.* London: Centre for Advanced Study in the Developmental Sciences, in press.

Insko, C. A. *Theories of Attitude Change.* New York: Appleton-Century-Crofts, 1967.

Labov, W. Stages in the acquisition of standard English. In R. W. Shuy, ed., *Social Dialects and Language Learning.* Champaign, Ill.: National Council of Teachers of English, 1965.

———. *The Social Stratification of English in New York City.* Washington, D. C.: Center for Applied Linguistics, 1966.

Lambert, W. E. A social psychology of bilingualism. *J. Social Issues* 1967, 23: 91–109.

Lambert, W. E.; Hodgson, R. C.; Gardner, R. C.; and Fillenbaum, S. Evaluational reactions to spoken language. *J. Abnormal and Social Psychology* 1960, 60: 44–51.

Lewis, M. M. *Language, Thought, and Personality in Infancy and Childhood.* New York: Basic Books, 1963.

Naremore, Rita C. Teachers' evaluational reactions to pupils' speech samples. Doctoral dissertation, University of Wisconsin, 1969.

Putnam, G. N., and O'Hern, Edna. The status significance of an isolated urban dialect. *Language* 1955, 31: Part 2, 1–32.

Rosenthal, R. *Experimenter Effects in Behavioral Research.* New York: Appleton-Century-Crofts, 1966.

Rosenthal, R., and Jacobson, Lenore. *Pygmalion in the Classroom.* New York: Holt, Rinehart, & Winston, 1968.

Schatzman, L., and Strauss, A. Social class and modes of communication. *American J. Sociology* 1955, 60: 329–38.

Shuy, R. W.; Wolfram, W. A.; and Riley, W. K. Linguistic correlates of social stratification in Detroit speech. U. S. Office of Education Cooperative Research Project No. 6-1347, 1967.

Strauss, A., and Schatzman, L. Cross-class interviewing: an analysis of interaction and communicative styles. *Human Organization* 1955, 14: 28–31.

Tucker, G. R., and Lambert, W. E. White and Negro listeners' reactions to various American-English dialects. Unpublished paper. McGill University.

Williams, F. Psychological correlates of speech characteristics: on sounding "disadvantaged." *J. Speech and Hearing Research,* in press.

Williams, F., and Naremore, Rita C. On the functional analysis of social class differences in modes of speech. *Speech Monographs* 1969, 36: 77–102(a)
———. Social class differences in children's syntactic performance: a quantitative analysis of field study data. *J. Speech and Hearing Research* 1969, 12: 778–93. (b)

Chapter 19

SOME VIEWPOINTS OF THE SPEECH, HEARING, AND LANGUAGE CLINICIAN

David E. Yoder*

Increasingly, persons concerned with educational intervention programs with the poor, or persons concerned with such populations in the schools have turned to the speech and hearing clinician[1] for advice or assistance on problems associated with disadvantaged children. The work of this specialist has mostly involved disorders of speech (articulation, fluency, voice), hearing (total or partial loss), and certain types of language problems associated with brain damage, mental retardation, and emotional disorders. More recently, however, this specialist has been called upon to consider what might be done for the disadvantaged child, quite apart from the types of detailed disorders mentioned above. Although the speech specialist works with individuals of all ages, this chapter will deal basically with communication problems of children.

If one turns to the research or applied literature of the speech and hearing profession,[2] he will find general agreement in the concern and definition with what above was labeled as *speech* or *hearing* disorders, although as might be expected, ideas on specific definitions, etiologies, and therapeutic strategies vary substantially. On the other hand, the current professional concern with problems of language, being a more recently developed interest, presents a less stable and agreed-upon range of viewpoints among members of the field. This

---

*Department of Communicative Disorders, University of Wisconsin
[1]The label might be *speech therapist, speech correctionist, speech specialist. Audiologist, speech pathologist, speech scientist* refer more to specializations within the field.
[2]The main journals in the United States are the *Journal of Speech and Hearing Disorders* and *Journal of Speech and Hearing Research.*

situation is all the more magnified when considering the language of the disadvantaged child.

Although the clinical mission of the speech specialist, by definition, is in the diagnosis and correction of disorders in speech behavior, research in this profession is as concerned with the description and explanation of normal speech behavior as it is with the abnormal. In fact, one might venture the observation that the growth of research into normal behavior within the last decade or so has engendered a broadening of concern from the details of particular speech or hearing disorders to an overall concern with communication behavior itself. Thus in recent years there has been frequent reference to disorders of communication rather than to speech defects, delayed speech, and the like. There is more of a view of the whole of a child's or adult's communication capabilities, and this, no doubt, has increased the interest of how language is a factor within this whole.

COMMUNICATIVE DISORDERS AND THE POVERTY CHILD

Too often, perhaps, what other chapters of this volume variously describe as language problems, differences, or deficiencies, is naively equated with the label *communication disorder*. As broadly construed from the literature of the speech and hearing profession, the usual application of this label would imply the presence of a deficiency somewhere within the functioning or acquisitional sequence of the child's communication behaviors. In the section which follows, we will examine some of the more commonly encountered disorders of speech, hearing, and language and see whether there appears to be any particular bias toward incidence in poverty populations.

Speech Disorders

Articulation. Problems of articulation are usually classified in terms of sound or phoneme omissions, substitutions or distortions. For example, in "I ——aw the——un——ine," the /s/ and /sh/ phonemes are omited from the child's utterances completely. In the case of a phoneme substitution, the child would say the same sentence by possibly substituting a /th/ phoneme for the /s/ and /sh/ phonemes, e.g., "I *th*aw the *th*un *th*ine." In the case of the youngster who would distort the production of a sound rather than omit or replace it for another phoneme, one might hear the same sentence spoken with an excessive amount of air escaping from the side of the mouth on the /s/ and /sh/ phonemes causing listeners to recognize something unusual in that child's speech. There may be a variety of reasons why a child has deviancies in speech articulation. These include physiological inability as a result of a paralysis, cleft of the lip or palate, severe intellectual disability, emotional problems, or a hearing loss which has not allowed him to learn the sound accurately in the first place.

There are times, too, when omissions reflect, not failure to articulate or to learn the speech sounds, but that the child has learned a language (system or dialect) that does not distribute the sound in that particular linguistic environment or else there is little communicative importance placed on it. One need turn only to examples of the omission of /s/ inflections in nonstandard Negro English as given in chapters by Baratz (2) or Labov (9) in this volume to see such instances. Certainly, unless the clinician can identify such instances, problems of articulation may be confused with dialect or language differences when some of the standard tests of articulation are given (e.g., McDonald 1964; Templin and Darley 1960; Bryngelson and Glaspey 1962).

Do poverty children have more problems of articulation than other children? This, as well as subsequent questions of this type, is difficult to answer unequivocally because much of the evidence on the matter is indirect and also is subject to dispute for a number of reasons.

With respect to the acquistion and frequency of speech sounds of infants between the age of eighteen months and thirty months, Irwin's (1948a,b) study is often cited as evidence of socioeconomic differences. He found superiority in the number of different sounds acquired and frequency of usage by infants whose fathers were in business or professions as contrasted to infants whose fathers were semi- or unskilled workers. One could interpret this to indicate that children from a lower socioeconomic group will be delayed over children from upper socioeconomic groups in speech-sound acquisition and use. However, before such a conclusion is made, we need to look more closely at the population samples Irwin used. In another paper (Irwin and Chen 1946b, p. 431), it was noted that despite the occupational distinctions, the infants were from middle-class homes. Accordingly, these developmental data may have little relevance to what we might find in infants from lower socioeconomic groups as defined today. Another important criticism is that many of the sounds produced by the infants were classified as individual phonemes when they may have been allophones of a larger phoneme class. In short, Irwin was not adequately defining phonemes.

Other evidence of social-class differences in articulation development frequently cited by speech and hearing specialists comes from the research of Templin (1957). She studied a sample of children, three through eight years of age, who were classified as low or high in socioeconomic status as determined by the Minnesota Occupational Scale. She found that articulation proficiency in lower-class children seemed delayed in development by approximately one year, as compared to upper-class children. There are several problems in generalizing from this evidence to today's poverty populations. First, the population was classed into different socioeconomic levels based only on the father's occupation. Second, all the children were white and monolingual. Third, the stimulus materials used for assessing articulation behavior were based on standards established for white middle-class children.

The more recent study by Andersland (1961) reports that kindergarten children in a low socioeconomic group (established by a six-point scale based on the quality of the home, furnishings, dwelling area, occupation and education of the parents) made significantly more speech and articulation errors than did their peers from upper- and middle-class socioeconomic levels. Results indicated that from a battery of tested sounds, the children from the lowest socioeconomic group scored 75 percent errors, as against 59 percent errors for the middle group and 33 percent for the upper one. Andersland does not report, however, the type or frequency of the articulation errors; consequently, we have no way of interpreting or comparing them.

As one might expect, subjective evidence on articulatory development in poverty- or minority-group children has accumulated. For example, subjective ratings on the language samples from Head Start children have been reported (Raph 1967, p. 205) as indicating a high frequency of omissions and substitutions in speech articulation, and these were interpreted as being symptomatic of a general insufficiency in speech development.

The foregoing is illustrative of the available information on the matter of speech articulation. There is no overwhelming evidence that children from poverty populations have highly serious problems in articulatory development, nor is there persuasive evidence that no problem exists at all. Unfortunately, when we look closely at what evidence does exist, there are problems of sampling (precisely who comprised the population?) and of description (precisely what were the articulatory distinctions and criteria?). There is the worrisome prospect that our testing procedures and instruments are sometimes revealing to us ethnic and social-class differences in language rather than distinctions in the speech capabilities or development of children.

Some progress in this area is shown in the work of Monsees and Berman (1968) who report evaluation and screening procedures based directly upon the norms of the individual's speech community (here, nonstandard Negro English). Such procedures may enable us to determine when a child's articulatory development fits the norms of no community (thus a genuine deficiency) as against being discrepant from the norms of one community (say, white middle-class) but not another (say, Spanish-American, Negro, Indian, or certain white ethnic groups).

Stuttering. Disruption of speech fluency, or stuttering, is a common disorder encountered by the speech clinician. Despite the fact that the phenomenon of stuttering is known to most people, researchers and theorists remain at odds about its definition, cause, and remediation (see, e.g., Bloodstein 1958; Glauber 1958; Van Riper 1963; Johnson 1967). Many normal speakers do not realize that everyday speech is replete with disfluencies and that these vary substantially depending upon our emotional and intellectual circumstances at the moment of speaking. The stutterer, however, is typically a person who has more, and a few different, disfluencies as compared with the nonstutterer; and, in particular, these are marked enough that they may seem abnormal to listeners. Beyond this oversimplified definition, the characterization of the stutterer becomes complex and varied, ranging all the way from detailed description of his speech symptoms to his emotional behavior.

Nobody has reported that more than the usual incidence of stuttering occurs in the poverty populations of the United States; at least, it has not become a salient topic in dealing with Head Start children, and the like. There are, however, two curious points that are worth brief mention. One of these is the "upward mobility" hypothesis which Johnson (1967) suggests, based upon his examination of an earlier study by Darley (1955). A similar conclusion is suggested by Morganstern (1956) who found after surveying nearly thirty thousand children in five areas of Scotland that the incidence of stuttering was somewhat greater among children from families of semiskilled workers as against unskilled ones. Accordingly, he reasoned that since the former families seemed to be more ambitious about their children's success, perhaps this pressure somehow increased the potential for stuttering. The other curiosity is the prospect that groups or cultures exist which have no stuttering, and thus may reveal by implication a social or cultural variable related to stuttering. Much of this notion dates back to Johnson's (1967) statement that he found no stuttering among the Shoshone or Bannock Indians of Idaho when he studied them in the early 1940s and his observation that these tribes even lacked a word for stuttering. No further evidence exists one way or another on this point, but perhaps one modest research project could clear up the issue once and for all.

Other disorders affecting speech. It has frequently been speculated that the incidence of congenital anomalies such as cleft palate and cerebral palsy may be higher among families from low socioeconomic levels due to poor nutrition, and inadequate prenatal and birth care. Since children born with cleft palate or cerebral palsy also have a high incidence of speech, hearing, or language disorders, these two populations are of concern to the speech and hearing specialist.

By estimate, we can expect that one child in every eight hundred born will have a cleft of the lip or palate or both (Brown 1967, p. 361). The incidence of cerebral palsy in the United States is considered to be approximately six per 1,000 births (McDonald and Chance 1964, p. 2). In the incidence studies of cleft palate and cerebral palsy reported in the literature, the discussions are limited to the variables of sex, type, and degree of involvement with no breakdown or information reported as it relates to socioeconomic level. The relative number of children found within lower socioeconomic groups having these congenital anomalies, then, is thought to be at least that found in the overall population. Even though in raw numbers one may find a larger number of children with congenital anomalies in such groups, this is probably a reflection of the higher incidence of births rather than the conditions which exist within the lower socioeconomic environment.

Just as there is some speculation about a higher incidence of congenital anomalies among the lower socioeconomic groups, we might speculate that children with congenital defects born into lower socioeconomic environments do not receive the amount and quality of rehabilitative care given to their counterparts in upper socioeconomic groups. This may be partially due to the lack of availability of the services needed in his community, the difficulty for transporting the child to an area where the service may be available, and lack of trained personnel to go into the lower socioeconomic environment to assist with rehabilitating the child. If this is true, then one might expect a larger number of adults from lower socioeconomic areas to have communicative disorders in need of attention.

One of the most salient features of the mentally retarded child is his impoverished verbal behavior. Prior to the 1960s, most of the language and speech research which was done with the mentally retarded was focused on the number of retarded children who had speech or language problems rather than on how the speech and language behavior of retarded children could be modified (Siegel 1964). More recently the literature (Schiefelbusch, Copeland, and Smith 1967; Lillywhite and Bradley 1969) has begun to focus more on language modification programs for the mentally retarded. However, considering the types of retarded populations involved in such studies, there is no direct productive relation for dealing with children in poverty populations.

In sum there is a range of other disorders which come within the purview of the speech clinician, but these disorders are only as pertinent to the problems of poverty children as in the incidence of the disorder to be found in that population.

Hearing Disorders

Acuity. As most readers already know, the problems of hearing may range all the way from a slight loss of hearing acuity to profound deafness. There is no evidence of the totally deaf being in any greater numbers among the disadvantaged. Moreover since most children in this category will receive specialized training anyway, we need not discuss them at any greater length here. It is estimated (Silverman, Lane and Doehring 1960, p. 416) that 5 percent of all school-age children will have a hearing impairment of some

degree, and that one to two of every ten children will require special educational attention as a result of his hearing problem. In the area of auditory
acuity as in other areas it is difficult to find incidence studies which provide
data by socioeconomic levels. One finds statements such as the following (Butt
1968, p. 27):

> . . . a recent speech survey has shown that speech and hearing
> problems in this area are triple the figure to be expected on the basis
> of national norms. One cause of the numerous speech and hearing
> problems is the prevalence of poor health and inadequate nutrition
> (seven out of ten poor children are malnourished).

No specific figures accompany or are referred to in this statement, consequently one questions whether this is an impression or based on specific data.
Too frequently such statements are readily taken and perpetuated without
further examination.

A study reported by Carroll (1967) from Sarasota County in Florida
indicates that in a screening test comparing regular kindergarten children with
those from a Head Start program, 4 percent of the kindergarten children failed
the screening test as compared to 6 percent of the Head Start children. Coming
to my attention, but yet unreported formally, was another survey conducted
in a large midwestern city (which cannot be named) which found that black
and white children from a low socioeconomic area had a lower incidence of
hearing loss than black and white children from a middle-class socioeconomic
area.

Although pertinent research is ongoing in the area of audiology, it is
difficult to obtain precise information on the relation of hearing acuity and
social status or ethnicity. Part of this comes, no doubt, from the problems of
defining a child's social status in a large-scale testing program. There is also
the newer problem of not being able to specify race in school, institutional, or
sometimes even research records. Another valid question may be raised about
the techniques for assessing the hearing of children in lower-socioeconomic or
nonstandard-linguistic environments. Do these children have more frequent
losses of hearing or is their unfamiliarity with hearing-testing procedures
responsible for their lack of appropriate response to the task? A final note is
that many studies which report information relative to speech and language
programs provided for poverty children include only children screened on the
basis of having normal hearing acuity. Consequently many of the children who
may have losses in hearing and also speech or language problems are not
reported in studies of programs with poverty groups.

Auditory discrimination. Due mostly to the writings of Cynthia Deutsch
(1964), which relate problems of auditory discrimination among disadvan-

taged children with problems of reading, difficulties in this behavior have already been deemed pertinent to poverty populations. An auditory discrimination test (e.g., Wepman 1958; Schiefelbusch and Lindsley 1958) requires a child to differentiate between two words which differ only by one sound or phoneme. The evidence presented by Deutsch is that poor children have deficits in this capability, presumably caused by excessively noisy environments, and so on. This capability is also of particular interest to the speech and hearing clinician since there is some evidence of its affecting speech-articulation learning (Weiner 1967) and applicability to programs of articulation therapy (Van Riper 1963).

As argued in Baratz's chapter (2) in this volume, tests of auditory discrimination, like articulation tests, are subject to a linguistic bias. Currently, the research challenge is to develop tests of auditory discrimination which are relevant to speech, yet will not be biased toward a particular language or dialect. Until we have the benefits of such research, what is currently discussed about auditory discrimination and the language of poverty children is largely at a stalemate (however, see Plumer Chapter 14). Do the social-class and ethnic differences point out deficits in discrimination capability per se, or do they point out an interaction between class and language, relative to test performance?

The Overall Perspective on Disorders in the Poverty Population

When evidence of speech, hearing, or language disorders is presented (or implied) for poverty groups, it is usually in the direction of imputing that important problems do exist in the population. However, we, as yet, have no major evidence from the speech and hearing literature that the problems are any more serious than with the general population. We can point, too, to the fact that programs such as those involved in Parent and Child Centers, Head Start, Follow Through, and the like, have not seemed to bring together an obvious concentration of children with speech and hearing disorders, or the more usual type of language disorders known to the speech clinician.

As mentioned, we do need more and better studies of the incidence of speech, hearing, and language disorders in the population, and the current restrictions upon keeping records of race, the problems of getting across class boundaries, and of conducting new studies with populations who already have been overresearched, make such study difficult. During the years 1970 and 1971, however, we may have available some of this much-needed information. At this time, results should be available from the National Speech and Hearing Survey which was commissioned by the U.S. Office of Education and is being carried out by the Department of Hearing and Speech Science at Colorado State University.[3] The survey has gathered data on the articulation, voice, fluency, language, and hearing-acuity characteristics of some thirty thousand school children representing a sample of grades one through twelve in the United States population. Data on speech production (articulation, etc.) have been gathered both in terms of responses to picture stimuli and to selected questions. Data on hearing acuity are based on responses to pure-tone audiometry. Hopefully, by computerized storage-and-retrieval techniques, it will be possible to generate summary data on segments of the population sample and aspects of the behavior tested. Unfortunately, it was not feasible (or possible in some cases) to record race or socioeconomic status of individual children; however, based upon the identification of sampling units (individual schools), estimates of such parameters could be found and used in interpreting the results.

Thus far we have discussed the usual speech and hearing disorders and only those aspects of language related to such disorders. In the next part of this paper we turn to the issues of language problems as they have presented a challenge to the speech clinician's viewpoint in dealing with poverty groups.

VIEWPOINTS ON LANGUAGE

It may be useful to give some description of the orientation, both theoretical and practical, which speech clinicians often hold about language. For a number of years, the developmental viewpoint of language has been influenced by both the learning-theory-based accounts of language acquisition (e.g., Skinner 1957; Mowrer 1952, 1960), and the well-known survey studies of McCarthy (1930), Day (1932), Davis (1937), or Templin (1957). More recently, however, contemporary theorizing in both psycholinguistics and sociolinguistics has had an impact upon the field, and increasingly one sees a concern with the concepts of linguistic competence and performance (Menyuk 1969; Carrow 1968; Lee 1966; Williams and Naremore 1969) and social class differences in dialect (Baratz 1968a, b, 1969; Shriner and Miner 1968; Shriner, in prep.). Much of the current empirical research in language, however, utilizes standardized tests —e.g., The Illinois Test of Psycholinguistic Ability (Kirk, McCarthy, and Kirk 1968), The Peabody Picture Vocabulary Test (Dunn 1959), The Ammons Full Range Picture Vocabulary Test (Ammons and Holmes 1949)—for de-

---

[3]This has been under the direction of Professor Forest Hull of that department. A brief description of the project's planning has been published by Hull and Timmons (1966).

scription or diagnosis of language behavior. When applied to poverty populations, these tests are subject to the cultural biases described by Severson and Guest, Chapter 15.[4]

The "Deficit-Differences" Issue

With the speech clinician's primary experiences in disorders of, or delayed, language behavior, it is not unusual that one of the first articles in a speech and hearing journal on the language of poverty children took this point of view:

> Disadvantaged children's pronunciation and articulation, vocabulary, sentence length and use of grammatical and syntactic structures resemble the language of privileged children of a younger age level. Such children lack the language facility required to do independent thinking and problem-solving. Unless new strategies of intervention are introduced at an early age, this gap in ability to manipulate symbols is seldom narrowed sufficiently to enable many of these children to succeed in school. (Raph 1967, p. 212)

Before criticizing this position, it should be pointed out that this was a view held by many outside of the field in the mid-sixties, and one congruent with what some other influential researchers had taken (e.g., Deutsch and Brown 1964; Bereiter and Engelmann 1966; John and Goldstein 1964).

At the time the Raph position was published, there were persons within the profession who questioned this deficit interpretation upon the basis of its being a confusion of language differences observed in poverty children. In subsequent issues of the same journal, Weber (1968) pointed to the obvious dialect distinctions found in such children (which might be erroneously interpreted as deficits when gauged relative to another dialect) and Baratz (1968a, p. 299–300) argued this same point as well as emphasizing the "well-developed, highly structured and grammatical" subcultural dialect, found in black children.

This issue of deficiency-difference interpretation has been a major challenge when the speech clinician has tried to formulate a viewpoint on the language behavior of poverty children. How can one best differentiate deficiencies from differences? If deficiencies do exist, how can they be dealt with? If differences are the key problem, is the speech clinician trained adequately to identify and deal with them?

---

[4]An example of this very point appeared in print (Gerber and Hertel 1969) after this chapter was prepared. As usual, disadvantaged children scored low on the ITPA. Unfortunately the researchers overlooked most of the hazards in using such a test on this population—hazards such as discussed by Severson and Guest in Chapter 15 of this volume.

Coping with the Issue

One position that may reduce some of the confusion raised by the deficien-cy-difference issue is to insist upon a more rigorous definition of what qualifies as a language deficiency. In a more theoretical sense, we could exercise the criteria discussed by Menyuk (Chapter 10 in this volume)—that the use of fewer generative rules, or more rudimentary ones, or deficiencies in capabilities related to language behavior (e.g., short-term memory capacity) would be a basis for calling a child's language deficient. But in a practical sense, we might arrive at this same position by determining whether a child is functioning normally in a speech community. If he is not functioning within the language norm of any community, then he is deficient. Even though he may not meet the demands for using some mainstream version of a language (as standard English would be), if he can meet the demands of another community (such as the use of nonstandard Negro English; see Labov Chapter 9), then we have a case of language difference. Based upon what we know about poverty children, the difference category may stand out as the situation of many of these children. But the issue is by no means closed. The great bulk of the evidence about language differences has involved research with Negro children. How do we know that the same arguments about language differences apply equally as well, for example, to the Appalachian child, the Chicano, the Indian, or even white children of the inner city? The fact is that we do not have the kind of evidence for these groups that we are accumulating for Negro children. In short, we need massive research into the different varieties of nonstandard English. Until we have the fruits of this, there is some hazard in saying that the language of all disadvantaged children is simply different.

Even if we call the poverty child's language different, this still does not alleviate his problem within our society. Something still needs to be done about it. The reformulated question for us now is: How might the speech clinician work with the linguistically different child? We can speculate on a few answers to this.

For one thing a different set of assumptions would underlie our work with the linguistically different as compared to the linguistically deficient child. Our focus on deficient language is primarily an etiological and developmental one. What so-called basics of language does the child possess, and what level of achievement might we hope to gain relative to his entrance into some speech community? This is the thinking which we most typically exercise with the mildly to moderately retarded child when the aim is to teach him enough language so that he can get along in the main society. In brief, the most one usually hopes for here is narrowing the gap between what a child has learned and what we think he is capable of learning, to move toward some of the requirements of a speech sommunity. The linguistically different child on the other hand, we assume already possesses the basics of language and has a normally developed system to meet the demands of his primary speech community. Thus our goal, rather than being one of basic development, is one of parallel development along the lines of an additional linguistic system. This is not a case of narrowing a language gap, so to speak, but simply closing it. Even the terms which we might use to describe the instructional activity with these two groups of children must be carefully differentiated. The speech clinician's everyday terms, "therapy," "remediation," "correction," "rehabilitation," and the like are applicable only to the child with language deficiency. Work with the linguistically different child is more a case of straightforward instruction, and should be so identified.

This type of distinction between deficit and difference carries weighty implications for the training of the speech and language specialist (perhaps a more appropriate term than *clinician*). To understand the basic capabilities of the language-deficient child one needs information in the etiologies of language deficits and the development of language, and in how to modify and change the behavior. By contrast, perhaps the most important thing for the specialist in language differences is a knowledge of the contrasts between a target language or dialect and the child's existing language or dialect. This calls for knowledge and information about the existing dialect being used by a child and the understanding that dialects by their very genesis may have evolved to accomplish different communicative tasks and thus are to be preserved.

Some Practical Implications

Obviously this line of reasoning presents a formidable challenge since the specialist in language differences will have to become knowledgeable (but not necessarily a user) of the details of one or more languages or dialects other than his or her own. Thus we need to know more of the contrasts between the communicative aspects of standard English and, say, the language of New York Puerto Ricans, of Chicanos, of American Indians, and of inner-city children, to name a few. The implication for recruiting minority-group members as speech specialists seems obvious here, as is the necessity of training the typical middle-class speech clinician to work with dialects.

Although persons such as Labov (Chapter 9), Baratz (Chapter 2) and Severson and Guest (Chapter 15) have pointed out that most of our strategies for language assessment are culturally biased, a careful consideration of the deficiency-difference contrast will enable us to use some of these strategies with less error. If, say, an articulation test were carefully used, it would allow us to see what linguistic differences on this level exist in a disadvantaged group, thus helping the specialist to plot the course of instruction. Moreover such tests could be used at various stages of instruction as an index of progress in developing the additional language or dialect system. Ironically, the more culturally biased such tests are, the more benefit they will be in this case, so long as they are used as a basis for describing differences instead of deficits.

OVERVIEW

Generally, we have argued first in this paper that the poverty child does not seem to be subject to more than the usual incidence of speech and hearing disorders as found in the general population. Nor do some of the disorders associated with language problems, as in brain damage and the like, seem to prevail more than usual in the poverty population. Although such a generalization would influence us against mounting some type of "speech correction" campaign with the poor, we must realize that we are proceeding on the basis of a negative case. Thus it may not be safe to consider the issue closed, and we should wait for the results of such surveys as the one discussed, before taking a final position on the matter.

We also have tried to point out that in the speech clinician's confrontation with the language problems of the poor, the issue of language deficiency as against language difference has come to the fore. To cope with this we have suggested that a more rigorous definition of language deficiency would reduce some of the confusion of the issue. This basis for differentiating language deficiency from language difference carries a variety of significant implications for the people in the field of speech and hearing. Out of our own feelings on this issue, we have reflected the position that the speech specialist may be working more with differences than with deficiencies. Nevertheless, we should remember that individual differences and capabilities do exist and that to assume differences where deficits exist would indeed be tragic. Thus, like the question of the incidence of communicative disorders in poverty populations, the issue of deficiency-difference is in need of substantial research.

REFERENCES

Ammons, R. B., and Holmes, J. C. The full range picture vocabulary test: III: results for a pre-school age population. *Child Development* 1949, 20: 5–14.

Andersland, P. B. Maternal and environmental factors related to success in speech improvement training. *J. Speech and Hearing Research* 1961, 4: 79–90.

Baratz, Joan C. Reply to Dr. Raph's article on speech and language deficits in culturally disadvantaged children. *J. Speech and Hearing Disorders* 1968, 33: 299–300. (a)

———. Language in the economically disadvantaged child: a perspective. *ASHA* 1968, 10: 143–45.(b)

———. Language and cognitive assessment of Negro children: assumptions and research needs. *ASHA* 1969, 11: 87–91.

Bereiter, C., and Engelmann, S. *Teaching Disadvantaged Children in the Preschool.* Englewood Cliffs, N. J.: Prentice-Hall, 1966.

Bloodstein, O. Stuttering as an anticipatory struggle reaction. In J. Eisenson, ed., *Stuttering: A Symposium.* New York: Harper & Brothers, 1958.

Brown, S. F. Retarded speech development. In W. Johnson and Dorothy Moeller, eds., *Speech Handicapped School Children.* New York: Harper & Row, 1967.

Bryngelson, B., and Glaspey, E. *Speech in the Classroom.* Chicago: Scott, Foresman, 1962.

Butt, D. S. Language development for disadvantaged children. *New Mexico Speech and Hearing Association J.* 1968, 1: 26–32.

Carroll, Anne W. Speech and hearing services in project Head Start. *Colorado Speech and Hearing Association J.* Spring, 1967.

Carrow, Sister Mary Arthur. The development of auditory comprehension of language structure in children. *J. Speech and Hearing Disorders* 1968, 33: 99–111.

Darley, F. The relationship of parental attitudes and adjustments to the development of stuttering. In W. Johnson and R. Leutenegger, eds., *Stuttering in Children and Adults.* Minneapolis: University of Minnesota Press, 1955.

Davis, Edith A. *The Development of Linguistic Skills in Twins, Singletons with Siblings, and only Children from Age Five to Ten Years.* Institute of Child Welfare Monograph Series, No. 14. Minneapolis: University of Minnesota Press, 1937.

Day, Ella J. The development of language in twins: I. A comparison of twins and single children. *Child Development* 1932, 3: 179–99.

Deutsch, Cynthia. Auditory discrimination and learning: social factors. *Merrill-Palmer Quarterly* 1964, 10: 277–96.

Deutsch, M., and Brown, B. Social influences in Negro-white intelligence differences. *J. Social Issues* 1964, 20: 24–35.

Dunn, L. M. Peabody Picture Vocabulary Test. Nashville: American Guidance Service, 1959.

Gerber, S. E. and Hertel, Christina G. Language deficiency of disadvantaged children. *J. of Speech and Hearing Research* 1969, 12, 270–280.

Glauber, I. P. The psychoanalysis of stuttering. In J. Eisenson, ed., *Stuttering: A Symposium.* New York: Harper & Brothers, 1958.

Hull, F. M., and Timmons, R. J. A national speech and hearing survey. *J. Speech and Hearing Disorders* 1966, 31: 359–61.

Irwin, O. C., and Chen, H. P. Development of speech during infancy: curve of phonemic types *J. Experimental Psychology* 1946, 36: 431–36.

Irwin, O. C. Infant speech: the effect of family occupational status and of age on use of sound types. *J. Speech and Hearing Disorders* 1948, 13: 224–26.(a)

———. Infant speech: the effect of family occupational status and of age on sound frequency. *J. Speech and Hearing Disorders* 1948, 13: 320–239(b)

John, Vera P., and Goldstein, L. S. The social context of language acquisition. *Merrill-Palmer Quarterly* 1964, 10: 265–75.

Johnson, W. Stuttering. In W. Johnson and Dorothy Moller, eds., *Speech Handicapped School Children.* New York: Harper & Row, 1967.

Kirk, S. A.; McCarthy, J. J.; and Kirk, W. D. *Illinois Test of Psycholinguistic Abilities (Revised Edition).Examiner's Manual.* Urbana, Ill.: University of Illinois Press, 1968.

Lee, L. Developmental sentence types: a method for comparing normal and deviant syntactic development. *J. Speech and Hearing Disorders* 1966, 31: 311–30.

Lillywhite, H. S., and Bradley, Doris P. *Communication Problems in Mental Retardation: Diagnosis and Management.* New York: Harper & Row, 1969.

McCarthy, Dorothea. *The Language Development of the Preschool Child.* Institute of Child Welfare Monograph Series, No. 4. Minneapolis: University of Minnesota Press, 1930.

McDonald, E. T. *A Deep Test of Articulation.* Pittsburgh: Stanwix House, 1964.

McDonald, E. T., and Chance, B., Jr. *Cerebral Palsy.* Englewood Cliffs, N. J.: Prentice-Hall, 1964.

Menyuk, Paula. *Sentences Children Use.* Cambridge, Mass.: M.I.T. Press, 1969.

Monsees, Edna K., and Berman, Carol. Speech and language screening in a summer Head Start program. *J. Speech and Hearing Disorders* 1968 33: 121–26.

Morgenstern, J. J. Socioeconomic factors in stuttering. *J. Speech and Hearing Disorders* 1956, 21: 25–33.

Mowrer, O. H. The autism theory of speech development and some clinical applications. *J. Speech and Hearing Disorders* 1952, 17: 263–68.

———. *Learning Theory and the Symbolic Process.* New York: Wiley, 1960.

Raph, Jane B. Language and speech deficits in culturally disadvantaged children, and their implication for the speech clinician. *J. Speech and Hearing Disorders* 1967, 32: 203–14.

Schiefelbusch, R. L., and Lindsey, M. J. A new test of sound discrimination. *J. Speech and Hearing Disorders* 1958, 23: 153–59.

Schiefelbusch, R.; Copeland, R.; and Smith, J. *Language and Mental Retardation.* New York: Holt, Rinehart & Winston, 1967.

Shriner, T. H. Sociolinguistics and language. In L. E. Travis, ed., *Handbook of Speech Pathology.* Rev. ed. New York: Appleton-Century-Crofts, (in prep.).

Shriner, T. H., and Miner, L. Morphological structures in the language of disadvantaged and advantaged children. *J. Speech and Hearing Research* 1968, 11: 605–10.

Siegel, G. M. Prevailing concepts in speech research with mentally retarded children. *ASHA* 1964, 6: 192–94.

Silverman, S. R.; Lane, H. S.; and Doehring, D. G. Deaf children. In D. Hallowell, and S. R. Silverman, eds., *Hearing and Deafness.* New York: Holt, Rinehart & Winston, 1960.

Skinner, B. F. *Verbal Behavior.* New York: Appleton-Century-Crofts, 1957.

Templin, Mildred C. *Certain Language Skills in Children, Their Development and Interrelationships.* Institute of Child Welfare Monograph Series, No. 26. Minneapolis: University of Minnesota Press, 1957.

Templin, Mildred C., and Darley, F. L. The Templin-Darley Tests of Articulation. Iowa City: University of Iowa Bureau of Education Research and Service, 1960.

Van Riper, C. *Speech Correction Principles and Methods.* Englewood Cliffs, N. J.: Prentice-Hall, 1963.

Weber, J. L. Conspicuous deficits. *J. Speech and Hearing Disorders* 1968, 33: 96.

Weiner, P. S. Auditory discrimination and articulation. *J. Speech and Hearing Disorders* 1967, 32: 19–28.

Wepman, J. M. Auditory Discrimination Test. Chicago, 1958.

Williams, F., and Naremore, R. Social class differences in children's syntactic performance: a quantitative analysis of field study data. *J. Speech and Hearing Research* 1969, 12: 778–93.

Chapter 20

AN ANNOTATED BIBLIOGRAPHY OF JOURNAL ARTICLES

Frederick Williams* and Rita C. Naremore**

This bibliography represents a revised and updated version of our earlier paper which was circulated under the Special Reports series of the Institute for Research on Poverty at the University of Wisconsin. We have centered this version solely upon journal articles for several reasons. One is that books are typically in the public knowledge and most in this area can be found cited in the chapters of this volume. Second, we have chosen to avoid references to unpublished items (including dissertations) because of the unfortunate unreliability of their availability. Additionally, most unpublished items of merit eventually find their way into print. In brief, then, the entries for the most part are restricted to only those items which may be found in printed and presumably available journals.

As in the earlier bibliography, inclusion of items was based upon the pertinence of each potential entry to the study of language and poverty. This has involved taking considerable liberty in determining what was defined as *language* and what was defined as *poverty*. To the educator, for example, language is apt to be reflected as scores on a standardized test of verbal ability, and poverty is defined in terms of parental occupation or is based loosely upon the type of neighborhood or ethnic group that a student represents. To the psychologist or sociologist, the description of language is sometimes extended

*Center for Communication Research, University of Texas
**Research and Development Center, Indiana University
Compilation of this bibliography was completed during the authors' affiliations with the Institute for Research on Poverty at the University of Wisconsin.

416

Classification Guide

Types of Materials
0-0-0-0-*

{
1 = conceptual, theoretical, review of literature
2 = specific description of a population
3 = general description of a population
4 = an experiment, technical report
5 = quasi experiment, demonstration report
}

Population Ethnicity
0-0-0-0-*

{
1 = white
2 = Spanish-American
3 = Negro
4 = American Indian
5 = other minority in the U.S.
0 = not applicable
}

Population Age
0-0-0-0-*

{
1 = infancy or preschool
2 = school years
3 = past school, adult
0 = not applicable
}

Linguistic Description
0-0-0-0-*

{
1 = formal linguistic description
2 = specialized or less formal description
3 = tests, measures
4 = other
0 = not pertinent
}

. . . .   Considered basic reading beyond standardized tests to the classification and measurement of verbal behavior either found or elicited in given situations; poverty is defined most frequently on the basis of social stratification indices. Although the linguist rarely looks at poverty per se, his studies of the dialects of certain populations and a knowledge of their social positions provide materials pertinent to the present topic.

For most of the entries the brief annotation is an attempt to capsulize the essence of the materials, but to do so with a biased eye toward showing the pertinence of the item to the joint topical criteria. In some cases where a regular annotation was not deemed useful, we have simply inserted special remarks. We have tried to augment the annotations with classificatory symbols below and at the right of the entry which are explained at the beginning of the listing. In addition to these symbols, we have marked with a star(*) a few entries which we have considered to be basic reading. The date of the bibliography is June 1969.

Anastasi, Anne, and D'Angelo, Rita. A comparison of Negro and white pre-
    school children in language development and Goodenough Draw-a-man
    IQ. *The J. of Genetic Psychology* (1952) 81: 147–65.

Measures of IQ and linguistic development were obtained from the following samples of five-year-old children: twenty-five Negroes and twenty-five whites living in uniracial neighborhoods, and twenty-five Negroes and twenty-five whites living in interracial neighborhoods. Sex and socioeconomic factors were relatively uniform in all groups. No statistically significant race differences were found for mean sentence length, although more "mature" sentence types were found among white children as compared with Negro children.

                                                        2-1,3-1-3

Anastasi, Anne, and deJesus, C. Language development and nonverbal IQ of
    Puerto Rican preschool children in New York City. *The J. of Abnormal
    and Social Psychology* (1953) 48: 357–66.

The language development and IQ of twenty five Puerto Rican boys and twenty five Puerto Rican girls were measured. Results were compared with the performance of fifty white and fifty Negro children tested by the same procedures. The Puerto Rican children spoke Spanish 98 percent of the time, while the white and Negro children spoke English. Although the educational and occupational level of Puerto Rican parents was lower than that of the parents of the white and Negro children, the Puerto Rican children used longer sentences and sentences with a more mature syntactic structure than did the white or Negro children of the same age. The researchers suggest that the greater extent of contact between between adults and children in Puerto Rican homes may account for their children's superior linguistic development.

2-5-1-2

Anisfeld, M.; Bogo, N.; and Lambert, W. E. Evaluational reactions to accented English speech. *J. of Abnormal and Social Psychology* (1962) 65: 223–31.

Jewish and gentile college students evaluated the personality characteristics of tape-recorded speakers, four using standard English and four having a Jewish accent. Students were unaware that the same speakers at one time used one accent and at another, the other. Differences in evaluation of the accented and unaccented versions were found, with the accented speech being generally devalued by both Jewish and gentile students.

4-1-3-0

Arnold, R. English as a second language. *The Reading Teacher* (1968) 21: 634–39.

(A reading program used with disadvantaged Mexican-American children is described.)

5-2-2-0

Ausubel, D. P. How reversible are the cognitive and motivational effects of cultural deprivation? Implications for teaching the culturally deprived child. *Urban Education* (1964) 1: 16–38.

The theory of "critical periods" in development of an organism, which maintains that the organism will be forever unable to take advantage of a given stimulus if it does not receive that stimulus at the time of maximum susceptibility to it, does not appear applicable to humans. However, it is possible for a learning deficit to accrue which can put an individual years behind in terms of cognitive development. Language is discussed as both a symptom and a factor of cognitive development.

1-0-1-0

Baratz, Joan C. Reply to Dr. Raph's article. *J. of Speech and Hearing Disorders* (1968) 33: 299–300.

The "deficit" position of a previous paper on the language of disadvantaged children is rejected in favor of a position based upon recognition of language "differences."

3-0-1-0

————. Linguistic and cultural factors in teaching reading to ghetto children. *Elementary English* (1969) 46: 199–203.

Language difficulties which interfere with the disadvantaged Negro child's ability to learn to read standard English are discussed, and a system using Negro dialect in beginning readers for such children is proposed.

1-3-2-0

————. Who should do what to whom . . . and why? *Florida Foreign Language Reporter,* in press.

The hypothesis that the language of black children is in some way deficient is dismissed in favor of a hypothesis that this language is instead different. Assuming that these children must learn standard English in order to function maximally in society, the author discusses the need for specialists to teach standard English in a quasiforeign language situation.

1-3-2-0

Bernstein, B. Some sociological determinants of perception. *British J. of Sociology* (1958) 9: 159–74.

Speculations are introduced on the social origins and implications of two different orders of perception, a distinction further relating to social-class differences. The working-class child is restricted to cues of "content" and is capable of only simple logical implications, whereas the middle-class child has the additional capability of perceiving cues of "structure" and is capable of recognizing relatively more elaborated implications. This difference of perception is manifested in a distinction between a *public* language (both reflecting and affecting restricted perception) and a *formal* language (reflecting and affecting elaborated perception). The working-class child has access only to the public language, whereas the middle-class child has access to both languages.

1-0-0-0

————. A public language: Some sociological implications of a linguistic form. *British J. of Sociology* (1959) 10: 311–26.

The earlier posed distinctions between *public* and *formal* languages are a perspective for deriving sociological implications pertaining to differences between working- and middle-class groups. Relatively detailed descriptions of the features of the two languages are given, along with their cognitive and sociological consequences.

1-0-0-0

———. Language and social class (research note). *British J. of Sociology* (1960) 11: 271–76.

In a detailed assessment of discrepancies between IQ and verbal test scores, it is found that language scores of a working-class group are depressed in relation to their scores at the higher ranges of a nonverbal IQ measure, and this depression is not found with a middle-class group.

2-1-2-3

———. Social class and linguistic development: a theory of social learning. In *Economy Education and Society*, A. H. Halsey, J. Floud, and A. Anderson. New York: Harcourt, Brace & World, 1961.

Reflecting Bernstein's prior theorizing on the distinction between *public* and *formal* languages and their manifestation as social class distinctions, a theoretical perspective on social learning is posed.

1-0-0-0

———. Aspects of language and learning in the genesis of the social process. *J. of Child Psychology and Psychiatry* (1961) 1: 313–24.

The characteristics of *public* and *formal* languages are seen as "modes of speech" which are differentially dominant across social strata. Such modes are presumed to be socially learned rather than to reflect some type of difference in innate capacities of children from different social classes. The social function of public language is examined in particular, and with a view to providing a lower-class child with programs designed to develop usage of formal language.

1-0-0-0

———. Social class, linguistic codes and grammatical elements. *Language and Speech* (1962) 5: 221–40.

Selected grammatical characteristics of the messages obtained in a prior study are assessed in terms of the theorized distinction between *restricted* and *elaborated* codes (originally *public* and *formal*).

2-1-2-2

———. Linguistic codes, hesitation phenomena and intelligence. *Language and Speech* (1962) 5: 31–46.

Theoretical distinctions between *restricted* and *elaborated* codes are investigated in terms of measures of pausal phenomena, word and syllable counts, and speech rate in messages obtained from working- and middle-class persons.

2-1-2-2

————. Elaborated and restricted codes: their social origins and some consequences. In *The ethnography of communication* , edited by J. Gumperz
and D. Hymes. *American Anthropologist*, special publication (1964) 66:
No.6, Part 2, 55–69.

The theoretical perspective of *restricted* and *elaborated* codes is outlined.
Within this perspective, language is defined as the totality of options for
expression, whereas speech reflects the options that are taken under actual
circumstances. Within this theoretical context, the social-class uses of restricted and elaborated codes are examined, and implications are drawn as to
their socializing and educational consequences.

1-0-0-0-*

Bernstein, B. and Young, D. Social class differences in conceptions of the uses
of toys. *Sociology* (1967) 1: 131–40.

Social-class differences are found in mothers' conceptions of uses of toys. An
index of mother-child communication relates to maternal conceptions in the
uses of toys among the three lowest social strata tested. These conceptions are
seen as related to the child's adjustment to school.

4-1-0-0

Bernstein, B., and Henderson, Dorothy. Social class differences in the relevance of language to socialization. *Sociology* (1969) 3: 2–20.

Samples of mothers from middle- and working-class areas were presented a
questionnaire designed to examine the effect of the social class of the mother
on her perception of the role of language as a socializing process. Results
indicated that middle-class mothers place greater emphasis on the use of
language in the person area, while working-class mothers place a greater
emphasis on the use of language in the transmission of basic skills.

4-1-3-4

Blank, Marion, and Bridger, W. Deficiencies in verbal labeling in retarded
readers. *American J. of Orthopsychiatry* (1966) 36: 840–47.

Retarded readers were found to be inferior to normal readers in the conversion
of visual-temporal to visual-spatial patterns. This deficiency was ascribed to
the difficulty retarded readers had in applying conceptual categories or correct
verbal labels to temporally presented stimuli.

4-0-2-0

Blank, Marion, and Solomon, Frances. How shall the disadvantaged child be
taught? *Child Development* (1969) 40: 47–61.

Examples are given of dialogue between a teacher and a four-year-old disadvantaged child in a one-to-one tutorial language program.

5-0-1-4

Bloomfield, L. Literate and illiterate speech. *American Speech* (1927) 2: 432–39.

The popular distinction between "good" and "bad" language is difficult to define scientifically. Presumably, good language is a "standard" version while bad language incorporates dialectical diversion. One viewpoint indicates that good language corresponds to a literary (written) standard, while bad language comprises spoken deviations from this standard. This viewpoint is questionable since written language is truly secondary to spoken language, and further, in societies having no written language, a good-bad distinction seems nevertheless to exist. The nearest approach to an explanation of the distinction seems to be that, "by a cumulation of obvious superiorities, both of character and standing, as well as of language, some persons are felt to be better models of conduct and speech than others."

1-0-0-0

Brazziel, W. R., and Terrell, Mary. An experiment in the development of readiness in a culturally disadvantaged group of first-grade children. *J. of Negro Education* (1962) 31: 4–7.

Significant gains in both reading and number readiness of disadvantaged Negro children are reported as the result of parent-child orientation activities and an intensified teacher-parent program to promote readiness.

5-3-2-0

Brittain, C. V. Preschool programs for culturally deprived children. *Children* (1966) 13: 130–34.

Selected programs and some of their preliminary results are briefly discussed.

1-0-1-0

Bromwich, Rose. Developing the language of young disadvantaged children. *The Education Digest* (Sept., 1968) 19–22.

Two approaches to the teaching of verbal skills to disadvantaged children—the prescriptive-instructional approach, assuming that the teacher knows best, and the developmental approach, assuming that the child will select experiences to meet his own needs—are rejected. The author proposes instead a third approach in which the child is encouraged to verbalize in an atmosphere in which his attempts to communicate are valued.

1-0-1-4

Brown, R. W., and Ford, Marguerite. Address in American English. *J. of Abnormal and Social Psychology* (1961) 62: 375–85.

The regularities and semantic implications of forms of address (i.e., calling a person by his first name, or by his title plus his last name) were studied in data taken from American literature as well as from actual and reported usage by given populations.

3-0-0-0

Burks, Ann, and Guilford, Polly. Wakulla county oral language project. *Elementary English* (1969) 46: 606–11.

The use of audio-lingual methods to teach standard English to Negro school children is discussed. A list of phonological variations between the Negro dialect and standard English is included.

5-3-2-2

Caldwell, Bettye, and Richmond, J. Programmed day care for the very young child—a preliminary report. *J. of Marriage and the Family* (1964) 26: 481–88.

A center to be operated as a special project is proposed, to study the influence of maternal deprivation on very young children while also providing quality day care for these children. The research literature dealing with maternal deprivation is reviewed, and the proposed center program and research are described. Language skills have a high priority in the center's training program.

5-1,3-1-0

Caplan, S., and Ruble, R. A study of culturally imposed factors on school achievement in a metropolitan area. *J. of Educational Research* (1964) 58: 16–21.

Factors inhibiting school achievement are related to the bilingual backgrounds of junior high school students in the southwestern United States.

2-2-2-0

Carson, A. S., and Rabin, A. I. Verbal comprehension and communication in Negro and white children. *J. of Educational Psychology* (1960) 51: 47–51.

Groups of northern-white, northern-Negro, and southern-Negro children, matched for age, grade, sex, and level of tested verbal comprehension, were compared on assessments of vocabulary ability in verbal communication.

White children were found advanced over Negro children, and northern Negro children were advanced over those from the south.

4-1,3-2-3

Cazden, Courtney B. Subcultural differences in child language: an inter-disciplinary review. *Merrill-Palmer Quarterly* (1966) 12: 185–219.

A key issue is to determine the ways in which the language used by children in various subcultural groups is simply different, and the extent to which such language differences can be considered as deficiencies by some criteria. Research bearing on this issue is reviewed under three main topics: (1) describing nonstandard English and assessing its possible deficiencies, (2) viewing language in terms of a developmental continuum, and (3) considering the different functions fulfilled by language usage.

1-0-0-0-*

———. Three sociolinguistic views of the language of lower-class children—with special attention to the work of Basil Bernstein. *Developmental Medicine and Applied Neurology*, in press.

Sociolinguists' descriptions of language differences between lower- and middle-class children are discussed, and some implications for education are presented.

1-0-0-0

Clark, Ann D., and Richards, Charlotte J. Auditory discrimination among economically disadvantaged and nondisadvantaged preschool children. *Exceptional Children* (1966) 33: 259–62.

The Wepman Test of Auditory Discrimination was given to economically disadvantaged and nondisadvantaged preschool children. Results indicated that the disadvantaged group was deficient in auditory discrimination. Suggestions are made for alterations in the education of such children.

2-0-1-0

Clasen, E. E.; Spear, Jo Ellen; and Tomaro, M. P. A comparison of the relative effectiveness of two types of preschool compensatory programming. *J. of Educational Research* (1969) 62: 401–405.

Children from low-income families were randomly assigned to two treatments during an eight-week Head Start program. One group received intensive language training based on the Peabody Language Development Kit, and the other group received more conventional, socially oriented training only incidentally related to language skills. The group receiving language training made superior progress during the training period, and their advantage persisted over a year of kindergarten.

5-1-1-3

Cohn, W. On the language of lower-class children. *School Review* (1959) 67: 435–40.

The general distinctions and respective roles of standard English and lower-class dialects are briefly discussed. Effective teaching of standard English to lower-class children must incorporate an understanding and respect of the nature and function of their dialects.

1-1,3-2-2

Conners, C. K.; Schuette, Corinne; and Goldman, Ann. Informational analysis of intersensory communication in children of different social class. *Child Development* (1967) 38: 251–66.

Information theory methods are used to determine the separate contributions of shape, size, and angle of stimuli to transfer of information in five-, six-, nine-, and twelve-year-old children from middle- and lower-class backgrounds. Social class was found to have a marked effect on all three dimensions, particularly for five-year-olds.

4-1-2-3

Conville, Mozella. Language improvement for disadvantaged elementary school youngsters. *Speech Teacher* (1969) 28: 120–23.

A summer reading program, designed to aid those students who were having difficulty learning to read in regular school is discussed. The author reports several activities, including dramatic play and use of tape recorders, which she used to improve the language performance of the students in her classes.

5-1,3-2-4

Coulthard, R. M., and Robinson, W. P. The structure of the nominal group and elaboratedness of code. *Language and Speech* (1968) 11: 234–50.

Linguistic analysis of the grammatical structure and vocabulary of six-year-old working-class girls was performed. Participation in a daily language program and high IQ were found to be associated with a higher incidence of nominal groups in clauses, compound modification, complex rankshifted qualifiers, and a wider range of adjectives.

2-1-2-2

Davis, A. L. Dialect research and the needs of the schools. *Elementary English* (1968) 45: 558–59.

A brief description is given of the existing studies in dialect research which aim for more efficient teaching methods.

1-1,3-2-2

————. Teaching language and reading to disadvantaged Negro children. *Elementary English* (1965) 42: 791–97.

The problems involved in teaching lower class Negro children are described, and suggestions are made for teaching programs and teacher training to overcome these problems.

1-3-2-0

Dawe, Helen. A study of the effects of an educational program upon language development and related mental functions in young children. *J. of Experimental Education* (1942) 11: 200–209.

A study was designed to investigate the effects of enrichment training on the language development and related mental functions of preschool and kindergarten orphanage children. At the end of fifty hours of training, the experimental group was found to be superior to a matched control group on tests of vocabulary, tests of general information, IQ, and reading readiness tests. Children receiving training had improved in language ability as measured by mean sentence length and sentence complexity.

4-1-1-3

DeBoer, J. J. Some sociological factors in language development. *Elementary English* (1952) 29: 482–92.

Research literature is reviewed on language development and the following topics related to language development: (1) social class and socioeconomic factors, (2) bilingualism, and (3) effects of mass media.

1-0-0-0

————. Oral and written language. *Review of Educational Research* (1955) 25: 107–20.

This review of research describes several studies in the area of language and social class.

1-0-0-0

Deutsch, M. Facilitating development in the pre-school child: social and psychological perspectives. *Merrill-Palmer Quarterly* (1964) 10: 249–63.

The situation which develops when the lower-status child encounters the school system is discussed, and some of the causes of this situation are posited.

A compensatory program for three- and four-year-old children is proposed in order to remedy deficiencies of the children at these ages and possibly prevent future difficulties in school. It is also suggested that such a program might serve as a bridge between the child's home and school environments, thus facilitating his adjustment to school requirements.

1-0-1-0

———. Social and psychological perspectives on the development of the disadvantaged learner. *J. of Negro Education* (1964) 33: 232–44.

The position is taken that there is an interrelationship between environment and psychological development. Suggestions are made for school curricula to aid in overcoming the influence of the environment for disadvantaged children.

1-0-2-0

———. The role of social class in language development and cognition. *American J. of Orthopsychiatry* (1965) 25: 78–88.

The major objective was to delineate the major dimensions through which environment is likely to inhibit linguistic and cognitive development. Interrelationships among language and selected demographic variables were based upon the assessments of 292 children. Membership in lower-class or minority groups was associated with poorer language functioning, as compared with groups having more favorable environmental circumstances. This distinction was more evident for fifth- than for first-grade children, a finding which suggests that environmentally deprived children are susceptible to a "cumulative deficit phenomenon." The differences in language functioning generally indicate that "denotative and labeling usage" characterizes an inhibition of linguistic as well as cognitive development, as contrasted with "abstract and categorical" usage.

3-0-2-0-*

Deutsch, M., and Brown, B. Social influences in Negro-white intelligence differences. *J. of Social Issues* (1964) 20: 24–35.

IQ data were obtained from a sample of urban public-school children stratified by race, grade level (first and fifth), and social class. Negro children's IQs were lower than those of white children and the differences were greater as groups of higher social-class level were compared.

2-1,3-2-0

Dillard, J. L. The English teacher and the language of the newly integrated student. *Teacher's College Record* (1967) 69: 115–20.

Descriptions are given of the background, development, and implications of Negro dialect, with an outline of school programs such as teaching "English as a second language."

3-3-2-1,4

Drazek, S. J. Training 30,000 Head Start teachers. *School & Society* (1966) 94: 130–31.

The conception and implementation of a specific Head Start teacher-training program are briefly described.

1-0-0-0

Dunn, Charleta. The characteristics and the measured language arts abilities of deprived youth in the School Desegregation Institute. *Elementary English* (1969) 46: 266–72.

The results of a pilot program in total school desegregation are discussed. Results of several language and achievement tests given to the students before and after the program are reported. Interpersonal relations among students and between students and teachers in the program are also discussed.

5-1,3-2-3

Edmonds, W. Sex differences in the verbal ability of socio-economically depressed groups. *J. of Educational Research* (1964) 58: 61–64.

In a study involving southern high-school students in economically depressed areas, it was found that the socioeconomic status of a child is a far more consistent index of his verbal ability than is sex. The differences between verbal ability of boys and girls are not statistically significant within deprived groups. The results of the study also indicate that there are different levels of ability among children of low socioeconomic status, just as there are among middle- and upper-class children.

2-0-2-3

Eells, K. Some implications for school practice of the Chicago studies of cultural bias in intelligence tests. *Harvard Educational Review* (1953) 23: 284–97.

The concept of cultural bias in intelligence tests is discussed in great detail. The purpose of measuring intelligence is questioned, as are the possibilities for developing "culture free' intelligence tests. Suggestions are made for developing "culture fair" tests.

1-0-0-0

Effrat, A.; Feldman, R.; and Sapolsky, H. Inducing poor children to learn. *The Public Interest* (Spring 1969) 106–12.

The authors propose that schools should offer rewards for achievement in terms of the values of the children involved. Since the values of the lower classes in America are primarily materialistic, they claim, schools should reward disadvantaged children's achievements with monetary payment. Advantages and disadvantages of such a situation are discussed.

1-0-2-0

Eisenberg, L.; Berlin, C.; Dill, Anne; and Sheldon, F. Class and race effects on the intelligibility of monosyllables. *Child Development* (1968) 39: 1077–89.

Negro and white school children from low and middle socioeconomic groups listened to Negro and white, educated and uneducated, females read lists of monosyllables. Educated speakers, regardless of race, were found to be most intelligible to listeners of their own race. Negro children showed generally poorer listening scores than whites.

4-1,3-2-3

Elam, Sophie. Acculturation and learning problems of Puerto Rican children. *Teachers College Record* (1960) 61: 258–64.

In a general (and subjective) account of the author's experience with Puerto Rican school children, language disability is seen as both a symptom and a factor of learning problems.

3-2-2-4

Ellis, D. S. Speech and social status in America. *Social Forces* (1967) 45: 431–37.

A review of several studies dealing with speech as a determinent of social status is presented. Several possible repercussions of lower-class speech are also discussed.

1-0-0-0

Entwisle, Doris. Developmental sociolinguistics: a comparative study in four subcultural settings. *Sociometry* (1966) 29: 67–84.

Linguistic development of several groups of children from four different subcultural settings is measured by the number of paradigmatic responses given to words of different form classes and frequencies. Although the sequence of development appears to be constant, it varies on the age continuum (ages five to ten) for different subcultural groups.

2-1,3-2-3

———. Subcultural differences in children's language development. *International J. of Psychology* (1968) 3: 13–22.

Paradigmatic responses on a word association task of first-, third-, and fifth-grade children matched for IQ were examined. Results were surprising in two respects: (1) Rural Maryland children fell behind suburban Maryland children, even when matched by age, IQ, and social status. (2) First-grade white children in the slums of Baltimore City, Maryland performed better than first grade-white suburban children, and first-grade Negro slum children equalled the performance of white suburban children.

2-1,3-2-3

———. Developmental sociolinguistics: inner-city children. *The American J. of Sociology* (1968) 74: 37–49.

Word-association responses suggest that first-grade white slum children are more advanced in linguistic development than suburban white children of the same intelligence level. Reasons for and implications of this finding are discussed.

2-1,3-2-3

Erickson, F. 'F'get you Honky!': a new look at black dialect and the school. *Elementary English* (1969) 46: 495–517.

Reports of a research project, "Sounds of Society" indicate, that if Bernstein's restricted and elaborated language codes are used to mean "high-context" and "low-context" communication styles, there is no indication that either inner-city black people or suburban white people are bound exclusively to either style. The data also indicated that the language used by the black speakers was adequate for communication of abstractions when the researcher shared the context of the speakers. It is suggested that allowing the use of the black dialect in the classroom would result in a high-context and thus more productive communication situation for the black child.

5-1,3-2-4-*

Fuschillo, Jean. Enriching the preschool experience of children from age three: II. The evaluation. *Children* (1968) 15: 140–43.

Children involved in a preschool program administered by Howard University were compared with a group of similar children not involved in the program.

The children receiving preschool enrichment were found to have greater gains in IQ than the children who had no enrichment.

5-3-1-3

Gahagan, Georgina, and Gahagan, D. M. Paired-associate learning as partial validation of a language development program. *Child Development* (1968) 39: 1119–31.

Children, ages 6.9 to 7.3 years, were asked to produce sentences linking the stimulus and response words of items presented pictorially. Children who had participated in a language development program produced more different verbs linking the stimulus and response items and took fewer trials to criterion than either of two control groups.

4-0-2-3

Gladney, Mildred R., and Leaverton, L. A model for teaching standard English to nonstandard English speakers. *Elementary English* (1968) 45: 758–63.

Recognizing the functional distinction between "school talk" and "everyday talk," the program attempted to elicit the former in informal settings. Results were assessed as favorable.

5-3-2-4

Goldfarb, W. The effects of psychological deprivation in infancy and subsequent stimulation. *American J. of Psychiatry* (1945) 102: 18–33.

Institutionalized children who had been transferred to foster homes at the age of thirty-seven months were found inferior (at age forty-three months) on a number of performance variables to a matched group of family-reared foster children. The language deficiency of the formerly institutionalized group seemed to be a specific retarding factor, a finding compatible with previous studies which indicated this effect even up to the age of eight-and-one-half years.

2-0-1-3

Gordon, E. G. Characteristics of socially disadvantaged children. *Review of Educational Research* (1965) 35: 377–88.

Some emphasis is given to reviewing studies which describe the language, cognition, and intelligence of disadvantaged children.

1-0-0-0-*

Green, G. Negro dialect, the last barrier to integration. *J. of Negro Education* (1962) 31: 81–83.

The speech of the majority of American Negroes is seen as the major obstacle to the Negro's successful entrance into a predominantly white world.

2-3-0-4

Gumperz, J. J. Types of linguistic communities. *Anthropological Linguistics* (1962) 4: 28–40.

Whereas the linguistic concept of a speech community is oriented toward defining speakers who share a language, with stylistic variants, dialects and the like often receiving relatively secondary attention, the present concept of linguistic community places stress upon intralanguage variation. The linguistic community is defined as "a social group which may be either monolingual or multilingual, held together by frequency of social interaction patterns and set off from the surrounding areas by weakness in lines of communication."

1-0-0-0-*

Harms, L. S. Listener comprehension of speakers of three status groups. *Language and Speech* (1961) 4: 109–129

Listeners from different social strata heard short recorded messages from speakers of different social status. After listening, the respondents attempted to replace words which had been systematically deleted from a written version of the messages. Based upon degree of word replacement, speakers of high status were found the most comprehensible. The same criterion also indicated that listeners were most successful in comprehension when responding to speakers of their own status rating.

4-0-0-3

———. Listener judgements of status cues in speech. *Quarterly J. of Speech* (1961) 47: 164–68.

Listeners from different social strata were capable of rating the social status of an individual after hearing from ten to fifteen seconds of his tape recorded speech. Listeners also rated the high-status speakers as more "credible" than low status speakers.

4-0-0-3

———. Status cues in speech: extra-race and extra-region identification. *Lingua* (1963) 12: 300–306.

Tape-recorded speech samples of Negro speakers from Washington, D.C. were presented to untrained midwestern college students who rated the speakers in terms of their suspected social status. Results indicated a significant correlation (.94) between these ratings and ratings previously obtained from listeners living in the same region as the speakers, as well a significant correlation (.88) between the midwestern ratings and an objective index of the social statuses of the speakers.

4-0-0-3

Hawkins, R. A speech program in an experimental college for the disadvantaged. *Speech Teacher* (1969) 28: 115–19.

A program in higher education for low-income youth is described, including problems encountered in teaching speech, drama, and poetry-reading in the program.

5-1,3-2-0

Herman, S. Explorations in the social psychology of language choice. *Human Relations* (1961) 14: 149–64.

A bilingual's choice to employ one of his alternative languages may be influenced by: (1) factors in the general or background situation, (2) personal needs (such as greater facility in one language than the others), or (3) demands of the immediate situation. His choice will depend on the relative saliency of these factors. It is suggested that the choice of language, once a choice has been made, may serve as an index of group preferences and social adjustment. Analysis of the determinants of the language choice may also have relevance to the problem of second-language learning.

1-0-0-0

Hess, R. D. Educability and rehabilitation: the future of the welfare class. *J. of Marriage and the Family* (1964) 26: 422–29.

An argument is presented that present welfare policies may be perpetuating a permanent "welfare class" because they overlook the possibility that behavior leading to social, educational, and economic poverty is socialized in early childhood.

1-0-0-0

Hess, R. D., and Shipman, Virginia. Early blocks to children's learning. *Children* (1965) 12: 189–94.

This research pursues the argument that early social experience shapes cognitive capabilities and that the most significant facet of this early experience is the mother-child interaction. Specifically, it is posed that the structure of early experiences shapes communication and language, and that language subsequently shapes thought and cognitive styles of problem solving. The study centered upon mother-child dyads drawn from Negro families representing four different socioeconomic groups. Results of various situations of mother-child interactions led to the conclusion that maternal teaching style was as predictive of children's performance as maternal IQ and social-class variables combined.

5-1,3-1-3

———. Early experience and the socialization of cognitive modes in children. *Child Development* (1965) 36: 869–86.

The research question is: "what is cultural deprivation and how does it act to shape and depress the resources of the human mind?" Three arguments in considering answers to this question are: (1) behavior associated with social, educational, and economic poverty is socialized in early childhood; (2) a key aspect in the effects of cultural deprivation is in the lack of cognitive meaning in mother-child communication; and (3) growth of cognitive processes is fostered by family control systems that permit a wide range of alternatives of action and thought in the child, as contrasted with systems that offer predetermined solutions and little freedom for alternatives. Mother-child interaction data were gathered from Negro families representing four different social-status levels, ranging from families with mother on public welfare to families with college-educated fathers. Selected measures of language behavior (e.g., number of utterances, sentence length, incidence of certain types of words) were interpreted with reference to Bernstein's theory of restricted and elaborated codes. Additional assessments included types of statements involved in interactions as well as accomplishment of certain types of cooperative tasks. Results are interpreted as supportive of the arguments expressed above and generally indicative of the overall generalization: "the meaning of deprivation is a deprivation of meaning—a cognitive environment in which behavior is controlled by status rules rather than by attention to the individual characteristics of a specific situation and one in which behavior is not mediated by verbal cues or by teaching that relates events to one another and the present to the future."

5-3-1,3-3-*

Higgins, C., and Sivers, Cathryne. A comparison of Stanford-Binet and Colored Raven Progressive Matrices IQs for children with low socioeconomic status. *J. of Consulting Psychology* (1958) 22: 465–68.

In a population of children of low socioeconomic status (ages seven through eleven) no support was found for the belief that the social bias in the verbal parts of the Stanford-Binet depressed IQ measures below a nonverbal, nonso-cially-biased IQ measure (Colored Raven Progressive Matrices test).

5-1,3-2-0

Hill, E. H., and Giammatteo, M. C. Socio-economic status and its relationship to school achievement in the elementary school. *Elementary English* (1963) 40: 265–70.

Third-grade children participated in a study designed to investigate the rela-tionship of socioeconomic status to vocabulary achievement, reading compre-hension, arithmetic skill, problem solving, and a composite of these skills. Tests used were: Otis Quick-Scoring Mental Ability Test, Iowa Tests of Basic Skills, and the Scott-Foresman Basic Reading Tests. It was found that children of high socioeconomic status were superior to children from low socioeco-nomic status on all measures.

2-1,3-2-3

Hockett, C. F. Age-grading and linguistic continuity. *Language* (1950) 26: 449–57.

Practically nothing is known about the transmission of linguistic habits from one generation to the next, but there are undoubtedly strong environmental influences at work. One of the most important forces at work shaping the child's dialect is the speech of other children.

1-0-1,2-0

Horn, T. D. Three methods of developing reading readiness in Spanish-speak-ing children in first grade. *The Reading Teacher* (1966) 20: 38–42.

Results were relatively inconclusive but revealed a spectrum of needs for dealing with the Spanish-speaking disadvantaged child.

5-2-2-3

Howard, D. P. The needs and problems of socially disadvantaged children as perceived by students and teachers. *Exceptional Children* (1968) 34: 327–35.

Fourth- and fifth-grade disadvantaged students and teachers from their schools were administered the SRA Junior Inventory to establish their under-standing of the needs and problems of the children. Teachers were found to differ markedly from students by suggesting that the home rather than the school was the source of student frustration. Other teacher-student differences are discussed.

5-1,3-2-0

Hunt, J. McV. The psychological basis for using pre-school enrichment as an antidote for cultural deprivation. *Merrill-Palmer Quarterly* (1964) 10: 209–48.

Cultural deprivation is seen as "a failure to provide an opportunity for infants and young children to have the experiences required for adequate development of those semiautonomous central processes demanded for acquiring skill in the use of linguistic and mathematical symbols and for the analysis of causal relationships." Such a position argues in favor of carefully guided enrichment programs for culturally deprived children.

1-0-1-0-*

Hurst, C. G., and Jones, W. L. Psychosocial concomitants of sub-standard speech. *J. of Negro Education* (1966) 35: 409–21.

The relationships of certain psychological, sociological, and attitudinal variables to levels of speech proficiency of Negro college students were investigated in order to establish the existence and extent of psychosocial correlates of environmentally induced speech and language deficiencies.

5-3-2-3,4

————. Generating spontaneous speech in the underprivileged child. *J. of Negro Education* (1967) 36: 362–67.

A situation is reported where, even with biracial workers, traditional methods for generating speech in three- and four-year-old underprivileged Negro girls were ineffective, particularly as compared with their speech among peers.

5-3-1-4

Hymes, D. Introduction: toward ethnographies of communication. In *The ethnography of communication,* edited by J. J. Gumperz and D. Hymes. *American Anthropologist* Special Publication (1964) 66: No. 6, Part 2, 1–34.

The argument is advanced that it is an "ethnography of communication" which "must provide the frame of reference within which the place of language in culture and society is to be described." This focus implies two main considerations: (1) the direct investigation of the use of language in the contexts of situations so as to discern patterns which escape more traditional linguistic, sociological, or psychological approaches, and (2) the consideration of the "community" as the frame of reference for study.

1-0-0-0-*

438   Bibliography

Irwin, O. C. Infant speech: the effect of family occupational status and of age on use of sound types. *J. of Speech and Hearing Disorders* (1948) 13: 224–26.

Infants (one through thirty months) from laboring-class families develop speech sounds at a slower rate than infants from families representing a business, clerical, or professional class.

2-1-1-2

————. Infant speech: the effect of family occupational status and of age on sound frequency. *J. of Speech and Hearing Disorders* (1948) 13: 320–23.

At the age of between eighteen and thirty months, infants from laboring-class families have a lower frequency of speech-sound utterances than do infants from families representing a business, clerical, or professional class. Prior to this age, the two classes show no difference.

2-1-1-2

————. Speech development in the young child: 2. Some factors related to the speech development of the infant and young child. *J. of Speech and Hearing Disorders* (1952) 17: 269–78.

The occurrence of types of phonemes and phoneme frequency was studied in the speech of various populations of infants ranging in age from birth to two-and-one-half years. Selected findings included: (1) no differences between white and Negro infants; (2) no difference according to occupational status of parents until the age of about eighteen months, then those infants reared in a home where the occupational status is unskilled tend to lag in development behind higher status counterparts, and (3) differences showing delayed development in orphanage children, as compared with infants living in their own homes.

2-1,3-1-2

Ivey, Sara; Center, W.; and Tanner, Nancy. Effect of cultural deprivation on language development. *The Southern Speech J.* (1968) 34: 28–36.

On the basis of testing forty first-grade children using the Illinois Test of Psycholinguistic Abilities, the authors concluded that cultural deprivation does affect language development, and that there is no unique relationship between race and cultural deprivation taken separately.

2-1,3-2-3

Jackson, J. A survey of psychological, social and environmental differences between advanced and retarded readers. *The J. of Genetic Psychology* (1944) 65: 113–31.

Approximately three hundred advanced and three hundred retarded readers (the upper and low quartiles based upon reading tests administered to children in grades two through six) were compared on various psychological, social, and environmental factors. Among the distinguishing factors were: (1) family economic status, poor readers tending to come from poor families, as compared with advanced readers who tended to come from families of relatively "good" economic status; (2) parental education, advanced readers' parents having more education than their counterparts; and (3) to some extent, father's occupation, tending toward professional classes for the advanced readers, as compared with unskilled classes for the poor readers.

2-1-2-0

John, Vera. The intellectual development of slum children: some preliminary findings. *American J. of Orthopsychiatry* (1963) 33: 813–22.

First- and fifth-grade Negro children from lower, upper-lower, and middle class homes were administered tests measuring language use. The first-grade sample showed no significant differences between social classes on any of the tests given. However, the fifth-grade sample showed that the middle-class children performed significantly better on the Peabody Picture Vocabulary Test, integration tests, IQ, and WISC vocabulary. In a sorting task, the lower-class fifth graders sorted illustrated cards into more piles, and were less able to explain the bases of their sorting than middle-class fifth graders.

2-3-2-3

John, Vera and Goldstein, L. The social context of language acquisition. *Merrill-Palmer Quarterly* (1964) 10: 265–75.

The hypothesis is advanced that the shift in a child's use of words for labeling specific referents, to his use of language for signifying categories of objects, action, or attributes varies in rate and breadth according to social context, and that this shift has consequences upon the child's cognitive development. The dynamics of language acquisition are seen generally in terms of two variables: (1) stability in experiencing word-referent relationships, and (2) frequency and type of verbal interaction during language acquisition. More specifically, the latter variable refers to "the amount of corrective feedback the child receives while learning a new label." The lower-class child is seen as lacking the opportunity to have as much experience with the foregoing variables as the middle-class child. Further topics include how language capabilities affect cognitive functioning and how all of the foregoing has implications for the preschool enrichment programs.

1-1,3-1-0-*

Kagan, J. His struggle for identity. *Saturday Review,* Dec. 7, 1968, 80–88.

The importance of the parent-child relationship to the psychological growth of the child is stressed. Informal reports of social-class differences in children's cognitive development are given, and these differences are explained by relating them to the parent-child relationship.

1-0-1-0-*

Karnes, M.; Hodgins, Audrey; and Teska, J. A. An evaluation of two preschool programs for disadvantaged children: a traditional and a highly structured experimental preschool. *Exceptional Children* (1968) 34: 667–76.

A traditional nursery school program and an experimental preschool program focused on specific learning skills are compared. The experimental program proved significantly more effective in promoting language abilities, intellectual functioning, perceptual development, and school readiness.

5-1,3-1-3

Katz, Phyllis. Verbal discrimination performance of disadvantaged children: stimulus and subject variables. *Child Development* (1967) 38: 233–42.

Performance of disadvantaged Negro boys on a discrimination task indicated that differences between good and poor readers were smaller for unfamiliar stimuli, suggesting that both perceptual skills and stimulus familiarity factors play a role in children's discrimination.

2-3-2-3

Kellmer-Pringle, M. L., and Bossio, Victoria. A study of deprived children. Part II: language development and reading attainment. *Vita Humana* (1958) 1: 142–70.

Here, "deprived" refers mainly to the effect of institutionalization upon the language and reading capabilites of children. Although pertinent international literature is reviewed, the concern is primarily with British children. Measures of language are typically standardized, commercially available tests. The general conclusion not only argues that institutionalized children are retarded in language skills, but attempts to define some of the details of such retardation.

3-1-2-3

Kellmer-Pringle, M. L., and Tanner, Margaret. The effects of early deprivation on speech development: a comparative study of 4-year-olds in a nursery school and in residential nurseries. *Language and Speech* (1958) 1: 269–87.

Preschool children represented two matched (age, sex, intelligence, family background) groups distinguished by the fact that the nursery school group lived with their own families while the second group lived in a residential nursery. Measures of verbal development included vocabulary and sentence structure, obtained under both controlled and spontaneous conditions, as well as rating of expressive ability obtained in social discourse. Results indicated that children in the residential nursery showed some retardation in all language skills as compared with the family-based group.

2-1-1-3

Kittrell, Flemmie P. Enriching the preschool experience children from age 3: I. The program. *Children*(1968) 15: 135–39.

A Howard University nursery school program is described. Procedures for selecting children are given, and activities designed to involve the parents in the child's education are outlined.

5-3-1-0

Kofsky, Ellin. The effects of verbal training on concept identification in disadvantaged children. *Psychonomic Science* (1967) 7: 365–66.

Although verbal training showed results in itself, concept identification did not improve as a result of such training.

4-3-1-3

Krauss, R. M., and Rotter, G. S. Communication abilities of children as a function of status and age. *Merrill-Palmer Quarterly* (1968) 14: 160–73.

Novel graphic designs were named by middle- and lower-status boys aged seven and twelve. A group of boys of matching age and status characteristics were then asked to identify the designs from the names. Results indicated that twelve-year-olds were superior to seven-year-olds at naming and at identifying. Relatively small differences were found between middle- and lower-status boys on both tasks, with middle-status boys superior. No support was obtained for the hypothesis that intrastatus communication is more effective than interstatus communication.

4-1,3-2-3

LaCivita, Alice; Kean, J. M.; and Yamamoto, K. Socio-economic status of children and acquisition of grammar. *J. of Educational Research* (1966) 60: 71–74.

Children from grades two, four, and six were tested in an investigation of the relationship between socioeconomic status and acquisition of grammar. The children were individually presented with six sentences containing nonsense words, and were asked to guess the meaning of the nonsense word in each sentence. Grammatical signals (such as "-ed" ending) and syntactic position were used as cues to suggest three parts of speech—nouns, verbs, and modifiers. Responses were labeled as either homogeneous or heterogeneous. Although children from the higher socioeconomic group were expected to have a linguistic advantage over those from the lower socioeconomic group, no difference was found between the two classes in terms of homogeneity of responses.

5-0-2-3

Lambert, W. E. Psychological approaches to the study of language. Part II: On second-language learning and bilingualism. *The Modern Language J.* (1963) 47: 114–21.

Social-psychological implications of second-language learning are introduced and discussed. Particular emphasis is given to the theoretical position that, as an individual successfully acquires a second language, he tends to adapt various cultural traits which characterize users of that language. His success in learning the second language is believed to depend upon his own ethnocentric tendencies and his attitudes toward the users of the second language. Discrepancies between the two cultures may lead the second language learner to "experience feelings of chagrin or regret as he loses ties in one group, mixed with the fearful anticipation of entering a relatively new group," a feeling referred to as *anomie*. Studies of various bilingual groups are discussed.

1-0-0-0-*

Larson, R., and Olson, J. L. A method of identifying culturally deprived kindergarten children. *Exceptional Children* (1963) 30: 130–34.

In an attempt to develop a working definition of cultural deprivation in children, four main aspects of contrasting behavior are defined: language development, self-concept, social skills, and cultural differences (i.e., norms). Language development is assessed by selected standardized tests (e.g., Illinois Test of Psycholinguistic Abilities).

1-0-2-4

Lawton, D. Social class language differences in group discussions. *Language and Speech* (1964) 7: 183–204.

An analysis of the oral speech of lower- and middle-class boys yielded results supportive of Bernstein's restricted-elaborated code distinction. Lower-class boys were found to use fewer "uncommon" adjectives and adverbs, fewer personal pronouns and passive verbs, and simpler syntactic structures than middle-class boys.

4-1-2-3

―――. Social class differences in language development: a study of some samples of written work. *Language and Speech* (1963) 6: 120–42.

In an investigation of Bernstein's restricted-elaborated codes distinction, language differences were found between lower- and middle-class boys in terms of vocabulary, certain form-class usages (adjectives, adverbs, pronouns, passive verbs), and sentence structure. In written essays, the lower-class boys were found to use a narrower vocabulary and simpler sentence structures.

4-1-2-3

Lerman, P. Argot, symbolic deviance and subcultural delinquency. *American Sociological Review* (1967) 32: 209–24.

In a study emphasizing the importance of verbal deviance (such as slang) in the identification of subcultural delinquents, it was found that the combined index of argot and peer values provides a means of identifying persons participating in delinquent subcultures. The sociological aspects of nonstandard speech are discussed, and the point is made that "people who share modes of verbal communication are likely to share participation in a social and cultural community as well."

1-0-0-0

Lessler, K., and Fox, R. E. An evaluation of a Head Start program in a low population area. *J. of Negro Education* (1969) 38: 46–54.

In an evaluation of Head Start programs in North Carolina, the researchers report gains in several areas for the participating children. The most significant of these were the increased sensitivity and receptiveness to the spoken word on the part of both Negro and white children in the program. Improved verbal skills are also reported.

5-1,3-1-2

Loban, W. Teaching children who speak social class dialects. *Elementary English* (1968) 45: 592–99, 618.

A program devised to teach standard English to children who speak social class dialects is described through use of examples.

1-3-2-0

Lorenzo, L.D., and Salter, Ruth. An evaluative study of prekindergarten programs for educationally disadvantaged children: followup and replication. *Exceptional Children* (1968) 35: 111–19.

Results of an enrichment program for preschool disadvantaged children are summarized. Gains in IQ, language development, and reading readiness are reported.

5-1,3-1-3

McCarthy, Dorothea. Factors that influence language growth: home influences. *Elementary English* (1952) 29: 421–28, 440.

Factors in the home that serve to influence the child's language development include: amount of contact between mother and child, kind of relationship between mother and child, active participation in conversation in the home, disciplinary methods used in the home, bilingualism, and attitude of parents toward books and reading. General suggestions are made for remedial work with children who have language difficulties.

1-0-1,2-0

McDavid, R. I., Jr. Variations in standard American English. *Elementary English* (1968) 45: 561–63.

A brief historical survey of dialect differences is given along with specific examples of present-day linguistic variations.

3-0-0-4

Marge, M. The influence of selected home background variables on the development of oral communication skills in children. *J. of Speech and Hearing Research* (1965) 8: 291–309.

In a study involving 143 preadolescent children and their parents, the children were evaluated on forty speech and language measures by classroom teachers and speech specialists. It was found that (1) children of permissive mothers were more mature in language usage, (2) high educational expectations on the part of parents were related to better speaking ability on the part of children, and (3) parental correction and emphasis on proper language usage, together with parent-child interaction in the home, lead to better general speaking ability of children.

4-0-2-3

Mattleman, Marciene, and Emans, R. The language of the inner-city child: a comparison of Puerto Rican and Negro third grade girls. *J. of Negro Education* (1969) 38: 173–77.

Data on language facility, syntax, and fluency were gathered from five Negro and six Puerto Rican girls. Analysis indicated that these two groups should not be lumped together in any discussion of language difficulties of the disadvantaged.

2-2,3-2-3

May, F. The effects of environment on oral language development. *Elementary English* (1966) 43: 720–29.

The home and the school are seen as important forces shaping the development of the child's language. In the home such factors as extent of adult contact, amount and kinds of parental pressure, and socioeconomic position influence language. In the school, language development of the child can be influenced by specific practice in voice control, articulation, and word usage.

1-0-0-0

Menyuk, Paula. Children's learning and reproduction of grammatical and nongrammatical phonological sequences. *Child Development* (1968) 39: 849–59.

Children, preschool through second grade, were found to have greater difficulty reproducing nongrammatical utterances, and took more time to process them. The author concludes that nongrammaticality of phonological sequences affects reproductions at an early age, but not perception and storage.

4-0-1,2-3

Milner, Esther. A study of the relationship between reading readiness in grade one school children and patterns of parent-child interaction. *Child Development* (1951) 22: 95–112.

Results of a study involving groups of first-grade children differentiated by parental social status indicated: (1) a positive relationship between social status and "language IQ," and (2) that children from higher status families had a richer verbal environment in the home than those from lower status families. Suggestions are made for origination and testing of preschool remedial programs.

5-0-2-3

Monsees, Edna K., and Berman, Carol. Speech and language screening in a summer Head Start program. *J. of Speech and Hearing Disorders* (1968) 33: 121–26.

A screening test was developed, and some general, practical experiences with it are reported.

5-3-1-2

Mukerji, Rose and Robison, Helen. A head start in language. *Elementary English* (1966) 43: 460–63.

Culturally and economically disadvantaged children in a New York City kindergarten participated in a training program designed to foster language development. The teaching strategies used in the program are described in general terms, along with suggestions for additional activities which might be used in such programs.

5-1,3-1-4

Nash, Rosa Lee. Teaching speech improvement to the disadvantaged. *Speech Teacher* (1967) 16: 69–73.

Describes a program of speech improvement undertaken in schools in New York City as a part of the More Effective Schools program.

3-3-2-4

Newton, Eunice. Section B: Verbal destitution: the pivotal barrier to learning. *J. of Negro Education* (1960) 29: 497–99.

Rather consistent patterns of substandard English usage as well as certain types of precollegiate personal and educational environments were found in case studies of "seriously retarded" readers drawn from a college-level remedial reading program.

5-3-2-3

———. Section D: The culturally deprived child in our verbal schools. *J. of Negro Education* (1962) 31: 184–87.

The language difficulties of the culturally deprived (low socioeconomic status, member of a minority group) child are described, and a language arts program for the school is proposed as a remedy for these difficulties.

3-3-2-2

———. Planning for the language development of disadvantaged children and youth. *J. of Negro Education* (1964) 33: 210–17. (Reprinted in *J. of Negro Education* (1965) 34: 167–77.)

The language difficulties of children from lower socioeconomic strata are described, and a language arts program designed to remedy these difficulties is proposed.

3-3-2-2

Noel, Doris. A comparative study of the relationship between the quality of the child's language usage and the quality and types of language used in the home. *J. of Educational Research* (1953) 47: 161–67.

Results of a study involving 124 students in fourth- through sixth-grade English classes and their families indicated that: (1) there was a relationship between the quality of parents' language usage and the quality of their child's usage, but (2) there were no differences in quality of usage across children grouped in terms of their fathers' occupational categories.

5-0-2-2

Olim, E.; Hess, R.; and Shipman, Virginia. Role of mothers' language styles in mediating their preschool children's cognitive development. *The School Review* (1967) 75: 414–24.

The techniques used by mothers from different social strata in dealing with their children are related to the cognitive development of the children. Correlations are found between social status and mothers' control techniques, mothers' control orientation and mothers' language elaboration, and both mothers' control techniques and language elaboration and children's cognitive development.

4-3-1-4

Osborn, L. R. The Indian pupil in the high school speech class. *Speech Teacher* (1967) 16: 187–89.

Reports the results of a poll of speech teachers in high schools serving Indian populations.

———. Speech communication and the American Indian high school student. *The Speech Teacher* (1968) 17: 38–43.

A high school curriculum for Indian children is formulated, emphasizing the need for understanding the special problems of Indian students. Special concern is given to speech skills and the need to maximize the identity of the student as "Indian."

1-4-2-0

Osser, H.; Wang, Marilyn; and Zaid, Farida. The young child's ability to imitate and comprehend speech: a comparison of two sub-cultural groups. *Child Development*, in press.

Two psycholingusitic tests designed to assess speech imitation and comprehension abilities were administered to lower-class Negro and middle-class white five-year-olds. White middle-class children were found to perform better than the lower-class Negro children, even when dialect differences were taken into consideration. Possible sources of group differences are examined.

4-1,3-1-3

Peisach, Estelle. Children's comprehension of teacher and peer speech. *Child Development* (1965) 36: 467–80.

First- and fifth-grade children, divided according to two social-class levels, race, and sex were subjected to the task of replacing words deleted from language samples obtained from first- and fifth-grade teachers. Generally, there were no significant differences found between first-grade children in terms of the division by social level, although this became a salient distinction in terms of fifth-grade children.

5,1-3,2-3

Piecris, R. Speech and society: a sociological approach to language. *American Sociological Review* (1951) 16: 499–505.

In a generalized discussion, examples from literature and several foreign languages as well as English speech are used to show that language changes generally follow or accompany social changes.

1-0-0-0

Prehm, H. Concept learning in culturally disadvantaged children as a function of verbal pretraining. *Exceptional Children* (1966) 32: 599–604.

In a study involving children living in a slum area with the lowest median income and educational level in a metropolitan area, it was found that verbal pretraining on the stimuli to be used in concept-learning tasks had a significantly positive effect on the child's performance.

5-1,3-1-3

Putnam, G. N., and O'Hern, Edna. The status significance of an isolated urban dialect. Language Dissertation, No. 53. *Language* (1955) 31: No. 4, Part 2.

The research comprises two parts: (1) a description of the dialect spoken by a group of Negroes having extremely low social status, and (2) a study of how persons would rate this dialect along with other Negro dialects in terms of a scale of social position. Detailed descriptions of the dialect phonology and lesser detailed descriptions of morphology and syntax are presented. The correlation between persons' ratings of social status and separate ratings based upon a socioeconomic index was .80. The latter finding is taken as evidence of the importance of speech as a mark of social status.

2-3-3-1,2

Rackstraw, S. J., and Robinson, W. P. Social and psychological factors related to variability of answering behavior in five-year-old children. *Language and Speech* (1967) 10: 88–106.

Children, differing in social class (in London), verbal IQ scores, sex, and an index of mother-child interaction, performed three language tasks and the linguistic structure and vocabulary of the responses were analyzed. Results indicated that middle-class children, especially those with high IQ, tended to use more abstract structure and words, less self-referential speech, more precise words, and were more likely to summarize in their answers.

5-0-1-2

Radin, Norma. Some impediments to the education of disadvantaged children. *Children* (1968) 15: 170–76.

Factors which interfere with the disadvantaged child's progress in school are discussed. Some implications for solutions of the problems are given.

1-0-2-0

Radin, Norma, and Kamii, Constance. The child-rearing attitudes of disadvantaged Negro mothers and some educational implications. *J. of Negro Education* (1965) 34: 138–46.

The lack of ability to verbalize and to think conceptually on the part of lower-class Negro children is seen as resulting from Negro mothers' child-rearing practices, which discourage discussion and communication by the child.

3-3-1-0

Raph, Jane B. Language and speech deficits in culturally disadvantaged children: implications for the speech clinician. *J. of Speech and Hearing Disorders* (1967) 32: 203–14.

The position is developed that the language of disadvantaged children often resembles that of younger-aged privileged children, and that intensive language and perceptual training should be undertaken by the clinician.

1,3-0-1-2

Reinecke, J. E. "Pidgin English" in Hawaii: a local study in the sociology of language. *American J. of Sociology* (1938) 43: 778–89.

The evolution and social implications of "pidgin English" in Hawaii are described. (Generalizations derived in this early paper can be compared in interesting ways with the generalizations of current studies of social class differences in language.)

3-5-0-2

Riessman, F., and Alberts, F. Digging 'the man's' language. *Saturday Review of Literature,* September 17, 1966, 80–81, 98.

A distinction between peoples' primary and secondary languages is described, including the implications of such language distinctions for educational programs.

3-0-0-0

Robinson, W. P. Cloze procedure as a technique for the investigation of social class differences in language usage. *Language and Speech* (1965) 8: 42–55.

In further testing of Bernstein's hypotheses concerning restricted and elaborated language codes, two aspects of the codes were investigated: (1) that there are differences in vocabulary between the two codes, and (2) that the structural elements of the restricted code are more predictable than those of the elaborated code. Results indicated that working-class boys used a more limited vocabulary than middle-class boys, and that the structural elements of working-class language were more predictable than those of middle-class language when a written task was involved.

4-1-2-2

———. The elaborated code in working class language. *Language and Speech* (1965) 8: 243–52.

A test situation was established in which working-class and middle-class boys were asked to write both a formal and an informal letter. According to Bernstein's theory, the working-class child should be at a greater disadvantage in formal situations which his restricted code is not equipped to handle. However, fewer language differences were found in formal letters written by working-class and middle-class children than were found in informal letters written by the same children.

4-1-2-2

Robison, Helen F., and Mukerji, Rose. Language concepts and the disadvantaged. *Educational Leadership* (1965) 23: 133–41.

This study emphasizes the need for an expansion at the kindergarten level of the disadvantaged child's vocabulary, concept formation, and symbolic representation skills through "true life" experiences, such as shopping and free play.

5-0-1-0

Rosenthal, R., and Jacobson, Lenore F. Teacher expectations for the disadvantaged. *Scientific American* (1968) 218: 19–23.

The effects of teachers' expectations on children's school performance are described. Results from several studies are incorporated into the report.

5-0-2-0-*

Ruddell, B., and Graves, Barbara W. Socio-ethnic status and the language achievement of first-grade children. *Elementary English* (1968) 45: 635–43.

The objective was to investigate the relationship between development of syntax and socioethnic status of first-grade children. The number of errors made by low-status Negroes was comparatively greater than high-status whites, although they scored relatively the same when given material unfamiliar to both. Several implications were made for the classroom.

4-1,3-2-2

Salzinger, Suzanne; Salzinger, K.; and Hobson, Sally. The effect of syntactical structure on immediate memory for word sequences in middle- and lower-class children. *J. of Psychology* (1967) 67: 147–59.

Urban Negro lower-status children, aged three to six, were tested for immediate recall of a recorded sentence. Recall ability increased with age and similarity to standard frequency characteristics of English. These results replicated similar findings with white middle-class children. Implications for language acquisition and effects of socioeconomic status on children's speech are discussed.

4-3-1,2-3

Schatzman, L., and Strauss, A. Social class and modes of communication. *American J. of Sociology* (1955) 60: 329–38.

Differences in modes of communication, as revealed in interviews with lower- and middle-class respondents are more than differences in intelligibility, grammar, and vocabulary. Differences are found in number and kinds of perspective, ability to take the listener's role, use of classifying or generalizing terms, and devices of style to order and to implement communication.

3-0-3-0-*

Schwartz, S.; Deutsch, Cynthia; and Weissmann, Ann. Language development in two groups of socially disadvantaged young children. *Psychological Reports* (1967) 21: 169–78.

Results of a prekindergarten-through-third-grade enrichment program for culturally disadvantaged children are reported. A group of children who participated in the enrichment program and a control group who had no enrichment were tested at the beginning of first grade and again at the beginning of second grade on the Illinois Test of Psycholinguistic Abilities. Differences over the two-year period favored the experimental group.

5-1,3-1-3

Scott, R. Head Start before home start? *Merrill-Palmer Quarterly* (1967) 13: 317–21.

The importance of preschool cognitive development for disadvantaged children as necessary for later verbal and nonverbal skill is discussed.

5-0-1-0

Seidel, H. E.; Barkley, Mary Jo; and Stith, Doris. Evaluation of a program for project Head Start. *The J. of Genetic Psychology* (1967) 110: 185–97.

An attempt to evaluate the success of a Head Start program in North Carolina is described. Four tests were administered to selected children in the first and eighth weeks of the program. The only significant change measured in this period was in reading readiness.

5-1,3-1-3

Shuy, R. A selective bibliography on social dialects. *The Linguistic Reporter* (1968) 10: 1–5.

This is a brief listing designed to acquaint readers with a representative sampling of literature in the area. Annotations are included.

1-0-0-0

———. Detroit speech: careless, awkward, and inconsistent, or systematic, graceful, and regular? *Elementary English* (1968) 45: 565–69.

The aims and methodology of the Detroit Dialect Study are briefly presented.

2-1,3-2-1

Sigel, I.; Anderson, L.; and Shapiro, H. Categorization behavior of lower and middle class Negro preschool children: differences in dealing with representation of familiar objects. *J. of Negro Education* (1966) 35: 218–29.

Lower-class and middle-class Negro preschool children were given three sorting tasks involving twelve familiar items. Form of presentation varied from actual object to color picture of object to black-and-white picture of object. Lower-class children differed from middle-class children only in ability to group the colored and black-and-white pictures. Differences were found in bases used to group the objects, with middle-class children classifying more often on the basis of common physical attributes, and lower-class children more on the basis of use.

4-3-1-3

Sledd, J. On not teaching English usage. *English J.* (1965) 54: 698–703.

The teaching of traditional standard English usage is deplored, and the author proposes that English teachers teach, in its place, a respect for whatever language a student has.

1-0-0-0

Spence, Janet T., and Dunton, Moira C. The influence of verbal and nonverbal reinforcement combinations in the discrimination learning of middle- and lower-class preschool children. *Child Development* (1967) 38: 1177–86.

Both lower- and middle-class children performed more poorly on a discrimination task when a candy-reward reinforcement was given, than when punishment or reward-punishment combinations were given. The verbal reinforcement "right" also resulted in poorer performance.

4-1-1-3

Strauss, A., and Schatzman, L. Cross-class interviewing: an analysis of interaction and communicative styles. *Human Organization* (1955) 14: 28–31.

Analysis of interviews gathered from lower-class (low income, little education) and middle-class (middle income, higher education) natives of Arkansas after a tornado showed marked differences in the communicative styles of the two classes. Lower-class respondents had difficulty giving connected accounts of the disaster, and were generally subjective and unable to answer questions calling for abstract answers or answers involving classification of persons or acts. The middle-class respondents gave well-ordered accounts of events, and were able to maintain the direction of the interview as set by the interviewer.

3-1-3-2

Taba, Hilda. Cultural deprivation as a factor in school learning. *Merrill-Palmer Quarterly* (1964) 10: 147–59.

The influx of children from lower-class slum backgrounds into a middle-class-oriented school system has brought about difficulties for both children and schools. The children suffer from the psychological effects of their lower-class status, i.e., lack of habits and skills necessary for meeting the expectations of conduct in school, lack of readiness for learning tasks, and negative attitudes toward school, teachers, and achievement. The discrepancies between the content of a curriculum designed for middle-class children and the meanings attached to the verbal cues of that content by lower-class children may often be unexpected. The school may add to the child's difficulties by failing to recognize these gaps, and by demanding a too-abrupt cultural transition of the child.

1-0-2-0

Templin, Mildred. Relation of speech and language development to intelligence and socio-economic status. *Volta Review* (1958) 60: 331–34.

Although the relationship between speech or language, and intelligence and socioeconomic status is a demonstrated and important one, it is a relationship which should not be overemphasized. There are several considerations which deserve attention: (1) it is necessary to state specifically what aspect of language is being related to intelligence and social class; (2) the use of an intelligence test inappropriate to young children may confound results; (3) the definition of socioeconomic status is a constantly changing one, and the basis on which such definition is made should be clear; and (4) the relationship between socioeconomic status and intelligence should not be overlooked.

1-0-0-0

Wasserman, Miriam. Planting pansies on the roof: a critique of how New York City tests reading. *The Urban Review* (1969) 3: 30–35.

An attempt is made to show that the nationally standardized reading tests used in New York City schools are unreliable and invalid when applied to poor minority group children.

1-0-2-0

Williams, F. Social class differences in how children talk about television: some observations and speculations. *J. of Broadcasting*, (1969) 13: 345–57.

Findings indicate that children from families of relatively high social status tend more to engage in relating the "story" of what they saw on television, whereas children from lower-status families tend to describe isolated instances of action witnessed on television.

4-1,3-2-4

———. Psychological correlates of speech characteristics: on sounding "disadvantaged." *J. of Speech and Hearing Research,* in press.

Teachers' ratings of children's speech samples are analyzed to determine their judgmental behavior and to determine what speech and language characteristics might predict variations in such behavior.

4-1,3-2,3-4

Williams, F., and Naremore, Rita. On the functional analysis of social class differences in modes of speech. *Speech Monographs* (1969) 36: 77–102.

Differences in how children respond functionally with language in an interview situation are assessed in speech samples of children from families of relatively high and low social status (including balanced subsamples of boys and girls, Negroes and whites). Social-class distinctions are interpreted in terms of a modified version of Bernstein's mode-of-speech concepts.

4-1,3-2-2

———. Social class differences in children's syntactic performance: a quantitative analysis of field study data. *J. of Speech and Hearing Research* (1969) 12: 778–93.

Types and degrees of syntactic elaboration are assessed in speech samples of children from families of relatively high and low social status (with balanced subsamples of boys and girls, Negroes and whites).

4-1,3-2-2

Williams, F., and Wood, Barbara. Negro children's speech: some social class differences in word predictability. *Language and Speech,* in press.

Teenage Negro girls from a poverty area school were less able to approximate the language (word predictability) in language samples from girls of a middle-class area school, than they were able to approximate the language of their peers. By contrast, the middle-class girls were equally able to approximate the language of their peers as well as that of lower social class girls.

4-3-2-3

Wood, Barbara. Implications of psycholinguistics for elementary speech programs. *The Speech Teacher* (1968) 17: 183–92.

The language acquisition process in children is described in psycholinguistic terms, and social-class differences which affect this process are discussed. Implications for speech education in the early elementary grades, and for teacher-training are made. Current texts in these areas are evaluated.

1-0-2-1

Wood, Barbara, and Curry, Julia. 'Everyday talk' and 'school talk' of the city black child. *The Speech Teacher* (1969) 18: 282–96.

Interview conditions (instructions to use "school talk" or "home talk") and social status were found to influence stylistic variations and various grammatical characteristics of Negro girls. Implications for the classroom teacher are discussed.

4-3-2-1,2

TOPICAL INDEX